MW00462657

So Say We All

ALSO BY THE AUTHORS

The Fifty-Year Mission:
The Complete, Uncensored, Unauthorized Oral History of Star Trek:
The First 25 Years

The Fifty-Year Mission: The Next 25 Years: From The Next Generation
to J. J. Abrams: The Complete, Uncensored, and Unauthorized
Oral History of Star Trek

Slayers & Vampires:
The Complete Uncensored, Unauthorized
Oral History of Buffy *and* Angel

SO SAY WE ALL

THE COMPLETE, UNCENSORED, UNAUTHORIZED ORAL HISTORY OF
BATTLESTAR GALACTICA

MARK A. ALTMAN
AND
EDWARD GROSS

TOR

A TOM DOHERTY ASSOCIATES BOOK

NEW YORK

SO SAY WE ALL: THE COMPLETE, UNCENSORED,
UNAUTHORIZED ORAL HISTORY OF *BATTLESTAR GALACTICA*

Copyright © 2018 by Mark A. Altman and Edward Gross

A Tor Book
Published by Tom Doherty Associates
175 Fifth Avenue
New York, NY 10010

www.tor-forge.com

Tor® is a registered trademark of Macmillan Publishing Group, LLC.

The Library of Congress Cataloging-in-Publication Data is available
upon request.

ISBN 978-1-250-12894-2 (hardcover)
ISBN 978-1-250-12895-9 (ebook)

Our books may be purchased in bulk for promotional, educational, or business
use. Please contact your local bookseller or the Macmillan Corporate and
Premium Sales Department at 1-800-221-7945, extension 5442, or by email at
MacmillanSpecialMarkets@macmillan.com.

First Edition: August 2018

Printed in the United States of America

0 9 8 7 6 5 4 3 2 1

FROM MARK A. ALTMAN

Steven A. Simak, without whom this book would not be possible and who is the biggest *Galactica* fan I know. He provided incalculable help and assistance in completing this volume. Can't tell you how many times I went to his house and watched *Mission Galactica* on Super 8. Of course, his wonderful mom Nilda's baked ziti didn't hurt either.

My parents, **Gail Altman-Orenstein** and **Michael Altman**, who let me stay up waaaay late to see how it all ended on September 17, 1978. (Spoiler alert: the Colonials escaped from Carillon, it was a cookbook . . . and Begin and Sadat signed the Camp David Peace Accords.)

Those who believed that there may yet be brothers of man who even now fight to survive somewhere beyond the heavens; our intrepid editor, **Brendan Deenen**, and Tor Books publisher and founder, **Tom Doherty**.

And, of course, all the charter members of **The Galactic Club of Science Fiction** (Kevin Costello, Ira Altman, Kenny Feinleib, Wayne Meyers, but not you Lance Schulman) in 1978 that nurtured my love of science fiction movies, television, novels—and especially *Battlestar Galactica*—for many years to come.

The East Coast Altmans: Ira, Becky, Tyler, and **Emily**, because they got left out of all the other books . . . and I never heard the end of it.

Ed Gross, the best collaborator one could ever wish for, despite the fact that I keep trying to get out, but he pulls me back in . . .

Finally, and most importantly, **Ella** and **Isaac**, my own Colonial Warriors. And **Naomi**, because she *still* tolerates me after all these yahrens.

FROM EDWARD GROSS

Ronald D. Moore, whose enthusiasm for this project mirrored the authors', and without whom this book would never have been possible.

Our Tor editor, **Brendan Deenen**, and Tor publisher, **Tom Doherty**—thanks for believing in *Galactica* as much as we do.

My coauthor, **Mark A. Altman**—what an incredible ride this has been; I appreciate your collaboration and your friendship.

My wife, **Eileen**, who, in a turn of a sports phrase, became a *Galactica* widow throughout the writing process. It was a long haul, but we got through it. I love you.

Our sons, **Teddy**, **Dennis**, and **Kevin**; daughter-in-law, **Lindsay Saier**; and, taking up the "hey you could be next" positions, **Nicole Plaia** and **Yumi Matsuyama**. Our own personal ragtag fugitive fleet on this journey through life.

Fleeing from Cylon tyranny, the last battlestar, Galactica,

leads a ragtag fugitive fleet on a lonely quest:

a shining planet known as Earth.

DATA LOG

SECTAR ONE: *BATTLESTAR GALACTICA* (1978)
THE ABC YEARS

THE BOOK
OF THE WORD

"I see the party is not a huge success with all my children."

BY **Mark A. Altman**

There are very few things about middle school (or, as we fashionably called it at the time, junior high school) that I can still recall. It was, in fact, four decades ago, so you can hopefully forgive me for my rather vague recollections. I sure do remember Ms. Radiloff, my toweringly tall and delightful science teacher, who was prone to breaking into bouts of the now very politically incorrect Randy Newman song "Short People (Got No Reason to Live)" in the middle of class. I recall Mr. Rubin, my rather dour science teacher, and his uncharacteristically impassioned lessons about quasars, which were apparently quite in vogue at the time (along with, of course, black holes), and Mrs. Rosen, my septuagenarian typing teacher, whom I will forever be indebted to for teaching me to type at warp speed on an old IBM Selectric; and, of course, I remember the loathsome Lance Schulman, who revealed to me that Darth Vader was Luke Skywalker's father in the Marvel Comics adaptation of *The Empire Strikes Back* before I saw the movie. Fuck you, Lance, wherever you are.

But the thing I do recall better and more clearly than anything that happened during those halcyon three years attending Roy H. Mann Junior High School in Brooklyn, New York, during the late seventies, long before Brooklyn was remotely cool, is Monday mornings. What was it about Monday mornings that even now continues to resonate in my ever-depleting synapses? Well, it was gathering in the schoolyard during lineup in the morning to discuss *Battlestar Galactica* from the previous night. And perhaps there is no more vivid memory of those years than our shared horror at President Jimmy Carter for interrupting the broadcast of "Saga of a Star

World"—just as the *Galactica* crew was arriving at Carillon—to speak to the nation about the Camp David Peace Accords. To an eleven-year-old, this all seemed extremely trivial compared to the fate of the survivors of the Twelve Colonies of Man, who were desperate to elude the clutches of the devious Cylons and survive an interstellar genocide. Thankfully, my parents let me stay up way past eleven o'clock to see how it all ended, for which I will be eternally grateful.

Back then, I certainly didn't get the fact that compared to *Star Trek*, with its laudably optimistic, liberal, progressive politics (ocassional right-leaning missteps like "A Private Little War" notwithstanding), *Galactica* was far more militaristic and neoconservative in its viewpoint. It's the liberal President Adar, played by Lew Ayres, who seems to be a thinly veiled Jimmy Carter analogue, who is easily tricked by Baltar into disarmament, and who pays an apocalyptic price for his naïveté (shades of SALT II—in fact, the series even inspired much outrage from the Soviet Union, which accused the show of trying to poison relations between the United States and the USSR). And it's the politicians, like the gluttonous and self-serving Sire Uri, who are as devious as the metallic automatons hell-bent on humanity's destruction.

But none of that mattered to me back in 1978; my friends and I sure dug *Battlestar Galactica* . . . a lot. Yes, even as preteens, we knew it wasn't nearly as literate or allegorical as *Trek* or as smart and sophisticated as *The Twilight Zone,* and the science was an utter mess with galaxies being confused with solar systems constantly and ships traversing the galaxy from week to week at sublight velocities among other things, but at a whopping $7 million, the pilot really delivered on its promise to be *Star Wars* for the small screen. With its glorious Frank Frazetta artwork in *TV Guide* beckoning you to watch along with its story of swashbuckling spacefarers, malevolent mechanical Centurions, and a robot dog, this was a show that promised a lot . . . and, for the most part, delivered. It was cool. As an eleven-year-old, I was utterly entranced with the magnificent space vehicles designed by *Star Wars'* Ralph McQuarrie, the stirring Stu Phillips orchestral score, and the even more stirring Maren Jensen.

Battlestar Galactica was also the show that prompted me to publish my first magazine, *Galactic Journal,* a fanzine that my junior high school friends and I started (and was covertly mimeographed by my mother at work, plowing through gallons and gallons of ink in the process—thanks, Mom!) and continued to publish till our college days, now completely typeset and printed in full color, with a substantially increased circulation. Our premiere issue, in 1978, had a drawing of a Colonial Viper on it, sketched by Galactic Club charter member Kevin Costello, still a dear friend. Man, we loved that show a lot.

Years later, as a co–executive producer of the TV series *Agent X* for TNT, I was lucky enough to work with the great Rod Holcomb, a veteran director who worked on such legendary TV series as *The Six Million Dollar Man, The Greatest American Hero, The A-Team, Wiseguy,* and *ER* (shooting the pilots of the last two groundbreaking series) as well as, you guessed it, *Battlestar Galactica.* Some of my favorite memories of working on that show are of chatting between takes with Rod about the lonely quest, working with everyone's favorite Alpo pitchman, living legends and lost planets of the gods . . . and, of course, Bigfoot, but that's a story for another book.

Given how important nostalgia is to me when it comes to *Battlestar Galactica,* it shouldn't surprise you to know that while we were writing this volume, what may have amused me the most was when *Battlestar Galactica* story editor Terry McDonnell, reflecting on his work on the series, said, "I went down to the stage a couple of times just by myself at lunch when they weren't shooting. If I could have only had this in my backyard when I was a kid playing pirates." At this recollection, I broke into a wide grin and confessed that as kids we would actually play *Battlestar Galactica.* He laughed, "Nobody has ever said that to me before." I didn't have the heart to tell him that we played *Space: 1999,* too.

Years later, when the reinvention of *Battlestar Galactica* was announced, I could not have been more ecstatic. I was particularly excited because the project was in the hands of a brilliant writer/producer like Ronald D. Moore, who had not only been responsible for *The Next Generation*'s greatest episodes, but later helped Ira Steven Behr make *Deep Space Nine* one of the most compelling and unique science fiction TV series of all time. That's why I'm embarrassed to admit now that when I first watched the miniseries, I disliked it intensely. I thought it looked cheap and was way too grim and lacked the fun of the original series. I particularly missed the Ralph McQuarrie visual aesthetic of the 1978 show's groundbreaking design and felt the allegory for 9/11 was a little too on-the-nose. Not to mention, I thought the new bridge was unimpressive compared to the stunning, massive one-million-dollar set of the original series (full disclosure: having recently rewatched it, I can now say that the miniseries is much better than it seemed to me at the time).

So when the show was green-lit to series, I remained trepidatious. I still had faith in Ron (who I knew had been showrunning *Carnivàle* during the miniseries production, which might have been part of why I found it lethargic and unengaging), but I wasn't sure Syfy Channel (still called Sci-Fi at the time) could and would deliver the goods. In my mind, they hadn't spent the money they needed to on the miniseries, and it lacked the iconic polish of the 1978 series, not to mention the malevolent metal machine robots that I had first fallen in love with as a kid. Fortunately, I was proved very wrong. With the brilliant debut episode, "33," a nail-biting pressure cooker of an episode, it was clear Ron Moore and David Eick had a powerful and original vision for the new series. For years, fans (myself included) had bemoaned why there couldn't be a sci-fi *Sopranos,* a genre series that was as complex, riveting, and sophisticated as the best of what is now branded "peak TV." *Battlestar Galactica* was finally it. It was a show that rightly belonged in the pantheon of television classics such as *Hill Street Blues, The West Wing, Twin Peaks, The Wire, Mad Men,* and, yes, the original *Star Trek.*

There were no daggits, no alien Ovions or Borays, no rip-offs of *Shane, The Dirty Dozen,* or *The Towering Inferno,* just morally complex characters and dynamic storytelling unlike any the small screen had ever seen in a sci-fi series, and that never changed over the course of its entire run, culminating in one of the most divisive series finales since *Lost.* For the record, I loved it.

That said, it's such a thrill to be writing the final volume in our trilogy of oral histories of legendary science fiction TV series ranging from *Star Trek* (*The Fifty-Year Mission*) to *Buffy the Vampire Slayer* (*Slayers & Vampires*) to *Battlestar Galactica* (in case you missed it emblazoned on the cover, *So Say We All*). These were all shows that changed the genre forever and will always remain touchstones for a generation of fans who grew up with them, including Ed and me. The 1978 *Battlestar Galactica* was the Rodney Dangerfield of sci-fi shows, never quite getting any respect, and the magic of 2004's incredible and groundbreaking reinvention has never been explored in depth. Until now, that is. I hope you enjoy this not-so-lonely quest to once again bring the battlestar *Galactica* home to Earth.

And finally, and most importantly, maybe the biggest delight of writing this book (and I must say a personal triumph) has been introducing my eight-year-old son, Isaac, to the joys of classic *Battlestar Galactica.* Isaac has had the sophistication and good taste to appreciate the oft-maligned genius of the original series that has (mostly) aged like a fine ambrosia (albeit *Galactica 1980* not so much). He is the living proof that this has all happened before and it will all happen again.

May the Lords of Kobol Bless You.

September 17, 2017

A LONG TIME AGO IN A GALACTICA FAR, FAR AWAY . . .

"It's been a while since I've had a woman throw me to the ground. Not quite as much fun as I remember."

BY **Edward Gross**

While conducting interviews with cast and crew from the reimagined *Battlestar Galactica,* I was the one who kept getting hit with a recurring question: Had I seen the *Galactica* episode of the *Portlandia* TV series? I replied that I hadn't, and in fact had barely even been aware of the show's existence, hardly a surprise these days.

Time was that I would know pretty much every new TV show out there, what they were about and when they would air. In fact, it was something I prided myself on—for years my wife (Eileen) and I would pick up two copies of *TV Guide*'s Fall Preview issue just so we could read about what was coming and check off what we would or wouldn't watch. *Now,* of course, the sheer quantity of television is so overwhelming that I'm suddenly hearing about a show in its third season that I've never even heard of at all.

We'll get back to *Portlandia* in a second.

During the writing process, there came a point where I felt like I needed a *Galactica* 2003 refresher, having not watched the show since its first run. I streamed the original miniseries, which made perfect "background noise" for the writing process, though I found myself paying attention to it more than I probably should have been. Next thing I knew, I was making my way through season one, with all the others streaming before me over the next couple of weeks. The writing of the book needed to continue, but *Galactica* wouldn't. It was over. They'd found Earth (and thank God *not* the Earth of

Galactica 1980), and now *I* was the one feeling lost. Searching. My first impulse was to start watching the original series, but *then* I remembered *Portlandia*. Or, more accurately, what I'd been told about it. A bit of searching on Netflix, and there it was: season 2, episode 2—"One Moore Episode." In it, characters played by the two lead actors, Fred Armisen and Carrie Brownstein, decide to check out an episode of *Battlestar Galactica,* which leads to another and another and another . . . to the point where they lose their jobs, electricity is turned off (briefly, but painfully), and they find themselves so obsessed that they decide to go this side of Kathy Bates in *Misery* on Ron Moore's ass to get him to write another episode. Won't spoil things from there, but you should check it out for yourself if you haven't.

Needless to say, "One Moore Episode" was pretty reflective of what I felt rewatching the series, its power once again completely capturing my imagination, and, it being one of the few shows (particularly in the sci-fi genre) to live up to the true potential of the medium, standing as the model by which others are still measured all these years later.

Personally, it's an ironic feeling to have, considering that I *wasn't* the biggest fan of *Battlestar Galactica* when the original series debuted, in 1978. I can still remember the excitement leading into the series—at that point I was a massive *Star Trek* fan and had been swept up by *Star Wars* along with everyone else—and I was pretty impressed with the three-hour event "Saga of a Star World." Unfortunately, with the exception of several two-parters, that feeling didn't last all that long. The series (at least for me) felt as though it quickly fell into a certain repetition, and drove home the notion that *Battlestar Galactica* was an incredible *premise* that failed to live up to its own potential. And when *Galactica 1980* followed as a failed apology from ABC, that feeling remained with me. For decades.

Which is part of the reason that rumblings over the years of a revival barely elicited a Spockian rise of an eyebrow. Oh, sure, talk of Bryan Singer doing a new version with Tom DeSanto was intriguing, but didn't inspire a tremendous amount of hope in me. And neither did Richard Hatch's attempt to get the show revived, which felt like it was going to be more of the same (not entirely fair, since I didn't know much about it). But when word came out that Ronald D. Moore was writing a new version, *then* I was interested. And to be perfectly honest, it wasn't because I was suddenly filled with hope of *Battlestar Galactica* being all that it could be (my bad), but more because I was already friendly with him, having interviewed him numerous times regarding his work on *Star Trek: The Next Generation* and *Deep Space Nine*. He'd always made me feel welcome to contact him, and my initial impulse was that I could have an interesting exclusive on my hands.

So I contacted Ron, and we chatted about how it all came about and what he was hoping to achieve. We probably spoke for about forty-five minutes, and afterward I thanked him, both of us figuring we'd talk again at some point. What neither of us expected was that my tape recorder would malfunction and the interview was *not* recorded. Just to show you what kind of a human being Ron Moore is, when I told him what had happened, he took a deep breath and we dove right back into it as though the first conversation hadn't occurred. End result was that I came away from that first chat—both of them—with more excitement in my heart for *Battlestar Galactica* than I'd felt since those days leading into "Saga of a Star World." And, as it turned out, for good reason. The show was *everything* that was suggested in the premise, the writers, cast, and crew pulling together to create some intergalactic magic.

And more than anything, it's that—speaking to all of those people— which has been the highlight of cowriting *So Say We All* with Mark A. Altman. Engaging in hour upon hour of conversation, gradually piecing the story together, and coming away from it all with not only a greater appreciation for the show, but a true understanding that when everyone who worked on it refers to each other as a family, you absolutely believe it.

Prior to this we've written three oral histories: the two volumes of *The Fifty-Year Mission,* which chronicle the first half century of *Star Trek,* and *Slayers & Vampires,* which takes on both *Buffy the Vampire Slayer* and *Angel.* But I'd be lying if I didn't say that there was something extra special about this book, the enthusiastic cooperation of *everyone* we reached out to bringing us into the fold in a way that the others haven't quite done. We've relived the entire journey in a way that few outsiders have, feeling as though we've stepped onto the CIC of the battlestar *Galactica,* fought for survival on Caprica and against Cylon occupation on New Caprica, experienced the sense of hopelessness upon discovering the nuclear wasteland that was Earth, fearing the loss of everything as mutiny threatened to tear the remnants of society apart, and, of course, settling on a new Earth to begin the saga anew.

It's been one frak of a journey and we'd be happy to do it all over again. So say we both.

October 11, 2017

DRAMATIS PERSONAE

FÉLIX ENRIQUEZ ALCALÁ is a director who has worked on such series as *ER, The Good Wife, Agent X, The Defenders,* and *Battlestar Galactica* (2004).

PETER ANDERSON is a visual effects cinematographer and supervisor who helped create the theme park attractions *King Kong 360 3-D, T2 3-D: Battle Across Time,* and *Captain Eo.* He was awarded an honorary Oscar for his technological contributions to the industry. In addition, he was visual effects supervisor for *Cosmos* and the original *Battlestar Galactica.*

MICHAEL ANGELI is a writer/producer who worked on such series as *Monk* and *Touching Evil,* and was co–executive producer of *Battlestar Galactica* (2004).

JAMIE BAMBER is an actor. He played Lee Adama in *Battlestar Galactica* (2004).

DONALD BELLISARIO is a writer/producer/director who created such hit TV series as *Quantum Leap, JAG,* and *NCIS.* He is a former supervising producer of the original *Battlestar Galactica.*

DIRK BENEDICT is an actor. He played Lieutenant Starbuck on the original *Battlestar Galactica.* He also starred as Face on NBC's hit series *The A-Team.*

PETER BERKOS is a sound effects editor whose work includes *Slap Shot, Car Wars, The Hindenburg* (1975), *Buck Rogers in the 25th Century,* and the original *Battlestar Galactica.*

BRANNON BRAGA is a writer/producer for television and films who was an executive producer of *Star Trek: Voyager* and *Enterprise*. He is currently executive producer of *The Orville*. Along with Ronald D. Moore, Braga wrote the screenplays to *Star Trek: Generations* and *First Contact*.

JAMES CALLIS is the actor who played Gaius Baltar in *Battlestar Galactica* (2004).

JIM CARLSON was a story editor on the original *Battlestar Galactica*.

TERRY CARTER is an actor and documentarian, best known for his roles as Sergeant Joe Broadhurst on *McCloud* and as Colonel Tigh on the original *Battlestar Galactica*.

ERIC CHU is an art director at Enigma Studios who worked on *Battlestar Galactica* (2004).

ALLAN COLE is an author, journalist, and television writer who was a story editor on *Galactica 1980* and wrote for such series as *Quincy, M.E., The Rockford Files, The Incredible Hulk,* and *Werewolf.* He is also author of the bestselling *Sten* sci-fi novels.

JOHN COLICOS was an actor best known for playing Count Baltar in *Battlestar Galactica.* He also played Kor in *Star Trek* and *Star Trek: Deep Space Nine.*

RICHARD COLLA was the director of the *Battlestar Galactica* three-hour premiere, "Saga of a Star World." He also directed *The Questor Tapes* for Gene Roddenberry.

STEVEN E. DE SOUZA is a writer/producer/director who wrote some of the most successful action films of all time, including *48 Hours, Commando, Die Hard,* and *Judge Dredd.* While a story editor at Universal Television, he worked for producer Glen Larson on *The Hardy Boys/Nancy Drew Mysteries.*

TOM DESANTO is a producer of such films as *Transformers* and *X-Men.* He developed an unproduced *Battlestar Galactica* TV series for the Fox network to have been directed by Bryan Singer.

JEAN-PIERRE DORLEAC was an Emmy Award–winning costume designer whose films and television series include *Somewhere in Time, The Blue Lagoon, Buck Rogers in the 25th Century, Quantum Leap,* and the original *Battlestar Galactica.*

AARON DOUGLAS is the actor who played Chief Galen Tyrol in *Battlestar Galactica* (2004).

ROBYN DOUGLASS is an actress who starred in *Breaking Away* and played Jamie Hamilton in *Galactica 1980.*

JOHN DYKSTRA is a legendary special effects artist and recipient of three Academy Awards. He is well known for his groundbreaking visual effects work on *Star Wars.* He later founded his own visual effects company, Apogee, which worked on *Star Trek: The Motion Picture* and the original *Battlestar Galactica,* for which he was also a producer.

RICHARD EDLUND is a visual effects supervisor and cameraman who worked with John Dykstra on *Star Wars* and the original *Battlestar Galactica* before starting his own visual effects company, Boss Films, whose credits include *Big Trouble in Little China, Die Hard, Ghostbusters,* and *Air Force One.*

VINCE EDWARDS was an actor and director who played Ben Casey on the TV series of the same name before becoming a television director for such series as *Police Story, The Hardy Boys/Nancy Drew Mysteries, Fantasy Island, The Fall Guy,* the original *Battlestar Galactica,* and *Galactica 1980.*

DAVID EICK is a former television executive and writer/producer for such series as the NBC remake of *The Bionic Woman* and TNT's *Falling Skies.* He was executive producer and cocreator of *Battlestar Galactica* (2004).

JANE ESPENSON is a writer/producer who has worked on numerous TV series, including *Buffy the Vampire Slayer* and *Battlestar Galactica* (2004), and was an executive producer on *Caprica.*

ROBERT FEERO was an actor best known for his work on *THX 1138* and *Fade to Black.* He played a Borellian Nomen, Bora, in two episodes of the original *Battlestar Galactica.*

DOROTHY FONTANA is a writer/producer who was story editor on the original *Star Trek* TV series.

JONATHAN FRAKES is an actor/director who played Commander William Riker in *Star Trek: The Next Generation* and was the director of *Star Trek: First Contact* and *Star Trek: Insurrection.* He also was executive producer of *Roswell.*

HARVEY FRAND was the line producer of *Battlestar Galactica* (2004).

JEFF FREILICH is a writer/producer who has worked on such series as *The Incredible Hulk, The A-Team,* and *Halt and Catch Fire.* He was a producer of *Galactica 1980.*

BRYAN FULLER is a writer/producer in television, and the creator of such critically acclaimed series as *Dead Like Me, Hannibal, Pushing Daisies, American Gods,* and *Star Trek: Discovery.*

MIKE GIBSON is a visual effects artist who was visual effects producer on *Battlestar Galactica* (2004).

JACK GILL has been a stunt coordinator for numerous films and TV series, including *Furious 7* and *The Hangover Part III,* as well as *Knight Rider.* He was a stunt double on the original *Battlestar Galactica* and on *Galactica 1980.*

TONI GRAPHIA is a Peabody Award–winning writer/producer who has worked on such series as *Grey's Anatomy, Alcatraz, Roswell, Outlander,* and *Battlestar Galactica* (2004).

LORNE GREENE was an actor who starred as Ben Cartwright on *Bonanza,* in such films as *Earthquake* and *Nevada Smith,* and as John Reynolds on the hit ABC miniseries *Roots.* He played Commander Adama on the original *Battlestar Galactica* and on *Galactica 1980.*

MARC GUGGENHEIM is a comic book writer and television showrunner who is the cocreator and executive producer of such series as *Arrow* and *DC's Legends of Tomorrow.* In addition to writing numerous comic books, he wrote the *Galactica 1980* miniseries for Dynamite.

RICHARD HATCH was an actor who starred as Captain Apollo on the original *Battlestar Galactica* and Tom Zarek on *Battlestar Galactica* (2004). He also produced and starred in the fan film *Battlestar Galactica: The Second Coming.*

NOAH HATHAWAY is an actor who starred in *The Neverending Story* and played Boxey in the original *Battlestar Galactica.*

TRICIA HELFER is an actress and model who starred as Number Six in *Battlestar Galactica* (2004). She currently stars on *Lucifer* for Fox.

MICHAEL HOGAN is the actor who played Colonel Saul Tigh in *Battlestar Galactica* (2004).

ROD HOLCOMB is a director who has worked on such series as *The Six Million Dollar Man, The A-Team, The Greatest American Hero, ER, Wiseguy, Agent X,* and the original *Battlestar Galactica.*

RICHARD HUDOLIN has been a production designer for such series as *Stargate SG-1, Arrow,* and *Battlestar Galactica* (2004).

GARY HUTZEL was the visual effects supervisor for *Battlestar Galactica* (2004). Previously, he oversaw the visual effects for *Star Trek: The Next Generation* and *Deep Space Nine,* as well as *Defiance.*

ALEX HYDE-WHITE is the actor who played Mr. Fantastic in Roger Corman's infamous *Fantastic Four* movie. He is the son of actor Wilfrid Hyde-White and starred in such films and TV shows as *Pretty Woman, Game Change,* and the original *Battlestar Galactica.*

RICHARD JAMES is a production designer who worked on such series as *Star Trek: The Next Generation* and *Star Trek: Voyager* and was an art director on the original *Battlestar Galactica.*

HERBERT JEFFERSON, JR. is the actor who was Lieutenant Boomer in *Battlestar Galactica* and Colonel Boomer in *Galactica 1980.*

MAREN JENSEN is the actress who played Athena in the original *Battlestar Galactica.*

CLAUDE EARL JONES is an actor who has starred in such movies and TV series as *I Want to Hold Your Hand, Miracle Mile, Dallas,* and the original *Battlestar Galactica.*

ALESSANDRO JULIANI is the actor who played Lieutenant Felix Gaeta in *Battlestar Galactica* (2004).

ROB KLEIN is a movie memorabilia and prop collector and former archivist for the Walt Disney Company.

WINRICH KOLBE was a producer and director of numerous TV series, including *Star Trek: The Next Generation, Star Trek: Deep Space Nine, Knight Rider, Hunter,* and the original *Battlestar Galactica.*

DAVID LARSON is the son of *Battlestar Galactica* creator Glen Larson. He also appeared in "Greetings from Earth" and as a Super Scout on *Galactica 1980.*

GLEN A. LARSON was a legendary television writer and producer who created such series as *Quincy, M.E., Magnum, P.I., The Fall Guy, Knight Rider, Buck Rogers in the 25th Century, Manimal,* and the original *Battlestar Galactica.*

KEN LARSON is a set designer and visual effects model maker who created numerous miniatures for the original *Battlestar Galactica* and for *Galactica 1980.* He also worked on *Buck Rogers in the 25th Century* and *Airport '79.*

PAUL LEONARD is a producer for television who has worked on such series as *Warehouse 13, Alphas, Defiance, Caprica,* and *Battlestar Galactica* (2004).

ALAN J. LEVI is a director who has worked on such TV series and miniseries as *The Incredible Hulk, The Bionic Woman, Scruples, Quantum Leap, Buffy the Vampire Slayer,* and the original *Battlestar Galactica,* including his uncredited work directing the three-hour premiere, "Saga of a Star World."

ANNE LOCKHART is the actress who played Sheba on the original *Battlestar Galactica.* She is the daughter of *Lost in Space* actress June Lockhart.

ANGELA MANCUSO is the former president of Universal Cable Entertainment, where she was involved in developing the remake of *Battlestar Galactica* (2004).

SCOTT MANTZ is the chief film critic for *Access Hollywood*.

RICHARD CHRISTIAN MATHESON is the son of legendary author Richard Matheson and has been a writer/producer for such films and TV series as *The A-Team, Hardcastle and McCormick, Three O'Clock High, Chemistry,* and *Galactica 1980*.

MARY MCDONNELL is an Oscar-nominated actress who has starred in such films as *Donnie Darko, Independence Day,* and *Dances with Wolves,* and in *Battlestar Galactica* (2004) as President Laura Roslin.

TERRENCE MCDONNELL is a writer/producer and was a story editor on the original *Battlestar Galactica*.

STEPHEN MCNUTT is a cinematographer for film and television who has worked on such series as *The Dead Zone, Helix, Person of Interest, Outlander, Battlestar Galactica* (2004), and *Caprica*.

RONALD D. MOORE is a writer/producer who developed and was executive producer of the 2004 version of *Battlestar Galactica*. In addition, he was a producer on *Star Trek: The Next Generation, Deep Space Nine,* and *Roswell,* and is executive producer of *Outlander* and *Philip K. Dick's Electric Dreams*.

MICHAEL NANKIN is a Peabody Award–winning writer/producer and director who has worked on such series as *Defiance, The Exorcist, Van Helsing, Battlestar Galactica* (2004), and *Caprica*.

BOONE NARR is an animal coordinator and trainer who founded Boone's Animals for Hollywood and worked on the original *Battlestar Galactica*.

CHRISTIAN I. NYBY II is a television director who has worked on such series as *Diagnosis Murder, Emergency, Hill Street Blues,* and the original *Battlestar Galactica*. He is the son of Christian Nyby, the director of *The Thing from Another World*.

MICHAEL O'HALLORAN is an editor who has worked on such TV series as *Cosmos: A Spacetime Odyssey, Banshee, Outlander,* and *Battlestar Galactica* (2004).

GLEN OLIVER is a pop-culture commentator who previously contributed to Ain't It Cool News.

EDWARD JAMES OLMOS is a writer, producer, and director who has starred in such films and TV series as *Blade Runner, Miami Vice, American Family,* and *Narcos,* and as Commander William Adama in *Battlestar Galactica* (2004).

GRACE PARK is an actress who recently starred on *Hawaii Five-O.* She played the role of Sharon "Boomer" Valerii on *Battlestar Galactica* (2004).

TAHMOH PENIKETT is the actor who played Karl "Helo" Agathon in *Battlestar Galactica* (2004).

H. JOHN PENNER was a director of photography on such TV series as *Quincy, M.E., Knight Rider,* and *Salvage 1* as well as the original *Battlestar Galactica.*

STU PHILLIPS is a composer for film and television whose scores include those for *Knight Rider, The Fall Guy, Buck Rogers in the 25th Century,* and the original *Battlestar Galactica* and *Galactica 1980.* He also composed the music for the *Monkees* TV series and *Beyond the Valley of the Dolls.*

ANDREW PROBERT is a production and conceptual illustrator who's worked on such films and TV series as *Star Trek: The Motion Picture, Back to the Future, SpaceCamp, Mask, Tron,* and the original *Battlestar Galactica.* He also designed the *Enterprise-D* for *Star Trek: The Next Generation.*

ROBBIE RIST is an actor and musician who played Dr. Zee in the three-hour premiere of *Galactica 1980.* He also played Cousin Oliver on *The Brady Bunch.*

CARLA ROBINSON is a writer for television who was story editor on *Battlestar Galactica* (2004).

DAVID ROGERS is an Emmy Award–winning editor and director for such TV series as *Seinfeld, The Mindy Project,* and *The Office.*

SARAH RUSH is the actress who played bridge officer Rigel on the original *Battlestar Galactica.*

MICHAEL RYMER is a producer and director for such films and TV series as *Queen of the Damned, In Too Deep, Hannibal,* and *Battlestar Galactica* (2004).

KATEE SACKHOFF is an actress whose projects for film and television include *Longmire, Oculus, The Bionic Woman, 24,* and *Riddick,* and who played Kara "Starbuck" Thrace in *Battlestar Galactica* (2004).

JANE SEYMOUR is an actress who has starred in such films and TV series as *Live and Let Die, Dr. Quinn, Medicine Woman,* and the original *Battlestar Galactica.*

REKHA SHARMA is an actress for such films and TV series as *The Core, Star Trek: Discovery,* and, as Tory Foster, *Battlestar Galactica* (2004).

TODD SHARP was the executive in charge of production on *Battlestar Galactica* (2004) and *Caprica.*

STEVEN SIMAK is a veteran journalist and *Battlestar Galactica* historian who has written extensively about both versions of the series.

MICHAEL SLOAN was a producer on the original *Battlestar Galactica.*

DOUG SMITH is a visual effects supervisor who has worked on such films and TV series as *Independence Day, True Lies,* and *Spaceballs,* and was a co–effects producer on the original *Battlestar Galactica.*

EMILE SMITH is a visual effects artist who was the digital effects supervisor on *Battlestar Galactica* (2004).

WAYNE SMITH is a miniature effects and special effects photography supervisor who has worked on such series as *Buck Rogers in the 25th Century, Galactica 1980,* and the original *Battlestar Galactica.*

DAVID SNYDER is a production designer for such films as *Demolition Man* and *Soldier.* He was also art director on such classic films as *Brainstorm, Pee-wee's Big Adventure,* and *Blade Runner,* and swing art director on *Galactica 1980.*

LAURETTE SPANG is the actress who played the role of Cassiopeia in the original *Battlestar Galactica.*

MARK STERN is the former president of original content for the Sci-Fi Channel and is currently president of IM Global Television.

DAVID STIPES is a visual effects supervisor who worked on such films and TV series as *Night of the Creeps, Real Genius, V, Star Trek: Enterprise, Star Trek: Deep Space Nine,* and *Star Trek: Voyager.* He was part of the visual effects team on *Galactica 1980* and the original *Battlestar Galactica.*

LEE STRINGER is a visual effects artist who was CG supervisor for Zoic Studios on *Battlestar Galactica* (2004).

MICHAEL TAYLOR is a TV writer/producer on such series as *Star Trek: Deep Space Nine, The Dead Zone, Defiance, Turn: Washington's Spies,* and *Into the Badlands.* He was a co-executive producer on *Battlestar Galactica* (2004) and wrote the telefilm *Battlestar Galactica: Blood & Chrome.*

BRADLEY THOMPSON is a writer/producer for television who has worked on such series as *Alphas, Star Trek: Deep Space Nine, Defiance, Falling Skies, The Strain,* and *Battlestar Galactica* (2004).

PHIL TIPPETT is a legendary visual effects artist and supervisor whose films and TV series include *The Empire Strikes Back, RoboCop, Starship Troopers,* and *The Twilight Saga.* He contributed creature designs for the original *Battlestar Galactica.*

MICHAEL TRUCCO is an actor in film and TV. He played Samuel Anders in *Battlestar Galactica* (2004).

BARRY VAN DYKE is the actor who played Lieutenant Dillon in *Galactica 1980.* He is the son of legendary actor Dick Van Dyke and costarred with him in the hit series *Diagnosis Murder.*

MARK VERHEIDEN is a comic book writer and writer/producer who has worked on such series as *Falling Skies, Hemlock Grove, Constantine, Daredevil,* and *Battlestar Galactica* (2004).

DAVID WEDDLE is a writer/producer for television who has worked on such series as *Alphas, Defiance, Falling Skies, The Strain,* and *Battlestar Galactica* (2004). He is also author of the acclaimed biography of director Sam Peckinpah *If They Move, Kill 'Em.*

SECTAR ONE

BATTLESTAR GALACTICA (1978)

THE ABC YEARS

There are those who believe that life here began out there, far across the universe, with tribes of humans who may have been the forefathers of the Egyptians, or the Toltecs, or the Mayans. Some believe that there may yet be brothers of man, who even now fight to survive somewhere beyond the heavens.

1.
THERE ARE THOSE
WHO BELIEVE

*"The final annihilation of the life-form known as man.
Let the attack begin."*

The year was 1978. Nine hundred and nine followers of Jim Jones did drink the Kool-Aid and died in a mass suicide at the behest of the tragically charismatic cult leader, while Louise Brown, the world's first test-tube baby, was born. The dominant New York Yankees once again won the pennant, while the Dallas Cowboys triumphed in the Super Bowl. Yet another reason not to mess with Texas.

On the radio, the Bee Gees dominated the charts, along with Billy Joel, Barry Manilow, ABBA, Paul McCartney & Wings, and Frankie Valli with his hit theme song to the movie *Grease,* which was a top-grossing film in theaters. Other films released that year were *Animal House, Heaven Can Wait, Halloween, Midnight Express,* and, most memorably, in late December, Richard Donner's revelatory *Superman: The Movie.* Keith Moon of the Who died that year, as did Nancy Spungen, who was violently stabbed to death by her boyfriend, Sid Vicious of the seminal punk rock band the Sex Pistols.

If you visited the bedroom of many a young teenager in 1978, you'd likely see Kenner's ubiquitous *Star Wars* toys, a 2-XL talking robot from Mego, and a poster of Farrah Fawcett thumbtacked to the wall. And not surprisingly, the video game *Space Invaders* continued to collect millions of quarters in arcades around the world.

Ironically, a different kind of space invader was about to take over ABC that year, *Battlestar Galactica,* a landmark series for television as well as a personal triumph for its creator, Glen A. Larson. Although not exorbitant by today's standards, the series' estimated price tag of one million dollars per episode was a turning point for the 1978–79 season and the industry as a whole. Millions watched as the most publicized series in history made its three-hour debut at 8:00 P.M. on Sunday, September 17, 1978, against the annual Emmy Awards (which prompted host Alan Alda to crack at the ceremony, "Don't you wish you were home so you could watch *Battlestar Galactica*?") and the television debut of the Dino De Laurentiis remake of *King Kong* on CBS and NBC, respectively. Wondering what was on Fox that night? There wasn't one—the Fox network didn't debut until 1986—nor was there any major network at the time other than NBC, CBS, and ABC, the so-called Big Three.

By the time of his death in 2014, Glen A. Larson would become one of the most successful and prolific television producers of all time, but in 1978, despite early triumphs, he was still at the beginning of an enviable career that would later include *B.J. and the Bear*, *Buck Rogers in the 25th Century*, *Knight Rider*, *Magnum, P.I.*, *The Fall Guy*, and many others.

Born on January 3, 1937, in Long Beach, California, Larson, a devout Mormon with eight children, already had several series on the air by the time he pitched *Battlestar Galactica* to ABC, among them *Alias Smith and Jones; Switch; Quincy, M.E.*, starring Jack Klugman as the curmudgeonly coroner; and *The Hardy Boys/Nancy Drew Mysteries*, based on the famous series of mystery novels.

A broadcast veteran, Larson began his early career in music, as a member of the musical group the Four Preps, for which he composed three gold-record-winning songs. Attracted to the film and television industry, he began writing teleplays for such series as *Twelve O'Clock High*. His talents were soon noticed by veteran screenwriter Gene L. Coon, who had just left late in *Star Trek*'s second season to run the Robert Wagner-toplined series, *It Takes a Thief*, and became a mentor to the creative young writer. Larson rose quickly through the television-industry ranks, advancing from writer to story editor and, eventually, to series producer and creator, showrunner, and fixer.

GLEN A. LARSON
(creator/executive producer, *Battlestar Galactica*)

Like most ideas, writing isn't writing, it's rewriting. You're searching and playing with your themes. One of the things you do as a writer is that if you have a story problem you reverse it; you find ways that if you can't make something happen one way you look at the opposite. It's a little trick of writing you use in mysteries or anything else. You find out that you don't force things by doing that.

DAVID LARSON
(son of Glen Larson)

My father always wanted to be a writer. When he was a kid, he was a page at NBC. He grew up surrounded by movies and television. That's what he wanted to do. I think he sort of fell into singing and the band. That's what you do. You want girls? You go form a band—and they just happened to make records and had a good time. But even when he was with the Preps, he would sit in his hotel room and write. He would turn on the faucet because he liked the sound of running water. It goes back to his childhood.

If we were filming a movie, we'd cut away to his childhood. There's some deep psychological stuff there. I think it had to do with his mother. She worked. She was a single mother. He was kind of a latchkey kid. He would know that she had come home because he would hear the bathwater turning on at night, so he loved the sound of running water. Years later, he would have a fountain, or he would turn on the bathtub when he wrote, which was terrible in a drought. He was not very conscientious about water usage. He would just turn the faucet on, and just let it go for hours.

GLEN A. LARSON

Most authors don't enjoy writing. It's a lonely, frustrating, demanding way to earn a living. What we enjoy is having written, and watching skilled actors bring it to life. For a screenwriter, the happiest words in the English language are "FADE OUT."

DAVID LARSON

In the Four Preps, they'd be touring around and he had one of those IBM Selectrics or something like that. He would sit there and write. I remember we were going through some of his old stuff, many years ago, and he had a script called "Finger Popper." I'm like, "What is this?" He goes, "This is the first thing I ever wrote." I didn't read it. I don't think he wanted me to read it, but it was the first thing he ever wrote.

JEFF FREILICH
(executive producer, *Halt and Catch Fire*)

I learned how to write television from Glen. He was the first person to teach me that as a writer, you lock yourself away from all distraction. You do not answer your phone, you don't care what's going on, you get people to do it for you. You go wherever it is where you find peace, which for him was his house in Malibu, and you work undistracted and create the most pleasant environment for yourself to write. He probably created more shows than anybody in the history of television, and successfully, too, because most of his shows were big hits during the seventies and eighties.

Larson's writing ability, coupled with his eye for the commercial requirements of the business, soon made him a star at Universal Television, which was his home for over a decade, until he left for 20th Century Fox in the early eighties. Although it wasn't without controversy, Larson's penchant throughout his career for extracting ideas for television series from popular movies at the time (*Alias Smith and Jones* was seemingly inspired by *Butch Cassidy and the Sundance Kid,* and *B.J. and the Bear* was clearly redolent of *Every Which Way but Loose,* among others) led to noted author and raconteur Harlan Ellison pejoratively labeling him "Glen Larceny."

GLEN A. LARSON

I like to think that you can do a lot of different things when you are part of a team organization like Universal. I was kind of Frank Price's [head of Universal Television] fair-haired boy in some ways; I would be his fireman. He originally made *The Six Million Dollar Man* as *Cyborg* and it didn't get bought. It just didn't work. So he assigned me to do two or three ninety-minute movies, from which we sold the series. I just brought a different approach to it; what I would think would be slightly more commercial. Ultimately, I do look for commercial value, because there is no great joy in having a victory in the studio that no one sees.

DAVID LARSON

My father worked a lot. He was gone most of the time. I didn't see him a whole lot, but he always made it a point to throw the ball around and to have special moments, and I think he did that with most of the kids, like going to a Dodgers game and things like that. Being a showrunner is a twenty-four/seven a week job, though.

Unfortunately, I wanted to be with him all the time. I could have just sat in his office, and I used to at 20th Century Fox. Just sit in his office and play with little car toys. He was working on like three or four different shows. That's when he had *The Fall Guy* on the air. He did so many pilots. Those were good times.

GLEN A. LARSON

When the president of NBC saw the *Quincy, M.E.* script [in which Jack Klugman, as a medical examiner/coroner, solved crimes using forensics], he didn't want to buy the pilot until it was pointed out to him that we already had a thirteen-show commitment. That's a fairly dark arena when you deal with death on a weekly series. But that's the way they think, they say, "Who will want to watch this?" Well, there is a lot of interest in forensics, and we used humor to slip the audience what you call "the flat end of the wedge," to get your foot in the door. The show got much more serious after it had been a mystery movie, largely because Jack [Klugman] liked to push it harder in those directions.

DAVID LARSON

My father was a type-triple-A personality. He was always going. He didn't stop. He was always working on many things at the same time. There was one year he had like five shows on the air at one time. I can't even imagine. Going from editing bay to editing bay, how do you keep it all straight? But he could. He loved that. He needed that.

BARRY VAN DYKE
(actor, "Dillon," *Galactica 1980*)

My impression of Glen when I first met him was he was like a big kid. He was so enthusiastic. I got along great with him. He really loved what he was doing. And had fun with it. I just thought he was a terrific guy.

JEFF FREILICH

Glen was a guy who liked a posse. He would call me up at ten o'clock at night on a Saturday, having had dinner already, sitting with my wife watching TV, and say, "Come out to Malibu and have dinner with me." And I always found it impossible to say no. I would drive out and there would be seven or eight or nine other people with Glen holding court. We'd all sit together and [*Galactica 1980* producer] Frank Lupo would come out and other people on other shows of his, sometimes actors, sometimes people who weren't even associated with him professionally but just people that he knew.

I enjoyed those days. I got to the point where I looked forward to those phone calls. It didn't happen all the time and it didn't happen frequently, but for me, it was entertainment and it was a glimpse into the world of a guy who drove everywhere in a chauffeur-driven stretch limousine, who had a three-quarter-inch videocassette deck in the back with a television, who had a plugged-in IBM Selectric in the back of his car. It was a traveling office. And he lived in this really beautiful house on the waters of Malibu.

DAVID LARSON

It must have been a lot of pressure to maintain his lifestyle. To maintain that house and having a jet and the cars and the limo. It's part of the costume that you wear. You have to keep up with all these other showrunners. People perceive you as successful and as at the top of your game. Other people don't have this. That's all I knew. You always went to the front of the line. You were standing in line for *Star Wars*. "Do you know who I am?" It was embarrassing, but also kind of cool. We just go right into the special entrance. He liked that. He liked the status that it afforded him. He liked being an icon, sort of.

Right when they first started the Universal studio tour, we went on a special VIP tour in a station wagon. I still remember this big, brown station wagon, and we had a driver. Somebody was driving us through and then we went through the ice tunnel from *Six Million Dollar Man*. As a kid, you're five, six years old, getting this type of experience. You really take that for granted.

WINRICH KOLBE
(associate producer, *Battlestar Galactica*)

Glen was a scream and a very interesting human being. I liked working with him—although he drove me nuts. He drove everybody nuts, because he just wouldn't let go of any product. It was hard to nail him down, but he had terrific ideas and he was good at what he was doing. It might not have been Shakespeare, but he had a very keen sense of story and was an interesting person to be with.

ALAN J. LEVI
(director, "Gun on Ice Planet Zero")

Glen was a man of ideas. He came in all the time with different ideas and then he was let go off most of the shows that he created. He was not that good as a continual producer, but he was a marvelous idea man.

RICHARD COLLA
(director, "Saga of a Star World")

Glen works to his greatest capacity to make the best product that he can make, usually based on some knowledge of a prior type of program that did work as a theatrical picture, and take that style and concept and apply it to television.

DAVID LARSON

He was creating, he was writing the pilot, getting it going, and then moving on to something else, which was his personality. He didn't like the day-to-day operation, year after year after year. I don't know how he would have been staying on a show for six, seven years. He just didn't have the attention span for that. He wanted to keep creating things. He had lots of ideas.

There were a lot of unsold scripts, just shelves full of stuff that he had written that he really believed in. Every single idea he ever had, good or bad, he was an absolute believer. He loved it. He could sell it to anybody. Back in the old school, he would put on a suit and tie, go into his network meeting.

He would sell something having nothing written. Probably something on a napkin or even just give a quick line and they'd be like, "Absolutely. We're going to order twenty-two." They don't do that anymore. It was a different time. He had the clout to do that for a time. Not many people did. There were a handful of people who could do this. You've got to be a salesman.

Along with Glen Larson's *Quincy, M.E.*, which began as an installment of the NBC Mystery Movie, many other popular Universal series dominated the Nielsen charts in the seventies, including *Emergency*, *Kojak*, *The Rockford Files*, *McCloud*, *The Six Million Dollar Man*, *The Bionic Woman*, and *The Incredible Hulk*. MCA/Universal, presided over by the legendary Lew Wasserman and Sid Sheinberg and which owned Universal Television, was one of the most successful television production studios in the business.

   With the last vestiges of the old studio system slowly on their way out, MCA/Universal had one foot in the old Hollywood and one foot in the new as the business was beginning a dramatic transformation. With a massive backlot and myriad stages at its Universal City home, while continuing to keep both above-the-line and below-the-line talent under contract, the studio was uniquely positioned to produce some of the most iconic shows of all time. It was here that some of Hollywood's most legendary movie stars found themselves in their twilight years as regular staples on television, ranging from Joan Crawford on *Night Gallery* to Bette Davis on *It Takes a Thief* to Ray Milland and Lew Ayres on *Battlestar Galactica*, among many others.

RICHARD JAMES
(art director, *Battlestar Galactica*)

Universal was always called "the Factory."

ALEX HYDE-WHITE
(actor, "Cadet Bow")

Universal was this big TV factory, producing maybe a dozen shows on a weekly basis to the three TV networks: ABC, NBC, and CBS. An analogy would be: If *Galactica* was a "counterinsurgency" in search of targets, then Universal was "the Pentagon." And, once you had clearance to be in "the Pentagon," you were fair game.

CHRISTIAN I. NYBY II
(director, "The Long Patrol")

Universal was almost like a college campus. They had anywhere from fifteen to twenty television shows in production at one time. So the stages were always full. There would be a couple of features going, so you kind of knew who everybody was. You'd see them in the commissary or around the lot. Everybody kind of knew everybody.

JEFF FREILICH

Universal had over twenty television shows going at the same time on the lot. This is way before anybody ever moved out of Los Angeles to make anything. It was wonderful. Instead of sitting down in a commissary to have lunch, I would just walk around from set to set and play with the monkey on *B.J. and the Bear* or talk to James Garner or go over and take a look at *Buck Rogers*. It was all there. It was terrific. It was a real movie studio. It was like a scene out of the end of *Blazing Saddles* where people were just walking around wearing different costumes and you felt you were in the movies, although the vast majority of what was being done there were actually television shows.

ALEX HYDE-WHITE

MCA founder Jules Stein was still on the lot, and I met him at the commissary one day, that was cool. He was one of the original "alpha" New Yorkers, an eye doctor turned music and band promoter-agent turned mogul, taking a moribund Hollywood motion picture studio of horror films and turning it into what became a huge conglomerate. Universal TV was still in its heyday.

CHRISTIAN I. NYBY II

It was kind of the last of the big studios. By then, Fox had sold off their backlot and it became Century City. Warner Bros. kind of had that kind of feel, but Universal still had actors and directors under contract. Actors would shift from one show to another. You'd see them on *The Virginian* and they'd go on *The Name of the Game,* then show up on *Ironside* or *Adam-12* or something.

TERRENCE MCDONNELL
(story editor, *Battlestar Galactica*)

Steven Spielberg had his offices on the first floor. Glen and [*Galactica* producer] Donald Bellisario were on the fourth.

ROD HOLCOMB
(director, "Murder on the Rising Star")

I thought *Battlestar Galactica* was really so timely and groundbreaking. It changed television and offered an opportunity to get out of the *Marcus Welby, M.D.* mode of doing series, and really got into doing adventure, and having control over it, on the stage. The work that they did was just stunning.

ALAN J. LEVI

Back then, we shot television. Head close-ups and masters, and over-the-shoulders. Today, every TV show today is a feature film. We began that transition. I think *Galactica* was one of the shows that was at the beginning of that.

With a string of television hits behind him, Glen Larson was probably one of the few people in the industry with the experience and clout to make *Battlestar Galactica,* an epic and expensive TV series with feature film aspirations, a reality.

SCOTT MANTZ
(film critic, *Access Hollywood*)

No conversation about *Battlestar Galactica* can start without talking about *Star Wars,* because the pitch for that show, the pitch that everyone was given, was imagine *Star Wars* production values on TV, and that's what it looked like. I'll never forget in the commercial for the premiere that shot of a Cylon Raider passing over the top of the *Galactica,* with that little tiny Raider, and you see the scope and the detail on the *Galactica* model.

STEVEN SIMAK
(journalist, *Battlestar Galactica* historian)

A successful producer always looking for the next big hit, Larson saw the achievements of *Star Wars* as an opportunity.

GLEN A. LARSON

Science fiction had been pretty dead up until *Star Wars* broke, and obviously when something like that comes in and fuels the market it makes a big difference. People did bring out their projects, including us. Clearly we came in early, and with such an ambitious project and with the Industrial Light & Magic group involved. This was a different generation of space project. It captured the new wave.

DAVID LARSON

Star Wars gave them license to say yes. It was a proven model now. They hadn't done anything like that on TV. *Star Trek* wasn't really like that. Very different show. *Star Wars* proved that people wanted to see this kind of thing. Let's do it on TV using John Dykstra. You had *Star Wars* as the boot camp which created all of these possibilities and these effects makers. It did a lot of the legwork, so you could do it on a much smaller budget on TV.

GLEN A. LARSON

Ours is a business and a world in which I guess every car has to look like a Mercedes and when you go in to sell something it doesn't hurt that one of the biggest blockbusters of all time is on the screen. I have to say that John

Dykstra and Richard Edlund and that group of young people from Long Beach City College had taken and moved the techniques of doing space effects into a whole new generation.

DAVID LARSON

He had the right idea at the right time. Without *Star Wars*, it never would have happened, but I think they were very different things.

A huge part of *Star Wars*' success, in addition to the groundbreaking special effects from Industrial Light & Magic, was the designs by legendary conceptual artist Ralph McQuarrie, who was also part of *Galactica*'s early development and helped sell the show, as Larson cagily included McQuarrie's stunning preproduction art as part of his sales pitch, even attaching McQuarrie's artwork in copies of the scripts he gave to the crew and actors.

GLEN OLIVER
(pop-culture commentator)

My layman, nonartistic eyes have always perceived a distinct difference between Ralph McQuarrie's preproduction aesthetic, and how those concepts and designs were ultimately visualized onscreen. While many broad strokes of McQuarrie's intent were grafted on the show, his developmental work suggested an overall aesthetic which was much sleeker—perhaps glossier— than what eventually went before cameras, which was grittier. His concept paintings are rather badass.

That said, I understand why the powers that be opted for a more grounded, gritty universe. *Galactica* isn't a terribly clean tale in terms of thematics— many stories were driven by explorations of treachery, greed, desperation, and struggle. These concepts often feel more accessible, and may even be amplified by, more "real world" and familiar settings. And, of course, *Star Wars* demonstrated that a universe doesn't have to be squeaky-sleek. Love or hate the show, it's impossible to argue that there's some mighty potent iconography present. For my money, the show's base aesthetic is a key reason the series has endured.

GLEN A. LARSON

We had pretty good response from the guys at ABC. We had very strong support from one of the top guys [ABC VP Stephen Gentry], who later died in a plane crash with [*Mission: Impossible* creator] Bruce Geller, and was really our mentor at ABC, a big fan. When we lost him, we lost some of our people who were most simpatico with us, who kind of knew what we wanted to do.

To make the ambitious project a reality, Larson teamed up with longtime associate Leslie Stevens. Stevens, a writer/director who had worked with Larson previously on *McCloud* and *It Takes a Thief*, joined the series as supervising producer. John Dykstra, fresh off his revolutionary work on *Star Wars*, was lured away from ILM, both to serve as a producer on the pilot and to supervise the visual effects.

STEVEN SIMAK

For *Battlestar Galactica*, Larson revived a series concept he had pitched unsuccessfully a decade earlier, *Adam's Ark*. The premise focused on the journey of a group of humans in search of a new home after the cataclysmic destruction of Earth. For *Galactica*, he reversed the idea, having our celestial brethren coming in search of us.

GLEN A. LARSON

It was a colonization theme and had a lot of interesting elements to it. At the time I was pitching it, *Star Trek* was on the air and *Star Trek* didn't last long so no one was interested in that area. In a way, it was the reverse of *Galactica*. It was inspired by the mysteriousness of Howard Hughes and all of his enigmatic dealings out in the desert in Nevada, where he was buying up hotels. Hughes had always been one of the pioneers of aviation. I noticed *Time* magazine had a cover anniversary issue which looked at the top five hundred people in our society. Anyone who had ever been on the cover of *Time* had been invited to a photographic session and so I had this sort of screwball idea, that Howard Hughes invites these people out to a major achievement ball in the middle of nowhere.

The building for the celebration is the most spacey-looking thing you've ever seen. Somewhere along the line someone realizes there's some odd sensations going on and you discover that this thing has taken flight. It turns out the Hughes computers have predicted that within a finite date a nuclear holocaust destroys Earth. We had variations on what the threat was, but the premise was Noah's Ark. The ship had left Earth with all of these incredibly important people to set sail. For *Galactica,* instead of leaving Earth with sort of a doomsday scenario, it was a little more optimistic coming from out there.

SCOTT MANTZ

It was the biblical story of Exodus. They're looking for Earth. What a great twist. I remember thinking, "Oh, I get it. They're looking for *us*." Does it take place in the past or the future or the present day? Who knows? We found out, and we regretted it, when we actually learned in *Galactica 1980.*

GLEN OLIVER

Given that *Galactica* was driven by so many conceits and thematics derived from outside material, Mormon beliefs and practices, for example, it's certainly feasible that Larson had conceived the overall thrust of the show far earlier than the late 1970s. Or, that the essence of the show had been generally shaped in his mind or via notes, without pen having been formally put to paper.

This said, considering the substantial amount of material which is available from *Galactica*'s development and production, including extremely early designs and unproduced scripts, it's hard not to raise an eyebrow at the notable dearth of material directly pertaining to *Adam's Ark.*

Knowing a bit about Larson from folks who worked with him over the years, my personal hunch is that some variant of *Galactica* was bouncing around in his head for quite some time, but was never fully formed. When it came time to coalesce these ideas—an opportunity enabled by the release *Star Wars*—it was impossible for him not to catch some sort of blowback given that franchise's immense visibility, popularity, and uniqueness.

DAVID LARSON

More than any other show, *Battlestar Galactica* was my father's legacy. He felt attached to that more than anything else, so he was really reluctant to let that one go. Back in 1977, he was successful, but he wasn't huge yet. They weren't just writing him checks to do whatever he wanted to do. He had to prove himself. *Battlestar Galactica* was his sort of magnum opus. There was a lot of that methodology from the [Mormon] church. There was just a lot of him that he put into it. It was a story he had been mulling over for a long time. Some stories just stick with you, and I think he knew this was going to be his legacy. He put everything he could into it.

ALAN J. LEVI

Glen's main force through all of that was he wanted to beat *Star Wars* to the theaters, because he had read the *Star Wars* script. When Universal turned it down [after George Lucas made *American Graffiti* for the studio], he and Leslie Stevens got together and formulated *Galactica.* That's how he got the idea of making it and he was determined to get it on before *Star Wars* came out.

Leslie was an alien expert and he wrote books on aliens, interplanetary travel, and the whole bit. Universal had turned down *Star Wars* and Glen had read the script somehow, and he said I'm going to bring *Star Wars* to the small screen, and that's how *Battlestar Galactica* got off the ground. It was he and Leslie actually speaking to put the initial thing together, not a lot of people know that.

The one thing about Glen is that Glen was always the star. There was a little bit of tension between the two of them because Leslie always felt that he had made more of a contribution toward the original *Galactica* being done than what he had been given credit for. He didn't get co-credit on much of what he wrote. He was such a kind, soft man. He was so brilliant. His books are almost a bible on intergalactic beliefs, alien beliefs, and so on. He believed it all! He was a very quiet man, a big soft-spoken man, but you listened to every word he said because he was that brilliant. My dealings with him were basically as a mentor that I owed a great deal of appreciation to. He never really got involved on set. He would come down and visit every once in a while, but Glen was the one who really ran the show and Glen hired most of the people who were working on the show. I never did forget that Leslie was really a good human being. A very talented writer and it was very sad when he died.

RICHARD COLLA
(director, "Saga of a Star World")

I first became acquainted with Leslie Stevens's work on a play that he had done in New York in the early fifties called *Bullfight*, which was kind of a dark piece about two brothers who are bullfighters, and the bullfight is done almost as a ballet on stage. He had a lovely poetry and a lovely sense of human value. He can also be very commercial and did plays like *Marriage-Go-Round* and TV series like *The Outer Limits*.

I had great respect for Leslie Stevens as a writer and he said, "Come on and do the pilot of *Battlestar Galactica*, 'Saga of a Star World,' because what we're going to do is we're really going to tell the story of mankind here, we're going to talk about human values." I said, "Okay, because it's really a comic book right now as far as the story is concerned and the people." He said, "Yeah, but we're going to work on that." It ended up being a really good craft exercise, but they ultimately never did fix the story. It never really did become the story of people. It was just a cartoon.

GLEN OLIVER

I see *Star Wars* as a literal and figurative "hero's journey," sometimes wrapped in sociopolitical allegory with hints of slavery, Nazism, World War II, Vietnam, etc. *Galactica,* to me at least, has always been about humanity trying to find itself and define itself, asking what is truly important when all is lost? How do we relate to spirituality and faith, when neither seems to be delivering exactly what we're seeking in a given moment? It's about the dangers of imbalance between political and military infrastructures, and how this lack of clarity can lead to uncertainty and even annihilation. *Galactica,* in many regards, is driven by harder, more tangible, more expansive themes than *Star Wars* often is. How fully, or smartly, it actually exploited these themes is an entirely different matter.

ALAN J. LEVI

You can't sue Roy Rogers for being a cowboy after Gene Autry, you know. This was a different kind of a show. He put Cylons in there because there were no Cylon types in *Star Wars* so there was a real threat there.

GLEN OLIVER

Does *Galactica* owe its green light to *Star Wars'* success? Without a doubt. But riding the wave of a popular trend—and exploiting genres and formulas which have recently proven successful—is a long-standing Hollywood tradition which is practiced even today. There's a long road between existing because another property proved successful, and actively ripping off that property.

ALEX HYDE-WHITE

Battlestar Galactica was my entry into TV in Hollywood. Like many of my generation, *Star Wars* was the catalyst. After numerous enthralled viewings on the big screen, I wanted to fly jets in space. And apparently, so did ABC.

TERRENCE MCDONNELL

Not only had I seen *Star Wars* a day or two before it opened but I had sunk a ton of money into 20th Century Fox stock based on the movie and it like tripled. I saw it at the Academy of Motion Picture Arts and Sciences building on Wilshire Boulevard and, like everyone else, I'll never forget seeing that ship coming over your head and it didn't stop and everybody went out of their minds.

Back then it was all doctor shows and a Western or two. It was just by the numbers. And then there was this weird space show they didn't know what to do with it. When we went off the air we were twenty-fifth in the ratings. They would kill to have that kind of number right now.

Of particular interest to Larson was the opportunity science fiction provided to explore theological and theoretical themes not possible in more earthbound programming. In the mid-seventies, long before the Kardashian daughters were even a glimmer in their parents' eyes, pop culture was fixated on astrology, the Bermuda Triangle (to wit: NBC's short-lived *Fantastic Journey*), and Erich von Däniken's *Chariots of the Gods,* first published in 1968, in which the author postulates that ancient astronauts (a.k.a. aliens) helped forge the great civilizations of the globe.

One of the more visually intriguing examples of this exploration is *Galactica*'s use of Egyptian symbols, such as in the helmets and costumes, to suggest a link between the citizens of the Twelve Colonies of Man and ancient civilizations of Earth as well as the signs of the zodiac. Larson was fascinated by the idea of an advanced civilization settling on Earth and leaving its influence, in the form of the pyramids, on developing civilizations. He married this to the tenets of his Mormon faith, creating such concepts as the Quorum of the Twelve, part of the Church of Jesus Christ of Latter-day Saints.

GLEN A. LARSON

It's fun stuff theoretically and philosophically to explore some of these themes. I actually used to sit with who I consider to be one of the great minds behind *Star Trek,* Gene Coon. Gene was a mentor of mine who brought me into television. He would sit with me at lunch and we would explore thematic issues about the Athenians and the Phoenicians and all kinds of migratory patterns of humans on Earth. We would talk about some of the theological things that the Mormons believed; that the Tribes of Israel scattered and many wound up in Central and South America with the pyramid influence. There's a kind of interesting contamination from what we perceive as the old world to the new.

DAVID LARSON

Even today, very few people are aware of some of the references to Mormonism in *Galactica*. He drew from some of the names, but they're not religious. The religion has been stripped away. You'd have to be pretty high up in the church to know about Kolob. The Council of Twelve is a very different thing in the Mormon church than it is in *Galactica*, but that's what he knew, and that's what made it so special and so different. Even today it's a very esoteric thing. A lot of people like it for that reason. They like that he infused his own beliefs. Nowadays everything has to be sanitized, cleaned up, focus-grouped to death. It's the corporate nature of entertainment these days.

GLEN A. LARSON

I also thought it would be great fun for all of the people who live and die and won't get out of the bed in the morning until they read their horoscopes. I thought they would have great fun in giving greater credibility to astrology and letting the mythology of the zodiac like the Picons and the Virgons spring from something far more tangible; that perhaps the origins of some of these things really precede these beliefs. What I was laying was the groundwork for further exploration of those themes and letting people's beliefs take a new form. Instead of nailing everything down, you just open up areas and discuss them in the genesis of these people that ultimately genetically wound up here.

RICHARD HATCH
(actor, "Captain Apollo")

Television back then was still into clichés of good and bad. It was only later that we began to find a hero can have a dark side. Obviously, *Battlestar* was a merging of a lot of Mormonism and a smattering of other religions.

GLEN A. LARSON

It really just comes from personal belief. Religion has played an important part of just about every tribe on this planet in one form or another. There are some wonderful books out like Graham Hancock's *Fingerprints of the Gods*. Every one of the ancient civilizations, and we mentioned the Egyptians, the Toltecs, and the Mayans and the others, had an incredible knowledge of the galaxies and the constellations and of mathematics, and there is no evidence that any of those societies developed that information on their own.

For me, the personal joy of this particular series was that we could explore the fact that there are far greater powers in the universe than we know. There is a passage in the Bible about Ezekiel, who saw a wheel way up in the middle of the air. A NASA engineer did an analysis of it and said he saw a spaceship because based on his analysis that ship would fly today. So all of those various underpinnings worked through my mind and made it fun to explore some of those theories. Not necessarily coming close to accuracy—but, at least, leaving that one element open, because the greatest scientists who ever lived, including Wernher von Braun and Albert Einstein, all believed in a god or something much stronger and more powerful than any of us.

JEAN-PIERRE DORLEAC
(costume designer, *Battlestar Galactica*)

The concept for *Battlestar Galactica* was all on the page; there was no question about it. Glen had originally conceived of the thirteen lost colonies as being Earth people. Since our projections of the earliest people on Earth were the Phoenicians and the Egyptians, we decided to take elements a step in a different direction and use them in connection with all the [Colonial] costumes. All the yokes on the uniforms were cut to look like the Egyptian neckpieces worn by the pharaohs. The helmets were specifically designed to look like the pharaoh's head covering. All of this was done very intentionally, but it was done in a stylized version of how the actual things looked.

ROB KLEIN
(*Battlestar Galactica* archivist)

I loved his work, but always thought the Colonial Warrior suit was literally pinched right out of a French comic book.

In original discussions, ABC programming executive Fred Silverman envisioned *Battlestar Galactica* being produced as a seven-hour miniseries encompassing the three-hour pilot followed by a string of two-hour episodes ("Lost Planet of the Gods" and "Gun on Ice Planet Zero") to be broadcast as special-event programming during sweeps, given the huge success the network had experienced with miniseries event programming such as *Rich Man, Poor Man* and the massive ratings juggernaut *Roots*.

SCOTT MANTZ

Originally, the plan was for them to do a series of TV movies. Now, once they went into series, they were always catching up, and the writing of the show suffered. They were basically giving wet prints to the network, because they were editing and scoring up to the last minute.

GLEN A. LARSON

That was one of the things [ABC president] Fred Silverman wanted to do, and he may have been right, because then we could have taken a lot of time on each one and just hand-built each one to some extent. We almost tried that in the first few episodes, because we did a couple of two-hour variations and I think they were some of our best shows.

STEVEN SIMAK

Although seemingly cashing in on the *Star Wars* space-combat formula, the premise for the series owes as much to television classics such as *Wagon Train* and *The Fugitive*—fleeing the destruction of their civilization by the Cylons, the battlestar *Galactica* leads a ragtag fleet of civilian ships on a journey to find a new home: Earth.

SCOTT MANTZ

Battlestar Galactica was different from *Star Wars*, because *Galactica* was on every week, every Sunday on ABC, and that repeat, that constant exposure to *Galactica*, endeared me more to *Galactica* than to *Star Wars*, because I was getting new stories every week. I didn't have to wait three years for a new episode of *Battlestar Galactica*.

RONALD D. MOORE
(cocreator/executive producer, *Battlestar Galactica* [2004])

[The 1978] *Battlestar Galactica* was the return of science fiction to prime-time television. I'd never witnessed that. To me, science fiction was something that only existed on those sort of five-day-a-week strip syndication shows like *Lost in Space* or *Star Trek*. There was nothing in the prime-time schedule that went there. So, when *Galactica* came around it was like, "Wow! This is a huge opportunity. This is a big deal. It's science fiction on a major network." I thought this would be sort of a new era of sci-fi making it into the mainstream because of the success of *Star Wars*.

2.
CAST OFF

"I'm designated a socialator. It's an honorable profession; it's had the blessings of the elders for four thousand yahrens."

With effects and set construction already under way on the three-hour movie of the week, "Saga of a Star World," Larson proceeded on the difficult task of casting the series. With an immense group of leads and supporting characters, it would be a long and arduous process that took many months, with casting continuing well into production on the premiere. The process was made even more challenging by the many parties involved in the decision making: Larson, of course, but also the executives at ABC as well as at the studio, Universal, whose head of casting, Mark Malis, was charged with assembling the interstellar ensemble.

In addition to the names most strongly associated with the series, *Galactica* is known, though less well, for the many now-familiar faces in its supporting roles, including a young Ed Begley, Jr., as Greenbean; *Magnum, P.I.*'s Larry Manetti as Giles; *The Next Generation*'s Q, John de Lancie, in a small role in "Experiment in Terra"; and the debut of Dennis Haysbert, who would later go on to play the president of the United States in *24*, as a nameless Cylon Centurion (as well as the Imperious Leader in *Galactica 1980*). And, of course, "Jessie's Girl" crooner, Rick Springfield, as Apollo's ill-fated brother, Zac.

GLEN A. LARSON
(creator/executive producer, *Battlestar Galactica*)

The casting process was like any process. It was like pulling teeth. Casting is subjective, because no one likes your choices and you don't like anyone else's choices, so it was very difficult.

STEVEN SIMAK
(journalist, *Battlestar Galactica* historian)

In an attempt to humanize the series, Larson elected to define the core group of characters as a family. He hoped that such an approach would provide greater opportunity to explore dramatic interpersonal relationships, while at the same time broadening the appeal of the series to a mainstream audience. In the case of Adama, Lorne Greene was a choice on which both he and the network could readily agree. Famous for his performance as Ben Cartwright on *Bonanza,* Greene's image as the classic patriarch seemed an ideal match.

GLEN A. LARSON

Lorne Greene was one of the easy ones. Having been a member of one of the biggest successes in the history of television, he was one everyone could agree on rather easily. In retrospect, he might not have been the best choice, because it makes people think immediately of *Bonanza,* but we did want a certain amount of warmth in there, so that was considered a good choice and it didn't come up for a lot of argument. The toughest thing was to find our fresh young guys.

For legions of televisions fans, Lorne Greene's fourteen-year portrayal of Ben Cartwright on *Bonanza* made him the archetypal father figure. Bitten by the acting bug at age sixteen, Canadian-born Greene studied at Queen's University before moving to New York, where he received a fellowship to study with Sanford Meisner and Martha Graham at the Neighborhood Playhouse. Two years later he returned to Canada to accept a job as a newscaster with the Canadian Broadcasting Corporation. After serving in World War II, Greene returned to Toronto, where he continued his radio work and founded the Academy of Radio Arts. Many point to Greene's years in radio as the foundation for his now-legendary speaking voice. Greene's film credits include *The Silver Chalice, Peyton Place, Autumn Leaves, The Gift of Love,* and *The Trap.* The actor was sixty-three when he accepted the role of Adama, for which he was perfectly cast.

TERRENCE MCDONNELL
(story editor, *Battlestar Galactica*)

Edward R. Murrow was the voice of America in World War II. Lorne was the Edward R. Murrow of Canada. He did the war broadcast. He also invented the backward clock that everybody uses in radio because he needed to know when to end his broadcast.

GLEN A. LARSON

People have always made a big deal out of the fact that it was Lorne Greene and they asked if we were trying to do *Bonanza*. Well, not really, but there's a show that even though it was a Western it really just dealt with human dilemmas from week to week. So one of the things we wanted to do was start pushing these people into situations where the people become important to us. Their existence becomes important and then the shows are playing on a human level or a heart level that transcends science fiction.

ALAN J. LEVI

I hadn't been in Hollywood too long and my folks, who were at the very first filming that I ever did in my life, when I was fifteen in St. Louis, had never been out to Hollywood, so when I said to Glen [Larson] I can't take over the pilot because my folks are due to come out here next week and I don't want anything to interrupt their visit, he gave me his limo and a driver and hosted them for an entire week. So I did the show and when we were in the launch bay, there were all these guys ready to climb into their ships and this was the first day my folks arrived in Glen's limo.

I was up on a crane and we had a crew of forty or fifty and another forty or fifty cast members. Everybody was getting in their fighters and I'm about to call "Action" when the door opens to our stage and in walked my mom and my dad. I called "Cut" and everybody takes ten. I got down and walked over and gave my mom and dad a hug and a kiss and Lorne Greene walked over, and he said, "I've got to meet the parents of the guy who just shut down an eighty-five-person crew for fifteen minutes to come say hello." He and my dad became friends for the whole week and it was great. Every moment that he wasn't on camera he spent sitting with my folks. He was that kind of gentleman.

TERRENCE MCDONNELL

My dad loved *Bonanza,* and he was in charge of the TV, so we watched it on Sunday nights. I remember with Lorne the first time we were introduced to him we were down on the "Fire in Space" set the day they were doing all the stunts and somebody said, "Have you met Lorne?" Jim [Carlson] and I said, "No." So they walked us over to him and he was very nice and tall. So, he looks at us after we're introduced and there was a lull onstage, they were resetting for something, and he says, "You don't have to give me *every* line, but what I do has to be imporrrrtant." And it was this long dragged-out "imporrrrrtant." Every time we'd go down to the set, which wasn't that often, and we saw Lorne sort of coming our direction, we'd get out of there. Just because we didn't want to get sucked into we're not giving him important lines.

I think it was when we were doing "Murder on the Rising Star," we were on a tight deadline, we're crunched, all of a sudden we look up and Lorne is in our office. I don't know what he was doing there. It was like two hours. He sat down and he started talking. And Lorne talked and talked and talked. If we had been at a cocktail party it would have been wonderful. And Jim is saying that's fantastic, now we just have to get to this act. And Lorne was oblivious to it. He just kept talking and talking. It was like, "My God, how are we going to finish this?" But apparently the actors adored him.

RICHARD HATCH
(actor, "Captain Apollo")

I was really thrown by his voice. It's like going to see James Earl Jones until you realize that, yes he's got this magnificent voice but he's just a human being behind it and in this case he's a very genuinely warm, loving, caring, down-to-earth human being who is actually very easy to talk to. I think that was the first thing that surprised me; after a few hours of kind of watching my manners, I realized that he was very much a very normal guy. He really was very personable.

He came to a Christmas party of mine and sat in the corner and I swear that everyone who came to my party, including most of my family, all spent time sitting in the seat next to him talking with him not just out of courtesy, but for hours. He would talk to everybody and anybody and that was the way he was. He was like a second father to me, and I felt genuine warmth and love for him. His death was very hard and very surprising. He looked like one of those men who would go on forever.

HERBERT JEFFERSON, JR.
(actor, "Lieutenant Boomer")

Lorne is still in my heart. He just did the perennial patriarch; that combination of strength and tenderness that he had as a human being always came through in his work. That is who Commander Adama was, and there will never be a replacement for him.

RICHARD HATCH

We always respond to family. The camaraderie, the bonding, the love, and also the infighting that goes on among family members. It always makes for an intriguing relationship, because that's where we all come from and that's what we all understand.

LORNE GREEN
(actor, "Commander Adama")

This was the first science fiction story I'd ever done. When I read the script, my first reaction was, "Wild." Then I thought, "But how in heaven's name are they going to bring it off?"

ROD HOLCOMB
(director, "The Man with Nine Lives")

He was like one of the very first real TV legends on *Bonanza*. Now, I've worked with a lot of Jack Klugman–type people, but they weren't necessarily known as television monsters, but Lorne was. A little pompous, sometimes, but I think it was just his voice and his presence. If you didn't recognize him for who he was, as that person, you would think he was trying to put on airs, but he was never doing that. He was always a good guy who knew he knew a lot more than you did—and he did.

TERRY CARTER
(actor, "Commander Tigh")

One of the nicest people I have ever met. A really warm individual, very professional actor, full of humor, very funny man. Even when we were not on the set or even in between takes, he was a very relaxed fellow. I think everybody loved him. He had a paternal quality. And he exuded a warmth and professionalism and set a high mark for everybody. He was a wonderful man.

HERBERT JEFFERSON, JR.

If you knew him, if you worked with him, he was very much like the man you grew to love in *Bonanza*. We all kind of gravitated to him. It was a chaotic work situation with fourteen-hour days, sometimes five, six, seven days a week. And we were all in orbit around Lorne, he kept us all chill. He was Poppa. I'm sure anyone who worked on the original show has a great admiration for Lorne Greene; he was sort of like an adopted uncle to you.

He was also a great chess player. We had an ongoing chess game on the set of *Battlestar Galactica*; we had a board and set it up on an apple box. I'd make one move, and maybe sometime during the day he'd come by and make his move. And the crew knew you were never to touch that board. We would leave the board sitting there all night and we'd come back and all the pieces were there.

SARAH RUSH
(actress, "Flight Officer Rigel")

We once went to lunch in our space suits for my birthday. We went to what became the Universal CityWalk area. Nowadays it's very big. It was smaller back then. I think there was only one restaurant. It was really special. I remember thinking, "This is a great birthday!" Lorne Greene paid for it.

LAURETTE SPANG
(actress, "Cassiopeia")

In the beginning, I was very awed by him because he was Ben Cartwright and that's all I could think of, but he was just so kind and his wife and daughter, Gillian, they just sort of took me under their wing. At one point, there was a People's Choice Awards show and they had only invited Dirk and Richard and, I think, Maren [Jensen] to go and Lorne came up to me—and his wife couldn't go—and he said, "Why don't you come up to my house and go with me in my car and you can sit with me?" It was so sweet. He knew I felt bad and so I went with him and we shared a car on the way over there and he was just such a gentleman. He was funny, he told the best jokes, and his family had the cast over a few times. He was a special favorite.

ALEX HYDE-WHITE
(actor, "Cadet Bow")

I remember Lorne had a nice big Christmas party for us at his house in Mandeville Canyon. That was fun.

HERBERT JEFFERSON, JR.

Lorne and I became very good friends and we spent a lot of time up at his house and participating with him and his wife in strategic war games, since she was a strategic analyst. I have lots of interest in world politics, and it was quite a blow and a loss for me when we lost Lorne.

LAURETTE SPANG

Right after I did *Galactica,* Lorne and I did a show in Hawaii together for Aaron Spelling called *Aloha Paradise,* and he played my dad, and Jayne Meadows was my mom. We went over there and it was sort of *The Love Boat* in Hawaii: I had just gotten married to Grant Goodeve in the show, and my parents show up, they've been traveling abroad and they show up on my honeymoon and they're just obnoxious and they want to play bridge, and

Lorne and I had great fun because he was so funny. It was a whole different side of him.

Unfortunately, I didn't get to see him the last couple of years, but I sent him a long letter when he was in the hospital and told him what he meant to me and how much at that time in my life he was a real grounding type of person. That he had this great family life and he was still in the business and I am very blessed with that now. I've got a wonderful family and not too long after *Galactica* I walked away from Hollywood.

With the casting of the paterfamilias of the *Galactica* family, on screen and off, an easy call and a triumph for the fledgling series, the casting of Adama's son, Apollo (originally called Skylar, but changed owing to its similarities to Skywalker), would prove more challenging. However, it found the ideal Colonial Warrior in the guise of the late Richard Hatch.

After growing up in Santa Monica, California, Hatch began his professional acting career on the East Coast. Not unlike the Colonial fleet, he and a group of actors traveled across the country in search of fame and fortune. Arriving in New York, they formed a repertory company in a rented ballet studio on Eighth Avenue and Fifty-fourth Street. The group eventually disbanded, but Hatch remained in New York and in 1969 won the role of Philip Brent on the soap opera *All My Children*.

After two and a half years on the show, Hatch went on to do an off-Broadway play, *Love Me, Love My Children*, which won an Obie Award in 1972. Returning to Hollywood, the actor worked as a guest star in episodes of series like *Hawaii Five-O*, *The Rookies*, *The Waltons*, *Cannon*, *Kung Fu*, and *Barnaby Jones*. One of his big breaks came in 1976, when he was offered the opportunity to replace the departing Michael Douglas in *The Streets of San Francisco*. The actor's other credits include the starring role in the Chicago stage play *P.S. Your Cat Is Dead*, and *Deadman's Curve*, about the rock artists Jan and Dean.

RICHARD HATCH

Science fiction has always had something for everyone. I don't care who you are, how old you are, or what nationality, science fiction bridges all those gaps. It bridges the gender gap and addresses issues that most television shows are afraid to tackle. Science fiction gets away with it because it's put out of context in a futuristic setting, so it's not so threatening. Yet the information that's brought forth is very inspiring and consciousness-raising. It really helps people to realize how to get along with one another and that we are all human beings. Science fiction contains some of the most incredible concepts and yet brings a tremendous humanity to it.

GLEN A. LARSON

Richard was one of the choices that came down from the network that I happened to agree with. We didn't agree on a lot of different people. When [casting director] Pam Dixon came up with Richard, I thought he was a good choice. I thought he was interesting.

RICHARD HATCH

I have to tell you, being as insecure as I was, with low self-esteem, whenever I had to play a role that was more heroic or a character that was confident and together it was very hard for me because I felt totally unconfident. I had no confidence as a person. I had no security as a human being, so it was a major challenge for me to be able to dig inside myself and find a way to connect to a part of myself where I could find that sense of strength and confidence to play any role that had those qualities, and obviously Captain Apollo had those qualities.

Right before getting cast I had a role in a play, *Class of '65,* where I played a coach. It was very much a similar character. He was very confident and he was wonderful with people and he was an inspired leader and he worked with this young kid to help him bring out his talent. I had played that role and basically within that time frame they were casting for Captain Apollo and I had turned down the initial reading for Apollo because I had loved *Star Wars* so much. I was very idealistic and I had seen television so many times rip off movies and do second-rate versions of successful movies. And not knowing that much about *Galactica* I just had the sense that they were going to do the same thing.

Usually when they do sci-fi I was disappointed, and I will say that most sci-fi fans all over the world are disappointed with most sci-fi movies, because they are done in a cheesy way, and so I basically turned down the reading. About six months later, after every actor in Hollywood had gone out for the audition, they were still searching for the perfect actor, and as we all know when there is a very big expensive project they are looking for perfection and nobody is perfect. So I think it was about two days or a week before shooting, something like that, and they had not cast Apollo. At that time, I was called Skylar. They changed that to Apollo about three or four days into the shoot.

GLEN A. LARSON

We were looking for sort of the traditional leading man, who was positive and straight heroic as opposed to being an antihero. Richard fit that mold very well.

Looking for leading men is a tricky thing. I have been very fortunate in picking some guys who did it, from Selleck to Hasselhoff to Don Johnson, and you pick them for different reasons. In this case, we were looking for the straight hero.

RICHARD HATCH

They were down to the wire getting ready to film and I guess someone saw my *Class of '65*, where I played the coach, and that was a difficult role for me because again I had to play a character that I felt so distanced from. I didn't feel confident, I didn't feel together, and, yes, those characters were in me but I hadn't yet really forged them or developed them as a human being. That's what I lacked in acting, because it forced me to deal with areas inside of myself that I was uncomfortable with.

They saw the *Class of '65*, and that very character that I forged was Apollo. After seeing *Class of '65*, Glen took me out to dinner and offered me the role.

GLEN A. LARSON

I don't think Richard [screen] tested at all, because that suggestion came from ABC, and when the network makes the suggestion, in many cases, you don't have to test because they're saying they already like him, whereas if we make the suggestion sometimes we have to test to prove our point. These days you do a lot more testing of everyone, since there's just a lot more insecurity.

RICHARD HATCH

Glen took me out to one of the nicest French restaurants [in town], and I was a starving actor, so why not? He picked me up in this big black limousine that Glen is famous for and took me to this wonderful restaurant. We had a great dinner, he got me drunk and told me what the show was going to be about. I remember a couple of lines he used. I basically was not sure I wanted to do it, but he said there is a lot of action but it's about family; it's about characters; it's about people. He said two things: he mentioned *Wagon Train,* an epic Western which blended action and character and that's perfect for an action piece to have.

Then he mentioned *Family,* which was a very highly esteemed show at the time, and that it was a combination of those two kinds of shows. Everybody loved *Family* and I loved the personal character stories they had on that show and when he said *Family,* I thought if they are going to have these types of relationships and in-depth profound connections, people-to-people-type stuff, that it was something I would like to do.

In fact, I actually think that for a sci-fi program it was a wonderful balance of action and character and plot, which was very rare, and that was one of the things that made *Battlestar* so special. I loved sci-fi, but as an actor I wanted something that would really challenge me, and I hate to say it but when they write sci-fi most of the time they don't write challenging characters. But when I got the script and I looked at the imagery, the pictures from Ralph McQuarrie blew me away—the little child in me was looking at this incredible vision being laid out. Having seen *Star Wars* and seeing these pictures and reading it led me to believe that the character was going to have depth and heart and there was going to be more going on there than just the cliché superhero.

So Glen told me the story and he showed me the script. The artwork by Ralph McQuarrie was stunning, and the vision that was laid out in that piece was absolutely extraordinary. I don't know how anyone could turn that down. I was wide-eyed. I was very much into science fiction actually as a kid, so I fell in love with it and said yes. Twenty-four hours later I was on the set filming and not knowing any of my lines.

GLEN A. LARSON

If Clark Gable was a leading man, as opposed to an Errol Flynn, who had more of an edge to him, Starbuck was the one that was supposed to have the pixie quality, a little more off-center, and Apollo was supposed to be the straighter, more all-American—or in this case, all-*Galactica*—kind of straight character.

In the case of Starbuck, a number of actors, including Don Johnson (soon to be Sonny Crockett of *Miami Vice* fame) and Barry Van Dyke, who would later be cast as Dillon in *Galactica 1980,* auditioned for the role. Growing up in White Sulphur Springs, Montana, Dirk Benedict had a very traditional upbringing. He attended Whitman College, in Walla Walla, Washington, where on a dare he tried out for the college production of *Showboat.* To his surprise, he was cast in a starring role, and as a result of the experience decided to change his major to drama. After college, Benedict went to Detroit to study with John Fernald, formerly head of the Royal Academy of Dramatic Art, in London, and went on to perform in repertory companies in Seattle, Washington, and Ann Arbor, Michigan, as well as doing summer stock. While on a trip to New York he auditioned for the Broadway play *Abelard and Heloise* with Diana Rigg and got the part. Benedict later replaced Keir Dullea as Gloria Swanson's son in the Broadway hit *Butterflies Are Free.* Film and television roles soon followed. The actor's film credits include *Georgia, Georgia; Sssssss;* the short-lived television series *Chopper One;* guest spots on *Hawaii Five-O;* and, following his starring role on *Battlestar Galactica,* five years on *The A-Team,* in which he, in a moment of meta hilarity, amusingly does a double take as a Cylon walks obliviously past him in the hit NBC series' opening credits.

DIRK BENEDICT
(actor, "Lieutenant Starbuck")

At that time I was kind of making a comeback. I had had a career earlier in this town but I was a stage actor from New York and before that I was in repertory theaters in Seattle and Michigan, so I had classical training. My dream was to be a stage actor and nothing more. Through a set of so-called coincidences I ended up in Hollywood doing a couple of films and series. Then I had cancer in 1975 and that went away for a couple of years so when I came back, of course, I did a couple of jobs and then *Battlestar Galactica.*

Although *Galactica* seemed to be my first real visible show, I had actually done a series before that and several films.

GLEN A. LARSON

I liked Dirk. I had always felt Dirk was a real natural for this. I was lobbying pretty heavily for him.

DIRK BENEDICT

It was a huge struggle with ABC, who did not want me in the show. So that went on literally for months.

GLEN A. LARSON

I tested a few other people that were interesting. The one that would probably be the most noteworthy was Don Johnson. He actually did a very good job, and from that point on I knew I wanted him in a series and kept trying to cast him. People around me eventually of course did, too. My protégé eventually put him in *Miami Vice*. I also tested him for *Knight Rider*.

DIRK BENEDICT

I had done a movie at Universal for Richard Zanuck, the movie about a kid that's turned into a snake. I had starred on Broadway, and when I recovered from cancer I came back and did a couple of episodes of *Charlie's Angels* and another show, where I met Glen Larson and found out he had me in mind for this part all along.

GLEN A. LARSON

I tested him twice and I didn't get it off the first one so I went back and did another version.

DIRK BENEDICT

That went on for months, and finally they had already started filming for four or five days, before ABC finally gave in and cast me in the show. I was forced to do a lot of screen tests, because they basically didn't want me because they wanted another actor who had an agent who they had a deal with. It's all about business and relationships, but Universal wanted me, and thanks to Frank Price, who was the head of Universal Television at the time, and Glen Larson, they were forced into giving in.

Their final reason for not wanting me was that I wasn't sexy enough. So that was the final reason that they gave and refused to hire me but they went ahead and started principal photography and then Universal told ABC that if you don't hire this actor we will stop shooting. I think that was one of the reasons that created bad feelings between ABC and Universal over that show. There were other things, but that was certainly one of them. ABC, at the time, was quite arrogant. They were the number-one network and I think that was one of the reasons they canceled us the next year.

DAVID LARSON
(son of Glen Larson)

Cigar-smoking ladies' man. Sure he had his issues, but he's the kind of guy every young man wants to be, right? Apollo had the weight of the world on his shoulders.

We all wanted to be Starbuck. Apollo was kind of a drip. Yeah, even today I wouldn't want to be Apollo. I don't want that responsibility. I'd rather be Starbuck.

SCOTT MANTZ
(film critic, *Access Hollywood*)

When I was watching *Star Wars,* my favorite character was Han Solo. Luke was a good guy, but he was kind of a wimp. Han Solo was the rogue and the pirate, he could fend for himself. Now, over the years, so many people have compared Starbuck to Han Solo. Starbuck wasn't a pirate. He was a loner. He was a womanizer. He was definitely a ladies' man. He was very confident. When I was a kid, I wanted to be Starbuck, but I was really Apollo.

They were a great team. Dirk Benedict and Richard Hatch had great chemistry together. Apollo was noble and honest. He was sincere. He was a good guy. Starbuck, his heart was in the right place, but he tried to hide his feelings, pass off like he didn't care. He was less Han Solo than he was Rick Blaine from *Casablanca*.

And he had a nice little love triangle going on with Maren Jensen, as Athena, and Cassiopeia, Laurette Spang. I remember that scene in the launch tube between Starbuck and Cassiopeia, they're fooling around and Athena's checking the monitor and she sees them in the launch tube and puts the steam on. He gets a little steam burn before they have to go into the Nova of Madagon.

LAURETTE SPANG

The network got overly sensitive about it, because Dirk and I had that scene in the launch tube and he had his shirt off and they flipped out about that. I was in Michigan visiting my family and I had to fly back to reshoot that scene with his shirt on. It was the exact same scene with his shirt on.

Dirk and I always had a very kidding relationship. He was always into health foods and I would always tease him about the birdseed he would eat and all that. I teased him about his dating life and he did the same with me. That was just sort of the relationship we had. It was easy.

DIRK BENEDICT

I modeled Starbuck on James Garner's *Maverick*. It was almost mimicry, but a lot of his attitude about situations, certainly in the card games, the reluctance to put himself in danger was very unusual to see. I was playing a hero but he wasn't crazy about getting into his fighter plane and going out and getting killed. He would rather, if he could, talk his way out of it and stay home and play cards or have a meal with an attractive girl. This was the hero, but it was a very unheroic thing, and this was 1978, and there hadn't been a lot of that. That was something that I added, him sort of shifting his feet and shuffling and that attitude. He wanted to have a good time, he wanted to party, but when he got into the situation he rose to the occasion.

I would have liked to have played Starbuck for another three or four years. It was a wonderful character. I would have paid them to have been part of that experience and it was one of the greatest experiences I ever had.

The casting of the stentorian Terry Carter as the ship's second-in-command, Commander Tigh—a part originally written for a Caucasian actor—helped make *Galactica* an early champion of diversity on television. Carter, born in Brooklyn, New York, attended St. John's University with hopes of becoming an attorney. Acting, however, spoke to him, and he joined the noted off-Broadway repertory company at the Greenwich Mews Theater in Greenwich Village. In 1954 he received his first leading role, opposite Eartha Kitt in *Mrs. Patterson*.

Carter began commuting between New York and California and made appearances on such television programs as *Combat, Breaking Point*, and *Dr. Kildare*.

TERRY CARTER

I was flying back and forth, like most New York actors were in the early sixties. I was living in New York but would be cast in California. Hollywood perceived that New York actors had theater training, so they wanted to get them out there.

In 1965 Carter decided to leave the industry and accept the challenge of newscasting at Boston's WBZ, where he was the first African-American news anchor in New England. He later returned to Hollywood, where a chance encounter at the Universal commissary led to him being cast in the role of Sergeant Joe Broadhurst in *McCloud*.

TERRY CARTER

I happened to be sitting there when the head of casting came through, and he knew me because I had done work through him before. He didn't know I was in town, and the same day my agent got a call and that was about *McCloud*. I don't think it would have happened had I not been sitting in that place at that particular time. I was offered roles in two other series as well, and the only reason I chose *McCloud* was because of Dennis Weaver. He, at the time, was one of my favorite actors. I had seen a lot of his work, including what he did for Orson Welles in *Touch of Evil*, and just the idea of working with Dennis Weaver was more interesting to me than the other stuff. As it turned out, I put my money on the right horse. I had worked for the producers, Leslie Stevens and Glen Larson, because I was on *McCloud* for seven years and both of them had been associated with that show.

What happened is when *McCloud* finished, they were putting together *Battlestar Galactica* and they thought of me in the role of Lieutenant Boomer. I think it was a mistake. Because Lieutenant Boomer is a kind of gung-ho, young fighter pilot and I was a little more mature. I'd been in the business for twenty-odd years or something like that. I was over fifty, but who's counting? So it was okay with me, I was willing to play it. But as luck would have it, I went roller-skating with my daughter, who was six years old at the time. We went out to Venice Beach, and as we were leaving the area, the sidewalk where we were walking was broken and there were holes in the sidewalk. I remember the last thing I said was, "Look out for the holes in the sidewalk," and the next thing I know, this hole reached up and grabbed my skate. I had shoe skates on and I lost my balance. I went over and my foot stayed in the same place. It broke my ankle, and it was the most painful thing I have ever experienced. I had to be carried off and put in a splint. So naturally I called my agent and I said, Jack, this is what happened, and he said, "What the hell are we going to tell the *Battlestar Galactica* people?"

HERBERT JEFFERSON, JR.

At the time *Battlestar Galactica* was being cast I was doing a play, an award-winning play by David Rabe called *Streamers*. Terry Carter had been set to play Boomer on *Galactica* and he had a great relationship with Glen because of his involvement with *McCloud* playing Sergeant Broadhurst. He took a bad turn, fell down and broke his ankle, which immediately took the role away from him.

TERRY CARTER

Well, fortunately for me they were still writing, and writing, and rewriting, and planning, and postponing the start date of the show. And we were just hoping that maybe my leg would heal. So they finally did call me for the show and I had designed with my agent what he was going to say. They said, "We're starting on Wednesday and we need Terry at seven o'clock Wednesday morning." And he said, "You know what, I just found out that Terry broke his leg," and they hit the roof! They said, "Why the hell didn't you tell us?" and he said, "I didn't know, I just found out myself." So there I was without a job and I just saw that the boat was leaving without me. And Leslie Stevens and Glen Larson got the idea: "Hey, what about Terry for Colonel Tigh?"

GLEN A. LARSON

I'd always enjoyed working with him, he's a very strong guy. Terry comes off without any ethnic baggage and I am not specifically talking black, I am talking anything that is regional, because we don't have a South in space. One of the problems with Donny Johnson's test is that he had quite an accent in it. It was very down-home and I had a little trouble with the idea that you're going to have someone in the middle of the *Galactica* fleet from Caprica or someplace with a Southern accent. It just contaminated us, and that was a factor in Terry's casting along with his strength. His accent is very neutral, because in radio you could never have an accent.

With Carter now aboard as Colonel Tigh (and wearing a cast underneath his uniform throughout the duration of filming the three-hour premiere), it fell to veteran actor Herbert Jefferson, Jr., to assume the role of Lieutenant Boomer, for which he was cast after Terry Carter was sidelined by his injury.

HERBERT JEFFERSON, JR.

I auditioned for my role in Century City at ABC's old headquarters along with about ten, twelve, or maybe fifteen other people. They were in the middle of shooting the series already and they were casting it as they went along. And out of that ten or fifteen people, I must have fit the boots or something. I was still in the play, so in the beginning of shooting *Galactica* it was in my contract that I had to be released by six o'clock so that I could leave the set, go back to Westwood, and perform in *Streamers*. It's an actor's dream to be working two jobs! I loved it.

The actor came to *Galactica* after ten years in theater, film, and television. He attended Rutgers University before going to study drama at the Actors Studio and the American Academy of Dramatic Arts. An accomplished stage actor, Jefferson's theater credits include *Electra*, Howard Sackler's *The Great White Hope*, *No Place to Be Somebody*, *The Dream on Monkey Mountain*, and *Murderous Angels*, the play about the deaths of Patrice Lumumba and Dag Hammarskjöld. His motion picture credits include *Detroit 9000, Black Gunn*, and *The Slams*. Jefferson's many appearances on television include such programs as *Rich Man, Poor Man, McCloud, Columbo, The Streets of San Francisco*, and *Mission: Impossible*.

HERBERT JEFFERSON, JR.

I was very fortunate that for the first week or two of shooting, the material I was given to do was for the most part action shots and filler, such as getting into the cockpit. So I had time to study Boomer and ask the writers how they perceived this character. They didn't spring the deepest emotional scenes on me the very first days. I was pretty much given free rein—of course, within the limitations of what the writers, directors, and producers wanted.

They did not even have the uniform cut at the time I was hired. They had the readings and the meetings and the decision was made. We all waited, and I was asked to step inside and spoke to casting executives and immediately was sent out to Universal wardrobe. At the time they only had the boots and the pants to fit me. So in the scene that we were shooting late that afternoon in the pilot, which was the pyramid game, I had no tunic.

We filmed the scene and they were cutting my tunic, so I did the scene with a towel around my neck. It wasn't because of style, it was because there wasn't anything to fit me. As far as Sergeant Jolly, Tony [Swartz] was a big fellow. There were no pants or a tunic for him either, certainly not for a man of his size, so he did the first day of shooting with a towel wrapped around his waist.

Boomer, like Terry Carter's Tigh, was an African-American character in a position of authority aboard the battlestar *Galactica*, a rarity in late-seventies television.

HERBERT JEFFERSON, JR.

That was another reason I was very, very happy and proud to be part of the project: because none of those characters were written as "black" characters. They were characters who were qualified and had a particular kind of expertise and attitude about their jobs as officers and happened to be black.

I think it was progressive for its time. I was honored with a nomination as Best Actor by the NAACP Image Awards. I lost out to Michael Jackson, but I was proud to be nominated.

Of all the characters in *Battlestar Galactica,* Laurette Spang's Cassiopeia probably saw the greatest change as the series progressed. Originally introduced as a seventh-millennium prostitute, a "socialator," Cassiopeia quickly metastasized into Florence Nightingale when it was decided to sign Spang on as a series regular after the three-hour premiere was shot.

LAURETTE SPANG

It was a guest-star part originally, and I was just like Jane Seymour. I was just going to be there for the pilot, and then they decided they wanted to keep me on. I had done *Streets of San Francisco* and I had played a young girl, the hooker who couldn't do it, so I was sort of the one with the heart of gold. Most of my parts had been the sweet girl next door, so this seemed like it was fun, because we go into space and I always loved science fiction. When I was a kid, I used to read Ray Bradbury and anything I could get my hands on.

The actress, who grew up in Ann Arbor, Michigan, first became interested in a career in acting after taking speech courses in high school. At seventeen, she traveled to New York and later studied at the American Academy of Dramatic Arts. After graduating and performing in summer stock, she decided to move to Los Angeles. Spang received a small role in *Airport '75* and started doing guest appearances on such programs as *Charlie's Angels, The Streets of San Francisco, The Six Million Dollar Man, Happy Days,* and *Lou Grant.* Her other credits include *Short Walk to Daylight* and *Sarah T.: Portrait of a Teenage Alcoholic.* Spang had been under contract to Quinn Martin Productions when she was offered the opportunity to guest-star as Cassiopeia on the three-hour premiere.

LAURETTE SPANG

Universal offered me the part to guest-star in the pilot, and it was originally going to be for the movie, and finally I went to Quinn Martin and he let me go and said, "Sure, go ahead, have a ball." By the time we were finished, they offered me a contract for the series.

SCOTT MANTZ

A socialator is a hooker. I didn't know that as a kid, but when I got older, I certainly did.

GLEN A. LARSON

It was an attempt to try and be a little more sophisticated. Cassiopeia was something like a geisha, in that tradition. It wasn't purely sexual. I don't recall us having any real problems with that, because we never hit that very hard. That was never a centerpiece.

LAURETTE SPANG

The network was not happy about the socialator. Glen had to do some changes, and all of a sudden I went from being a socialator to being a med tech and being able to do heart surgery. We had to make it work, so I had my costumes go from being short with cleavage and all of a sudden my dresses were down to my feet with fur vests and everything up to my neck. It's a little disconcerting, but I think everyone eventually accepted it. I was the nurse with a heart.

DAVID LARSON

I think I may have had a crush on Cassiopeia. I sort of remember Jane Seymour. We went to stay at her house in Bath, England, back when she lived there. Kurt Russell was there with Goldie Hawn, skeet shooting. You can't forget memories like that. Goldie Hawn walking down the hall with a green mud mask on and a robe. That's Private Benjamin walking by!

SCOTT MANTZ

Both of those characters were wasted. When they made Cassiopeia go from being a socialator to a nurse, it kind of took away her edge. It could have been more dynamic with both Athena and her in love with Starbuck, but it was never fully realized.

LAURETTE SPANG

What I wanted to bring to it was a sense of fun. I loved the relationship between Starbuck and Cassiopeia, because I think what came out was how intelligent she was. She knew very well that this was a guy that wanted to be free in one way and the only way she could catch him was to be as smart as he was.

Athena was another vital member of the bridge crew, played by the stunning Maren Jensen. Shortly after appearing in the series, Jensen starred in Wes Craven's *Deadly Blessing* with a young Sharon Stone, and has largely disappeared from public view after reportedly developing Epstein-Barr syndrome, which prompted her retirement from acting. When hired for the series at twenty-one, the former model, who had been featured on the covers of *Cosmopolitan* and *Seventeen*, had the least amount of acting experience of anyone in the cast, having only appeared in college productions and a guest-starring role on *The Hardy Boys/Nancy Drew Mysteries,* another Glen Larson production on ABC.

MAREN JENSEN
(actress, "Athena")

I did absolutely nothing professional, not even the California equivalent of off-off-off-Broadway. No matter what you think you've learned in school, when you face a camera—a real camera—for the first time, it's different. There's no way to teach what I've absorbed simply playing scenes with people like Lorne Greene and Ray Milland.

ALAN J. LEVI

Maren was a very sweet young gal. She was a model and she had never acted before. She was always very receptive and always there. A very pretty gal. Her presence never became a central focus for anybody. It was a minor role to a certain degree, and she never did anything afterward that I know of.

DIRK BENEDICT

They realized that women didn't want to see Starbuck attached to one woman. The intellectuals, the network, all the people who sat there saying, "Well, he's a chauvinist," they wanted him to be married and have a child, I guess, but that was Richard's character.

SARAH RUSH

Maren Jensen was just precious, Anne Lockhart was a doll, and Laurette Spang I adore. I don't think there was any kind of competition in there. It was just lovely and we all got along so great. Only with Jane Seymour there was definitely a little bit of an aloofness there.

There once was a scene where we were all on set—I believe it was the wedding scene. The makeup artist put a little glycerin under her eyes or something. I was standing there and was supposed to do a little weeping or something. Jane said, "Oh, our little actress . . ." It made me feel really small, but it was okay because she's wonderful. So she was a little bit more aloof, but the other girls were just great.

When I was younger I was so very serious and committed. So I came in, I auditioned, and there was Glen Larson and all these people and I had to say something like, "Red alert! Red alert! One hundred microns and closing, ninety-nine microns and closing." I sat in the middle on a chair with everybody around me and I used my fist as a microphone, said my lines and then looked at everybody. They all burst into laughter! I was so serious about it. We laughed and I got the job. It was wonderful and a blessing, even though my role was so small. I wished I could have been around more. I was just twenty-two years old and this show was so fantastic. I got to work with Terry Carter a lot and talked to him about acting. I don't even know if he knows how important he was for me. He was so supportive. It was such a great cast and it was a blessing to be on the show.

Also a significant member of the ensemble was Boxey, the son of Jane Seymour's Serina, who becomes an important part of Apollo's family after the death of his mother. The role was played by a six-year-old Noah Hathaway, who is best known for his starring role in 1984's *The Neverending Story* as Atreyu.

RICHARD HATCH

They weren't so sure they wanted to keep Apollo with a son. I asked if we could, because these shows tended to lean very heavily sometimes on the action and I wanted to be able to play more dramatic scenes that would allow for some sensitivity. I knew that having a child would allow me to play some meaningful dramatic scenes. Glen Larson was very insightful in keeping the child, because it allowed me to bring in a little more of the vulnerable side of my character. Captain Apollo had this stern, strict commanding presence, and I think that child really helped me to also show other dimensions to him.

NOAH HATHAWAY
(actor, "Boxey")

When I was three, I did a Pepsi commercial, which was my first job. I probably did ten to fifteen commercials up until I did *Battlestar*. I screen-tested for the part. It was just between me and one other kid.

RICHARD HATCH

We were a family in space and we didn't make some kid the genius like they did in *Galactica 1980*, which fans hate. We let the kids be kids and they didn't dominate the show.

LAURETTE SPANG

I babysat for Noah. I remember taking him to see *Saturday Night Fever*.

Many years later, the actor visited his TV mom, Jane Seymour, on the set of her hit TV series *Dr. Quinn, Medicine Woman*.

NOAH HATHAWAY

I said, "I had the biggest crush on you; you were so beautiful!" She blushed.

And, of course, equally memorable was Boxey's companion, Muffit II, the daggit, a robotic dog created by Dr. Wilker at the behest of Apollo to replace Boxey's beloved puppy, killed during the Cylon attack on Caprica.

SCOTT MANTZ

When I watch the original "Saga of a Star World," and the Cylons are attacking Caprica, and Boxey is running and Muffit, his daggit, is killed by the building falling on top of him, that scene still upsets me to this day. It's like, you can watch people get killed left and right on Caprica, but that stuff happens to the dog and it's upsetting.

For the mechanical daggit, John Dykstra recruited animal trainer Boone Narr to help bring Muffit to life, using a chimpanzee inside the suit married to the sound design of Peter Berkos.

BOONE NARR
(animal trainer, *Battlestar Galactica*)

Originally they wanted a dog to put in that suit, but we felt that a dog wouldn't have the flexibility to do the stuff we needed to do, and we wanted it to be as comfortable as possible. Besides, the chimp liked dressing up anyway, so it just worked out.

SCOTT MANTZ

This was just a year after they put a man in a little tin can to be R2-D2, but they really went to another level here, putting a monkey in a suit to be a mechanical daggit. I remember watching it for the first time when Dr. Wilker brings out Muffit II. It's this mechanical dog, and the mechanical barking sound. Muffit was actually a really great character. In "Fire in Space," he saved everybody.

BOONE NARR

The suit was lightweight and ventilated and made to look like metal but it wasn't, and the mouth was remote-controlled, radio-operated so you could move the mouth up and down, and then the tail was on a spring, which gave it a little more movement when she walked. We taught her a lot of doglike behaviors.

There were two we used, Doc and Evie. Doc was the male but she did the majority of it. Doc was her backup. He liked it and was pretty outgoing. In fact, he was much more outgoing than she was. She was pretty laid-back and he was full of piss and vinegar. He loved running and jumping and climbing in that suit. She loved just hanging out, so we alternated to do the different scenes we had to do.

CHRISTIAN I. NYBY II
(director, "Fire in Space")

It was a lot fun to film, because you were never sure how the chimp would react. I did one where there was a big fire on the battlestar *Galactica*, and I remember we had the daggit in an elevator coming down with Boxey or something like that, so we started to smoke up and had the fire effects and closed up the elevator doors and cut the slate and everything, and the special effects man opened up the doors and the only thing that was there was the daggit's head. He had taken off and was in the rafters of the stage.

HERBERT JEFFERSON, JR.

When we were shooting "Fire in Space," there was a scene where we have to send the daggit through the air-conditioning ducts to retrieve breathing gear for the impending explosion. I am supposed to take it away and cut the bag and pass out the breathing gear to the crew. But what you have to do to get the chimp accustomed to it is you have to let her play with it for a while so she'll drag it; that way it becomes hers. So on action we now have the chimp pull the bags through the air duct and pull them out and I run over to get them. Well, have you ever tried to take a toy away from a two-year-old? "No, no, mine, mine." The daggit went at me. It's got this whole suit on now with the ears going round and round and the mouth which is being run remotely. But inside there is one ticked-off chimp. The thing is standing on two legs and swinging and trying to kick and take it away from me. Finally, we had to cut. So what we had to do was Boone came over and took off her helmet and put this fistful of grapes in her mouth to shut her up and pulled the helmet back on and then she'd go back to work.

GLEN A. LARSON

She never did learn her lines. For me to watch that and realize there is a little chimpanzee inside that suit and running around. That was great fun. I don't think she got enough credit.

BOONE NARR

Evie liked Noah a lot. He used to come and spend the weekends with us out at our ranch. I remember when Noah first came out, our little star kid, I made him clean up behind the elephants one day. My son was out there and he was doing it and at the time my son was visiting from back East, so that was the first thing he said to his mom when I took him back on Monday to the show: "He made me shovel elephant poop." They had a really good rapport and they really got along and that was why I made sure Noah spent a lot of time with the chimp, so they would have a good rapport.

NOAH HATHAWAY

We had the same birthday. I was November thirteenth; she was the fourteenth, so we would have our birthday cake together. She was my best friend while we were shooting. She was wonderful. I chased her the whole damn movie.

BOONE NARR

She went off to breeding in Florida and she has had babies. The experience on the show was actually quite unique for me. It was early on in my career, and to work with John Dykstra to develop that daggit suit was great. We ended up doing Johnny Carson with that, and a lot of people were fascinated by it; they could not believe there was a chimp inside that suit.

The show featured a large ensemble of supporting characters, like Jack Stauffer's Bojay, Tony Swartz's Jolly, and Ed Begley, Jr.'s Sergeant Greenbean (one of his earliest roles), as well as George Murdock's Dr. Salik and John Dullaghan's Dr. Wilker. In some cases, the same actor could be called on to play numerous roles over the course of the series, as was the case with Alex Hyde-White.

ALEX HYDE-WHITE

On *Galactica*, I felt like I was part of a prestige unit of "freedom fighters." We would go from episode to episode, sometimes playing a different character, and at the end of the shooting week they would see what they had and put the episode together. We were a "counterinsurgency" with a big military budget.

My father, British actor Wilfrid Hyde-White, played the head of the Council of Twelve in the pilot. He and Ray Milland [who played Sire Uri], who at his heights had been a *big* film star, enjoyed their time and my dad got a few laughs. Glen liked him. I was nineteen years old, selling real estate in the desert, when he called to say he was going up to Universal for ten days or so and his usual "man," Mike Lally, was unavailable because he was working with Peter Falk. So I was my dad's "assistant" for the pilot. It's nice having somebody with you when you're sitting around a set waiting to do your scenes. Otherwise, especially for the older character actors, it can get a bit lonely. So I was hanging around, too.

My dad's agent, a character himself named Abby Greshler, who had been sending my head shots around town for a few months prior because, like I said, I was selling real estate in the desert, called and told me to go see Mark Malis, the head of TV Casting at Universal. Abby calls and says to me, "Punch, this is Abby Greshler." I think, "Duh." He says, "Is your father behaving himself?" I couldn't see him at the time, as I was on a pay phone outside the stage, so I said, "Oh yeah, he and Ray Milland are having a good time." Then he says, "Go see Mark Malis at the Black Tower [where Universal's executive suites were located and the most iconic building on the lot], I just spoke with him and he wants to see you." I thanked him, said I was on my way, checked that Dad was good. He was. Ray Milland and he were enjoying their "Styrofoam cups" while sitting in canvas chairs waiting for the next setup. It was around noon on a late spring day in 1978.

Mark Malis was an efficient, easygoing "cog in the wheel" company guy. He couldn't have been more receptive and seemed genuinely interested in giving me his time. After a few minutes he asked if I had time to do a "cold reading" for him. I did, thank you, so he gave me a two- or three-page scene and I went back out in the reception area and read it over a couple of times.

"That was quick," he said, when I was let back into his office, where he introduced me to Alan Levi, the director on the next episode. We read the scene. It was a scene where my character was literally "flying JETS in SPACE." It was fun, and I swear I hit every beat. After the ninety-second "audition" scene was over, Mark says, not really asks, "You've never done this before?" Then he says, "Do you know about our Contract Players program?" I stopped selling real estate in the desert the following week.

I signed on a Monday for three hundred and fifty dollars per week guaranteed, and the next day was in Griffith Park telling Jack Klugman as Quincy to "leave my mother alone." USC Heisman running back Charles White was one of the extras, as an LAPD uniformed officer at the funeral scene.

Two days later I was on stage twenty-seven sitting on an apple box in front of a blue screen with the Viper-pilot helmet wiggling around my head. I think the only direction Alan Levi gave me was to not move my head too much. Wow, it was quick. And . . . I was flying jets in space!

Within no time I was staying in Westwood, and driving over to Universal as needed. The contract program lasted two years, alongside actors Sharon Gless, Lindsay Wagner, Andrew Stevens, George DelHoyo, Rick Springfield, Alan Stock, Larry Cedar, Sarah Rush, Leann Hunley, and others. We were, indeed, a band of brothers and sisters, a happy, happy few. The then SAG president Ed Asner led the union in a militant strike that lasted over six months. The contract system was done.

3.
I'M IN CHARGE HERE...

"Commander, we're picking up some attack signals between Purple and Orange Squadrons. We don't have Purple and Orange Squadrons."

Although *Battlestar Galactica* visual effects supervisor and producer John Dykstra, fresh off his revolutionary work on *Star Wars* and lured away from ILM to work on the series, had been toiling away for almost a year on the telefilm's elaborate special effects before production even began, the three-hour premiere finally began filming in mid-1978 in what was planned as a twenty-nine-day shoot and had stretched to fifty-two by the time it was finished. Director Richard A. Colla was hired to helm the ambitious movie, but by the time it wrapped, Colla had long since been replaced by director Alan J. Levi. Associate producer Winrich Kolbe (who would later direct extensively for the *Star Trek* series *The Next Generation, Deep Space Nine,* and *Voyager*), a veteran of the Marine Corps who served as a point man in Vietnam, was charged with keeping the troops in line for a star war unlike any that television had ever attempted before—or has since—with some of the cast not even being finalized well into production.

The immense and ambitious production tells the story of a thousand-year war between man and machine and the betrayal of the humans by the president of the Twelve Colonies' trusted advisor, Baltar, who helps facilitate a Cylon sneak attack, à la Pearl Harbor, against the human fleet, which is obliterated along with its home colonies. Only the battlestar *Galactica* survives, leading a ragtag fugitive armada in search of the mythical planet of Earth, home of the legendary Thirteenth Tribe, pursued by the Cylons intent on eliminating the last vestiges of humanity.

DIRK BENEDICT
(actor, "Lieutenant Starbuck")

I have the original script that Glen gave me. It was a three-hour pilot, so the script is almost two hundred pages. It's full of these beautiful paintings and artistic concepts of the show and how it would look. The part of Starbuck was wonderful but he really was something of a supporting character. He only became more a part of it as the show went on. Originally, he was just one of the pilots, but I loved it because he was such a bad boy.

RICHARD HATCH
(actor, "Captain Apollo")

After three days of negotiation, we finally came to a deal, and it was the very day they were filming, so I got the agent calling me up and saying you've got to get over there now. I drove over to Universal, ran into wardrobe and hairdressing and then onto the set. And it's not like some quiet set; there is publicity, there are news crews. From the moment I walked on, it was this huge deal. There were no read-throughs or time to get to know anybody and I'm thinking, "Oh my God, what have I done?" The deepest insecurity hit me. It was a really terrifying day.

Hatch, who had literally just been handed his pages for the day, shot the scene in front of the giant glass map on the bridge with Boomer and Starbuck as they constructed a plan to destroy the mines in the Nova of Madagon, allowing the fleet to escape the Cylons and safely reach the planet Carillon, where they could refuel.

DIRK BENEDICT

It was first class all the way and it was exciting to be around all this artistry and all these wonderful creative people, from sets to wardrobe. The costume designs by Dorleac were all handcrafted that he made specifically for each character, and then you had the special effects of John Dykstra and hundreds of extras all made up of creatures from various galaxies. We had all these huge soundstages and the front projection and all the back projection. Every day was just like getting up and going to Disney World—only better. You never knew for sure what it was going to be like. It was this fantasy.

RICHARD HATCH

I must say, with each day it became quite an incredible experience, but it was like going to war. We had no time off. It was eighteen-hour days. You lived on the backlot. You lived in your motor home; you barely had time to even go home. They were working overtime to do this theatrical-style television series which had never been done before. Most shows were shot in seven days; this show took ten to twelve days per episode.

But we did survive and I must say this: After I read the script I realized this was not a *Star Wars* clone. It was inspired by *Star Wars* because the success of *Star Wars* opened the door for sci-fi to come on television, but it was a totally different story and in many cases I thought it was an even better story because the epic story of it was like Moses and the Israelites. Even though everything was not thought out, the potential of that story was phenomenal.

People don't realize this and they judge *Galactica* too harshly. First of all, it came out with all this hype; then it went into a series format without the proper time to set up for a series format. We were up against the wall getting production done in time when it was still getting all worked out. If you look at every first-year show, including *Star Trek,* most are notoriously bad because most times they haven't worked out the kinks and flaws and they don't know how to use each character properly and the stories are not fully thought out. It's in the second and third year that you have the time to really begin to focus in on the characters, to use them the right way, to find which plotlines and storylines work, and to bring out the best in the show.

We were trying to do something that had never been done before. We were attempting to do theatrical-style effects and a theatrical-size show for television—and it had never been done—without even the proper preparation. They didn't want to lose the momentum *Star Wars* had created in terms of sci-fi being successful, so they didn't give Larson enough lead time to develop it properly.

WINRICH KOLBE
(associate producer, *Battlestar Galactica*)

My first contact was when I got a two-page outline for the pilot *Battlestar Galactica,* which was in 1977, and then it just took off from there on a level that I was not included in. I was an associate producer for Glen Larson on most of his shows, including *McCloud, Switch, Quincy,* and *Hardy Boys,* so then I was scheduled to be associate producer on *Battlestar.*

I felt that, given the state of the art of special effects at that time, there was just not enough time to do the necessary amount of special effects on a weekly basis. Especially since episodic television per se is a very short-prepared medium, and with Glen being a five-minutes-to-twelve person, it was even less preparation. He kept fine-tuning the script and writing elaborate scenes and expecting quality work, but there was not enough time to do all that compared to what we have today, where we have a digital system and video blue screens which at that time didn't exist since everything was done on film.

As far as the special effects was concerned, they were all done by John Dykstra, so they had to fight that battle. My job was to take the finished version and shove it through postproduction, make sure that the editing was done on time. The dubbing and all the inserts that had to be shot was my responsibility.

RICHARD COLLA
(director, "Saga of a Star World")

I just finished a movie and I went into George Santoro's office [the head of production for Universal Television], and I would sit down and chat with him. We got to be friends. He was really my mentor. He was a guy who had worked in the crew, and had worked his way up to the [Black] Tower, into his position, so he really knew how to make movies. He knew the ins and outs, the ABCs of it, the craft of making movies, so I found great insight and great wisdom from this man.

I went into his office, and I said, "What do you want me to do?" and he said, "Well, I've got a couple of scripts, what would you like to do?" I said, "I'd like to do a picture on a warm beach with a lot of pretty girls," and he said, "Well, you know I've got this pilot with Dennis Weaver to be made in Hawaii." [*Pearl,* 1978] He said, "Would you like to do that?" and I said, "Well, gee, Dennis and I get along really well, that's kind of a nice idea," and he had this other thing sitting on his desk, and I said, "What's that?" He picked up this fairly thick script, and he said, "This is *Battlestar Galactica.*"

RICHARD JAMES

(art director, *Battlestar Galactica*)

It had a lot of talented people on it. You had Leslie Stevens, who I admired a great deal, and you had John Dykstra, who is a very talented man but he was out of control. He was using his clout coming off of *Star Wars* to do everything.

RICHARD COLLA

I knew that Johnny Dykstra was attached to work on it, and he said, "Would you like to do this?" I said, "I don't know, let me read it," so I took it back with me, and I read it, and I came back and I said, "So George, you're going to make this movie?" And he said, "Oh yes, we're going to make this." I said, "Boy, this is really ambitious. How much is this movie going to cost?" He said it was going to cost one million and eight. I said, "It's going to cost one million and eight?" We were making movies for seven hundred and fifty thousand, you know? He said, "Yeah." I said, "I don't know, George, are you sure?" and he said, "Well, sure. But, if you want to do it, you've got to let me know because we've got to get started." I said, "George, can I have another day?"

I took the script back to my office, and I read it again, and then I started going around all the department heads that I knew—to camera, to editorial, the grip guy—and I sat down with everybody, at different times, and I said, "So you guys have this script? What's it going to cost in the camera department to do this?" And they would dig out their estimates, and I asked, "Can I have a copy?" and they said, "Sure." So they'd give me a copy of this thing, and I took all of these estimates from all the different departments back to my office.

I sat there, and I looked at them all and I read the material and I added them all up, and I thought, "Oh, that's really interesting." So I went back to George's office and I said, "George, what's the budget for this movie again?" He said, "It's a million eight. We sold it . . . Glen [Larson] sold it to ABC for one million and eight. That's what we're going to make it for." I said, "George, I just spent a couple days going around talking to all the department heads. You can't make this movie for one million and eight!"

And he said, "Sure you can. I've got the budget right here in my drawer," and he opened his bottom drawer, and he pulled out this budget for one million and eight. I said, "George, I've got the budgets from all the departments. This picture is going to cost you twelve million dollars!" He said, "No! It's one million and eight!" So he called all the guys, all the department heads from all the different departments, and we had a meeting in George's office. George asked, "What's this going to cost us to make," and they gave him their budgets, and it was twelve million dollars. Well, they sold it to ABC for one million and eight!

He was stunned! What were they going to do? They'd already made the sale. Glen had sold this thing to ABC for one million and eight, and committed the studio to make this thing for a budget that was going to be twelve million dollars. And I said, "Wow! Goodness!" Now, everybody else left, and George and I sat there with a cup of coffee, and I said, "You know, I'll help you any way that I can possibly help you here, but how can we do this?" And he said, "I'm going to need a lot of help here." I said, "George if I can help you, I will, but this picture can't be made for a million eight, whatever it's going to be made for." And so he got the budgets from a lot of the departments, like the stages and sets. How do you build the inside of a starship [and] how do you do the hold of a starship when you haven't any money to build a set? What do you do with the bridge? How do you do all the special effects?

ALAN J. LEVI
(director, "Gun on Ice Planet Zero")

John [Dykstra] is still a friend and we see each other at Super Bowl parties. We became very close because I understood and appreciated what he was doing and on set he was just so bloody helpful it was unbelievable. He was right there all the time. He was an active producer on set. Even though he was doing all of the effects with Apogee.

RICHARD COLLA

By the time we got it cast and started shooting this picture, the studio was about twenty-four hours ahead of us in getting things ready. [We] never knew for sure what sets would be ready, or what sets wouldn't be ready. I would turn sometimes, and I'd say, "George, you know in another day or so I've got this huge scene to do and there's no sets for it." And he said, "Well, have you any ideas?" I said, "Well, I tell you what. Let's go over to stage twelve," which was the biggest stage there. "Get me a bunch of the steel shipping containers, the forty-foot containers. Let me stack those up, just have them go in there and stack those things up. Let's take the green beds from up above, on their chains, and just drop them down so that they're like ramps all through this thing." I said, "I don't even care what's on the other end. I'll get the other end of the stage," which was their biggest stage, "and I'll start shooting everything on three-hundred- and six-hundred-millimeter lenses to get some sense of size to this thing." Well, that's what we do. We pump a little smoke in to confuse things, and give a sense of depth, of scale to these things. It got to the point where George and I used to have these wonderful conversations.

I'd be out making something, and he'd come down after dailies and he'd chat with me about it, and I'd say, "So how does it look, George?" He said, "It looks just fine. . . . It looks just fine." I used to kid him about the place just being a factory, and that we were churning out automobiles. I'd say, "So, does it look like a Chevrolet, or does it look like a Cadillac?" And he'd say, "in this case I need a Volkswagen." I said, "George! I can't give you a Volkswagen here. We both know the only way the studio's going to get out of this is by making a picture that's good enough that you can release it theatrically first. That's the only way you're going to make your money back."

While that would indeed eventually happen, *Star Wars* veteran John Dykstra and his crew were already working on the visual effects. Universal art director John E. Chilberg II began designing the numerous sets envisioned by Larson's script, which went through numerous rewrites. Chilberg worked with assistant art director Richard James, set designers John Warnke and David Klassen, and set decorators Mickey Michaels and Lowell Chambers. When Chilberg left the project early on owing to health problems, James (who later worked on *Star Trek: The Next Generation* and *Voyager* as a production designer after Herman Zimmerman left for *Deep Space Nine*) was promoted to lead art director, alternating episodes with Mary Weaver Dodson.

STEVEN SIMAK
(journalist, *Battlestar Galactica* historian)

At its height, the standing sets for *Battlestar Galactica* spread across eight soundstages at Universal, the largest number of stages ever utilized for a single television program. The most extensive set was the *Galactica* bridge.

Built at an estimated cost of eight hundred and fifty thousand dollars, the bridge set was the centerpiece on which much of the action and drama would take place. To create greater visual complexity, the set was designed with multiple levels and a rotating circular command pedestal.

RICHARD JAMES
(art director, *Battlestar Galactica*)

We thought in terms of a captain standing on an upper deck and looking down. That was the driving influence. You are on a ship and it sort of goes back to the time when you look back and see a captain on board ship. He is always elevated and so you have those levels. That was the development of it, and the levels create an interesting set because it gives something for the director to do with the people.

SARAH RUSH
(actress, "Flight Corporal Rigel")

It was incredible! It was like a three-million-dollar set and at that time that was enormous. The set looked brilliant and it really was wonderful to work on it. I had never been a big sci-fi person, but I loved the thought of real people in this kind of atmosphere. It was one of the reasons why the show was so successful. People were very human and had human experiences in the perspective of space.

STEVEN SIMAK

One goal was to create the illusion that the bridge controlled every function on the *Galactica*. With this in mind, set decorator Mickey Michaels contacted computer giant Tektronix, Inc. In return for a prominent screen credit, Tektronix donated some three million dollars of computer hardware to dress the set. A large number of television monitors, worth an estimated thirty-five thousand dollars, were also used. Computer schematics generated by the Universal art department were fed to the computer terminals to make them appear functional. In addition, effects shots—such as a Viper launching—were looped to the television monitors from a series of Betamax players hidden offstage. Stage twenty-seven, known as the "swimming pool," was selected for the bridge set, because it contained a tank below the main floor that was used to conceal the equipment necessary to run the Tektronix hardware.

RICHARD JAMES

In the beginning, it was hurry-up-wait. There came a very lengthy delay in shooting from the time we first started designing everything. And then they just put us on hold and all of a sudden it was go, go, go. And then everything had to be ready overnight. The main push up front was the bridge set. At one time, *Battlestar Galactica* had more stages involved than any production had ever had at Universal.

Tektronix furnished millions of dollars' worth of computers for the set. The lowest level was multiple stations and all the electronic equipment, and the computers had all been preprogrammed. We had people in the art department who worked with programming the computers so they could pull up images that were for on camera so they didn't burn into the screens.

CHRISTIAN I. NYBY II
(director, "Fire in Space")

As far as the computer effects, we had everything set up on the bridge; someone was very clever. The extras in the background that were part of the crew, on their computer screens, had early computer games. They were really playing *Artillery* or whatever. They had three or four games so they were actually working the computer and they were having fun at the same time. We just told them that if they won, not to show great excitement or anything.

RICHARD JAMES

The set was built so they could pull the back panels out of those stations so you could get reverse shots of the people at the stations and there was room down there to go behind the set. The command station rotated, and there was room underneath that. It was complicated, and a lot of the directors complained it was probably too complicated and too ambitious. It was just time-consuming to film.

GLEN OLIVER
(pop-culture commentator)

I've always thought the *Galactica* bridge, which presumably Ralph McQuarrie was involved in shaping, was an astonishing set—even though it feels illogical in some ways and probably wasted a great deal of space when considered practically. But the essence of it, the busyness of it, the sense of power and functionality it conveyed, were invaluable to the scale and energy of the show. It looked fantastic on camera.

RICHARD JAMES

The bridge set was a long time in construction, and Jack was very nervous to get it built, because of all the working electronics involved. We really pushed to get that set going; it would be the one set that we were going to need and it would also give us the cushion to get the other sets done. That set was able to be started before there was final approval, because they knew once they got final approval they needed to have somewhere to go to film.

Although the bridge set had been approved early on in the production process, changes had to be made once the effects work began taking shape so that the interior matched the design of the miniatures. Initially, designers had envisioned a more streamlined approach for the bridge and interior sets. However, the model for the *Galactica,* designed by Ralph McQuarrie, with its heavy industrial detailing, required James to make a midcourse adjustment.

RICHARD JAMES

We had some stuff that didn't look like it would go in that ship at all. We had to scramble to make modifications so we didn't get such drastically different looks. We actually had the bridge design before John Dykstra got it. It was pointed out that we had curved designs. We did things to reinforce the ability to eventually come out of the models and so forth with the rivets.

There was a lot of discussion of those issues. In reality, spaceships wouldn't have rivets, but Dykstra was the hero of the day for doing *Star Wars* and we had to take the lead from him in that situation. He wanted that hardware look and not the clean *Star Trek* or *2001* look. I remember I just told the shop to make lots of rivet runs because we were going to add rivets to everything. We added lots of support beams. I got Universal finally to buy a vacuform machine so we could do vacuform [panels] to give a machinery look to the walls. It really helped us out a great deal to have that.

STEVEN SIMAK

The multilevel set proved to be a double-edged sword for most directors. While it afforded them many great opportunities for dramatic shots, it proved to be a time-consuming process.

RICHARD JAMES

Any time you create the levels, it makes it harder, because you have to do camera platforming. That takes time to set up, and when you get into shooting a series they don't want that kind of time spent.

ALAN J. LEVI

It was a difficult set, but it lent itself to some wonderful camerawork. It was a three-level set, and using a crane I was able to go over the side and do a bunch of stuff. It was almost a practical set in that there were very few wild [movable] walls, which made it very difficult. I found it amazingly challenging to get good shots, but when you did they were terrific because you had great scope. It wasn't just a little tiny cabin—it was bigger and broader and more interesting.

ROD HOLCOMB
(director, "Greetings from Earth")

Unfortunately, it was a little too quiet for my tastes on the bridge. I felt that they needed more people on the bridge and more sound effects. I felt that in some ways, the bigness hurt it. If you look at the *Star Trek* bridge, it's not that big and yet you had tons of people coming and going, so there's a real sense of movement and life in it.

TERRENCE MCDONNELL
(story editor, *Battlestar Galactica*)

The set that had the bridge also had one of the hallways, the generic hallways. I think it had a swing set that also had the Imperious Leader. There was a little room alongside the bridge that had to have over fifty Betamaxes with a different tape in it that was going on to the individual screens. I remember being over there when they did "Fire in Space" because they were doing a lot of gags there with the explosions like blowing up the screen. There was a big piece of Plexiglas that was wired from the back, and the stage was packed with people watching it. There was no sound. It just disintegrated. But onscreen, it's this big thing. They had the wrap party on the bridge. It was so cool.

The directors would work closely with the series' initial director of photography, Ben Colman, a veteran cinematographer whose work included several previous shows for Larson, and later John Penner, to maximize the possibilities of shooting on the ambitious set.

ALAN J. LEVI

I said to Benny [Colman], I tell you what I want to do on this set, I want an Atlas crane. So they brought in a crane and I shot the bridge set with a crane, because I could take one wall out of the stage on the left side and stick the crane in there on a big platform so it could come in and I could go from the bottom all the way to the top and go all the way up to the map. I shot eighty percent of everything on the bridge from the crane. And it sped it up. I don't know what they did before, because that set wasn't even completed until I came on.

Benny Colman was a gift to me. We could set up shots that would follow them all around the set, and he never missed a beat; it was amazing. I remember this unbelievable scene where Maren Jensen was down on the bottom and there was an attack coming, and she ran up the rear ramp to the middle portion of the set up to the top of the set, and Apollo was right up there and there was some kind of problem. I turned to Benny and said, "Did you get it?" He said, "Wasn't I supposed to?"

RICHARD JAMES

We had so many stages tied up with standing sets that the studio kept saying to us, "You have to relinquish some of these stages, because we need them for other productions." I don't recall for sure, but we had seven to eight stages tied up at one time and as many as eight standing sets. By comparison, on *Star Trek: The Next Generation* we only had two stages tied up with permanent sets, and then I had one large stage for turnaround. Seven to eight stages is a lot of stages to have tied up for a TV show.

WINRICH KOLBE

Stage twenty-seven was always underwater when it rained.

ALAN J. LEVI

In fact, at that time Universal was so busy that we had to rent general-service studio space over on Las Palmas, because there were too many shows and we didn't have enough stages.

DAVID LARSON
(son of Glen Larson)

Walking through the sets—I think that's where I began my love affair with doughnuts. There was always the smell of doughnuts in the air. I still smell it. It was amazing. I think I was a little entitled brat walking around set. "Do you know who my daddy is? Do you know who my daddy is?" There's a story, I kicked Vince Edwards, who was directing one of the episodes, because he wouldn't let me see my dad. I don't think he liked me very much after that. I don't blame him.

DIRK BENEDICT

I remember talking to John Harker Wade, who was our unit production manager. He used to come to me and he'd just shake his head, because we built a set once where we played a game on the show called triad, which was a basketball-meets-handball kind of game that was a forty-thousand-dollar set which we used in one episode for two or three scenes.

WINRICH KOLBE

Battlestar *Galactica* was a warship, so everything was in the tradition of the American navy and was gray. Everything was gray inside, and since everything had to be shot on stages with a few exceptions when we went outside, it was an eerie atmosphere on set. At seven o'clock in the morning every day you entered another world, all gray and dark. After a while, I think it began to bear down on me, because I was ready to do something else after the pilot. I think I had done enough gray hallways as associate producer on the pilot that I decided, Okay, now I am going to go out and see the world and enjoy flowers.

STEVEN SIMAK

Another complex set piece was the life-size Viper. One full mock-up as well as a two-dimensional cutout profile were constructed. In addition, a partial cockpit was created for two-shots of the Vipers in space. The back wall of the launch bay set was adorned with a forced-perspective painting depicting a series of Vipers ready to launch.

TERRENCE MCDONNELL

They had another stage that they used at Universal where they had two Vipers and the launch bay. The Vipers were made of wood, but the one in the back was just a flat—it had no three dimensions to it at all. It was just guys sitting behind a piece of plywood.

If you pull in on Jimmy Stewart Avenue and go a little bit to the left and head toward where DreamWorks used to be on the Universal lot, there is a little café. Right next to it is this other stage, and that's where they had the two Vipers. They put up a felt star field with little twinkly lights in it. The front one was all wood, and there was a place for the actors. The second one was a completely flat board. The one that was in the back, somebody just sat in a chair behind it.

On lunch hour, I wandered down there and they were shooting some Starbuck and Apollo scenes in the Vipers. There was nothing really to do, and there were these big huge velvet drapes that were hanging down as baffles, and out of curiosity I walked around behind these drapes and all of a sudden I just kind of stopped and it absolutely took my breath away, because I am standing onstage looking out at a magnificent opera house from Lon Chaney's *Phantom of the Opera,* and the rumor was and still is that if that set falls, Universal Studios will fall, too. It was there and they used it for a number of pictures and used part of it for the remake with Claude Rains in the forties.

But, I've been told that within the last year they've moved it to somewhere else safe and that it's going to be part of the studio tour.

RICHARD JAMES

We had a very difficult time with the way the fighter planes were designed. They were just letting model builders come up with them, and it became an issue with the union, because the designs are supposed to come from the art department, not from the model makers. When we tried to generate the drawing of the Vipers after the models had already been made and they were taking them from model kits and putting them together, we still had to build sets that people had to get into. You have to be concerned that a person can get in the set and work.

What we had to do with those Vipers was do a forced perspective against that nose, because the nose was so far out of proportion to the cockpit that if we had built it the way it was on the models, it wouldn't have worked. If you started with the cockpit and increased the size of the cockpit to scale, then the nose became something like thirty-eight feet long from the cockpit windshield to the tip of the nose. It couldn't have been done, so we did a forced scale on that. Even then it was still quite long [eight to ten feet].

It was just very time-consuming, and we had to have design engineers drafting those sets. I actually worked on the Apollo missions at NASA, so I had some background in design engineering, and it was a very complicated issue in some respects, with those models that had been generated without first coming to be designed in the art department. It was a very backward situation that was kind of out of hand and was one of many issues.

CHRISTIAN I. NYBY II

It was so hard shooting the Vipers. I had done rear projection and we used that occasionally for some of the cockpit stuff, but I don't even think we used any blue or green screen. We didn't have time. In fact, Lorne had such blue eyes that we could never shoot him in front of a blue screen.

HERBERT JEFFERSON, JR.
(actor, "Lieutenant Boomer")

We were rarely in the life-size Viper. Most of it was a tiny mock-up cockpit with process screen going past us. We'd sit there basically just wearing our tops and the helmet because it was so hot inside.

ANNE LOCKHART
(actress, "Sheba")

The first day that I did the cockpit stuff, I remember, they said we need to shoot some shots of you launching and said on action push yourself back into the seat like g-forces shooting out of the launch tube. So the first time I did it, I hurled up and pushed myself back into the seat and the helmet slips up and hits me in the nose. They printed it, and it was used repeatedly throughout.

DAVID LARSON

I remember my father would do pickup shots in the living room. He had a mock-up of the Viper. He had the canopy brought in and set it up on the pool table and he would have a crew come in and they would shoot some stuff. It was the full-size canopy. I was too young to understand what he was doing, but it was cool. To see the process like that made it this very magical thing. It has a mythical status to the people who watched it growing up, but it was the same thing for me. I was just a little bit closer to it, and I saw some of the behind-the-scenes stuff.

RICHARD COLLA

We didn't have time for a lot of takes. We did it very efficiently, very quickly, and we knew pretty much what we were going to shoot, and what the coverage was, and what I needed to have to get to the editor, and really did not have the luxury of being able to shoot things from a lot of different angles. Just to get a second camera was like pulling teeth.

There were times when we would get into trouble, and we would just have to work around it. We never had time to shut down and say, "Let's get a writer in here and fix this." We just did it. If the actors had a problem, we would find a way. If they would get frustrated because they wanted to say "Fuck!" and you can't say "Fuck!," I said, "Well, then say 'Frak'! Let's just say something else. Let's stop saying, 'Gosh darn it!,' because isn't that stupid in the middle of it? But some other guttural kind of expression that you can just use and it'll feel okay." So, in television, you go out and you capture moments. It's much more like the Jackson Pollock approach to filmmaking—looking and waiting for the happy accident, giving the actors freedom to do what they do as well as they can, encouraging them to surprise you and surprise the audience. It isn't like Mr. Hitchcock. When Mr. Hitchcock was asked one day who his favorite director was, he thought for a moment and said, "It's Walt Disney. If he doesn't like his actors, he tears them up and throws them away." But we, in television, don't have the luxury of a lot of takes. We don't have the luxury of rehearsal. We didn't get rehearsals.

DAVID LARSON

At five, not much registers. You've got doughnuts. You've got a robot walking around. You have a mock-up of the spaceship. It was amazing walking through that. I remember a sense of being just awed. It's kind of that sense you get when you're walking on a backlot alone. I once had to make some deliveries as a gopher for a few years. Just walking onto the Warner Bros. lot and they were shooting *Batman* and had built Gotham City. You really get a sense of awe of the magic of moviemaking. It took me back to when I was a kid. I'm kind of glad I never really lost that. You get really jaded growing up in L.A.

However, midway through production, tensions between Colla, who had been Universal's first choice for the telefilm, and Larson came to a head, and the all-too-familiar "creative differences" arose, which led Larson to fire Colla in the middle of shooting.

RICHARD COLLA

Once we had a movie, Glen [Larson], I guess, felt that he needed more control than he had. He then also had occasion to be able to go back and add a scene and rewrite some things. I think it was my outspokenness and anger at Glen [for] coming in at that point, with a lot of little complaints, or unhappiness, or things that he found fault with.

ALAN J. LEVI

What was wrong with it [Colla's direction], I don't know. I do know that Glen is a very exacting producer, and when he asked for something, you delivered it to him. Television is more of a producer's medium than a director's medium. In features, the director is in control; in television, the producer is in control, and that may have been part of it. He did say that he wanted things done one way and Richard did them his way. That was it.

RICHARD COLLA

George [Santoro] had always been very good to me, and when he needed help, I was there for him. So it wasn't about Glen. It was about making this thing work for George, and when in the end Glen kept finding little faults, I just told him he was an ungrateful bastard, because everybody was working so hard to pull his ass out of the fire here, and now he's in there pretending like he's the one who has all the ideas. It was his idea originally. Nobody can fault him for that. You know, it's him and the Mormon church. So if you say, "Okay, this is mine, well that's just fine," and I applaud his ability for all of the work that he's able to do in television, all of those opportunities that he saw in movies and then made television shows out of, all that stuff that he was able to convert. So I could even understand where he would want to feel like he was back in control of it once the major roaring fire of this thing was out, and some hope was in the air, but I just found him very ungrateful to all the people who worked so hard for him.

HERBERT JEFFERSON, JR.

It was personally shocking, because we missed him, but as it is with the nature of this kind of show, we just picked up and did what we were told. It isn't as though we didn't know the storyline and what was expected of us, but we certainly missed Richard and went back to work.

RICHARD COLLA

Glen is the kind of producer who wants the piece to be a reflection of his point of view. And would like the director to supply to him the material with which he can take that material and put it together in a way that satisfies him.

ALAN J. LEVI

Richard Colla, as you know in the credits, has credit for directing that show. But about halfway through, the chasm between him and Glen Larson grew. Larson said, "You do have other things to do, don't you?" And I think Richard said, "Yeah, I do." He said, "Good, you're off." So, he hired me to complete it. Richard shot twenty-five days, I shot twenty-seven days.

I knew of Glen. We'd occasionally say hi, but he didn't know who the heck I was, but Leslie Stevens was a mentor of mine. He was a beautiful human being and a man of his word. He first came to me in 1972 and said, "I've got a pilot that I'm financing myself." It was a talk show. He said, "I can't pay you, but will you direct it for me?" We discussed it and I said I'd love to. I didn't know Leslie but you hear that all the time. So, I directed the show for him, and the pilot didn't sell but it was a very good show and he was the interviewer. It was a mostly technical thing, because he was into space and alien beings and it was a forum for the intergalactic and the extraterrestrial.

In 1975, he called me and he said, "I'm part of the original crew who put together *The Invisible Man,* the pilot has sold and I'm going to be on it as a consulting producer and I want you to come over and meet Harve Bennett and go up and meet the guys at the Black Tower [at Universal]. If they like you, I want you to direct the first episode, and if you do well then you're part of the team, and if you don't, good luck."

So, I went over and met Harve and some of the other people, and Harve said, "Okay, direct the first show." I did, and then I did every other one, and Harve was a great mentor but it was all because of Leslie. So when there was a rift between Richard and Glen, Leslie came in and said, "I think you should talk to Alan about taking over." And so I came in and talked and he wanted me to take over the show. I said, "Glen, I can't." He said, "Why not?" I said, "Because I'm set to direct something else, and my parents, who have been my biggest supporters all of my life, are finally coming out from St. Louis to visit me next week, and they're going to be here for a whole week, and that's more important to me than anything." He said, "I'll tell you what. I will give you my chauffeur and my car and they will be treated like king and queen and chauffeured all around and they'll be brought to the studio, they'll have lunch here, they'll be on the set with you."

I thought to have my mom and dad, who are sweet Midwestern folk, to be squired around as though they were queen and king would really be fun for them. So, I said, "Okay, I only need one thing from you, and that is to promise that you will support a dual credit." And he said, "Absolutely I will go to the Directors Guild and support that." So, I took over the show. I called Richard after he had already been told that he was being let go and I said, "I hope you will come in, this was nothing of my doing, I'll be happy to sit down and chat about where you were going with it so I follow the same thing so no one can tell it was you who directed a scene or me and that I hope you'll come in and edit your scenes." He said, "Listen, just do your job, don't worry about it. Don't worry about me. You have final cut of the picture as far as I'm concerned. I'll come in and edit my stuff and if you find out you want to alter it, don't worry about it, do it." He didn't want anything more to do with Glen. Glen felt the same. So, basically, I came in, I saw all the dailies, and I saw the cuts, which was about a little less than half of the show.

But he prepped it.

I'll be real honest about it: Glen and I had a rift toward the end of the show, because two things happened. Number one, he had me reshoot a number of scenes that Richard had shot, which was okay. But then he had another list of scenes that he wanted to do, and the Tower put the kibosh on it and said, "No, we spent enough money on this." So, the Tower pulled me off the show and said, "No, Glen, Alan can't shoot anymore, he's already shot twenty-seven days, put the show to bed," and they put me on what they were talking to me about doing next. Glen thought that was my doing. So, he didn't talk to me for a while. When it came time to take the negotiation to the Directors Guild for my credit, he reneged. He did not talk to them and he told me basically that he never said that to me. And because Richard had prepped the show and shot twenty-five days, and I shot twenty-seven, the Directors Guild gave him total credit. I had a third of the residuals. But, the credit was more important to me than the residual.

At that point in his career, Levi was already a seasoned director in his own right, and had a reputation at Universal in the seventies as a troubleshooter, having taken over on several television productions that the studio perceived to be having problems. Subsequently, Levi has directed for such series as *JAG*, *Buffy the Vampire Slayer*, and *ER*, among many others in a long and enviable career.

ALAN J. LEVI

Before directing [the miniseries] *Scruples*, I had directed *The Immigrants*, which was a miniseries as well. I liked doing movies of the week and miniseries almost more than episodic, because in episodic the director is really not the molder of the show, the producer and the showrunner and the writer are. Whereas with *Scruples* I had to come in and take over four days into the shoot. They walked me through the sets that were designed and so on, and some of them I did not like, and I sat down with them and told them why. They totally agreed and rebuilt the sets. Most of it was cast already. As was *Battlestar Galactica*.

There were a number of people at that time who were under contract. I was the only pure director under contract at Universal. There were producer/ directors, writer/directors, and so on. The executive producers who became directors and so on, they were not hired as directors. They were hired as showrunners and producers and so on. I became their fix-it man. I was sent down two or three shows, including *Miami Vice*, because one of the directors who went down there just did not get the style of the show. So I was on a plane to Miami on Sunday night and started directing Monday morning. I read the script on the airplane. That was always very interesting and a great challenge and I enjoyed that.

ROD HOLCOMB

Alan did a great job. I always wished he had gotten more recognition for his work and had done more pilots. Couldn't figure out why I was doing it and he wasn't. He was really good and a nice guy.

For the telefilm, Levi's first directorial call for "Action" was made on the sequence in which the Cylons attack the Carillon gambling casino. Hired less than a week before assuming control of the pilot, Levi had little time to prepare for the massive production logistics.

ALAN J. LEVI

I had spent a lot of time with Glen just discussing [it] before I officially took over. I didn't do a lot of storyboards, because I didn't have time to, but I did do a lot of prep. If I have a whole day of shooting on one set—let's say for Monday—then on Saturday or Sunday I will go in and spend between three and five hours on that set, walking it, planning it, thinking about it, etc. I do a huge amount of homework that way. So I had the weekend to plan the first five days, and then I got into the swing of it.

The scene takes place on Carillon, the mysterious homeworld of the insectoid Ovions, who run an enigmatic casino resort on the deep fringes of space, where no one ever seems to lose and humanity is on the menu.

GLEN A. LARSON

I've always thought of Las Vegas, with its dazzling decor, glittering lights, and feverish atmosphere, as another world. So when I let my imagination wander into outer space, it seemed appropriate to put it there. Among the attractions at the mythical casino is a vocal trio, the Android Sisters. Each of the girls has two mouths and two sets of vocal cords, resulting in fabulous six-part harmony. That idea was inspired by my own checkered past. As a member of the Four Preps, I wondered how to make our sound bigger, without enlarging the group. The Android Sisters offer one answer.

ALAN J. LEVI

I was very fortunate in the first day that I shot, it was an extremely difficult night. It was the attack at the casino at nighttime, with all the tanks outside and everything else, and I was extremely lucky that that was it. Because that night went so well, I was accepted into the crew immediately. If it had just been a day of over-the-shoulders and close-ups and stuff, it wouldn't have been the same, but it was a difficult night because I had the Cylons, I had most of the cast, I had Boxey, and tanks, and shoot-'em-ups—the whole thing! I had the monkey in the daggit costume. I had everything piled onto that first night that went very well thanks to all the people who were there.

We shot almost all night, because we were outside of the studio. Inside was the gambling parlor and then the doors opened up and they ran outside and tanks were coming and so on. A lot of people were pulling to make that night work. We had to do it at night because of the pyrotechnics, which don't show up very well in the daytime. I mean, if a pyrotechnic goes off in the daytime, and you're shooting day for night, it's a little sparkler. At night, that lights up the entire field, and that's basically what we did when the Cylons finally came outside.

It wasn't until many years after finishing the pilot and the two-part "Gun on Ice Planet Zero" that Levi finally reconciled with Larson after their falling-out.

ALAN J. LEVI

We finally patched things up on the baseball field. I was playing for Universal and Glen was coaching for 20th Century Fox, where he was doing *The Fall Guy* with Lee Majors. We were on opposite teams. I said, "I've got a bet for you. If we win, you and I start talking, and if you win, you never have to talk to me again." He shook hands on that; at the end of the game we won. Bygones be bygones, and Glen was Glen. If you knew Glen you accepted Glen.

4.
BY YOUR COMMAND

"When Commander Adama sees this, he's gonna go crazy!"

Surprisingly, the period just after the release of *Star Wars* was one of relative inactivity in the effects industry. That would soon change. In the interim, however, John Dykstra was able to bring many of the key players on *Star Wars,* including effects pioneers Dennis Muren, Richard Edlund, and Joe Johnston, directly onto the *Galactica* production. Universal also made arrangements with 20th Century Fox to lease the same facility and original equipment used by ILM on *Star Wars.* The new effects unit was loosely called "MCA-57," derived from the name of the Universal parent company, MCA, plus the last two digits of the facility's phone number. MCA-57 would eventually be renamed and was the foundation for what would later become John Dykstra's privately owned Apogee effects house. With the team and facility in place, effects work on *Battlestar Galactica* began during the summer of 1977, and the majority of visual effects work on the pilot (three hundred shots in all) was completed before principal photography even began.

GLEN A. LARSON
(creator/executive producer, *Battlestar Galactica*)

John Dykstra is a genius. No one else could have done what he did in the time he had to do it.

JOHN DYKSTRA
(producer/visual effects supervisor, *Battlestar Galactica*)

Within the confines of the reduced resolution and format size of television, we were trying to make effects that weren't there to fit the bill but were in fact themselves a piece of the story. Instead of just saying they were going from point A to point B, which can be handled by a flyby, we attempted to do what is done in features, which is to create an environment which was attractive to look at and special. It set the piece apart from a master, a two-shot, and coverage.

CHRISTIAN I. NYBY II
(director, "The Magnificent Warriors")

In those days we didn't have CGI yet. We could do matte shots, but they were time-consuming and laborious. They did do some miniatures, but they were so much more ambitious than *The Rockford Files* or a show which would just use present-day stuff—a guy would get in his car and just drive off. We had to get in a Viper and take off, but I truly enjoyed it, because it was a challenge to create a real world with that.

RICHARD COLLA
(director, "Saga of a Star World")

The timetable to make it to television and get it made and on the air was a tremendous task. How to accomplish the effects? How to build all that stuff? How do you do it? I certainly would sit with John [Dykstra] and all of that stuff was storyboarded, so we knew all the pieces. We knew where the wide shots were, what the close-ups were, and where the actors cut into that stuff—in the cockpit of the Vipers, or on the bridge of the battlestar. All of that was choreographed, so we all knew who's on first. But we didn't have a lot of time to think about it, or second-guess, and Johnny was really good at this.

STEVEN SIMAK
(journalist, *Battlestar Galactica* historian)

The number of miniatures that were created and shot for that two-hour alone is staggering—the ragtag fugitive fleet and all the special effects that turned up time and time again through the use of stock footage of the Vipers and Cylon Raiders. It's pretty extraordinary.

Built at a cost of $50,000, the seventy-two-inch model of the *Galactica* was constructed on a series of steel tubes, which both provided structural support and served as mounting points for the motion-control model movers. Bulkheads on the vessel were created from plywood and covered with a Plexiglas skin. As was the custom of the day, the surface was detailed from individual parts scavenged from wholesale model kits purchased in bulk. Gang molds—detailed sections of a surface that can be recast and rearranged (such as on the Death Star)—were not used. All the parts were individually and painstakingly applied from various armor and ship kits.

For POV shots approaching the landing bay, one of the bays contained a backlit forced-perspective matte painting depicting the interior. For reverse shots inside the bay looking out as a vessel approached, a larger model was constructed. This consisted of a floor section with lights and a separate roof section. The roof piece was flipped and doubled as the battlestar's surface for later shots in which two Vipers pursue and destroy a Cylon Raider flying over the *Galactica*'s hull.

The Viper launch tube was created using a piece of Sonotube (a tube used in construction for pouring concrete). It was detailed with girders and lit practically with halogen lights hidden behind the bulkheads. One half of the tube could be pulled away for side shots with the camera and Viper traveling simultaneously down a motion-control track.

STEVEN SIMAK

At least two versions were created of the Colonial Viper—which measured approximately sixteen inches long. The "hero" version was complete with lights and a clear canopy containing a pilot figure. It also featured a gas jet system used to create the "turbos" effect. A lesser, secondary version sans the lights and jets was also used. To create the turbo effect, the hero Viper was equipped with brass tubing, which would spray liquid nitrogen under pressure out of the rear engine of the vessel. Lighting was also built into the engine to illuminate the turbo effect. Shot as separate passes, the dramatic turbos proved to be problematic for the filmmakers.

RICHARD EDLUND
(special effects director of photography, *Battlestar Galactica*)

It was hard to shoot, and it had to do with the temperature on the stage. If it was in the morning and it was cold on the stage, it looked one way. Later on in the afternoon, if it got warm, it looked another way. It was a pain to do.

That's an idea that we wished somebody had never come up with, because in the days of motion control you shoot a beauty pass on the model against blue screen and then you have to turn the lights off and shoot an engine pass without the smoke. Then we had to feed liquid nitrogen through a tube [in the Viper model] and shoot that separately as a motion-control shot. Of course, as the temperature of the stage changed during the day, so did the nitrogen. So it was a nightmare—nitrogen-mare.

DOUG SMITH
(camera, miniature, and optical effects unit, *Battlestar Galactica*)

Everything would freeze up and start sputtering. And chunks of ice would start flying out.

STEVEN SIMAK

By comparison, the Cylon Raider models were much simpler to execute. Measuring approximately thirteen inches long, with a seventeen-inch wingspan, the hero Raiders had lights in the front and engines but did not feature any of the turbo mechanics. Estimates are that half a dozen Vipers and Raiders each were initially created, with duplicates being cast from molds as needed. Measuring four feet across, the structure for the Cylon basestar was created out of Plexiglas with steel tube mounting points. Unlike the *Galactica*, the basestar utilized a series of patterns, which repeated on the surface.

Approximately a dozen vessels were created to represent the ragtag fleet. Sizes ranged from hero ships of approximately sixteen inches in length to the much smaller trailing vessels seen only as spots in the distance.

WAYNE SMITH
(production and special effects consultant, *Battlestar Galactica*)

There is a lot of good stuff that came directly out of the model makers' hands without going through any design process, like the giant ragtag fleet—things that had to be done quickly.

ANDREW PROBERT
(conceptual designer, *Battlestar Galactica*)

I only worked on the two-hour pilot movie. I do remember being excited and impressed with seeing the famous Dykstraflex camera system, revolutionary, at the time, and knowing it was the one used in filming the spaceship flying scenes in *Star Wars* . . . and it was very cool to see working cinematic history.

DOUG SMITH

There were times when the model makers were left on their own to just build something without going through any design process. Depending on their talents, it turned out either brilliant or unusable.

ANDREW PROBERT

At one point, the call went out for everyone to come up with additional spaceship models, for shooting various parts of the "ragtag fleet," carrying the remaining survivors of the Cylon attacks. So, being a hobby modeler, I thought it might be fun to contribute to this collection, and I came up with a little winged flier. Somebody really liked it, and it ended up being featured in the show's opening credits, showing ships evacuating various planets, which I also ended up painting.

RICHARD EDLUND

One of the sequences I really liked was the mine sequence with that red laser stuff. I think I may have lost a quarter of my optical nerve shooting that by not wearing yellow glasses. We had a one-watt laser, which doesn't sound like much, but you could light your cigarette on that laser. We were scanning it around on the stage and bouncing it off things like Saturn Awards trophies. The surface of that was really good for bouncing a laser off of.

GLEN A. LARSON

It was all an experiment. Half the time they were looking for what would work. I remember when we showed the surface of Caprica, I asked how they got the look of that city and they said that's just a bunch a sugar on a table lit just right to look like billions of lights.

RICHARD EDLUND

In the *Guns of Navarone* show ["Gun on Ice Planet Zero"], we blew up a mountain that was really powder. There was a lot of really great stuff. We used microballoons, these little miniature glass bubbles to simulate snow. I probably still have some in my lungs. But it worked so great and that's what it's all about.

STEVEN SIMAK

Motion-control technology (MOCO), pioneered by Douglas Trumbull during *Silent Running* and perfected on *Star Wars,* would be the foundation for the effects work on *Galactica*. Motion control allows for computer-controlled movement of the camera and models along a repeatable programmed path. This precision photography allows filmmakers to separately photograph a series of elements which would track and match exactly when optically composited together later. The Dykstraflex camera, the motion-control track camera system pioneered on *Star Wars,* would also be utilized.

One area of departure was the film format. All the effects for *Star Wars* were shot in VistaVision. VistaVision is an eight-perf [eight perforations per frame] film format that yielded twice the image area of a standard four-perf thirty-five-millimeter frame. Four-perf film runs vertically through the camera and projection system. In contrast, VistaVision runs horizontally, creating a larger film format. As a cost-saving factor, for *Galactica* the entire facility was converted from VistaVision to four-perf thirty-five millimeter.

RICHARD EDLUND

It did affect the quality of the image. In thirty-five-millimeter, you are basically intercutting a dupe [duplicate] with the original, and that's the reason
we went to VistaVision on *Star Wars.* We had an image quality advantage
so that when we duped it, it would cut like an original negative shot; whereas
when you dupe a thirty-five shot and cut it with the rest you have that kind
of dupe effect.

DOUG SMITH

All the equipment, from the stage cameras to the animation camera to the
optical printers, had to switch to four-perf. There was a whole shift from
the field charts and how things lined up. As far as shooting things on the
stage, it actually got a little easier, because a four-perf field of view is smaller
than a VistaVision field of view. So the areas that you had to cover with
blue screen behind things got a little easier, but the grain issues were worse
and it made the lineup of mattes as critical as ever. It was a trade-off there,
I guess, in relation to the size of the format. The camera stayed the same size
even though the format got smaller, so you wouldn't have the same feeling
that you were as close to the particular model as you did before.

When we shot the models, frequently we were so close we were hitting
the models or scraping the paint off. We got really close with the miniature
photography in order to feel the sort of closeness that you want—the feel of
a dramatic shot. . . . Because of the format it was harder to make the model
feel as big on television as it did when you were shooting it in VistaVision
for a feature film.

RICHARD EDLUND

Visual effects have come a long way in forty years, and I apologize for some
of those matte lines. In fact, if you look at many of the shots and compare
those to the shots of *Star Wars,* the choreography of the shots was better. Of
course, we could play the violin better because we had had a little more time
on the instrument. It was a lot of fun for us on the effects crew to work on
this project. We did change the whole system over from VistaVision to
thirty-five millimeter because of budgets and, frankly, I didn't expect it to

go to a feature. But, all of a sudden, it was a feature and I was kind of cranky about it because the work wasn't as polished technically as it could be.

SCOTT MANTZ
(film critic, *Access Hollywood*)

You want to talk effects? The scene in the Nova of Madagon where they clear the Cylon minefield and get to Carillon is another great scene. Everybody's having a big party, but wait, the Ovions want to eat the humans, but they're not running from the Cylons, who just want the humans dead and exterminated. They're going to feed off of them. The humans can't get a break. So what do the humans do? They blow up the fucking planet. It was brilliant. They're laying fire to the tylium mines with their little laser pistols, because the fire's going to spread like wildfire, and they blow up the freaking planet.

There's a lot going on in "Saga of a Star World." You've got the power struggle between Adama and Sire Uri, and Ray Milland was great. He was wresting control of the fleet. They just got out of the Twelve Colonies, with their butts intact, and now Adama has to worry about a power struggle, because Sire Uri wants to negotiate peace with the Cylons? It's like, "Are you kidding me?" Adama was smart. He played his cards close to his vest, he gambled, and he won because he did a brilliant switch to protect most of the Vipers so they could be ready in case the Cylons attacked. Adama was right. "The Cylons lured me into their deception once, never again." Then after they discover the secret of Carillon, and the Cylons are closing in, Adama has a little smirk on his face. He's like, "I knew it, I fucking knew it."

When the Vipers engage, there's a great shot of the three Vipers going down, with the turbos and the Cylons, and they engage. It's a great shot. Even given today's standards, the special effects of *Galactica* were great. So many people have said, "Oh, well, they used the same shot over and over again." Yeah, they did, but I don't care, because they're great shots. There's so much detail to that *Galactica* model that no matter how close the Cylons get, it still looks great. Remember, this was 1978, it was only nine years after the original *Star Trek,* which doesn't hold up, but even by 2017 standards, what John Dykstra did with the effects of *Galactica* still works great, even on the big screen. It really was one of the best pilots ever done for television.

PHIL TIPPETT
(creature designer, *Battlestar Galactica*)

Somewhere in my archives I have pictures of the original designs I did for these little antlike people [Ovions] on *Battlestar Galactica*. The only person I ever dealt with was producer Glen Larson. It was on the Universal lot, and he hired me to do some design work. I made this small clay maquette, which was the basis for the design of the suit and the manufacturing of it. I did some other characters as well but I can't exactly remember, but there was some big cloaked alien, a dark overlord [the Imperious Leader]. I just worked on the very initial design phase.

Costume designer Jean-Pierre Dorleac had been brought to Universal specifically for *Galactica*. His prolific career in the film and television industry includes such projects as *Barbarella*, *The Bastard*, *Mae West*, *Quantum Leap*, *Somewhere in Time*, and *Buck Rogers in the 25th Century*.

JEAN-PIERRE DORLEAC
(costume designer, *Battlestar Galactica*)

I had worked on lots of other different types of science fiction movies in the past, and this was an opportunity to do something that was not the plastic and chrome and high-tech costuming that I had done before.

I decided that I wanted the uniforms to look like they were made out of suede, because it has a very soft natural texture. Glen liked the idea and we looked for suede costumes in earth colors and that's how the warrior costumes got started. We wanted something very dignified for the uniforms worn by Adama and Tigh, so we went for the midnight blue.

ROB KLEIN
(*Battlestar Galactica* archivist)

Battlestar Galactica's Colonial wardrobe for the bridge officers and battle suits were made with extreme quality and durability, with the assumption that the show would go on for many seasons. The battle jackets had interior pockets and were fully lined on the interior. Dirk Benedict's Colonial jacket and sweater worn in "The Magnificent Warriors" had custom-made pockets on the inside to accommodate his cigars.

STEVEN SIMAK

Dorleac's sketches went to Glen through supervising producer Leslie Stevens. The two of them would then review the concepts and make decisions on the proposed designs. The designer, who began his career as a sketch artist on *Barbarella*, welcomed the opportunity to create the unique type of costuming *Galactica* required.

Some of the most memorable design work in the entire series was the Cylon Centurions and their hardware, the iconic Cylon basestar, and, of course, the Cylon Raiders. These were all developed by legendary conceptual designer Andy Probert, who, along with Joe Johnston (future director of *The Rocketeer* and *Captain America: The First Avenger*), would later go on to design even more iconic vessels for *Star Trek: The Motion Picture* and the *Enterprise 1701-D* for *Star Trek: The Next Generation*.

ANDREW PROBERT

I had met Ralph McQuarrie earlier, and interviewed him for our college newsletter, showing him my work in the process. He recommended me to John Dykstra, heading up ILM at the time. He was doing the special effects for the show, and I was subsequently hired to provide concepts for the Cylons. Ralph had provided the initial design for the Cylons, along with other preproduction illustrations, to get the project started. That was my starting point, with the helmet-scanner idea already in place. I continued creating variations of the robots, while starting to emulate the face of the Imperious Leader from an already-cast mask of that character. Then Glen Larson asked for the helmet to have a "skull-like" look, so additional helmet designs were generated by myself as well as concept genius Joe Johnston, who had already been in place on the production. Once I had started sketching skull forms, I created a "snarl" in the mouth area, adding a horizontal grille between, rather than teeth.

The grille was also to have been a design echoing of the Cylon Raider spaceship cockpit window area, for subliminal design continuity. The mouth-side snarl forms reminded me of an ancient Greek helmet, so I added a top piece to complete that look. About the same time, as I recall, I started exploring Egyptian-motif ideas for the Colonials' helmet look. My thinking was that maybe the Cylons were ancient astronauts who influenced the Greek armor and helmets. With the Thirteenth Tribe reaching Earth later, their helmets could have influenced the Egyptians.

Mr. Larson liked my Cylon helmet but wanted to see additional ideas for a full-body suit from both of us. Joe Johnston's concepts were heading more toward a Japanese samurai feel, while I stayed with the Greek-armor look, complete with a rear half cape, broadsword, and spear. Mr. Larson chose that Greek style, adding the requirement that their proportions be "high-waisted" with chromed armor. I added a "grille" motif into the rib cage area, visually repeating the lower helmet look, added a life-support pack on the back, an equipment belt, and also an arm-mounted gun to the final sketch, which Mr. Larson approved, but when the costume designer added big hockey gloves into the mix, the arm gun was unusable. Joe Johnston, meanwhile, provided the beautiful final look for the Colonials' helmet design.

JEAN-PIERRE DORLEAC

The Cylons were a reptilian race and they were robots. We came up with the chrome plating to give them the real high-tech look as opposed to the *Galactica* Warriors and the people of the fleet.

ANDREW PROBERT

Mr. Larson only came into the Art Department, which was Joe Johnston and me, on occasion, so I didn't have a lot of contact with him. When I did, it was brief, but quite pleasant, as I recall. Sometimes, he would bring along one of his teenaged sons as a consultant, wanting to get a younger take on everything. *Star Wars* was, indeed, discussed, with the goal of avoiding similarities. You can see that those "snarl" side pieces, in my sketches, is curved and tapers toward the bottom. When the helmet was constructed, by one of the modelers, that area was changed, making it look more like Darth Vader's helmet, unfortunately.

ROB KLEIN

Apogee not only produced the special effects for *Battlestar Galactica,* they designed and built almost all of the Colonial props initially seen in the show's pilot, including Viper helmets, Colonial lasers, and Cylon rifles. Originally the weapon on the Cylon Centurion was supposed to rise from its wrist on the right gauntlet, something that was resurrected decades later in the Ron Moore version of the show. The producers felt that the Cylons needed to carry weapons, which would make it possible for the good guys to use the rifles, etc. The Cylon rifles needed to be produced quickly to accommodate this late change in the production. Some members of the crew felt that this is why the Cylon rifles were not as elegant as the Colonial pistols were. Joe Johnston was both on the *Battlestar* Apogee crew and later is given credit for designing the fan-favorite bounty hunter Boba Fett for *The Empire Strikes Back*. Knowing this, it is not surprising that the Cylon gauntlets are very similar to Boba Fett's armor.

STEVEN SIMAK

The Cylon costumes, worn only by stuntmen on the series, were designed for individuals who were six feet tall. The boots Dorleac designed had extra-thick soles and contained lifts inside the shoe to provide additional height. The bodysuit itself was made out of a corded vinyl that was then slatted on very heavy buckram, a coarse cotton cloth stiffened with glue, so that the costume wouldn't give. The final touch on the costume was the forbidding metallic armor that covered the head, neck, and chest. These pieces were vacuum-formed from a lightweight plastic, chromed, and then attached to the bodysuit with a metallic silver tape manufactured by 3M.

ROB KLEIN

The Cylon suits were entirely made of fiberglass at first for the pilot by Apogee, but were destroyed beyond repair during filming because there were no stunt-grade pieces of Cylon armor made. Eventually, Universal took over the fabrication of the Cylon suits and used vacuum-formed plastic, which was chrome-plated using the same process as the original fiberglass pieces. There are only a few examples of the fiberglass pilot-made Cylon parts that survive to this day. The Cylon eyes were powered using a movie-camera battery belt. Apogee disguised them by making chrome squares that fit over the battery cells on the outside of the belt.

STEVEN SIMAK

Galactica's first season provided few clues as to the origin or society of the Cylon Empire. Except for a vague reference to the fact that they were once living beings overrun by their own technology, costume designer Jean-Pierre Dorleac had very little to go on when visualizing the series' chief antagonist. Based on his reading of the script, the designer had two pieces of information—the Cylons were once reptilian and they were now machines. Although the chrome gave the Cylons a stunningly sinister look, it did create complications for the cinematographers working on the series.

JEAN-PIERRE DORLEAC

The reflections were terrible for the cameraman. It was very hard to light them, but this had been discussed. Glen was very specific in what he wanted and he knew of the problem and still insisted that they be high chrome. They were aware coming in the door; it wasn't something that surprised anybody by any means. It just was a difficult situation for lighting.

The difficulty was to avoid seeing the reflections of the camera and crew in the highly reflective Cylon armor when doing close-ups. Director of photography H. John Penner used lenses and clever camera placement to resolve the problem.

H. JOHN PENNER
(director of photography, *Battlestar Galactica*)

I usually used the stage lens and a 5:1 zoom. If I wanted a close-up angle on the Cylons, I would just get a little further away and change the angle a tiny bit.

WINRICH KOLBE
(associate producer, *Battlestar Galactica*)

That was a pain in the ass. Originally, we wanted to have them in shiny reflective garb, but during the pilot that would really interfere with all the optical work that we had to do, because it picked up every glint of reflection, and not only that, but every time they were coming into camera you could see the camera in their armor, so there were major discussions as to what we could do. We all liked the original shiny, very glossy surface, and then we had to tone it down because it was prohibitive and we just didn't have the time and money to shoot them from the angle where you wouldn't see the reflection. We did endless tests and finally found the right compromise.

ROD HOLCOMB
(director, "The Lost Warrior")

There was a little bit of overlighting, because they had to kind of even it out with the reflections. They did this with cross-lighting, single lights, and stuff, even though that's what they were doing outside. You never saw me take the Cylon [Red Eye] off the front steps in my episode. Those guys were just blind inside. They actually had to go as slow as they did, not because they just couldn't move, but because of the reflectivity. You couldn't get up really close. You had to be back and you had people, extras in the background, hiding things and stuff like that. So it took a little time to shoot.

CHRISTIAN I. NYBY II

They could kind of see where their feet were but that was about it, so the poor guys would fall over all the time.

JEAN-PIERRE DORLEAC

The first day we shot the Cylons on horseback on Carillon, the Cylons kept falling off the horses because they couldn't see where they were going. It was really very funny. Despite repeated attempts, removing the horses and having the Cylons advance on foot ultimately solved the problem.

CHRISTIAN I. NYBY II

Generally, you would get everything working and then two of them would fall flat on their face, because they couldn't see where their feet were going.

So that was always a problem. Eventually we would get a few of them that could actually work in the suit pretty well, and those were the ones that played the Cylons most often.

JACK GILL
(stunt double, *Battlestar Galactica*)

The only reason they stuck us in the Cylon suits was that they already had us on salary to double the leads, so it was cheaper for them to also put us in the Cylon suit while we were on set anyway. Most of the guys that were in the Cylon suits were really big guys. The tall guys were mostly background extras and weren't allowed to do stunts. Every now and then they'd bring in two or three really big stunt guys, but sometimes you had ten to twelve Cylons, of which a bunch had to be killed or blown up. That's why they put us in a suit and had us wear lifts.

I did Cylon suits like fifteen to twenty times I was on the series. Every time I did, that suit pinched the crap out of me. When you fell down there was always a shard that would pierce down in my armpit or somewhere else. It really was a very uncomfortable suit.

The problem with playing a Cylon was that you couldn't put your hands down when you fell. You had to fall straight to your chest. It sucked, because if you did put your hands down, the director would come over and say, "No, no, no. You've got to remember that you are a robot and you have to fall like a robot would fall. You can't put your hands out." So you'd fall face-flat to the ground with no protection and all the plastic breaking.

SCOTT MANTZ

What I loved about *Galactica* at the time, the thing that really struck me, was the Cylons, the way the Cylons sounded. When they talked, I couldn't get enough of it. I loved hearing them talk. When you first hear their voices in the gas cloud when Apollo and Zac are ambushed, I just thought, "Wow, that's so cool."

STEVEN SIMAK

Dialogue for the Cylon Centurions was never actually spoken on set, but recorded later by actors in postproduction. Using a device called a vocoder, sound effects artist Peter Berkos mixed the actors' voices with mechanical and electrical sounds to create the robotic Cylon tongue.

PETER BERKOS
(sound effects editor, *Battlestar Galactica*)

The vocoder's purpose is to disguise sounds. There are twenty-seven combinations that take a sound and change it. It creates a mixture of sound and dialogue. In fact, we [also] did that with the daggit, Muffit. We fed mechanical dog sounds into the vocoder and an actual dog barking, and we came out with the toy-dog barks.

The Cylon Imperious Leader, built for a then-exorbitant $50,000 and yet ultimately kept in the shadows, was envisioned as a reptilian creature with a cobra head. Dorleac was responsible for the costume, while Carlo Rambaldi, the man responsible for bringing E.T. to life, designed and built the head itself.

JEAN-PIERRE DORLEAC

Glen told me he wanted him to be reptilian, but still very imposing. He wanted him to be somewhat inscrutable, so we built a frame and put a huge cloak over it. The hood was a piece that was cast out of wire and sculpted. Scales were individually attached to both the cloak and hood. The costume was then coated with resin and metallic effects to provide an unearthly quality. It was a very involved costume, but there wasn't any costume on the show that wasn't to some extent.

For the voice of the Imperious Leader, the Cylon ruler, Berkos once again relied on the vocoder. Initially, Larson's instruction to the sound editor was to create "the most evil voice in the world." With that in mind, Berkos sought out actor Lou Ferrigno (TV's Incredible Hulk).

PETER BERKOS

He had a deep, resonant, good clear voice and so we had him record the dialogue. Then I got the sound of a cobra hissing and we sent the cobra hiss and the dialogue through the vocoder. These two sounds intermixed so that when you finally heard the voice, it had the distinct hiss of a cobra, as if the cobra was talking. Once we got that into the picture, Glen thought that it was almost too frightening and he wanted to go in a different direction. He was a little worried because we gave him too much of what he wanted, so instead we got Patrick Macnee.

RICHARD JAMES

We didn't have a lot of information—certainly no development of who the Imperious Leader was other than the fact that he was evil. It was one of those cases where less was more. It's kind of like Satan speaking from hell. How are you going to define the location graphically? You keep it in the dark, put a strong light over him, and again we went for that speaking from on high. Also, money was an issue. There was not a lot of money spent on that set, because he was going to be seated, so there was no need. They also had that red laser beam for the Cylon eye, so I reinforced it into the set.

In the theatrical version of "Saga of a Star World," the Cylon Imperious Leader executes the traitorous Baltar (John Colicos). A similar fate was planned for the television premiere, when it was decided that the character would make a good recurring villain and Colicos was granted a merciful reprieve.

GLEN A. LARSON

He was just such a good heavy. I don't recall if the pressure came from the network or what, but they simply liked him. When you're earning your sustenance from the network you certainly do keep an open eye to what they like, and if they like something and you don't dislike it, then you don't have a fight. I certainly liked Colicos. He had come out of *Anne of the Thousand Days* not too long before that, and he was high on my list of very fine actors. I always believe you want the strongest heavies you can get. It certainly validates your heroes.

JOHN COLICOS
(actor, "Count Baltar")

When he sells out to the Cylons you could read all kinds of little connotations—moles in secret service agencies and things like that. Yet he was fighting for his own, warped, integrity. One doesn't know why, because we never got that far. But that was the line in which I wanted to go. For him to say I am not wrong; I am not destroying the human race, I am trying to survive. It's a survival story in a strange kind of way. I'm the Benedict Arnold of the distant future, a kind of galactic Judas. Baltar is the fallen angel, and you can carry that through all the religions you want to think about. He's the ultimate Judas, the betrayer of mankind.

SCOTT MANTZ

He was brilliant. I knew him as Baltar before I knew him as Kor [in *Star Trek*]. Here's this guy who sold out the human race so he could lead the Cylons. What an asshole. But he was the perfect dastardly, mustache-twirling villain that you love to hate. John Colicos chewed the scenery among the best of them, and he played the role perfectly. He was so over-the-top, but he was over-the-top in all of the right ways.

JOHN COLICOS

There was an episode that Vince Edwards directed ["The Living Legend"] in which he said he wanted to get me down off that bloody chair. Of course, they polished the floor so tremendously that I nearly fell on my ass. But I welcomed anything that got me off climbing that ladder, because it was difficult to have a dynamic performance when you are rooted literally to one spot.

It was more than two decades earlier that Colicos first starred with Lorne Greene in *Hamlet* for the Canadian Broadcasting Company, with Colicos as the Danish prince and Greene as King Claudius.

JOHN COLICOS

That was before Lorne became a hero in *Bonanza* and I discovered that villains, like blondes, have more fun. Inevitably we both wound up in Hollywood, where we renewed our friendship. But by then, the die was cast. Lorne was a Western father figure. I was on the side of evil and injustice.

ROBERT FEERO
(actor, "Bora")

John was one of the funniest. I socialized with him quite often, after the shows, became pretty good friends with him. He was probably a genius. His wit, and knowledge, was vast, and he was a greatly entertaining fellow.

JOHN COLICOS

I went to a science fiction convention and they asked me one very perplexing question, "What does Baltar do when his chair turns around?" and I said, "He reads Marvel Comics," which brought the house down.

Just as *Star Wars* clearly influenced *Galactica*'s visual aesthetic, so, too, would the success of John Williams's music define the approach to the series' score, the last major component of the massive three-hour telefilm. To create the grand dramatic music audiences expected from their space operas, Larson sought out longtime associate Stu Phillips. Over the course of their fourteen-year partnership, Phillips composed the music for numerous Larson productions, including *The Six Million Dollar Man, Quincy, Knight Rider,* and *Buck Rogers in the 25th Century.*

Phillips is justifiably particularly proud of the main title, on which he shares credit with Glen Larson, for its combination of heroism and pastoral motifs. With the exception of the main title and some thematic material, which he had begun earlier, Phillips was allocated a scant thirteen days to score the entire three-hour telefilm.

STU PHILLIPS
(composer, *Battlestar Galactica*)

In thirteen days, I can tell you, a lot of it wasn't inspiration, it was hard work. A lot of it was, "I'd better decide on something, because I've only got thirty-six hours left."

Although the series itself was scored with a studio orchestra, the pilot was recorded in five days with the Los Angeles Philharmonic, an opportunity that was very exciting for Phillips as a conductor.

STU PHILLIPS

A space adventure like this is a composer's delight. It's the kind of thing that opens you up, because you're on ground where you can justify anything you do. It's the big career thing you do that you love—the opportunity to do a *Lawrence of Arabia.*

The theme as far as I know has been recorded about seventeen times with seventeen various orchestras. Years ago, I went to Scotland and rerecorded the entire score. Some of it wasn't in the original soundtrack album and we added some cues. I did it in Scotland with the Royal Scottish National Orchestra, and that was very exciting, to suddenly revisit all that music after all that time.

A very funny thing is we had to get the music from Universal. The librarian said great but this was a different librarian than was there when we did the show and he called me up and told me they could not find the music to *Battlestar Galactica.* They had looked through the entire warehouse and could not find it. It was ridiculous. They were about to cancel the entire trip to Scotland to go rerecord this and I called up the original librarian who used to be there, who was my neighbor. And I asked him why can't we find the music to *Battlestar Galactica,* and we thought and thought, and while I was on the phone it suddenly occurred to me that this originally was called *Saga of a Star World.* We were looking under "B" and it was in the warehouse under "S." I barely got the music to Scotland in time for the recording. So nothing has changed after all these years.

With production in full swing, Universal, in what was hoped would be a merchandising bonanza, signed licensing agreements with Mattel Toys in 1977. By July 1978, almost two months before the premiere, model kits of the Viper and

Cylon Raider were already selling well past their quota. Future merchandise plans included action figures, clothing, electronic games, stuffed daggits, playing cards, a soundtrack album, and a Marvel comic book.

SCOTT MANTZ

What I remember about the merchandise from *Battlestar Galactica* was I had all of it, because there wasn't that much of it. The show started, and it was very popular. It kicked the floodgates open for merchandising. I had the Topps trading cards, and I still have them, mint condition, the same condition I bought them in. I had the *Battlestar Galactica Photostory,* which I still have in mint condition next to all my *Star Trek* Fotonovels. I also had Battlestar Galactica the game. I don't remember what the objective of the game was.

RONALD D. MOORE
(cocreator/executive producer, *Battlestar Galactica* [2004])

I remember getting the *TV Guide* in the mail at our house that had *Galactica* on the cover. It was the Fall Preview issue, which I always looked forward to as a kid. I read *TV Guide* obsessively. They were on the cover as the big, new, flashy series on ABC that fall. I was like, "Oh my God, they're doing a full-blown sci-fi epic on television. This is amazing." And then I went out and bought the novelization and read it before the show was on the air and I was really excited to watch it.

I think that I was surprised that it was campier than it read on the page in the book, which had a rougher-edged quality to it in my memory. The things like the death of Zac and political aspects of the dialogue and the human colonies were more deeply explored in the novelization. In the filmed version, I remember feeling they went for the humor more than they did in the book, and I was a little bit disappointed by that, but trusting that it's all going to be fine. Even at that kind of young age, thirteen I think, I was becoming somewhat aware of tone and style and that kind of thing.

SCOTT MANTZ

I also had the plastic Colonial Viper, the one that shot a little missile from the front. Technically, the missile should have been shot from the side to the wings, but it was a missile that came from the front of the Viper. I got the thing, and I would play around with it and fire the missile, and then I heard on TV that a kid died because he shot the missile into his mouth and choked on it. Everyone in school was talking about this toy. My mom immediately took away my toy and took the missile and said, "Here, now you can play with it." I had the Cylon fighter, too. But that cast a very bad shadow over the series itself.

JAMES CALLIS
(actor, "Gaius Baltar," *Battlestar Galactica* [2004])

Growing up in the seventies and watching that show as a seven-year-old, I'd say Richard Hatch and Dirk Benedict were kind of heroes of mine. I thought they were amazing and they looked amazing. The premise of the show seemed pretty dark to me, even as a kid, that there were millions of people who would have been killed, their planets destroyed. I remember the scene where Apollo comes down in his Viper. There's all these people at his side in background, slightly out of focus, and there's evidently only room for him and maybe one more in the Viper, and there's hundreds of people behind him. I just remember as a kid thinking, "Wait a minute. What's going to happen to all of them?" And that upset me, because I'd not seen that before. It was, like, not only does that happen in the real world, it also happens on TV. I was like, "No, no, somebody's got to come and save these people. Are they just going to be left there to die?" It was upsetting.

RONALD D. MOORE

It was pretty amazing for network television. It was far beyond what *Star Trek* had been able to do ten years before that. So, I was pretty impressed with the production quality. I remember just feeling, "Wow, this is a big, giant, epic show that's willing to spend some real money and is gonna do big things!"

5.
LAUNCH WHEN READY

"They're waggling."

The September 17, 1978, *Battlestar Galactica* three-hour premiere on ABC drew an estimated audience of over sixty-five million viewers, finishing with a 27.8 rating and a 42 share. The stellar ratings success, however, would not last. By the critical November sweeps, the series hailed by *Newsweek* as "The Son of Star Wars" dropped dramatically to a 28 share. Over the course of the season, *Galactica* would ride a wave of popular highs, spiraling budgets, and, mostly, critical lows.

Transforming *Galactica* from event programming to a weekly television format would present a series of almost insurmountable challenges for the producers and may have ultimately sealed its fate as a short-lived but beloved cult TV series. Time and budget would be key considerations. With the pilot, "Lost Planet of the Gods," and "Gun on Ice Planet Zero" already in production, it also became necessary to rethink the dynamics of the show on a smaller scale as midway through the filming of the pilot, ABC and Universal made the decision to expand *Battlestar Galactica* to a weekly series.

RICHARD HATCH
(actor, "Captain Apollo")

It was originally supposed to be a seven-hour miniseries; then, halfway through the opening three-hour pilot, which they told us was also going to be a movie, they picked it up as a series. The hard part was that it was not constructed to be a series. They hadn't thought it out; they didn't know where they were going with it. They hadn't developed the sets, the shots, the special effects, and so they were working overtime. They had to just cram it.

LAURETTE SPANG
(actress, "Cassiopeia")

In the beginning, it was always exciting. We were on the cover of *Newsweek* and *People* and *Us* magazine. It was coming on the coattails of *Star Wars* and it was a great thing. I think everybody was sort of in awe of the project. It was wonderful. All of us were just thrust in there.

DIRK BENEDICT
(actor, "Lieutenant Starbuck")

A lot of that buildup and hype worked against it. If an athlete comes in and he is the number-one draft pick, he is going to save the franchise. If the franchise isn't saved, even though he has a good year and by any other standards it would be an exceptionally good year if not spectacular year, and he doesn't win the MVP, then he is a disappointment. Going to the Super Bowl and not winning it, you're a failure! We went to the Super Bowl and we didn't win it. Although we did very well, we were a failure in some eyes.

Joining Glen Larson to help launch *Galactica* as a full-fledged television series was Donald Bellisario, a former advertising copywriter and a protégé of Larson's who would later go on to create such hit TV series as *Magnum, P.I., Airwolf, Tales of the Gold Monkey, Quantum Leap,* and *JAG,* and the *NCIS* franchise. He got his start as a story editor and, later, producer on *Baa Baa Black Sheep,* starring Robert Conrad. As a young man in the Marines, Bellisario had served alongside Lee Harvey Oswald, who would later be arrested for the assassination of President John F. Kennedy and be shot by Jack Ruby.

CHRISTIAN I. NYBY II
(director, "The Long Patrol")

Glen was really pretty hands-on, particularly in the beginning, but [supervising producer] Don Bellisario became very involved as the series went on.

DONALD BELLISARIO
(supervising producer, *Battlestar Galactica*)

That pilot started off so dramatically and so big and there was an enormous amount of money spent on it that could never be spent on subsequent episodes. Some of the two-hours that followed did have a decent amount of money spent on them. Then when you got to the one-hour episodes, they had to start pulling back, and that affects the types of stories you can tell, the type of scenes you can write, and that affects the dramatic quality, the look, the tone, everything.

DOROTHY FONTANA
(story editor, *Star Trek*)

I pitched verbally on the original *Battlestar Galactica* once. Not hired, never tried again.

RICHARD HATCH

The hard part was that it was not constructed to be a series. They didn't know where they were going with it. They hadn't developed the sets, the shots, or the special effects, and so they were working overtime. Here is the biggest production ever on television and all of a sudden it's thrown into a series format without any lead time to develop scripts, story arcs, or plotlines. That's why the first year was such a conglomeration of good and bad. There were wonderful things, there were cheesy things, and there were horrible things.

MICHAEL SLOAN
(producer, *Battlestar Galactica*)

Once it got down to an hour, it became more difficult to maintain that production value. What we would do is take a lot of the cockpit shots and some of the fighter shots and try to use different parts of them and flip them and put them in different places. We had to take a lot of stuff from the movie and the two-parters and use that like stock footage, because there was only so much we could spend on it and we were always waiting for opticals. We had no video effects, so every effect was a major optical. I remember John Dykstra saying to me that trying to maintain this on an hour is going to be really rough, and it was.

In addition to the challenges of mounting such an ambitious series on a weekly basis, Larson and Bellisario also had to contend with a situation not unlike one that had developed on *Star Trek* ten years earlier: two unhappy lead actors, one of whom—the presumptive lead actor (and number one on the call sheet)—resented the growing popularity of the other.

DIRK BENEDICT

Richard was always intended to be the star of the show. It was him and Lorne, father and son. I was just one of the pilots, but the audience loved Starbuck and they got a lot of mail, so they brought that character more into the show.

DONALD BELLISARIO

I remember Richard having a problem with Apollo being so square, so to speak, and so morally straitlaced, whereas Starbuck was this character who smoked cigars and drank liquor and loved women. He's a fun character, but the difference was that Starbuck had no stability to him, which came out in a show that I wrote with Fred Astaire ["The Man with Nine Lives"], where you found out that his father had disappeared and left him and he really was looking for a father. That kind of explained his instability. The Apollo character played by Richard Hatch had stability. He was the one you want at your side when you really get into trouble.

DIRK BENEDICT

Much of the problems and the fighting, the egos that went on, happens with any show, and it went right by me. I didn't get involved with any of it, and there was a lot of it. When I went to work the first day, I was in a tiny little dressing room the size of a broom closet. I never said anything. After a while my character got popular and I got a lot of fan mail, but I was still in a broom closet. Richard and Lorne were in big motor homes, Jane was in a beautiful dressing room and I was in a broom closet. My agent wanted to say something, but I said, "No, no, no." One day I showed up to work after about four months and I had a motor home. Somebody decided we should give him a motor home, because I was working every day and I was doing the same amount of work and was contributing to the show. But I never asked for anything. I didn't get paid much, because the network didn't want me, and so I never made much money doing that show, but none of that bothers me.

RICHARD HATCH

I just felt like I was always there to drive the throughline with the main A-story and that it allowed the other characters to have a lot more fun, especially the Starbuck character. I don't want to take anything away from Starbuck, he is a great character. You want to give every character as much as you can, but then I felt you also need to balance that off with the Apollo character—he isn't just a straightforward leader.

TERRENCE MCDONNELL
(story editor, *Battlestar Galactica*)

Starbuck was a fun character to write. That kind of thing is always fun. I think that given the fact of where Apollo was when we came on board I am not sure there was anything we could do with the character.

ALAN J. LEVI
(director, "Gun on Ice Planet Zero")

Richard and Dirk were both nice guys. They were competitive. If Richard had four words more than Dirk he'd say, "Why didn't I get those four words?" I think they liked each other and they were respectful of each other but there was a little competition there. Dirk had the lighter character, but he was the character that everyone wanted to be. He had the girls, he had the romances, he had the fun. If it had been twenty years later, he would have been the one in the corner smoking dope.

RICHARD HATCH

My question wasn't about doing more, it was about my character having a little more dimension and challenging me more as an actor to bring out more of the layers and levels of this character. In the first year a lot of characters get neglected, and looking back, had they had a second or a third year, I am sure they would have worked out those kinks like they did toward the end of the first season. They started doing interesting things again and giving my character dimension. In fact, they started to give the Starbuck character more serious things to do, to show the other side of his nature, to balance his laid-back cigar-swaggering character by giving him some emotion, and they were trying to loosen my character up and give him a little bit more romance and a little bit more of a sense of humor. I had told Glen that I felt a little frustrated.

ANNE LOCKHART
(actress, "Sheba")

Richard was *very* frustrated.

TERRENCE MCDONNELL

He was the first actor that ever came to [story editor] Jim [Carlson] and myself that wanted to sit down with us, the writers, and talk about this character. How we could improve the character, what little pieces we could give him, little things like that, and he was very concerned, as any good actor is to get the most out of who they are portraying. He would come up to the office from time to time, and we would have little chats. I remember he had complained because Dirk was getting all the comedy lines. Well, that's the character of Starbuck. And he wanted some funny lines; that's not the character of Apollo, but we took it in stride.

RICHARD HATCH

Many people said that after the first couple of episodes, where I was very strongly positioned in the show, my character kind of moved to the side.

That was frustrating to me. Looking back, it just takes time when you are dealing with that many characters. And yes it is hard for an actor's ego when writers tend to lean toward one or two characters that they seem to have more fun writing for, but if I was the writer I probably would have had fun writing the Starbuck character or the Baltar character, too, because it's the bad boy and the bad guy.

In order to save time and money and take advantage of the expansive Universal Studios backlot, Larson decided to expand on the *Wagon Train* thematics and set many of the storylines in frontier towns. "The Lost Warrior"—a thinly veiled knockoff of George Stevens's *Shane* in which a damaged Cylon under the thrall of an evil rancher faces off against the mysterious stranger who's come to town—and "The Magnificent Warriors," a ham-fisted homage to *The Magnificent Seven,* both utilized Western motifs, right down to the swinging barroom doors.

GLEN A. LARSON
(creator/executive producer, *Battlestar Galactica*)

If you can then treat space and its environments more as frontiers, you're preparing a setting for a kind of drama that traditionally has a larger audience than science fiction. I had a certain concern about dropping down to a soundstage and finding some creature. I always wanted to try and find themes that allowed us to be much larger.

Star Trek was always at its worst when it was monster of the week. I wanted to avoid the pitfalls that might narrow the appeal of the show. People have always made a big deal out of the fact that it was Lorne Greene and were we trying to do *Bonanza*? Not really. We just wanted to push these people into situations where the people become important to us and their existence becomes important and that the shows are playing on a human—or heart—level that transcends science fiction.

GLEN OLIVER
(pop-culture commentator)

Battlestar Galactica often felt like a series fueled by atypically lofty ambitions: to explore the human condition, survey the importance of spirituality versus pragmatism, examine our tendency toward greed versus a far more elusive altruism—but it was sometimes marginalized by not remaining a hundred percent dedicated to this exploration. Its uneven fusion of genres undermined its own core intent. I think *Battlestar*, on the whole, was very much headed in the right direction. There's some great spirituality and truthful, genuine drama to be found in it. But it was often clumsy in its balance, and failed to smoothly merge disparate visions.

ALEX HYDE-WHITE
(actor, "Cadet Bow")

The set had a collegial, soap opera feel to it. Kind of like a nice big community preparing for a long haul of a run. No one really knew that the stories were too thin to justify the big production value, because it was a new show, with high expectations, supervised by veterans but produced, actually produced on a daily basis, by this fraternity of creatives, some of whom were used to the other shows on the lot like *Rockford Files, Quincy,* and *The Hulk* that were built around the alpha male lead and had a strong central authority figure. Richard Hatch was supposed to be the star; he was a kind and gentle man. The set was well run under Don Bellisario's command. Glen Larson had a lot going on and he left the day-to-day to his lieutenants.

CHRISTIAN I. NYBY II

First thing in the morning, all the actors come in, the crew reports in—whatever scene it is, ex: scene fourteen on the bridge of *Galactica*—and then you get Lorne [Greene], Terry [Carter], Dirk [Benedict], and Maren Jensen or whoever you've got in the scene. You've all got your scripts, you've got the cameramen with you, and the assistant director, and then you very carefully go through the scene. Generally, I had it blocked out in my mind to a certain extent, but I allowed the actors the freedom to move where they would like to move. I usually started them where I liked them to start. Often in the script, there was a scene where it would dictate to them where to go. During that time the cameraman or the director of photography will determine with me where the best place is for the camera to go. Maybe at a certain point we'll move the camera with them, or decide that this is a great time to use a crane, or a great time to maybe do a dolly shot. Or maybe it's a very tense scene and we'd like to do it handheld.

All of those are determined when you are rehearsing, and then the actors go away. They continue to get made up, and get in their costume, and so forth. Then the director of photography with the gaffer, the key grip, and the stand-ins light the scene. You rehearse the camera moves with the stand-ins and get as close as you can to shooting it without the actors. Then of course you bring the actors back in and refine it all. By then everyone, the actors and the director, has contributed to the construction of that scene.

ROD HOLCOMB
(director, "The Man with Nine Lives")

I used to spend hours and hours on homework. Sometimes never going to sleep, getting ready for the next day because I was insecure. At the time, I didn't have a lot of experience, but I watched a lot of episodes when I was a producer on *Harry O.* The other thing I learned was how to cover so many characters in a scene. Sometimes there could be ten speaking characters in one scene, so you really had to work out who you would spend time shooting and who you didn't. You'd need to decide who had to work in a three-shot as opposed to getting a single. You always paid homage to Lorne and made sure you gave Lorne his close-up, and Richard as well. The other times, you could use nice two-shots. The material itself required work on your part to find the nuances. The forward motion of most of the episodes was fairly straightforward. It was a really simple three-act play. And Glen did a good job of writing, since he never wrote from a whole outline. It was a big operation. How they got it on the air every week was beyond me.

CHRISTIAN I. NYBY II

My dad [Christian Nyby, director of *The Thing from Another World*] put it best when he said, "Do your homework before you go to work the next morning and plot out every scene," which I always did. He said, "But leave it on your desk, because when you get to work, you don't want to be locked into something because if an actor says, 'You know. I don't feel right sitting in this chair. I'd like to sit over here,' it throws everything off. So the best thing is to know the scene as best you can, know how you'd like to do it, and then as best you can cope with the actors." In my career it worked ninety-five percent of the time.

Once you were set on a scene, you could do multiple takes, obviously, because you wanted to get the best take. You had a little time for coverage because you wanted to get in closer, or do the reverse angle, or so forth, but you just didn't have that much time. In television movies, you do have more time. Instead of doing eight or ten pages a day, you might do four or five. There are a number of ways to film any sequence, but once you make your mind up you just go forward with that.

You shoot a master of some sort where you're establishing where you are and who the characters are, and the position they are in and where they're moving to first. It doesn't have to be perfect all the way through, because you can fix that in coverage. Where you'd have problems is if you're going to do one take, where it's a long kind of walk-and-talk and you have two characters walking down a long corridor and the camera is in front of them. If a mic shadow pops in there, or if somebody blows a line, you have to go back to number one, because you don't have anything to cut to. Unless you're really hard up and try to cover it, but it's hard when you have two people in a corridor they're walking down. You can't get too much closer to them or you'll see just two heads walking.

However, the biggest challenge for the fledgling series remained the punishing production schedule. With the rigors of filming a visual-effects-intensive series in the seventies, pre-CGI, and mounting a massive production with a large ensemble, it became more and more difficult to make the episode airdates, in some cases necessitating episodes being flipped in broadcast order and often overlapping shooting schedules among multiple episodes.

DIRK BENEDICT

It took us sixty-nine days to do the pilot, which was supposed to be done in twenty-nine. I remember, by the end of the first season, we were shooting two episodes simultaneously to try and make it. Richard and I would be in both episodes and we would go from soundstage to soundstage with two crews, two directors, two of everything. I'd say the last couple of months it went like that. It was very intensive twelve- or thirteen-hour days.

HERBERT JEFFERSON, JR.
(actor, "Lieutenant Boomer")

It was a lot of fun, a lot of work. We put in fourteen-, fifteen-hour days under the hot lights in hot uniforms and all kinds of physical discomfort here and there, but it paid off in the fun that we had.

ANNE LOCKHART

It was sixteen- to eighteen-hour days.

HERBERT JEFFERSON, JR.

Some episodes they were writing as we shot. We would get rewrites on the spot.

LAURETTE SPANG

I had been doing guest-star parts for a while, so I just wasn't prepared for this sort of thing. I wasn't unhappy, because it was just too exciting. It's a very overpowering thing for someone in their twenties to be thrust into all of a sudden. Dirk was being chased by the *National Enquirer* and I gave him the keys to my house a couple of times when I was out of town so he could stay there and they'd leave him alone. There was just a lot of that. There were interviewers on the set a lot and there were fans, but beyond that the hours were long and there was night shooting and going overtime. I think it ended up being thirteen months of straight shooting.

GLEN A. LARSON

I used to have a reputation, which may or may not mean anything to the layperson, but you know at some point you have to turn over a film. We had very pressing airdates and difficult effects and I had a reputation for having heel marks all the way to the lab: "Give it back to us, we can still fix this,

this, and this." I'm still making notes on some of the things I would fix even now.

VINCE EDWARDS
(director, "The Living Legend")

Long hours but it was enjoyable. Everyone was into the space craze at that particular time and it was fun doing it. We had *a lot* of set visitors.

ANNE LOCKHART

Our shooting schedule was really loopy. I remember one night watching the show and what they showed as coming attractions for the following week were the dailies of what we'd shot on Friday, which literally made no sense. I had no social life. One night, I fell asleep on the phone with a guy I was dating.

LORNE GREENE
(actor, "Commander Adama")

We started up as a miniseries and all of a sudden it became a full-fledged series. We didn't have enough lead time. We didn't have four or five months to prepare for the series itself. It takes time. Sometimes you get one line in a script that says that the battlestar *Galactica* is on fire, and four days later that one line has been filmed.

So each show has its own schedule. You can't say a show is going to be done in seven days, because sometimes it's done in ten days or twelve days.

LAURETTE SPANG

There was a period of time there in the middle of the season where I was really worn out and I had a week off and I went to Mexico myself. I had never been out of the country before. We were all doing a lot of talk shows like Mike Douglas and Merv Griffin and Dinah Shore and doing *Hollywood Squares*. It was terrific, but it all took its toll.

ANNE LOCKHART

I have also heard stories of the picture being delivered to the network in New York four minutes before airtime. We got rewrites two days *after* we'd shot a scene. We'd go, "We already shot this."

TERRY CARTER
(actor, "Commander Tigh")

It was very difficult to develop the scenes as you might have if you had more time with things. I am from the old school. When I started working in television, it was live back in New York with *Playhouse 90* and *Kraft Theatre*. We rehearsed for weeks before we shot, because it was live. Live TV meant you had to know what you were doing, so we would rehearse and you would develop your relationship and your character. You would have a chance to think about things, and that's, of course, based on the whole theater tradition of rehearsal and development. Hollywood had a whole different way because they had a movie tradition and in movies they didn't do a lot of rehearsal. In television they did even less. They would say, "Let's do a rehearsal for camera," and you would walk through and hit your marks and then we'd be ready to shoot. They do give direction, I don't mean to imply otherwise, but if it looks good the director will just shoot it.

CHRISTIAN I. NYBY II

It was difficult, because we tried to achieve something that was only achieved in film. We were cranking out eight or nine pages a day. I really did enjoy it, though.

PETER BERKOS
(sound effects editor, *Battlestar Galactica*)

We sometimes reached a point where executives from the Tower [Universal corporate] came down threatening to pull the plug on us Sundays because we were taking too long. Yet, we were not going to release anything that was not ready for the general public.

STU PHILLIPS
(composer, *Battlestar Galactica*)

Before I even got on the scoring stage I was over budget. Even though they gave me thirty-eight or forty-two players, they still budgeted the thing like it was *The Rockford Files*. As far as they were concerned at Universal, it was still a one-hour dramatic show and every one-hour dramatic show gets the same budget, so none of the producers bitched. From the very beginning I was over budget. When I asked what I should do, they said do nothing— just continue being over budget. In three days there was no way I could write twenty-five minutes of music. It was the worst.

Phillips's solution to the rigid time constraints was to restructure cues that had been used in previous episodes so they would fit the new story in terms of length and dramatic intensity. Tracking, a practice no longer permitted by the musicians' union, was another alternative, which involved using the actual music recordings from previous episodes to fill the series' current needs.

STU PHILLIPS

The union went to a hundred percent no tracking a little at a time. When we did *Galactica* we were on ninety percent no tracking. However, even to this day when you have no tracking, if you petition the union for reasons beyond your control that you have to track, they can give you permission. Exciting and next to impossible but it got done. Somehow all these things and all these deadlines get done eventually. You suffer. You don't sleep a lot but you get it done and if you are lucky it comes out reasonably well.

STEVEN SIMAK
(journalist, *Battlestar Galactica* historian)

The music for the pilot was recorded in five days, with some additional work done after revisions were made to the final edit.

Art director Richard James faced similar budget and time problems. Although a substantial amount of money was allocated for the construction of the standing sets on the premiere, once *Galactica* went to series, the art director saw his budget for new sets drop to an anemic $17,000 per one-hour episode.

RICHARD JAMES
(art director, *Battlestar Galactica*)

Here I was spending a hundred thousand dollars on sets and suddenly when we went to series, my budget was seventeen thousand dollars per episode. You can't do that show on that kind of money.

GLEN A. LARSON

Television is restrictive and when you're on fairly early Sunday night it can be even more restrictive and it takes a lot of pressure on your creative juices, but probably the most inhibiting of all of them was just simply time.

Maintaining the Cylons as a credible threat also became problematic, owing in large part to the relationship the series had with ABC Standards and Practices. Utilizing a point system, Standards and Practices would review each episode to ensure it was not overtly violent for network broadcast. Although an action show, because of its 8 P.M. Sunday nighttime slot *Galactica* was also considered to be family viewing. As such, the series was allowed only six acts of violence per episode. Because the Cylons were depicted as essentially alien robots, there was no limitation on how many of them could be destroyed in an episode.

DONALD BELLISARIO
(supervising producer, *Battlestar Galactica*)

The problem with that is that all you could do was kill machines and show no consequence of it. The machines couldn't kill anybody back. It soon became a bit ludicrous to the watching public, who did like the show, but your hero was never in any jeopardy. No one was ever in any kind of jeopardy in this trek through space to find Earth, and I think that was very detrimental to the show.

STEVEN E. DE SOUZA
(story editor, *The Hardy Boys/Nancy Drew Mysteries*)

The network tortured them on violence. The shows had not aired yet. They were filming the third episode and some junior underling at the network was in the room and they had this long memo from the censor. "You can't do this?" she asks. "I don't understand why they're giving you such a hard time about killing the Cylons. Aren't they just robots?" Somebody started to say, "No they're rep . . ." Then Larson kicked that person hard under the table. As we all left and got into the car, Glen said, "The Cylons are robots from now on!" They had been lizard people, but now they were robots.

Somebody said, "We already showed the leaders." He goes, "The leaders are lizards but the Cylons are robots." They had already filmed a scene in the snowram for "Gun on Ice Planet Zero," where they go to a planet of clones and they're all wearing OshKosh B'gosh overalls where Boxey says, "Why do the Cylons hate us?" Apollo says, "They're cold-blooded creatures. They have a natural enmity toward mammals." It was a whole biological thing. They reshot that entire scene to explain they're mechanical life forms instead because they were getting so many notes about killing them.

Censors are horrible. I had one guy that had the misfortune of constantly being my guy at ABC. I was always good. I would say, "What about this? I don't want to spin my guys' wheels here, so on next week's episode I took your note about guns seriously so we're only going to kill one bad guy, we're going to crush him under a collapsing house. Another guy we're going to have cut in half by a steel cable. We're also going to have somebody fall into a commercial oven."

He says, "Are you out of your fucking mind? It's a 7:00 show." I said, "A-ha! I just described *The Wizard of Oz, Captains Courageous,* and *Hansel and Gretel.*" Anyway, I battled with this guy on *The Hardy Boys* and then it was *The Spirit* and then I had him again when we did the television series of *Foul Play.*

GLEN A. LARSON

You'll have the network pushing you to do certain things, but a prototype for me on this was *The Fugitive.* A lot of the guys at the network weren't familiar with that show, but I was, because I was weaned on it as a kid. Lieutenant Gerard, as opposed to being a constant threat unlike in the movie, didn't show up very often. You talked about him a lot and he shows up maybe every third episode for a quick pop and that was a good idea. When you're running, there's a threat, but very much like *The Fugitive* you've got these fugitive people running through space and are constantly under pressure and afraid of people who will betray them. So if you combine *The Fugitive* with space and *Wagon Train,* you're exploring some fairly successful shows.

TERRENCE MCCDONNELL

Part of the problem initially was the Cylons looked so cool and their ships were great and at least in the first episode they were actually a threat; but when you got into eight o'clock on Sunday night they were no longer a threat. They couldn't kill anybody. So it became a joke and I think at least to some degree that's why they started shifting the focus of stories to what other kind of villains can we have. That's why you got the neo-Nazi thing ["Greetings from Earth"] and Count Iblis ["War of the Gods"].

GLEN A. LARSON

What was great was *Galactica* sets out to find Earth but we have no way of knowing if this is a thousand years in the past or a thousand years in the future because there is no clock. They could have advanced a lot faster than us or a lot slower. Earth could have been a futuristic world when we got there, so what I was trying to avoid in the first season was nailing certain things down just to keep our options open. You could have discovered Earth and found a planet filled with prehistoric monsters or come back in the distant future. That might have been better than what ultimately became *Galactica 1980.*

There's a point where you can't bring in writers to do too much. That just bulges out and pushes out the parameters of the series until you have gotten your feet on the ground, especially when you have the network hammering you every day for different things. We actually had a lady come in from the network who was a coke addict. I didn't know at the time, but she would have these hyper ideas where she suddenly comes racing in and have this brainstorm. You'd look at her and say, "Gee, that's a great idea." Her idea was—and this was in the third week of the show—"Let's have the *Galactica* discover Earth." It's like let's have them catch the Fugitive or let's find the One-Armed Man in the third episode. I don't know how she got her job, but she certainly didn't have a great sense of theater.

The scope of the series, like the telefilm, remained unlike anything previously attempted for episodic television. Costume designer Jean-Pierre Dorleac estimates that once the show went to series, his team was producing close to 125 costumes every seven to eight days. Also, some thirty Cylon costumes, at $3,500 a piece, were also created, and, in many cases, destroyed.

JEAN-PIERRE DORLEAC
(costume designer, *Battlestar Galactica*)

Galactica was quite an undertaking. There was a lot of money spent. All of the various pieces on the show were made to order. All the boots, all the holsters and all the guns, everything that was in the costumes was all made. We only had eight days to do the episodes. During that time, we were supposed to be preparing for the next show, but inevitably, because the scripts weren't available, we would end up using probably five of those days actually doing the show we were working on, and then three days prepping the next show, and then five days on the next show finishing it off. We were constantly overlapping on shows, and after a while they all ran one into the other. But I have always been proud of the fact that no production has ever had to wait for my costumes. Sometimes we did not get the scripts until two or three days before the shoot, but the costumes, no matter what they were, were always there.

ROD HOLCOMB

I was just so blown away by all the creativity that was on that set.

Leaving the show was an aggrieved John Dykstra, upset over Universal's sudden decision to release "Saga of a Star World" theatrically, when he had only designed the visual effects for the smaller television screen (the telefilm played in theaters in Canada and Europe prior to its U.S. TV premiere in 1979 and was later released in America, in 1979, after having already played on television). Dykstra and his team had never designed the shots for the big screen and was unhappy with how the visual effects translated onto film screens. In addition, he was also anxious to realize the many post-*Star Wars* opportunities that existed in feature films for him, ankling *Galactica,* and soon found himself in an even more chaotic situation, taking over visual effects on the troubled *Star Trek: The Motion Picture* from Robert Abel & Associates, along with visual effects legend Doug Trumbull. As a result, the newly formed Universal Hartland took over production of *Galactica's* extensive weekly visual effects work.

STEVEN SIMAK

Dykstra's company, Apogee, was only contracted to create effects for the pilot and the two-hour episodes "Lost Planet of the Gods" and "Gun on Ice Planet Zero." After these were completed, many on the crew elected to return to ILM, newly relocated to Northern California, to work on *The Empire Strikes Back*. After *Galactica*, Apogee continued as a separate entity and created the effects for new projects including *Star Trek: The Motion Picture*.

RICHARD EDLUND
(special effects photography, *Battlestar Galactica*)

The funny thing about the show was there was no George [Lucas] there. There were different directors on the three [episodes] and they didn't really know how to deal with effects. It was kind of interesting for us who were doing it because I think a lot of us felt on *Star Wars* that we could have done more far-out shots, but George wanted very specific stuff, so we shot exactly what he wanted. On *Galactica*, we had kind of free rein to develop our own shots, so I think a lot of the shots in *Galactica*, dynamically and so on, are superior to *Star Wars*. Partially, it's because we had already learned to use the equipment and we had our chops together when we did *Galactica*. So the shots are better, but how they worked in the show, I don't think they are as good as how George put *Star Wars* together.

JOHN DYKSTRA
(visual effects supervisor/producer, *Battlestar Galactica*)

The work that I did on that show, although I think it could have been better if I had organized it differently, was really hard on me. You have to remember, too, that at that time, because there weren't many effects houses in town, there were some pretty tasty offers in the air. So it really came down to, as much as anything, a decision based on what I wanted to do rather than this was too hard to do. There was no real animosity. It was simply an issue of saying I don't think I can keep doing this. Also, I won't say I was young, but I was young. That was a new experience for me and I was learning and trying to do at the same time. It was a formidable task.

After Dykstra left *Galactica,* special effects would be handled by the Universal Hartland effects facility under the supervision of Wayne Smith and David Garber. Unlike Apogee, Universal Hartland was a wholly owned subsidiary of Universal Studios. Hartland (named after the street where the facility was located, in North Hollywood) was initially created to design and produce the visual effects for a theatrical version of *Buck Rogers*–a project stalled in development at Universal. Eventually, Glen Larson became involved, and *Buck Rogers in the 25th Century* moved forward as both a feature and a television series for NBC. Special effects development for *Buck Rogers* progressed at Hartland simultaneously while Apogee was creating the visuals for the *Galactica* TV series. After *Galactica* moved to Hartland, the facility was doing the effects for both series.

PETER ANDERSON
(visual effects supervisor, *Battlestar Galactica*)

We had actually started off at Douglas Trumbull's Future General; we had taken over—David Garber, Wayne Smith, Richard Yuricich, myself, and a few other people. When it went down we sort of semi-dissolved, but kept going and building the computers, the technology, and the *Draconia* for *Buck Rogers.* The *Draconia* was about two years in building. Three weeks to shoot it at the end of two years. During the hiatus, we realized that we were going to have to create our own environment to carry this, and by that time *Battlestar Galactica* was fairly far along. We knew we would be picking that up as well as *Buck Rogers,* which was going to be a series. So we put together this incredible facility that Universal owned and operated but was off-site in North Hollywood. It was about a hundred and thirty people; some of the best technicians, the best-educated people, the best designers and electronics came together and, as you can see, we were allowed to have fun. We were allowed to deliver images that just had some magic to them. The editors would say we need a shot and we would put personality into it. We built our own star fields; we built everything. Everything was delivered in-house, including the designs.

We had three different sections of models shops, full machine shops, full editorial, full processing, optical department, and a matte department.

[Matte painter] Syd [Dutton] did the marvelous work on the feature, and on the series we set up our own [matte painting] shop. So it was a full-service facility, and the contract with the network was we had to deliver a finished print, same as a theatrical print. So what we saw here was the feature release, and every week we delivered two films [*Battlestar Galactica* and *Buck Rogers*] on print. Oftentimes it was thirty to forty different shots under motion control and a lot of animation effects, but we didn't miss an episode and we didn't miss a shot. So sleep was not an option, generally speaking, but what a great team, what a great facility, and what a great series of shows to work on.

WAYNE SMITH
(co-effects producer, *Battlestar Galactica*)

What they asked us to do was almost impossible, because none of the equipment existed. We had to pull stuff from all over the place, and at the same time there was a grab for people in the industry because there was a lot of effects work right then. We didn't know who was going to show up sometimes for work. The first six months was unbelievable when I think about it. We tried to set it up so we had a library of shots and we would add to those every week. So in optical we would put existing elements together with new elements for a story and we just set up an assembly-line kind of process.

DAVID STIPES
(special effects, *Battlestar Galactica*)

We had ridiculously long hours, but it was delightful and really wonderful to work at. Peter Anderson was a bit of a jokester. He knew it was stressful, so he would at times bring food in, but if Peter ever walked out with his rain slickers on, you knew you were in trouble. He actually had a set of rain pants and overcoats, stuff like that, for rain and wet stuff, because . . . he loved to "pie" people—hit them with pies or food fights. Stuff like that. Basically it blew off a lot of tension, plus we all got a certain level of camaraderie that came of all that silliness. We finished a shot or got some accomplishment done and he'd bring in some food. Usually Peter also wound up throwing something. It was always an interesting time.

PETER ANDERSON

Our record was about two hundred and fifty separate passes for one shot [on *Buck Rogers*] but we were up to speed at that point and rather streamlined. We had fine-tuned our own blue screens and our own MOCO units so we were able to take the workload and run with it.

Universal Hartland never missed an airdate on either show. However, with an average of four to six weeks to produce visuals for an episode, it became necessary to use stock elements to save time wherever possible. Generally, the Hartland team received a first draft of the script for an episode one to two weeks prior to the live action shoot. Meeting in the facility's "war room," they would plan their strategy for the upcoming show.

TERRENCE MCDONNELL

They were doing *Buck Rogers* at the time, too, so Hartland was doubly busy. They could do little things, but if you needed a big effect you probably weren't going to get it and had to figure out another way to do it.

PETER ANDERSON

We would create a list of shots and oftentimes we would deal with the editors directly or indirectly to find out what they thought they really needed, because if they were going to cut something out it wasn't worth putting that much energy into it. Or, if they felt they had a big hole [effects-wise] coming up we would go back and shoot new elements, pull a couple of shots out of library, recomp them, or figure out something else appropriate to create for them.

The marvelous thing was that we had a season budget—we didn't have a show-by-show budget—so we knew how much money we had to spend. Therefore we could balance out the staff and materials, the purchases, and the gear we needed as a global, and at the end of that season we had to stay within that budget. In a couple of cases we had go to NBC or ABC when we were going to do a couple of two-hour shows and we would have them kick in a little extra bit of change to make them special.

Occasionally, we would sit up with the corporate people and do a little negotiation, but basically we knew by the end of the season that we would have spent our money properly, and how we did it was to deliver the best show possible. We had a strategy, we knew the shots, and we knew we had to have a couple of hero shots in each show. Each show was hand-approached, basically, and depending on how much lead time we had and how much magic that was in there, we would run with it.

DAVID STIPES

If all of the motion-control setups were tied up, I would wind up doing the shots stop-motion-animation-style or something. They were just amazed how I could do that without having motion control, because they were locked into that technology. Most of these were guys, even then, who were younger than me. They knew the motion-control technology, but didn't know any of the other more eclectic obscure stuff and approaches to things. So I got the chance to work on a lot of really weird projects. like doing the little shots of things that nobody could figure out how to deal with.

I saw the pilot for *Battlestar Galactica* that Dykstra had done. I thought it looked glorious and I thought, "Wow! Great stuff." So I was really stoked and excited in being on the show. At the same time, I was a little bit intimidated and concerned, because I didn't know how to do motion control. But what was important, and actually the point I wanted to go to here, was that this was one of those liberating moments or pivotal experiences that a person has—where I finally got to realize what I knew. At that point I had already been working for almost ten years; even though I had the years of professional work plus I'd done all that effects experimenting in high school, I was thinking, "Well, I don't know if I can measure up to these guys." As it turned out, I knew a heck of a lot more than most of these guys. This is not a place of ego, but it was actually one of those moments where I realized, "Damn, I actually know more than I thought I knew." It made me more confident to really jump in to get more projects. And I'd like to feel that I made a contribution and helped get some shots done that otherwise never would get done without my approach to some things. It was pretty neat.

STEVEN SIMAK

As a time- and cost-saving factor, as the series progressed it was also not uncommon for modelers to create new ships from existing models. For example, in the *Battlestar* episode "Greetings from Earth," the Eastern Alliance cruiser was adapted from a minor member of the ragtag fleet. The pumpkin shuttle from the same episode (named for its orange color) was a re-dressed version of Buck's shuttle from the theatrical version of *Buck Rogers in the 25th Century*.

KEN LARSON
(model maker, *Battlestar Galactica*)

Usually we would go out into the cupboard and grab one of the ragtag fleet ships—things which we didn't build; the stuff we inherited from Dykstra. These were all very crude, for the background. They were never featured, so they were all sitting there in the cupboard. Dave [Jones] would just go out there and say, "This one." He'd go through the kit boxes and he'd pull out an F-16 engine or something like that and say, "Put this engine here and add some piping there and put a dome here," and that's how we would build the ship. The chassis was already there, and it had an armature in it.

We would maybe spend two or three weeks on a model, and meanwhile someone else would spend two or three weeks on a model for a different show, so there was that leapfrogging. I would maybe finish the model on Tuesday and it would be painted. By the end of Thursday night, they would be shooting it. We would see dailies on Friday or Monday. It would be comped on Tuesday and I would see it on TV on Thursday. I am not exaggerating. More than once, I would see my model less than two weeks after I finished it. It was a very good learning experience for me.

DAVID STIPES

The shot count started going down. You start recycling stuff. There was one episode of *Buck Rogers* where they had to go from one place to another in the show. In one shot it's Princess Ardala's shuttle and in another shot in the same sequence it's the *Battlestar Galactica* shuttle. I was just going like "Oh my God, guys!" and they said, "Don't worry, nobody will notice." Well, everybody noticed! It looked horrible. Then they have this ship going into this cave and you see its engines blazing as it goes in. Then there's a shot of it coming out and they just printed it backward, so now it's flying backward, with its engines blazing backward. They were so desperate for money that they would do crazy stuff like that, right toward the end. I was just rolling my eyes, "Oh my God!"

Universal Hartland continued on after the cancellation of *Battlestar Galactica* and *Buck Rogers in the 25th Century*. The facility contributed effects work for such projects as *Airport '79, Cosmos,* John Carpenter's *The Thing,* and Disney's 3-D *Captain Eo* before disbanding in 1984.

WAYNE SMITH

Everything has changed. What you see now on television is just incredible. We couldn't even come close to it before. I don't think it's any faster and, probably, it isn't any cheaper—but you can do it.

One of the things I learned is, again, about not taking things personally. It's not my show. I need to be responsible for the shots I do and do the best that I can for those shows. If the producers or the directors or somebody else wants to drop the ball and that's out of my realm of control, well, that's out of my realm of control.

Also out of control were the series' reviews. Even legendary science fiction author Isaac Asimov lambasted the new series. "Well, I liked *Star Wars.* I thought *Battlestar Galactica* was such a close imitation of *Star Wars,* emphasizing the less attractive portions, that I was a little impatient with it," Asimov said at the time. While the comparisons to *Star Wars* were inevitable, matters took a dramatic turn when 20th Century Fox filed an injunction to prevent ABC from airing the three-hour *Battlestar Galactica* pilot. Claiming copyright infringement, Fox was subsequently joined by coplaintiff Lucasfilm Ltd., which charged that ABC and Universal had also infringed on the company's copyright to the *Star Wars* novelization.

SCOTT MANTZ

The lawsuit was bad PR for *Galactica.* Lucas tried to stop it because there were too many similarities. Fighting spaceships, lasers, droids; he felt it was a rip-off of *Star Wars.* It kind of was, in terms of the tone of what they were looking for, but storywise, it was different. This lawsuit went on long after *Galactica* was canceled.

In the suit, Fox charged that a comparison of the two franchises revealed at least thirty-four similarities, ranging from the overall visual design of the series to various plot points. The trial judge was presented with a copy of the *Star Wars* film and book, videotape of the *Galactica* premiere, and, for comparison, a video montage of prior science fiction works. Universal countersued, claiming Fox had infringed on its *Silent Running* property—with R2-D2 and C-3PO being reminiscent of the robots Huey, Dewey, and Louie—as well as on the *Buck Rogers* property the studio controlled.

According to court records, Fox charged that, like the vehicles in *Star Wars,* the vehicles in *Galactica* "are made to look old contrary to the stereotypical sleek, new appearance of space-age equipment." The suit alleged other similarities, including that "the central conflict of each story is a war between the galaxy's democratic and totalitarian forces" and that "a leading character returns to the family home to find it destroyed." Fox also argued that the Carillon gambling casino plagiarized the renowned *Star Wars* cantina sequence, stating that both featured "entertainment by bizarre, nonhuman creatures."

GLEN OLIVER

I wasn't necessarily surprised by the lawsuit, but I was disappointed by it. To my eyes, *Galactica* didn't rip off *Star Wars* any more than *Star Wars* ripped off—or rather was "inspired by"—a substantial quantity of outside narratives and source material like *Dune* and Kurosawa. For *Star Wars'* powers that be to take aim at *Galactica* wasn't necessarily a shock given *Battlestar*'s proximity to the original *Star Wars* film, but it always felt like a bit of a crass double standard to me.

JOHN DYKSTRA

Personally, I didn't think that there was something sacred that was being violated here. I felt that there was a technology that had opened up, an opportunity or genre for television that wasn't available before.

Ironically, Larson had attempted to avoid any problems over *Star Wars* initially by consulting with George Lucas and producer Gary Kurtz before production began on *Galactica* and made several changes as a result of those conversations in order to avoid a lawsuit.

GLEN A. LARSON

I was only surprised because I thought we had agreements with all the people involved by which we weren't going to have any litigation. It was counterproductive given the fact that, even though they lost the lawsuit, the amount of time I took to devote to that was probably destructive to the series. It's the same with the coroner from New York who sued us over *Quincy* because I guess he decided any coroner show has to be about him.

SCOTT MANTZ

Lucas had already said, "Well, if you're going to have laser battles with guns, I don't want you to see the laser being fired." They had the flashing lights on the pistols instead. "Don't call them droids, call them something else." Larson called them drones. Then, there was word that the next *Star Wars* movie was going to be done on an ice planet. Well, *Galactica* beat them to the punch with "Ice Planet Zero."

STEVEN E. DE SOUZA

I was working with Glen Larson at that time on *The Hardy Boys/Nancy Drew Mysteries* and I was there the day that he was served the lawsuit from George Lucas. He was really in a panic and I go, "I can't believe the nerve of this guy [Lucas]." Glen starts going through a list of what they're saying in the lawsuit and I go, "Two suns [is an infringement]? Go look at the cover of *Farmer in the Sky*. The paperback cover of *Farmer in the Sky*."

Glen said, "What's that?" I go, "The Robert Heinlein book." He turns to an underling and says, "Go buy that book right now." They were back in twenty minutes. He goes, "This is bullshit. What else do you know, Steve?" He starts grilling me about stuff and then he has a secretary come in and take notes and he calls Don Bellisario in and says, "Come and listen to this guy." As I'm going through this, I said, "Listen, you don't need me. I got a book in my desk, *The Encyclopedia of Science Fiction*. It has every sci-fi book cover going back to 1930." As a result, they ended up re-cutting the premiere. They had creatures, they started cutting out the creatures. They were such pussies. I remember being in the editing room with Glen and he'd say, "Cut out that creature, it's too *Star Wars*–y." They ended up cutting some of the early episodes to ribbons, which was ridiculous because Fox had no case.

GLEN A. LARSON

It was a body blow that was like dropping a newborn on its head. It's not real good for the child and you find yourself distracted and preoccupied and it sort of imposes a certain kind of censorship on yourself. Not even using the laser streak is kind of ridiculous when they had been used before in *Star Trek* and stuff like that. It made us look a little old-fashioned but we went along with it. That was really the least of our worries at that point, because the costs of the show were so enormous. The problem was we were on a network that was very spoiled. Had we been on the number-two or number-three network at that time we undoubtedly would have been on a lot longer.

6.
I AM LEGEND

*"Cain, the greatest military commander who ever lived.
He was my idol!"*

On the heels of the three-hour debut, "Saga of a Star World," *Battlestar Galactica* aired another massive two-parter the following two weeks, on September 24 and October 1, 1978, "Lost Planet of the Gods." The episode is stuffed with multiple storylines in which, as Apollo and Serina prepare for their wedding, the Viper pilots are sidelined by a pernicious, life-threatening virus, forcing the women of the fleet to be trained as fighter pilots. At the same time, Apollo and Starbuck discover a magnetic void that, according to legend, hides the mysterious planet Kobol, the origin of all human life in the universe. Given its vast scope, the episode is nearly as ambitious as the three-hour debut that preceded it.

GLEN A. LARSON
(creator/executive producer, *Battlestar Galactica*)

I think the network was so nervous about this show being a hit and because it's science fiction, they kept front-loading us. I got this letter once and it said the idea of a disease coming on the ship and knocking out all your pilots is a good idea for an episode. And the idea of discovering the planet you came from, that's a great idea for an episode. And the idea of them getting married and then her dying is also a great idea for an episode. But all in the same episode? The truth of the matter is those were all on my list of three different things we were going to do and the network pushed to get them all going at once because they were so nervous about whether we'd be a hit. It's called front-loading. You put too damn much in there, so you don't have a chance to explore any one of them appropriately.

SCOTT MANTZ
(film critic, *Access Hollywood*)

"Lost Planet of the Gods" was a good episode to better establish the characters and the dynamics introduced in the premiere. What I liked about it was the way it really played into the mysticism of Egypt. When you're watching the pilot episode, a lot of the buildings on Caprica look like pyramids. Then, they get to Kobol, and it's Egypt. It's the pyramids. But Jane Seymour, who is Apollo's love interest, she was just going to do the pilot episode. They asked her to come back and she said, "Well, I'll do it if I can have a good death scene," and she did. That was a really sad ending to that episode.

I would say that of all of the episodes of *Battlestar Galactica*, "Lost Planet of the Gods" is the one that's the most dated, because of the storyline involving the female fighter pilots and that you can't have a woman flying a Viper. They're not shuttle pilots, but they had to do it because the male fighter pilots contracted a disease on an asteroid that has a Cylon base, and the only hope for the fleet was to train the women to fly Vipers fast. They flew erratically, but they still beat the Cylons.

The episode called for the cast to explore the ruins of the desert world of Kobol, eventually entering one of the ancient tombs under a massive pyramid. To ensure authenticity, a second unit was sent to Egypt to shoot exteriors of the Sphinx and Great Pyramids at Giza, while principal photography continued in Hollywood.

Doubles, dressed as Adama, Apollo, and Serina, were photographed in long shots walking among the ruins for sequences depicting the surface of the ancient planet. Because local religious doctrine would not permit a woman to wear a man's clothing, a young boy was used to double for Jane Seymour.

GLEN A. LARSON

They hired some little boy to put on the outfit, and he had the biggest butt. He was walking away from the camera and I knew if Jane saw that, she would kill me, so I had to cut around some of those terrible shots.

STEVEN SIMAK
(journalist, *Battlestar Galactica* historian)

For close-ups, front projection was used to create shots of the principal actors standing in front of the ruins. To achieve these images, the Egypt unit photographed a series of stills of the pyramids. These "plates" were transferred to large transparencies for later use on the soundstages at Universal. The north wall of stage twenty-eight—the old *Phantom of the Opera* stage—was outfitted with a huge 3M screen. The actors would perform a scene while a transparency, in this case an Egyptian temple, was projected onto the screen behind them.

H. JOHN PENNER
(director of photography, *Battlestar Galactica*)

You have to balance the whole front stage with the images that you're projecting. Front projection is a very tricky thing to do, because the 3M screen has multiple reflective microscopic beads as a surface, and the optical axis has to be dead center to that. If you're off half a degree one way or another, the magnification of light completely falls off. It's rather tricky and you can't really hurry.

SCOTT MANTZ

When they get to Kobol and they have to go through the tomb, it's like *Indiana Jones and the Temple of Doom* for a little bit. It was a great moment when Baltar goes to grab the staff from the tomb and then it starts shaking. Adama and everyone in the tomb thinks it's a supernatural force because you've disrupted the tomb, and Adama turns to Apollo and says, "What do you think?" Apollo says, "About fifteen-megaton loads," and you cut to the Cylons firing on the freaking pyramids of Egypt. This was 1978, and it still looks amazing.

RICHARD JAMES
(art director, *Battlestar Galactica*)

In building the tomb, I took a lead from the Egyptian designs, and I came up with the idea of the eye Adama was wearing so when he stands up there is a light beam that comes from the upper window. When his medallion hits it, it makes a triangle with the sphinx guarding the tomb and it would open and reveal the room below the slab. They liked that idea very much and we did do that.

I recall they were trying to get prices out of me and I said don't put any detail in these drawings because they get more expensive. Leave off as much as possible and I will say I am not finished. The way they worked at Universal was you had estimators. You were not allowed to turn in your own estimates. I had to submit my drawings to the estimator and they would say how much these sets would cost and I would go in and haggle with them over it. Their prices were outrageous.

HERBERT JEFFERSON, JR.
(actor, "Lieutenant Boomer")

I got one of the great lines from [writer/producer] Don Bellisario. It was after Boomer and Jolly bring back a virus to the *Galactica* and they end up in suspended animation until they could find the cure. The girls end up on the planet and the Cylons have attacked and they're losing the battle and the next thing you know there's Boomer and Jolly and all of the [male] fighter pilots, who were in very bad shape, staggering up and I say, "Lieutenant Boomer, reporting for duty, sir." And Colonel Tigh looks up and says, "You can't even stand." And Don wrote the great line for me where Boomer leans over and he says, "I believe the Viper is flown from the seated position!"

For the cast, the first season proved to be one of change as well. Starbuck and Cassiopeia, initially supporting characters, would emerge to the forefront, while others—such as Athena and Boxey—would see their roles slowly diminish, with the two disappearing altogether after the airing of the midseason two-parter "Greetings from Earth." Baltar, who was killed in the initial three-hour pilot, would later be spared in the first two-part episode when producers, now tasked with taking *Galactica* to a weekly series, felt the need for a villain with greater dramatic potential than the monotone Cylon robots. Leaving the series was Jane Seymour, whose role was short-lived. Serina was originally killed off in the pilot, but the subplot was omitted from the three-hour premiere and a new demise was plotted for the character in the following episode.

RICHARD HATCH
(actor, "Captain Apollo")

She didn't feel she was going to get enough to do on that show as an actress, because it was a very testosterone-oriented show. I loved working with Jane. I think we really had a chemistry together, and I was extremely sad to see her go.

JANE SEYMOUR
(actress, "Serina")

I was only supposed to be in the pilot and die of galactic cancer. Then they called me up and said that I had tested better than their regulars so they wanted me in the series. I told them I was dead, but Glen Larson said, "We've done some reshooting." They cut in anywhere I looked like I was dying or ill. Sure enough, I was still alive. I said no about a hundred times and they doubled, tripled, and quadrupled my fee. I finally said I'd do two more hours on the condition that I die. They had me fly battleships, marry the guy, and I got to do everything I would have done if I had been in the entire season. It was pretty wild.

SCOTT MANTZ

The common myth about *Galactica* is true. The two-part episodes are much, much better than the single-part episodes. "Lost Planet of the Gods" is not the best two-part episode, but after that you had "The Lost Warrior," which is a Western with a Cylon. It's *Shane*. I thought it was chilling to see a Western setting, and in the corner was a freaking Cylon sitting with his laser pistol. When Apollo goes over and he starts making conversation with the Cylon, he goes, "You want to destroy me?" He goes, "No, I don't." He goes, "You're lying." I was scared. It was a great moment, but it's not a great episode.

In the episode, after running low on fuel, Apollo is marooned on a frontier planet. There, he discovers that a single Cylon under the control of the local bad guy, Lacerta, threatens the town. In an homage to Alan Ladd's iconic (and laconic) character, Apollo goes mano a machine with the Cylon in a classic Western showdown.

GLEN A. LARSON

I am not sure we pulled off the *Shane* story as well as I had hoped. Maybe we had built an appetite for only the big shows. With the smaller episodes, I guess I worried that they might have been disappointing. You lose some of the people who are only there for the events. We were certainly reacting to the fact that we couldn't hold the kind of audience you get on a premiere big night, but then Sunday night is a cutthroat night for television. You're competing with an awful lot.

RICHARD JAMES

The episode was filmed on Western Street at Universal Studios' backlot. I built a frame and stretched canvas over it and we painted them to get these strange shapes. I would cover the windows and get these strange looks to Western Street to make it look a little foreign. For the swinging barroom doors, out came the silver paint. The whole series was *Wagon Train* in space. It got to that point during production meetings where our guys are walking down a strange street in an alien town and they would say Western Street and I would say, "Western Street? You have to be kidding!"

The thing that was so frustrating with Universal was they invested all this money and then they slammed the door on you. I would see these scripts come out and it was obvious they hadn't thought about where these scenes are going to take place. Where is this strange alien street that they are walking down? That would be the original description [in the script]. It was not Western Street. Western Street [on the Universal backlot] came up because that's what they could afford.

GLEN OLIVER
(pop-culture commentator)

When taken on the whole, the writing wasn't particularly *bad,* especially when compared to other genre entries of its era—even when compared to other Glen Larson titles of that era. If you step back to compare the metaphysics and mythology of *Battlestar*'s "Ship of Light" conceit to fucking *B.J. and the Bear* or *Sheriff Lobo, Battlestar* looks Kubrickian by comparison.

It should also be noted that the late seventies/early eighties was a strangely pregnant time for science fiction storytelling on television. *Galactica* pre-dated the "made for cable" series revolution by many years. Other science fiction shows which were shaped by big networks? Many of them were fun, to be sure, but at their core they were often a bit dodgy and narrow in scope and vision and execution. I don't think it's hard to argue that *Galactica,* for all its eccentricities and warts, was easily the most boldly conceived and ex-pansive television concept out there at the time—as well as being the big-gest risk commercially. I wouldn't say it ushered in the megaseries like we see today—like *Game of Thrones, Westworld,* or some of the current costly and high-profile Netflix shows—as too much time passed before those came around. But I do think it portended their existence in terms of anticipating a scale and thought process we'd eventually see more frequently on TV.

Battlestar . . . and *Space: 1999* before it . . . went shamelessly "big" in a way which didn't feel self-conscious or apologetic. It would be many years before we'd again see such audacity evident in small-screen science fiction.

JOHN COLICOS
(actor, "Count Baltar")

I got so sick of that goddamn child and that stupid dog. That was sentimen-tal slop shit as far as I was concerned. When Don [Bellisario] wrote the scripts, they were very much in line with what we had all discussed. When other people were involved in writing the scripts with other directors, then we would concentrate on the daggit.

RONALD D. MOORE
(cocreator/executive producer, *Battlestar Galactica* [2004])

I remember being sort of disappointed over and over again. There were in-teresting moments, interesting episodes in isolation, but the story—the overall arc—just wasn't carrying me any place that I was interested in going. I mean, right in the first episode, when they went to the casino planet, even as a kid I was sort of like, "This feels really disconnected from everything else in the story. Didn't they just have this giant, terrible thing happen? And now they're jumping around and, you know, gambling." I just thought that was so weird and I didn't really get it. And I really detested the daggit. I hated all that when I was watching it in its first run.

I was interested in all the pilots. I wanted to see more stuff with the pilots and Adama. I remember liking all that. When they did the Western episode, that was basically *Shane* done as a *Galactica* episode. I remember going, "God, this is so bizarre. It's like we're doing a Western, and not a very good one, on this show." I just remember feeling less and less like the show knew what the hell it was doing. This kind of went on. But I think, when I was a kid I just kept having this faith that it was gonna all work out, they're gonna figure it out.

My dominant influence was *Star Trek,* and as a *Star Trek* fan, I guess, I was comparing it unfavorably to the way *Star Trek* would do these shows. But I just kept feeling like it was going to be a really great show eventually.

DONALD BELLISARIO
(supervising producer, *Battlestar Galactica*)

If you look at my shows, I always do character shows. They may have action or something but they are character-oriented shows. They tell heart stories. That's what I like to do. I like to have twists and do the unexpected by the end of the show. I think I put a pretty good twist in "The Hand of God," where they pick up the *Eagle* landing on the moon. It was typical of the shows I like to write and that's the direction I would have liked to have taken the show.

When I joined *Galactica,* Glen was struggling with all the problems of the show. It was a massive show to mount, it was an incredible accomplishment to get it done on a television budget since it was so expansive and large. It was an enormous undertaking. People expect to see what they see in feature films, and that's very hard to do and turn it out every week. Glen deserves a helluva lot of credit just for pulling it off. But it was a little bit like an oil tanker; you had to make an adjustment five miles back in order to make the turn you want, and what we were doing was trying to take the show and make some adjustments and take it in a more personal direction in a way that we could make it and mount it. We were beginning to accomplish that and take it in a direction that viewers would have loved and would have continued to make good television instead of just hardware stories, but by that time it was too late.

RICHARD HATCH

In the first-year show, they tended to go toward the Baltar character, and the Starbuck character got played up a lot. By the end of the season, they actually started giving my character more stuff to do, which I think was the direction the show needed to go in. By the second season, there would have been a chance to take Apollo out of that box of basically being the straightforward leader. That character always tends to be the most boring, but I was looking in every way I could to bring humanity to that character. Having my son helped sometimes, and some of the scenes with Sheba allowed me to show a little bit of that, but I was searching to find a way out of being the straightforward, ultraserious leader guy.

Following on Colla's and Levi's work on the pilot and Christian Nyby II helming the "Lost Planet of the Gods" two-parter, young director Rod Holcomb, who remains active as a television director today, shot what would be the first of several episodes of the fledgling series with "The Lost Warrior."

ROD HOLCOMB

I didn't start my career until very late. I graduated from San Francisco State when I think I was twenty-seven or twenty-eight. I didn't know anybody and I was throwing my sixteen-millimeter films over the fence, hoping somebody would pick it up and go look at it and say, "Oh, this is good," because you didn't have the internet. I actually got a job in the mailroom at ABC over on Prospect and Talmadge in Silverlake, and from the bottom, looking up, you can really learn a lot, fairly quickly. Then, after I went through that for about a year, I think, I got a chance to go over to the promo department, and somebody gave me a chance to do some of the writing and producing of the promos, which I thought was a great thing. Then, I did some main-title kind of stuff for *Kung Fu*. I got the idea of the titles in the bathroom, so that's where I got my inspiration, and they were nominated for a Clio Award.

Then I got offered to be the associate producer on *Harry O*, with David Janssen. Jerry Thorpe was the executive producer, and a really wonderful director himself. I got to learn what postproduction was all about. It was a short-lived journey over at *Harry O*. My next job was actually doing the pilot for *Wonder Woman* with Lynda Carter, and then I got a job at *The

Six Million Dollar Man as an associate producer. I went to dailies and always had something to say, so I guess they heard a few things they liked and said, "Well, you want to try it?" In those days, that's the way you got to direct. They thought the young guy has a few good ideas, let's give him a shot and see what happens.

My first shot, it was all set up to go. The camera was running. I was so enamored by the camera and with the noise of the film I never called action. Somebody behind me yelled, "Action," and I turned around, then I went back, and a Jeep drove by. It was a simple Jeep drive-by we were shooting. I said, "Gee, that was pretty good." Then, somebody called, "Cut. Print that, and we're moving on." It was Lee Majors with the crew, laughing their asses off. I forgot to say cut. I reminded him of this when he called me to congratulate me on the Emmy, a long time ago. I reminded him of the story. He says, "Well, I guess you learned something since then, huh?" Always a ballbuster. That was back when you were doing twelve pages a day on a six-day show. I watched it recently, it was terrible.

I was on a producer's contract with Universal, after *Six Million Dollar Man* went down, when I got a call to do *Galactica*. There was a big learning curve for a director on that show. The big thing was that I always wanted to get wider on the cockpits of the Vipers. I wanted to get back to where I could see the wings, but that seemed to be a little bit out of their ability to do, because it was costly. I felt we were always tight and doing close-ups. I was glad that I had "Lost Warrior" as my first episode, because it was actually kind of a real heroic moment for Richard Hatch.

I'm not so certain I saw him as the lead, as much as an ensemble with Dirk and everybody else. But I thought this was a very good opportunity for Richard to do some kind of good stuff. I liked the actress a lot, I let the kid get a little bit broad, because I hadn't been used to working with kids very much, but it seemed to work, for the audience. I loved some of the actors. There were a couple of the actors, they got a little big.

CLAUDE EARL JONES
(actor, "Lacerta")

I had done a show with Rod Holcomb before, and so, apparently, when this role came up on *Battlestar Galactica,* he sent for me. He had the casting director call my agent and said, "I want to see Claude on this." So I went in and read for it, and Rod told the producers, "I want you to experience

Claude. He's quite a special actor." I'm not an ordinary actor. I'm different, and I'm unique, and I don't play the same thing twice. I'm a true character man in the sense that I play what's written, not what they don't write for me. I adapt myself to the script. At least, that's what I assumed he meant. The point is that I had played a very strange thing for him, off-the-wall kind of role, and Lacerta was certainly off the wall.

ROD HOLCOMB

That was my Sydney Greenstreet character. That went too far, and how they even hired me back after that is beyond me. But it was such a great learning experience to be able to have all these great toys. I remember walking in with my first agent and he said, "Jesus, Rod, they're really putting some money into this, aren't they?"

CLAUDE EARL JONES

Rod is a very fine director, and he's one of those smart directors who hires good actors and gets the hell out of their way. That's one of the reasons why I liked to work with him. He entrusted me to do my job and he didn't really direct me so much as he just points me in a way. The episode was a kind of takeoff on *Shane*. I played him, at least I tried to play him, with a great deal of humor, but I didn't set out to make him funny either. He was a very lethal man, and one of the things that I found in playing heavies and playing bad guys, and I played a lot of them, is that the ones that I find most frightening are the ones that are very quiet, who don't rage and scream and yell and all of that. Some of the most lethal real people that I've known in Hollywood are Medal of Honor winners like Audie Murphy. The quiet, soft-spoken people don't have to prove they are tough. They don't have to prove they are rough and mean and that they can kill you. They know they can.

GLEN OLIVER

The greatest challenge facing the original series was that it was too often a hodgepodge. Whether that was because of time or talent or both, my sense of the matter is that writers were struggling to balance and refine the flavor of the show.

By "flavor" I mean: *Galactica* sported a distinctive vibe, a "flavor" if you will. There was an aesthetic, an atmosphere, a cadence of dialogue and tone which defined the series very succinctly from its earliest moments. This "vibe" was one ingredient in its "flavor." But they often added other ingredients. For example, many episodes then proceeded to intermix this preset "*Galactica* vibe" with clichés and conventions from other genres: bedroom comedies, pseudo-fantasies with unicorns, World War II "squad on a mission" tales, lost-pilot gags, Westerns, the building-on-fire saga, even a murder mystery centered around sports. This, in itself, wasn't necessarily an ill-considered approach—many movies and TV shows have utilized similar "genre potpourri" philosophies. And I'm sure the thinking at the time was that exploring the potential of so many genres would broaden the breadth of story ideas which *Galactica* could consider telling, which is a reasonable and fundamentally correct assertion.

But where *Galactica* went wrong, in this regard, was that writers chose to exploit some of the most trite moves from the genres they were incorporating—instead of mining less literal elements, or tweaking literal elements and having fun with them. Instead of using genres as inspiration to steer in unique and unpredictable directions like in the original *Star Trek,* they often choose the path of least resistance. This approach often did not create a fresh-feeling mash-up which people would be excited to see, but instead delivered something that people would expect to see. Something which felt more familiar than it probably should've and more stale. This resulted in something of an identity crisis for the show.

After Apollo was stranded on an alien planet in "The Lost Warrior," Starbuck found himself marooned on his own as well in "The Long Patrol," in which the hotshot pilot tests out a new long-range Viper to escape the date from hell with Cassiopeia and Athena. Outfitted with extra thrusters and a flirtatious computer named C.O.R.A., the recon Viper is twice as fast as a normal fighter but is unarmed. Outwitted by a criminal, Starbuck is captured and trapped on a penal colony where the inmates are imprisoned for the crimes of their ancestors.

CHRISTIAN I. NYBY II
(director, "The Long Patrol")

I liked the story on that one a lot. It was an interesting concept, that these people were generations of prisoners and there were generations of guards.

SCOTT MANTZ

I loved the flirty banter between Starbuck and C.O.R.A. Not a great episode, but the beginning of that episode is fun, because it deepens the dynamic of the character of Starbuck.

CHRISTIAN I. NYBY II

Jimmy Whitmore, Jr., who played Robber in "The Long Patrol," and I were up on the backlot at Universal. He was in the cockpit of a Viper and I was on the big Titan crane. It was a night shoot. I was just lining up the shot and we were rehearsing. I was just having the grips moving the crane in for a close-up or something of him and he just kind of looked at me—since we were kind of rehearsing it—and he said, "Isn't this great, Chris? It's like we're twelve years old and we were given all of these great toys," which was true. The patient is not going to die and nobody is going to lose the lawsuit or anything and it was a lot of fun.

"Gun on Ice Planet Zero" was directed by returning helmer Alan J. Levi and was the final two hours of what had originally been conceived as a series of TV movies. "Gun" had the most torturous development of all of them, going through many extensive rewrites and iterations before it was finally broadcast. In the episode, the *Galactica* recruits a band of convicts and infiltrates an ice planet to destroy a Cylon superweapon created by a human inventor, Dr. Ravashol (Dan O'Herlihy), in order to continue their journey through space and avoid annihilation.

ALAN J. LEVI
(director, "Gun on Ice Planet Zero")

It was the original *Rogue One*. The focus was on destroying the giant super-weapon that had to be stopped before it could destroy us.

SCOTT MANTZ

"Gun on Ice Planet Zero" is basically *Ice Station Zebra* in space. Great setup; they had to recruit these murderers and cutthroats and go down to this ice planet to destroy the Ravashol pulsar, with the help of Ravashol's clones. You get into some provocative stuff about what it means to be human, because the clones are greedy. It is an exciting episode. I've heard people say that they don't really like that episode, or it's too much of a rip-off of *The Dirty Dozen*, but you know what? It worked.

The conflict between the warriors and the prisoners was great, and you have one convict who used to be a Colonial Warrior who's trying to regain his lost honor.

The fleet can't turn back because they're being tailed by a Cylon basestar, they have to move forward. The only way to move forward is if they go past the pulsar. If they go past the pulsar, they're never going to make it, which is why they have to send these people down to destroy it.

MICHAEL SLOAN
(producer, *Battlestar Galactica*)

We did talk about *Guns of Navarone* and that s how the genesis of that came about. You don't so much rip them off as say, let's take that idea and give it the spin of this particular show.

ALAN J. LEVI

I had a different crew on the second movie. Benny [Colman] had left and I brought in Enzo Martinelli, who I learned more from than any other DP I've worked with. Enzo was just fabulous. I worked with him on *The Invisible Man* and then *The Gemini Man*. We were really good buddies. Enzo started making movies before the laboratories and before sound. He really knew how to make a movie, and fast, and just marvelous.

HERBERT JEFFERSON, JR.

It was all done on a set. We were all in the big quilted winter gear that we were wearing for that show when in reality we were on a soundstage with huge klieg lights, so every fifteen to twenty seconds someone would have to come over to mop our brows so we didn't look like we were sweating in the middle of an ice storm. We had to act cold.

ALAN J. LEVI

We were halfway done with the day and we had lost three hours due to makeup runs. I called upstairs and I said, "Guys, I've got my crew and cast in parkas and snow gear and I can shoot for maybe five minutes before every-body is drenching wet. I've got to get another air conditioner on set, we've got to bring the set down to forty degrees." They said, "You're not going to need it. You're at sixty-five degrees now with this one."

I'm shooting on set and sure enough we have to dab every ten minutes. I called the front office and I said, "Please come down here as soon as you can, I've got a big problem and I don't want it to go any farther and you can help me." They came down to set, walked on set, and saw everyone was just drip-ping wet. The next morning we had two big air conditioners, which got it down to forty degrees and we could shoot. We were on that set for days and days because of all the snow.

HERBERT JEFFERSON, JR.

They had these big bins that were made with wooden cylinders that had chicken wire wrapped all around it and inside they had this chipped-up white plastic, and what they did is they'd turn these bins around so that it snowed. This stuff is plastic, we're trying to act and we're breathing in all this plastic stuff. But, of course, the director and the crew were wearing masks while we're inhaling all this.

RICHARD JAMES

For the pulsar, I wanted these big cylinders going up and down and they had to rig those. They were massive. They were framed and actually lightweight and faceted, they just weren't built on curves. I had that narrow split-lighted area in them. There was a big fight going on over that, because I had gotten this set, which is the one where I said it's not finished and you have to give me the money to finish it. I probably came very close to getting fired over it.

For "The Magnificent Warriors," after a Cylon attack destroys two Colonial agroships and damages a third (utilizing the miniature and some stock footage from Universal's *Silent Running*), Adama leads a team down to a nearby planet in search of new seed for crops. Once there, the Colonials come to the aid of the local inhabitants, who are being terrorized by the piglike Borays after Starbuck is made sheriff. A would-be comedy, with some truly cringe-worthy moments, it's the first of the one-hour episodes in which the production values really suffer despite an amusing coda in which Starbuck negotiates a deal with the Borays after Adama fails to come to terms.

SCOTT MANTZ

One of the worst episodes, with Brett Somers guest-starring. It is terrible. It's sort of like slapsticky kind of romance between Lorne Greene and Brett Somers. At another point, it's exactly like the Old West. It's like, "Really?" It felt very rushed.

Shooting this episode proved to be a difficult prospect for director Christian I. Nyby II. One key sequence required that the Borays, mounted on camels, ride dramatically into town. Short on camels, the producers added horses galloping toward the back to add greater size to the charge. Cowboys, wearing pig masks portraying Borays, were hired to ride the animals.

CHRISTIAN I. NYBY II

These cowboys hated these camels. I remember we were having trouble getting them to charge, because the horses were balking at the back. They didn't like the smell of the camels. We did this charge down across the bridge.

We had done it a couple of times and we finally got a good take but I had to do it again because one of the cowboys lost his pig mask as he came by. We all saw the mask go off, but he was trying so hard to be a good trooper about it that he had his face all scrunched up like a pig because he didn't want to do it again. The lead Boray was actually a publicity agent that used to walk around the studio all the time. He just sort of had the look. He was an actor, too, and was always looking for a part, so we brought him in and had a mask made for him. We had two or three masks that we could have in the foreground and then we had others of cheaper quality in the background.

In "The Young Lords," after a battle with enemy fighters, Starbuck is forced to crash-land (again!) on a planet under Cylon control and commanded by the cunning Cylon robot Specter, an acerbic and quick-thinking member of Lucifer's IL-series. Starbuck encounters a group of child warriors who have been attacking the Cylon battalion that abducted their father. He leads the children on a raid to rescue their father and destroy the Cylon garrison there. Unfortunately, the production destroyed numerous Cylon costumes as well when they were marched through the swamp and the water seeped into the armor, damaging them beyond repair.

DIRK BENEDICT
(actor, "Lieutenant Starbuck")

Don Bellisario was directing and we were shooting at night on the backlot, which, of course, is where we always were, since we never left Universal. We were in this fortress and the Cylons were up on the upper level of the fortress and we were in the middle and there was kind of a shoot-out. There were eight or nine of them in a long line marching and coming down the wall of the fortress and then down the steps, and twenty feet up, the first guy stumbled and of course the second and it was dominoes. You had twenty Cylons go down these steps, and when you're watching it it was terrifying and yet it was unbelievable—it was like a bowling alley.

HERBERT JEFFERSON, JR.

In those outfits you could only see through a little slit, and it was angled so you could only see about two or three feet in front of you, so you had to keep your head up and angled and watch where you were going, because you couldn't see straight ahead. So we had a whole phalanx of Cylons just piled all lying on the ground with their scanners looking up in the air with little red dots going.

DIRK BENEDICT

Nobody got hurt, so we laughed a long time about that.

ALAN J. LEVI

I do remember that they had to set up a repair set somewhere because we had a lot of pyrotechnics on the Cylons and we would burn a lot of them. They were getting expensive as hell to make, and there were a lot of them. I remember we had to be very careful about putting on the pyrotechnics for a while because we were destroying suits left and right. In the second half of the pilot we must have destroyed forty of those suits.

ROB KLEIN
(*Battlestar Galactica* archivist)

They were filming out at Fox Ranch in Malibu and they had the life-size Viper in the marsh from Ape City [from *Planet of the Apes*] and it got stuck, so they were cutting up Ape City to put underneath the crane to get the Viper loose.

With production continuing to fall further behind and budget overages mounting, Donald Bellisario, on the recommendation of ABC, approached writers Jim Carlson and Terrence McDonnell as potential story editors. No strangers to series television, the writing team had contributed scripts to such hits as *The Six Million Dollar Man* and *The Bionic Woman*.

TERRENCE MCDONNELL
(story editor, *Battlestar Galactica*)

I got into game shows early on, and one of the guys that I was working with at Jack Berry Productions' name was Ken Johnson, and Ken was doing *Juvenile Jury* or something like that, and he had also written a few episodes of *The Six Million Dollar Man*. He comes in this one day and he says very excitedly, "I think they're going to offer me producer of the show." I didn't even wait for him to finish the sentence when I said, "If you get that job can I come in and pitch?"

I called a friend of mine that I knew, Jim Carlson, and said, "Do you want to team up and go in and try and do this?" I had never done it before, but he had. He was from *Laugh-In* and had done *Emergency, Adam-12, The Jeffersons,* and stuff like that. We just clicked from the get-go, so that's how it all started. They started handing us scripts and all of a sudden we were a team.

On *Six Million Dollar Man,* the first episode we did was a trial by fire. I thought it was going to always be like this. They wanted to shoot it up at Mount Shasta in the snow, so we wrote the script and then we turned it in. It was a good script and they said, "Oh, great, but we can't go there. So, don't do it in the snow now." This was a page-one rewrite. The second one we did for them we wrote in the mountains somewhere, but it was local. The next one we wrote was about a Japanese Zero that shoots down an experimental aircraft and we discover the bad guys have a hologram they are using to bring planes down. They want to bring down Air Force One with the president on board. The network came to us and said, "We can't do this. We don't want kids duplicating this." I said, "Really? They're going to build a hologram to bring down Air Force One?" They were worried about replication. It was total insanity. The other thing was they wanted to change Steve Austin's friend with whom he is flying the plane to Farrah Fawcett. So, it's another page-one rewrite, because the whole relationship changes. I thought it was always going to be like that and it wasn't. It seemed like every time we did a script, it was a page-one rewrite.

Because of our background on *Six Million Dollar Man* and *Bionic Woman,* we also did a series called *Gemini Man* with Ben Murphy. People liked our work, and apparently there had been some conversation at ABC about getting somebody in to help them at *Galactica*. Don Bellisario and Glen were writing the scripts and they couldn't do it because they needed a third wheel to keep the machine churning, so the guy that was in charge of prime time, my ex-girlfriend was his secretary and she recommended us. We got called in out of the blue to meet with Don. And he says, "We'd like you to go home and figure out 'Patton in space.'" I said, "Okay." He said, "Bring me act one in the morning." We said, "Okay." We just thought we were getting an assignment. So we beat out the outline and we wrote the first act and the next morning we turn in act one. And Don says, "What's this?" And we say, "That's act one," and he says, "Already?" So he looked at it and he says, "Go home and write act two." So, we went home and we beat out and finished act two and we brought it in the next morning. He says, "Okay, let me read this and I'll get back to you." I remember going out to Jim's house that night because we hadn't heard from him and we figured we better start on act three just in case he forgets.

So, I pulled in the driveway to Jim's house and I knocked on the door and came in and he handed me a glass of wine. And I said, "What's this for?" He says, "Welcome, Story Editor!" I said, "Are you kidding me?" We were ecstatic. The story editor job today would be the equivalent of producer of some type.

We got hired based on the first two acts. So did Annie Lockhart [Sheba], because they used that half of the script to entice her to be on the show. She read it and accepted it. That particular script, by the way, was taken away from us. We called it "The Last Legend" [later renamed "The Living Legend"]. In the script, we called him Jedediah, but Glen always used to use the Bible, so he called him Commander Cain. Glen decided he wanted to do a two-parter based on this idea, so our two acts were thrown out. Instead we went on to "Fire in Space."

GLEN A. LARSON

"The Living Legend" was probably one of the purer shows in terms of the two-hour epic with some of the feel of the pilot. Patton was blood and guts and Cain was really our Patton in space. Cain was driven by his own ego and point of view. Everything was simple for him, you know, you kick ass. There are deliberate parallels there again, because a show like *Galactica* really gives you a chance to explore the basic conflicts and predicaments we experience in our world, even though we're looking at it through a mirror world.

TERRENCE MCDONNELL

This was my introduction to Glen the first day we're there. We have parking spots on the lot where the *Jurassic Park* ride is now. We'd walk past Alfred Hitchcock arriving in the morning and [legendary costume designer] Edith Head being dropped off. So we get there and they don't have offices for us yet. So we're put in the basement of the commissary. Don [Bellisario] took us down to the set where they were shooting the Boray episode. Barry Nelson, the first guy who played James Bond [in the CBS TV version of *Casino Royale*], was in it and this was all very exciting. Now Glen wants to take us to lunch. We said, "Oh my God, we're living the dream!" So we go up to Glen's office and it's during the World Series. We get on the elevator to go down into the garage and we get into his limo. Does it get better than this? I wonder who we're going to see next. He's got his own driver. We pull out of the producers' building down to the guard gate to Lankershim Boulevard and across the street into the restaurant. He had to show off that he had a limo. We couldn't just walk across the street. And the whole time we're in the limo he's watching the World Series on a little TV, which he then takes into the restaurant.

SCOTT MANTZ

Of the two-part episodes, there were two that stand out as among the very best. The first one is "The Living Legend," with Lloyd Bridges as Commander Cain. He was a guy who was a World War II vet, Mike Nelson from *Sea Hunt,* one of the early choices to be Captain Kirk. He didn't want to do sci-fi, go figure.

I loved the beginning of the episode. Starbuck and Apollo are being chased by two Vipers. They're Vipers, but they're firing on Starbuck and Apollo. We hear from the *Pegasus,* and Starbuck goes, "Wow, that really is the *Pegasus*," but it's supposed to be like a great moment of relief. Not only did we find more human survivors, they're on a battlestar, we just doubled our power and increased our chances to survive. This should be a piece of cake from here on in until we get to Earth.

There's just one small problem. There is a massive power struggle going on, because of the very different commanding styles of Adama and Cain. Adama just wants to escape. Cain wants to attack. Right there, you've got a big problem. It got to the point where Adama had to relieve Cain of his command.

VINCE EDWARDS
(director, "The Living Legend")

It worked very well for Lloyd, it was right up his alley. I don't mean it arrogantly, but he plays a forceful figure well. Lorne is forceful and the script was well written. There was no problem of equating the two. It was a much better picture if you have two forceful characters instead of one totally dominating. It makes for interesting conflict.

JIM CARLSON
(story editor, *Battlestar Galactica*)

Adama was cautious but rightfully so, as opposed to Lloyd Bridges's character, Cain, who was a bull in a china shop. Not that there was anything particularly wrong with that, except that in this case you could get people killed.

LAURETTE SPANG
(actress, "Cassiopeia")

Early on I felt that I just wasn't getting anything to do, so I went into Glen's office and asked to be given the chance. A week later he wrote the two-part Lloyd Bridges episode. He was terrific that way. He listened and was reasonable. He was a nice guy.

SCOTT MANTZ

One big addition to *Galactica* that came out of "The Living Legend" was Anne Lockhart as Sheba. Laurette Spang, she was great as our favorite socialator turned nurse. Maren Jensen, I thought she was a knockout, but she really didn't have much to do. Now, Sheba was a great character. She was one of the boys, and she was also very feminine, vulnerable. She was terrific. Anne Lockhart just nailed her performance as Sheba.

TERRENCE MCDONNELL

For me she was a utilitarian character who was a member of the fighting-forces group. A woman who obviously would have intuition that would enable her to possibly look at things differently. She would throw out the other possibility. It couldn't always be Starbuck and Apollo. Hers was another point of view we could get across and keep that antagonism alive. She respected Apollo. There was absolutely no question about that. But she was her own woman.

ANNE LOCKHART
(actress, "Sheba")

I loved this character. I liked that she had great gumption and she was very good at what she did. She was a warrior equal to the men. In fact, I loved that gender was not made an issue of at all. I also very much liked her vulnerability and her awkwardness with personal situations. She never wavered from her convictions or her intelligence as a warrior and as a military character, but she was very awkward emotionally. I really loved that dichotomy of a young woman who is so in control and on top of her game in the military aspects of her life and just as clumsy but trying desperately to cover it and be cool.

TERRENCE MCDONNELL

I think it was the first time we ever saw a woman in combat in terms of science fiction. Personally, I love strong women, so it was fun to write her character where she gives as good as she gets. She is one of the boys and she was probably raised with brothers. So she doesn't back down from anyone. Besides that, she was Cain's daughter, for crying out loud, with that charismatic personality, so all of that has to be a big part of who she is. I loved getting my teeth around that character.

SCOTT MANTZ

That great scene on the bridge of the *Galactica,* where Cain says, "You were right, I was wrong." At that moment, they were working together. Their strengths worked in their favor. Cain pulled out the *Pegasus,* Baltar and the Cylon fleet attacked the Colonials, and Baltar was wearing this ridiculous Cylon helmet. It was so stupid, but it was funny. The Cylon says, "Sir, if I may," and he goes, "Not right now, I don't want to miss another moment of the last battlestar's destruction." And the Cylon goes, "I really think you should take a look at the other battlestar." "What are you talking about? That's impossible," and then he panics as it approaches: "Turn, turn you fool, it's coming straight at us. . . ."

To Be Continued. *That's* how you do a cliffhanger. It's a lot of good con-flict in this two-part series, and then Cain attacks two Cylon basestars that explode, but what happened to the *Pegasus*? You don't really know. The door was left open for Cain to return.

GLEN A. LARSON

We would have brought Lloyd Bridges back. I deliberately obscured what happened in that battle so it wasn't definitive that we had killed them off. I figured that Cain was too good. It also gave you a chance to go off and do episodes with just him and his group.

LAURETTE SPANG

It was fun. We had one scene where Anne Lockhart and I had on these black leather suits and they strapped us to some contraption to make it look like we were coming down by parachute—we were on a crane at night. It was very exciting and you revert to being eight years old running across your backyard with a laser gun. I had done a lot of TV in the years before but I really think that was a highlight. It was just great fun.

ANNE LOCKHART

We were so excited. We shot that at Cal State Northridge. Laurette and I went go-karting that morning. We weren't in a soundstage. It was such a thrill.

When we all stepped out of our trailers we were like, "Hey, ain't we hot?" The outfits were fabulous but we were in black sprayed hockey helmets.

SCOTT MANTZ

With Sheba, there was something about her that they were setting her up to be Apollo's love interest. I don't see Apollo going for a girly girl, like Starbuck. Sheba was such a great addition, you forget that she was only in half the series.

Interestingly, Anne Lockhart, the daughter of *Lost in Space* star June Lockhart, had actually turned down a different role in the original pilot when Glen Larson first called her about appearing in *Battlestar Galactica*. This time the answer was different.

ANNE LOCKHART

To this day is still amazes me, the nerve I had for doing this, but I called him up on the phone after I got this script about eight months before they shot and I said, "Thank you, I am really flattered that you think enough of me, but I have to make a decision based on what you have given me at this point." And I said no. He was very nice about it, and I just figured that was that. The show went on and the pilot was shot and it was a huge success, but something inside told me I had done the right thing. It was purely a gut instinct that I did that, and something told me that sticking to my guns was a good idea. I guess it turned out in the end that he respected me for that, because he called me up when Jane Seymour did not want to do a series.

He called me again and said, "I have the opportunity to write a new character and I would like to write it for you." I said, "I'd love to read it," and he said, "I'll send you what I have," and within about four hours a messenger arrived with the first twenty-five pages of "The Living Legend." I read those and I called him up and I said, "When do you want me to start?" I loved

182   **SO SAY WE ALL**

this character and I think Sheba was far more suited to me and I was far more suited to Sheba.

They all thought that I was there as a guest star for a two-parter. They did not know when I started working that I would be a series regular, and I actually couldn't say anything, because the deal was still being done. The only person who knew was Lorne Greene, who said something to me my first day. He kind of winked at me and said this will turn into something good for you, and I knew he knew.

SCOTT MANTZ

The episode that followed was *The Towering Inferno* in space. It's a potboiler episode, it's entertaining, it's fun while you're watching it, but you don't really remember it when it's over.

In "Fire in Space," the Cylons launch a deadly kamikaze attack on the *Galactica*, causing devastating damage to the bridge and a raging fire. Apollo and Starbuck place charges on the hull, hoping that the resulting detonation will expose the fire to the vacuum of space and smother it before the *Galactica* is destroyed.

TERRENCE MCDONNELL

Jim and I were down on the set for that particular episode more than any other episode of any show that we have ever written, especially when they blew up the bridge. It was terrific. There were a lot of cuts in there. The ceiling would collapse and then they would clean that up. They would fire these guys off of trampolines to go flying and then we'd get a shot of the glass map shattering. Everyone was standing around applauding.

CHRISTIAN I. NYBY II

I had directed like thirty-five *Emergency* episodes, so I have a lot of fire experience, I guess. We planned that fairly carefully. I don't think we storyboarded it but we had all the effects pretty well figured out. A little of it was the seat of your pants.

TERRENCE MCDONNELL

Apparently before we got there one of the other people who had worked on the show was Michael Sloan and he had written a script that was also called "Fire in Space." We never saw that script until a week or two before the series was over. There was a lot of anger on Michael's part, because he thought we'd stolen it from him. It was a two-hour two-parter, and the fire did not occur until the second half of the script, and there was a murder in it. But Glen wanted to break it up, so he talked us through what he wanted in "Fire in Space" and then we gave that to him—although the original ending that we wrote was a thousand percent better than the ending that ABC demanded.

At the beginning of "Fire in Space," there is a suicide attack by the Cylons, and we thought that was great, because already friends of mine were complaining that the Cylons were no threat. They couldn't kill anybody, so we had a suicide attack and the ship slams into the *Galactica* and causes this huge fire that is raging on board. At the end, Starbuck and Apollo go out on the hull and set these charges. In the finished product they are out there and they are climbing up these rungs that are attached to the hull and one of them breaks loose coincidentally and goes sailing out into space as the charge is about to go off.

The other launches himself bodily into the other one, and that propels them out of the way as the charge goes off. That was hardly what should have been the ending. ABC did not understand drama. In the original they were back out on the hull and the Cylons come back for another suicide run and they are firing at them. One ship is getting through, and Apollo and Starbuck set the charge just as the Cylon ship comes in for another suicide crash, and it takes out the ship and puts out the fire simultaneously. ABC said, "Well, they did that at the beginning, so we don't want to see it again." It would have been so dramatic and intense. It's unbelievable drama, because we know what is going to happen if it gets through. But you're talking to empty suits.

RICHARD JAMES

They would write things like our guys are on the outside of the ship planting explosives, and this was a Friday-night production meeting. We were getting the first two acts in pencil and we were going to start shooting the episode on Monday. This is the way it went. Literally, we were working on two acts that weren't even finished at a late Friday night production meeting, and then Universal would say you can't work overtime on Saturday and Sunday. How are we going to shoot this? We went through that line—you know, our boys go out on the exterior of the battlestar and plant bombs to snuff out the fire—and they just continued on with the meeting. My hand shot up and I asked, "Where exactly is the exterior of this ship? It's vast." I'd run into the office and say, "I've got to have another stage," and they'd say you can't have any more stages.

Under tight budget and time constraints, James set out to create a hull set that would match the intricate surface detail established by the six-foot miniature of the *Galactica* used in filming the special effects.

RICHARD JAMES

I finally got an empty stage, painted the walls all black, did the floor like the surface of the ship, and painted it battlestar gray. I ran around the backlot and got pieces of junk that I planted on the stage that became the exterior of the ship. I did rivet runs all over everywhere and went out and found big hunks of machinery on the backlot. I painted the machinery all the same gray and stuck it around on the stage so that it kind of looked like ducts to match the miniature as close as possible. The studio could have fired me any day if I was going over budget, but Glen did not care. They ended up I don't know how many millions of dollars over on those shows, but Glen was telling them, this is what I want and then the studio would say you can't. And, of course, they had to bring in the guy who did the wiring to wire the actors like they were floating in space.

CHRISTIAN I. NYBY II

The weightless thing was tough. Filming that was very difficult then, but today you could just CGI out the cables. We ended up with two large wires and you could really see them and we couldn't get rid of them. We had to do front projection, because we were putting up the stars and stuff on the back, so we had to reshoot. Oh, it was awful.

BOONE NARR
(animal trainer, *Battlestar Galactica*)

We had this elevator scene where it fills up with smoke. The effects guys put a little too much pressure on the smoke, so it made a real loud hissing sound. When we opened the doors up and the smoke cleared, Evie was up in the rafters.

CHRISTIAN I. NYBY II

You couldn't quite predict what the chimp would do. Often to me it would steal a scene doing something goofy off in the background, because it was a chimp. I would have to bite my tongue to not laugh during a shot. So, we had to send this poor little chimp down these tubes that we had and, of course, we had the fire effects and light effects and stuff. The first time the chimp got in there it came running toward us. We shot up some flame in the foreground and it just spun around and disappeared at the other end. It took its helmet off and climbed up to the top of the scaffolding of the stage. We had to give him a little acting lesson, I guess. Anyway, poor thing. It was completely safe but I think we just startled it a little more than we expected.

By the middle of the first season, Larson's series had begun to evolve. Driven by cost and the realization that greater attention needed to be given to character for the series to survive, *Galactica* moved in a new direction. As planned, the role of the Cylons was diminished and new adversaries, such as the Borellian Nomen and the Eastern Alliance, were introduced. Episodes such as "War of the Gods" and "Experiment in Terra" explored the spiritual foundations established earlier in the pilot. Stories began to focus less on combat and more on character-driven solutions to create drama.

TERRENCE MCDONNELL

I wanted to find out more about these other ships in the fleet and who was on them. What were they doing and how were they contributing to the whole process? There could be drama as you got to know these characters. You can't really compare the first version of *Galactica* with the second version of *Galactica*, where everything was opened up. Cylons were legitimately dangerous. We couldn't kill anybody on the show. We did an episode called "Take the Celestra." It starts out with a firefight going on aboard the *Celestra* because there is a mutiny. Then we cut back to Starbuck and Apollo, and they are doing something on the *Galactica,* and by the time they get over to the other ship the firefight is still going on. And we're going to cut back and forth. ABC at the time had this weird Standards and Practices rule where you can only have between four and six incidents of violence per episode. So they were claiming that this one had like twelve, because you're in a firefight and then you cut away and then you come back and that's another incident of violence. We're going, "It's the same firefight!" We finally won that, but that took a long time. It was nuts the notes we'd get. They'd say, "She's wearing a revealing costume. No nudity." Seriously? Really?

GLEN OLIVER

I've always felt the show's gimmicky use of goofy terms to denote time and distance measurements also undercut dramatic intent quite a bit. "Centon," "micron," "centar," and "secton" were often vague and undefined, and not always easy to intuit on the fly, in the heat of a sequence. Some of these time units could be inferred, maybe, kinda, sorta, but clumsily. I never felt they were clear. So much so that, in one of the show's few meta moments, a newly introduced character, Randolph Mantooth's Michael, a more recognizably contemporary human from "Greetings from Earth," actually ponders what such terminology means. Tellingly, he doesn't get an answer from our leads.

TERRENCE MCDONNELL

If you watch the show the terminology is so inconsistent. It's just all over the place.

So, there was no bible. Nothing that we could refer to except the other scripts. Glen's first drafts on a number of episodes made no sense, and pages would be going down to the set all the time to clarify things. That was the way he worked. He'd write two-part episodes and knock 'em off relatively quickly and there were problems.

I made some notes, because Glen had a proclivity for calling the same things different things in various scripts, like a centon was a micron.

I went up to Glen's office and I stuck my head in and said, "Could I see you for a second?" He nodded and I went in. I said, "I've got some notes on your script." And all it was going to be was the terminology, but all I could see is Mount Vesuvius starting to move up his chest into his face, and I realized this was a really bad idea. I never went back into his office again unless I was called, and I never had any notes.

So if there are things that don't work in various scripts, it's not because we didn't find them. It's because those kind of things were unwelcome. I wanted to print out a little bible of the terms, but we thought that would be rubbing Glen's nose in it. He was furious with me. So we kept our distance for quite a while, but we still did our work. He was very nice to us, don't get me wrong, it was just one thing that I absolutely remember because this was my first job as a story editor and I didn't want to screw it up, so I learned a big lesson that day.

GLEN OLIVER

How close are those attacking Cylons, exactly, and how worried should we actually be? How much time do our characters really have before "X" calamity strikes? How long have our heroes actually been looking for Earth, anyway? Orientation and immediacy are lost, and that's not a reasonable obstacle for any story to overcome. Those kind of questions shouldn't be obscured in a narrative about desperation, struggle, and life and death. I'm all for some mysteries being left vague for the sake of audiences discovering as they go, but to not have a clear sense of time flow simply deflates or convolutes tension unnecessarily.

However, one aspect of *Battlestar Galactica* that is rarely written about, and is often overlooked in this age of "binge TV," is how much it preliminarily paved the way for the serialization that is de rigueur in television today. While series like *Lost in Space* and even the original *Star Trek* rarely connected the dots between episodes or the emotional stakes therein (Kirk isn't fazed by the death the previous week of Edith Keeler as he confronts the death of his brother in "Operation: Annihilate" a week later), *Battlestar Galactica* would often elaborate on elements from previous episodes even though it sometimes bungled its own continuity.

In "Lost Planet of the Gods," women are finally allowed to become Viper pilots. In future episodes, we would see female Viper pilots fly missions. Later, in "War of the Gods," Apollo, Starbuck, and Sheba would be given a clue to the location of Earth, and in the following episode, "The Man with Nine Lives,"

Adama would pick up on that thread. The fate of the disappearance of the battlestar *Pegasus* would be an ongoing concern, as well as the evolving love triangle among Starbuck, Cassiopeia, and Athena and the relationship between Apollo and Sheba, although character drama was less likely to be explored in depth. Another plot thread that was serialized through the latter half of the series was Baltar's fate after he surrenders to Adama in "War of the Gods," and still another was the disposition of his Cylon fighter in "Baltar's Escape," which plays a key role in "The Hand of God."

TERRENCE MCDONNELL

It wasn't like where you do big story arcs like you do now. That's not the way television was. It would have been so much more interesting to see people grow and develop. I remember when I was writing *Six Million Dollar Man* the one episode I kept pitching was where Steve discovers that there was a guy before him and everything is going to shit in his body. I thought it would be such a fabulous episode and it was like, "Oh my God, what's going to happen to me?" But they wouldn't let us do it, because the characters were the characters. They never had moments of doubt.

7.
LET THERE BE LIGHT

"Isn't he wonderfully evil? We can learn much from him."

Every science fiction series tends to have the one seminal episode that defines it. In the case of the original *Star Trek* it was "The City on the Edge of Forever," for *The Next Generation* it was "The Best of Both Worlds," for *The Outer Limits* it was "Demon with a Glass Hand," and for *The Twilight Zone* it was "The Monsters Are Due on Maple Street." In the case of the original *Battlestar Galactica,* it was "War of the Gods," a clever, mysterious, metaphysical two-parter introducing *The Avengers'* Patrick Macnee as the enigmatic Count Iblis.

In the episode, a Viper patrol vanishes after encountering a mysterious Ship of Lights. Apollo, Starbuck, and Sheba are sent out to investigate, and discover the wreckage of a vessel on a nearby planet. There, they meet Count Iblis, an elusive stranger, who returns with them to the *Galactica.* Iblis quickly rises to prominence by performing powerful miracles, such as delivering Baltar to the Council of Twelve for justice. Adama questions his true motives as Iblis comes closer to gaining control of the fleet while Apollo tries to unearth the sinister secret of Iblis's true identity on the planet where they first discovered him.

GLEN A. LARSON
(creator/executive producer, *Battlestar Galactica*)

I think I started to lose the network executives. I don't think they knew what to make of the series. They had been trying to overlay all of these basic soap opera principles on us, but at that point we were writing faster than they could keep up with us. They didn't know what to do with us at that point, and I think some of them had written us off.

TERRENCE MCDONNELL
(story editor, *Battlestar Galactica*)

Glen would generally write big, two-part episodes and then he'd use up all the money in the special effects for those shows. What we'd wind up doing is little bottle shows. They're self-contained in the fleet, with stock footage we've used before.

ANNE LOCKHART
(actress, "Sheba")

There is a famous line which is cut [in "War of the Gods"] because the censors cut it and it is the end of the scene where Iblis kisses me in the agroship. I am in a pretty pink dress—the only time I got to wear a pink dress, which Jean-Pierre designed which was gorgeous, and I am in a trance and moony-eyed because he had me in his spell. I am afraid and Iblis says, "What are you afraid of?" and I tell him I don't know. He leans toward me and is getting ready to kiss me and says the scripted line, "Oh Sheba, nothing can harm you as long as I am inside you." Well, I would just lose it every time he said this to me. We got a bad case of the giggles. He was this dear man, a professional trained man, who would say this to me and I would lose it. I tried looking at the top of his head. I tried looking at his ear. I tried everything I could to compose myself, and I couldn't. I have never done this before or since in my life, I excused myself and I went to the telephone on the set and I called Glen and I said, "You can't have this man say this to me, we can't even look at each other and do this scene," and he said he'd be right down.

Glen said there was nothing naughty about it. It's just the intent of Iblis taking your spirit and he's possessing you and all this stuff. Glen insisted on it, and we finally pulled ourselves together and actually shot him saying the line, my reaction, and the kiss. They edited the show and sent it to ABC's Standards and Practices and they cut it.

Fans of the series have long questioned a mystery raised in the episode's conclusion. Returning to the planet to investigate Iblis's ship, Apollo, Starbuck, and Sheba make a shocking discovery in the debris which is "as big as a battlestar," leading many to speculate that it could be the wreckage of the *Pegasus*. What the characters saw, however, was never shown onscreen, and the intention of the writers was never revealed.

JIM CARLSON
(story editor, *Battlestar Galactica*)

What you were going to see there was a cloven hoof, but the network wouldn't allow that. We were going to have a very stylized hoof so it would look like some unearthly being.

ANNE LOCKHART

It was supposed to be something malevolent and deadly-looking when I go in there. Apparently it was on short notice, and this was the best they could come up with, to suggest this Mephistopheles character—but they couldn't show anything, so they had to cover it. It looked like a dead sheep under a blanket with its feet sticking out. It was about the most unthreatening thing you have ever seen. It was far more effective to not ever show what we saw, because ever since people have been asking about it. I guess I am a better actress than I thought, because what I was reacting to was a furniture pad with four phony feet sticking out of it. It was horrible.

GLEN A. LARSON

In retrospect, I don't think I minded that, because going the other way sort of nailed it down to one specific thing limited to accepting a biblical position which may be as apocryphal as when someone stands up and says, "I died and before the surgeons brought me back I saw heaven and the streets were paved with gold." And you want to say, "Well, maybe, but what value is gold in some other dispensation?" People tend to interpret things in terms of their own references, and those references could be quite meaningless on some level. I think the hoof thing might have been a limiting factor.

TERRENCE MCDONNELL

They didn't know what to call him, so I went back through Arabic mythology and found that Iblis is a name for Satan, so if you knew that, and I don't think a lot of people would have known that, they would have been on to it right away.

GLEN A. LARSON

I had been influenced by the fact that the top ten scientists in the world at the time all believed in a greater power and a Godlike creature.

JIM CARLSON
(story editor, *Battlestar Galactica*)

We all agreed that we couldn't just have the Cylons in there every week with those computer voices missing everything they shot at. We were looking for other kinds of villains to bring in.

SCOTT MANTZ
(film critic, *Access Hollywood*)

This was the episode where Glen Larson, the creator and writer of this episode, wore his faith on his sleeve. This episode is about his Mormon faith. A line from that episode is lifted from Mormonism, "As you are now, we once were, as we are now, you may become." That's direct from the Mormon faith, but this was an episode that brought religion and belief into the fore.

GLEN A. LARSON

We were very careful to keep it sort of theologically neutral. It was a bit of a stretch to some people probably to even consider the existence of a belief in God in outer space in the first place.

SCOTT MANTZ

That was the best of the bunch. This episode was *Galactica*'s finest hour. There are a lot of reasons for that. First of all, up to that point, every episode was more or less a threat from the Cylons. Every episode was the humans winning, getting away, escaping. Week after week, you did that; the Cylons stop being a threat. They become laughable. When you're watching the pilot, the Cylons just wiped out the Twelve Colonies. They are a force to be feared. But by halfway through the first season, you stopped really worrying about them. They were establishing good dynamics with characters, bringing in someone like Commander Cain and Sheba, but "War of the Gods" was the first story of *Galactica* that went outside of the box.

Because they're moving further and further away from the colonies, we're getting further into deep space, we're going into the unknown. What's out there? This was the first episode that really brought in a new force, but is it good or bad? It starts off with the Ship of Lights and the pilots that totally disappear and Starbuck, Apollo, and Sheba go to a planet where there's some seismic activity. They think it might be the pilots who crashed, but it was something else that crashed. I'll never forget the image of when they get down to the planet, the cinematography of that episode, they're all red.

One of my favorite scenes of that two-part episode is where Iblis meets Adama for the first time and they're sizing each other up. They are on the same level playing field. They're both older and wiser, and they both have paths. Adama's trying to be a gentleman and say basically, "Are you sure you want to come with us? We've got problems." Then, Iblis says, "Let me bring you a more optimistic appraisal. You're searching for a tribe called Earth. Your tribes are scattered. The thirteenth journeyed to Earth a millennium ago," and Adama, in a moment of vulnerability, plays it perfectly. He's like, "Tell me about the civilization." Iblis goes, "They have known great rises and falls." It's chilling, because it's true. That sums up the Earth perfectly.

Then, Adama composes himself. "Is our technology strong enough to help us defeat the Cylons?" Then the bomb drops when Iblis says, "I've come to prepare your way to Earth, but I have to lead you." When you have a vampire, you have to invite him into your house. He has to be asked to lead them, and Adama is resisting that. The Council of Twelve has basically made up their minds. This is the guy, he's got these special powers. He's got this very interesting, romantic connection with Sheba, because she sees a lot of her father in this guy, but he is charming, and that moment where Baltar surrenders, that was like a sweeps story. The guy who just fucked over the human race just surrendered to us. Whoa!

HERBERT JEFFERSON, JR.
(actor, "Lieutenant Boomer")

It touched on the good-and-evil theme and the morality of the Cylons and that there is a higher power that controls everything. You don't find many science fiction films in general that touch on that point.

RICHARD HATCH
(actor, "Captain Apollo")

I believe that a lot of the ancient stories and mythology contain some degree of truth and that life must exist on other planets and on other dimensional frequencies. Therefore, it's interesting to deal with an entity or someone that man has built into a powerful figure and put him in a science fiction framework.

GLEN OLIVER
(pop-culture commentator)

"War of the Gods" has always spoken to me loudly, as it's the first full-on indicator that the show had the potential to go far bigger than seemed possible at face value.

The Ship of Light concept and mythology—and the possibilities it opened up—lay a tremendous groundwork. The Count Iblis character is fascinating in that he so pointedly represents a greater struggle in the universe—and greater danger—than viewers had previously been aware of. I've always wondered how or if the show would eventually have paid off his overt relationship to the Cylon backstory.

SCOTT MANTZ

Baltar is pacing in his cell, and then on the other side of the prison door, Iblis says, "Sit, Baltar, don't pace." Baltar just says, "I know your voice. I remember that voice." Iblis goes, "Do you?" And then it hits him, he knew. And John Colicos's delivery of that line is brilliant. He's already figured it out before we got to that scene. He says, "I know you. I know it. I've figured you out. That's the voice of the Imperious Leader." And Iblis says, "If that's true my voice must have been implanted into the Imperious Leader a thousand yahrens ago. I have to be thousands of yahrens old." Then, Baltar turns his back on Iblis and Iblis is suddenly in the cell with him. "Do not fear, my friend. All is not lost." Whose side is this guy on? It's such a great episode.

RONALD D. MOORE
(cocreator/executive producer, *Battlestar Galactica* [2004])

We briefly thought about doing something with Count Iblis [in the 2004 *Galactica*]. Couldn't find a way to work it into our version of the mythology. We talked about the Ship of Lights, which he's connected to. There were ideas kicked around here and there, but we never quite landed on something that felt satisfying, so it never got very far.

GLEN OLIVER

In "War of the Gods," the *Battlestar* mythology went full-tilt, and it's a damn shame the show never had a chance to revisit the notions these episodes set forth.

SCOTT MANTZ

In addition to the battle of wits between Patrick Macnee and Lorne Greene, another great moment is when Apollo confronts Adama, and he sees Adama moving the figure with his mind. He's telling how he did it, back with his wife and everything, and it drove him mad. It's so deep. This is like mature, philosophical stuff dealing with religion and faith, and how is it that after all these years, I'm finally still learning things about my father? How is it after all these years, I'm still learning things about my son? It's such a great moment. Lorne Greene and Richard Hatch were so good together. They have believable chemistry as father and son.

HERBERT JEFFERSON, JR.

I enjoyed that. I am very religious. When I look and listen it put into the hearts and minds of the viewers, especially the children, that there is something bigger than the war with the Cylons, it's a struggle between good and evil, which is universal and covers the universe.

SCOTT MANTZ

The music for that episode is probably one of the best scores that Stu Phillips ever did. The episode is so emotional when they revive Apollo, and the fact that the pilots that they found before are going to be returned with no memory of what happened. Then they're back on the *Galactica,* with very little memory of what actually happened, and suddenly Apollo walks over to the window and remembers the Ship of Lights and talks about a battle between good and evil. Adama says, "It'll be that way until we find Earth," and then they start expositing on the coordinates of where Earth is. It starts with nine planets and one sun, and they're all like, "Whoa, what is that from?" If nothing else, *Galactica* would still be a monumental achievement because of the strength of that one two-part episode. It's after "War of the Gods" that they start going through the motions.

In the following episode, legendary actor/dancer Fred Astaire guest-stars as Chameleon in "The Man with Nine Lives," an aging con who may or may not be Starbuck's father (spoiler alert: he is). The energy on the set was electric in anticipation of Astaire's arrival. For cast members, working with Astaire was a once-in-a-lifetime opportunity.

DONALD BELLISARIO
(supervising producer, *Battlestar Galactica*)

I received a phone call one day, and my secretary said Fred Astaire was on the phone, and I said, "Yeah, right." So I got on and said hello and it was really him. He said his grandchildren loved the show and they were after him to be on it. He asked, "Do you think you could give me a little part?" And I said, "Mr. Astaire, I will write an episode for you." And I did.

He was a charming man, a really wonderful guy. So professional. I can still remember when we were shooting that. I was just standing there next to the camera and Fred would not leave the camera. He would put his chair right behind it so that he could sit there and be available the instant you needed him. He was so professional. It was one of the best experiences I ever had.

ROD HOLCOMB
(director, "The Man with Nine Lives")

I got to go to his house, and I noticed something I thought was really odd. His belt was actually a tie that he wrapped around his waist, and he tied it into a really pretty knot that hung off to the side. Almost a gaucho kind of thing. I thought, "That's freaking cool."

Of course, there was a fairly big party scene where he danced with one of the actresses, but he didn't want to dance. He said, "No dancing." I said, "Fred, what we'll do is a little bit more of you hiding. Let's think about what you're doing, that you're really basically moving and looking around to avoid the Nomen. Let's make sure that's the object." And he was so appreciative. Those are great memories.

TERRENCE MCDONNELL

That was the last time Fred Astaire ever danced on film. I grew up watching his musicals. My mom loved the standards, in terms of music, and she had a Hammond organ in the house. At night I'd go to bed and she'd be playing music and in the morning I'd ask her what was that song and she showed me Fred Astaire. I'd never seen anybody dance like that before. It was just astonishing. I was always a huge fan of his. I still am.

Laurette tells the story about coming back from lunch while we were shooting. And Fred, a consummate professional, always had everything memorized. Everything was prepared. He was just ready to go. She came back from lunch and I guess there was nobody on the stage but him and he was off in a corner. He was trying different ways of sitting down into a chair. Trying this way, trying that way. Didn't think anybody was watching. That's the detail that he would put into a performance.

LAURETTE SPANG
(actress, "Cassiopeia")

The sweetest moment that I had with him was the scene where we were talking about whether Starbuck and Cassiopeia will one day be together. Fred was supposed to sit down into a chair for me to do this test on him. We were rehearsing and talking and he would turn and sit in the chair from one direction, then he got up and went to the other side and kind of spun around and turned and sat down in another way. I thought this is the way he works. I have always heard that the way he danced he was a technician. He was incredible about practicing and trying different things, and here he was just going to sit in a stupid chair. He was just kind of looking for the most comfortable way to sit, and I just was so delighted talking to him.

DIRK BENEDICT
(actor, "Lieutenant Starbuck")

It was my favorite episode, and Fred and I consequently were friends for the rest of his life. He was a wonderful human being and a hard worker and I learned a great deal about a work ethic which no longer exists really in television. The guy just showed up, worked hard, and did his job. A living legend, but you would think he was a guy on his first bit part, as hard as he worked. No star temperament or anything. That was a wonderful script and an interesting story and I loved playing it.

LAURETTE SPANG

A couple of months later, at Christmastime, I had sent Fred an invitation to a Christmas party my husband and I were having. One night, I ran to answer the phone and it was Fred. He said, "I got your lovely invitation and I am going to be out of town that weekend." I thought, "Oh my God, it's Fred Astaire," and it was sweet that he called personally. He said he was invited to a lot of functions, but he was very touched by my invitation.

HERBERT JEFFERSON, JR.

It was wonderful. You couldn't find a more gentle and easy-to-work-with individual. I was awestruck.

ROBERT FEERO
(actor, "Bora")

Between setups one afternoon, they were resetting the camera and I sat down next to Fred. I asked him for an eight-by-ten glossy of himself for my mother and I said, "Could you please put 'Love from Fred'?" He paused for a moment and looked at me and said, "I never sign 'Love' on my photographs. I save that for [something] special." He was a man of great, great integrity. It was a pleasure working with him.

TERRENCE MCDONNELL

The guy who played the leader of the Borellian Nomen, the villains of the episode, was an actor named Lance LeGault. He had done a lot of stuff at Universal. He was in Elvis Presley's comeback special dressed in black leather and playing the drums. He was in a bunch of Elvis movies. He was a stuntman and stuff like that. One day, Don comes into our office and I'm trying to come up with names for these guys who are like nomads and Jim [Carlson] goes "Nomen." That worked. Then we needed a weapon they use, and we figured they were a little behind technologically, so maybe we could find an older weapon, and we came up with the laser bola.

As the countdown to the end of the season continued, story editors McDonnell and Carlson found themselves stuck writing a series of bottle shows—a term used to describe episodes that occur primarily on standing sets with minimal expense. Bottle shows are traditionally done late in a season to save on production costs. They seized on that as an opportunity to focus on the members of the fleet in such episodes as "Take the Celestra" and "Murder on the Rising Star."

JIM CARLSON

Terry and I were sitting in our office kicking things around and trying to come up with something when we thought, "All these people get along so well, and that wouldn't really happen that way." When you're boxed in under trying conditions, people tend to get a little feisty.

STEVEN SIMAK
(journalist, *Battlestar Galactica* historian)

Although time is always a factor in short supply on any television series, it was particularly true for the writers working on the episode "Murder on the Rising Star." After waiting to learn what the next script would be, Carlson and McDonnell were given notice at 4 P.M. on Wednesday to write a teleplay and have it in mimeo by seven o'clock on Friday morning. With little time, the writing team fleshed out a mystery story in which Starbuck is accused of murder.

TERRENCE MCDONNELL

We had no story; nothing was worked out. We had submitted a bunch of stories on Monday and we were sitting around waiting and waiting and we needed to go ahead because we knew we were up to bat next. Then at four on Wednesday afternoon we get word from Glen, who used to write in Hawaii on the beach, to go ahead and do the script off a little logline. He did that on a lot of scripts. We had about thirty-six hours to do an outline and write. Whatever came out of the typewriter was pretty much that script. We didn't sleep for two nights. So, when I look at that script, all I remember is the pain and the hallucinations.

In "Murder on the Rising Star," a game of triad leads to a violent confrontation between Starbuck and Ortega, a pilot with anger-management issues. When Ortega turns up dead, Starbuck becomes the lead suspect. Apollo, confident that Starbuck is innocent, sets out to discover who really committed the murder.

TERRENCE MCDONNELL

We did the outline together, so we knew exactly where we were going. Jim generally did the teaser and the first two acts. And I did the last two acts and the tag. But we had a different writing style. Then we would get together and edit it so it all had one voice. And it worked. We were always able to knock an hour script out in five days.

SCOTT MANTZ

"Murder on the Rising Star" is okay. "Take the Celestra" is pretty good, another power struggle in the fleet, with Paul Fix as Commander Kronus, another *Star Trek* veteran.

TERRENCE MCDONNELL

When I first came out to Los Angeles, I got a job in the mailroom at ABC and my best friend at the time was Rod Holcomb. We were both working in the mailroom and we would go see movies and discuss film. We often fantasized about how I wanted to be writer he wanted to be a director and "Wouldn't it be cool if I wrote something that you got to direct?" And that was "Murder on the Rising Star." It was cool. It was one of those very lucky moments.

Director Rod Holcomb returned behind the camera for "Greetings from Earth," a two-hour episode that served as a backdoor pilot for a spin-off series. In the episode, Apollo and Starbuck intercept a shuttle-like spacecraft (a re-dressed version of Buck Rogers's space shuttle from the "Awakening" pilot of Glen Larson's *Buck Rogers in the 25th Century*) containing a man, woman, and four children and return it to the *Galactica*. Believing that the shuttle may be from Earth, the Council of Twelve orders that the inhabitants be detained even though the *Galactica*'s atmosphere is harmful to their health. Adama has Apollo and Starbuck arrange for the shuttle's escape and follow it back to its original destination, Paradeen. The episode guest-starred Ray Bolger, the scarecrow from *The Wizard of Oz,* and legendary vaudeville performer Bobby Van, as two incredibly annoying robots, Hector and Vector. Randolph Mantooth, star of the hit NBC series *Emergency,* played Michael, and Kelly Harmon played his wife, Sarah.

ROD HOLCOMB
(director, "Greetings from Earth")

Mark [Harmon] came on the set and visited his sister, Kelly. She was a little difficult, but she was good. I liked her. She was a nice person. The learning process for me was trying to manage the overwhelming elements of trying to direct creatively in a gigantic business of making your day and staying on budget. I came from advertising, where everything was about making it as good as you possibly could.

TERRENCE MCDONNELL

It's "Little House on the Planet." It's awful. It was all Lorne's and Glen's kids who were in that episode. I think Glen had seen the writing on the wall that maybe the show wasn't coming back or he was trying to head it off and he was trying to do something that was real family-friendly.

RANDOLPH MANTOOTH
(actor, "Michael")

Ray Bolger was getting along in years and he was pretty grumpy, but grumpy in the neatest way. I loved being around him. It was hard for him to keep those kind of hours. But I thought, "Oh my God, Ray Bolger, he's the Scarecrow." Bobby Van was the exact opposite, so they made the perfect team. They wanted to do a spin-off and have it be me and Kelly and then the show got canceled. How can you do a spin-off of a canceled show? So it didn't happen.

ROD HOLCOMB

Bobby Van was suffering from a brain tumor at the time I was working with him. He would get there late once in a while, and I think he may have had a little bit of a fainting spell. I really tried to take care of him. We were asking him to do a lot of things, and I didn't realize what a strain it must have been for him.

GLEN A. LARSON

The only thing I regret about that episode, something no one really knows much about, is that Marvin Antonowsky, who was Frank Price's right-hand guy at Universal, criticized a dance number in the middle of the episode as being something the kids wouldn't like, and so I cut it down to the minimum. I think I lost the wide shots just to appease him. I shouldn't have even asked his opinion, but at that point we were really trying to get everyone on our side. It was a classic with Ray Bolger and Bobby Van and it was a wonderful piece of theater. I got talked into pruning it, and Bobby Van died shortly after that.

DAVID LARSON
(son of Glen Larson)

I was one of the kids in "Greetings from Earth," when I was five years old. There was one scene where we're all in these little, cryogenic sleep chambers when they find us. They wanted to stick me in one of those little sleeping pods and I just started screaming, "No, I'm not doing that. I'm not doing that. I'm not doing that." They could have fired me right then, but I was the producer's son, so they built something special for me. They had to take it off the hinges, take it off out of the set, put it on cinder blocks on the floor, lay me on the floor, put the thing over me, and told me to push a button to open it. I'm like, "What?" It would lock, but they explained if you just a push a button it will open from the inside. They accommodated me for my entire role. I still remember that. You remember the fearful memories more than you remember some of your best memories.

Meanwhile, art director Richard James had had enough and was ready to leave the series after being asked to work the impossible week after week.

RICHARD JAMES
(art director, *Battlestar Galactica*)

They called me in to the Black Tower, and there were quite a few people in on the meeting. It was rather intimidating in a way, because they were grilling me on why I wanted to quit. Universal didn't pay anything but scale and

I had for fifteen months knocked myself out and no one came to me and said, "Would you like fifty dollars per week over scale?" I almost had the impression that no one knew who I was. Then they offered me something ridiculous over scale and I basically said, "It's too late. I am wiped out." It was just that there didn't seem like there was any appreciation, and I did feel a certain sense of satisfaction when I left. When I went back to visit Universal and they had about three or four art directors doing *Battlestar Galactica*, they each said, "I don't know how you did it."

For "Baltar's Escape," all of *Galactica's* bad guys are featured in a single episode: Baltar, the Eastern Alliance, and the Borellian Nomen plan an escape from the prison barge and take the Council of Twelve hostage.

ROBERT FEERO
(actor, "Bora")

I can hear Lance LeGault's voice now, saying, "THE BLOOD HUNT! THE BLOOD HUNT!" The blood hunt was never explained and they didn't give us any background on it. I always thought of it as "We're going to go out and whack somebody." Someone has broken the code, perhaps, so they have to go on a blood hunt and whack the guy.

WINRICH KOLBE
(director, "Baltar's Escape")

Sometimes you stand there and wonder how can you tell someone they are going overboard and looking campy without pissing the guy off. I remember we had a lot of fun doing that show. Yes, John Colicos was a campy actor and yes we had to tone him down occasionally but he was an excellent actor with a great sense of humor and he could handle it.

In "Experiment in Terra," the celestial aliens from "War of the Gods" return. Apollo and Starbuck meet John, played by *The Ghost & Mrs. Muir's* Edward Mulhare, who asks for their help in averting a war between the militaristic Eastern Alliance and a pacifist Terra.

STEVEN SIMAK

Had *Battlestar Galactica* continued, viewers would have seen more stories using the Light Ship to explore the religious and moral underpinnings fundamental to the series.

GLEN A. LARSON

I always felt we had to go very carefully there for two reasons. One, of course, was that the network would go crazy if they thought we were going to get stuck in one groove. But also, I didn't want to run the risk that we were going to suddenly lose the Bible Belt or have fundamentalists telling people not to watch the show. We had enough trouble trying to keep a science fiction audience without having someone banning us on religious grounds.

SCOTT MANTZ

That's basically an episode of *Quantum Leap*. The Eastern Alliance was sort of introduced as a potential new threat, but they weren't really much of one. It's kind of fun, but again, here's where they went right. Starting with "War of the Gods," they more or less made you forget about the Cylons. Maybe we got rid of them.

TERRENCE MCDONNELL

Richard [Hatch] went to Glen and was upset. He wanted more fun stuff to do. And what Glen did was he took the script that he had already written ["Experiment in Terra"] and gave all of Starbuck's dialogue to Richard and he gave all of Richard's dialogue to Dirk.

RICHARD HATCH

I was very thankful for that. I had told Glen that I felt a little frustrated. I felt that my character had been painted into a box.

ROD HOLCOMB

It was the best choice. Richard, by far, had all the right elements for the character to be what he was. It was a certain kind of sense of innocence with Richard. There was a sense of you knew that he was supposed to be the best fighter. You weren't worried about his strength, yet you were able to enjoy his mystified "Who am I? What am I doing here?" kind of thing, and he actually played it very well.

I don't think Dirk would've been right for that part. Dirk has got a certain edge to his humor and a certain edge to who he is, and it's sometimes Dirk that gets in the way of Dirk. That's what my thinking was. Now, I love Dirk, but I don't think for that role he would've been right, because he was too self-conscious of who he was as a person.

GLEN A. LARSON

We went to a white suit on the guys because that's a translated form at that point, impervious to death. It's beyond death and that's an interesting area. It deals with the higher level of creation. That episode is actually a resurrection theme in many ways. It's translating the spirit into the purest form and has some theological underpinnings. I remember when I was growing up as a little boy and they say, "Say your prayers." I wondered how could anyone listen to all your prayers, but then I realized as we hit the computer generation you should never try to interpret some superintelligence based with your own intelligence because it's pretty ridiculous.

The season finale, "The Hand of God," which is almost universally considered the strongest of the one-hour episodes, is indicative of where many of the cast hoped the series would go during the second season. After an absence of several episodes, the Cylons return to threaten the fleet. With the help of the imprisoned Baltar, Apollo and Starbuck concoct a daring mission to infiltrate a Cylon basestar. Although action-oriented, the script focuses largely on the character relationships between Apollo and Sheba and between Starbuck and Cassiopeia, with a memorable tag involving the origin of a mysterious transmission.

DIRK BENEDICT

I liked that show, too, and it was kind of prophetic that that would be the last episode we ever shot, because of the nature of what that story was about. They didn't trust the characters in the beginning, because, of course, everyone is just enamored with special effects and they're very exciting until you realize that special effects are only interesting when its connected to the human personality.

ANNE LOCKHART

It was kind of where Apollo and Sheba both admitted their feelings, because we spent the whole season playing oil and water, but it was definitely set up as an opposites-attract thing. And we both finally admitted that there was something here in that episode. That's my favorite episode, because the characters were very well fleshed out. We all had very true and real emotions that were very valid that we were playing. It also had one of the most interesting science fiction concepts, which was getting the transmission of the LEM landing on the moon. That concept was very cool.

LAURETTE SPANG

It just started to open up. They started realizing they had to put more into the characters and put the Cylons a little bit more in the background for a while.

GLEN OLIVER

I'm a sucker for "hapless dudes on a suicide mission" stories, and this one was a fine one. It was nice to see *Battlestar* get back to a more rousing adventure motif after getting bogged down midseason. The final sequence, in which the *Galactica* receives Apollo moon-landing transmissions, is a doozy. The show felt like it was finally finding its footing toward the end of its first season. The disparate elements writers seemed to have difficulty juggling early on felt much more deftly conceived and smoothly integrated. Its existential and mythological arcs had been firmly locked into place, and for the first time the series suggested a narrative which could head in any number of interesting or insane directions, while also remaining true to itself. The show, on the whole, felt more balanced, more self-assured, more mature.

SCOTT MANTZ

When you get to "The Hand of God," which was written and directed by Donald Bellisario, and it starts off with this double date, Starbuck and Cassiopeia, Apollo and Sheba, and they go to that dome and start getting the signal, which to you and me is clearly a transmission from Apollo 11, you *know* it's going to be a great episode. And the Cylons are back. We missed you.

What was great is there was no Imperious Leader, Baltar wasn't on the ship, and you had the gold Cylon talking. When Adama says "I'm tired of running, we could attack" to Tigh, who replies, "We haven't tangled with a basestar since we left the colonies," it was a great moment. But what would get them an edge? They could knock out their scanners from inside, easy, and they use Baltar's captured Cylon fighter.

Then, there's that great scene in Adama's quarters, where Adama is looking at the Cylon basestar, which is the model that they shot for the show. Baltar doesn't lose a moment of his charm, toys with Adama, and goes, "Playing with toys, Adama?" But now, for the first time, Adama is the one holding the cards. He's the one pulling the strings. "What do you want, Adama?" It's great. Adama goes, "Information," and walks away. Baltar goes, "They found you," drinks up. Adama goes, "We found them." "It's the same thing, isn't it?" Adama goes, "We're going to destroy them, with your help." "Why should I help you?" Pulling the strings: "You'll regain your freedom." It's brilliant, but what's great about that episode, too, is the emotional stakes. It could have just been Starbuck and Apollo go off in the Cylon ship, but there's the emotional pull of Cassiopeia and Sheba.

The character development in "The Hand of God" was the best of the series. It was brilliantly, sensitively depicted. It was fully realized. It was deep. It made you care more about the characters you've known for a whole season. I've heard Anne Lockhart say, in an interview one time, "We finally got it, and the show was over." It was the perfect last episode, and if they had come back for a second season, who knows? I was so sad when *Galactica* was over.

DONALD BELLISARIO

We were beginning to take the show in a direction that the viewers would have loved. We would have continued to make good television instead of just hardware stories, but by that time it was too late.

8.
BURN, GALACTICA, BURN

"Your battlestar is quite impressive, but it is still just a single ship. We will dispatch it the way the wolf pack does the bear."

Maintaining moderately strong ratings all season long despite myriad pre-emptions and facing off against CBS's still formidable *All in the Family*, *Battlestar Galactica* finished in the Nielsen Top 25 shows of the year. But even with a loyal fan following and solid, if not stellar, ratings, *Battlestar Galactica* was unceremoniously canceled at the end of the 1978-79 TV season by ABC. It came as a shock and a surprise to cast, crew, and fans, but no more tragically than to superfan Eddie Seidel, Jr., who committed suicide over the show's cancellation. Unlike *Star Trek,* no amount of fan fervor would convince the network to continue the series, at least not in its existing form as an epic space opera about the Colonial fleet's search for a shining planet known as Earth.

SCOTT MANTZ
(film critic, *Access Hollywood*)

When the first show premiered, it was a massive hit, a hit that could not be sustained week-to-week. Now, when the show finished its run at the end of the season, I think it was in the Top 25, which today anyone would kill for, but *Galactica* was an expensive show. It cost a million dollars an episode. For 1978–79, that was a lot of money. And it was on ABC. And you know what else was on ABC? *Mork & Mindy, Happy Days, Laverne & Shirley,* and *Three's Company.* Those were hit shows that cost a lot less.

When the show finished out the season, the excitement, the anticipation, leveled off. It still had a steady place in the ratings, that was still pretty damn successful, especially for a sci-fi show, but they didn't think long-term. If they would have renewed it for a second season, had that show gone on for like three or four years, it would be just as popular and relevant as *Star Trek,* but it didn't have the chance.

GLEN A. LARSON
(creator/executive producer, *Battlestar Galactica*)

I could handle the network or I could at least get a truce out of a lot of the things they wanted. I lost the battle and wound up with three themes in one show and I knew better, but at the time I felt I had to bite the bullet. Anyone with less power would've written that *Galactica* discovers Earth because they would have been pushed around.

WINRICH KOLBE
(associate producer, *Battlestar Galactica*)

What ultimately worked against the show was we could not keep up with the hardware. The audience had been promised *Star Wars* for the small screen and I guess they wanted to see *Star Wars* for the small screen. The problem is that the moment you introduce any type of action or hardware you take away from the dramatic element, because it takes so much longer to shoot. So you can't develop stories to such a degree and still try and shoot it in seven or eight days.

It came out immediately following *Star Wars*, so everybody automatically assumed that Glen Larson was ripping off *Star Wars*, which worked against him. Glen also had a certain reputation as a "screw you" guy as far as the studio was concerned. He wanted to do the stories his way, and being the consummate writer he was, he wouldn't let go, which was another thing that was a strike against him. I kept saying that Glen writes until they tear the show away and air it. Even in postproduction for Glen, he was writing and was perfectly capable of sitting there and reediting shows until finally the studio said, "Glen, it's airing tomorrow, you have to get rid of it," and I think that worked against him. There was a certain dissatisfaction on the side of the studio with his working process.

Glen also had a reputation for lighter material with shows like *McCloud* and *Switch* and *Quincy*. There's a certain touch of humor in there that is rather intriguing but it put him in a nice place that wasn't either hard drama or comedy at the time. The moment somebody was out of the ordinary, especially in television, people have a tendency to say, "Oh God, he doesn't know how to write drama and he doesn't know how to write comedy," which I think is false because looking back at the shows now I think they stand up quite well to time.

ROD HOLCOMB
(director, "Experiment in Terra")

You walked into that building and it immediately affected you. I did the Jack Klugman thing when he was the coroner, *Quincy,* and it was the same place, same office, walking, talking, that kind of stuff. You walk into the *Galactica* set, it was like another world. You're almost overwhelmed by it. Then in the end, you walk out of it and you take it home with you because it made such an impression on you. I lived that through all that time. I wasn't doing anything else other than just doing *Galactica.* It must've been maybe over six months, I just stayed with it, and I had a great time. When you're young, you're just doing it. That's what's fun about it. You're just doing it. By the way, nobody was thinking about Emmys and shit like that. I wasn't. I was just there doing the job. I don't even know if I was watching any of the Emmy shows, to be honest, because I didn't watch television at night. I found this to be a wonderful grade of entertainment.

SCOTT MANTZ

The other thing about it that makes the original show stand out is the show is timeless, other than the hairstyles. There's nothing that really gives away when the show is filmed, or when it takes place, because Glen Larson imagined this star system in a way that, while the influence of Egypt and pharaohs was there, it could have taken place in our past or in our future.

He was creating another civilization from scratch, one that was timeless. Compare that to the other show he had going on at the time, *Buck Rogers in the 25th Century.* The reason why that show is very dated is because he was imagining the twenty-fifth century from the disco era. That show looks like disco in 1979, so that show has not aged well. It's also not as good, but the original *Galactica* holds up and still stands out today, because of everything that went into it. Yes, it was rushed, sometimes the writing suffered. Some episodes are much better than the others, but when *Galactica* was good, it was as good as any sci-fi series ever got.

With the series canceled after one season, the studio needed to find a way to recoup their massive investment in the series. With ABC paying only $750,000 an episode, it was Universal that financed the large deficits incurred by the series' massive overages. That helped prompt a theatrical release in the United

States following an international release in Europe and Canada, where the movie had been surprisingly successful. Interestingly, it was the last film ever to be released in Sensurround, the gimmicky low-end bass format, which had been introduced to audiences with the release of Universal's film *Earthquake,* also starring Lorne Greene. Despite *Battlestar Galactica*'s having already aired on television, the theatrical release earned over $10 million at the box office in 1979, an impressive sum given its pedigree.

GLEN A. LARSON

Someone asked for a screening up on the twelfth floor at the Universal Black Tower [the studio's executive offices]. [Chairman] Lew Wasserman and [studio president] Sid Sheinberg saw it and said, "Do you want to release this as a feature?" So, we did go back and do a little more work, but it was really the work that everyone had already done.

In addition, the studio created a syndication package for local channels as well as international distribution, which combined pairs of episodes into multiple two-hour blocks. In the case of *Mission Galactica: The Cylon Attack,* it also received a wide release overseas in theaters, as a reedit of "The Living Legend" and "Fire in Space." (Another edited movie, *Conquest of Earth*—which was a combination of several episodes of the critically reviled *Battlestar Galactica* sequel series, *Galactica 1980,* including "Galactica Discovers Earth," "The Night the Cylons Landed," and "Space Croppers"—was released on VHS in the United States and got a limited theatrical release internationally. It featured ham-fisted ADR (automated dialogue replacement), or looping as it's commonly referred to, in order to explain the presence of two actors playing Dr. Zee by creating a second child genius, Dr. Zen. In addition, Robyn Douglass's looping was done by another actress, which made the actor who looped Gene Hackman's lines in *Superman II* seem authentic by comparison.) The remaining telefilms were created exclusively for television, and in some cases featured footage cut from the original airings as well as a new wraparound, directed by Glen Larson, in which an astronaut discovers the logbook of the battlestar *Galactica* (along with, apparently, a bevy of preproduction art), which also finally explains the original Cylon war. For the insatiably curious, it is easily accessible on YouTube despite never having been released on home video.

The syndication package included the three-hour premiere, *Lost Planet of the Gods, The Phantom in Space, Space Casanova, Gun on Ice Planet Zero, Curse of the Cylons, Murder in Space, The Living Legend, War of the Gods, Space Prison, Greetings from Earth,* and, most intriguingly (and inexplicably), *Experiment in Terra,* which married parts of the "Return of Starbuck" episode from *Galactica 1980* with the original *Galactica* episode "Experiment in Terra" along with a bevy of deleted scenes to reach the requisite running time.

JEFF FREILICH
(producer, *Galactica 1980*)

Budget was the last thing that Glen Larson ever cared about. If anything, Glen, in a way, delighted in making some of the most expensive episodes of television, ever. But he rationalized it in an actually pragmatic way. *Conquest of the Earth,* for example, was a combination of a couple of episodes, and they were written specifically to do that. He would sell that through Universal Distribution as a feature all over the world and as a cassette throughout the United States and make back way more than whatever the overages on the episodes were. That's something that I took with me when I created *Dark Justice,* because I was short. CBS gave us a lower license fee, and I needed more money. So I proposed to Warner Bros. Television that I do a two-part episode that shot in Barcelona the first season and that I would make it into a movie, and they would be able to distribute it. I wouldn't have even thought about doing that until I woke up one day and went, "Well, Glen used to cover his overages by making two-part episodes that could be turned into movies, and I'm going to do the same thing."

Ironically, planning for the anticipated second season of *Battlestar Galactica* had begun before the show's inauspicious cancellation. An early detractor, sci-fi author Isaac Asimov had agreed to join the series as a script consultant. There were also several unproduced scripts from the first season sitting on the shelf that would have likely been produced. In addition, substantial cast changes were being considered. In a proposal to ABC, the character of Sheba was to be written out, foreshadowing a darker and less kid-friendly show.

TERRENCE MCDONNELL
(story editor, *Battlestar Galactica*)

They had six episodes planned, and it wasn't very good. It all felt like stuff I'd seen before. There was a script that was floating around called "I Have Seen Earth." It was a pretty good episode. It was basically *The African Queen* about a miner who's going from planet to planet and claims he's seen Earth.

We thought Jack Elam would have been great for it, he's full of tall tales and Boxey loves this guy and stows away with him and, of course, they land on the planet where the Cylons are.

In the first episode, they were going to bring back Cain with the *Pegasus* and they were going to kill Sheba. It was probably an effort to open up with some kind of big moment. That would have been the impetus for Apollo to become this brooding "I don't care" type of character. He would risk everything and would have nothing to lose. Apollo picks Starbuck to be in charge of the fighters. Cassiopeia was going to be there, but her relationship with Starbuck would be over. How would I feel about characters I had come to like in this way going in another direction? I don't know. I really don't know.

STEVEN SIMAK
(journalist, *Battlestar Galactica* historian)

Other proposals include the elimination of Colonel Tigh and the possible recasting of Athena with another actress.

TERRENCE MCDONNELL

We had been approached by the network about doing a script based on *The Captain's Paradise*, a 1950s Alec Guinness movie where he is a sea captain and he has a wife in port A and another wife in port B. We said sure, so Jim [Carlson] and I wrote a script called "Two for Twilly." It did not get produced. It was basically about the chief mechanic on the fleet and he was married to this woman and all of a sudden, the agroship starts listing and it's heading toward a megastar and they can't do anything about it and they're going to lose the food. So they get Twilly over there to start fixing it and we discover that yeah he's married to this woman, but he's married to *this* woman, too, who's on another ship. So he's going to jump the boat because he's so confused that he can't get everything right, and at the end when he's finally confronted with it and they're back on the ship, they get a divorce, and he's very upset. And so he calls his other wife, and that was the ending. They had a casting session for that and one of the people they were looking at was Jamie Lee Curtis. She came in and read for it. And she got the giggles in the middle of the audition, and my partner looked at me when we got back to our offices and said, "Poor kid, she's never going anywhere in this town."

Second-season plans became academic when ABC canceled the series after only seventeen episodes. The ratings, while considered strong, were not sufficient to justify the series' million-dollar-per-episode price tag, despite the fact that the network was only paying a $750,000-per-episode license fee.

RICHARD HATCH
(actor, "Captain Apollo")

I didn't expect it. I was very frustrated as an actor after the first season, because I felt that, despite all the promises that had been made in terms of having really interesting things to play, I wasn't getting a chance to really act. I was very idealistic and I just felt a little neglected as a character. I wasn't sure if this was something I wanted to continue doing.

ANNE LOCKHART
(actress, "Sheba")

Galactica suffered from the network having input, and it was too many cooks spoil the batter. We were really close to hitting our stride at the end, and then they canned us.

GLEN A. LARSON

I wasn't surprised, because I knew the realities of the numbers and of ABC. The costs of the show were enormous, time was a problem, and we were on a network that was very spoiled. Had we been on the number-two or number-three network at that time, we undoubtedly would have been on a lot longer. There were some very good guys there and I think there were one or two that were not helpful to us. Some egos got in the way. This is a business of egos and it's very difficult to balance all these things. *Quincy, M.E.* was on NBC and its numbers were just okay but Jack loved to scream at everybody and he sort of got into a groove. That show went on about three years longer than it probably should have because they didn't have anything else to put on the air that was better even if it wasn't in the top ten. It was a nice show, but it would have never lasted on ABC when they had all those hits. ABC knocked themselves from number one to number two the year after *Galactica* because of their stupidity. My fantasy was to do a spin-off about Starbuck, a gambler and maverick fighter pilot who travels the Wild West of the Universe.

MICHAEL SLOAN
(producer, *Battlestar Galactica*)

Everyone hoped that they were going to do a second season and not, after all the money they spent, abandon the show. A network has to get behind a show like this and help it out, particularly when we did this in the seventies, because it was very expensive. It needed what Brandon Tartikoff did with *Hill Street Blues*. That show did not come on strong in its first year, but he was not about to cancel it, and then suddenly in the middle of the second season it became a hit. That's what *Galactica* needed. It needed to go for another season, and then I think it really would have grabbed hold.

LAURETTE SPANG
(actress, "Cassiopeia")

It was very sad. Glen Larson was going to write some new scripts for the second season. We had just gotten to a place where Don Bellisario had written the last episode and it just started to open up and they were realizing they had to get more into the characters and put the Cylons a bit more in the background for a while. It takes a season for any show that's worth its weight to get going, and they buried it before it had a chance to happen.

It seemed that we were sabotaged at every corner. We aired opposite the Emmys, we aired opposite *Gone with the Wind*, we were preempted all the time. The other networks were brutal, they just threw stuff in our path every time, and we were kind of pulled from time slot to time slot and that's what did us in. We went to the Rose Bowl, and Michigan was my hometown. I am from Ann Arbor and the band was playing and they asked the whole cast of *Galactica* to go onto the field at halftime. The band formed a giant spaceship that played the *Galactica* theme song, but it was on NBC and not ABC and they cut away from us because it was promoting another network. It never made it on the air. My whole family was watching and I was just devastated.

GLEN A. LARSON

Ironically, the thing that really did the most damage to us was a show called *Mork & Mindy*. ABC had a major hit night going on Thursday with *Mork & Mindy*. They thought that this was science fiction being done the way it should be done and that if *Mork* were on Sunday night then ABC would be in the top ten on Sunday night, too. They didn't realize that Sunday night was going to get split regardless of what was done. So they moved *Mork & Mindy* to Sunday. That show went down to numbers that were not as good as ours, or at least comparable, and destroyed the night that *Mork & Mindy* had been on. They had to eat crow, retreat, and go back and rebuild that night by putting *Mork* back where it had been and find something else for Sunday night because they had already canceled *Hardy Boys* along with us. They never got back to those numbers. They were so spoiled that they didn't appreciate how good our numbers were.

DIRK BENEDICT
(actor, "Lieutenant Starbuck")

It wasn't a show that was a failure in the ratings. It was [canceled] because they expected it to be the number-one show in the country against *All in the Family*, and I thought that was asking too much.

GLEN A. LARSON

It had been too much of a television saga, between the simple logistics of doing it, the lawsuit, and the tremendous success the series had enjoyed at given moments, along with the general feeling that we were doing fine. Not perhaps holding the high numbers that we could like to have held and not doing the kind of numbers a *Mork & Mindy* was doing—but it should have been enough to guarantee our success. At that point, ABC was spoiled. *Mork* cost nothing to produce, because it was a three-camera show and look at the enormous numbers it got.

If you rated us for the whole season, the phenomenal thing was that there were shows that were picked up that were in the sixties like *The Rockford Files*. It started a feud between me and Brandon Stoddard [ABC's then head of programming] that never ended, because there was a lot of petulance and pettiness in that cancellation. There was no excuse for canceling a show with that high ratings.

RICHARD HATCH

With a first-year series you are basically trying to stay afloat. You're trying to get through each episode and get it done on time. The fact that we accomplished as much as we did was a miracle.

DAVID WEDDLE
(producer, *Battlestar Galactica* [2004])

Ironically, my writing partner, Bradley Thompson, and I were in an acting class after we got out of USC. One of the people in the class was Richard Hatch, and he was doing the original *Battlestar* at that time. And so, he was the big star in the class. All the women were in love with him. And here I was, starving film student. So, I wasn't really happy with how all the women were, you know, enraptured with Richard Hatch. I watched a couple of the original shows, which I didn't like. I don't like it now, I didn't like it then. The jealousy was all on my part, though. Richard was a very nice man. He was very down-to-earth, he didn't act like a star in the class. He was really serious about developing his craft. Here he was, big star in a big series. He could've just said, "Hey, I've made it. I know what I'm doing," and yet he was going to class every week trying to deepen his craft.

ROBBIE RIST
(actor, "Dr. Zee," *Galactica 1980*)

Battlestar Galactica, historically, sociologically, might be the last of the post-sixties television shows. Here's what I mean by that. In the 1960s there's all this youth culture and by 1969 the man has pretty much ensured that the foothold of youth culture sunk into the culture wasn't going to take. So the kids got their asses kicked. Their heroes are dying. During Vietnam, a bunch of these disaffected kids are in college during that period and they, of course, graduate college, and some of them are theater majors and writers and things like that. It seems like there is a huge theme of entertainment in the

seventies about people who can't go home. *The Incredible Hulk,* every episode of the show is him walking down the street, lonely. *Man from Atlantis*
was sad, *Land of the Lost. Battlestar Galactica* seemed to be a part of that
continuum. There is no "you can't go home" television now.

ALAN J. LEVI
(director, "Gun on Ice Planet Zero")

Television was different back then. I remember I was doing *The Bionic Woman*
with Forrest Tucker, who was the star of *F Troop.* They said you better go
over and meet him. He lived in Studio City and I went over to meet Tuck. I
walk in and I said, "Mr. Tucker, I'm Alan," and he said, "It's Tuck." We sat
there and chatted and he is a very nice man. Before I left, he said, "Listen,
I've got to tell you this, I have an assistant who follows me around all day
and he holds my glass of bourbon, I will take a sip of bourbon all day long.
Many sips, don't worry about it, I'm fine. At five o'clock at night I won't be
able to say a word—at five minutes to five, I'm perfect." "Okay," I said, "you
got it."

And goddamn that happened twice! Five, ten, fifteen minutes to five I
would be shooting something and at five o'clock, he's out, he had to go home.
I just loved that.

One of my favorite stories was in *The Immigrants.* Barry Sullivan was
playing this old anti-Semitic, angry, pissed-off guy who owned a shipping
company that was being challenged by these younger men. They meet at a
wedding and I rehearsed the scene, we shot it, and I said cut. I was sitting
on the dolly and Barry looked at me and said, "Alan, what's wrong?" I mo-
tioned for him to come over and I said, "Barry, there's a tension between you
and the character of Levy that comes out of anti-Semitism as well as the
young squirt who's trying to take over your ownership of the world with
your shipping company and I didn't get that tension." I asked him what he
wanted to do and he said, "I would like for you to go back and roll the camera." I went back and rolled the camera and it was like roses, it smelt of such
anti-Semitism and hate, without being mean at all. I said cut and I went up
to Barry and I shook his hand and I said, "Barry, thank you so much." He
looked at me and said, "No, I thank *you.*" Oh, I loved that.

HERBERT JEFFERSON, JR.
(actor, "Lieutenant Boomer")

There's something about the way that *Galactica* was written and produced. Tune in to the original *Battlestar Galactica* and you know who the good guys are, who the bad guys are, you know what the objective is. And somehow this all started with a vision, a vision that one Glen A. Larson had for the story. Forty years later, people don't want to know anything about my other body of work, I've worked on Emmy Award winners, no, they want to talk about *Galactica*. I've done work in the theater, that's nice but I want to talk about *Galactica*. I love it but there are less than thirty hours total, including the three-hour pilot. Something must have clicked with the fans.

ALAN J. LEVI

It's not that it was a new genre of filmmaking where there is a story about a family. It was one of the first family shows, especially in space.

TERRENCE MCDONNELL

This is about a group of people who are looking for their home. It's like *The Wizard of Oz*, only sideways. They lost everything and I'm sure that lots of people can relate to this. Some people don't have a home. So, I think that just subconsciously it's there in the background. Nobody talks about it other than in the beginning when they say they are looking for a planet called Earth. But I think it tugs at your heart for that reason.

DAVID LARSON
(son of Glen Larson)

It was the scope of the story that made it enduring. It had a cinematic scope shrunk down to TV, but didn't seem small. It seemed big and iconic, and the story that they were telling was a human story. It was about humans fleeing an oppressive regime, heading to Earth, our home. It just somehow resonated with kids and adults. I think that's kind of uncommon. Because it was personal to him, it became, I think, the best of his writing. If you're writing from a personal place, it's going to resonate with other people. People are going to hate it. There are people who like the Beatles and people who like the Who.

Maybe it's when they grew up. That's another big thing. Who are you talking to? *Galactica* people grew up at that time. That era with *Star Wars* and *Galactica*. There was nothing else like it. My father was a family-friendly kind of writer. There was nothing very complicated about it. It was pretty simplistic stuff, but I think that's part of why it resonated. You have laser battles. You have robot men. It's the same thing you had back in the thirties, forties, fifties in classic sci-fi. It wasn't complicated. You can root for the good guys. He liked heroes that were heroes. He did not like antiheroes. He didn't like flawed heroes as much.

JAMIE BAMBER
(actor, "Captain Lee 'Apollo' Adama," *Battlestar Galactica* [2004])

I loved it. I was a child of the early eighties. It was Vipers flying out of these slightly phallic tubes, but nonetheless flying into space. It was the joystick with the three buttons, it was the sort of pharaoh-like, sphinx-like helmets. It was Richard Hatch's great hair, it was Starbuck's cigar, it was Lorne Greene's—also great—silvery hair. It was just that life aboard the ship with all these people and these cool sort of different shades of brown leather and suede attire. It was all the surface of the show.

ANDREW PROBERT
(conceptual designer, *Battlestar Galactica*)

I think it stands on its own as a fun series that had a lot of good stories and lots of "classic" visual effects . . . warmly remembered today by fans around the world. Working on the series had its ups and downs, like any other show, but, generally, the memories are good. The people I met were all great. That said, the experience, my first, in the movie business, taught me some things about the business while the design side of it became my confidence base with which to move forward.

DAVID ROGERS
(director, *The Office*)

I grew up on shows like *The Six Million Dollar Man*, *The Bionic Woman*, *Battlestar Galactica*, and *Knight Rider*. They taught "Fire in Space" in my screenwriting class at Ithaca College. I'm a big fan of *Battlestar Galactica*. I'd worked on a bunch of things like *Seinfeld*, and a producer from *NewsRadio* said, "I have a pilot for you to work on." I watched the pilot of *The Office* and, in it, Steve Carell does an impression of the Six Million Dollar Man and I said, "I'm doing this show!"

So, I met with [creator] Greg Daniels and we talked about the show and I said, "I just love this environment and these characters," but I felt that Dwight Schrute's love of *Star Trek* was too mainstream for him. He should like *Battlestar Galactica*. I said, "I can picture him at his desk with like a Viper just sitting in the background." And Greg took this in and I got hired on the show. I edited a ton of episodes and directed a bunch. I got started on the first episode after the pilot. Well, the next thing you know the reimagination of *Battlestar Galactica* took off, and instantly the writers started writing that for Dwight. Bears beats *Battlestar Galactica*. It just kind of took off and he became a fan of the show.

For my birthday Greg Daniels bought me an original model of a Cylon baseship. I directed the second-to-last episode, and in it we have a plot point where Dwight is painting the *Galactica* and later he hangs it up in his office. Now, he has possibly had a son with his paramour Angela, who says it's not his son, and there's a scene where the kid is looking and pointing to the *Galactica* hanging up in his office and Dwight goes, "That kid looks at the *Galactica* the same I way I look at the *Galactica*."

I had to choose which props I wanted, the new series or the original. They didn't have to finish the sentence, I'm like "I want the classic *Galactica*." And sure enough, that's what we got. To me it all came full circle, to be able to get to direct this episode, this second-to-last one, and to have the *Galactica* in there and just wrap it up. I have the *Galactica* from the show and Rainn Wilson signed it to me. It says, "Galactica loves you, Rainn Wilson— Dwight." And it's hanging up now in my apartment.

DAVID LARSON

I'm sure the cancellation was extremely upsetting. He was always, always writing, always taking meetings, always selling. Until the late eighties, early nineties he was just constantly selling, constantly working, and then you get to a certain point where the calls stop coming in, and they're not buying pilots anymore. That was really hard for him. Every once in a while he would get something like *One West Waikiki, P.S.I. Luv U, Night Man,* that seemed to come out of nowhere, right at the right time.

I'm sure he was affected by things, but I've never asked him what he thought about what Harlan Ellison said about the show. I'm not sure that he would have cared. I think he knew what he wanted to make. He was very proud of the things that he did. He did not let other people's opinions sway him. I had a very contentious relationship with him at times. We would argue. He would throw things across the restaurant. I was very strong-headed, and so was he. He did not like to lose an argument. He believed what he believed, and so I don't think critics affected him. I think he wanted the respect of his peers, but if somebody called him out on something, he was just doing what he was doing, and that's who he was. My father could have done a lot with CGI back in the day. He would have gone crazy with it, but they had such a small budget, you kept seeing the same spaceships exploding. Watching it now, that's one of the things that sticks out in your head, didn't I just see that shot five seconds earlier? What he could have done now would have been unbelievable.

TERRENCE MCDONNELL

There were so many stories to tell and so much more we could give them.

DAVID ROGERS

Seinfeld was a situation where they did the pilot and got picked up for four episodes after that and then the network said let's do thirteen and the next thing you know it runs for seven years and is a hit. *The Office,* same thing. We did six episodes season one, we got picked up for another six, it went to thirteen. Something caught on and then the show runs for nine seasons. Everything about *Galactica*—the writing, the directing, the chemistry between the actors, their skill, their talent, the realism, and how much they believed and put into it—was so amazing. The only people who were short-sighted were the network executives, because this show should have run five, six, seven seasons. Today that's what would happen, with merchandising, with toys you figure out how to subsidize, with Netflix and everything. I wish we were talking about season five of *Galactica*.

DAVID LARSON

I was very proud of it, because I watched his shows. It was kind of cool that my dad's shows were some of my favorite shows. I loved *Battlestar*, even though I watched it being made and was only five years old. I think walking through those sets started my love of science fiction, seeing it all come together.

GLEN OLIVER
(pop-culture commentator)

Another part of its legacy is a bit more circuitous, but also more tangible. Without the original *Battlestar*, Ron Moore and David Eick's *Galactica* would have never have been conceived of. That series laid the groundwork for bolder, tougher, grittier, more mature narrative shifts throughout the genre . . . and on TV in general . . . that we're still enjoying today in shows like *Game of Thrones* and *Westworld*. If you can accept that the remade *Galactica* series resonated in this way, and I think there are strong arguments to support this notion, then one could legitimately view the original series as the Sarah Connor of modern genre television.

JAMIE BAMBER

It was escapism, it was fun, and it was heroes fighting against bad guys in space. For me, it was part of *Star Wars;* part of my early experience of viewing adventure. So it was purely that. Obviously, I left that in my childhood, and the surprise I felt when I heard there would be a new version was more like, "Why would you make that now when television and tastes and things have moved on?" But obviously I didn't realize what Ron Moore intended to do.

AARON DOUGLAS
(actor, "Chief Tyrol," *Battlestar Galactica* [2004])

I was seven or eight and I thought the original *Battlestar Galactica* was great. It was like *Star Wars* on TV every week. Spaceships and Cylons whose voices are cool and all of that. It was just so campy, but at that age you don't realize just how campy and goofy it is. You look back on it now, and you have those nostalgic little things, but other than that, you go, "Man, this is *really* bad." Having said that, you couldn't do our *Battlestar Galactica* in 1995, let alone 1978. No way. It wasn't until *The Sopranos* or *The Wire* came along that you could get away with some of the things that Ron Moore and David Eick ended up doing in the show.

GLEN OLIVER

There's an argument to be made that the functional "legacy" of the original *Battlestar Galactica* series is relatively negligible. Many people make fun of the show, many people dismiss it or deride it entirely. In my personal experience, they're often doing so without having actually seen much of—or any of—the series. They're attacking based on preconceptions—without understanding what it actually was, and how it worked on the whole. Even its own remake eschewed many of the tenets which vividly defined the original series.

So, on the one hand, the original series, which does have a loyal fan base, by the way, brings with it a cloud of preconception which, in the eyes of many, relegates it to the status of being a kitschy, and often bludgeoned, footnote from the *Star Wars* era.

On the other hand, the series has endured. It is still known—still in demand.

Fans are spending immense quantities of time and resources fabricating gargantuan and extremely impressive ship replicas. Costumes are available. Soundtracks are being issued. Vintage *Galactica* props still cycle through auctions and online sales. A rather nice Blu-ray set was issued. Despite the stink brought upon the franchise by *Galactica 1980,* and despite the retrospective drubbing the show often receives, *Galactica* has comfortably evaded obscurity. And, sometimes, this in itself is a triumph.

This was the case even before Moore and Eick brought it back in 2004. Considering how many other shows have emerged, and been consigned to the ether, to be completely forgotten and never again resurrected or spoken of? That we're still talking about *Battlestar* today is a miracle of considerable proportions.

GLEN A. LARSON

In some ways I still think of *Galactica* as a success even though it didn't enjoy years on the air. We managed to accomplish a great deal; it was just unfortunate they wouldn't let us do more. It's like the Jack Kennedy of television shows—we didn't know what would have happened if we had been allowed to live.

9.
I HATE THE EIGHTIES

"You must have us confused with somebody else.
My name's not Turkey, and neither is his."

With a respectable theatrical take at the box office for the 1979 release of the pilot telefilm and interest in *Battlestar Galactica* merchandising continuing unabated, it's not a surprise that ABC reconsidered their rash decision to sideline the series. What was a surprise was the decision to instead bring it back with a new cast, a new premise, and a diminished budget in one of the most ill-advised spin-offs in television history. Premiering on January 27, 1980, *Galactica 1980* told the story of the battlestar *Galactica*'s arrival at Earth, retooled for a younger audience and utilizing a myriad of recycled props from the original series, extensive stock footage for space battles, and an almost entirely new cast of characters while telling a considerably earthbound fish-out-of-water story (which was handled far more adeptly by *Star Trek IV: The Voyage Home* several years later) with slapstick comedy, heavy-handed indictments of prejudice and pollution, and, in one case, a sci-fi-infused version of *The Bad News Bears*.

STEVEN SIMAK
(journalist, *Battlestar Galactica* historian)

After a series is canceled, it's standard practice for producers to shop the property around to other networks—usually with little success. In the case of *Battlestar Galactica*, Glen Larson decided on a course of action he had never taken before. In a letter to all three networks, Larson called for a television movie continuing the saga of the Colonial fleet.

GLEN A. LARSON
(creator/executive producer, *Galactica 1980*)

I had written a letter right after the cancellation. I said for all the effort and for all the people and the manpower and the accomplishments and the accolades around the world, this was a shabby way to end something this magnificent. It was a letter that my boss at the studio said he'd wanted to write all his life. I got an immediate response from everybody at ABC, especially at the top end. They said, "You are absolutely right, this was not the way to do it," and they wanted to do a two-hour special. Of course, as soon as we put it together, it validated everything we wanted to do. I wish I had quit there and we hadn't done the rest of them.

RICHARD HATCH
(actor, "Captain Apollo")

I could never believe that with the phenomenal potential and such incredible publicity and signature name value that they threw it away. Then they came back a year later, when they realized they did make a mistake, but decided to make *Galactica 1980* and ruined the whole story that everybody loved; which tells me that networks don't get it—they don't understand what fans love about a show.

DAVID L. SNYDER
(swing art director, *Galactica 1980*)

I was there when *Battlestar Galactica* was canceled and the permanent sets struck and demolished then dumped in the Barham Boulevard landfill on the backlot. Ooops. Then it was alleged that ABC had changed its mind and called Glen Larson to renew and pick up the series. When it was discovered that some key sets had been destroyed, Glen came up with the brilliant idea to have the next season of the series set in the present, 1980, and time-jump, back and forth.

HERBERT JEFFERSON, JR.
(actor, "Colonel Boomer")

By the time we got to *Galactica 1980,* most of the sets had been cut up, and if you look really closely at *Buck Rogers in the 25th Century,* you'll see a lot of their sets are *Galactica* sets that had been repainted.

GLEN A. LARSON

The revival of *Galactica 1980* gave us a small measure of satisfaction. It was the network somewhat admitting they were wrong. Unfortunately, it was a very small reward, but it was something. There was quite a feeling of disappointment and failure when the show was canceled. Afterward, I tried to take time with those that were involved to think about it a little bit. I realized that you tend to say, "Okay if we're off then we did fail," without looking at the numbers and without really realizing that we did accomplish much of what we wanted to accomplish. We just didn't make the cut. Ordinarily, on any other network I think we would have. You don't like to blame yourself but you do wonder what you might have done differently.

RONALD D. MOORE
(cocreator/executive producer, *Battlestar Galactica* [2004])

I was bummed. There was no science fiction left on TV anymore. *Space: 1999* had come and gone at that point, so there was really nothing else out there. I watched *Galactica 1980* and remember just hating it. I was going, "Oh my God, this is so completely misconceived." I knew right away it was a failure. Terrible.

With the exception of Lorne Greene and an occasional appearance by Herbert Jefferson, Jr., as newly promoted Colonel Boomer, none of the original cast returned. Apollo and Starbuck were replaced by new fighter pilots Troy (*Adam-12*'s Kent McCord) and Dillon (Barry Van Dyke). The real stars of the show, however, were the Super Scouts—the superpowered children of the *Galactica*—who were featured prominently in several episodes.

Promoted heavily by ABC with misleading footage of Cylon Raiders attacking Los Angeles, *Galactica 1980* appeared to be a continuation of the original in which a contemporary Earth finds itself on the front lines in a war with the Cylons. In reality, the series was designed to appeal strictly to children.

HERBERT JEFFERSON, JR.

I kept hoping that *Galactica 1980* would get better as we went along, but it didn't.

MICHAEL SLOAN
(producer, *Battlestar Galactica*)

It was a valiant attempt, but it wasn't the same show and, to be fair to Glen, ABC didn't want it to be the same show. They wanted it to be different and they pushed it in a direction which I didn't feel was a direction the show should go.

MARC GUGGENHEIM
(cocreator/executive producer, *DC's Legends of Tomorrow*)

When you're nine years old, time moves slower than it does now. In the version in my memory, *Galactica* was canceled, there wasn't going be any more *Galactica*, and suddenly there's this commercial. Not only is there going to be more *Battlestar Galactica*—but they're going to find Earth. This is amazing. It's going to be incredible. In the commercial the Cylons attack Earth and it looked like it was going to be the greatest thing ever.

SCOTT MANTZ
(film critic, *Access Hollywood*)

Before it premiered, they aired these commercials for *Galactica 1980*, which showed Cylons attacking downtown Los Angeles and a Cylon fighter firing on the Cinerama Dome. Turns out that was just a what-if scenario. Right from the first episode, I was crushed. This show was nothing like the *Galactica* that I loved. I was old enough to know that it felt like a kiddie show, which is what it was.

MARC GUGGENHEIM

Even at ten years old, I came to the slow realization this is not what I was expecting. By the time we get to the Super Scouts playing baseball, I just surrendered. It didn't match anything that was in my head when I first saw that commercial where I imagined all these great things I was going to get to see—and didn't.

DAVID STIPES
(visual effects artist, *Galactica 1980*)

There were some things that we just couldn't do, because we didn't have enough time to do them and we didn't have enough resources to make them happen. But sometimes there was something really spectacular that we got to do. That attack on Earth, the Cylons firing on Hollywood Boulevard, was one of those little things. That was pretty cool.

RONALD D. MOORE

It just felt cheap and it felt half-baked. I remember specifically when they were promoting *Galactica 1980* they showed you the Cylons attacking Los Angeles and flying down Hollywood Boulevard and blowing up buildings and cars and the Cylons attacking Earth. That was the promotion and you're like, "Whoa." So then you watch it and that whole sequence turns out to be a computer simulation of what *would* happen if the Cylons ever attacked Earth. That is so lame and such a fucking lie. It just pissed you off. It was such a bait and switch.

DAVID STIPES

My favorite thing about the Cylon Hollywood attack is that they had a bunch of extras . . . I guess they told the extras to show up in street clothes, and there was one lady who, I think, had a really big yellow hat on. She was running across the street as the Cylons are supposedly strafing the street and everybody is yelling, running back and forth. They'd run them across the street and then the assistant director would turn them around and run them back. So you see this lady run back and forth. That was really funny. I guess they didn't bother to tell the extras where the spark squibs were on the street because you'll see these people running and just as they're running, they're leaping, taking a big long step in their run, because these squibs were going off right under them. We're all just going like, "Oh my goodness," because we're filming this and are watching these people getting shocked and are thinking they should have known where the squibs were. They're all just screaming and all of a sudden these long strips of spark hits go off and are running down the street, right under this crowd.

DAVID LARSON
(son of Glen Larson)

Finding Earth was the worst thing that they could have done. It's like *Lost* if you figured out they were all dead at the end of the first season. I refused to watch that show for years.

Among those new to *Galactica* behind the camera was series producer Jeff Freilich, who, along with Frank Lupo (*Hunter, Walker, Texas Ranger*), oversaw script development. Freilich, like many a *Galactica* alum, was a veteran of NBC's *Quincy* and CBS's *The Incredible Hulk,* both popular Universal Television series. Freilich has had a long and successful career in television since and remains active in producing TV today as an executive producer on AMC's *Lodge 49,* following on the heels of producing the eighties-set *Halt and Catch Fire* for the network.

JEFF FREILICH
(producer, *Galactica 1980*)

I was under contract at Universal and had worked on *Quincy, Mrs. Columbo, Baretta,* and *The Incredible Hulk.* In those days, it was a lot closer to what we knew as the studio system for actors, where they would simply transplant you from one project to another at their whim and it didn't matter if it was something you were interested in doing or not. In my case, they never asked me to do something that I wasn't interested in doing. I got to go from police procedurals to science fiction, fantasy shows, and medical procedurals, which I liked because I'd gone through medical school at USC years before.

I was told that Glen Larson was really interested in me for a new show called *Galactica 1980*. I had never actually watched *Battlestar Galactica*, but I knew that it was loosely borrowed from *Star Wars*. I was a big fan of that and I liked sci-fi and Glen Larson to me was the godfather of television. He had put more shows on the air than anybody that I'd ever heard of. There were various stories about him as a person. I never choose to believe anything I hear from anybody until I experience it.

But I knew that the guy had to have an incredible imagination. I had already worked on a show he had created, which was *Quincy*. I watched other shows of his. They were always clever and entertaining and smart. Sometimes they were very transparently lifted from other material. I knew he had a nickname of "Glen Larceny." On the other hand, I went and met him and he said, "You worked for Kenny Johnson [on *The Incredible Hulk*]." I said, "Yeah." He said, "Well, now I want you to come and work with me." And we became very quick friends.

The story editors for the show were the writing team of Allan Cole and Chris Bunch, who had vociferously demanded *not* to be hired on the show. Despite their misgivings, the writers, who were a staple of Universal Television shows of the era, were brought aboard by Freilich and Frank Lupo on *Galactica 1980*, as they were under contract to the studio and had little say in the matter when the studio's chief of production, Peter Thompson, insisted they take the gig if they wanted to continue to find employment at the studio.

JEFF FREILICH

Bunch and Cole were anomalies in the television business. Chris Bunch had been the highest-decorated noncommissioned officer in the army during the Vietnam War. He was a sergeant, who grew increasingly more antiwar the longer he served. He came back and was put on *The Joe Pyne Show*, who was a right-wing talk-show host on television, and began to tear the war apart, to Joe Pyne's complete embarrassment. Chris had been a Hells Angel and went on to be an editor of a biker magazine.

Allan Cole was the child of a CIA intelligence operative who did a lot of traveling as a child. He wound up becoming the editor of the *Santa Monica Evening Outlook*. The two of them met in high school and wrote some science fiction books together and also wrote a pretty good book from both sides, the Vietnamese side and the American side, about the war in Vietnam.

ALLAN COLE
(story editor, *Galactica 1980*)

Chris [Bunch] and I broke into the business at an ideal time. In late summer of 1979 we sold our first TV script for *Quincy*, and our first novel—book one of the eight-volume *Sten* series. We quit our jobs and dived right in and never looked back. It was a time when there were only three networks and most prime-time shows had orders for twenty-two episodes per season. Almost all of them were written by freelancers, perfect for two guys who wanted to carve out careers as novelists—not TV writers. Most of our fellow writers were after studio contracts—the typical term was for seven years—to work on staff. They'd try to negotiate deals for two scripts per season and a weekly salary. That meant there was lots and lots of work for hungry young freelancers, and in a short period of time we had written so many scripts for so many shows that we were old-timers even though we were just a few years into the business. Chris and I decided early on that we'd only take staff jobs when it was absolutely necessary. For example, because of our science fiction expertise we were greenmailed by the head of production at Universal into signing on as story editors at *Galactica 1980*. We thought the show was awful and wanted nothing to do with it. But it was either take the job, or get cut off from the Universal Studios episodic teat.

JEFF FREILICH

Alan Godfrey, who was the executive producer of *Quincy*, had brought them in for that show. He said, "I want to bring in these two crazy guys. You'll love them." And in they came; they were nuts. Allan was much more grounded than Chris. I liked them both. They were really off-the-wall guys who had unique ideas. And what I like the most about them was that they had a dedication to detail and reality, and had an incredibly vast bank of knowledge to draw from. They delighted in the research process, which is why [Chris] Trumbo and I both liked them. We immediately clicked with them and I think we hired them to do a couple of *Quincy*s.

When I arrived at *Galactica 1980*, we needed writers. There were a couple of writers Glen had suggested, but he basically said, "Bring in who you want who you can work with and who you think can do a good job." So I introduced Frank Lupo to Bunch and Cole, who I knew had a love of science fiction and fantasy, and this amazing knowledge bank.

ALLAN COLE

Glen was shameless about ripping things off and making—mostly—successful TV series out of them. *Galactica* was a *Star Wars* rip-off. *B.J. and the Bear,* the Eastwood orangutan buddy movies, *Every Which Way but Loose* and its sequel, and a whole host of others. As for *Galactica 1980,* we were told that Glen didn't want to do the show after the cancellation of *Battlestar.* But ABC kept throwing money at him and eventually he relented. Unfortunately, they put him next to *60 Minutes* on Sunday night, which made it a kids' show. If there was ever any chance of the show succeeding, that move alone doomed it. Making things worse was that Glen insisted on writing most of the episodes himself. And he was a terrible writer. He'd start a script and when he hit sixty pages he'd type "to be continued" and then write part two—all without outlines or notes.

Also, *Galactica 1980* existed in many ways for him to pay back favors to people. Friends were made producers, who didn't even have to show up at work. ABC gave him a lot of money and he spent like a sailor. He even got a condo in Hawaii, where he'd run off to rest with a bevy of beauties. Then it'd be back to Malibu, with those same lovelies—and more. At least, that's certainly how it looked to us and everybody else. Each week more producers' names were added to the roster. Chris and I joked that entries kept getting pushed down and down and down by this big producer pile-on and that the writers' names were now below the janitorial staff.

JEFF FREILICH

The problem that Chris and Allan had was similar to the problems that all of us had. Every time we thought we knew what the show was, either ABC or the studio was redefining it. Universal, in its fear of losing a show, would try to redirect it, and so Chris and Allan pitched to us stories that they thought were perfectly great, which in my mind were just too hard-core for that audience and that time slot, and they found themselves frustrated with it. They stayed on after I left, and it was good practice for them, because they had never really learned what it was like to rewrite other people's stuff.

Galactica 1980 abandoned the epic adventure of its predecessor in favor of cheap (or at least cheaper) gimmicks and simplistic action fare with an almost entirely new cast. And repeating the mistake made with the original series,

ABC put "Galactica Discovers Earth" into production as a movie of the week only to decide midway through production to green-light a weekly series, which would leave virtually no time for script development, with the episodes being rushed into production and airing weeks after the three-part telefilm had debuted.

In "Galactica Discovers Earth," the Colonial fleet finds Earth in 1980 and learns that its technology is not at a sufficient state to protect them from the Cylons. As a result, Adama, in consultation with resident child genius (and genetic mutation) Dr. Zee, decides their best hope is to quickly advance the technology of Earth by working with the planet's scientific community, led by Dr. Mortinson, played by *The Brady Bunch*'s Robert Reed. Matters are complicated when a rogue member of the Council of Twelve, Xaviar (originally written as Baltar in early script drafts), played by seventies überbaddie Richard Lynch, hijacks an experimental Viper and travels back in time to share their advanced technology with the Nazis. Why, of course, if the Galacticans can now go back in time thanks to Dr. Zee they didn't return to Caprica and stop the Cylon sneak attack against humanity from happening in the first place is never broached.

RICHARD HATCH

They asked me if I wanted to do it and I read the script. I don't know if they made a mistake, but the character names had already been changed to Dillon and Troy. I thought that if they are offering me this part, why are they already changing my name and Starbuck's name? I thought that on some level, they had already moved on.

DIRK BENEDICT
(actor, "Lieutenant Starbuck")

I read the script. I didn't want to do it and I couldn't do it. If it had been *Battlestar Galactica* and they wanted to do that show again, of course, I would have done it. But it was very cheap.

GLEN A. LARSON

It didn't look like we were going to be able get Dirk. We might have been able to get Richard [Hatch] back. My impression was that we probably could have gotten a lot of the cast but maybe not all of it so, at that point, what we really should have done was change the entire cast and we were going to. The truth is that I got a call from Lorne Greene that broke my heart because it meant a lot to him to go back on the air. So I bit the bullet and put Lorne back on without the rest of them and that was a bad judgment call. I should have gone with a whole new group.

JEFF FREILICH

The first day I walked onto the set as the new writing producer of *Galactica 1980,* I met Lorne Greene. No one told me Lorne was hard of hearing. So I introduced myself. And he said, "Well, Fred, welcome." And I said, "No, it's Jeff." He said, "Fred, let me talk to you about the show." He called me Fred all day. Everything I said he misinterpreted. He couldn't hear. A couple of weeks later, Glen Larson called me up and it was opening day at Dodgers Stadium. Glen had first-row seats behind the Dodger dugout. He knew that I liked baseball and said, "Do you want to come to the game with me and Lorne and Dirk Benedict?," who was not on *Galactica 1980,* but who had remained friendly with Glen and was a big baseball fan.

So the four of us go to the game. Lorne did not know baseball at all, was not a baseball fan. He thought [Dodgers manager] Tommy Lasorda was a player. Didn't know what a ball versus a strike was. But the best part was somewhere in the middle of the game, a gaggle of children surrounded Lorne with their scorecards and asked for his autograph. And he was flattered and as he was signing these scorecards he says, "*Bonanza*?" And they went, "No." And he said, "*Galactica*?" And they said, "No." And he said, "What then?" They said, "Alpo." The Alpo dog food commercial made Lorne Greene more famous than anything else he did.

ROBBIE RIST
(actor, "Dr. Zee")

It's been my experience that the people that have been doing it the longest and have the least amount to prove largely tend to be the coolest people. Aside from being super pro and always nailing his shit, Lorne was super sweet and super nice, not just to me, but to everyone. It was the second time I worked with Robert Reed since *The Brady Bunch* and he was also a very sweet, wonderful man. It seems the people that I run into who are jerks are the ones who are on their first ride up or their first ride down.

ROBYN DOUGLASS
(actress, "Jamie Hamilton")

Lorne was a pro. Sometimes they had cue cards for him to read. No big deal. He's entitled. He's Hollywood royalty. But he and I clicked because he asked me some questions about my background. I'd lived in Chicago and done a lot of work with the Humane Society rescuing horses and he went on my board at the Humane Society. He was just A-plus in my book. He would never be grumpy. Always rock solid like you would expect from a professional like him.

ALLAN COLE

One day Lorne dropped by our office for a visit. We mixed him a drink, chatted awhile, and then he got directly to the point of his visit. Lorne said, "Boys, what the fuck are we going to do about this show?" He let this sink in and then went on: "The scripts are awful. The directing is awful. The acting is as good as it can be, under the circumstances. But we're getting stinker lines that Lord Lawrence himself couldn't rescue from the lavatory." I flashed on our mentor, Al Godfrey, who'd once told us, "A good actor can make a shitty script better. But it'll still smell like shit."

HERBERT JEFFERSON, JR.

Of course every actor loves to work, I was happy to be pulling in a paycheck, but at the same time I missed my team. I missed that quality of work in front of and behind the camera. It was a true family.

BARRY VAN DYKE
(actor, "Dillon")

Kent [McCord] and I both tested for the original *Galactica*. Universal wanted one combination and ABC wanted a different combination. Kent and I lost out, they took Richard and Dirk. It was right on the tail of *Star Wars* being a huge hit and I said, "I don't get it, I don't want to do something like that." But they sent me the script and it was so good and then I met with Glen Larson and saw the sets and it was just mind-boggling. It was like a huge feature, not a TV show. I was like "Oh man, do I wanna do this!" So when they hired Dirk and Richard I was quite disappointed.

They called me back in for *Galactica 1980* and made an offer and they cast another actor I had read with as Troy and said, "Okay, we want you guys for wardrobe." This was only a few days before it was going to start. I came back from wardrobe and the other actor was gone. I said, "Well, what's going on?" They said, "It's not going to work." I guess they saw us together and someone didn't like it and they called Kent [McCord] right away. Kent got the offer on a Saturday and we went to work on a Monday. I remember Kent called me Sunday night and introduced himself on the phone and I really liked him right away and we started work Monday.

Playing the role of the enigmatic Dr. Zee, a brilliant child prodigy in the pilot (albeit dubbed), was *The Brady Bunch*'s Cousin Oliver, Robbie Rist, who today is a successful musician. Rist was replaced in subsequent episodes by another child actor, James Patrick Stuart, who continues to work today as an actor on *General Hospital* as well as the voice of intergalactic bounty hunter Dengar on *Lego Star Wars: The Freemaker Adventures* for Disney XD.

ALLAN COLE

Zee was a Larson creation to satisfy the FCC's children's hour dictates. The character was supposed to be a child in body and age, but very wise, very adult, but with really, really long sideburns. A disco-era hairstyle on steroids. Zee was played by a twelve-year-old named James Patrick Stuart. He was a nice kid. His father was Chad Stuart, of the sixties pop group Chad and Jeremy. His mother, Jill Gibson, collaborated on most of the group's albums. We all assumed the kid had the part because his dad was a friend of Glen Larson from his days in the music business. The kid's voice was starting to change, so it cracked at every other syllable. When he said "Adama," for example, it came out "ah-Dam!-ah." Low at the start, cracking high in the middle, back to low at the end. Making things worse, he was plainly terrified.

Another addition to the new cast was Robyn Douglass, a veteran of director Peter Yates's critically acclaimed film *Breaking Away,* playing Jamie Hamilton, a nosy reporter who inadvertently learns about the existence of the *Galactica* in orbit and becomes an important ally to the Colonials as they navigate the strange, mystifying world of twentieth-century Earth.

ROBYN DOUGLASS

I was really a novice, so this is all wide-eyed and I was naïve. It's my first television series. I had only done the pilot of *Tenspeed and Brownshoe* and *The Clone Master,* which is probably why they saw me in the venue of the whole sci-fi thing. Frankly, I was thrilled to get the show, but I lived in Chicago, where I had bought a house, so I thought I would just commute. That's how naïve I was.

MARC GUGGENHEIM

I love Jamie Hamilton. I really loved that character. She had a nobility to her and an idealism and she was really funny.

ROBBIE RIST

I had a crush on her. She was cute and I was sixteen, but there was no way I'd be like "So Robyn Douglass, ever want to have sex with Paul Williams? Got any weird John Denver fantasies?"

ROBYN DOUGLASS

Barry [Van Dyke] and Kent [McCord] were delightful on the initial show. So, that didn't give me any alarm. But later, it turned out sort of to be the agony and the ecstasy of doing the show. Barry was real sweet and terribly funny because he does these pratfalls, just like his dad [Dick Van Dyke]. He's got no phoniness. Very genuine. Very generous actor. I considered him Hollywood royalty on account of his dad. He was wonderful all throughout the show. Then, after the series got green-lit, Kent McCord was different. He would hide my props before a scene and I would mess up my take and he would criticize me for not paying attention to my key light.

BARRY VAN DYKE

Kent was the consummate professional and a super nice guy, but very set in his ways. He had his ideas of how to work, and Robyn was more like a method actor. She really thought about the characters, what her motivation was. Kent kind of thought that was bullshit. She would get mad because she would really, really rehearse and lock in to what she was going to do and sometimes when you get on the stage, it's different. He didn't have a lot of patience for people like that. I remember them butting heads. There was just friction from the beginning. They were just different types that approached their work differently. I get along with everyone, so I didn't care.

If everyone says their lines and it looks good, all right, it was time to move on. As an actor she felt, "I can do better, I can always do better. I need another one." If it was a scene with Kent, he was done. "You can have another take, but you'll have to do it by yourself."

ROBYN DOUGLASS

Kent's jokes on the set caused pain with me. I just thought, "If this goes on for year after year after year, I'll be in therapy just on account of this relationship." I tried to stay away from Kent. I just didn't understand where he was coming from. I think he thought, "We don't need the girl. We've got the two guys, we've got the ship, we've got the adventure with just us—what do we need this girl for? Jamie Hamilton, the Earth reporter that bails us out," right?

Happens all the time, with big movie stars in big scenes. But anyway, it was good to get a huge taste of reality up front, because in some ways, it toughened me up for the rest of the road.

ALLAN COLE
(story editor, *Galactica 1980*)

She was treated horribly on the show. Larson never could figure out what to do with her character. We used her in our "Earthquake" script, but it was never shot. We had a second script guarantee and that would have offered her some meat. But nobody ever even saw the outline. They just paid us for both shows and that was that. We resented it, of course. But our recourse was to work on our first *Sten* novel.

ROBYN DOUGLASS

To this day, I don't understand why Kent went to such lengths being a professional that was on *Adam-12*. It's no different than what was going on with *The A-Team*. They went through a lot of girls on that. They really wanted me to do that show, because they couldn't hold on to the girls, and they thought I was tough. I heard George Peppard and Mr. T didn't want a girl on the show either, but you need balance. You've got to have the broad on the show so that both audiences, male and female, can identify with a character.

After the three-part premiere, the much-loathed superpowered Galactican kids are introduced in "The Super Scouts." With Earth's gravity being weaker than on board the *Galactica* and the fleet, the Super Scouts, stranded on Earth after the school barge is attacked, are endowed with super strength, allowing them to win at baseball in "Spaceball" (against a team that featured "Little Frankie Lupo and little Jeffrey Freilich") and help a band of financially strapped farmers in "Space Croppers" who are being put out of business by a racist landowner among others in some truly dreadful hours of dramatic television.

JEFF FREILICH

In targeting it for a younger audience and a family audience, it was Glen Larson who decided to introduce the Super Scouts and to give them basically two counselors to go with them and to bring them to Earth because you can do more with kids on Earth than you can in a spaceship. There are just many more stories to tell. In fact, his whole concept of the show was to see the world through the eyes of children who've never seen it before.

In "Spaceball," the kids demonstrate how a television camera works. The purpose of the scene was to show the Galactican kids' advanced technological capabilities and their knowledge and their understanding. But to Glen, it was a comedy scene because he had a bunch of kids, and he always loved the capricious nature of children. Because the show was geared for a younger audience, he thought it might be fun to show kids basically misbehaving in an incredibly intellectual way and getting away with it.

However, *Galactica 1980* did make one significant contribution the *Galactica* mythology when it introduced humanoid Cylons long before 2004's reinvention, in "The Night the Cylons Landed," in which the Cylons crash-land on Earth on Halloween and look for a radio station to transmit Earth's location back to the Alliance. It further cemented the series' schizophrenic reputation: Was this a show about superpowered children, was it about the search for a rogue Colonial Warrior intent on changing Earth's history, or was it about preventing the Cylons from finding the location of Earth?

JEFF FREILICH

The first experience I had with Glen as a writer was when he saw [producer] Frank Lupo and me one Friday night, and he said, "I want you guys to come out to the house for the weekend, because this script we're going to shoot on Monday is terrible and the three of us are going to rewrite it." Mind you, this was an entire television script written over a weekend.

ALLAN COLE

The Suits were all over Larson. Out of desperation he pitched them a story about the evil Cylons finding the school ship. After a furious fight, they blow the ship up. But our heroes rush in and get the kids off just in time.

JEFF FREILICH

Glen had three IBM Selectrics and several really excellent bottles of red wine, and a couple of guitars. He had the guitars because he was a member of the Four Preps and the coauthor of "26 Miles," the song about Catalina that was a big pop hit in the fifties or the early sixties. What he didn't know was that I both played guitar and I used it as a method of procrastinating when I write, and that I also did a really spot-on Bob Dylan impression. So we're sitting there and we're each at a typewriter. Glen sat down at the typewriter on his deck looking out at the ocean. He was outside with a long extension cord. Frank and I were in the living room. He asked us to come out on the deck because it was so pretty out and the sun was going down. I was in awe of the fact that when Glen wrote, he never looked at the page. He looked straight out at the ocean with this idyllic expression and he typed without stopping, page after page. He knew when he would get to the bottom of the page and he would just pull it out of the typewriter and put a new one in and keep going. Glen managed to write two complete acts of a television show overnight. It was I'd say twenty, at least twenty, twenty-eight pages maybe, while Frank wrote an act, which was probably twelve or thirteen pages, and I was stuck in the middle of mine.

Glen looked and he said, "Look, don't struggle. Let's have a glass of wine." I picked up a guitar and I started doing Bob Dylan impressions and that's all he wanted me to do. He was laughing, he was singing along. Then he picked up the guitar and we sang "26 Miles," and he found a use for me that I actually wasn't hired for. It loosened me up enough for me to be able to continue to write, and although I never really got a handle on the show, I could certainly tell the stories. The dialogue for that show was very difficult for me on a variety of levels, because I didn't really know the character of either the Cylons or the Galacticans as well as Lupo did, and certainly as well as Glen did, but I knew the stories that we should be telling. I had a lot to do with arcing all the stories and all the permutations of the plot throughout that first season.

"The Super Scouts, Part One" was directed by actor turned director Vince Edwards, who had done such a magnificent job with "The Living Legend" on the original series. This time, however, the highly touted episode, in which the Galactican kids are stranded on Earth and find themselves poisoned from the runoff of a local manufacturing plant into a nearby lake, would be a misfire of dramatic proportions, filled with a heavy-handed, eco-friendly message, slapstick humor (Dillon accidently robs a bank in a scene that no one would confuse with Woody Allen in *Take the Money and Run*), and the introduction of Allan Miller's Colonel Sydell, who begins his relentless (and buffoonish) pursuit of the marooned *Galactica* children.

ALLAN COLE

It was a complicated episode that needed a director experienced in handling lots of action, stunts, explosives, fire—all that scary, expensive stuff. And so they hired Vince Edwards, former brooding Marlon Brando wannabe, who starred in *Ben Casey* years before.

BARRY VAN DYKE

I almost got arrested on that episode. We were shooting at a bank on Sherman Way [in the San Fernando Valley] and Vince Edwards was across the street from the bank with the crew where the camera was set up. He said, "Can you run out of the bank and run through traffic? I'm not going to stop traffic." I said, "Yeah, if you're willing to wait to make sure there's no cars coming or anything." He said, "Just take your time and run straight to the camera." So I said, "Fine." Then they rolled and I had a bag of money in each hand and I ran out. As I got to the curb, I saw a cop car coming. I thought, "Oh man, should I do this or not?" They were rolling so I just ran through traffic. They slammed on their brakes. Both guys jumped out of the car with their guns drawn and started yelling, "Freeze." I'm trying to point at the crew so they'd see we were filming. I said, "We're filming a TV show." The headline in the next day's paper was "Cops Steal Scene as Van Dyke's Son Robs a Bank": "Crack team of L.A. cops swooped down on the twenty-eight-year-old son of actor Dick Van Dyke yesterday while the fledgling actor was filming a bank robbery scene for his upcoming TV series *Galactica 80*. They mistook him for a real-life bank robber and it took some fast, glib talk to keep him out of the slammer."

ALLAN COLE

The true disaster unfolded one day at dailies. There were Suits in attendance from every Universal Studios department, ABC Television, and advertisers who were chained by contracts for the run of the show. And then there were the hordes of producers from *Galactica 1980*, including Glen, who sat at the command station in the center of the screening room. Directly in front of the command group was Vince Edwards, the director of the episode. He didn't look well. But maybe it was the lighting. Chris [Bunch] and I found a place out of the line of fire where we could see both the screen and the Suits. The footage rolled. It was herky-jerky at first but soon settled down. The next bits were supposed to portray the aftermath of the Cylon attack on the school ship. The corridors were filled with smoke and flames. Alarms were blaring. Meanwhile, in a series of shots, our heroes are shown walking casually through the chaos as if they were on a Sunday-school outing. Later footage showed them leading the kids to safety with equally slow calm. If this was an emergency, you sure couldn't tell it from our actors. Plus, if any of them started to quicken his or her steps, you could hear Edwards's offscreen voice commanding, "Slow down." We heard Larson's booming voice: "What the fuck is this? Who directed this turd? Who? Who?" We heard someone whisper something to Larson. "I don't care if he is here. He's ruining my show."

Not unlike the original series, *Galactica 1980* was rushed into production, which led to a chaotic shooting schedule, with multiple episodes being written and shot at the same time, which created immense problems for both cast and crew.

ROBYN DOUGLASS

This whole adventure of *Galactica 1980* was really a baptism by fire for me. They started early on in this series shooting two shows simultaneously. I thought it was going to be temporary that I'm being handed rewrites for two different scripts, and things are changing every day. You think you're going to shoot one scene and it's changed at the last minute.

BARRY VAN DYKE

Before we even aired the TV movie, they picked up the initial order, so we never got a day off, not even weekends. We were just punchy half the time, because we didn't know what the scripts meant. We were shooting scenes from two different segments at the same time and running from one set to another, all in different episodes. So half the time we didn't even know what was going on. But the fun was since we were supposed to be on Earth and our characters were the fish out of water, everything worked. We had to play dumb since we didn't know what was going on either in real life or on the show.

ROBYN DOUGLASS

At first, I thought, "Oooh, this is great," since they were paying me so much overtime. I then realized I'm not getting any sleep. I called the union, and I said, "How can they possibly work me eighteen straight hours?" And they said, "They can. They pay you overtime." I said, "Yeah, but they're setting my hair and doing my makeup while I'm sleeping." They'd do my face from one side. Do one side, and turn my face to the other, and I'm still sleeping. I would ask other people, "Is this normal?" And they'd go, "No. This is not normal." And I would say, "Oh my God. I don't think the money is worth this."

BARRY VAN DYKE

A lot of the space stuff where we sat in the Vipers, they would just put you in the cockpit and light the whole thing and you'd shoot all your scenes from different episodes. Our pages were taped on the dash, so we were just reading some of this stuff and had no idea what we were talking about. But it was so much fun; I don't know if I've ever had so much fun on a show.

ROBYN DOUGLASS

You can't get out of a contract like this, so I had to figure out how to pace myself for something that's two shows simultaneously, two different scripts, two different rewrites coming at me each day, and sometimes locations would change at the last minute. Sometimes I would confide with fellow actors and say, "Oh my God, this is really stressing me out," but I felt very isolated, because it seemed like everybody I ever talked to was either drinking alcohol or on drugs or seeing a therapist, and I was the only one that was kind of normal.

DAVID LARSON

My father stuffed me in there [as a Super Scout] for whatever reason and I was really shy. I have outtakes from *B.J. and the Bear* of me where I'm supposed to order a cheeseburger and hid under the table for like fifteen takes.

"Can't you just order a cheeseburger?" I don't think I ever really grew out of that shyness. It was good, though, because it paid for some of my schooling. I couldn't touch the money until I was eighteen years old, so it paid for some of my college. That money just sort of accrued over the years. All I remember is unlike *Battlestar Galactica* we shot outdoors a lot . . . and the flying motorcycles.

BARRY VAN DYKE

I'm a motorcycle nut. I was into desert racing and dirt bikes and everything before that. The turbo cycles were Yamahas—MX 175s, which is kind of a small dirt bike—and they built the retractable wings and everything around them. They were the most awkward things in the world to ride to even go ten feet on them.

JACK GILL
(stunt double, *Galactica 1980*)

I remember they were always trying to make it look cooler since they didn't have the effects the original show had. One thing I was involved with, since I have a motorcycle background, were the flying motorcycles. They built these motorcycles with a button on them, so the wings dropped out at the front and back of the motorcycle.

BARRY VAN DYKE

In the pilot, we were on the motorcycles going down the freeway. It was way out at the end of the Valley and they closed the whole freeway for this. A gang of bikers start chasing us and say, "Let's see those bikes," and start yelling at us. Kent's going, "We can't get caught, we can't be seen on these bikes." And we fly off, up into the air. Our stunt coordinator actually took one of the bikes and strapped it to the skids of a helicopter and shot out where you could just see the bike and the road, and then put a guy on it and took off with the bikes on the skid of the helicopter. There's no way on Earth they would let you do that now. It's totally illegal.

JACK GILL

The helicopter first flew close to the ground and then took off. They'd film me sitting on the motorcycle, so it looked like I was taking off on the motorcycle. Since the camera was inside the helicopter looking over me, it looked like I was flying. It was a little scary at first since we weren't sure if the motorcycle would stay on the skid. It was rigged on the side. It worked really well, so we used that a lot.

BARRY VAN DYKE

I remember I got in the van that morning to drive out to set that day and Bud Ekins, who was Steve McQueen's friend, and actually did the motorcycle jump in *The Great Escape,* got onto the van. He's famous in Southern California for desert and TT racing, he's one of the top racers. All the stunt guys were getting in, and he got in the van and I sat next to him. He was my hero, and I was so intimidated. I never said a word. I could not get a word out. It drives me nuts now, because my God the things I could've asked him.

New Colonial helmets were also created for *Galactica 1980* owing to safety concerns regarding the actors and stuntmen riding the turbocycles.

ROB KLEIN
(*Battlestar Galactica* archivist)

The Daggit Squadron pilot helmets exist due the fact the stunt drivers refused to ride the turbobikes using the prop Colonial Viper helmets, which were made of thin fiberglass and were not made for safety. New helmets were made using a real motorcycle safety helmet, adding the familiar Egyptian/Colonial styling. The round shape of the motorcycle helmet caused the helmets to look ugly, and not as elegant as the popular Colonial Viper helmets were.

JACK GILL

We also did this episode where we were leaping through a cornfield ["Space Croppers"]. They had this real six-feet-high cornfield and they wanted to make it look like we were weightless and we were leaping, making big jumps through the field. They put us up on this thing called the Russian Swing and we would hit airbags in the middle of the field. This swing would throw you thirty feet high in the air to this airbag. I was doing this with this other guy and while jumping I looked over to the left and saw he was missing his airbag. He broke his shoulder and punctured a lung. He was pretty messed up.

We did some wire jumping into thirty-feet-high trees in white tuxedos ["The Night the Cylons Landed"]. They also wanted us to jump from the top of this tree onto this building. They had us on piano wires—a really thin wire that was attached to each hip, going up to a crane. They'd lift you up out of the tree, you'd throw your arms up and act like you're jumping from the tree to the top of this roof. They were taking us from a thirty-foot tree to an eighty-foot building. I doubled for Barry Van Dyke, and this other guy doubled for Kent McCord. While we were doing this jump one of his wires broke and he was going sideways. I thought for sure he would fall sixty feet and get killed, but he made it fine. The only bad thing about that was that we then had to do it again. Back in the eighties you had to have these really thin cables [because you couldn't erase them digitally] and they were very dangerous, most of the times.

While the original series had largely eschewed laser beams as a result of the agreement they had made early on with Lucasfilm and 20th Century Fox to minimize comparisons to *Star Wars*, *Galactica 1980* reintroduced traditional animated laser effects to the proceedings, utilizing a smaller and less production-challenging prop.

ROB KLEIN

The original effects of the Colonial laser and Cylon rifles were achieved by adding a "star filter" on the motion picture cameras used during filming of *Battlestar Galactica,* and Apogee built the laser guns and Cylon rifles with camera strobes inside that would fire off in sequence when the triggers were activated. The strobes required a 510-volt battery to power them. These batteries were large. The cumbersome batteries would fit inside the stock of the

Cylon rifles, but were obviously too large for the Colonial pistols. The Colonial actors had to wear a fanny pack around their waist with a wire running up their sleeves into the handles of the pistols. If you look for these fanny packs, you can sometimes catch a glimpse of them onscreen. Due to the expensive and fragile nature of the pistols, a safety strap was used to go around the actor's wrist in case an actor dropped the pistol to avoid it being dropped and damaged. One of the only two known surviving hero strobe Colonial lasers was dropped on set late in the series' production, and was never put back into working service on the show.

For *Galactica 1980,* the strobe effect was dropped as well as both of the Colonial laser pistols, and new, smaller "laser derringers" were designed for *Galactica 1980,* rigged with one simple incandescent lightbulb powered only by a nine-volt battery. The nonworking dummy Colonial laser prop pistols left over from *Battlestar Galactica* were cut in half and altered by adding a single incandescent lightbulb to become "working" *Galactica 1980* prop pistols, as the strobe laser effects were found to be too complicated for *Galactica 1980*'s modest production.

BARRY VAN DYKE

Universal, when they did the first season of *Galactica,* thought it was kind of dark and heavy, which appealed to a lot of people in the long run, but at the time they were thinking, "It's too much, and we have a young audience." So they decided, "We're gonna lighten this up and put a little comedy in it and appeal to kids more than anything," which appealed to me, because I was doing some comedy at the time but I loved to do action stuff. These guys are thrown into a world they know nothing about and they've got to walk around and pretend like they fit in.

We had a wristband where we could punch stuff in and if an Earthling were talking, we could look it up. It was so funny it got to the point where we started to laugh every time we did it. We were working so many hours, twelve, fourteen hours, seven days a week, every single day for weeks, and you get a little punchy.

So we were on the mock-up 747 for "The Night the Cylons Landed" and a guy jumps up to hijack the jet. He says, "Everyone stay in your seats, I'm taking this plane to Cuba." But he was Hispanic and correctly pronounced it "Ku-ba." So I have to repeat the way he said it back to Kent when I punch it in, and I look at Kent and I can see his eyes starting to go and I said, "Ku-ba?"

And we both just went to pieces. We started laughing and laughing. It's late, the crew is tired, everyone just wants to go home, but we couldn't get through it. Every single time I had to look him in the face and say "Cuba," we went to pieces. The director finally yelled at us and told us to get off the plane and said, "You guys go get it together. I expect you to act like professionals." It was so unlike Kent. He just lost it. We just couldn't stop laughing. It must have taken ten takes before he said, "Just don't look at me." And I said, "I'm not looking at you." And then trying to say "Cuba" and we finally got through that one.

However, the biggest problem for *Galactica 1980* remained ABC's Standards and Practices department under the aegis of Susan Futterman, the head censor, who some felt took great pleasure in tormenting the series writers in order to maintain the sanctity of the 7 P.M. hour, which was mandated by the government as an educational hour for television at the time.

GLEN A. LARSON

ABC made it impossible, since one of their prerequisites for going on the air was going on at seven o'clock, which was an educational, not an entertainment, slot, so the odds were enormous. If we had walked away from it, we probably could have continued to do two-hour movies. The mistake was in not turning down the series order, because if we couldn't do it the way we wanted to then we shouldn't have done it all. But there is a certain arrogance in power, and you feel that you're going to get your way. It turned out that Standards and Practices at ABC was more effective than we were. I guess we just desperately wanted that chance.

JEFF FREILICH

We were on against *The Wide World of Disney* and *60 Minutes,* two of the biggest shows on television, and it was the "family hour," so there were rules that governed content. *Galactica 1980* was a spin-off and a continuation of *Battlestar Galactica,* which was always intended to be more of an adult show.

ALLAN COLE

Because it was a seven o'clock show it had to either educate kiddies, or be of value to the general public, like a news program. In episodic TV, you had to have "educational beats" in every episode for the kiddies. So, for example, in the middle of car chase, you'd have to stop and explain the mysteries of the internal combustion engine.

BARRY VAN DYKE

It always stuck out like a sore thumb because they had to work it in somehow. In the pilot, Kent starts asking how does the car run and Robert Reed describes in detail how the internal combustion engine works out of nowhere. We used to laugh because every episode had to have a message that was educational for the younger audience. We would take bets who was going to have to give the speech. With the kids who could jump high into the air, we had to describe what gravity was.

ALLAN COLE

It was an action-adventure shoot-'em-up, but we were only allowed so many "violence beats" per episode. Susan's definition of violence included cutting down a tree to save a school bus from crashing. Making a tree a victim was considered a violence beat in her book.

BARRY VAN DYKE

The violence was very limited. You could kill a Cylon, I think.

GLEN A. LARSON

They were ripping and tearing at every script that didn't come down to a certain level. They stripped everything out of that show. It was virtually a replacement for *The Hardy Boys*.

JEFF FREILICH

It became a lot more about the Galacticans as the Fugitive: the air force was Lieutenant Gerard and the Cylons were the One-Armed Man. It was all ripped off from the TV series *The Greatest Show on Earth,* where somebody in hiding would still go out of their way and risk their own freedom and safety to help people in need. The Galactican kids and their adult counterparts would get involved in situations where they could. It was just like *The Incredible Hulk,* where David Banner—whose name they changed from the comic book because the network thought Bruce sounded too gay—would risk his own safety to help somebody in need using his expertise in those situations to do the greatest good.

That was certainly true for the Hulk and it certainly was true on *Galactica 1980.* The Galactican kids can do everything from hit a ball that goes for miles and leap high fences to make amazing catches to help save the community. The way we made the show into a family-oriented, child-friendly show was to show the Galactican children as good samaritans who bring goodness with them to the Earth. But along with it came the baggage from *Battlestar Galactica,* which is the violence, and the constant ongoing war with the Cylons, who were robotic and not human beings. We got into constant battles with ABC Standards and Practices over the number of violent moments in the show. We were limited to ten. If we shot a tree with a laser gun, that was one. If we shot a Cylon out of the sky, that was one.

ROBYN DOUGLASS

Every time somebody would come down to my trailer, I would always think I was in trouble. For some reason, I always feared when a writer or a director or somebody would come knock on my door. One day somebody came down and said, "We need to talk to you about something personal," and I'm like, "Oh, crap." And they said, "When you're in the *Galactica* uniform, you're too sexy. You're too curvy. So, we're going to change some of your wardrobe." It was not a question of dieting. I was curvy with a small waist. So, they started dressing me a little more schoolmarmish because of the children's hour. It fell to me to be the cool teacher.

JEFF FREILICH

There is one time I remember vividly where the Standards and Practices person, who was over-the-top in her diligence, would not allow an episode to air. The champion who helped us get the show made is now president of Warner Bros. Television, Peter Roth. He was the vice president of ABC for current television at the time and oversaw *Battlestar Galactica*. He was a huge fan of the show. He got the show better than I did, certainly, and he would intercede for us when Standards and Practices would come in. He interceded and was correctly claiming that the additional Cylon that got shot out of the sky was just a piece of metal and nobody got injured and kids knew this and she should know that and we saved that episode. There was no thinking in a lot of these decisions. The other thing that kind of frustrated everybody who was working on that show was that it was a capricious approach to determining morality, both for adults and children.

STU PHILLIPS
(composer, *Galactica 1980*)

They were evidently unhappy with the sampling of viewers they had. They kept leaning toward the fact that they wanted to pick kids up and when they did *Galactica 1980* they wanted young stars and a lot of children in every episode. They wanted to see the children of *Galactica*. It got sterile, it had no heart, it had no balls. It was typical network interference. If they were so smart, when they put on eighteen new shows every season they wouldn't have sixteen of them flop.

Standards and Practices' heavy-handedness was typical of that era of television and not exclusive to *Galactica*. It was often the result of powerful stars pushing the boundaries of their clout and was often a way to tweak the network suits as well.

JEFF FREILICH

There wasn't a lot of questioning things on most shows in those days, except on *Quincy,* where Jack Klugman pretty much refused to read any line of dialogue without taking complete credit for it. For whatever reason, Jack thought it was important to say that he rewrote everything, which drove me a little bit crazy. Robert Blake was like that, too. The day after I wrote my first script for *Baretta,* I got a call the next day from Robert Blake directly, saying, "Kid, I want you to come and work for me." As I was driving in the Universal gate, driving out was the executive producer, who had hired me to write the script. He yelled back, "Good luck." And left. I got to the building and Blake took me down the hall and showed me all the empty offices and said, "I got rid of Donald Duck, I got rid of Goofy, I got rid of Mickey, it's just you and me."

I had to write all of the scripts or rewrite the ones that had already been started. Blake would change dialogue on the set and insist on changing it in a way that Standards and Practices rated it as unusable. He delighted in doing combat with [ABC network president] Fred Silverman and Al Snyder, who was the head of ABC's Standards and Practices. He was renowned for doing things that perpetuated his bad-boy reputation. I was always kind of on his side, because I thought it took a tremendous amount of chutzpah to do what he was doing. No two people share the same sense of values, and I never believed, nor did he, that anybody should dictate any of that stuff.

In one episode, two jewel thieves were driving around in a fur-lined van, which was very popular in the seventies. It's a little pimped out. Baretta pulls them over and opens up the back of the van and proceeded to say, "Where did you get the muff-mobile?" ABC hit the roof. Called me to the dailies screening to look at it. They asked me if there was any coverage of the scene and there wasn't. I told them, "I didn't write that line, Bob made it up." And they went crazy. Blake shut down the show by saying, "If you don't leave that line as is, find a new Baretta." Which is something he did several times. We would end up in a closed conference room with Fred Silverman. At the time, shows were sent by satellite to air on the West and East Coast separately, so we dubbed it for the East Coast feed so that Fred Silverman could say he got the better of Robert Blake. On the West Coast, it stayed in so Blake could say he got the better of Fred.

ALLAN COLE

Glen's scripts started drifting down to our level, where we'd plug in educational stuff to make the censor happy. Then it became a big part of our job, because we were the guys Futterman went after first. We'd have to defend the undefendable. She'd piss and moan, until finally we'd tell her—"Susan, you're asking to change things that our boss already told you he wasn't going to change."

JEFF FREILICH

There was a Halloween episode we were writing where the Cylons get picked up in a car by this couple who bring them to a party where they're serving Swedish meatballs or something ["The Night the Cylons Landed"]. They thought the Cylons were going to a costume party. So they give them a ride to this costume party, and they get there and the host opens the door and they say, "I see you made your famous meatballs."

ALLAN COLE

Futterman refused to believe that Glen was not up to something filthy. She insisted there was some hidden meaning. Although she couldn't explain what nastiness she thought Larson was trying to slip past her. Eventually, she made Larson so mad that he took the script back and inserted meatball references willy-nilly everywhere.

JEFF FREILICH

Standards and Practices called us up and said that it had sexual connotations. Frank and I looked at each other like, "Are they on another planet? What are they thinking about?" So Frank said, "Well, what if we say wieners?" They said that would be fine.

For Larson and many of those involved, there was one episode, however, that made *Galactica 1980* worthwhile. "The Return of Starbuck" reunited viewers with the spirit of the original series and answered a few questions as to the fate of the character. The episode chronicled the experiences of Starbuck after he crash-lands on a barren world. For companionship, he repairs a damaged Cylon that pursued him down to the planet, and together they face being marooned there. With a nod to the mysticism of the original series and episodes like "War of the Gods" and "Experiment in Terra," the episode reveals that Starbuck is actually the father of Dr. Zee.

GLEN A. LARSON

It was something from my heart. I wrote the simplest little story, and to me it had all the dynamics of some of our biggest pictures. Maybe it sounds egotistical to talk about an episode like it's something great, but it's great in my heart. They even wanted to make that a play in England. They wanted to do virtually a two-man show with Starbuck and the Cylon.

DIRK BENEDICT

It was a wonderful script that Glen wrote. It was basically me and a girl on a planet with a Cylon. It was only a year after *Battlestar* had been canceled, so the wonderful thing for me was that all those episodes seemed like years of being chased by Cylons. Here I was having this wonderful show where I built a Cylon to have company; taught him how to gamble, taught him how to cheat, and he ends up saving my life. It was great fun.

TERRENCE MCDONNELL
(story editor, *Battlestar Galactica*)

My heart goes out to the guys who were on that show. The writers in particular. But, it certainly wasn't what I would have done. They toned it down and made it G-rated. The only episode worth a damn was "The Return of Starbuck." And that was the last episode.

DAVID LARSON

That was the best *Galactica 1980* episode. It was a bottle show, basically.

MARC GUGGENHEIM

It was just this constant slow level of disappointment. I wish I could say that I stopped watching, but I didn't. Quite frankly, I'm glad I didn't. For one thing, "The Return of Starbuck" is a really great hour of television. The rest of it is like Wolfman Jack and Mike Brady and Cousin Oliver.

SCOTT MANTZ

Glen Larson wrote that for the fans, and basically, it was an episode of *Battlestar Galactica*, just framed with this dream that Dr. Zee had. The beginning of that episode is pretty chilling, when Zee tells Adama about his dream about a great warrior, "Starbuck." Adama is horrified. He's just like, "Tell me your dream." "There was a great battle," and it's basically lifted from stock footage and Boomer has to abandon Starbuck and he says, "Starbuck, take care of yourself," and he speeds off and Boomer goes, "My friend, my dear, dear friend, if I could trade places with you, I would."

The next scene is lifted from the original show with the Cylons attacking the *Galactica* and a scene on the bridge, which isn't really the bridge because that set was destroyed, where Boomer tells Adama they can't just leave Starbuck behind.

Lorne Greene has one of the best scenes that he had to act in. "You think I want to leave him behind," Adama says. "Someone I love like a son? Our enemy pushes us on and on. It can never turn away or look back." Boomer just turns his back and walks away and says, "Thank you, sir, I appreciate your honesty."

Then, they just put Starbuck on the planet, and he's so desperate for companionship that he builds a Cylon. It was *Enemy Mine*, before *Enemy Mine* was out as a movie. They're teaching each other. Cy calls him out on cheating at pyramid. Then, this girl, who is she? Is she from the Ship of Lights? Probably. Angela . . . Angel. She's caught, and Angela is calling Starbuck out. "Haven't you just worried about yourself all this time?" Basically, she makes him look inward at himself, to be a better man, to be a better person, to be selfless instead of selfish.

DIRK BENEDICT

That was my second-most-favorite experience playing that character [after "The Man with Nine Lives"]. It was a wonderful script that Glen wrote. It was *Robinson Crusoe*.

ROB KLEIN

The detonator built for Baltar in "Baltar's Escape" was later reused in the episode "Return of Starbuck" as the control that turns Cy on and off, and again was put into use in *Buck Rogers in the 25th Century* and can be seen on Frank Gorshin's belt in "The Plot to Kill a City."

ALLAN COLE

Chris [Bunch] and I thought that Larson finally had just had it and threw up his hands and wrote what he fucking felt like writing. It turned out to be not only the best but the only good episode in the series. It was basically a two-person radio episode. We thought it was Larson's *Galactica 1980* swan song. He knew he was going to get canceled. So there was no reason not to just do what he pleased. It scared the hell out of some of the young regulars. But they were all still fooling themselves.

Galactica 1980 was canceled after airing only ten episodes. Another time-travel episode was already in production and several days into filming when ABC pulled the proverbial plug on the series. Called "The Day They Kidnapped Cleopatra," the episode marked the return of the nefarious rogue Council of Twelve member Xaviar, who travels back in time to 48 BC proclaiming he is a god only to return to present-day Earth with Cleopatra as his prisoner after being poisoned in search of an antidote. Although the role was played by Richard Lynch in the pilot, when Xaviar returned he was now portrayed by *My Fair Lady* and *Sherlock Holmes* actor Jeremy Brett. The episode was mercifully never completed, and footage from the episode has never materialized on DVD or the internet.

JEFF FREILICH

I left *Galactica 1980*, not at the end, but maybe a few weeks in advance of it. Glen had hired me to work on a show called *Battles*, starring William Conrad as a campus security chief at the University of Hawaii. He said, "You're really good at plotting mysterious stories, and maybe *Galactica* is not exactly right for you, but I think this is. With your medical background and your police-procedural background, you're going to like this. And you'll get to go to Hawaii." He got me all excited about it. At that point, I only witnessed the cancellation of *Galactica* secondhand, because I got it from Glen and from [producer] Frank [Lupo], who came into my office and said, "Well, that's that. You got out while the getting was good."

ALLAN COLE

"We're having a little party at my office," Freilich told us. "A wake, really. To say good-bye to the other people on the show. Come on over and drink a little champagne with us." Chris got out the Metaxa and we had a couple of shots of that fiery Greek cognac, then headed for the wake. Lorne was there. I'm pretty sure Kent McCord and Robyn Douglass were as well. They'd been in the middle of filming an episode titled "The Day They Kidnapped Cleopatra" when word came down to not only cut, but to cut forever.

ROBYN DOUGLASS

I was doing a scene in that episode and I fumbled it like a dozen times. I couldn't get the words right. Whatever it was, it was one of the worst days and I was really stressing and they had to do take after take after take. Right after another flub, someone said, "We're stopping the show." I burst into tears, thinking it was all my fault and that I will be immediately fired and they were stopping the show because I couldn't get it right and it was all my fault. I was inconsolable. I went immediately to the makeup person because I could not stop crying. I didn't want to do that with the whole cast and everybody seeing me. It could easily have been misinterpreted as "They're canceling the show and Robyn's very upset that they're canceling the show." They had no idea that, in my mind, I thought it was all because of me.

ALLAN COLE

Lorne greeted us with a wide smile. "We gave it our best, boys," he said. "Pity we didn't have more support from on high." Someone else muttered, "It was that fucking Susan Futterman's fault." Well, maybe our network censor was a little at fault . . . but only a little. The show was simply a very bad idea, guided by a lousy producer/writer who insisted on writing all the episodes himself, believing all the while that his words were golden. As Mark Twain said, "Ignorance is like bad breath. You don't know you have it."

The party ended almost as soon as it began. When we took our leave, Lorne slapped our backs and said, "Cheer up, boys. Maybe we'll get a chance to work together again." We worked with him again a couple of years later on Irwin Allen's fireman show, *Code Red*.

JEFF FREILICH

I think that the problem with *Galactica 1980* was, in part, because of the restrictions of family hour. Some of the stories that people wanted to tell, like Bob McCullough or Bunch and Cole, all wanted to go darker, more action and emphasize the war between the Cylons and the Galacticans, and deemphasize the kids because nobody knew what to do with the kids when you got into a threatening situation in the story. You couldn't put the kids in danger. You couldn't have them fight. All you can have them do is clever things based on their knowledge of technology. It was like *Home Alone* on a weekly basis. Whereas what you really wanted to do was all the things that you could do in *Star Wars*, which is to get into a ship and blow other people out of the sky.

ROBYN DOUGLASS

Galactica 1980 had a little bit of momentum, but it never got all of its ducks in alignment. Like with a lot of sci-fi shows, it really tapped into the universal dreams of humans to be the hero and stop the evil person with nonlethal means, because of the nature of the audience we had. So, it was great. There's no blood and guts on our show. How odd for today's world. It wouldn't fly.

But back then, how great that you could stop evil people without killing them. I think that's in the dream of humans. To fly, obviously, is in all of our dreams, and to have those special abilities that the *Galactica* children had. And to travel back in time, to fix the past so that you could have a better outcome for the present. Who doesn't have that dream while we have Trump? There are a lot of people in this country who would like to go back in time and fix this mess.

ROBBIE RIST

What I learned at seven years old was don't be too attached. When the *Battlestar Galactica* job goes away after I was recast, there's a moment of "Aw, it sucks," but ultimately in entertainment, there's always disappointment. Like my-girlfriend-has-had-sex-with-someone-else disappointment. I actually just did a low-budget movie with Barry Van Dyke last year, and now I'm wondering if I brought it up to him that we worked together before. I don't think I did. I don't think he remembered. He's got a real career, why would he remember me?

GLEN OLIVER

Galactica 1980 is bad news. Like Ned-Beatty-meeting-the-hillbillies-in-*Deliverance* bad news. Having recently rewatched both series in quick succession, I can say that the contrast between them is shocking, bewildering, and more than a little depressing. *1980* is far more than a retooled series concept. It feels like a cheesy spin-off nobody really wanted, yet somehow it made it through a nearly impossible network gauntlet, only to be shitcanned unceremoniously several episodes in. *Galactica 1980* was the *Joanie Loves Chachi* of science fiction television.

STU PHILLIPS

The thing about *Battlestar Galactica* originally was that it had no time period. It could have been the year 1000 or 3000. That allowed you so much latitude to do things, because you're not locked into a particular period of time. Nobody knew when these people were in those ships looking for Earth. Now you take it and you call it *Galactica 1980* and you've locked these people in a particular time period and I think that the mysticism and magic of everything that was going on suddenly got lost.

GLEN OLIVER

There's so very much wrong with this series, not the least of which was it was barely recognizable as *Galactica*. The series' reorchestrated, downgraded score was painful, accentuated by "hipper," modern music, which today reads as stereotyped and kitschy compared to the original series' score. Stories were utterly devoid of gravity, and were generally geriatric in their urgency. There was a timelessness to the approach of the original series—while *1980* was very much a product of its time, and came across as much less mythic. It felt this way from the outset. The death blow here was that show was just plain dull.

Other episodes developed but never made for the series include a bullfighting script by Chris Trumbo, former writing partner of Jeff Freilich and the son of Dalton Trumbo—screenwriter of *Spartacus* among other classics—who was blacklisted by HUAC in the 1950s. Another episode would have featured Troy and Dillon going back in time to the Trojan War to stop Xaviar from altering the past. In "The Money Machine," Troy and Dillon would have used their ability to counterfeit money to help a precocious band of orphans. Cole and Bunch's "Earthquake" script presaged fracking (the process of extricating oil and gas using high-pressure liquid, not the Galactican expletive) by two decades. And what would a 1980s TV series be without the requisite biker episode? In a script by Richard Christian Matheson and Tom Szolossi, Troy and Dillon would have mixed it up with a band of bad-guy bikers.

RICHARD CHRISTIAN MATHESON
(story editor, *Quincy, M.E.*)

Tom and I were under a seven-year term deal at Universal, assigned as staff writers to different series, as needed. Those included *Cliffhangers, The Incredible Hulk, Quincy, The Misadventures of Sheriff Lobo, B.J. and the Bear, Simon & Simon,* and *Galactica 1980.*

As to *Galactica*, we were assigned to write for the show. We knew about Glen Larson, who was a major TV producer on the Universal lot along with Stephen J. Cannell, Steven Bochco, and Levinson and Link. Tom and I were the head writers of *Quincy* right after *Cliffhangers*. I was twenty-one and Tom was twenty-three. It was very exciting and *Quincy* was a prestigious show; for a couple of punks like us to be the head writers was a big deal. Even then, we had never met Glen and were essentially hired by Donald Bellisario, who was the executive producer of *Quincy* at the time. He heard about us, around the lot, I suppose. Anyway, we met with Don and hit it off and he liked our writing and hired us. We met the great Stephen J. Cannell in our *Quincy* offices and he offered us an assignment on his show *Stone*—but we didn't meet Glen until we were writing for *Lobo*, as I recall it.

ALLAN COLE

Trumbo was a good friend, who edited our first sale on television, *Quincy*. The late Chris Trumbo was the son of Dalton Trumbo, one of the most famous of the blacklisted writers. Famously, Kirk Douglas demanded that he get screen credit for *Spartacus*. Chris had a strange life on the lam with his father, who was being chased by the FBI, and then as the son of that guy in prison for being a dirty communist. Chris was a wonderful writer in his own right. He basically wrote the movie *Papillon* on location in the jungle while his father was going through alcoholic tremors.

They pitched a biker story. Now, [my partner] Chris [Bunch] was an expert on bikes and bikers. He once had a public-relations contract to represent the Hells Angels. It was a good story that did a good job dodging most of the many logic problems inherent in the series. But they had to sit there patiently taking copious notes while Chris nitpicked motorcycle and gang-behavior detail. We had great fun with Richard and Tom. First off, they were our very friendly rivals. When freelancing, we pitched—and sold—the same shows they did. Later, we were on the other side of the desk at *The A-Team* pitching them.

RICHARD CHRISTIAN MATHESON

My best memories were meeting the amazing Frank Lupo, who'd just been hired as story editor and then producer [for *Galactica 1980*]. His gift for story was remarkable. I liked him right off and I remember the two of us, at the advanced ages of around twenty-one, walking around the Universal lot and talking about a million things together. We struck up a friendship that has lasted a lifetime, and I suspect it was Frank who really got us in as story editors when Steve [Cannell] started Stephen J. Cannell Productions, since we'd be working with Frank, up close, on *The A-Team*.

We loved Steve, and over the years he became one of my dearest friends. While on *The A-Team*, I do recall, while walking to the set, often being mistaken for Dirk [Benedict], since, at the time, we kind of resembled one another. I might have even signed his autograph, once or twice, for someone who thought I was him. Working with Dirk was a blast. He had a winning knack for light comedy.

GLEN OLIVER

The most interesting of the episodes involved the use of time travel to reengineer Earth's history so that modern humanity would be better prepared to grapple with Cylons should they show up—a conceit which was originally to have driven *1980* if I understand correctly. But, by the end of *1980*'s opening installment, even that concept felt muddy, sloppy, and inconsistent, and proceedings pretty much plummeted downhill from there.

JEFF FREILICH

The time-travel element was born out of an attempt to just extrapolate on the original *Battlestar Galactica* and also to make it different. *Star Trek* did it a lot. One of my favorite *Star Trek*s was when Kirk and Spock go back in time to the thirties and make a decision about whether or not to kill Joan Collins. It was a great moral dilemma. How much do you want to change history without fucking everything up is basically what that story was about. Time travel was used in *Star Trek* very effectively. Glen just felt that when you launch a new incarnation of an old idea, which is what *Galactica 1980* was, that you have the freedom to take it a step further. And what was the natural step further other than time travel because, for the most part, we were going to be stuck on Earth on that show. So we weren't going to be able to fly through space that much. Space travel on that show was always a sidebar story, since it all took place on Earth. So I think the time travel was just a new toy.

ALLAN COLE

Glen just kept throwing shit at the wall to see what would stick. He sort-of-kind-of dropped the archvillain Xaviar, early on. Dropped the time-travel angle, only to revive it again for the last episode—"Cleopatra"—which was never finished.

Even with the series cancellation, *Galactica* continued to live on for another decade at Universal Studios with the two-minute-and-forty-five-second theme-park tour attraction, The Battle of Galactica, which opened on June 9, 1979, in which guests are attacked and taken aboard a Cylon basestar to be fed to the Ovions until a Colonial Warrior comes to the rescue and the tram escapes unscathed. The popular ride was featured briefly in the 1980 *Get Smart* movie, *The Nude Bomb,* for those who want to relive the, um, excitement. The attraction was closed permanently in 1992.

ROB KLEIN

Many of the original props for *Battlestar Galactica* were used for the Universal Studios tour tram attraction The Battle of Galactica. This impressive show featured a live actor portraying a Colonial Warrior. Initially the actors were able to use original Colonial wardrobe and Colonial pistols, but the original items eventually went missing as most of the wardrobe and props were taken home by employees.

Universal sold off their sci-fi wardrobe along with their Western costume collection in the early nineties to make room for rentable wardrobe. Among this sale was the wardrobe from the *Back to the Future* trilogy, *The Wiz, Battlestar Galactica, Heartbeeps, Buck Rogers in the 25th Century, The Reluctant Astronaut, Otherworld, Brave New World,* and *The Harlem Globetrotters on Gilligan's Island,* to name a few. Sci-fi wardrobe does not usually rent too often, and Westerns were going out of favor, so Universal has little use for this type of wardrobe.

However, Universal's wardrobe retained for some odd reason a few Warrior tunics and Warrior pants as well as most of all of the Earth Directorate dress jackets that Western Costumes made for *Buck Rogers in the 25th Century.* The studio retained a six-foot rack of Warrior pants in the wardrobe department until 2005. According to one of the original founders of the Universal Archives Department, the studio eventually threw these pieces of *Galactica* history away, sending only one example of a Warrior tunic and a pair of Warrior pants to their archives. The studio didn't even bother to go through the remaining wardrobe to save a star costume such as an Apollo or Starbuck. This oversight makes Warrior pants one of the rarest costume items to obtain today. What is someone's trash is someone else's treasure.

The model of the battlestar *Galactica* was sent to Universal Studios Florida in the late 1980s and was put into a storefront window for decoration. The sun and humidity caused severe damage to the model. The managers of Universal Florida had no idea of this miniature's history or its value, and it was soon after conned out of the studio by a fast-talking opportunist. This fan restored the beloved battlestar and held on to it for many years. It was sold at auction with a few other miniatures made for *Battlestar Galactica* and *Buck Rogers* in 2017 for one and a half million dollars.

As for the full-size Viper itself (which had been expanded for *Galactica 1980* to accommodate a two-seat cockpit and a larger canopy, despite the fact that it didn't match the copiously used stock footage from the original show), it also met a sad fate, back in the days when studios undervalued and quickly disposed of their iconic props following a series cancellation.

ROB KLEIN

Many rumors circulated for years after the show's cancellation that the Viper still existed, but [former *Battlestar Galactica* grip] Mike Smith confirmed that the Viper was stripped and the metal frame was cut into pieces and scrapped. The rear engines of the Viper can be seen in the fourth-season *Knight Rider* episode "The Phantom of the Studio" on the back of a flatbed truck. No surprise, as *Knight Rider* was also a Glen Larson production.

Despite the revulsion many fans still feel over *Galactica 1980,* comic book writer and *Arrow* and *DC's Legends of Tomorrow* cocreator and showrunner Marc Guggenheim wrote a revisionist version of the series for Dynamite Comics. In his version of events, Dr. Zee is a power-mad zealot intent on taking over Earth, Baltar craves immortality courtesy of the Cylons using cybernetic implants, and Adama lands the *Galactica* over the White House in an attempt to make first contact with President Jimmy Carter, who nukes the battlestar. To say things don't go well would be an understatement.

MARC GUGGENHEIM

The *Galactica 1980* comic book was basically just a brain dump of the stuff I thought I was going to get to see in the series with a slightly more adult, more mature point of view. Of course, if *Galactica* enters our solar system, the first thing they're going to encounter is *Voyager,* which had just been launched two years before. It wouldn't have even made it out of the solar system. You're going to go, "Oh the people who made this are from the United States of America. They're the ones who have their shit together. We're gonna go there." Of course, if a massive ship were to show up over the White House, you're not going to think aliens in 1980. You're going to think it's the Russians and you're going to fight back.

A lot of my ideas come about from questions. I had a question, in the case of *Galactica,* which fueled the story, which is why does Baltar betray humanity? That's kind of dumb unless there's something in it for him. Well, what could possibly be in it for him? These are robots that don't age, so I realized he wanted to be immortal. For me, it's always about coming up with the answer to the question.

Also, I guess it's the writer in me, but I always appreciated the biblical story of Moses not being able to enter the Promised Land. He's the protagonist of the story, he leads the Jews to Israel, but isn't allowed to enter it. That always struck a chord with me as a writer, and as a person. It made a lot of sense for me that Adama doesn't get to the Promised Land. It's part of the whole biblical inspiration that inspired Glen Larson, who worked a lot of religion into *Galactica.*

I thought I was not only being artsy-fartsy with it, but really was also writing in the style that quite frankly Glen Larson was writing in because there are these parallels between the situation with the Colonials and the people of *Battlestar Galactica,* their biblical forefathers. All these things sort of came together for me. That was a blast to write. Also, Ron Moore's *Battlestar Galactica* had come out, and I wanted to use that approach to *Galactica 1980.* It was fun to be able to incorporate some little nods to Ron's *Battlestar,* because it was so amazing. It also always bothered me as a ten-year-old that they were taking orders from Dr. Zee. I was ten years old when I watched it, and no one listened to me.

ROBBIE RIST

I don't get recognized nearly as much for *Galactica 1980* as I do for a television show I did when I was thirteen called *Big John, Little John.* It ran for a year. It was producer Lloyd Schwartz's first show after *The Brady Bunch.* That thing gets more juice than *Galactica 1980.* They released the DVD set of *Galactica 1980* in Germany a few years ago, and I did an interview for that and they sent me the package and none of it is in English, so maybe if I want to get recognized for *Galactica 1980,* I have to go to Germany.

BARRY VAN DYKE

I have very, very fond memories of *Galactica 1980.* You know the funny thing is I still hear from people about it. Not long ago I went to one of those autograph shows with my dad [Dick Van Dyke] when they had the *Diagnosis Murder* cast there and people came up to me with all this stuff from *Galactica:* jackets, posters, pictures. Half the people there came for *Galactica 1980* and I couldn't believe it.

ROBYN DOUGLASS

It sounds a little silly, but one of the highlights I remember from doing *Galactica 1980* was that I got to do the original *Battle of the Network Stars.* I know it sounds a little juvenile, but I got to get chauffeured around and treated like a movie star and met Howard Cosell. I got twenty thousand dollars for having a great time. It was a perk, and I got one huge, yummy, yummy perk. But that's one of the real highlights for me of doing the show.

GLEN OLIVER

It's hilarious to think the powers that be felt *Galactica* needed reformatting into *this,* when the show which has most successfully endured, and inspired remakes, is actually the show they were attempting to reformat. *Galactica 1980* somehow, almost impressively, manages to be a double wasted opportunity: not only did it effectively castrate its progenitor season, it failed to satisfactorily exploit the "what if they find Earth?" scenario driving the whole damn concept. I fully realize it's incredibly difficult to make a TV series, and even more difficult to realize onscreen what is in one's heart or mind. But, on the whole, *Galactica 1980* feels like little more than hackwork. Everyone creatively responsible for it should be ashamed of themselves. Except for Dirk Benedict, Robert Reed, and possibly Wolfman Jack. It's hard to get pissed off at Wolfman Jack.

JEFF FREILICH

Until human beings actually have civilizations and societies on other planets, I don't think they will ever tire of the fantasy of making contact with ETs, let alone ones that present themselves as humans and have human emotions and characteristics. The other thing that *Galactica* did that *Star Wars* didn't do was to bring to Earth the story of people who live in other worlds. And as opposed to being in a galaxy far, far away, a long time ago, this was contemporary and it involved our own military. And we were basically as human beings, let alone Americans, being dragged into a war of the worlds. That's what the theory of *Galactica 1980* was, when they finally made contact with Earth. The original series and the remake were more space shows, so *Galactica 1980* is unique. I still think it strikes a chord in the heart of a lot of generations. There was something about *Galactica* that even the original, which was not on at family hour, was one of those shows that the whole family could sit down and watch.

ALLAN COLE

The only reason people are still talking about it is because of the success of the final incarnation [*Battlestar Galactica* (2004)]. Real science fiction people produced and wrote that show, and they had fine actors to deliver the lines. Boiled down to its simplest line—human beings returning to Earth pursued by another civilization—*Battlestar* became the hit it would have been if Glen Larson had been forced off the show, like Klugman forced him off *Quincy*. Even so, we were told Larson collected a hundred grand per episode as the creator. Nice job if you can get it.

JEFF FREILICH

There was a charm that was very Glen Larson about *Battlestar Galactica*, because all of his shows had that charm. Even *Quincy,* which was a pretty dark show about a forensic pathologist in an era where that was just really being born as a science. The opening credits have Quincy doing a dissection and half of the people at the table, all medical students, fainted. And it got a laugh. The theme was a whimsical piece of music that tells you from the very beginning of the show that you're going to be entertained, but you're not going to be shocked beyond your comfort level. You're going to be engaged with the characters, and you may laugh. That was a lot more the goal of entertainment in those days than it might be now.

You've got less restrictions on you now. The viewer has to make a choice about whether they think it's appropriate for them and their families versus the network. And that's why I think that *Galactica* in a way was a fairy tale told back in 1978 and 1980, not unlike the Grimms' fairy tales and others that will never really die. When I was working on *Grace and Frankie* in Los Angeles or *Burn Notice* in Miami, a large majority of the people that I work with are half my age, if not younger, and they all know *Battlestar Galactica*.

MARC GUGGENHEIM

Both these stories are a postapocalyptic story where the thing that caused the apocalypse is still a constant danger, which makes it unique. Other than *The Walking Dead*, I can't think of a series that's done this. It's a super clever idea where you do a story about an apocalypse, and what caused the apocalypse, the Cylons in this case, are still your primary villain.

JEFF FREILICH

These shows live on for years after their original run. Whereas television shows today don't. They're on, they're gone. They live on streaming networks, but they don't live on reruns on local and national television broadcast networks. You have to go to Hulu or Netflix to see shows that are from many years ago. And then they have a half-life on those streaming services. But they all recognize *Battlestar Galactica* right away. Like horror fans recognize *Freddy's Nightmares,* which was from 1988 that I worked on. Every horror fan alive knows that show. And it's appalling to me, actually. What parents allowed their kids to ever watch that show? It's the goriest show in the history of television. And yet, when I did *Wrong Turn 2* with first-time director Joe Lynch, who was a horror geek beyond description, I walked in the room and he bowed to me, and told me that his childhood was basically sculpted by his viewing of *Freddy's Nightmares*. So it's funny, there are many shows from those days that have long shelf lives that have become legendary. And *Galactica*, I think, is the most unique among all of them.

SECTAR TWO

BATTLESTAR GALACTICA

THE MINISERIES (2003)

All of this has happened before.
And all of this will happen again.

10.
WHAT ABOUT
THE OTHER BATTLESTAR?

"I really think you should take a look at the other battlestar."

Maybe it would have been better for us to have died quickly back on the colonies with our families instead of dying out here slowly in the emptiness of dark space. Where shall we go? What shall we do?

—Commander William Adama

The seeds for the new *Battlestar Galactica* were already being planted as the *Star Trek* television series *Deep Space Nine* came to an end in June 1999. By that point, writer Ronald D. Moore had spent a decade writing in the world of *Trek,* having begun as a freelancer for *The Next Generation* and gradually moved up to the position of coproducer. With that series concluding—and after cowriting the first two features based on it with Brannon Braga—he shifted over to *DS9,* eventually becoming coexecutive producer.

As a part of the *Star Trek* franchise, *Deep Space Nine* was unique. It embraced serialized storytelling, delved into a darker dramatic territory that was atypical, and tried its best to create and sustain a reality among a future landscape with humans interacting with various alien species. It pushed the envelope at a time when few shows were, and yet for Moore it still wasn't enough.

One of the members of the *DS9* writing staff, which included showrunner Ira Steven Behr, René Echevarria, Robert Hewitt Wolfe, and Hans Beimler, Moore felt a creative freedom on that show that he had never felt on its predecessor, *The Next Generation.* And *still* he believed that things weren't pushed hard or far enough; that there was untapped potential yet to be explored. When the series ended following a seven-season run, he joined the next installment of the franchise, *Voyager,* which at the time was getting ready to enter its fifth season.

It *should* have been the perfect match. After all, the show's newly in-stalled showrunner was Brannon Braga, Moore's friend and frequent col-laborator. However, in this particular hierarchy he was co-executive producer *under* Braga, an important distinction to be made compared to their previous collaborative working relationship, where he had been the "senior partner" of the writing team.

Upon joining *Voyager*, Moore had some very clear notions in mind on how he wanted to evolve the *Star Trek* franchise, updating the format for the soon-to-begin twenty-first century. Unfortunately, he was pretty much the only one who felt that way.

BRANNON BRAGA
(executive producer, *Star Trek: Voyager*)

Ron came aboard as a writer and he came aboard wanting the show to do all sorts of things. He wanted the show to have continuity. When the ship got fucked up, he wanted it to stay fucked up. For characters to have lasting consequences. He was *really* into that. He wanted to eradicate the so-called reset button, and that's not something the studio was interested in, because this thing was a big seller in syndication. It wasn't until season three of *Enterprise* [the next spin-off] that we were allowed to do serialization, and that was only because the show needed some kind of boost to it, because it was flat. I made a big mistake by not supporting Ron in that decision or in supporting Ron in general when he came aboard the show. That was a dark chapter for me and Ron and [executive producer] Rick Berman. It was a bad scene.

RONALD D. MOORE
(cocreator/executive producer, *Battlestar Galactica* [2004])

One of my few regrets with my association with the franchise is that brief, but very unhappy, period at *Voyager*. It was just a very unhappy experience and a mistake I shouldn't have made. I should not have taken that gig. I think I took it for the wrong reasons and went into it with the wrong expec-tations. When it went south, I clearly wanted to get the hell out of there. I remember when Brannon said he really wanted me to do it and we had talked about it through that last season of *Deep Space Nine*. I did it because I just didn't want to leave *Trek*. I had been there for ten years. I was comfortable there. I was making a lot of money. I loved *Star Trek*. It was just what I did. It's weird to think of now, but it was ten years of my life and it was my first ten years of being a professional writer. Every year I just kept coming back. I took my two weeks' vacation and showed up and started the next season. That was my life. That was part of my routine, and it was hard to imagine not doing it. I didn't really want to go out and I didn't have a pilot I was desperate to go pitch and I didn't exactly want to learn another show. And not one of those reasons was, "Oh my God, I'm so intrigued by *Voyager*."

If anything, I stepped into it feeling like I was going to fix *Voyager*. I felt it was flawed and problematic and wasn't working very well. And in my hubris at the time, I thought, "Well, I'm going to go and I'll show them how to do a *Star Trek* show. I'll fix that show. Brannon and I, we've worked together for years. It'll be fine. He and I together—we'll turn this into a really great show." I came in and tried to change things, tried to play with the concept, but it was all different. Brannon was in a different space. He was in charge.

BRYAN FULLER
(cocreator, *Star Trek: Discovery*)

I'll give you a personal angle into the story. I'm the youngest of five, and I watched my parents play my sisters off of each other to the point that they haven't spoken to each other in forty years. I saw that happening with Rick Berman playing Brannon and Ron off of each other in a way that caused them both to behave outside of their natural states, because insecurities were played on, exposed, manipulated. What happened between Brannon and Ron boils down to bad parenting on Rick's behalf.

Rick would taunt Brannon, saying things like, "I should have hired Ron to run *Voyager* instead of you." So of course Brannon is going to be insecure and vulnerable. Brannon is a very complicated guy, but an amazing storyteller and a good guy ultimately. Both Ron and Brannon are good guys. But when you're in a situation where you are feeling vulnerable and insecure and you're having somebody essentially say "I wish you were more like that guy," you're going to resent that guy. And when *that* guy is told, "I wish

Brannon was more like you," then you're going to feel like you should come in and you should be in a position where you're exerting a certain sense of control over the story. So I feel like both of them were victims of bad parenting in that scenario.

BRANNON BRAGA

Ron came in with a very strong point of view, and I was irrationally resistant, because I felt that I had just earned my keep as a showrunner. I felt a little threatened by my old colleague, which was silly of me. Ron is always one to push the boundaries, and I wish I'd listened to him.

RONALD D. MOORE

I think at the heart of it is that when we were partners, I was something of the senior partner, because I started a year before him. And in our relationship as people, I took somewhat of a more dominant role. It was a marriage and a partnership. I'm not saying I was number one and he was number two, but there was a certain dynamic between the two of us that I was used to, saying what I wanted to do and not the other way around. And then I was going to work *for* him and he was a different person running that show. This is from my perspective, but he seemed less willing to take chances. He seemed more afraid of changing the show, and his arguments were feeling a lot like Rick's arguments about what *Star Trek* was and what it wasn't. He still had his Brannon ideas about weird science-fiction things and strange concepts and bizarro time travel. Things that were kind of his signature at the time. But the character work, he was not as receptive to really challenging the characters. A lot of things I eventually put into *Battlestar Galactica*, I started pitching to him originally.

But the bottom line is that it was his show and I acted like it was my show, which was not the smartest move. I really underestimated what it would be like to go work with him again. In my heart, I was ready to move on. I should have left *Trek* at the end of *Deep Space Nine* and taken on other challenges. Instead I went for comfort and ease and it blew up on me.

BRANNON BRAGA

Now I think it was best he left, because he was frustrated with me. On the one hand I wish I had responded differently, because I think the show would have been better for it. But then again, if he had remained, Ron might not have gone on to do *Battlestar Galactica*—which, in my view, is what he wanted to do with *Star Trek*. Every show creator has their moment, their show, and I really think *Battlestar* was Ron's best work. It was what he was yearning to do with *Star Trek,* but was constrained by the premise.

DAVID WEDDLE
(executive story editor, *Star Trek: Deep Space Nine*)

We were privy to his frustration on *Star Trek*. We were still in a box of things we couldn't do on *Deep Space Nine,* because of all of the rules that had been put in place. Ron was always very vocal in the room and saying to Ira Behr, "Are you gonna take this?" And Ira responded as best he could. And as you know, Ron went over to *Voyager* and really tried to change it, and Rick Berman didn't like it and he ended up leaving and eventually created *Galactica*.

BRADLEY THOMPSON
(executive story editor, *Star Trek: Deep Space Nine*)

There's a beautiful story that illustrated what Ron was trying to do on *Star Trek*. On *Deep Space Nine* there was an episode called "One Little Ship," and in it the Jem'Hadar take over the ship the *Defiant*. They say, "Okay, you're going to do X, Y, and Z. You're gonna get these engines up, and we're going to go do something really, really bad. And if you don't do it, we're going to shoot this young ensign." The stock version we gave to Ron was the captain says, "Don't worry, Ensign. Everything's going to be fine." Because it's our captain, we're keeping him strong. And Ron took the pass, he took the same line, "Don't worry. Everything will be all right." And the Jem'Hadar blows her head off and says, "No it won't."

DAVID WEDDLE

And then that had to be taken out.

BRADLEY THOMPSON

The studio just totally freaked out when they saw that.

DAVID WEDDLE

And *there* you can see the beginning of the birth of *Battlestar Galactica*.

"Our goal is nothing less than the reinvention of the science fiction television series."

Those are the words that begin the "series bible" for *Battlestar Galactica,* as written by Moore on December 17, 2003—completely born out of frustration with the conventions of the genre in which he had spent his career.

"We take as a given," he continues, "the idea that the traditional space opera, with the stock characters, techno-double-talk, bump-headed aliens, thespian histrionics, and empty heroics has run its course and a new approach is required. That approach is to introduce realism into what has heretofore been an aggressively unrealistic genre. Call it 'Naturalistic Science Fiction.' This idea, the presentation of a fantastical situation in naturalistic terms, will permeate every aspect of our series.

"Visual: The first thing that will leap out at viewers is the dynamic use of the documentary or cinema verite style. Through the extensive use of hand-held camera, practical lighting, and functional set design, the battlestar *Galactica* will feel on every level like a real place. This shift in tone and look cannot be overemphasized. It is our intention to deliver a show that does not look like any other science fiction series ever produced. A casual viewer should for a moment feel like he or she has accidentally surfed onto a *60 Minutes* documentary piece about life aboard an aircraft carrier until someone starts talking about Cylons and battlestars. . . .

"Editorial: Our style will avoid the now cliched MTV fast-cutting while at the same time foregoing *Star Trek*'s somewhat ponderous and lugubrious 'master, two-shot, close-up, close-up, two-shot, back to master' pattern. If there is a model here, it would be vaguely Hitchcockian—that is, a sense of building suspense and dramatic tension through the use of extending takes and long masters which pull the audience into the reality of the action rather than the distract through the use of ostentatious cutting patterns.

"Story: We will eschew the usual stories about parallel universes, time-travel, mind-control, evil twins, God-like powers and all the other clichés of the genre. Our show is first and foremost a drama. It is about people. Real people that the audience can identify with and become engaged in. It is not a show about hardware or bizarre alien cultures. It is a show about us. It is an allegory for our own society, our own people, and it should be immediately recognizable to any member of the audience. . . .

"Character: This is perhaps the biggest departure from the science fiction norm. We do not have 'the cocky guy,' 'the fast-talker,' 'the brain,' 'the wacky alien sidekick' or any of the other usual characters who populate a space series. Our characters are living, breathing people with all the emotional complexity and contradictions present in quality dramas like *The West Wing* or *The Sopranos*. In this way, we hope to challenge our audience in ways that other genre pieces do not. We want the audience to connect with the characters of *Galactica* as people. Our characters are not superheroes. They are not an elite. They are everyday people caught up in enormous cataclysm and trying to survive it as best they can. They are you and me."

RONALD D. MOORE
(cocreator/executive producer, *Battlestar Galactica* [2004])

There is definitely truth in the idea that *Battlestar Galactica* was a means for me to do things I wasn't allowed to do on *Star Trek*. As much as *Deep Space Nine* pushed things, there were things I wanted to do, and fought for, but just couldn't in a *Star Trek* universe when you're doing a war story. That I was frustrated with, and I wanted a chance to do it. When I went to *Voyager*, there was a storyline that came up that did have *Voyager*, for a time, escorting a group of alien civilian ships through a war zone or something. We talked explicitly about the fact that it was like *Battlestar Galactica*. I thought, "Oh, that can be a great, gigantic arc where you explore how Janeway deals with the other people and that civilian fleet. Don't they get a vote and a say in sort of what happens with them? Don't they have a culture? And isn't this some kind of society at a certain point?" I just was really intrigued in exploring those aspects of the story.

I had a lot of ideas about making it its own culture, and was really pushing hard for a lot of the things that, ultimately, I ended up doing in *Galactica*.

So, yes, a lot of the early thinking about how and why different aspects of *Galactica* would come into being were done at *Deep Space* and that brief period of *Voyager*.

One of the things I kept saying was if *Voyager*'s really on the other side of the galaxy and they're off by themselves, by the time the ship gets back home it should be unrecognizable. They should develop their own culture, they would deal with things on their own. Why is Janeway going to be the captain of the ship forever? Shouldn't there be some elections? Shouldn't there be some political thing that should come up? Do they have any other rights? Wouldn't they start customizing the ship in certain ways? Why can't we have battle damage from last week's episode last for a bit? Maybe there's areas of *Voyager* that you can't go into anymore because they've been too damaged? I was looking for some kind of grounding in some kind of reality.

In response, I got a lot of "That's not the show. That's not *Voyager*. We don't want to do that. That's not *Star Trek*. *Star Trek* is . . ." They had this idea of what *Star Trek* had to be, and it's adventure. "We don't want to deal with damage to the ship, and no one should ever question Janeway's authority. And Janeway doesn't have to vote." You just had to accept the heroism of the characters, and they couldn't be morally questionable.

Even on *Deep Space,* during the Dominion War I wanted more ambiguous stories that made the characters more flawed; have them make bad choices or difficult ones in wartime. You know, having more dark endings and having a sense of the devastation; that this is wrenching throughout the entire Federation in that quadrant of the galaxy. They were just unwilling to go to those places.

I was also butting up against the style of the show itself. I wanted to do a lot more handheld work, wanted to make it grittier. And the show, stylistically, in terms of the way it was shot and produced, absolutely refused to compromise. They were like, "This is not how we shoot *Star Trek*. *Star Trek* is shot in a particular way," which I thought by that point was a boring way and a very stilted way. They wouldn't make it rougher and edgier. They just absolutely refused to go there.

When we were doing *Deep Space,* we definitely felt like the redheaded stepchild. We felt like they were not supporting the show. Paramount was *not* a supporter. They were disappointed in the ratings and sort of felt like, "Well, this whole thing has been a flawed experiment. The next show has to be a starship and all of the usual things." So, we kind of felt like we were not taken seriously. That said, we did just push it—push all the boundaries as far as we possibly could—and we felt proud of what we were doing. And now, looking back on it, you can go, "Wow, that's really unlike anything else that anybody ever did." At the time, we loved the show so much. We were *so* enamored with the characters that we just wanted to keep going further and further. And any kind of limitation, and any kind of boundary, frustrated us, because we just kept feeling like, "There's so much more if you let us keep going. Come on, don't slow us down."

All of that was the beginning of my thinking, "If I had to do this show my way, what would I do?" I would edit it differently, and I would shoot it differently. I would rough up these characters even more, and I would be riskier in a lot of ways than what we were willing to do in *Star Trek*. And I'm tired of the big viewscreen, and I'm tired of the captain's chair, and I'm tired of the way the ships move in space. Why can't they move more like ships in space would really move? It was a lot of that sort of thinking all through those years that later, when I had the opportunity . . . well, now you really can do a show. All those things were ready. I'd already thought deeply about them. I was ready to just implement them.

Ronald D. Moore, born on July 5, 1964, in Chowchilla, California, developed a love for science fiction early in life. He was obsessed with the space program when he was a kid, a love that spread to the science fiction genre in general and *Star Trek* in particular in the years to come.

RONALD D. MOORE

Lost in Space was the first space show that I fell in love with, and then I started seeing *Star Trek* and *that* became the show for me. It was on five days a week at four in the afternoon, and after I got home from school I would watch *Star Trek* every day. I saw it as where NASA was going someday and where we could all go someday. I read it as a prophetic show; that this was what was going to happen. I remember thinking, "When are we going to have one world government and start building starships?"

Moore dabbled in writing and drama while in high school, but by the time he went to Cornell University he'd decided to study political science, attending based on an ROTC scholarship. Although he would leave school in his senior year (completing his degree later), during his freshman year he spent a month serving on the USS *W. S. Sims*, a frigate. In the fall of 1986 he was working a variety of jobs, among them receptionist at an animal hospital, while awaiting his big break as a writer.

RONALD D. MOORE

I would tape *Next Generation* every week on VHS and watch it, and told myself someday I'm going to write for it, but I was still sort of at ground zero in terms of actually having a writing career. I worked different jobs and along the way I started and stopped scripts. I wasn't really pursuing a path to get me through the doors of Paramount, which is so odd in retrospect. I was just kind of being a young guy in L.A. and telling myself I was going to write for the show someday.

That opportunity ultimately presented itself thanks to the show's open-door script policy, which meant that the producers would look at virtually any script that came its way as long as it was accompanied by a legal release form, not necessarily through an agent or attorney. It was the belief of executive producer Michael Piller (who joined the show in its third year) that this would be the best way to find talented young writers, back when television series still relied on freelance pitches and spec scripts. Moore joined the show and stayed with the franchise for a decade, cowriting (with Braga) the *Star Trek* feature films *Generations* and *First Contact* along the way. Following the *Voyager* debacle, he took a year off to, as he says, recharge and get his thoughts together.

RONALD D. MOORE

Leaving the *Star Trek* universe after ten years was a pretty big deal. First step was I consulted on a show called *G vs E* for the Sci-Fi Channel. Jonas and Josh Pate were the showrunners and creators of the show. It was a funny, off-kilter, eccentric show, and the Pates were a couple of guerrilla go-getter guys. They made that show for a song; for nothing, and it was fun and really just goofy and interesting. It was also the experience that introduced me to David Eick.

And then I got a call to do *Roswell* with Jonathan Frakes, who was one of the executive producers. They were looking for someone to come in and kind of bring a deeper mythology to the show in the second year. *That* was a real growing experience. I learned a lot about postproduction and editing.

You know, a lot of the things that I wasn't allowed to get involved with at *Trek,* I was able to do at *Roswell.* And then Jason Katims handed the show over to me in the third season. So that was my first real experience running a show.

JONATHAN FRAKES
(executive producer, *Roswell*)

First of all, Ron and Brannon wrote *First Contact,* which I directed. They were an incredible team. Ron's passion about the Klingons was unsurpassed. One of the reasons I recommended Ron to Jason Katims on *Roswell,* besides the fact that he was a brilliant writer, was that he had created so much mythology of the Klingons, both on *Next Generation* and *Deep Space Nine.* We really needed to ground the mythology of the aliens on *Roswell,* so there would be enough backstory, enough consistency. It was a situation where Jason Katims was the relationship guy and Ron ended up, I think without having been in the writers' room with them, balancing that with a grounded mythology. Ron's other show, *Outlander,* is a perfect example of it. That's a romantic, surreal sort of magical realism, but also almost sci-fi and very much in his wheelhouse.

Moore nearly had a second showrunning experience with an adaptation of Anne McCaffrey's *Dragonriders of Pern,* which was far along in the development process: sets were being built and roles cast, but a severe difference in opinion on the eve of production on how the show should be approached resulted in Moore departing and the project falling apart.

RONALD D. MOORE

During that period I pitched a pilot called *Dragonriders of Pern.* And actually a lot of the *Galactica* style of handheld photography in space was born on *Pern.* Because, as I started thinking about how we would do dragons on TV, I got this notion of doing it very handheld and making it very realistic, because I'd developed this theory that if you're asking the audience to sort of believe in something that is fundamentally unreal—and you're asking them to believe that these dragons are really flying around and people are sitting on them—the only way to really convince them of that is to shoot it handheld and to shoot it like you had to actually go out and do it in a real environment. So, if we're going to see a shot of the dragons flying through the air, it couldn't just be a steady pan watching them fly by camera. I wanted to make it feel like a helicopter had to go out there and chase this dragon down. And you have a cameraman sitting out the side of the helicopter, trying to hold focus, losing the dragon in frame, and there would be fixed cameras on the neck of the dragon shooting back at the rider. So, I had this whole sort of idea, in order to convince the audience that something that was fundamentally unreal was real, that the way to do that was to make them feel the presence of the camera. There were a lot of conversations with VFX artists.

FELIX ENRIQUEZ ALCALA
(director, *Dragonriders of Pern*)

That style was something I'd also done on *The Shield,* just because of the time period. I interviewed to direct that show and I went in to talk to the writer and I said, "This is a documentary. Do two-camera, handheld, and you just don't light anything. You just shoot the shit out of it and that's how you make the show. And you don't do two takes, you just go for one take here and there, and let it be a mess. It'll be cool." I think I scared the writer, like I was going to try and take over the show or something, which I didn't, of course. So they hired another director to do the pilot and, of course, they did everything I told them to do. And then a year later, they called me and said, "Would you just come work on the show?" I came in and everybody said, "Look, we have a way we're doing the show," and I said, "You know what? I know *exactly* how you do the show."

RONALD D. MOORE

One of the ideas of film is that, theoretically, the audience should never be aware of where the camera is. You should never think about the camera, because you're pulling them out of the drama if you do. But I kind of went the opposite way and said, "If you're trying to convince them that doesn't exist, actually, it's not going to work."

FELIX ENRIQUEZ ALCALA

Ron and I were on location in Santa Fe, and we were told a script from Warner Bros. was coming and they said, "Look, we made some changes and we want you guys to read them." And Ron says, "Who made changes on the script?" "Well, they want to polish this and that." And I told Ron, "Look, let's just read the script. No big deal. Let's just keep working." And then we got the script and it was a *total* rework. It was not anything he wrote. It was like somebody had been writing on this thing for a while. It was a totally different thing.

RONALD D. MOORE

I *hated* it. We all hated it; it was just not the show. They had done a WB on it, all right—it had become a teenage idiotfest. They were trying to be hip and cool with these dragons, man. And you're like, "What *is* this?" And it was so far from what Anne McCaffrey had written. So I said, "I don't want to shoot this. Let me go back and rewrite my own script. I'll rewrite it the way you want, but I can't shoot this." WB said, "No, this is the script we're approving. So this is the script you have to shoot." And I said I wouldn't do it and they said, "Well, now we've got a big problem. A very serious problem. Let's get on the phone tomorrow."

FELIX ENRIQUEZ ALCALA

We're standing there, like, what do we do? I guess I instigated, but I said to Ron, "Look, let's mark the line in the sand and we'll say we're going to do the show that we came to do," which Ron wrote. We were just going to produce the show and shoot the shit out of it. And that we weren't doing the other script. He should say, "If you make us do the other one, we shut production down." I said to Ron that if we didn't draw a line and do that, we would be dead meat. We would end up doing a piece of shit we're all going to hate and we're going to get blamed for it when it failed.

That night Moore had to be in Beverly Hills for a panel at the Museum of Television and Radio featuring a number of science fiction writers, among them J. Michael Straczynski and Harlan Ellison, the latter of whom would, whether he realized it or not, have a profound impact on Moore and his dealings with studios from that point forward.

RONALD D. MOORE

At the end of the panel, the moderator said, "Last question is, 'What advice do each of you have for young writers starting out in the business?'" We go down the line, and each of us answered the question. Then they give the mic to Harlan, who leans forward into the mic and says, "Don't be a whore. You know what? These people will rape you, and they will take all your talent and use it for their own shit. You've got to stand up and have some principles. Don't whore out your talent to *anybody;* show some balls in this business. Be *about* something. What does it really mean to be a writer if you can't protect your talent?" And it was just, like, "Whoa!" And I was literally in the car driving home that night and was like, "Don't be a whore, don't be a whore . . . oh my God, I'm having this call tomorrow." It was a movie moment.

So the next day on the call they put it to me again: "This is the script we approved." I said, "Well, I just don't want to shoot it, but I will rewrite the script. You can give me all the notes and I'll rewrite it. But this is not the show." They said, "Well, Ron, *this* is the show. And here's the deal. I guess if that's the way you feel, we should all just say good-bye right now and just let it go." I took a deep breath and said, "Okay, then let's do that." And there was dead silence. I heard a network exec go, "All right, then, I guess that's it." Click, click, click—everybody got off the phone and all hell broke loose. The phones are ringing, they're calling my agent, they're calling each other, they're screaming. People are freaking out, because New Regency was on the hook for a million or two . . . whatever they had spent. Basically the whole thing had just blown up and it was my fault and I was afraid that no one would hire me again.

But by the time I got to *Battlestar,* I had gotten to the point where I realized that moment was a really important one for me, because I had been willing to walk away. I learned that I could walk away and it meant that there was a line I wouldn't cross, and if you tried to push me over that line, I would quit or walk away. That knowledge gave me a tremendous amount of security in two ways. One, it told me I knew what the battles were that I could fight and that there were hills to die on, and I knew the difference. In a weird way, it gave me permission to compromise, because I wasn't afraid of conceding ground anymore. I wasn't afraid of changing my mind, or giving the network a victory, because it didn't mean I couldn't stand up to them. I knew when I could say fuck off.

As *Dragonriders of Pern* collapsed, Moore was approached by former Universal executive David Eick, who had transitioned into producing. They had previously worked together on *G vs E*.

RONALD D. MOORE

David had read my scripts and we'd had a couple of interactions during *Good vs Evil*. And we liked each other; we had lunch a couple of times and he just kind of remembered me. Then when he left the network to go work for Universal as a producer, they came to him and said, "Hey, we've got this property with *Battlestar Galactica* that various people have tried to get off the ground. Nothing's really worked. Do you want to take a crack at it?" And I think David said yes, and then he called me—he might have called a couple of other people, too, but he called me.

Behind the scenes at Universal, a reborn *Battlestar Galactica* had been discussed for a while. Among those involved from the start of that process were Angela Mancuso, then president of Universal Cable Entertainment, and production executive Todd Sharp.

TODD SHARP
(production executive, *Battlestar Galactica* [2004])

In most cases on most shows, you will have a studio and you will have a network. In most cases, those are separate entities. The thing that's probably confusing is that Universal owned both Sci-Fi Channel *and* our studio. And the reason why I say "our studio" is it had so many different names over the years. At one point it was Studios USA. At one point it was USA Cable Entertainment. At one point it was Universal Cable Productions. It changed names repeatedly through the years, because we kept going through corporate reorganization. Barry Diller owned us. Then Universal owned us. Then NBC came in and took us over. The current version of that company is called

Universal Cable Productions. Basically the studio was the group within Universal that was producing shows for the owned cable networks USA Network and Sci-Fi. We were making the show. I was the executive of the show *Monk* for USA Network, and I was also the executive on *Battlestar*. Both USA and Sci-Fi, as well as the studio, were all owned by the same parent company, but we were all separate entities. So on the studio side you have Angela Mancuso, who runs the studio. I'm the production executive.

I would say Angela was probably the most responsible for the show existing, because there was a big push at the time to kind of mine the Universal library and figure out what shows in the library we could rekindle and make some money on.

ANGELA MANCUSO
(former president, Universal Cable Entertainment)

I was the one who pulled *Galactica* out of mothballs. Barry Diller had bought the company and he said, "I want to go through the entire library. I want you to find *anything* that might be something we could remake." He was pushing us to do stuff that was already a title that we owned. One day I got a call from Scott Greenstein, who was the chairman of USA Films at the time, and he said, "Bryan Singer wants to do *Battlestar Galactica*." And I said, "That's great. So he wants to do it as a feature?" "No. I'm calling you because he wants to do it for television." I said, "That's fabulous, because we've been thinking about doing *Battlestar Galactica* and if Bryan wants to do it, that's amazing."

TODD SHARP

At Universal, there were two sides of the television group that were completely unrelated to one another. There was the cable side, which was us, and there was the network side, which was a different group of people. And Bryan Singer was developing a faithful adaptation of the original show. Totally, spiritually, very much a redo with Tom DeSanto.

TOM DESANTO
(executive producer, *X-Men*)

Initially it was a decision between me and Bryan Singer on whether to do it as a continuation or not. My thing was always to do a continuation and keep it in continuity, sort of as *The Next Generation* was to *Star Trek*. Keep it almost in real time, twenty-five years later. The great thing about the first *Galactica* was that it was symbolic about the story of the Exodus. It's this group of people fleeing, being pursued by the Egyptians, which were the Cylons, and the Israelites are fleeing, looking for the Promised Land, which was Earth. There was something about that theme which was really resonant, and it was wanting to keep the fact that they *didn't* find Earth, and the way that we had described it became "What if the Israelites stopped at Mount Sinai and it was Las Vegas?"

ANGELA MANCUSO

So now I was in charge of the cable studio, David Kissinger was in charge of the network television end, and I brought it to the television staff meeting and said, "Bryan Singer wants to do this. This is fabulous." And David said, "Well, then we'll do it for Fox. Why would we do it for Sci-Fi Channel? Fox is a bigger network, they'll pay more money." I started literally jumping up and down, saying, "But we own the Sci-Fi Channel. This is the biggest sci-fi title that we have in the library. We should do it for Sci-Fi." But I got vetoed and they developed it with Bryan Singer at Fox. The short story is they had a handful of writers who wrote a handful of scripts no one was happy with. I don't remember much about it, except that it was *not* dark and was a little closer to the original. It was nothing like Ron Moore's version. It didn't have the social resonance that I think Ron's had about, you know, how precarious our lives are. It definitely didn't deal with a woman head of the universe dying of cancer. It didn't have any of that gravitas. It was much lighter and much more tonally like the original.

TOM DESANTO

What we wanted to postulate was that twenty-three years ago there was a great battle between the *Galactica* and the Cylons, and they won but it wasn't decisive enough to fully defeat the Cylons. There was no contact with the Cylons after that point, so the humans come across this massive asteroid belt and it's filled with raw materials and ice and gold and everything they need to hide. And that's what they want to do. It's not a planet, but they start to mine this asteroid field and build this massive—for lack of a better word—white elephant. This space colony is filled with pleasure domes and business centers and gambling areas and everything that is shallow in life and that becomes their focus.

But, of course, those who do not remember the past are doomed to repeat it, and there is the decision made by the Council and the president to decommission the *Galactica,* their reasoning being that they haven't had any contact or any word from these things in over twenty years. So they turn the *Galactica* into a historical tourist attraction, but, of course, that doesn't last long when the Cylons pull another Pearl Harbor and attack the *Galactica* and the Colony again. They come out of this and defeat the Cylons with a renewed sense of purpose and repledge themselves to finding Earth.

TODD SHARP

My recollection is that version went down because Fox had just had a bit of a hit with *X-Men* and they had decided that making a sequel with Bryan Singer was a far more financially lucrative decision than doing the season of *Battlestar.* They were deep into prep. They had already built some ships. They had already built some sets.

AARON DOUGLAS
(actor, "Chief Tyrol")

I was told it was a continuation. He wanted to have the same clothes, the same everything and he wanted to have Richard and Dirk, but obviously not Lorne Greene. Then they had their kids or something. So it wanted to pick up where the original left off, which I thought was a pretty challenging thing to do given that everybody's thirty years older.

ANGELA MANCUSO

When Bryan Singer bailed to do the next *X-Men* movie, I said, "Give it back to me, I want to do it for Sci-Fi Channel." So I finally talked them into giving it back to me, and the next battle was, "It's so expensive, how can we pilot this?" The answer was "Let's do it as a miniseries." So, literally, I marched around halls like the minority whip at Universal, trying to garner support to do it as a miniseries.

TODD SHARP

When that version went down, and simultaneously Ron and David are putting this *Battlestar* together, we were actually told that we shouldn't see any of the stuff from the other show, because we don't want to taint it in any way, either creatively or legally. I didn't see the sets that they were building from that original *Battlestar*. Ours was a totally separate animal. I'm sure Bryan Singer would've made something perfectly wonderful that would have had fans—he's certainly a talented guy—but it was much lighter and more optimistic than what it would become. Ron and David would embrace the dark, embracing the zeitgeist of the time, which was that things are not so good. There's a lot of instability. A lot of uncertainty. To do what the best science fiction does, which is to be able to comment on today, comment on the world that we know.

RONALD D. MOORE

The network was of two minds. They were kind of predisposed to do it and they were predisposed *not* to do it. They were predisposed to do it, because they had done a lot of market research for various titles and had found that even though not many people remembered the show as such, a lot of people remembered the name. Early on they said to me, "We've already done the research that proves that we could get eyeballs on this. So it's an easy lift for us to sort of sell this series." Added to that, because of the previous attempts, they were already a little bit pregnant; they'd already put some time and money toward doing it internally.

But the part of their brains that *didn't* want to do it was they were having a bad experience with *Farscape* and the money with the Jim Henson Company.

They felt like they got screwed, and it was too expensive and it wasn't worth it. They were starting to have a philosophical change in terms of where they wanted the network to go in that they were saying, "We want to get out of the spaceships. We don't really want to keep doing space programming. We want to start doing things that are set up on Earth." Ultimately things like *Eureka.*

ANGELA MANCUSO

And what really saved us was that the merchandising department said, "If you can get this off the ground, this could be giant merchandising-wise." So we got our estimates together and we finally were able to talk everybody into doing it as a miniseries for Sci-Fi Channel. And there was a lot of opposition from the ridiculous comments that the original audience is going to feel cheated by a new take on it. It's ridiculous, because I'm in my fifties and *I* don't even remember the original one.

Eventually I brought on David Eick, who had a deal at the studio, to produce it.

Born in 1968, Eick graduated from the University of Redlands with a BA in political science and a minor in business administration. Prior to *Battlestar Galactica,* he worked as a producer with Sam Raimi and Robert Tapert on such shows as *Hercules: The Legendary Journeys* and *American Gothic;* during the show he was executive producer of the remake of *The Bionic Woman,* and since then was consulting producer of *Touch,* executive consultant of *Houdini,* and executive producer of *Falling Skies* and *Beyond.* Inspiring him into Hollywood was the experience of watching films like *Dirty Harry* and *The Exorcist.*

DAVID EICK
(executive producer, *Battlestar Galactica* [2004])

The Exorcist sort of shocked me into a state where I had to believe that it was possible to really traumatize and upset people through filmmaking. I knew you could tickle them, I knew you could delight them, I knew you could surprise them. I didn't realize you could actually upset them.

If you come to my house and look at my home office, the posters on the walls around my writing station are *Manhattan, Taxi Driver, All That Jazz,*

Lenny, Jaws, The Exorcist. But *not* outer space, not sci-fi really at all. So my roots are not necessarily genre, except for *The Exorcist,* this kind of separate bit of trauma that kind of forced me into the industry. I guess I responded to a kind of masculine protagonist who was strong in spite of his obvious foibles. I liked that flawed hero. I liked Dirty Harry. I liked the priest in *The Exorcist.* I liked these strong male figures who were flawed, who had corruption inside them, yet could overcome it. That probably wound up being applicable to some of the stuff I would do later, versus more atmospheric or aesthetic inspirations like outer-space shows and stuff like that. That wasn't where I was coming from. But, like I said, *The Exorcist* and even something like *Dirty Harry* were traumatizing—I guess I saw them too young—and in chasing the solutions to the trauma, I got dragged into the business. And, fortunately for me, because my early sort of mentors were also irreverent, subversive types, rather than having my instincts diluted or shamed or put in the corner, they were encouraged.

I got sort of dumped on Sam Raimi and Robert Tapert's doorstep in 1992, and six years later we had done six TV shows and it was a lot of happy luck and a lot of good fortune, but a lot of it had to do with my desire to tell stories from the point of view of an irreverent subversive protagonist, and here I am at a company where that's all they do. So that combination got us some early success and it was through that success that I was able to spend a couple of years as an executive. Sort of a kamikaze experiment to see what the other side of the coffee table was like. I did that at USA and Sci-Fi. I ran development for those two networks after my days with Sam Raimi. So I spent six years with Sam, two and a half years working for Barry Diller at USA and Sci-Fi Channel, realized that was not where I wanted to be and that I wanted to get back in the trenches. I was able to get—I wouldn't say a golden parachute, it was more of a nickel parachute—out of the executive ranks and into my own overall deal.

Which is about the time that *Battlestar Galactica* made its potentially renewed presence known in his life.

DAVID EICK

Shortly after putting the finishing touches on my office furniture, the phone rang and the head of the studio asked if I was interested in rebooting this *Battlestar Galactica* title as one of the early projects under my new overall deal. And, I, of course, said no, because I heard the title and thought it was ridiculous. Being friends with Shaun Cassidy—we did *American Gothic* together with Sam Raimi—I learned a lot about the seventies on the Universal lot. Shaun was, of course, very close to Glen Larson, who had done *The Hardy Boys,* which Shaun had starred in, but also had done the original *Battlestar Galactica.* So when it was first presented to me, the echo chamber in my head was, "Oh, this is the goofy space show that Shaun Cassidy told me about." That was my only reaction to it: that it was Shaun's goofy seventies story of the time that Glen Larson ripped off *Star Wars* and they had this one-season kind of expensive flop.

It wasn't that I had never heard the title, but I didn't have an opinion about it. I'd never seen it. What I *had* seen was the Universal Studios Tour with those Cylon robots. I just didn't know anything about it. In one regard it was the training from running Sam Raimi's company that came back. When I was running Raimi's company, it's, like, the studio came to us and said, "We have the title *Hercules* as public domain. You want to do something with it?" "Well, no, not if we have to do it the normal way. But if we can do it in a completely crazy way in New Zealand with girls with breast-plates and all kinds of crazy monsters, well, sure. You know, we can make it kind of funny, too." So it was a little bit like that. The appeal to me had nothing to do with the title.

This was 2001 and there were five gazillion space shows on TV—at least two *Star Trek* shows, *Farscape* had just gone away, Joss Whedon had his show *Firefly* coming, so to say you were going to do a space opera was to say you were going to do a superhero show. I was like, "Who gives a shit?" But I felt if I could cut left every time *Star Trek* would cut right, and if I can subvert and demean the expectations of the contemporary TV space opera, then *that* might be fun in a sneaky kind of dirty way. It could be fun to upend the whole infrastructure of what everyone is used to. But I had a problem: I didn't really watch *Star Trek*, I didn't really watch *Farscape*, I didn't really watch *Firefly*.

To solve that particular problem, he turned to writer Matt Greenberg, with whom, as he describes as part of his "kamikaze moment at the network," he developed a show called *The Invisible Man*, which had been a minor hit for Sci-Fi.

DAVID EICK

Matt is a hilarious and great action-adventure sci-fi writer. *Invisible Man* was irreverent in taking the Claude Rains heaviness of *Invisible Man* and kind of punking it. I didn't want to do a spoof with *Battlestar,* but I thought, "Well, this guy knows how to think outside the box. He just has kind of a kooky perspective." So I sat down with Matt and said, "They've given me the title, but I don't really know what I want to do with it except I want to cut against all the fucking *Star Treks.*" And he *didn't* like it. He came back to me with a whole weird pitch about a Cylon planet. It was a little more fantastical, I guess. Too much like *Star Trek.* Neither one of us knew if it was something we should be working on.

ANGELA MANCUSO

David really didn't have a take on it. What it ended up being came largely from Ron Moore.

DAVID EICK

I'd had two experiences with Ron Moore. One was—again, back in the kamikaze days—I'd hired him to be a consultant on a little punk rock show called *G vs E,* created by these Sundance punks, the Pate brothers. They were great, but they were young kids. They didn't really know what they were doing when they were doing the show, so I brought in this guy Ron Moore, who I'd had a general meeting with and really liked. He'd come off *Star Trek* and he'd come off of *Roswell.* So he came in for a general meeting, and I was very reluctant to ask him about *Galactica,* because I thought that nobody who's spent the bulk of his life immersed in fucking *Star Trek* is going to want to go back into another sci-fi space opera thing. So I was very tentative and that was a reason I didn't go to him first.

So we sat down. Now we're just after 9/11; it's just happened. I think this was December of 2001. We start talking about it and, to my surprise, he recalls that the pilot of the original involved this holocaust, and at that moment we were bleeding raw from 9/11. We're thinking, what if we took it really seriously? That was sort of the linchpin.

DAVID WEDDLE

Ron used to have a house out where I lived and I saw him a weekend after 9/11. He poured me a glass of champagne and he said, "Here's to being alive." I mean, we were all totally shaken by what happened. And that's an element of his genius, that he took that event and would fuse it into *Battlestar Galactica*. I don't think I ever could have made that kind of leap or seen that kind of potential, but *he* could.

RONALD D. MOORE

There's a good chance the show would've happened even without 9/11, because they were just looking for someone to capitalize on the title in the library. And it wasn't because of 9/11 that they saw value in it. It was just a market title. So I think that was on a separate track. I believe that it definitely would have gone in a different direction no matter what if not for 9/11 and the aftermath—the war in Afghanistan and then Iraq, the Patriot Act and Guantánamo and all those things—were such a heavy influence in the show that, if none of that had happened, it's hard to imagine the show would've developed in the same way.

BRADLEY THOMPSON
(producer, *Battlestar Galactica* [2004])

9/11 was definitely in our consciousness, but did we say, "Let's make this like 9/11"? Not particularly consciously, except there's a photograph that our guys slap when they're going out to battle leaving the ready room, which is a deliberate homage to the ones with the firemen and the flag, and the shattered buildings of the towers. We wanted to do that to say, "Yes, this is what this is about." But this was America *after* 9/11. Without it, the show would have been different. It wouldn't have been as "scared"; I don't think our audience would have had the same reaction to it, because that informs everything in the country, not just us.

MICHAEL RYMER
(director, *Battlestar Galactica* miniseries [2003])

We were on the tail end of the September eleventh tragedy, and that was a big positive to me, because I lived through that experience like everyone else on the planet and it was a very shocking, surprising, transforming experience, where you started communicating more deeply with strangers; strangers started to make eye contact. It felt like there had been some sort of paradigm shift, so immediately, as an artist, you're trying to interpret and process that experience for yourself. I happened at the time to be working on an espionage story and immediately became embroiled in reading everything to deal with this problem of how to protect our civil liberties. That's all I was thinking about at that time, so it was great to have a story that was an outlet but at the same time it was a little close to be making movies about. Then again, you're dealing with the other side of the galaxy, and it is clearly fiction.

MARY MCDONNELL
(actress, "President Laura Roslin")

We were so fresh from September eleventh, so we had a sense of our mortality as a nation, as a people. We were suddenly threatened. All of it was threatened. We understood what that was for perhaps the first time, even though I was old enough to remember "duck and cover." But as an adult I hadn't really felt what we felt that day. And that was in the script.

MICHAEL ANGELI
(co-executive producer, *Battlestar Galactica* [2004])

Right from when I read the script for the miniseries and saw it, I realized this was going to be an adult show that is dealing with the types of issues that we deal with every day. 9/11 was three or four years earlier, but it certainly did resonate. We talked a lot about that in the writers' room. The first time we all got together, we just sort of riffed on the zeitgeist and of course that came up. What I thought was really ahead of the curve is what we're seeing now a little bit: the possibility of a nuclear strike that could devastate the planet. And having people find a way to survive with our Agent Orange president. I went back and watched some of our episodes a couple of weeks ago, and it felt *so* relevant. It sort of transcended the time in which we created the show.

GRACE PARK
(actress, "Lieutenant Sharon 'Athena' Agathon / Lieutenant Sharon 'Boomer' Valerii")

The allegories to 9/11 were the key for all of us, because it was *so* fresh and it put us all into space where everything was a lot more serious, for lack of a better word, than, just, "Oh, there's an attack with a robot race and, ooh-la-la, we're running through space." That doesn't sound compelling, but the real world we live in is pretty scary. I don't know how it affected the evolution of the story, but it certainly affected the execution. I do think that the two races and the war between them brought a lot of resonance with genocide and racism; how we divide people amongst almost any line that we can think of. If it's race, it's race. If you're the same race, then we're going to do countries. If you're in the same country, we're going to do towns. Or religion. It's still the duality, the us-versus-them.

AARON DOUGLAS

The show's response to 9/11 was a little bit of, "Hey, World, let's stop lying to ourselves and take a look and see what we're doing to each other here. How many planes do you need to get flown into buildings before we all wake up and stop watching *Dynasty* and *All My Children* and *Law & Order*? Come on!"

MICHAEL RYMER

During the shooting of the miniseries, I kept saying to everybody in the cast, "You're coming to conclusions too quickly. Remember how long it took you to process 9/11? It took weeks before you even understood. It was beyond our imagination. This is what it's like for these guys." The miniseries is slow, but I love it for that in that it takes time to let the reality of that situation sink in in a more realistic way. It's quite different in tone, and a different piece to the series, where we start with "33." But in the way that 9/11 is the great mythological story of our life span, that was the goal, to try and touch that mythic stuff, which is why the rituals were so good—the funerals and the pageantry of their culture. We did a good job on that, because it resonates with people that, "Oh, okay, yeah, our funerals don't look like that, but I know what that *feels* like." The goal was to make something as gritty and real and adult as we could make it. To move away from the broad strokes of the cartoon sci-fi shows that we all love and bring it closer to *2001, Blade Runner* . . . the gritty, real good classics that we all admire and which are the reason we're in this game.

DAVID EICK

When I sat down with Ron, I was relieved to learn he knew how to do everything differently than it had been done before. Like I've said, he knew how to cut right every time *Star Trek* would cut left or whatever. We could talk about what that meant in terms of the lighting and the camerawork. "What did Rick Berman tell you that you could never do? Let's do that all the fucking time. What did he tell you you had to always do? Let's *never* do that."

RONALD D. MOORE

I got the call from David in January/February 2002. I was still on *Roswell*. *Dragonriders* had fallen apart, and David called and said, "What do you think?" I was intrigued, but it had been a while since I'd see the *Galactica* series, because the series wasn't available on VHS and it was way before streaming or anything like that. I just said, "Give me the weekend, let me go track down the pilot." So I went to Blockbuster and rented the pilot, watched it over the weekend. And watching it a couple of months after the 9/11 attack, it just had a completely different resonance for me than back in the seventies. I just saw the opportunity. I was like, "Okay, if I remake this now, in today's world and about this attack, and what it does to these people, and the questions that would come up, and the survivors—what they would do. And military versus the state authority. And freedom versus security. My God, this is an enormous opportunity and I could put in effect these ideas about shooting a new kind of sci-fi story and not having a big viewscreen, and not doing a captain's chair. Being more documentary-style in production and doing this naturalistic approach." I just got excited about it, and I said, "Okay, David. I'm in."

DAVID EICK

For a director, I called this guy Breck Eisner [son of former Disney head Michael Eisner]. I had done a drama pilot with Shaun Cassidy as the first thing in the overall deal I'd gotten. The pilot didn't get picked up, but I really liked Breck. I figured because his father is so deeply in the business, I'm sure Breck may know things about the original *Battlestar*. You know, he might have been able to inform some things.

So we all go home over the weekend. Ron watches the three-hour pilot. I watch *SportsCenter* and the Dallas Cowboys. We get back on Monday, Ron's done his homework, I have not. But this dynamic in a weird way sort of serves as a model for how we all end up working over the next four years, because, by knowing what the old *Battlestar* show had done, Ron was always going to have a sense of a wink and a nod, and even an homage to certain either structural or characters or just kind of thematic ideas that the old show dipped its toe in. At the same time, there would be a counterbalance to that, with no allegiance to any of that shit. Someone who didn't give a fuck about any of that, didn't understand any of it. And if it worked for both of us, meaning in terms of *Battlestar* and the "knower" and first-timer virgin, then we figured it was good. So that's not an excuse for not doing my homework. In a weird way, it gave us kind of a yin-yang advantage so neither of us were too inside it.

For example, when we got to the season-two *Pegasus* arc, which was greatly inspired by one of the original-series episodes ["The Living Legend"], it had to mature and evolve enough to work for someone who had no context for the old episode. And because that was the circuitous obstacle course any idea had to navigate, it meant that we forced it to be better than it might have been. So our version of *Pegasus* had a female antagonist who usurped Adama's authority, would be torturing—Abu Ghraib style—a Cylon prisoner. All of these kinds of things that spring from having a sense of what came before, but not being bound by it at all.

RONALD D. MOORE

The development process was relatively easy. Angela Mancuso, who was an executive at USA Networks at that point, was a big proponent of it. I pitched our take to her with David and Breck Eisner, who was originally going to be the director for the mini. The three of us kind of did the preliminary groundwork on developing the fundamentals of the show and how we were going to pitch it. We pitched it to Angela and she was like a bull terrier, man. She just went in there and fought for it and wasn't going to take no for an answer. Angela is kind of the forgotten player in all of the stories of how *Galactica* got made, because she really believed in the project. She fought for it and she just wouldn't let it go. She made it happen.

ANGELA MANCUSO

Bonnie Hammer, who's my good friend and at the time was president of Sci-Fi, finally got behind it and said, "Okay, we're gonna do this."

RONALD D. MOORE

When I went in to pitch it, they were like, "Yeah, we kind of want to do this. This isn't really where we want to go, but we're open to it." I pitched it to Bonnie Hammer. She was on a big TV; I was pitching in a conference room in L.A., and Bonnie was on the big TV. All of a sudden it's like I was in *Star Trek*, because I'd never done a video conference. It was really bizarre, because I'm getting distracted by seeing myself at the bottom of the screen. Like, "Am I leaning too far forward?" It was that kind of shit. But Bonnie liked it. I remember the moment that I thought I had her was the moment I said that we were going to make Starbuck a woman. I remember Bonnie specifically clenching her fists and going, "Yeah!" I was like, "I've got her," you know? She was intrigued by it and pulled in, even though the idea would be controversial to some people.

MICHAEL RYMER

I find it curious this controversy over Starbuck being a woman. It's quite bizarre. When the original show was made, in 1978, there were no women in the military, or very few. And now there are lots of women. There they are fighting wars and dying. We were watching it happen as we were shooting and they were very young, fresh-faced women.

ANGELA MANCUSO

The vision was totally Ron's. The only place I can say I honestly pushed was really wanting more diversity and strong women. Otherwise, a hundred percent of it was Ron.

RONALD D. MOORE

One of the first things I thought about when I was rewatching the original premiere was what to do with Apollo and Starbuck. One of the things I'd forgotten was, when the original show was starring Richard Hatch and Dirk Benedict, they were the stars. It wasn't Lorne-Greene-as-Adama's story with the focus on the captain of the ship. The stars of the show were the two pilots. So I was like, "Okay, what do you do with this relationship? What do you do with the straight-arrow son and his roguish, cigar-smoking, gambling, womanizing friend?" I was like, "Wow, that's such a cliché. I've no idea what to do with this. How do you possibly update this?" And the thought just occurred to me, "What if we made Starbuck a woman?" I just realized that would change *everything*. It would change the whole dynamic. She would be an interesting character. It was right at the point where we were starting to get familiar with the idea of women in combat in the United States. So it was kind of a fresh and new character to play with. That was an early idea that then came to be a big influence in the show.

I started looking at the old show and said, "All right, I'm going to keep everything that works and lose everything that doesn't." You know, aircraft carrier in space? Keep it. Civilian fleet? Keep it. Cylon attack? Keep it. The Adama family? Let's keep it Apollo as Adama's son. I think that works. That's a strong, interesting relationship. In the original series there's Athena, his sister, and as I looked at the original series, she had no real role to play. She just wasn't a vital character. She was in love with Starbuck and that was about it. So I quickly decided to lose that character from the show, because it didn't serve a purpose. They did have a Council of Twelve and a civilian president, but in the old show the civilian president was just such a stick figure that was always suggesting the wrong thing to do so that Adama could be smarter. I thought that there was an opportunity to make that a real character so that she could play the tension between the military and the civilian authority. I was fascinated with the idea of what the survivors would try to reconstitute as part of their society.

I really liked the idea of, once the Cylon attack happens and they were cut loose and there's only these people that happened to be on these ships, what are the aspects of their culture that they choose to hang on to? Do they try to maintain their democracy? Do they try to remain true to the concepts of their republic? What do they think of civil liberties in this context? Is it all just what Adama says? Is there any power to balance? I was fascinated with all of those elements that are of the series.

It was just one of those things where you kept finding more and more places to go. And you know, you just took this construct, but then you kept enriching it and finding more levels to it. It was just something so great about the premise, the fundamental jumping-off point of what the show was going to be. I did have an attitude from the beginning that the original *Galactica* was a missed opportunity. That it had such a dark, challenging idea at its core, but that it was forced to sort of become a popcorn show by ABC in 1978. The pilot is emblematic of everything that was good and bad about it. It had this dark premise, this apocalyptic attack that wipes out human civilization. Oh my God. But they go to a casino planet, you know? Therein lies the conundrum of the original show.

I felt that filmed science fiction started to become all popcorn. That it was all just silly escapism and that it had no relevance to the world I lived in anymore. And at that moment in time the world I lived in had just been upended, you know? The 9/11 attacks changed everything in so many ways. Suddenly we were in a long war that wasn't going to end for many, many moons. And we were passing things like the Patriot Act. It was just like, suddenly my world had shifted and I deliberately set out to comment on and talk about that environment in *Battlestar Galactica*. I was like, "This is going to be the format in which we're going to discuss those questions." And I was also pretty adamant that it was not a place we were going to get answers to those questions. I said, "These are really complicated questions and complicated issues, and my job on the show is *not* to say, 'Well, here's the easy answer.' Captain Kirk is not gonna show up at the end of the episode—or Captain Picard—and say, 'And here's the moral of the story . . .' It's always going to be difficult, it's always going to be ambiguous, and you're never going to be quite sure if our characters have landed on the right answer or not. But it's going to be in their struggle to find the right answer that you're letting the audience see." I just wanted the audience to be engaged and think about things in the world around them by allowing them to watch a show that took place in another place, another time.

DAVID WEDDLE

I saw the 9/11 reflections that made *Battlestar Galactica* such a very relevant show. But I didn't, at the beginning, see how much we were going to explore the issues that America was struggling with after 9/11.

MICHAEL RYMER

Look at the miniseries. The opening show very much describes where America was pre–September eleventh. We were very lackadaisical about any sense of threat. There was a lot of finger pointing that went on *afterward,* but the truth is none of us took any of that stuff seriously. We were caught off-guard. That's the world—they are pulling back on the military. They are closing the *Galactica* and making it into a museum. It's very clearly not a relevant force in the world anymore, because the powers that be have decided that there is no threat and the human race had disconnected its computer network so the Cylons couldn't compromise them. They said life's too hard now. It's ridiculous to deprive ourselves of the convenience and comforts of network computers for some paranoid right-wing vestiges from the past. That really struck a chord in terms of the parallel between that and September eleventh.

RONALD D. MOORE

Drawing analogies to 9/11 was certainly fraught ground, but I kind of felt like that was my job; what I wanted to do. And I wanted to delve into the emotions the audience was feeling, and their personal experiences, and put them into a piece of entertainment. The thing is, I never had serious conversations with the studio or the network about any of the political/socio stuff that we were doing in the show. They kind of gave us a pass on all of it, because everything that I'd always heard about the original *Star Trek* series—it's not real, you can talk about Vietnam and racism and all that crap because it's all Vulcans and Klingons and Romulans and no one took it seriously—was true. I got a similar pass. It was all Cylons and the colonists and I could do all kinds of things that gave the audience permission not to get upset about it.

The feeling was similar to *Deep Space Nine*. We felt like we were the red-headed stepchild that nobody gave a shit about. We were always struggling to get our pickup and our renewal. But at the miniseries stage, we just felt we were doing something different and something unusual. People say we're crazy, but we really think it's going to be amazing. And when I looked back at it and watched it, I was just really surprised and impressed by what we were able to pull off. We really didn't compromise, we really didn't bow to pressures and make it silly or tongue-in-cheek. I remember specifically there was a point after I turned in the draft for the miniseries to Ian Valentine, who was running Sci-Fi Channel at that point. He said, "We are never going to end an act with a child and the teddy bear with a nuclear weapon going off and destroying her and all these ships. That's never going to happen." I was like, "Fuck you. This is what we're going to have. We *are* going to do this." And sure as shit, we did. We just held to our guns. And then Ian got slowly wedged out and then Mark Stern came in, and somehow Mark didn't pay attention to it and it ended up in the show.

Complicating the situation on the miniseries was the fact that at the same time it was green-lit, Moore, who had started writing the project, received a phone call from HBO asking if he would be interested in running their series *Carnivàle*.

RONALD D. MOORE

Carnivàle at that point was just a pilot and they were looking for a show-runner. So I went in and interviewed with HBO's Chris Albrecht as a potential showrunner and talked about what I would do for the series, and this and that. At the end of the day, they decided *not* to make me the showrunner. They went with Henry Bromell, but they really liked me and they asked if I'd be interested in coming aboard as a consultant, so I said, "Sure."

So I joined the staff as a consultant, which meant I would probably contribute a couple of episodes, but I wouldn't be there every single day. In the meantime, I was writing the *Galactica* miniseries. So there was a period of time where I rented an office for myself in Glendale, and I was writing the *Galactica* miniseries, like, two to three days out of five. Then on the other days I would drive to Santa Monica and go to the *Carnivàle* writers room and participate in their story break and start writing my own episodes.

DAVID EICK

We pitched *Battlestar Galactica* and sold it, and then—I want to be clear—
Ron got a fucking office and took the stacks of notes written on cocktail
napkins and shit, and went in and broke a story. Broke a fucking outline.
And we obviously discussed it several times before he presented it, but when
it came time to go in a room and figure out how these great ideas became a
story, that was Ron by himself. It's interesting how the nucleus sort of got
narrower and narrower—shrunk and shrunk and shrunk as we kind of pursued it and narrowed it down. It was a really healthy process. We had gone
through the *Battlestar* script development together and the notes from the
network and that kind of stuff, but then it just sat there while they mulled it
over and debated it. It was there for months, believe me.

RONALD D. MOORE

What happened is that just at about the same point that I finished the *Galactica* miniseries draft, and it had been approved and they were going to
do it, and the show was getting green-lit to at least a miniseries, HBO, on
the other side of the fence, decided to make a change in showrunners. They
let Henry go and they asked if I would take over the show. It was an enormous opportunity to suddenly run a show for HBO. And the *Galactica*
thing was only sort of a pickup for the miniseries. It wasn't a commitment
to a series yet. So at that point in time I said I would run *Carnivàle*. I had to
step back from *Galactica* and hand off production of the *Galactica* miniseries to David.

DAVID EICK

I don't remember what the exact specifics of the situation were, but eventually, after we had been waiting, Ron was like, "Look, I've got to take this
other gig." The upshot was that, by the time we started shooting, he was
gone. I was sending him dailies. We would talk on weekends, and on the
occasion when we'd hit snags in production, I would do a rewrite and shoot
it over to him and hope that at night he would get to it. He didn't vanish
completely, but he wasn't able to be there for the production. He wasn't able
to be full-time on it.

RONALD D. MOORE

At that point I was still involved, but he was really the guy. He really produced the *Galactica* miniseries. You know, I chimed in from Valencia periodically and we had various meetings with production designers. I did all the script rewrites along the way, but they were sort of in my spare time while I was doing the showrunner duties on *Carnivàle*. But we had gotten a "go" on *Galactica*.

MARK STERN
(former president of original content, Syfy)

It's become part of the lore now, but when Bonnie Hammer heard that Ron and David were going to turn Starbuck into a woman, apparently she raised her hands in joy. But all of that happened prior to my arrival. Now, the reason they had hired me, and the reason that I wanted to go there, was I was excited about reinventing what science fiction was on television. I know it's grandiose to say that, but I wanted to do things that were different in terms of science fiction and not what had been done before. They were all on board with that and I was very excited to do it. At the time they had some fairly traditional science fiction on their air. They had *Farscape* and *Lexx* and *Tremors*. So, for me, it was really exciting to go in there and figure out what the next iteration of science fiction was going to look like, but the first thing they did was say, "Oh, we just green-lit this miniseries around *Battlestar Galactica*." My first reaction was, "Oh, shit."

I grew up on *Battlestar Galactica* and I love it in all its kitschiness. But the last thing I wanted to do was preside over this kind of old-fashioned space opera. It was like the antithesis of what we were talking about doing, so I was like, "Okay, great. So this'll be the last thing before we kind of get on to the new agenda?" Then I read the script, and I was like, "Oh, this is awesome." The script changed my mind. Plus the manifesto, their statement, of what they wanted to accomplish and how they didn't want it to be a traditional space opera. When I read both of those things, I was like, "Okay, we're on track. This is great." I got very excited about it and was on board.

The next challenge was getting a director and crew on board. The answer was found in the form of Michael Rymer, who had come off of directing the films

Angel Baby (1995), *Allie & Me* (1997), *In Too Deep* (1999), *Perfume* (2001), and
Anne Rice's *Queen of the Damned* (2002).

RONALD D. MOORE

We started with Breck Eisner at the beginning, but he left because, I believe,
there was a feature in development that got the green light.

DAVID EICK

He left to do *Sahara* with Matthew McConaughey, so we can make fun of
him for that. But when Breck left, we were without that third partner, and
that's where I think Ron and I really began to connect, because it felt less
like a forum or a committee and more like a partnership. So in a way it was
good to kind of force us to focus.

RONALD D. MOORE

But when it came time to do the miniseries, we were back to square one in
terms of finding a director.

DAVID EICK

Remember, at the time the name *Battlestar Galactica* suggested a cheesy
seventies show. I know its fans and disciples adore it, but if you mention the
title to a lot of people in show business, they would roll their eyes. It wasn't
exactly a great calling card to say, "We're looking for a director for *Battlestar Galactica*." On the other hand, we were a basic cable network. This is
2003 when we started sending up the flares. You're still many years before
the cable world was viewed or the off-network world was viewed as the land
where all your dreams come true. It was viewed as, "Oh, you mean it's
cheaper than if we did it for NBC? Okay, got it." That was about all it meant.
Cheesy title, cheap network, right? We were getting action directors. We
were getting *Star Trek* guys and guys who had done *Stargate* and anything
with the word "star" in the title, but nobody who I had any certainty or

promise was going to understand what we were trying to do, which is that we were taking this title and turning it inside out. Then, Michael Rymer came around.

MICHAEL RYMER

I had just finished *Queen of the Damned* and was in Los Angeles. From there I went into a TV pilot called *Haunted,* and I found the medium to be a very interesting experience. The rhythm of it was quite different and gratifying, and even though there was a lot of green screen in *Haunted,* there were certainly a lot of set pieces. Because I come from the indie world, I said to my agent, "No more special effects, no more action. I just want to do character stories. People talking in rooms. Relationships. Things like that, because those are my favorite films." And the first thing he sends me is *Battlestar Galactica* [*laughs*]. He just said, "Read it," which I did. I sat down one afternoon to read it and didn't put it down. It was a *really* good read. Ron Moore hooked me in completely, and that's sort of tricky when you read a lot of scripts. When I did put it down, I said to my wife and my friends that it was a strong character piece, the emotions are all there, that it really was what I was looking for. I was quite surprised by it. This is not your standard space opera. So that was pretty much it, but then I was not offered the show originally. I went back to Australia and got on with my life, working on my independent stuff. Then I got another call saying they wanted me to do it, so I was back on a plane for Los Angeles.

RONALD D. MOORE

David had seen *Angel Baby,* which Michael Rymer had written and directed. Then we had a great meeting with Michael and all got along really well. It felt like a really good fit.

DAVID EICK

On a project like this, you need a sounding board. It would have been a lot more catastrophic losing Ron if we didn't have someone like Michael Rymer there to continue working with me and working with the cast and crew. Just

SO SAY WE ALL

someone who was so like-minded, I think is my point. Could have been Ron left and I was stuck with some yo-yo. That would have been a lot more difficult.

TODD SHARP

Michael was a visionary, and in concert with Ron and David, they really crafted a beautiful vision for the show.

DAVID EICK

Rymer was a guy who had this interesting combination of a very high-profile sci-fi feature film. I know features always got the brass of the network excited if you could bring them a director who had done big movies. It was *Queen of the Damned*. It was the right genre and it was large in scope. The only problem was, it was a piece of shit, which Michael hated, because the Weinsteins recut it. On the other hand, Michael had this award-winning celebrated little indie film that had gotten him legit.

One of the earliest things he did was called *Angel Baby,* which was about these two homeless Australian people who were mentally ill and fall in love and get pregnant. I would *struggle* to find anything less applicable to *Battlestar Galactica* than that. Yet the movie was filled with humanity. It so compelled you to relate to this culture that you really didn't have any natural access to. It's Australia, it's homelessness in Australia. Don't really know what that's all about. All these different ways in which it could have been distancing, just like science fiction can be.

MARK VERHEIDEN
(co-executive producer, *Battlestar Galactica* [2004])

Michael Rymer brought a lot to the show just visually, but also in terms of thinking through the dynamics of character in each individual script. We had some other great directors, too, and they're the ones who had to figure out how to shoot an episode in seven days.

RONALD D. MOORE

His interactions with the cast, and the pilot, just formed so much of the fundamentals of the characters, and how they behaved and the style in which the show was shot; the way it was lit. The whole aesthetic of the show was something Michael brought to the party, along with Richard Hudolin, obviously, our production designer. But Michael was the man on the scene. He was really captaining all of that, and his relationship with the cast was amazing. They spent a lot of time together and he helped them form those characters, and so many of the actors were so very young and very green and very early in their careers. It's hard to overstate the importance of the work that Rymer did with them to craft those characters and make those relationships work.

TRICIA HELFER
(actress, "Number Six")

Michael is a part of *Battlestar,* because he was one of the people that started it. He directed so many of them and finally came on as a consulting producer. Even if he wasn't directing it, he had his stamp on it. Not only is he incredibly artistic and knows exactly what he wants, but he's extremely collaborative as well. He comes in knowing what he wants, but he also, sometimes to the crew's dismay, would really take time to discuss it with anybody in the scene that wanted to discuss it or had questions or had thoughts or whatever. The crew would be like, "Can we go home?"

We did extremely long hours on *Battlestar,* and he was all about making the best product and was one of the directors where his ego was out of it. If somebody had a better idea about something, it was something that ultimately became what we used. He was open to that. He wasn't somebody who would say, "My way, that's it." He was also somebody who would just come right out and say, "Now, that was shit. Do it again."

MICHAEL HOGAN
(actor, "Colonel Saul Tigh")

When you're doing a play, you rehearse for weeks and you do the play every day and you live in each other's skins every day. And a theater rehearsal space is the safest space in the world. It's like a cocoon. You make a fool of yourself, you laugh, you cry, you do it again. You try everything and it's safe, because nothing's going to go wrong. Rymer was kind of like that with the miniseries and with the work he did with us before. And he did it with "33," the first episode, and after that. So there's the dress rehearsal, and there's the first preview, where you're letting people come in and see this baby that you're creating, and by the time of opening, yeah, let's go. You can fly. You've got wings like a bird coming out of the cocoon, and away you go. That's what Rymer created for us on *Battlestar Galactica* and we were safe enough to do what we did there.

RONALD D. MOORE

Michael brought a strong visual sense. He really embraced the docu-aesthetic and a naturalistic sense of shooting it. *And* he's really good with actors. He really spent time thinking about each scene, talking with the actors involved in each scene. He's an actor's director, and so he really concentrated on that aspect of it. David and I impressed on him at the beginning that this was really a character piece. It was all about character, character, character. We had to believe these people. We're doing this character internal drama. There's a lot of backstory, there's a lot of jagged edges to these characters. It's a complicated story, but don't get lost in the sci-fi action aspect of it. It's all about the people. Michael really embraced that, and so he embraced the cast and worked with them intensively. So his work with the cast, and his visual sense as a cameraman and a cinematographer in his own right, gave it a certain dynamism on the screen. He was a huge part of the show. It was David and Michael and myself, the three of us. It was that chemistry that really sort of delivered the whole product.

DAVID EICK

We twisted ourselves into a pretzel to make the argument that he was right for it. That he could handle the effects and the scope, because he had worked on that canvas but he could also handle terrific performances and texture and detail and really create a world. Bonnie Hammer, the head of the network, to my surprise, was very supportive. I think she saw in Michael a name she could promote, meaning he'd done a big sci-fi movie and somebody who's worked on low budgets and so wouldn't have an appetite to only understand how to make huge and expensive.

He became critical to the process. He had done other movies about subcultures, too. He's a Robert Altman type, and very interested in diving nose-first into these subcultures and exploring them. He did the movie about the fragrance industry. He did a movie about modeling. He does movies about worlds. He would struggle over things like how the helmets would have to have a visible oxygen source, but somehow understand even without a big scene about it, would just intuitively understand how the ship moved from the landing bay and into the hangar dock and how the pilot would be removed from the cockpit and how the helmets would work, and how they would get down and how there would probably be three assistants who would gather around that Viper when it came in. Each of them would have their own job.

These are things that you'd say, "Well, that's what directors do." You'd be shocked at how many directors *don't* do that. They don't do their homework, they don't think it through, they don't have a sense of building a whole world where every detail is figured out. You get into the editing room and you start panicking. Michael just obsessed over how everything would work. The only thing we gave up on, meaning we obsessed about it for a while and then said, "Fuck it," was gravity. I think for a while we were pretty caught up in the idea that we would need a rationale, an explanation, some sort of exposition scene—an "Irving the Explainer" scene—where you say, "Here's why everyone can just walk around flat-footed and not be bouncing around like in the space station." Then we basically said, "Fuck it, who cares?"

Helping to bring the look of *Battlestar Galactica* to life was production designer Richard Hudolin, whose prior credits include the TV series *Profit, Stargate SG-1, Haunted,* and *Dead Like Me,* and whose inclusion was considered surprising to some, given that the intent was to avoid people who had operated within the sci-fi genre previously, out of fear of a familiar design aesthetic.

RONALD D. MOORE

I was involved with the production design and had met with a few different production designers, looking at different ways of going at it.

MARK STERN

Angela Mancuso was running the studio at the time. I had been there, I want to say, maybe two or three weeks at most. I walked into a meeting where they were talking about production designers. They basically had three different people in mind they were considering. The studio's position was, "All right, we're going to make a decision on one of these three designers, period." One of them had just done a sword-and-sandal epic, and one of them was an art director—not production designer—from *Titanic*. I can't remember the third, but they were all very much *not* right, in my opinion. I remember it being really intimidating, because here I am with the guys and the head of the studio, and I'm like, "Um, I'm not really okay with any of them." And it got *heated*, because it became a bit of a thing. I remember at one point I think David said, "Well, if we don't make a decision on this now, we are probably going to have to push production."

RONALD D. MOORE

Richard Hudolin came in and he had come off of *Stargate*, I believe. At first I was a bit skeptical, because I was trying to stay away from pieces like *Stargate*, but Richard had a very strong sense of design and was very enthusiastic, and I quickly got sold on him.

MICHAEL RYMER

Richard Hudolin was a bit of a genius magician. I don't know how he built what he built with the money and time that he had, but he and his art director, Doug Drexler, had this knack for just repurposing sets over and over and over, and rebuilding them.

MARK STERN

I had been a really big fan of Richard Hudolin's for a while, and in fact he had worked on this *Painkiller Jane* pilot, and I was familiar with him because he had also done the pilot for *Dead Like Me*. He had a really great background in this kind of genre. And so I said, "What about Richard Hudolin?" and they thought that was a great idea. That was my first real meeting on the project.

RICHARD HUDOLIN

I met with David Eick and Michael Rymer and we talked about the project. When I walked out of the room, David said to me, "By the way, we will need to see a presentation by January sixth." I turned around and said, "Are you nuts?" because it was, like, two days before Christmas. He wanted to see conceptual drawings for the battlestar *Galactica* and all the major sets. I took Christmas Day and the legal holidays off, and spent those with family. I had people in from out of town. They showed up and I said I would be at the studio and would be back in twelve hours, but it worked out okay. Myself and three others worked over the holidays at Lionsgate Studios. It was actually kind of strange, because there was no one on the lot. You would show up and there would be three other cars there and that would be it. So we worked over Christmas. On January fifth I flew down, and presented on the sixth. After everybody had their holiday, they were all nice and refreshed and I showed up. I showed them our drawings and concepts and they all bought into them.

In that first meeting, they certainly had some idea as to what they wanted, but I had only had one pass at the script at that point, so I was listening to what they had talked to their people about. I am like a sponge at that point, because obviously they had sold something to somebody to get the project up and running. I was listening very carefully to what they said they would do and what they would provide, and out of that mostly was coming that they wanted to see something that nobody had ever seen before. It was, like, stay away from any of the conventions of sci-fi and spaceships and control rooms and stuff like that. They didn't want to have things like a viewing window, for example, or a commander's chair. There were a number of things that sometimes weren't said, but it was obvious that they didn't want. So it was more a matter of what you leave *off* the screen as opposed to what you put on it. What I put on it was totally up to me and there were certain functions we had to address, but other than that it was do what you want; show us something that we haven't seen before so the audience will see it as something fresh and new.

Following that first presentation, Hudolin had to make a second one for Bonnie Hammer, whose comments, like those of the producers of the show, centered more around the unconventional.

RICHARD HUDOLIN

We got into a very interesting geometric form and formality in reference to some American architects. There were many subtle references to Frank Lloyd Wright; his attitudes and theories were applied to a lot of designs. You won't see it. In terms of the philosophy of the design, some of the subtleties you might notice if you knew the man's work and most Americans do, whether they know it or not. That was a big influence.

TODD SHARP

There was just such a connection between Richard and that show. He understood what Ron wanted and he lived it. And by the time we were done with the series, because we kept adding on little bits and pieces to sets, we had built so many miles of corridor around our stages. I, who had spent dozens and dozens of days there on the set over the course of the series, would get lost in the middle of that set. And not know how to get out, because it was so massive. Richard was a genius at creating modular sets, the ready room turned into the conference room turned into this room turned into that room. All of our sets with minor modifications would become a different set.

RICHARD HUDOLIN

With the CIC, when you start with the premise that you don't want it to be like anything you've seen before, you're left in a big scary void and you don't know where to go. I started thinking what is essentially the bridge as the nerve center. What we were trying to bring together was the physicality of the ship, the machine and Commander Adama and the crew—man and machine, basically. I tried to create almost an operating theater. It's in the round. It's got two levels, so you have the upper gallery and the lower gallery. Everything is focused to the center point. Usually in a set like that you are looking out to something. While in this they are looking *inward.* Adama doesn't even have a chair to sit in. He's constantly walking or he's at the central table and the table has its own lighting source. A lot of the lighting sources are coming *from* the tables and underneath.

It's got what I call the periscope above it, and nobody really got the periscope even in the concepts. I was saying it will come down, like a periscope in a submarine, and you can see space. Basically it's information from all the sensors around the ship. Until I actually showed it to them on the set during construction, and said we can drop this thing into frame on camera and we can present this—once we got it there, everybody loved it and used it constantly. But getting it there was the laughingstock of the show. Basically, like I said, it was like an operating theater in the round. I thought of Shakespeare in the Round.

One thing that did change was the degree of aging on the ship. Because the ship was going to be mothballed, they had pretty much restored it so it would be very pristine. It would almost look brand new, because it's scheduled to become a museum. As we went into building the sets and people would come up and look, they would say maybe it should have a little more aging; maybe it should be like the older rust bucket. So we went back and forth a little bit on that and found a compromise where we aged it a little bit. Some areas weren't so much aged, but others were. There was a concept at one point—prior to my involvement—where the ship was basically going to be *Das Boot* in space, but we went away from that.

In the design of the exterior of the *Galactica,* Hudolin worked closely with the late visual effects supervisor Gary Hutzel, a veteran of several *Star Trek* series.

RICHARD HUDOLIN

When I was presenting the interiors in L.A., Gary was presenting some exteriors. When we did the second presentation, we hit upon a design that he had in the back of his book and said, "That's it! *That's* the look we want for the *Galactica* exterior." They were basically going to maintain that pontoon kind of thing and integrate it into the design, but that was not the primary motivation of the design. The surface treatment is fabulous. It had a very thin feeling to it. It was very cool-looking, and I said to Gary, "I can work with that." We worked very closely on it, and I made a big effort to integrate that, especially into the hallways. So all of the hallways reflect this thin-like sealant. Gary and I talked about concepts and what the show would entail and how we like to work. It's such a collaborative industry. I can't imagine designing something that is not going to match the interior to the exterior. I would say, "Gary, here is what we are doing, just so you know and build this into your design." We did it on things like the transport ship. A lot of that is going to be the exteriors totally visually done. The interior we went to a location and then we did some work on the location. So his exterior has to reflect what we were able to find and what we were able to do with it.

There were about forty sets built early on, all of which were built at Vancouver's Lionsgate Studios. There were three stages that were "flipped" (in rotation for different sets). That last stage was turned into a green-screen stage where, among other things, cockpit work for the Vipers was filmed.

RICHARD HUDOLIN

We built the Vipers in a whole different way. We didn't use the traditional building techniques, the ribs and stuff like that. Our construction coordinator came up with a great idea. We drew them up and we'd get these huge blocks of foam that come in at four-by-four-by-eight-feet blocks. He would get a template from one end to the other, keep in mind that the Viper has that long sleek nose. Well, he cut that shape really quickly. Once we had the spaces cut, we would build some structure into it. It's easy to cut it out and split it and then put steel structure in it, because we have people in it. That's the easy part. The hard part is getting the nice finish. So we started with the nice finish and built everything else inside of it. We sprayed a hard coat over it. Sanded that and then you paint that and it comes out with the finish you need. You can drop this thing, you can throw hammers at it and it won't break.

For the miniseries, we built one complete exterior/interior, one complete exterior and partial interior so it could be a background ship. We built a partial Mark VII and that included the cockpit and enough of the engines behind it so you could shoot it without green screen and the nose. We did a shot coming into the bay and even though it's a partial, people would swear it's a full ship, because of the way Michael Rymer directed and shot it. We built a full Raptor exterior and interior that was actually flyable. We had a hundred-foot crane and we lifted it off the ground. It's actually based on an Apache helicopter. It's a surveillance ship. It goes out there and gets all the information, so it could be a little more clunky.

RONALD D. MOORE

The second-season episode "Valley of Darkness" was a tough one. It had Cylons board the ship and we're fighting up the corridor. It was on our standing sets, which helped. Doing a lot of action on a TV budget and on a TV production schedule is always really tough. And this one had CG Cylons on top of it. So I remember really struggling with all the logistical problems with this. You know, how much fighting could there be in the corridors? Trying to set up the CG Cylons and Centurions coming through the corridors. Where Lee Adama was going to be, where were the people that he was trying to protect. Then there were sort of practical problems in terms of filming the big standing sets of the *Galactica*—but we needed them to feel like multiple corridors on different decks and be able to track it coherently for the audience so that you could track, "The Cylons came in here, the good guys are over there, the bad guys are trying to get to this location," and do it all within the same basic run of corridors and ladders and actions that we'd had since the beginning of the show. And then you're fighting time and money: How much money is this going to be? How much stunt players and live firing all these weapons? It was really complex.

RICHARD HUDOLIN

The interior of the ship itself was based on the figure eight. Remember the scene in the miniseries where Kara is running? She's basically running a figure-eight course, and the camera guy just wanted to kill me, because I had designed it that way. It just took a lot out of him. But the whole figure-eight concept for the entire ship gave you continuous walks-and-talks and that kind of thing. And then the detailing was us getting in there and saying, "Well, what's that thing?" "Oh, that's an air scrubber, or this and that." It took a while, but I had the time to design it properly. I also had the talent of people around me who were really into it, and excited about it. A lot of people brought a lot of things to that design and that set.

The real challenge was creating a cross between military and science fiction, because we have so many years of science fiction now in film and television, that there are common things that people rely on to say, "Oh, this is sci-fi, right?" Everybody's trying to be a little different, but the military is the military and sci-fi is sci-fi. So I'd come up with the basic ideas, do some sketches, do some drawings of them, explain the whys and wherefores. But the thing is, this isn't a full-on army or air force of space kind of thing. This is a people thing. So the blending of the military, the people, and the space thing is quite difficult, and it takes a long time to do it. Well, it took me a lot of time to do it.

Like everything else, the visual effects for the show were intended to be different from the types of effects shots that had been utilized previously in the genre on television. The answer came in the form of Hutzel, whom Moore had known from his *Star Trek* days on *The Next Generation* and *Deep Space Nine*.

MICHAEL RYMER

It was a stroke of genius on David Eick's part, first for hiring Ron Moore. He just intuitively understood that everyone involved in this show was completely burned out on this genre. Not that there was anything wrong with them, but that vein had been mined pretty thoroughly, and there was a generation of very highly skilled people looking to push the boundaries in other directions. Ron and then Gary Hutzel fit that beautifully. Gary turned out to be a great asset, and *so* enthusiastic. He appreciated what we were trying to do more than anyone. This is his world and we were in a way opening up other areas that all visual effects designers could build on. I'm not saying we started anything, but we were trying to be part of a progressive thing.

GARY HUTZEL
(visual effects supervisor, *Battlestar Galactica* [2004])

I had originally worked with Ron Moore on *Star Trek*, and I had heard he was doing *Galactica*. I had originally heard about it when it was Tom De-Santo's production. I had actually talked to someone in his office at that time and they said they were not hiring a supervisor right now. And then that eventually just petered out. So I sent Ron an email saying hi, it's great to hear that you're doing more space stuff, hope things go well. He emailed me back literally five minutes later and said, "Send your résumé over immediately." So I did and met with David Eick and Michael Rymer and we hit it off, and all of us agreed as a group as to what was to come out of this. The new look, the new approach to the way the visual effects should be shown.

RONALD D. MOORE

Gary Hutzel came in sort of unexpectedly for visual effects. I had gotten a call from David saying, "There's this guy, Gary Hutzel, who we're talking about for VFX. He says he worked with you on *Star Trek*. What do you think of him?" I said, "Oh, shit, why didn't I think of that? Gary would be perfect." I had actually had early conversations with Gary about the handheld style and sort of naturalism-in-space approach, and he was really enthused about it. Gary had made the transition from model-based visual effects work to full-on CG, so he was really excited about the possibilities of what could happen in that staged reality.

MIKE GIBSON
(visual effects producer, *Battlestar Galactica* [2004])

Up until this time, visual effects were done like this: an establishing shot, especially in space, of a planet or a spaceship, and then maybe you've got some laser fire or some burn-ins, wire removal and whatnot. People were not making fully animated CGI characters that have their own personality. People were not making large fleet spaceships and then doing multiple dog-fights. You've got your *Star Trek*s, and that's where Gary comes out of. You've got to remember, Gary comes out of the miniature world, where you actually make models and you shoot them, and you light them, and you do multiple passes of them on film, and then you begin to composite these things all together. And one shot could be anywhere between fifty thousand and a hundred thousand dollars. So our show comes in at the right time, when the prices begin to drop to do CG.

So you go through this process and you break it down: What is the most important element that we can bring to help tell the story? One thing that Gary always said is, "We never fear the render." In the visual effects business, if you said, "Hey, we're gonna put a full CGI robot and it's going to interact in this scene, and we're going to have all these shots," a lot of people get a little nervous and begin to run from that, because it takes a lot of calculation of computers to put that together. So when we started, the pricing had started to come down, and when Gary would say "never fear the render," what it means is, "If you have to put that shot in and it's going to cool out for three or four days to render, well, we're going to wait, because we're going to get a really good shot." In a lot of our business, people will maximize, cut things out to try and reduce that time to make it manageable. "Never fear the render."

The other thing he said was, "Never fear the amount of shots. Never fear the volume of shots." When you go into any project, there's goals that your bosses have, like Ron and David and the Mark Sterns of the world, but you have to also have your own personal goals. Every season, Gary and I would set those goals out. The first season was that we needed to tell dynamic visual-effects-storytelling sequences. Not shots. So this gets back to old types of visual effects series, space series. We did not want to tell our stories with establishing shots.

GARY HUTZEL

Fundamentally, one of the things we were striving to do on the show is to go beyond the regular integration of visual effects, where all the set extensions have a great, natural look. The idea was to take the overall feel from the camerawork and style of the show inside the *Galactica* to outside the *Galactica* as well. Some of that falls into the purview of specific rules. There are no magic platforms for camera. We don't swoop through space. We are hitchhiking with other ships. We stay with the ships just as a chase camera would in a live-action show. So that changes the texture of a lot of what we were doing. Also, we were following real physics—we were not cheating.

ERIC CHU
(art director, Enigma Studios)

At the very beginning, *Battlestar Galactica* was going through many different approaches. At one point they were aiming for a rusty, old, smashed-up metal battleship kind of look. At other times they were thinking of giving it a very closed and antiseptic *2001* look. So initially our designs were quite close to the original show's designs. In the case of the *Galactica*, we started by doing an updated version. We experimented with the landing pod bays and how many struts it had—mainly cosmetic changes very similar to the way the *Enterprise* was updated for *Star Trek: The Motion Picture*.

GARY HUTZEL

Then they said, "Come back with a totally different look. We don't want to be that strongly related to the original design." Of course, there were considerations. The story was written around the original design, from the launching tubes to the landing bays and all of that. So we had to take into account all those elements.

MIKE GIBSON

We were drawing spaceship after spaceship. You had to give a nod to the original *Galactica,* certainly, because the design and the shape is amazing. But we also wanted to set it apart. One of the things that I find invaluable when you're working with a creative team and get into a kind of stumbling block, is walk away. Go think about something else. The facility is in Chinatown in Vancouver, so I said, "Let's walk down to the Vancouver Public Library and go to the art section and open up some books." And that's what we did.

ERIC CHU

We started with a trip to the library to look at different architectural styles. Specifically Frank Lloyd Wright and retro starting points. During my research I discovered a photo of a set of vases created by industrial designer Andrea Branzi. These vases, with their distinctive steel-ribbed exterior, were the inspiration for the new *Galactica'*s modernized surface treatment. Just as a suggestion, I scanned the picture into Photoshop and quickly put together a makeshift spaceship. At that point it didn't look anything like the *Galactica,* but more like a 1950s rocket ship. We showed it to the network and they jumped on it. They liked that a lot and once that was approved, then we started to pull it back. We used that same surface treatment, but tried to make it look more like the *Galactica* so the fans wouldn't kill us. I would say the new design looks quite a bit more industrial. It's much more military; more hard-edged.

MIKE GIBSON

One of the reasons we justified the ribs is if the ship took a nuclear hit, it was stronger. That the force of that blast would be taken over the whole superstructure of the ship. We were trying to build in a certain amount of science. One of the things that was always really important to Gary is that he would say, "Even though we're living in science fiction, let's try and make the science work as best as we possibly can."

The ship didn't change a lot. Besides the ribbing, we knew we needed to have retractable pods. Well, the retractable pods were kind of new, right? In the old *Galactica* from the previous series, they kind of hang out on the ship. We wanted the sense that, because when you deal with our world of visual effects, any time you can animate or move something, it adds life to it. Gary called the ships potatoes—that we didn't want it hanging there like a potato. We needed it to have its own language in its life. So the retractable pods became extremely important. The idea of the faster-than-light jumping, which did not occur in the original series. The idea of being able to jump through space and time—that these pods would come into the ship and then the ship would jump.

We worked very hard with David and Ron to create what the optical look would actually be. We didn't want it to look like *Star Trek* or *Star Wars*. It really had to have its own language. In terms of designing dogfight sequences, we watched tremendous amounts of World War II, Black Sheep, Zeroes . . . all kinds of airplane footage. That wing cam hooked on to the Vipers was a style that Gary was really developing with Zoic Studios, our partners up there for the miniseries and season one of the show.

Richard Hudolin and [art director] Doug McLean, from there their interior design of all the ribbing and whatnot totally began to jibe with what we were doing. Richard was an extremely giving production designer; his attitude was, "Guys, here are some things that I'm concerned about, but go with it and have some fun and come back." We had a little bit of liberty working with Richard. Working with some production designers, they want immense control over that. That was not Richard. Richard was like, "You guys do visual effects. That's not my business. I want some input, but go, go, go." He was an amazing partner to work with in terms of beginning to flesh out the visual style of the show and what the ships were going to look like.

Unlike the original series, no physical models were created for this production. Artists at Zoic Studios, chosen to handle the effects for the miniseries, used

3-D models built in LightWave to create all the computer-generated effects. Back in 1978, the model builders detailed the original *Galactica* miniature with pieces from various military, Earth spacecraft, and aircraft model kits. This intricate detailing—commonly referred to as "nurnies" in the industry—added scale and weight to a model when photographed. CG supervisor Lee Stringer, the lead modeler for Zoic, who also worked on the Tom DeSanto production, borrowed on those techniques by creating a library of CG model parts to detail the revamped battlestar and the fleet.

LEE STRINGER
(CG supervisor, Zoic Studios)

When you just do something in CG, often it's just too sterile and a little bit too precise. When you do a physical model, if a piece doesn't quite fit, you can cut it or twist or whatever. When you do it in CG, you can make it fit precisely, and that preciseness gives it a more CG look. One of the things we tried to do was not make it look quite so natural. So when we built the models, the area details were built from a lot of new CG model kit pieces thrown in here and there to give it that kind of chaos. That kind of randomness.

GARY HUTZEL

Fundamentally, I credit the director for that and, in all fairness, David Eick. David was a very strong proponent of embracing what was good about the original show. Obviously the *Galactica* was important, but the Viper was the ship we were most intimate with.

MICHAEL RYMER

Most spaceship shows are shot on very wide lenses, perfectly posed cameras. Our cameras are panning and crashing around the sky looking for Cylons.

On the advice of several CGI professionals, Hutzel approached Pierre Drolet, a 3-D modeler at Eden FX, about designing the series' signature fighter. As it turned out, the artist had already modeled a Viper for the then-in-production *Battlestar Galactica* Sony PlayStation 2 video game, and promptly emailed Hutzel the file.

GARY HUTZEL

It was a great rethinking of the original Viper. He had some of the elements that we had discussed, like multidirectional engines, already incorporated into his design. So this was a marriage made in heaven. When the art department built the full-size props, they took their own artistic license, so the ship changed quite a bit from Pierre's design, but still has all the same tones. It's not the departure I would have made for a spacecraft, because there is very little detailing on the surface, but the Viper plays beautifully.

MARK VERHEIDEN

We would ask for three ships coming together, and when we got it back from Gary and his team, there would be twenty. They would constantly amaze us. They did so many great effects, but the standout for me was in part two of "Exodus" where the *Galactica* comes through the atmosphere on fire. Just an awesome visual image, and I've got to give those guys credit. Some of them would say, "I'm coming in on the weekend just to add more, because we want the show to be better." Things like that would happen, and it doesn't happen often. The quality combined with the emotional place that it came in that episode was just so powerful. The effects were in service of the story at all times, and they were so dead-on perfect for what we were trying to accomplish. I think they hold up incredibly well. It's amazing how fast effects look dated, even when you look at movies from the early 2000s, but *Battlestar* effects hold up *really* well.

MIKE GIBSON

The show is called *Battlestar Galactica,* so the ship itself is in the name of the title. Therefore it needed to feel like a real living character within the show in terms of how Gary wanted to express flybys, how we wanted to express moving around the ship. All very important things. As well as the snap zoom . . . I'm going to call it verité kind of style. Once again, no one had really seen it. It kind of had been explored in *Firefly,* but taken to a whole new level as Gary really began to develop that aesthetic and that look.

GARY HUTZEL

When I did *Deep Space Nine*, I did dogfights sixteen ways from Sunday and at a certain point you have to step outside the parameters. The battle scenes on *Galactica* are very messy. They are very sloppy. You have cameras picking up the battle from obscure places. We'll be looking at the battle from a camera placed on a ship outside the battle monitoring what's going on and then cut into the midst of it, and *then* travel to the enemy lines. So what you end up with is something that fits into the style of the rest of the show, which is a very documentary kind of look.

David Eick wanted to be involved in everything. A lot of execs don't; they just want to hear about it. He wanted to know and he wanted to be informed at every step. He wanted to be involved with the actual designs of the ships. In fact, he was more involved with the designs than Michael Rymer was. Although Michael had a lot of great input as well, but he was like, "As long as it does this, this and this, you guys take care of the rest." So we had a great team going for that reason. It was literally the greatest collaboration I have ever experienced.

TODD SHARP

There's lots of good reasons to go with facilities for your effects, but what you're really doing is paying for overhead. You're paying for the real estate. You're paying for the coffee girl. You're paying for the other shows over there that are losing money for them. You're paying for lots of things at a facility when you're basically just paying for artists and equipment. But once you own the equipment, you never have to buy the equipment again. Now you're just paying for artists. There's huge economies of scale. You can see, as the series goes on, our visual effects numbers did not go up, even as the ambition of the shots that we were doing did.

RONALD D. MOORE

By the time we got to the season-one episode "Hand of God," that was a heavy visual effects episode. That's where Gary Hutzel was starting to slowly build the team that would be our complete *Galactica* unit. At the outset when we did the miniseries, Zoic did the balance of visual effects. We continued with them into the first season, but Gary started using other visual effects houses as well. He was also slowly building an internal team that would ultimately just take over all the visual effects work for the show, and you can kind of see the transition. We do start doing more and more visual effects work, and, ironically, the cost kept coming down and down. So you kept being able to put more of them into the show. And there was a huge amount of stuff in that show. There's a bit where Lee finds himself alone and he's sort of inside the Cylon base in his Viper. He literally stops the ship and is hovering, turning around and trying to figure it out. That's one of those things that people just don't do. There's no X-wing stops in *Star Wars*, because everybody treats them like airplanes, you know? So suddenly you see one of our supposed airplanes stop and hover and turn around; it's kind of startling and cool.

Every department utilized on the show was united by the desire to bring something unique to the mix, and that included cinematography. The miniseries employed Joel Ransom (*The X-Files, Band of Brothers, Taken*), though the series itself would be shot by Stephen McNutt, whose credits at that point included *SeaQuest DSV, Spy Game, American Gothic* (where he worked with David Eick), and *The Dead Zone*.

RONALD D. MOORE

Joel Ransom did the miniseries. If you look at the miniseries carefully, you'll see that we were still a little on the fence about it. Like the handheld quality of the interiors was not quite as aggressive as it became in the series itself. Because there was a sense from Michael Rymer of "I don't know how well this handheld exterior work is going to go." If the handheld quality of the fighters and the battles isn't that good and has to go more traditional, he didn't want a really huge disconnect between the interior scenes and the exterior scenes. As a result, the miniseries is a little more formal. It's not quite as aggressively handheld as where we went with the show, because no one was quite comfortable with, were we going to be able to pull off the exterior stuff? And then after the miniseries was done and we thought about what was possible in the CG world, then we went much more aggressively into that territory in the show itself.

MICHAEL RYMER

I hired a wonderful cinematographer, Joel Ransom, who had coincidentally just finished shooting the American version of the English miniseries *Traffic*. He had three operators, and the director would set up three cameras and shoot everything, and he would be crossing the axis. I sort of inherited a crew that was on their game. But capturing that documentary look is a fine line, because the network was very shy about the idea. *Firefly* was sort of a touchstone to *avoid* as far as the network was concerned, because it had done so poorly. I had watched the show and it was quite well done with a lot of good ideas and good things about it. Maybe the overarching concept of the Western in space is a little odd and audiences weren't buying it. Who knows why people didn't flock to it, but I thought that they had attempted some of the thing we wanted to attempt.

STEPHEN MCNUTT
(director of photography, *Battlestar Galactica* [2004])

I met with Ron and David and it was a nice meeting and they basically gave me the job. They were going to switch to digital, which is one of the things that was going on in the industry at the time. Everything at that time was still being shot on film, but what they didn't do was tell the network or the studio that they were doing this. Todd Sharp, who was the main guy on the studio side, said, "If you can shoot on digital and no one notices, you're the guy that we want."

Ron's a great friend of mine, and my first meeting with him was great, because I remember we were up at the Sutton Place Hotel in Vancouver and we were sitting there talking about the look of the show. He said, "I want it to be gritty. I want it to be dark. I want it to be edgy, and I don't give a fuck if I see anybody's eyes." And I said, "Okay, I can do that," because it's a need quite often—which is the failure of *Voyager* and the failure of the *Star Trek*s and the failure of television dramas—they demand that everyone look beautiful and everything is attractive to everyone. *This* was not meant to be that.

TODD SHARP

Although Joel created the look of the show, it's one thing to create that look when you have sixty days and multiple millions of dollars to shoot it. It's another thing entirely when you're making a show on an episodic basis for an episodic budget, to be able to achieve that look. That we have to thank Steve McNutt for. The man is a genius. Frankly, I don't know that we would have jumped headfirst into high-def television photography if it weren't for people like him doing what he did on *Battlestar*. By the way, that look he established— the grainy film look—he did that by boosting the gain and doing all sorts of tricks with light. There are a lot of shows on TV that look the way they do because Steve McNutt did what he did on *Battlestar*. I firmly believe that.

STEPHEN MCNUTT

Celluloid is a chemical process, so when you photograph it, you have to send it to the lab and process, develop, and print it, and the negative gives you a work print. They cut it that way. Whereas the digital world is all internal in the computer system, and the image capture is on a sensor, not on the film, so essentially you're not using the chemical base anymore, you're using the computer's ones and zeroes, and basically you're creating your images that way. That does change your approach quite a bit, because in the film world you're pretty much relying on your eyes and your meters. The other thing is that with film you don't see dailies until the next day, and quite often you're surprised by what you *do* see and you say, "That turned out really well," or "I wish I had done *that*." Whereas in the digital world, with the monitors what you see is pretty much what you get.

Taking on the role of editor of the miniseries was Dany Cooper, who had worked with director Michael Rymer on the feature film *Queen of the Damned*. She did not ultimately remain with the television series, focusing instead on feature films. She would be succeeded by Andrew Seklir and, then, Michael O'Halloran.

RONALD D. MOORE

Dany established the style of editing. You know, we weren't afraid to jump the line. The thing that Dany said to me that I always remembered was,

"This is the kind of show where we're on people's backs for really important lines." I thought that was kind of cool. Michael came up with the whole thing of the really supertight shots on Adama's eyes, his glasses. Dany would cut to Adama's hands randomly in the scenes. Or she'd cut around the room or just find something to look at. So her style of editing the show was very influential. We took her style and kept expanding on it.

MICHAEL RYMER

I remember when we were editing the miniseries and trying to get the show down for time; it was quite long and we had to lose some visual effects, like a dogfight sequence. We were all feeling extremely pressured about everything in the show, because we loved everything. So I tried to delete this dogfight sequence and it suddenly made the whole act feel more realistic, because we were staying with the politics and the circumstances of real people dealing with a real scenario. Suddenly the Buck Rogers part of it was removed, and it was just something much more real and grown-up.

RONALD D. MOORE

When I pitched the show, I wanted the sense of "you are there." I was obsessed with it at the time. With editing and photography, we emphasized in both of those worlds that kind of rough style where we weren't going to be too precious about continuity in between shots. It just had to feel like it was really happening and it was happening right now. That came from the handheld quality.

If you look at the second episode, "Water," that was the show that we kind of went too far with it. The handheld style was too jerky and too disorienting, and we started losing actors in too much shadow and had to digitally adjust. We had to try to take some of the shake out of the camera in post. There's a scene in the episode where they're in the conference room and Adama is talking and he's on his feet, and Eddie [James Olmos] just literally walked out of the light and walked into a corner where there was no light at all and we just had to keep it, because there was no other coverage of it. Eddie would just wander through set periodically and find a place that was sort of not expected, or the place that the actor should not be, and then he would go give a speech over there.

TODD SHARP

On the series, we had an editor named Andy Seklir, and he and coproducer Paul Leonard were able to work with this huge amount of footage. We were shooting shows that were extremely long. Michael Rymer is a very prolific shooter. He'll do a lot of takes and shoot a lot of film. To be able to comb through all of that and find the show, and achieve the creative vision as evidenced by the script, takes an adept post team and an adept editor. You'll find no better than Paul Leonard as a postproducer and Andy Seklir as an editor.

MICHAEL O'HALLORAN
(editor, *Battlestar Galactica* [2004])

I've learned an incredible amount about storytelling from Ron, and just the way he approaches editing is different than anyone else I've worked with before or since. He has this amazing ability to see the forest through the trees. Often on *Battlestar* in the editing room we didn't stick to the script all the time. We would change the script quite a bit in post from what the original was. If you saw some of the first assemblies, say where we actually reassembled it just the way the script is, the directors would come in and make some changes, but for the most part they stuck to the script, too. *Then* Ron would come in—and he's said this to me a few times—and he considers the edit the third and final rewrite. The first is the script on paper, the second being what they actually shoot, which changes somewhat from what is scripted. Then the third is the final rewrite and polish in the edit bay. There's quite a few episodes that I did that are dramatically different from what was on the page.

PAUL LEONARD
(coproducer, *Battlestar Galactica* [2004])

"Mikey O" was hired by us as an assistant editor season two. He assisted an editor on the episode "Scar." Ron Moore sat with her and Mikey to give some challenging and abstract notes for his producer's cut. I was busy with another session off lot and missed that meeting. The editor took too long to execute the notes and was putting the episode in jeopardy of not being completed in time for air. I ran an idea past Ron and David, then executed it. I fired the editor and bumped up Mikey to editor to complete Ron's notes and help lock the episode for air. I had sat with Mikey working on sequences before then and knew he had the chops to be an editor. We ended up hiring another editor to replace the one I let go, so Mikey went back to assisting.

MICHAEL TAYLOR
(co-executive producer, *Battlestar Galactica* [2004])

I was new to the show in the third season, and I was in the room with Ron when I had the idea for "Unfinished Business." There was a lot of tension on the ship, so what if they kind of blew it off with boxing? He liked that and said I should combine it with some flashbacks, and that was that. That became one of the best episodes of TV I've been associated with.

PAUL LEONARD

With "Unfinished Business" we ran into a similar problem. The script, although one of my favorites, was challenging, with the shifts between time frames and trying to find the right emotional balance to properly tell the story. The director, Bob Young, gave some notes remotely for his director's cut and wasn't able to join us in person right away due to other conflicts. I looked at the work in progress and thought it was completely "at sea." I asked Bob if I could put some fresh eyes on it for fear of never getting the episode where we needed in time for air. He, David, and Ron agreed, so I suggested putting the original editor on another episode and asking Mikey to start over assembling "Unfinished Business" from dailies.

MICHAEL TAYLOR

Michael really took it over and it was great. It was a very different experience than I had working on almost anything else. I think Mike would attest to that as well as an editor. It was a very organic writing process. We didn't write very detailed outlines. We wrote little short stories that sort of summarized the flow of the episode and the scenes and the character dynamics and then we just sort of wrote just moment to moment. Ron likes to say that you write an episode once when you write it and you write it again in editing.

MICHAEL O'HALLORAN

It was good, but wasn't great in the first assembly. A lot of it changed when I put the music in. We had all Bear McCreary's great music to use for the rough cuts. I put in more orchestrated stuff in the beginning for the first flashbacks where we see Kara and Lee lying down out in the grass alone. A lot of slow motion also is used. The first time I showed that version to Ron, he really took to it. I think it even inspired him a little bit and, in a matter of about twenty minutes, he laid out a completely different structure for it. He said, "Let's take this part here and we'll move this up front. We'll start with this. And then this part that is now the beginning, let's move that to the middle. We'll get to that some point in the middle." And he created this entire new structure and as he's leaving, he goes, "I really liked the music. Just make this whole thing a lyrically orchestral love poem." And I understood what he meant. I did that and that was one of the stories where I was cutting with the music as I went.

MICHAEL TAYLOR

Michael picked up the ball and ran with it and just really experimented with the whole vibe. I had been a big fan of movies like *The Limey* by Steven Soderbergh, which was a relatively straightforward, but wonderful, script by Lem Dobbs, but Soderbergh just chopped it all up and threw in all sorts of flashbacks and played with time. It just pulls you in in that much more of a lifelike, organic way. That's sort of what I hoped to do with that episode, because we were flashing back to begin with. It was just really cool.

MICHAEL O'HALLORAN

The first cut we were almost short. I think it was forty-three minutes, because we left a lot of stuff out that Bob Young had included. But he shot a lot of extra footage. When you have the extra camera there, he would make sure the guy, even though there wasn't a real plan for it, would shoot angles and things that might be useful later. Then, when I finally did Ron's lyrically orchestral love poem, it came out to something like sixty-eight or seventy minutes. There was an extra thirty minutes added to it. A lot of that was playing out beats much longer than we would ordinarily do. Ron also told me, "Don't worry about the time." Usually, especially on a network show, we have the exact time of whatever it was, forty-three minutes and forty seconds. Once he told me not to worry about it, that changed everything, because then I was free to just make a movie out of it. Eventually, of course, a lot of that stuff had to come back out, but what we ended up with was so much stronger than what we started with.

When Roslin and Adama are smoking pot, she starts talking about how she wants to build a little cabin, a nice place to retire. That wasn't in the original. That became a thing he referred to several times later in subsequent episodes. In the final episode, "Daybreak," they obviously weren't going to build the cabin, because she was too sick, but that was their hope—that he was going to take her off and go settle in their little cabin together by the stream.

PAUL LEONARD

His work was so good on the editor's cut that Ron asked home video to include the editor's assembly in the box set. We gave Mikey the full promotion to editor for season four. One of the directors he worked with in season four was Anthony Hemingway. He clicked with Mikey and ended up suggesting to George Lucas that Mikey edit *Red Tails*, the feature that Anthony was prepping. Ron Moore stepped in with a hearty recommendation, and Mikey was off to the races.

MICHAEL O'HALLORAN

I owe Paul a great debt of gratitude always for that. Ron was very much, "Oh, yeah, of course, let's move him up. Love Mikey," but it was Paul that put the thought in his mind. Paul took a chance and, thankfully, it paid off.

TODD SHARP

All the pieces came together in terms of the crew. The one hiccup was that we had hired one of my favorite go-to producers, Michael Joyce, who worked in features. He had produced *Raising Cain* and *No Escape*. He was an executive at Fox on *The Abyss* and *Die Hard 2*. So we brought Mike in, and about four weeks before we hit camera, he became ill and had to leave the show. So here we are without a captain at the helm in Vancouver. We're on the ground, prepping at the studio in Vancouver. We're building sets and ships and we don't have a producer. I actually reached out to an old friend of mine, Harvey Frand, who I had worked with a number of times. I called Harvey and basically said, "Help us save the day," and he came in. Everything instantly clicked; it was like Harvey had been there all along.

HARVEY FRAND
(producer, *Battlestar Galactica* [2004])

My agent called me to say that a script for the miniseries was being sent out to my house and I had a meeting with Eick and Rymer at 9 A.M. the next morning. I fell into a deep despair, because I remembered the original before Ron Moore reimagined it. Had my career fallen so far so quickly? By 10 P.M. the script had not yet been delivered. I called my agent, who somehow tracked it through Universal Transpo, who claimed it was left at my door at 9 P.M. I went outside with a flashlight and by 11 P.M. discovered it in my neighbor's flower bed. My agent said that I should just read the first two hours. I couldn't put it down. I read the whole thing and couldn't put a script down for the four years. And that's where it starts—with the extraordinary material. Add to that a cast with incredible talent and a crew that I've never met the equal of.

DAVID EICK

There were many times Todd Sharp came to the rescue for *Battlestar* in a whole host of categories, and he happened to know Harvey. So this guy comes in, he's got a strange sort of limp and, because I've already lost a guy to illness, I'm worried. I look at his résumé and we start talking and he's an odd character. He doesn't look the part, meaning he kind of looks a little more blue-collar in his general countenance. He doesn't behave like a slick guy who's done a lot of Hollywood stuff, which actually appealed to me, and he seemed to really understand the material. So from a creative standpoint— "Wow, this would be so great and I love it"—but also from the standpoint of, "How the hell are you gonna do this?" So I appreciated the fact that he seemed to have a real passion for it and I appreciated the fact that he wasn't bullshitting me about how hard it was going to be to pull off.

So I asked him two questions: Can you commit to me that I will be the first call when there's a problem and not the studio? He said, "Yes, that's how I always operate." Which is how *I* operate. We're a team and we don't go around each other and all that kind of crap. The studio, of course, loves access to its line producers, because they figure that the executive producers are going to bullshit them and they want that end-around relationship. And, in fact, that end-around relationship winds up having to exist just as a function of time and efficiency. But what your line producer says, and how he says it or she says it, is crucial. Because if you have a line producer who's trying to lay a lot of blame and cover his ass, that's when the exec producers start having trouble with the studio, but if your line producer's on your side, you don't have to worry what he or she says to the studio, because you know you're controlling the information.

The second question I asked him, because he hadn't worked in about five years, is *why*? "I'm looking at your résumé, and it's been a while . . ." He says, "You know what? It's cold out there." I knew I liked this guy.

MARK VERHEIDEN

I can't say enough about what an amazing person Harvey was to work with, but also what an amazing conductor of this orchestra he was, keeping everything working together on this really tight schedule. We had some advantages in that most of *Battlestar* was set-bound and that makes life a little simpler, but it was still a good, complicated show. A lot of moving parts. A lot of actors. Where on a lot of shows the line producer will tell you something is impossible, we can't do it, forget it, Harvey was the guy who said, "Well, that's going to be challenging, but you've got to keep that because that's the core of the episode." He was an enormously important piece of the *Battlestar* family, and it's tragic that he passed away. An amazing guy.

RONALD D. MOORE

He was one of the best line producers I ever worked with. A genial guy with a real backbone of steel. There was a gentleness to him and a sense of humor.

He smiled and laughed pretty easily and was easy to get along with and very personable, but unyielding when he had to be. He could really whip the production schedule into shape and draw lines with departments when he had to, and wasn't afraid to say no to directors and push back. He pushed back with me at times. Not in a bad way, but he'd be like, "Ron, we just can't do the show. It's just not possible. I just can't do it." And if he said that, I knew he meant it, because he wasn't one of those producers that just sort of cried wolf all the time and threw up his hands. I've run into a fair number of those kind of producers, where they're just, like, "Oh my God, the sky's falling every week and the episode's out of control. What happened?" After a while you start filtering that out. Harvey wasn't that guy. He'd look at a script and go, "Well, it's big. We'll have to make some changes here, but we'll figure it out." He was always up to figuring it out in one way, shape, or form.

DAVID EICK

It was an unlikely assignment. I never would've looked at or met a guy like Harvey Frand and thought that he could've helped us realize a show like this—and I say this out of ignorance. But I learned a lot about how *not* to do that through my relationship with Harvey, because not only did he do a good job of bringing it on budget, but the only time my phone rang was when it was urgent. Unlike many line producers, he didn't feel the need to justify his existence by reporting every micro accomplishment of his day. That's a disease some line producers suffer from. The other promise he kept was to love the show, and you can't fake that for four years, twenty episodes a year.

TODD SHARP

Harvey was the producer of the miniseries and, of course, we brought him back for the series. He worked his tail off. He was like the train engineer, the school guidance counselor, the voice of reason, the adult in the room. The one who would tell Ron and David, "You can't do this." The one who would tell Ron and David, "I can't afford this, but we're going to figure it out, because I love what you're doing." He was the one who would roll up his sleeves with David and Ron and figure out how we were going to put this gigantic show into the box every week.

HARVEY FRAND

The miniseries was hard. We were creating a new world and we banged heads often. But mostly because all the departments cared so deeply about the show. I particularly remember a network note that we age down the CIC. Mark Stern came to check the set and Eick hid to avoid a confrontation with him. When he hadn't heard from me after several hours, Eick called my cell phone to ask about Stern's reaction. When I told him Stern was giggling like a little kid, Eick came out of hiding. There were a few other times we had issues, but we worked together for years and the head banging decreased but not the passion. It's a world and journey we all shared.

DAVID EICK

It was just so evident in so many ways where he went the extra mile, went overtime, got in trouble with the studio—he knew he'd get yelled at. But when faced with those decisions, I felt like he *always* chose the show. Before covering his ass, before saving another nickel, before whatever. That is *so* rare in men and women who do that job. That job tends to invite people who maybe struggle to be creative, or people who maybe struggled to not want to cover their ass. Harvey was not only someone we didn't have to keep an eye on, but was someone who really kept an eye on the show for us.

When *Battlestar Galactica* went into production, there were two very different visions of what was being created. For Sci-Fi, it was a miniseries: a standalone event that could potentially be revisited if success warranted it. For Ron Moore and David Eick, the view was that this was a pilot for a new television series, and that's the way they approached every aspect of it.

RONALD D. MOORE

Sci-Fi was saying that *Galactica* was a miniseries, but David and I planned it like it was a pilot. That meant we would establish sets that would then later be used in the series. We'd set up the characters that would later be in the series. Even though the network wasn't making any promises, we looked at it as the beginning of a series. We knew the miniseries story was going to be about the Cylon attack and the escape of the *Galactica,* and the end of it was going to be, "and we're heading to a forgotten tribe that went to some place called Earth."

In the miniseries, it's established that the Cylons were created by Man. Intended to replace human soldiers on the battlefields of the Twelve Colonies, they came to resent their masters. Fifty years ago, they rebelled, starting a decade-long war that ironically united the Colonials together under one flag. When the Cylons suddenly ended the war and disappeared deep into space, the battle-star *Galactica* became a relic of an era when humans feared technology.

On the fortieth anniversary of the Armistice, *Galactica* is being turned into a museum (a concept that Moore initially came up with for the starship *Enterprise* in the "All Good Things" series finale of *Star Trek: The Next Generation* and appropriated for *Galactica*). Her commander, William Adama, is about to enter retirement. Lee "Apollo" Adama, Commander Adama's estranged son, is assigned to participate in *Galactica*'s decommissioning. Lee is unwilling to forgive his father for the accidental death of his brother, Zak. Kara "Starbuck" Thrace, *Galactica*'s resident hotshot pilot, was engaged to Zak and has become a surrogate daughter to Commander Adama. Lee has a tense reunion with Kara in the brig, where she's held for punching *Galactica*'s alcoholic XO, Saul Tigh. Secretary of Education Laura Roslin is also on board for the ceremony, despite her recent breast cancer diagnosis. Belowdecks, Galen Tyrol (*Galactica*'s deck chief) is in an unauthorized relationship with Sharon "Boomer" Valerii, a rookie Raptor pilot. Their affair is overlooked because of the impending decommissioning.

On Caprica, Dr. Gaius Baltar is one of the leading proponents of advancing artificial-intelligence technology. The Cylon War is forty years in the past, and he believes that it's time for humanity to move on. Baltar is responsible for creating the Command Navigation Program, a networked defense system that will automate many functions in the Colonial fleet. A mysterious blond woman was instrumental in the creation of the program, and in return he gave her access to the defense mainframe. She reveals herself to be a Cylon agent just as the first nuclear bomb detonates outside Baltar's window. The machines have evolved to take on human form, and of the twelve models, she is Number Six.

The Colonial fleet is disabled by Baltar's CNP code, and unable to repel the attack. Only *Galactica* survives the onslaught, saved by her antiquated technology. Boomer and Karl "Helo" Agathon are forced to land their damaged Raptor on Caprica, where they recognize Baltar among a crowd of refugees. Helo gives up his seat for Baltar, and Boomer reluctantly leaves him behind. Baltar's overwhelming guilt is manifested in the haunting form of Number Six, a specter visible only to him.

Galactica retreats to Ragnar Anchorage to rearm. There, Adama discovers Leoben, another of the humanoid Cylons. After Leoben is killed, Adama consults with Dr. Baltar about uncovering other Cylon operatives in the fleet. Baltar's "Head" Six prods him into accusing Doral, the public-relations director for *Galactica*'s museum. Meanwhile, Roslin, forty-third in line of succession, is sworn in as the new president of the colonies. She and Apollo gather the surviving civilian ships and rejoin *Galactica*. Adama plans to attack the Cylon force, despite the overwhelming odds. Roslin believes that, to survive, humans have to start having babies. Adama ultimately, reluctantly agrees, and announces that they're crossing the Red Line into unknown space. They're going to find the home of the fabled Thirteenth Tribe—a place called Earth.

Roslin calls Adama on his bluff. He doesn't know where Earth is, or if it even exists. As *Galactica* travels toward an uncertain future, a group of Cylons converge on Raptor Anchorage. They find Doral waiting, ready to report on *Galactica*'s movements. Baltar's test turned out to be accurate, but another Cylon agent still lurks in the Colonial fleet: Sharon Valerii (Boomer) is also a Cylon.

For Moore, the moment he began seeing dailies from miniseries footage directed by Rymer, he recognized that everyone involved was achieving everything that he had envisioned.

RONALD D. MOORE

There wasn't a big difference between David [Eick] producing and me producing. I was really impressed by what he did on the miniseries. I mean, he truly realized everything that was in the show and then more so. I was at *Carnivàle,* and one day this big box came to the offices, and in this box were, I don't know, fifteen or twenty VHS cassettes of dailies of the first week of production, and I went, "Oh my God, here we go." And with great trepidation I put it in the VCR and turned it on, and the first thing I saw was Katee Sackhoff as Starbuck jogging through the *Galactica* corridors, and I was just *there.* I was like, "Wow, this is even better than I thought." He totally got what we were going for. We were so on the same page of what the vision of the show was, the realism of it, not making it hokey sci-fi, really being honest with it. Michael Rymer was dedicated to it. What they produced, I don't know that I would've done any differently in that miniseries. It set the tone and set a marker for really what the show is.

That being said, one of the early ideas jettisoned was the notion of doing split screens during key moments, particularly during dogfights.

RONALD D. MOORE

I was afraid that the dogfights were still going to look a little too traditional. That they were still going to look like what *Star Wars* had done twenty years before. So I was playing around with the idea of split screens; here you'd have one corner of the frame being in the cockpit, one would be out on the wing, another would be from the enemy's point of view. And you would just play them simultaneously as a way to reinvent the dogfight. As a result, there was a lot of time and energy spent in editorial trying to pull that off, and ultimately couldn't. We decided to side more on just the docu-style hand-held approach in space battles, and treating ship and the fighters as true spacecraft as opposed to fighters. Because what George Lucas had done in the original *Star Wars* was treat them all like airplanes. They were all sort of like World War II fighters going at each other, and we said, "No, these are spaceships. A Viper can clip around and shoot backward while it's traveling forward. You know, don't tie them to aerodynamics in the atmosphere. Make them spaceships." And that, combined with the style of cinematography and the advancement of CG, was enough to make the dogfights fresh and bold and different without doing the sort of elaborate split-screen idea that I had originally. So that had already gone by the wayside.

I'd like the show to take credit for really inventing that style of photography, because I see that used a lot now. There was a TV show called *Dogfights* that was CGI re-creations of classic World War II, Korean War, and Vietnam-era dogfights. And they were *all* using this sort of handheld photography that we did in *Galactica* just a couple of years before. I think people just got into it, because they kind of realized that it did draw you in and it did make it feel real to the audience in an intuitive way.

Once the miniseries went through production and was waiting for its airdate, there was a growing sense of apprehension over how it would be received by the television audience, as well as by fans of the original ABC show, from which the new series diverged substantially.

RONALD D. MOORE

A big moment in the life of the show was, what were the ratings going to be on the miniseries? Traditionally what had happened—or what used to happen—was night one of the miniseries we have one number, and then night two would be a lower number. The big question was, how big of a drop-off is there on the second night? Now, there'd already been a test of the miniseries in Houston, where they had brought people in as the focus group, showed them the miniseries and done a whole focus group on it, and they *hated* it. I mean, they, like, *really* fucking hated it. The cover sheet said something like, "This is one of the worst testings we've ever had. We see no reason why you would want to pick this show up as a series." And analytics were even worse. They sort of liked Eddie Olmos as Adama, but he was the only one, and even *that* was kind of a mediocre number. Sci-Fi went into a full-blown panic, but they were already so pregnant with the show. The show was done. We were completing visual effects. There wasn't much they could really do. We were only a few weeks away from broadcast, so they were kind of screwed. It took all the air out of the momentum of the show. Sci-Fi was essentially at this point saying, "This is a fiasco. *Fuck.* Let's hope it's not a total money loser." It was kind of that attitude at that point.

MARK STERN

Nerves before it aired were enormous. You have so much money and time and effort and resources put into something like that. It was the first big project of the new regime, as it were. It was the first big thing that I had taken on. It was a big statement, I think from Bonnie to the rest of management. I want to say it happened right after we'd gotten bought by GE, so there's a lot of corporate stakes there as well. And just everything you feel when you're mounting a big tent pole like that, and you're hopeful that people will show up. And, you know, there's a certain amount of whistling past the graveyard when everyone's just kind of not talking about it. Or they're looking for all the scraps of sunlight that they can find.

RONALD D. MOORE

We went into the ratings conversation on the miniseries with a sense of, "Oh, if we could just get a good number. It's our only hope." Night-one numbers come in. They're okay. They're fine. Now, what's the night-two number going to be? And the big surprise was that the night-two numbers *went up.* And it was shocking. No one had ever seen that before, and no one had a case to compare it to. No miniseries ever went up in the second night. So that changed *everything.* Suddenly you were in a different conversation, where there's a possibility that ordering the show to series was really on the table.

But there was so much head-scratching about how the test was terrible and people hated it, yet the numbers went up. The critics were positive; they didn't warm up to it as they did later on in the run of the show. The critics on the initial broadcast were good, but it wasn't acclaimed. I remember there being negative reviews, mediocre reviews, and then some very good ones. But it wasn't really until the show was on the air and had the weekly series that we started to really become a critical darling.

DAVID EICK

Even before the press got a hold of it, we knew the miniseries was a success, because we had a big screening at the DGA and everyone came and you saw it on the big screen. You'd have to contort yourselves into a stage of phony humility to not acknowledge that it was definitely a pretty successful piece of work. Of course, by that point in time I had already been through all kinds of despair over the cut and the split screens and all of that. The first time I watched it I had asked my whole family to leave the house for the weekend, so I could writhe in pain and hit my head. But that's just me. I just didn't know how to watch it. It's not because of anything that was necessarily bad or wrong about it, but, just like anything else, it needed a lot of work. It was four hours. It was something like fourteen million dollars. You open up a first cut of something like that, you're opening up a big old can of worms. There's no getting around it, but after all that work, we knew we had something really good. How it was going to do, we didn't know. And whether anyone would agree with us, we didn't know.

Prior to the airing of the miniseries, Moore and the new *Battlestar Galactica* most definitely found that they were not the critical darling of fans of the original series or actor Richard Hatch, who had been actively trying to get a continuation of the original series off the ground when word came out that a reboot was in the works.

Much like the fictitious journey to Earth, the route back to prime-time television for *Battlestar Galactica* was a tortuous one. Although throughout the 1980s Glen Larson vowed many times, "*Galactica* will return," it wasn't until Richard Hatch, who played Captain Apollo during the program's original run on ABC, produced his own trailer for a new series that a serious revival campaign took shape.

Hatch, long the series' sole champion, created a trailer prior to the Tom De-Santo/Bryan Singer–proposed version, titled *The Second Coming*, which he hoped would prove to Universal the amount of interest there still was in the property to pick up where the original series left off. Although Hatch did not own any rights to the series himself, he spent more than $50,000 of his own money to complete the two-and-a-half-year project. Yet despite the fact that *The Second Coming* played to standing ovations at various conventions around the globe, the studio remained firmly apathetic.

RICHARD HATCH
(actor, "Captain Apollo")

When I was going to do the *Battlestar* trailer, I had people laugh in my face at how stupid that was, and I heard rumors about people in the industry laughing at me. Who would spend money on something they don't own? But they don't understand the value I got and the love and the feeling of accomplishment and the learning and the growth that came from believing in something so much that you are willing to go the distance. I have never in my life done something like that; I'd always wondered if I would ever love something so much that I would be willing to step into the fire and step out of my comfort zone and risk it all. It didn't happen at once, but it was a step-by-step process and before long I realized that I believe in this so much that I was willing to do *anything* to make it happen. To bring it back.

SCOTT MANTZ
(film critic, *Access Hollywood*)

There's been so much talk over the years that they were going to revive *Battlestar Galactica*, and then Richard Hatch made it his mission to the point where he created a trailer. He even had Richard Lynch and John Colicos in it, and a bunch of dumb, hotshot Viper pilots. It was a pretty good trailer for a show that hadn't happened yet.

RICHARD HATCH

I didn't set a budget, but I maxed out my credit cards and spent something close to $50,000. I never intended to spend that much; it started off as a small thing that grew into a big thing. I remember shooting at a big hangar where they used to have the *Spruce Goose,* but being the neophyte that I was, I didn't realize that a location is wonderful but then you have to light it and dress it, and this costs money. Then you have to fill it. It was one monumental challenge after another. Filming these eighteen-to-twenty-hour days with no sleep and everyone singing songs and having the best times of their lives, because they are part of a new *Galactica* project, was the most extraordinary experience of my life.

I thought, "My God, we're just doing a presentation in order to demonstrate to Universal what can be done with this series." Obviously I couldn't sell it and I couldn't make money from it. It was just a presentation, and we kept thinking we could just continue and make the whole movie and just show up at Universal and say, "You may hate us, but here it is. Take it or leave it."

Toward the end of production of the trailer, word got out that Glen Larson had heard about what Hatch and company were doing and started claiming he had all rights. *And* that there were plans for a movie focused on the battlestar *Pegasus* (to be produced by Todd Moyer, who at the time was producing the film adaptation of the *Wing Commander* video game). Hatch contacted Larson, questioning why he would want to do a film based on the *Pegasus* storyline rather than *Galactica,* all of which became a moot point, as the critical and financial failure of *Wing Commander* ultimately resulted in the project collapsing.

RICHARD HATCH

We didn't challenge them about doing *Battlestar,* but they didn't want to do the original show. We spent two and a half years at Universal putting the trailer together in order to lay out our case for doing the original show with the original actors plus a new generation of our kids born in space, all serving as a bridge between the past and the future and demonstrating how we could bring the show back. And here's Glen Larson coming in saying we're going to do the *Pegasus* story and we are not going to use the original cast. From there it became a fan war in all the publications.

And then, a couple of years later, as information on the new *Battlestar Galactica* series reached the fandom, there was a growing anti-reboot fervor growing among them, not unlike the fervor of the anti-*Next Generation* fans who had said about the fledgling series in 1987, "Without Kirk, Spock, and McCoy, you don't have me."

RONALD D. MOORE

The script for the miniseries had leaked, and there was a lot of fan reaction about making Starbuck a woman. You know, "What are they trying to do?" Glen Larson, who I didn't have a lot of happy feelings for, came out and said, "They're just doing a show with a lot of dirty words in it." What the hell does *that* mean? A lot of dirty words? So it was a fan backlash that we were starting to get, which I didn't really care about because I knew that the *Galactica* fan group was a pretty small one and I was convinced that what we were doing was going to work.

MARK STERN

There was some concern on our part about *Battlestar Galactica* on the Sci-Fi Channel, that people would say, "Oh, it's just another Sci-Fi thing," and it was going to feel limiting to people. There was also the other side of that, which is people were *not* going to come because they remembered the old one. And then there was the concern that the people who did remember the old one wouldn't come because they don't want to see it reinvented. There *was* a relatively big outcry—certainly from the fanboys and the fan base—about turning Starbuck into a woman. In fact, we had a panel at Comic-Con, a small panel in one of the smaller rooms, the summer before the miniseries aired that December. So not a lot of people really knew about it. But there was a whole conversation about how people were going to throw popcorn at the stage, because I guess Ron had made some comment about the old version being very popcorn-y. They were going to protest the Star-buck thing and we were like, "Man, we have this real potential to alienate *everybody.*"

RONALD D. MOORE

I got this invitation to appear at Galacticon, which was going to be at the Universal Hilton about a month before the miniseries was on the air. They invited me to come. It was a con put on by Richard Hatch and some other people that was dedicated toward celebrating the original *Battlestar Galac-tica.* So they invited me to come talk about the new one. And let's face it: I kind of knew I was going into the lion's den on this, but I said, "I want to take a bunch of clips." I wanted to take the entire first act, but Universal wouldn't let me. So I pulled together five or six minutes of material from the miniseries. Full scenes, like the poker scene where Starbuck punches Tigh, and the first battle. Some other key scenes. Cobbled them together in a five- or seven-minute piece.

DAVID EICK

I didn't attend the convention, because I thought, "Fuck those guys." I said to Ron, "I think it's great you're extending an olive branch, but I think they're going to throw it right back at you. I don't know why you'd want to hang around those people, but have fun."

RONALD D. MOORE

So I got up onstage at Galacticon. I was with Terry [Dresbach], she was my fiancée at that point, and was still trying to figure out what the hell I was involved with. We were in the elevator and there's a guy, a gigantic man in a homemade Cylon suit, and she's looking at me and going, "Where are you bringing me? What *is* this?" We go into the main hall and I go up onstage and I said, "Well, this reminds me of a scene in *Patton* where Patton gets up in front of the crowd and says, 'I just thought I'd stand up here and let you people see if I'm as big a son of a bitch as some of you think I am,' which got like virtually no laughs. Maybe a couple of titters. Not much. This is *not* a friendly crowd. I said, "Well, let me show you some clips. No one has seen these before. This is exclusive to you, and then we'll talk about it afterward." So I brought the house lights down, played the show, played it all the way through, and then the house lights come up and they booed and hissed. They really did. I'm not making it up. I'm like, "Holy shit." And then it was, "All right, time for questions." So I'm taking questions from the audience and they were unremittingly hostile. Didn't like it, thought it was an affront, thought it was an insult to the original show and terrible. And they *hated* Starbuck.

I'm fielding questions as best I can, and at some point somebody got up and finally said, "Well, I think you can see our reaction and our feelings about what you've done. If you actually go to series with this, will you make a commitment today to do a show that's more in keeping with the *Galactica* that we know, and that we love, that would be a true *Battlestar Galactica*?" And I said, "Well, how honest do you want me to be?" And suddenly people are yelling, "Be honest! Tell the truth!" And I went, "Well, the truth is, no. If we do the show, it's going to be *this* show. You don't have to watch it and you don't have to like it, and that's fine. But this is the show we're going to do."

Now people are *really* upset and they're standing up and they're yelling. Suddenly, out of nowhere—and I hadn't even noticed him in the audience— Richard Hatch stands up like Moses and goes, like, "O children of Israel." Everybody shuts up and he's standing in the audience and says, "Look, this isn't what I would do with the show, but this isn't fair to Ron. He's our guest here and we have to treat him with respect. I don't like the things said today, but I just think we have to stop this. You know, he's an artist. It's not my vision of the show. I really disagree with some of the things he's doing, but this isn't right." And it just took the wind out of the audience and it was an amazing thing.

RICHARD HATCH

I was producing the twenty-fifth *Battlestar* anniversary convention for mostly the original fans at the time, and they were very angry that I was inviting Ron Moore. It was a very, very difficult convention, because of all the controversial feelings, and people had gotten bags of popcorn to throw at Ron Moore because Ron had made a statement—he'd taken so much criticism and had gotten a little frustrated with everything—and said, "If you don't like it, throw popcorn" or "eat popcorn" or something like that . . . I can't remember the exact wording, but I was sort of terrified that they we're going to throw this popcorn at Ron.

RONALD D. MOORE

Later, I went backstage and met Richard for the first time in the green room. And I said, "Wow, I really appreciate you doing that." He was like, "Well, I meant what I said. I mean, I really don't like what you're doing here; I don't think it's the right way to go. But that just wasn't cool and I just couldn't stand that."

RICHARD HATCH

I didn't change my mind. People mistake changing your mind. To clarify that, I have always been for a continuation. I think the most viable way of going with the series would have been a continuation. If I was Universal I would have even hired Ron Moore and Tom DeSanto and those people to do the continuation. Because I think Ron Moore is an incredible visionary, a talented, gifted writer. The only difference would have been, he would have kept the same backstory. He would have evolved the story forward twenty-five years. And then you could have evolved the Cylons and you could have got into the cutting-edge, provocative storylines that the new show [did]. But you would have had a continuation. That would have been the difference and obviously, that was my preference.

But they, Universal, made a decision not to do that. So for me, it wasn't about being against the new show, because I didn't know what the new show was. It was always for the original continuation. But I always was fighting to get into the darker, more provocative storylines, getting into the struggle to survive in space, getting into the *meat* of what *Battlestar*'s story is all about. But we couldn't do that, the network [ABC] wouldn't let us. I was always frustrated as an actor and also as a creative artist. I felt it was such a great story, but we were *barely* touching the surface of what that story was all about. The network, the studio, everybody was afraid of science fiction. Everybody was afraid of rocking the boat. Everybody was afraid of getting too deeply into something that might alienate somebody, so they played it very safe.

RONALD D. MOORE

When we were backstage at that con, I said to Richard, "You know, I have a lot of respect for that. I really admire you. If we actually do get picked up to series, I want to talk to you about appearing in the show." He says, "Well, we'll see. Let's just talk about that when the time comes." So I just kind of filed that away in my head, and once we got picked up to series, then I was going to find a place to bring Richard Hatch into that show.

DAVID EICK

There was a time, not too soon before hiring Richard Hatch, when both Ron and I would've absolutely scoffed at the idea of bringing *anybody* from the original *Battlestar* into the show. We were trying to stake out our claim, because we knew the fans of the old show didn't like what we were doing anyway, and some of the stars of the original show had said really nasty things about what we were doing, so we were like, "Fuck them." We'll have our nods—we designed the *Galactica* to kind of evoke the original, we kept the Viper sort of the same, we reinvented other stuff. We thought, "We're nodding enough; we don't need to be bringing in Lorne Greene's daughter or something." You know, give me a break.

RICHARD HATCH

Battlestar Galactica has played such a huge part in my life, from playing Apollo in the original version up to the new version, where I would get to play one of my most challenging and favorite characters ever: the complex and unfathomable Tom Zarek. It is rare in an actor's life that he gets the opportunity to play two such diverse characters in the same story so many years apart that not only speak to the heart of who I am as a human being, but who I have become as a result of the trials, struggles, and tribulations that follow all artists in their journey to find meaning and their place in the world.

DAVID EICK

When Ron came back from that convention and said, "Look, I spoke to Richard Hatch, and I think we should offer him a job," it was still a shock to me. But at that point in time I could see some wisdom in it. I could see that this guy, who's been the most outspoken about this version of *Battlestar,* and Starbuck . . . whatever his name is; Dirk Benedict . . . was just sort of nasty and dismissive, but Richard Hatch had tried for years to do his own version. He had made a short and tried to pitch and sell it. He wrote novelizations and did a bunch of conventions, so to me it almost became ironic. And then I started to love it, because I thought if we get the most outspoken critic, the guy who was the most vociferously against what you're doing, to be on your show, that's so insidious and underhanded that I love it. It's like we went and robbed their bank.

I think Ron had very different reasons for liking this idea. Mine were probably much more childish and subversive. I loved the idea of subverting all of that nasty blogosphere stuff about what we were doing by taking one of their own.

RONALD D. MOORE

When Richard *did* appear on the show once it went to series, I think it absolutely changed the view of some of the fans. The thing about it is, it could've gone either way. If he had been a rallying point for the fans as someone from the show saying terrible things about it, it could've really kept a core group of people that were opposed to what we were doing. I don't think it would have affected the sense of the show overall, but there would've been more of a negative core to some elements of the fandom. But Richard's endorsement and participation in it, and then advocacy of it, I think went a long way toward just saying, "Hey, look, they're not shitting on the original. They're just saying, 'Hey, we're doing a different version of it,' and they're actually trying to celebrate the original in some ways." And everybody just kind of got on board. There's that moment in the miniseries where the ships are flying to the original theme. I never wanted to pretend that it was completely original. I'd always wanted it to be *Battlestar Galactica.*

DAVID EICK

After the decision was made about Richard, and we're on set, I'm *terrified*. Now that we've gotten past the schadenfreude of it, now I'm terrified, because not only do I not know if this guy can act, I'm pretty sure he can't. I mean, I've seen enough little bits of the original *Battlestar* that I was like, "Well, that doesn't really even apply to what we're doing." And then you look at his credits and go, "Well, what has he done that speaks to an ability to just be naturalistic and real and vulnerable? And to kind of be able to sustain what we're doing with the rest of the show?" You know, to not be in another movie the whole time. But I've got to tell you, I was there for a great deal of his first episode, and during that time I'm kind of getting to know Richard Hatch. And what I'm discovering is that he's *really good*. Much better than I would've thought.

Richard and I talked about the character that day, but I think he knew or sensed that we were naturally going to be worried that he wouldn't be able to carry this kind of material. I could tell he was very intent, asking the director, "Is that too much? Do you want less?" He was aiming for naturalism and minimalism. And I thought, "He's here to be a team player. He's not here to sabotage, he's not here to badmouth, he's not here to just show us up. He's here to be a member of the team and really try to make this good." I just developed immediate respect for him, right then and there.

KATEE SACKHOFF
(actress, "Kara 'Starbuck' Thrace")

Richard had the most uncanny ability to make whoever was standing in front of him that he was speaking to feel like they were the most important person in the world in that moment. It was absolutely beautiful to watch, and he truly cared about every single person he came in contact with and what they were doing with their life, and he was interested to hear about it. He wanted to talk to everyone, because it motivated him to keep working.

RICHARD HATCH

This epic and profoundly moving story called *Battlestar Galactica* has always gone light years beyond its deceptive moniker and sci-fi nomenclature, delving deeply into the human condition and exploring mankind's greatest strengths and weaknesses. As an artist, I have always been just as interested in the story as the characters I'm asked to play, and the underlying story and subtext of *Battlestar* has provided me a powerful opportunity to look into my own soul and learn the most difficult lesson for all of us: to not be afraid to explore, embrace, and forgive our proverbial dark side, our flaws and imperfections, which we all have and need to come to terms with if we are to fully utilize our God-given talents and find our true path in the world.

RONALD D. MOORE

He was a true believer and *really* trying to get a new version done. So this was a blow to him. I understand that, and I can't say enough about what it takes to then stand up and protect me from that crowd, and then to come all the way and be on the show and be an advocate for it. He had an investment in *not* going that route, and he was able to sort of change his mind and embrace what we were doing. I give him a huge amount of credit for that.

DAVID EICK

From my point of view, during his first episode I was watching Richard and Jamie Bamber very closely, because I was worried about it. But I thought Richard was very gracious to Jamie and vice versa. I thought they didn't tiptoe around each other, but they both really seemed to be sensitive and compassionate about the other's awkward position to each other. I really respected Richard for that, because I thought it would've been easy for him to come aboard and then find little ways to undermine the job that the new Apollo was doing. I'm sure that would be the obvious soap opera version of what could happen. The fact that none of it did, and I never even sensed that it got anywhere near that, is a real testament to both of them, but I think particularly to Richard, because he had the harder job there.

RONALD D. MOORE

To be honest, I felt that Richard really stepped up his game a bit, and he was embracing this character that I think was just complex, dark and kind of different. Certainly completely different than Apollo, and different than other things I'd seen him play. It was a complex character, and I think he enjoyed finding those darker corners and playing against his own type, and the image people had of him as a person and the characters he had portrayed. Suddenly he got to play a villain, a charming one, and a guy with levels and smarts and running circles around other people. I think he just really enjoyed it and I was always really happy he was on our show, which is why we kept using him. It *wasn't* because we wanted to keep getting the PR value of it. The PR value was in the first one, and the subsequent episodes it was because we started really liking having him on the show. We could do more with Zarek, and Richard would be fun. As writers, you just started looking forward to things you could give him.

Things did not go as smoothly with *Battlestar Galactica* creator Glen Larson, who had tried over the years to relaunch the franchise himself and was fairly vocal in his disdain for the new series, despite the substantial fees and screen credit he was receiving for the reboot.

RONALD D. MOORE

I had no interest in direct interaction with Glen during development of the show. The first time I had any awareness of him was when I started reading things that he was being quoted as saying. You know, the show was being developed and he was starting to say snarky things about it, which I thought was kind of shitty and not cool. So I had a sort of predisposition. I would ask, "What is it with this guy? Like, we haven't even talked and he's already slagging on us in the press."

DAVID LARSON
(son of Glen Larson)

That show was my father's legacy. Ron didn't make an arbitrary decision to change Starbuck into a female, but that was an iconic character for my father. To just say we're going to gender-swap, we're going to do this, we're going to move this around, and we're going to change some of the mythology, was painful for him. I imagine any author, any writer, would have the same instincts. You want to protect your story.

RONALD D. MOORE

The biggest thing that stuck in my craw was he arbitrated for credit on the miniseries writing. If you look at the miniseries writing credit, it's not written by me. It's written by me and "Christopher Eric James." It's Glen Larson's pseudonym. And what happened was he actually took things to arbitration with the WGA that he wanted part of the credit. I thought, "All right, yes, I'm adapting the original." My point of view was, "I'm perfectly happy to give Glen complete story credit. Let him have the 'story by' credit, but I think I deserve the teleplay credit, because nothing in this script has anything to do with the original." Glen felt otherwise. So it goes to arbitration committee and somehow they agree with him. That's the decision I have to abide by and that's fine. So the final writing credit was shared by him and me. But what stuck in my craw was that after he wins the fight, he doesn't put his own fucking name on it. So it's not written by Ronald D. Moore and Glen Larson, which at least sort of would acknowledge the roots of it and my contribution versus the creator. It's my name and some other guy's name, which makes it look like I was either rewritten or someone else contributed in some way. I never quite forgave him for that. My speculation is that he was hedging his bets. Like he thought it was a piece of shit and he didn't want his name associated with it, but he wanted to cash the check. With *Galactica*, I always tried to talk about what we owed the original and that our show would not exist without it. I never took anything away from Glen, but when he took something away from my writing credit, I took that personally.

After the success of the *Battlestar Galactica* miniseries, a new waiting game began on whether or not it would be picked up as a weekly series. And during that process, neither Moore nor Eick could afford to sit around idly while corporate decisions were being made.

RONALD D. MOORE

We had a very troubled, very difficult first year on *Carnivàle*, which taught me even more about running a big, giant, complicated show. By the time that year one was over, I had had such an unhappy experience, I didn't want to go back. And Sci-Fi hadn't quite made up their minds whether they were going to do *Galactica* as a TV series, but they *were* willing to offer me a deal—an overall deal to be at Universal. If *Galactica* did become a series, they would have a deal there and would I take it? I said yes. So I left *Carnivàle*, went to Universal, and then took my chances. I wanted to see what was going to happen. I was there for a few months before they ultimately pulled the trigger. It was a lot of drama back and forth in the interim period where I was on that deal. You know, are they going to make the *Galactica* show as a series? Are we not? How much money was it going to be? It went up and down and up and down. David at that point had gone back to being a studio executive. He wasn't a producer anymore. But ironically, because he *was* a studio executive, then he was able to work the inside track to make the *Galactica* series happen, and *then* he could go back to being a producer again. A lot of machinations in those days.

DAVID EICK

While we were waiting, I needed a job. I got hired to be the senior vice president of the cable division of Universal TV, which means that I was suddenly reporting to Michael Jackson [the British studio executive, not the musician] and I'm able to work on the cut of the miniseries in my spare time on nights and weekends, and quietly whisper into the ears of the people who were going to be picking it up to actually pick it up with an understanding from my immediate supervisor that if I got it picked up, I could resign and go make the one-hour series.

RONALD D. MOORE

I can tell you that while I was at Universal waiting for them to pick up the show, for a brief period of time I went off and did a couple of scripts for a show called *Touching Evil,* which is a cop procedural based on a British show. So, suddenly I'm doing cop scripts while I'm waiting for *Galactica* to get picked up. It was just Maril [Davis, Ron's former assistant who now runs his company] and I in an office at Universal waiting for a word, and meanwhile we were farming me out to other shows. And David Eick's working on the inside to kind of get the show made.

There was a moment when it did not look like Sci-Fi was going to pick it up, and UPN got involved. UPN was saying they were looking for a science fiction series. They'd seen the *Galactica* miniseries and were possibly interested in picking it up to do a series. This is like Christmas. David calls me and he says, "Okay, there's a shot at UPN, but if UPN is going to pick it up, they need to have the first script in January. Could you just write the first script of the series by then?" I was like, "Uh, okay, if I have to, I will." But at that point there was no outline. There were no stories. There was nothing. I had written the bible for the show and I had also written loglines for potential episodes. Just literally one-liners of things that could've happened. In one, there's a serial killer loose in the fleet, and Apollo and Starbuck have to find out who it is. There's an uprising on a prisoner ship that they have to put down. The fleet has to keep jumping every thirty-three minutes, because the Cylons keep chasing them.

I looked at the loglines and I thought, "All right, I'll do the '33' idea, because that's just kind of intriguing." And it's the only time in my career I've ever sat down with a blank page and just started writing. I didn't break the story. I didn't write an outline. I didn't get it approved by anybody. I sat down and started writing from "fade in," and I just wrote the script. And it was an amazing, wonderful experience I've never been able to replicate. Where I just wrote one scene to the next, to the next, to the next, just in the spur of the moment, and wrote "33." And I loved the episode. I loved it in its first draft. David was blown away and they were all convinced. Sci-Fi liked it so much that then it kind of tilted the balance to pick up the show instead of letting it go to UPN. It was amazing. Suddenly we had the first episode. No one had even approved it; I just started to live with it.

DAVID EICK

With *Battlestar,* when we had Ron's first script, "33," I just knew at that point we were going to have to try to fuck this up. If Ron can dash off with relative speed our first episode, and it's this fucking awesome, there's no way this thing's *not* going to work. But, again, at this point I'm working for the studio. I report to David Kissinger, and Michael Jackson is our boss. I have a lot of face time with Michael Jackson, and after seeing the miniseries' ratings, he says, "Pass." Kissinger's telling me, "Dude, you've got to let it go. He doesn't think the ratings were good enough. He thinks the show's budget looks too expensive." Eventually he says, "Okay, if you recast the whole thing, I'll let you go make a series."

RONALD D. MOORE

It did come to a point where we had a meeting with Mark Stern at Sci-Fi. He had just kind of taken over the network at that point and they were saying, "You know, we are seriously considering picking up *Galactica* to series, but we probably want to recast the show with cheaper actors." We were like, "No," and they said, "What do you mean, no?" "If you don't want to use the original cast, then we don't want to do it." And they were all kind of, like, "What are you talking about? Are you crazy? Come on, you don't really mean that." We responded, "No, we really mean it. The cast is a huge part of the show. Letting go of Eddie and Mary for God's sake, not to mention anybody else, and doing a cheaper version of *Galactica* with subpar actors is out of the question. This is the cast." And they *really* got kind of upset and were annoyed, but we just held our ground, because there was no way we were doing it without them.

DAVID EICK

First of all, the idea of recasting is asinine. Second of all, half our cast was already Vancouver dinner theater players who've never worked before. How much cheaper do you think it's going to get?

TODD SHARP

The way it works is that the network pays the license fee and the studio finances the rest. And, even though we got adequate funding for the miniseries, the network was used to paying a much lower license fee and doing shows that were in the million-dollars-an-episode range. It's unfathomable now that TV costs anywhere between three and six million an episode. That was a time when Sci-Fi was making ambitious genre television for a million, two million, or three million an episode. And that's what they wanted to make *Battlestar* for. I'll take credit as the guy who would say to the network, "If you want to make this show, it's going to cost you X dollars. If you're going to spend less than X dollars, don't make the show, because we cannot do it justice. We cannot deliver every week what people will expect based on the miniseries." They had already aired the miniseries before they made a decision to go to series. God bless 'em, the corporate gods went out and found a financial partner.

DAVID EICK

When it looked grim and like we were just not going to get there, this woman, Belinda Menendez, the head of the international TV group, said to me, "Hey, I can make a deal with Sky [TV in Britain] where they'll pay four hundred thousand dollars an episode in exchange for world premiere rights on Sky in the U.K." I was like, "Well, will Jackson allow the studio to have a worldwide premiere in another country?" She said, "Well, he's leaving anyway and it's the U.K. where he's from." The whole scheme completely worked.

RONALD D. MOORE

Premiering in the U.K. market before it premiered in the U.S. market was really unusual. But they were able to put up a big chunk of money, and it bridged the gap between what Universal and Sci-Fi were willing to pay and what the show would actually cost. When they stepped up and made that offer, Universal jumped. David made the deal happen and they got it. So as a result, the actual premiere of *Galactica* was in the U.K. by several months. So back then you started seeing the reviews from people who had seen it in the U.K. first, and there were certain piracy issues with people pirating the show. It was the beginning of all that stuff on the internet.

DAVID EICK

Once the deal was made and Jackson said, "Okay, you've got a show," I promptly sat down with David Kissinger for lunch and resigned. He thought I was nuts, because I had this brand-new deal as a senior VP at a studio. He was like, "You're going to walk away from stock options and a car allowance and free insurance and all that for thirteen producing fees?" I was like, "Yup." By that point we had Ron's script for "33," and I just knew there was no way I was not going to at least give this thing a fucking try. It worked. They picked up the show and I quit. Oh, and one footnote: By that point in time, Ron had left *Carnivàle,* and suddenly the only way we could make *Battlestar* is if we have an overall deal with Ron Moore. I made him an overall deal to come back to the studio so that I could quit and join him in working on *Battlestar.* That thing was *so* incestuous.

RONALD D. MOORE

I look back at that miniseries, and I'm really impressed by what we did and the boldness of what that vision is. It's just still kind of mind-blowing what we got away with. You know, everything from the building of the characters and the world before the big attack happens. The style of how we shot it, the quality of the acting. It's just all of those pieces are just phenomenal. The music and the set design and the visual effects . . . I remember watching it again and going, "Wow! We just captured lightning in a bottle from the very beginning," and how just fully formed an idea this was. Looking back on it, I just remember that spirit of, "We're all in this together." That was always on the show, and always on the set, where we just were such believers.

SECTAR THREE

BATTLESTAR GALACTICA (2004)

THE SYFY YEARS

11.
THERE ARE *STILL* THOSE
WHO BELIEVE

"Let's get this genocide started."

Having achieved what seemed to be the impossible—taking a short-lived sci-fi show from the 1970s, with all that that era for the genre in television suggests, and reimagining it in such a way to make it one of the medium's true standouts by which all others would be measured—the *next* challenge was to figure out how to do so again, week after week, year after year.

RICHARD HUDOLIN
(production designer, *Battlestar Galactica* [2004])

While I was designing the miniseries, I said to Ron and David, "Look, are we going to series or is this just a one-shot deal? 'Cause I'll design and build it differently if it's for a series." "Oh, it's definitely a one-shot. No problems there. One show." And then they came to me, really late on, to make the changes in the drawings and said, "What do you think about storing some of this stuff?" So we stored a lot of it. We didn't store the monitors and all that kind of stuff, but the bulky pieces, complicated building pieces, we stored. And that's a couple of warehouses. Anyway, we finish the miniseries and it did very well, apparently, and I get a call later on, I don't know how many months later, "What do you think about doing a series?" Naturally they called me, because I was the guy who took it all apart, so I would know how it went together. They said, "Give us an estimate of what it'll take and we're gonna do a series." I said, "How many are you doing?" "Thirteen." Well, holy Christ! So off we went and set it up again.

We had to get all new monitors, and this time it was going for a longer run, so you're buying stuff, right? You're not just renting all of it. The thing is, we shot the mini on thirty-five-millimeter, so we fired up all the monitors in the set. And it looked like a jukebox, because digital in those days wasn't as good as it is today. So I had to have our painters come in and wax down all the monitors, to crush the colors. It took three or four months to put it back together, and it was a lot of money. And then we continued on. And the greatest thing was having the run that we did. It was a dream job, because everybody was smart. Everybody was talented. They parked their egos somewhere else and had a great time. The writing was fantastic, I have to say.

RONALD D. MOORE

(cocreator/executive producer, *Battlestar Galactica* [2004])

Probably the difference in the series, when I got involved as the showrunner, is that now I'm the writer. And the writer's involved more day-to-day on an ongoing series than the mini. On the mini, it's more like, "Here's a big movie," so you can hand it over to the producer and director, because it's a one-off story that's taking place from here to there. When you get into the series, now you're dealing with not just the needs of this particular episode, but the needs of *all* of the episodes. What was before, what was after it, and how it's all going to interact in this sort of complicated story.

David didn't really sit in the writers' room. That wasn't his thing and he didn't really like it. He sat in maybe one or two sessions. At that point in time, in season one, he concentrated more on the actual production up in Vancouver. I was down in L.A. more in the writers' room.

The truth is, in season one David and I had to kind of figure out how we dealt with each other. There were definitely times when we were butting up against one another just in terms of who got final say on what. Sometimes his story sense didn't match up with my story sense. Sometimes my sense of editorial and how to cut a show didn't match up with his. We definitely had some healthy debates, and sometimes just flat-out arguments and yelling matches with each other. But we both loved the show and we both liked each other and respected each other, so we never got to a point where there was an open break. But we definitely went at it to sort of creatively argue through the show.

DAVID EICK

There were definitely hills and valleys, you know? As the show wore on, like any partnership, our differences, which in the early days were ninety-nine percent of the time valuable, risked having more liability to them, because you get deeper into a show. Your agenda becomes narrowed by definition. Just because you know who your fans are, the pressure to be attracting new viewers goes down, the network settles into what kind of audience share they can expect from the numbers that you're pulling, and it's easier to just sort of focus on the folks who are already watching your show. And that certainly created tension, to the extent of, "How narrow do you go?" That is always going to be a point of conflict between creative people.

RONALD D. MOORE

David has an encyclopedic knowledge of film. He can quote specific shots and specific cinematographers from many motion pictures. He brings a tremendous visual sense of how film is put together, and telling stories visually. I had very much a writer's background and so the two of us could marry those two perspectives really well. But other times there just was a disconnect and we'd have to kind of wrestle it through.

DAVID EICK

That's not to say it ever got to Dean Martin/Jerry Lewis levels, but certainly there were points at which Ron and I stopped working as closely. But we started to really cook deep into the first season. I would say the last two episodes of season one were probably my and Ron's deepest creative collaboration on a specific piece of material. Episodes twelve and thirteen are my favorite episodes emotionally, because I feel they represent maybe the best of what Moore-plus-Eick meant, if that makes any sense. Beyond that, it always felt like it was a partnership, but if I had to hang a couple of episodes on my tombstone, it would probably be those two.

RONALD D. MOORE

I know in season one there were definitely times when the production would wonder which of us to listen to, because maybe he was telling them one thing and I was telling them something else. We'd have to circle back to each other and argue it out and move it forward. It got better. David and I'd never worked together on a show before that. He was a network exec when I met him. Then he moved over to the studio, then he became a producer. He produced the *Battlestar* miniseries. But then he left to go be a studio exec again, and then he came back to the production. So I was very used to running my own shop at that point, from *Roswell* to *Carnivàle,* and having to sort of figure out how David was going to fit into that and how he and I were going to work it out as partners when we'd never really talked about it. We never really had the discussion ahead of time. I think we just sort of walked into it and then went, "Wait a minute, what do you mean you're saying no? You don't get to say no." We both kind of say that. "What are you talking about? I'm the one who gets to say no." So it just took us a while to work it through. Pretty much by the end of the first season we knew what we were doing, so we felt we were both fantastically defensive of the show, and it was two of us against the world. It's like there was no daylight between us—fighting with the studio and the network. By the time we had finished that first order of thirteen, we were just in a better place and whatever flare-ups there were afterward were relatively minor.

DAVID EICK

There were points where I think both of us agreed to disagree. When you got to season four, most of the time it was my acquiescing not nearly as much as Ron did. I think I acquiesced because his vision was stronger at that point. He really had a strong sense of how he wanted to end it. He had reasons for it. It wasn't arbitrary at all. I didn't agree with all of them, but in a situation like that you have to abdicate to the one of you who's got the vision. So while I didn't agree with everything, I wanted to support the vision and did. It wasn't difficult at all. In the final analysis, I don't regret it at all. But season four was different from the first three seasons, make no mistake. That was definitely a time when I got shifted into a more supportive role. I stand behind everything that was done. Things just got tense in our interpersonal exchanges. But only because we're both passionate and we both care.

RONALD D. MOORE

At one point David said he wanted to write. I said, "Okay, but you're going to have to write it," helping him through it. Helping him on the first draft.

I rewrote him, which is never a fun moment for any writer, but he took it like a man. And it was fine. And then he wrote another one. And then he's taken that writing and gone off and become a showrunner. He writes and produces things in his own right now. Every once in a while we still get together for dinner, to chat, or we'll send each other goofy emails or whatever. But we were able to laugh about it. That's why they did the cartoon thing at the end of each episode, each of us arguing with each other, killing each other over and over and over again. That was our inside joke, but we loved each other and it was fine. It was like two brothers just going at it. By the way, those endings were David's idea. He had a friend in Arizona who did animation and things like that, and David had the idea to do these little gags at the end of the show. My participation in it was basically they took my picture and Photoshopped it. I never saw it until they were on air. I just always thought they were hysterical.

DAVID EICK

Ron and I got drunk the other night. It's not like any of it was bridge-burning. You have to remember, those were the days of twenty episodes a year. That's *a lot* of episodes. That's a lot of pressure.

On a more personal level, there had been some pressure stemming from the fact that during the show's run and particularly afterward, Ron Moore was heralded the one true guiding force of the show, with David Eick's name frequently being left out of the mix.

DAVID EICK

I'd be lying if I said it tickled, but I also don't obsess over it, because occasionally when I see a blogger write something or I catch something in an entertainment magazine where it says, "Ron Moore is *Battlestar*," I think, "Ah, well they didn't do their homework." But when the big shots—*The New York Times, The New Yorker, Rolling Stone*—came along and wrote about the show, it was fair and I was in there. There was a *New York Times Magazine* thing where Ron was on the cover and that bruised a little bit, too. Not so much the cover, but the fact they called it Ron Moore's show.

RONALD D. MOORE

I was aware of it and I felt uncomfortable about it. There were moments when I felt bad. At the same time, it was a tremendous ego boost, frankly, in that people regarded it that way and still do to this day. I don't deny that I accept those accolades, but there definitely are moments when I feel like, "Oh, shit," and it's not fair if he really was my partner in the whole thing, which he was.

DAVID EICK

The reason I didn't obsess and I don't obsess now is because of two things. One, the people who get the show and who know the show and write about the show, I've never felt shirked by. I've always felt very much evenly and fairly represented. The other reason is that Ron's always been really sensitive about it. He's said to me a number of times, "I think I get more credit for this than you do, and I don't think that's always fair." So I think the fact that he's always been sensitive to it and understands that might be a little more difficult, has also allowed it to not be the kind of thing that will be a rock in my shoe or something like that.

RONALD D. MOORE

The New York Times Magazine did a profile, and it was originally going to be a profile piece of David and I, so the writer spent a lot of time with me and a lot of time with David. Terry and I came to the set and dinner, and he picked our brains early in the run. Just before it was published, he sent me the article, or called me or something, and he had decided that he just thought that the story was me. The article became "Ron Moore's Deep Space Journey" or something. There was a big picture of me and I felt *really* bad. I sent him an email and was like, "I don't think this is right. David's a big part of it and I don't feel good about this." He was understanding: "I get it, but this is just the journalistic decision I've made." I made a point of sending David a copy of the email to make sure he knew that I didn't angle for that, and that I objected to it. David said he appreciated it, but it was hard. Part of it does have to do with the fact that I came from *Star Trek,* so there was an easy thing for a lot of journalists to latch on to. To connect from *Star Trek* to *Battlestar*. It was in the time before people were really using the term "showrunner" per se. That word was out there, but it wasn't really a thing like it is now.

DAVID EICK

Battlestar Galactica is going on my tombstone regardless of whether people thought it was mine or not. When I get annoyed is when it feels like it's just a matter of someone being sloppy or not looking under the hood. I also know that in sci-fi there's a tendency to kind of want the singular visionary like Chris Carter, George Lucas, George R. R. Martin, Joss Whedon, Gene Roddenberry. We don't tend to think of them as partnerships like we are a little more willing to think of other types of creative endeavors. I remember saying, as a joke, when I got the call from a reporter warning me about the fact the headline wasn't going to include me, I said, "Ask your editor, when he orders ice cream, does he order Ben's? I bet he says Ben and Jerry's." It *is* possible for more than one person to be responsible for a creative endeavor.

Beyond all of that, some of the pressure facing Moore and Eick was built into the show from the fact that it was considered by its creators to be much more of a character drama than a story-driven vehicle, which, while common today, flew in the face of the medium at the time and oftentimes was reflected in the ratings.

MARK STERN
(former president of original content, Syfy)

Part of revisionist history is that *Battlestar Galactica* was always just a big blockbuster. It wasn't. I've always believed if it had been on AMC instead, or any other network, including our sister network USA, it would've found a bigger audience. I do believe that having it be on Sci-Fi always kind of gave it a certain taint of being just for the fanboys, and obviously it wasn't.

RONALD D. MOORE

At that point, it still required a push to do a show so focused on character. I mean, again, Sci-Fi Channel was coming off of *Farscape*. That was their other big space case sci-fi show that they were just ending. So that was kind of what everyone was still talking about. *Quest* had just been on the air. And then you had the *Star Trek* franchise. So it was a push to move it into this other territory that was really a character drama that happened to be in a sci-fi universe. It was a really big, perceptual shift. In the television environment in general, this is when *The Sopranos* was on the air, but it was just happening. *The Sopranos* was becoming a big deal, you know? And *Sex in the City* and *Six Feet Under,* these pieces that HBO was doing. But people were kind of writing them off, like, "Well, only HBO can do that kind of stuff." And the rest of the work in cable wasn't going there yet.

There was still a mandate that everything had to be episodic. They did not want serialized storytelling, because they were afraid that if the audience missed episode three, they would be lost in episode four and they would never come back to the show. So there was a demand that any series you pitched had to have an episodic quality to it. They all had to be stand-alone stories. As we got on the air, then *Lost* broke through. But they were a *true* breakthrough. The television landscape was changing all around us, but the networks themselves were still kind of conservative. And even though there were these pockets of success in doing alternate kinds of storytelling, their instincts were still going much more toward, "Ah, that's too risky. What do you mean, 'It's all about the characters'? There have to be ray guns, and things have to blow up every week. It's too complicated, and we don't want it to be dark." There was still a conservatism just in terms of basic storytelling.

DAVID WEDDLE
(producer, *Battlestar Galactica* [2004])

On the last season of *Deep Space Nine,* Ira Behr, through just sheer force of will and audacity, started a continuing storyline even though we weren't supposed to do it. That's when I suddenly realized that science fiction and television shows have this potential for storytelling that is much bigger in scope and much more exciting than movies, because you can tell a story the way Tolstoy or Dickens did—a sprawling epic with many zigs and zags and ups and downs for the characters. That's when I began to fall in love with science fiction as a genre. In science fiction you can tell any kind of story. You can tell a metaphysical story, a moral drama, a personal/psychological drama, a political story, religious theme—we did all of those in *Battlestar.*

No other genre really offers so many story opportunities or dimensions, and serialized storytelling became an important tool, though back then no one wanted to hear it.

JAMIE BAMBER
(actor, "Captain Lee 'Apollo' Adama")

We were really one of the first cable TV serialized shows. *The Sopranos* obviously set the mold and we weren't long after that. But that also shot us in the foot, because I remember talking to Ron at the time and the networks and even cable channels at that time, and they really wanted something they could syndicate, that could be sold anywhere like an assortment of chocolates that didn't matter which order you ate the chocolate in. And we were before streaming and before all the models that really celebrate the binge. We were also, I think, one of the most pirated shows at that time, and people watched it through illegal downloads. They desperately wanted to watch it.

RONALD D. MOORE

To be fair, that's also indicative of the technology, because before the DVR it was really hard for the audience to catch up on it. It was kind of impossible. Yes, with VHS you theoretically had the ability to tape episodes and watch them, but for whatever reason the VHS industry never quite cracked making it simple. Nobody could program their clocks, you know? The VHS recording just was always a joke. And then when DVDs came, you could catch up on last year, but that's last year, so it didn't help audience numbers week-to-week. It wasn't until the DVR penetration started to become significant that you had an opportunity for the audience to record them as a season. You'd have networks broadcast them more than once and they could record the multiples and could actually bank them and watch them together and then get on board the show. Once that happened, the whole landscape kind of shifted into another style of storytelling. It's like the networks were not completely unjustified in that philosophy that they had of making everything standalone, because the audience just wasn't able to really catch up even if they wanted to back in the days of *The Next Generation*.

MARK STERN

I think the show was about three or four years too early in terms of the internet. If people had been able to catch up on Netflix or even iTunes, which at the time was still pretty nascent, it would have been a much bigger audience. Although it was always a hit on iTunes. I remember when you'd go on the site and see the top ten episodes that were being bought, it was always in the top ten. Sometimes number one. At the same time, iTunes made us nervous. In the beginning it was like, "iTunes is going to take our viewers away from us." And what you quickly realized was the opposite: that iTunes allowed people to actually catch up. We got to the point where we went from "How do we *not* air this on iTunes?" to "When can we get this on iTunes?" Now you see those streaming services actually become part of a strategy for the way networks roll projects out, but at the time there was a lot of concern about cannibalizing the audience. So there was always a lot of appetite for it for people who were trying to catch up. But the serialized nature of it made it a bit difficult if you came in late.

DAVID WEDDLE

Back on *Deep Space Nine,* during the last season *The Sopranos* was airing and all of the writers on staff, Ron Moore included, were *Sopranos* fans. I didn't have HBO in those days and they kept talking about it, and they were having a screening of the first-season finale. All the writers were going, so Brad and I went, too. When I saw that episode, my eyes opened because I realized that *Star Trek* was going through the door that *The Sopranos* had kind of opened with continuing storylines. I saw the genre changing in front of my eyes. And then, lo and behold, we got the opportunity to be on *Battlestar Galactica,* which was right in the red-hot center of that second Golden Age of Television. The *real* Golden Age of Television, actually.

BRADLEY THOMPSON
(producer, *Battlestar Galactica* [2004])

I think we were pretty successful in making it so that if you come in with a reasonable amount of intelligence, so to speak, you could figure out who were the good guys, who were the bad guys, and what was going on. Of course, the opening about the Cylons, that there was a war and all that good stuff at the beginning, sets you up with each episode. Kind of in the way that the old TV theme song set up the whole premise of the show so you could just pick it up.

RONALD D. MOORE

I sold *Battlestar,* in part, in saying we were doing a version of the structure of *Hill Street Blues.* I said, "Look, we're going to do an old show in terms of story structure. It hasn't been done in a while, but this is the idea: There's an A-story every week that has a beginning, middle, and end. But there's a B-story between characters that might run two, three, four episodes. And then there's a C-story that'll run throughout the whole season. So every week, even if you missed last week, there's always a story you can hook into this week." And if you look at *Galactica,* we really held on to that for quite a while. The whole first season in particularly always has an A-story that has a beginning, middle, and end, and then there's runners and the bigger mythology story that's going throughout and building it into the larger framework. But that was the way I sold it to them. They were structured and broken as individual episodes. In the writers' room we wanted each episode to build on each one, but each of them had its own individual story. At least until the second year we started to really break that down. And by the time you get into the third and fourth years, it's almost a straight-up serial.

The rise of DVRs eventually had one of the strongest impacts on the show, and the way that it would be able to unfold.

RONALD D. MOORE

The DVR penetration was growing and altered the ratings system by the third and fourth seasons. At the beginning they were collecting that data on season one and season two, where the ratings reports from the networks would have an addendum that said, "With DVR viewership, when you add that in, the show actually grew by almost twice as much over the course of the next week." David and I would get really excited and adamant and say, "Look at the show! I mean, people are recording it and they're watching it." But Sci-Fi was saying, "None of that matters, because advertisers won't give you a cent for it; we're just collecting this data to have it. All that means anything to us is the live numbers. Nobody cares how many people watched it on DVR." DVR Live Plus Seven hadn't even been invented. But by the last year of the show, that was shifted and DVR penetration had gotten to the point where advertisers were having to take it seriously. Networks were demanding to get paid for some of it, and that data was starting to actually influence whether shows got picked up or not. It's a whole different world now. That and streaming. *Everything* is different now. I mean, they'll send me visual effects shots and I can watch them on my phone. That's *crazy*.

The pace of technological change in the last twenty years is unbelievable. When I started on *Star Trek*, there was no internet. The computers weren't even networked together in the same office. You had to take a big four-and-a-half-inch floppy downstairs to get a printout of your script. We did most of the changes in pen and ink on the physical pages themselves. Now I'm in an environment where we're writing scripts and shooting them off. It's a whole different world.

The same could be said for *Battlestar Galactica*, which represented world building from the outset. Referring back to the series bible, the history of humanity on the show begins on the planet Kobol, described as "the quasi-mythical world which in *Galactica*'s universe is the cradle of homosapien. The location of this planet has been lost in the mists of time, but our characters have presumably been raised with various myths and legends. . . . Kobol seems to be an Olympian setting in which gods or god-like beings cohabited the planet with mere mortals. At some point in the distant past thirteen 'Tribes of Men' left Kobol never to return again. Why they left is open to conjecture. . . . The thirteen tribes travelled far away from Kobol and eventually twelve of them settled in a star system with twelve planets capable of supporting human life. The remaining thirteenth tribe broke off in a different direction and legend has it that it found 'a bright shining planet known as Earth' . . . The people of the Twelve Tribes colonized twelve different planets and each colony was named according to what we here on Earth would regard as the Zodiac: Caprica (Capricorn), Picon (Pisces), Gemenon (Gemini), etc. By the time of the pilot, the Colonials have lived on their worlds for several thousand years and yet their technology is not that much more advanced than our own. . . ."

In terms of religion, the Colonials have "a poly-theistic belief system that worships at least some of the God-like beings on the planet Kobol . . . The [Lords] are roughly analogues to the Greek and Roman gods of Earth (this linkage also helps tie Earth's belief systems and roots to those of Colonial society, remembering that we are all supposed to come from the same homeworld, namely Kobol) . . . Colonial society is very similar to 21st Century Earth society and can be considered a parallel world for all intents and purposes. . . ."

The flip side of the Colonists, of course, is the Cylons, described in the bible as "originally simple robots which grew increasingly complex with more and more powerful artificial intelligence. They eventually were used for danger work such as mining operations and they were used as soldiers in the armies of the 12 Colonies. As the Cylons became faster and more powerful, they also became smarter and more independent and there came a point at which the Cylons developed true sentience and self-awareness. . . . They rebelled against their humans masters and the Cylon War began. The war quickly became a desperate one for both sides as they came to believe that their own survival was dependent on annihilating their enemy. . . . The Cylon War finally ended in an armistice, the terms of which required the Cylons to leave the Colonial star system for a world of their own. . . .

"One of the more interesting aspects of the Cylons today is that they have consciously modeled themselves in the human form. Twelve forms to be precise—each of them embodying valuable aspects of the human body and personality. Just as western Man believes himself to be created in God's image, the Cylons molded themselves into the likeness of their own creator. To be sure the Cylons believe humanity to be deeply flawed, but they also acknowledge its positive traits and have striven to preserve what they believe to be the worthy aspects of mankind into their only culture. Deciding that only twelve models of Cylon were necessary suggests that the diversity of humanity is overrated and that there are relatively few physical attributes worthy of preservation . . . The fact that the consciousness of one Cylon can be transmitted from a dying body to another Cylon body also suggests that the Cylons place a tremendous value on life itself." It should be noted that, while there are only twelve models, there are likely millions of Cylons out there.

For forty years there was no contact between the Colonials and the Cylons. Then all hell broke loose in the *Battlestar Galactica* miniseries. . . .

RONALD D. MOORE

The big thing that came up between David, Breck Eisner, and me in the development of the miniseries was, "What do you do about the Cylons?" We were struggling with it. There was a restaurant that's no longer there called Chinois Hollywood, that we were having lunch in. Long working lunch trying to figure out the Cylons. The assumption at the beginning was that they should be like the original Cylons, guys in suits. Then we started talking in practical terms, because in today's environment the audience expectation of a guy in a suit was different than what it was in 1978. It couldn't just be silver suits. They were going to have to be more elaborate. They were going to have to be really cool and specialized to have all this stuff, and we kind of quickly came to the conclusion that, "Shit, how many of those things are we going to really be able to afford to make? Maybe one or two, and how's that going to work? We can't have just one or two Cylon suits that we're going to have to do, like, an entire series of. That's not going to be practical. Okay, what are the CGI possibilities?"

The Cylons and their technology proved to be the greatest challenge for the design team. In a significant departure from the original, it was decided early on that the Cylon hardware should reflect an organic aesthetic. Eric Chu's design for the basestar, for example, was inspired initially by images of seedpods and insects as viewed under an electron microscope. And then there was the Cylon Raider, which, more than any other vessel, was a combination of numerous elements that the director, producers, and network executives all wanted to see. Overall, producers wanted to maintain the signature oval shape of the original, but updated with the organic quality utilized in the basestar.

ERIC CHU
(art director, Enigma Studios)

What I intended was to come up with something that looked somewhat organic from a distance, but as soon as you started to come in closer, you could see it was made up of mechanical struts and circuits and that sort of thing. In fact, that was the first design that was unanimously liked and subsequently the first design that was approved. This approach created an innovative visual dichotomy between the series' two protagonists—making Colonial technology and vehicles more mechanical in design than their cybernetic adversaries'.

GARY HUTZEL
(visual effects supervisor, *Battlestar Galactica* [2004])

One of the underlying elements of our story is the Cylons are searching. They are, in a sense, searching for God and what God wants them to do. The

Colonials, on the other hand, have a long history of fighting with each other and generally not being very nice. So, to me, giving the Colonials this mechanistic design, while the Cylons are very artistic in nature and seek to understand those elements, is a good note for the story.

And with the Cylon Raider, in the original script it was described as a "squashed Cylon in space." David Eick very much wanted to stay with that idea, but to be honest, I did not understand what the hell he was talking about. None of us understood what he was talking about, but he kept after it and kept saying this is not a squashed Cylon. So we kept at it and it eventually grew into this organic ship. Charles Ratteray, a Zoic designer/illustrator, created the approved design, which later received some minor revisions from Eric Chu to make the vessel appear slightly more organic. Literally, it has swept-forward wings that are menacing. It is more of an artistic choice than it is a mechanical, practical choice, but what comes out of that is the fact that in some shots it *does* look like a squashed Cylon. It has this strength, almost as if it has this kind of Superman pose to it. It's a very strong visual design that I think worked very well in the show.

RICHARD HUDOLIN

When I approached the Cylon Raiders from a production design standpoint, I thought about the fact that the Cylons are mechanical beings, but they're alive. So how do you show that? If you remember, it was Kara who came out of the Cylon fighting ship, and she dropped through what was like a birth canal kind of thing, because they were evolving. In my mind, they're trying to be human and practically are human, and what happens when humans give birth? I had to have some sort of parallel. It doesn't have to be exact, but there should be a parallel process.

Moore wrestled with the concept of the Cylons, ultimately envisioning two distinct types—a humanoid agent that would be able to infiltrate Colonial society, and a second, more deadly, mechanical Centurion. Several considerations weighed heavily on the latter design. Specifically, producers wanted their new adversary to be more menacing than the original. It was agreed upon early on that the iconic red eye would be retained and, in a nod to the hard-core, its parallel movement timed frame by frame to match the 1978 version. Although the Centurions are featured only briefly in the miniseries, producers were also always aware of the strong possibility that *Galactica could* go to series. Not wanting to limit their possibilities, they realized that they needed the movement and articulation that only a completely virtual character could perform.

GARY HUTZEL

There is always an issue if you put guys in suits. How are we going to create the right tone? How are we going to execute it? Is it *RoboCop*? We can't have the guys in the chrome outfits that were obviously grips storming around, not being able to see. CGI eliminated all of those problems.

RONALD D. MOORE

Yes, we could do some CGI Cylons, but at that point in the game they were still very expensive and very limited. Even in the miniseries we only used the CGI Cylons for a couple of scenes in the very beginning. You didn't see a lot of them. We kind of said, "Yeah, but if they're the antagonist every week, you're going to want to do scenes with them. You're going to want to have more than just walking in and shooting. They're going to have to be characters." *That* wasn't practical on a TV budget at that point in time. But what else could we do? We were just throwing out ideas. Somebody threw out the idea, "Well, what if they were to look like human beings?" I dismissed that at the beginning. I was like, "Eh, that's *Blade Runner*, you know? That territory's been mined. Forget about that."

GARY HUTZEL

Eric Chu was asked to incorporate an unfeasible anatomy to the Cylons, specifically an extremely small waist to illustrate that this was a machine and *not* an actor in a suit. One of his earlier concepts featured an elegant "sci-fi retro" humanoid form with articulated sections. It was very feminine, and I rather liked that idea. It was a completely different take on them, very stylish. It was a great design, but nobody wanted it. So we turned about and went back to Eric again. I gave him a horrible little drawing that I had done. I said, "This is the idea." It's kind of like a death shroud—the Cylon design with a spiderlike face—and he created the Centurion the first time out. He sent it over and we said, "This is it. *This* is a Cylon."

EMILE SMITH
(digital effects supervisor, Zoic Studios)

We decided not to use motion capture to animate the Centurion, preferring instead to keyframe a unique walk cycle that would incorporate both humanistic and robotic traits. We were trying to give it a unique look. We felt motion capture would be too human. We referenced a lot of movies—from *RoboCop* to *The Terminator* to *Nightmare on Elm Street*—to get a heavy but evil movement devised for them. We have one shot of it unfolding its hands, which I reference Freddy Krueger unfurling his bladed hands for.

GARY HUTZEL

People should know that we spent a lot of time trying to reintegrate the original Cylons into the show. But ultimately it was decided we needed something more deadly-looking and something that would be more articulate. So by rethinking and redesigning it, we have a creature that has a lot of articulation and can move in lots of impressive ways.

MIKE GIBSON
(visual effects producer, *Battlestar Galactica* [2004])

Gary's feeling was that they had to be menacing, right? And they had to look deadly. He said, "Let's make them taller. Let's make them tower over you," which is how they ended up being about seven feet tall so that they would be quite impressive standing there next to a human form. You have to remember, when we started, you made ten CG shots a show. It was a very different world back then compared to the savvy viewer that, today, expects, like, one hundred or one hundred and fifty effects on a show.

The other thing Gary said was we should consider moving them in the direction of insects in terms of look. Working with the face, we began to look at mantises. In some of the early designs, you began to see the arms had that kind of upright position with longer talons and were almost mantis-like. We began to pare that down and that's where you got these very large hands with very sharp fingers, the idea being that it doesn't even need a weapon. It just needs to get near you and touch you, and it can rip you apart. It's *that* big.

The other thing we wanted, coming out of Glen Larson, is the oscillating eye, which needed to be worked in. We didn't want something that just felt like it was moving across, so the way that we then designed it is it almost came down as a "V" on one side, and came to a point in the center of the forehead, where the eye would be on a human, and then up the end. So we kind of angled that a little bit. It needed to have a human form, because you had to identify that in the evolution of that Cylon that it was imitating arms and legs, but still had this real deadly presence. In the next evolution we kind of shrunk the hands and made them clawlike. We wanted something that looked mean, with heavy weight, which is always very difficult to do with CGI characters, and putting them into real-life environments.

DAVID EICK

We knew we couldn't sustain CGI Cylons, and realized we would need to go with humanoid Cylons. I remember that coming up while Breck was still involved, and I remember pitching them the Manson Family as sort of an analogue for how the Cylons view their ancestors. Remember how the Manson Family believed that they were releasing you to heaven by killing you, because they were the rightful next stage in evolution? The Cylons therefore really didn't have to have any malice, you know? They didn't have to hate us, they just need to be done with us. Finished with us. Almost ambivalent. That came up during those early days.

RONALD D. MOORE

So maybe they look like human beings. How is it *not Blade Runner*? As we were sitting there, I started to come up with this sort of, "Well, what does that say? Why would they look like humans if they're robots? Why would an alien robot species look like human beings? Well, maybe if they were created by humans, it's sort of a Frankenstein thing?" Well, *that* starts to get interesting. Maybe they didn't always look that way. Maybe they used to look like traditional mechanical robots. Then they went away and on their own evolved into looking like human beings. But why would they do that? Could it be an existential thing? Could they believe that it's a religious thing? That they're making themselves more like human beings because that's what they think God is like or something? We were starting to feel all this depth and that there was something interesting about this. It became a way to solve a production problem.

DAVID WEDDLE

Early in the first season, we felt that we didn't want to explain them, we didn't want to be in their world. We thought it would demystify them and take away their power. That it would be better if they were more enigmatic. Of course that changed, but I don't know that we planned on them becoming so complex as they eventually did. None of that was envisioned.

RONALD D. MOORE

If you go back and look at the original writers'-guide bible that I wrote, there's very little about the Cylons. In fact, Number Six's bio consists of one line. It just says, "The woman as machine." I just embraced the idea that it was going to be an organic process to figure out the Cylons and what kind of society they had and how they operated, what their rules were, and all that just came out of the writers' room. It was really a completely improvisational process. You know the Hybrid that controls the basestars and talks in that sort of crazy word-salad? That was inspired by a drawing that [production designer] Richard Hudolin did of a hybrid Cylon and a tank. He was like, "I think we could build something like that, and doesn't this look cool?" I said, "Yeah, it does look cool. What is it?" "I don't know what it is. What do *you* think it is?" "Well, let me think about that. It looks like a hybrid. . . . Hmm, I wonder if we could make this into something that is half Cylon/half machine, and maybe it controls the basestar?" It was literally inspired by that drawing.

And from there, we always talked about the idea that the Hybrid could look into a level of existence above our own and just the mere fact of rising through the surface of the water and seeing something greater drove her mad and that she couldn't really explain it to us in any rational terms. So there was a sense of there being something else that human beings could sort of perceive on certain levels and not understand. And that we in *Galactica* were going to see sort of small shafts of light that came down from this other plane. We would see them and experience them imperfectly and never be able to truly understand what that was all about. Again, all of that was from a drawing.

BRADLEY THOMPSON

We were reaching into "What could be weird and different about this?" and something halfway between the Cylon and God. I don't know, something's got to run the ship that they can interface with. You *don't* want to see some guy sitting there flipping switches, because we've seen our guys flipping switches. So how would they do it? Do they need to read the dial that says, "There's this O_2 component in the atmosphere in these various sections," or do we just have something that monitors it the whole time and corrects it, because we've mastered the ability to create consciousness and put that in our various models' heads? Couldn't we make a ship that basically *is* a Cylon?

DAVID WEDDLE

In the miniseries, there's a woman with a baby and Six asks if she can see it, and she ends up snapping the baby's neck. That happened because they needed an act out. They called Ron up and said, "We need an out for the act; it's too soft the way it is." He didn't really know why he had her break the baby's neck either when he wrote it. He even said, "I don't know why she did, but let's find out."

BRADLEY THOMPSON

We would ask questions like that. "Why does she seem sad when she broke the baby's neck?" Ron at that point had said, "Well, I'm not exactly sure." It just seemed kind of cool. Or, in the opening of the miniseries, why would she kiss that guy in the beginning and ask the question, "Are you alive?" Why would *that* be an issue? Those are things that with Ron's instincts were intriguing to him. Let's say it and *then* figure it out later was a part of the fun of that. It was also saying, "Okay, we've got a war between these essentially killer robots and humanity. What are the weaknesses of the robots? What are the weaknesses of humanity? What do the robots envy about humanity? Do they want to be alive? Is that what they're testing?"

DAVID EICK

Ron was shooting *Carnivàle* and I called him up saying, "Rymer feels we need something to kick this off or we need to punctuate it." It was literally like one of the last things he wrote for the miniseries. By that point in time, there was a good-natured acceptance that David and Ron are going to go dark as fuck and the network is constantly going to be fighting them about it. To their credit, the network didn't make it an ongoing war, which I suppose they could have, although there were some skirmishes. At that point they were just, like, "Guys! Really? Really, guys? Is *nothing* sacred?" I think the effectiveness of it and the fact that it came to some sort of production rescue that I just can't remember, was part of the reason they let us get away with it.

TRICIA HELFER
(actress, "Number Six")

There was a lot of discussion about it, and the network didn't want it in there. But I liked the fact that it *was* in there. Michael Rymer and I talked about it, and Ron talked about it, being more of a mercy killing. To me it was important to have that moment, because the bombs were going to go off. This baby was going to die shortly, but it was the first time that she had actually held a baby. For her to take that moment and kind of be fascinated by the baby, and want to pick up the baby, and being kind of taken in by its innocence, and then make the choice to end its life quickly and painlessly as opposed to suffering hours later. To me that was a very integral moment of showing that there is some empathy, even if it's not something you believe in, and there's these robots that can have these emotions and feel. That's the first moment that we really saw a glimpse of it in the show that there's more depth to her and to their side. Sort of foreshadowing that there's a lot more to this side, the Cylon side, than you're expecting in the beginning.

RONALD D. MOORE

At the beginning, I really wasn't planning on seeing a lot of the Cylons as people and finding them in the show too much. I kind of thought that they were going to be more of a shark; they're off camera, they come in periodically, they catch up every once in a while. You know, you meet up with them one-on-one in discrete situations. There's some sleeper agents in the fleet out there, we'll play that for a long time. We're not going to play multiples of these guys very much. I think I had sort of an instinctive prejudice against it, because in *Star Trek* that was what we called the "evil twin scenario," where there was a bad Data, there was a bad Riker, the Mirror Universe and all of that. So I kind of shied away from it and didn't want to go down that road too deeply. But you just kind of found that you were able to do that. Look at Grace Park. She was playing both Sharon on Cylon-occupied Caprica, and the other Sharon on *Galactica*. The audience realized that there's two of them and they were two different people. Suddenly you realized you could do more of that stuff.

DAVID WEDDLE

At first we felt like we never wanted to really see much of the Cylons, because our thinking was that if they remain kind of an enigma, they're scarier. So we stayed with that for a while, but really Ron started blowing that apart with the episode in which he has Cally shoot Boomer, and we see her kind of deprogramming and resurrected in a new body in the second-season episode "Downloaded." Really what it is, is you have to develop more story. What are we going to do? We started to realize that our initial thought to keep the Cylons a mystery wouldn't work. As a show goes over four seasons, you can't be repetitive. You can't just keep telling the same kinds of stories, so how do we make it more interesting as they're being pursued across the galaxy, being attacked by the Cylons?

DAVID EICK

The only three Cylons we knew about for sure in the miniseries were Leoben, the PR guy, and Sharon, so anybody who became Cylons or were revealed as Cylons—the Final Five and all that stuff—developed later. All of them have their own origins in terms of folks on staff who had ideas and weird shit Ron and I would come up with, or stuff the network said they wanted more of.

DAVID WEDDLE

It was starting to fall into a repetitive pattern, so "Downloaded," and then from there on really starting to expand on things. It even started in the first season where you have Six and Doral talking about Athena running off with Helo, and that she thinks she's in love with him. Six admits that she envies them, which shows that they're conflicted about humans having love and they don't have it. And they're haunted by some insecurities. So it started in the first season, but "Downloaded" was really cracking it open into the Cylon world, and then we just embraced that. It turned out to be fantastic, because it not only gave us story material to explore them, but it amplified all our themes. You know, the human beings think the Cylons are not legitimate life forms, that they're just machines, but we began to see that the Cylons and the humans were really not that different. That they had some of the same common struggles.

SCOTT MANTZ
(film critic, *Access Hollywood*)

I thought it was interesting that you had Cylons that looked like humans. Among other things, the show really posed a four-year-long question of what it means to be human. Also, the brilliance of the new *Galactica* was this: In the beginning, the Cylons were bad, and the humans were good. As the series progressed, naturally, organically, over those four years, they became more alike than not alike. You had Cylons that were good, and humans that were bad. That happened gradually. It was a gradual shift that worked.

Moore admits that the idea of Cylons among us in human form was inspired by the Changeling storyline on *Deep Space Nine*. In that *Star Trek* scenario, the United Federation of Planets was being infiltrated by shape-shifters intent on destroying humanity from within in a creepy and effective take on the *Invasion of the Body Snatchers* sci-fi trope, which had also been effectively mined in the first-season *Next Generation* episode "Conspiracy."

RONALD D. MOORE

I like those storylines in *Deep Space* and I wanted to play more of that in the show. But I think one of the reasons why I limited it right in the miniseries—where I said there were only twelve models—was because I didn't want it to be everybody. I wanted to kind of put some kind of governor on it that would keep us in a certain box. That it wasn't a Changeling that could be anybody in the entire fleet and in the entire show, because I just thought that would overwhelm it and you would never be able to escape it. It would be so omnipresent. It also meant that you would have to get into a situation where eventually you're going to reveal them all and the game is over. And that would be a good thing.

To keep those same models returning, there had to be a "resurrection" ship, in which the consciousness of a fallen Cylon would download into a new body. The concept of that vessel was depicted in a second-season two-parter.

RONALD D. MOORE

The concept was something that David and Bradley had in the room prior to the episode. We were talking about how the notion of resurrection worked so far away from the Cylon world. You know, now they're pursuing us and we're very far away from the colonies and very far away from wherever the Cylon homeworld was. How does their resurrection happen so far afield? David and Bradley came up with the idea that, "Oh, well, maybe they have a ship. There's literally a resurrection ship that sort of goes out with them, sort of like a tanker would go out with a fleet to supply them with oil or fuel." Which is kind of a cool idea.

TONI GRAPHIA
(co-executive producer, *Battlestar Galactica* [2004])

Part of the idea for the resurrection ship came from my Catholic upbringing, plus I remembered the cover of that Michael Crichton book *Coma*. The cover had a picture of all these bodies suspended on ropes or something. It was a very visceral-looking picture. We also had some kind of strategic dilemma, story dilemma, of how we were going to make this happen. These

Cylons, how are they going to regenerate? We needed some kind of method, or base. I remember thinking, "If they just had tons of bodies, kind of like this *Coma* picture, just hanging on the ship, and they're resurrecting them." Because I'm Catholic, I was, like, we'll call it the resurrection ship. I remember that was one of my contributions.

MARK VERHEIDEN
(co-executive producer, *Battlestar Galactica* [2004])

Essentially the Cylons can't be killed, because they download into another body and come back. That evolved—this idea of the download and the bodies coming out of the pools on the ship—as we were going forward, looking for a story and looking for interesting new change-ups, and things to do as the series progressed to shake things up. It's following the stories along a track that feels logical to you, but being open to those side trips and to new ideas and inventions that possibly change how the series feels, which is great. That's the fun of it, the challenge of it, the joy of it—to have that opportunity to evolve a show like that. We always had a schematic of where to go, but it was getting there that was the fun for writers; figuring out *how* we get there in the most interesting, torturous way to our characters possible.

RONALD D. MOORE

In dealing with Cylon religion, I broke the story for the miniseries myself in my office in Glendale. Put cards up on the board and broke down each scene just like I had learned to do at the writers' office, and just started writing it. There was a moment when I wrote the scene between Baltar and Number Six at the beginning of the mini where she turns to him at one point and says, "God is love." I just sort of wrote that in the moment and didn't know what the hell it meant, but kind of thought, "Well, that's an interesting thing for a robot to say." I kind of liked it and it fed into some of the conversations that David and Breck [Eisner] and I had had. I said, "Okay, let's try it out."

TRICIA HELFER

There were moments where I was utterly confused about Six and the Cylons. I was like, "I don't understand what this 'God is love and we have a plan' is. What *is* the plan? I don't even know what I am, and I don't know why Gaius can only see me in his head." My character in particular, I think, had to kind of just go with the flow quite a bit. It started from the beginning in the series bible, where all the characters had a two- or three-page backstory—*except* for Six. Her backstory written by the creator of the show was "the machine as woman." I go to Ron and I'm like, "I am the newest actor of the show in terms of experience, and you've given me the least to work with." He's like, "I haven't decided everything on the Cylon yet. And because you are the Cylon, I don't know what else to say." Boomer became a known Cylon fairly soon, but she was a sleeper agent; her backstory was all the sleeper agent information. From the beginning, I had to just kind of make my own backstories.

MICHAEL RYMER
(director, *Battlestar Galactica* miniseries [2003])

When I first read the script for the miniseries, the religious angle didn't exist. The whole allegory of al-Qaeda was clear and strong to me. They added a lot of stuff to make the allegory more pointed, which I didn't think was necessary. I actually had a hard time getting my head around the God stuff, because I didn't feel like it had been realized specifically enough. Okay, robots are going to have a god, but we need to know what it is. But as we did the show and it was put together, I think that I was wrong and that the whole aspect of their spirituality is quite fascinating and is something that's not defined clearly, but certainly something that adds a complexity to them that makes me want to know how did this evolve. What does this mean? What do they believe? So I do see parallels to fundamentalism—not just Muslims, but people who have a clarity of belief.

DAVID EICK

It was certainly part of the Cylon mythos that they had adopted a monotheist religion. That was in the underlying material about the Cylons, but the emphasis on using it in the pilot as part of Six's character and actually making it part and parcel to her discussion with Baltar . . . that came very late. I don't know that we had intended to make it an overt character point in the miniseries until very late. "God is love" was just a weird line to end the scene on. It didn't mean anything.

RONALD D. MOORE

When we turned in the draft, Michael Jackson—who was a network executive, he really liked it and he gave back a specific note saying, "And you know the thing you have about the Cylons talking about God is fascinating. You've got all this other stuff in here that's sort of reminiscent of al-Qaeda and religious fundamentalism. I just think you could really go further in this direction in the script." I remember getting that note and saying, "Wow, I'm *never* gonna get the note that you can do more religion in the show again, so I might as well take it and seize on it and make it a bigger philosophical construct."

DAVID EICK

On the next rewrite, Ron was like, "Well, if the goddamn suit is telling me he wants me to be this subversive and to risk flirting with sacrilegious, who am I to say no?" I started thinking at that point more in terms of the Cylon religion versus the human religion. Since there were all these names in the human culture drawn from Greek and Roman mythology, that sort of implied a belief in a pantheistic—or a polytheistic—point of view, so it became, "What if I made the humans polytheistic? And they believe in the many gods, and then the Cylons could believe in the one true God and this is a way to sort of do a replay on Western civilization; of the one God coming to drive out the many, except we're on the other side of that story now." And I started really feeling like this is really rich and interesting territory.

RONALD D. MOORE

And then there's Cylons having sex with humans. It's part of what I thought was a mature science fiction piece. It was weird to me that most science fiction on TV and in movies was very sexless. I mean, there's no sex in *Star Wars* to speak of. The original *Star Trek* had a sexy quality to it. You know, Kirk had many women in his life. And then it all kind of went away from that. *The Next Generation* was pretty chaste, and it all just felt weird that human sexuality was not really a part of the conversation anymore in science fiction. So I just felt like this was also a part of making a mature show. It was an adult show. It was not a show that was meant for kids. They were adults and adults have sex, so we were going to have sex from the very beginning. Baltar and Six were going to go at it right in the first episode. And in fact, day one of shooting was Baltar and Six having sex. That was the very first scene.

DAVID WEDDLE

In that miniseries scene where Six kills the baby, when she walks away there's a sadness in her eyes, as though she resents the fact that human beings can procreate. So that led us all to brainstorm that, yes, there can be endless amounts of duplicates of Sharon or Six, but they're limited to certain prototypes. They can't sexually reproduce. They can't combine their DNA and create something totally unique and different. And maybe there's an insecurity beneath all of that.

BRADLEY THOMPSON

The idea developed that if you got two human beings, you can populate the universe if things go correctly. If you've got two Cylons, you have to build all the downloading equipment, you have to build all of this gear that makes Cylons. They don't replicate. That is a thing to say, "Well, if we were really alive, we could just do this ourselves." We also wondered what would it do if we had essentially a human consciousness. You're going, "I'm not really human, because I can't make more of me, unless I build all of this machinery. Do I feel somehow inferior?"

Then does this become a rage against the people that created me in the first place? You built a faulty thing. How could you do this to us? That was why it was, "You are flawed and we are not. We are the next step in evolution." It's also that thing where you're never really free until you've killed your parents. All of those things were floating around. Those are the discussions that went on at length, trying to figure out who these guys were and what they wanted. That brought in the whole aspect of love. Can you really have love? Which eventually got the question of what is human and who are we? By looking at them, we got a little bit of definition of what we are and what we are not.

RONALD D. MOORE

Something we got a lot of questions on was why Six's spine glowed red during sex with Baltar. That was something that David came up with and I, frankly, never particularly liked. But it was one of those concessions of, "Look, we've got to bow to some genre tropes here and there. Let's have the spines glow, because they're kind of cool. That's kind of sci-fi-y." I was sort of like, "Really? It seems so hokey." But I went with it, because it was more like, "All right, whatever." That's not a hill to die on for me. I really hated the ad campaign that had Six's eyes glowing, because that never happened in the show and I thought it was ridiculous and silly. So the glowing spine thing was just a concession to giving everybody something weird to talk about. It doesn't really mean anything, but okay. You know, in case you're worried that it's not a science fiction or fantasy piece, here's proof.

DAVID EICK

The question I was asking myself is, How do we show that the Cylons are seeking love? In other words, if you just say this person having sex is a robot and up to no good and that's it, it's one thing. But that *isn't* it. They're not just bad guys. They're complicated. They have yearning and they have needs and they have desires, and one way to show or press that humanity is an orgasm. I just thought, "Well, that's sort of an echo of the oscillating red eye from the Cylons in the original, and what if their orgasm is an oscillating red backbone?"

12.
LESS IS MOORE

"Grab your gun and bring in the cat."

The very foundation of the success of the new iteration of *Battlestar Galactica* was its ensemble, a cast of characters comprised of veteran actors as well as far less familiar names, many Canadians who were Vancouver locals at the beginning of their careers. The resulting ensemble became a powerful tool to allow the writers myriad opportunities for character exploration and innovative storytelling unlike any the genre had ever seen.

RONALD D. MOORE
(executive producer, *Battlestar Galactica* [2004])

We kind of knew we had gold as soon as we saw the miniseries. Think about that poker game. Helo's great. He's sucking on that lollipop. Kara's tossing Tigh and Tigh's anger is boiling over. Wow, that's a great little scene. And you got Adama and his son. Just fantastic. We had lightning in the bottle with that cast, because you could just see it in the miniseries. We were so excited about the actors that we had and the chemistry among the cast that when Sci-Fi started talking about, "Well, maybe we'll pick up the show, but we would want to recast," David and I were adamant that we wouldn't do the show if they were going to recast. You would never be able to recast those roles again and come anywhere near the quality of what we had.

MARK VERHEIDEN
(co-executive producer, *Battlestar Galactica* [2004])

I've found in so many cases when you're on a show and you think you know the characters really well as the writers and creator, but the people that inhabit those characters, who have to play them every week, bring insights that are often surprising. You're not always able to take their ideas, but you're wise to listen, because they inhabit the roles. That's what they do. If they have a feeling that doesn't feel like something their character might or might not do, or they have a strong opinion that this is something their character might do, then it's always wise to listen. The scripts were, I'd say, fairly well worked out before they hit the stage, so there wasn't a whole lot of argument and discussion at that point, but they definitely brought their attitudes toward those characters to the show. You'd always want to listen very carefully to what is it that's bugging them about this line or troubling them about this relationship, or where this is going. A lot of that would have happened on Ron and David's level, frankly, but when you're on set, you hear it, too.

Commander William Adama is the man at the helm of the battlestar *Galactica*. In Moore's bible for the series, he's described as follows: "Adama is a bit of an anomaly. He is both a career military officer and a passionate civil libertarian. Adama believes in the military, believes it's a noble profession. He's also a fierce advocate for liberties and freedoms on which the colonies were founded. This duality in his personality have often put him at odds with military establishment and has definitely held him back and prevented him from making admiral. He's a bit of a historian, versed in the classics from a young age by his mother, and views the world through the prism of larger historical content. He's also an avid sports fan and lover of the great outdoors, often spending his leave in remote wilderness campsites alone."

Bringing the character to life is Edward James Olmos, whose credits include acclaimed roles in the TV series *Miami Vice*, the original *Blade Runner* (1982) and its sequel, *Blade Runner 2049* (2017), *Stand and Deliver* (1988), *Selena* (1997), and *Jack and Marilyn* (2002). To this day, he considers playing Adama, and the show itself, to be one of the greatest experiences in his life.

RONALD D. MOORE

The first thing I've got to say about Eddie is that he was the one who came up with "So say we all!" in the final scene of the miniseries. I had written it into the script as just a line, but in the moment on the set, when Eddie said "So say we all" to the cast, he thought that they didn't give him very much back. So he said it again. You can see it in the take; they all kind of glance at each other and go, "So say we all." And then he insists. He says it louder and he just pushed them and pushed them until it became this big thing on the soundstage. But it was just something Eddie came up with on his own in the moment, and then it became a signature line in the series after that. That was a big thing.

MICHAEL HOGAN
(actor, "Colonel Saul Tigh")

If you remember, that was a gigantic scene with hundreds of extras, and Adama gives his speech . . . and it took *forever*. We set up for hours, of course, and it was the beginning of *Battlestar Galactica*'s long dolly shots, Steadicam, shaky cam. It was blocked and Eddie was up at the podium, and then as we were rolling, Eddie walks down and you could see the director of photography and people going, "What the frak is happening here?" We weren't saying "frak" steadily yet.

DAVID EICK
(executive producer, *Battlestar Galactica* [2004])

Michael Rymer and I had a different reaction to that scene being shot initially. Eddie says his speech, which ends in the script with "So say we all," but he says it in a solemn way, and everyone else says it in a solemn way. But Eddie, in the moment, didn't like it. He just didn't like it. He thought that their performance could be better, so he said it louder and it becomes kind of like a football game of "I can't hear you!" Michael Rymer is about to cut, because he figures Eddie doesn't like the performance, and I'm going, "No, no, no, no." Because I can see this is all going to build in real time, and *then* Michael got it after a couple of seconds. But that was all improvised and driven by his need to get them into it. It really is a metaphor about Eddie sort of leading the spirit of the show in a way that says, "Hey, I'm up here doing this, and I love it, and I'm giving it everything I've got, so don't you guys fail me." And they didn't.

MICHAEL RYMER
(director, "33")

It was written that everyone's very downtrodden, and so he inspires everybody, right? But Eddie went into a rage and started shouting, and attacking, and we're all like, on the day, going, "Oh my God, what's he doing?" And as soon as he did it, all the cast and extras burst into spontaneous applause at the end. That happened spontaneously as a result of Eddie, the actor in the room, taking a group of people to a place emotionally for real. David Eick is a big football fan or something. He's like, "Can you get them to cheer and high-five?" And I'm the Australian going, "Oh, please. Let's not be so gauche." But it happened and I turn around and David's grinning like a cat. I can't deny a spontaneous emotional response that occurred in front of me. Now, that's challenging and exciting stuff to be on set with as a director. That's what you want. You've got a great script. You just want to take it up those extra notches and you want to find the friction and the intensity and you want to capture that in a bottle. Particularly on a show like this, where we just didn't ever want it to be too clean.

EDWARD JAMES OLMOS
(actor, "Commander William 'Bill' Adama")

Now, you've got to remember that was the very first time we all were together. It was frightening. It was very intense and it caught everybody by surprise, because no one knew that I was going to repeat it. When we broke off of that scene, I remember David Eick talking to me about it, and I saw him shaking, because it was incredible. We all felt it. We all went there. That was, to me, probably the most penetrating moment, because it really set the whole tone for the rest of the five years.

MICHAEL HOGAN

You can watch the scene; you can see people looking around, going, "What the? . . . Oh!" So we were all on the same page by the end of that, you hear "Cut!" and you're like, "We are in for quite a ride here." And that certainly came true.

MARY MCDONNELL
(actress, "President Laura Roslin")

I want to comment on that moment. First, I found out that my character was dying, and then it's "So say we all," and I was, as Laura Roslin, going, "*This* is the man that I have trying to save the rest of the human race? Oh my God." You know, such an interesting revelation as to what that was going to be about. Learning his power. Learning his rage. It's, like, "Where *have* I landed? This paramilitary nightmare." Yet it was just extraordinary.

ANGELA MANCUSO
(former president, Universal Cable Entertainment)

Eddie brought a seriousness to the part that it needed. We didn't want to make a joke. I mean, the first *Battlestar Galactica* was a knee-jerk response to *Star Wars*. That's all it was. When we hired Ron, we knew we were going to get something that had a little bit more believable, this-could-happen characters in it. Eddie represents that, and we all agreed on him right off the bat. Everybody wanted him.

TAHMOH PENIKETT
(actor, "Captain Karl 'Helo' Agathon")

He's one of the first people that ever made me want to act. I remember my father taking me to *Blade Runner* when I was, like, five or six and being absolutely captivated by his character onscreen. His character in that film is so small, but so relevant. It's so enticing, provocative and compelling. You can't take your eyes off of it. It's amazing what he did with so little. And from that moment on as a kid, I was always attracted to Edward James Olmos's projects. I've told this story a million times, but to ultimately see and to end up working on a project with the man, and to call him a dear friend and a mentor, I can't express to you how much that means to me. He's family. And his work ethic, his loyalty, his character, never ceases to amaze me. Anyone who knows Eddie well will tell you that.

JAMES CALLIS
(actor, "Gaius Baltar")

When I first met Eddie, I was pretty scared, to be honest. The *conviction*. . . . Eddie knew exactly what he was doing and where he was going, which I must say was totally opposite to me. I remember we were all called into his trailer. It wasn't the first day, but it was in the first week or something, and that was the day Eddie sat us all down as the cast and went, "The show's going to go for five years. Five years. Every episode is going to be like a movie. Keep your powder dry. We're in here for the long haul. Nobody's to make fun of this. There'll be enough people anyway who want to cut a swath in us some way or rubbish the idea, or they're not going to be fully on board, because we've got this title. *Battlestar Galactica*—that's a blessing as well as perhaps a bit of a poisoned chalice. Nobody needs to take this as seriously as we do." I thought Eddie was raving mad. I was like, "*Five years?* I may not be here five minutes." The thing that I really did get was the passion and the commitment. For all of us, we were really led through example by Eddie and Mary. These two incredible professionals who gave us *everything*.

EDWARD JAMES OLMOS

For some of the younger kids it was their first time and it was heartbreaking to tell them, "I'm in my fifties, guys. Michael Hogan, Mary McDonnell, myself—we've had a lot of experience. We've been very fortunate and we're proud to be part of this with you guys, but I've got to tell you, this has never happened to us, and we never felt this way about anything we've done in television like that. And I've got to tell you, it's once-in-a-lifetime. I've never had it before and I don't think I'm going to have it again."

It was hard, because a lot of them were starting their career. They had never been on television, had never done an episodic television show, and if they had it's been just playing minor roles. None of them had ever done a recurring role. So they had no experience on what was going to happen, and I'd tell them, "We're going to be here for five years. And we're never going to receive any kind of recognition as actors, because they will never give it to us. But we will receive the highest awards possible in the understanding of the electronic worlds and video and cable and the usage of television." And we did. We won the Peabody, and that is so unusual and we were very grateful we won it. We also won so many Primetime Emmys, and we're grateful for it, but won them in special effects and that kind of thing. None of us won Emmys as actors. We weren't even nominated. Neither were the writers or directors.

RONALD D. MOORE

Meeting Eddie Olmos for the first time, I was still working at *Carnivàle*. David and I had put down names of who would be the dream cast. Eddie Olmos was the top of the Adama list. There were a couple of other Oscar winners. You kind of put those lists together and they're usually bullshit lists. Like, this is the dream list and you're never going to get any of these guys, but let's start there. David calls me up and he says, "Okay, I got a meeting. We're going to actually meet with Eddie Olmos." I was like, "Oh, shit. Really?" "Yeah, so come down to my office after *Carnivàle* or get off early and let's have a meeting with him."

EDWARD JAMES OLMOS

I had a strong understanding of the [sci-fi] world, but I had gotten it through *Blade Runner,* so, really, when I talked to them, I said, "Listen, guys, if we're going to really have an aesthetic, let's go after the aesthetic that was brought forth in *Blade Runner.* Let's at least, if nothing else, hit that understanding and not try to do something that's so outlandish where we'll be fighting Creatures from the Black Lagoon. You know, two-lipped, four-eyed, three-eared people."

RONALD D. MOORE

So I go to the meeting and Eddie's an interesting guy. He's quickly talking about, "If there's any green-eyed aliens in the script, I'm just gonna turn and walk off the set, you know?"

EDWARD JAMES OLMOS

Actually, I said, "I'm going to faint on camera and you're going to have to write that he died of a heart attack. Thank you."

RONALD D. MOORE

At some point we started talking about *Blade Runner,* and Eddie started telling a story about how he came up with the whole Japanese influence, using Japanese language and the Asian influences. I remember thinking to myself, "Okay, so he's *this* guy. He's just going to make up shit and take credit for an amazing thing in this classic movie." So, all right, file that away in your head that that's who Ed James Olmos is. I'd think that for a very long time. And then, many moons later, I'm watching the DVD special edition of *Blade Runner* and going through the supplemental stuff. And there's an interview with Ridley Scott, and Ridley starts talking about how, "Yeah, you know Eddie Olmos is the one who came up with the Japanese . . ." I went, "Holy shit! I've been judging Eddie all this time. Like, he actually *did* that and I thought he was full of shit. Oh crap!"

EDWARD JAMES OLMOS

What got me in it was the writing. I think what got us all was the writing. It was brilliant from the first page. You open it up and the manifesto that Ron Moore wrote—a three-page manifesto to how you're supposed to look at the script and what would be happening, and the way to read the script. He had three pages before you actually opened the script to get into the script and it was just beautifully written. I just said, "Well, this is really beyond."

RONALD D. MOORE

What had happened is I was still at *Carnivàle,* and we're trying to sell the draft. The first draft of the miniseries. David called me up and said, "Can you just write a one- or two-page document that sort of talks about your vision for the show and what we're trying to do?" I was like, "Really? I've already pitched it to you. Why do I have to do this?" He's like, "Just trust me. It's a sales document. It helps the executives. Executives don't remember any of this shit. Just write, like, a two-page thing. Just don't spend a lot of time on it, just tell us your vision of the show." "All right, what the fuck." So I sat down and pounded out this thing called "Naturalistic Science Fiction, or Taking the Opera out of Space Opera." And it just kind of went through the whole overview of the series. How we're going to do it, and shoot it, produce it, the philosophy behind it and the various aspects. It was two or three pages.

I sent it off with the draft of the script to the network executives. But then what happened, unbeknownst to either of us, was that it was essentially appended to the script from that point forward. So when the script was sent out to actors like Eddie and Mary, that document went along with it. Eddie read that first and it informed his idea of what he was about to read. The same with Mary. They both mentioned it when I met with them in person. They were, like, really taken by that document. At first I was like, "I don't know what the hell they're talking about. What are they saying?" And then it kind of dawned on me that somehow they got their hands on that sales thing that I wrote for the executives. But they were both really impressed by it. They both really took it to heart. And then when they read the script itself, it gave them an idea of what the goals were and all. It was just one of those great bits of serendipity that it all kind of really worked together.

EDWARD JAMES OLMOS

Not even *Blade Runner* was this well-crafted, because the story was very deep, very quick, and it was so long. I mean, it was four hours. That's a lot of writing, and a lot of story, and it just held true from the beginning to the end. Now, I had said no at the beginning. I said, "Thank you very much, but I'm working. You know, I have things to do rather than do a *Battlestar Galactica* remake. It's not for me. Thank you very much." You know, thinking, "Jesus." But they asked me to read it and immediately I said, "I want to meet with them. Let me do this." When we met, we got into it right from the very beginning. There was no two ways around it. It was right just into the aesthetic, into the understanding of what the power was, and he had it. He really meant what he said, that he was going to reinvent the journey, and I believed him. I said, "Okay, I'm in," and that was it.

ANGELA MANCUSO

There's a naturalness to Eddie and the believability of him as a leader, as a father ... He brought a life experience to the character that was partially him. A depth of emotion. The great thing about someone like Eddie doing television is that they actually bring all of that feature belief in character; digging deep into the character that they're trained to do.

RONALD D. MOORE

But Eddie and Mary were the only two real casting pieces that I have to talk about. I met Aaron, met Eddie, had that meeting. Went very well. Had breakfast with Mary and David, just a get-to-know-you meeting to talk about the character and the idea. And we scored and signed them both. David and Michael Rymer cast pretty much the rest of the show. They kept me informed of who they were looking at and I would see audition tapes and this and that. But they get the credit for casting pretty much everybody else.

DAVID WEDDLE
(producer, *Battlestar Galactica* [2004])

One of the most amazing lead actors I've ever worked with. He is an incredible leader on the set and he knew from the beginning, and was very articulate about it, that this is a series for all time. He said over and over again, "This is the best thing I have ever worked on, bar none, and I have worked on a lot of great things." Which is such an amazing statement. He said it particularly to the younger actors: "You don't realize it, but you will never experience this again."

MICHAEL ANGELI
(co-executive producer, *Battlestar Galactica* [2004])

He was the one who constantly talked about family. He told me a number of times when we'd be together, "You know something? You are on a show that many, many people wish they could be on. You're on a show that's going to be historic. Catching lightning in a bottle twice is really difficult. Live it up." And he was right. A lot of times you would think, "What a blowhard," but he was right. He's right about a lot of things.

DAVID EICK

Eddie isn't afraid to be a little corny. He's not afraid to make speeches that maybe, if you're a teenager, you'd roll your eyes at or you might snicker at a cliché. But he just goes for the heart. When he would talk about the show and talk about us as a family and talk about how we'd never have this experience again. When you're willing to speak with such vulnerability, it shows you're not playing games or holding things close to the vest hiding agendas. It's just infectious and kind of contagious.

RONALD D. MOORE

Eddie was a consummate pro. It's hard to say enough about it, you know? His integrity as a person . . . He and Mary both just kind of became the parents of the cast. They set a certain tone of professionalism and dedication that then the rest of the cast picked up on. Because, if you remember, most of the cast was very green, especially compared to Eddie and Mary. I'll never forget, during the shooting of "33," I came to the set. We were shooting in Colonial One, and there's a scene where Laura's on the phone and talking to Adama on *Galactica*. And usually how that scene plays out when you shoot it is she's on her own side of the phone talking and then the script supervisor is giving her the line from Adama on the side. But we're sitting there getting ready to set up the shot and Eddie walks into the soundstage. I was a little surprised, because I knew he wasn't on the call sheet that day and he didn't have anything to do. But he was there. He showed up just to give Mary the other line, to play his lines to her off camera. That was a big thing and everybody kind of noted it. It filtered out to the whole production that that's how seriously he took it, that was the respect he would show for the other actors. They set a certain bar of professionalism that then really became the way we did business. Everybody took it very seriously. Nobody goofed off. I mean, there was a lot of joking around. It was a very fun, very loose set, but they all took the work very seriously.

DAVID EICK

The obvious answer of what Eddie brought to the role is gravitas, and belief that there's a guy who could actually handle all of this shit. And at the time,

an understanding that there's no such thing. And that even the most courageous, accomplished, ambitious leader is human. What Eddie shows, and
what he showed over the course of the seasons, was that he was both. He
could be every bit the George Patton, the most martial leader of leaders that
you would ever want, and you would also see him sobbing so hysterically,
drooling on his son's uniform. That was played by the same guy, and that's
the same character. I don't think one obviates the other.

I think if you look at him in the first frame of the first episode, you recognize both the command and the vulnerability. And maybe even a bit of something broken. Something that's not well. And something therefore that needs
to be taken care of. And that's a lot, man. The pockmarks and rivets in his
face, which he'll talk about freely, aren't just his signature, his trademark. In a
way, they kind of symbolize exactly what I'm talking about. It's the command
and it's the vulnerability, and it's that something is maybe hurt in there
somewhere. And it's not that we could have ever predicted that, because we
couldn't have. We were certainly thrilled at the opportunity to work with
him, but I would be lying if we said we knew any of what I just said.

MARK VERHEIDEN

I've got to give him all the credit in the world. He went to some pretty dark
places with that character, especially in season four, and he was fantastic.
He really showed the rawness of how command had eaten at him, and how
discovering his best friend was his worst enemy impacted on him. He had a
gravitas to him that was unmistakable and so fun to watch when you're on
set. He's an amazing actor, and it was really just interesting to watch multiple takes and to see how he would evolve the scene a bit. Actors always try
to do their best, but they really brought it to *Battlestar*. Some of that comes
out of a pride in the material. That they were trying to be true to the material they were given, and you don't see that on every show.

MICHAEL ANGELI

Toward the end of the show, the ship is just a mess. It's on its last legs. Adama
goes out there and starts painting. He's got a roller on a roller stick and
he's painting. The script called for him to just sort of paint and have
people come in and see him, like, "Holy shit, look, it's the admiral. He's

actually . . . working. He's doing manual labor." But Eddie sort of ad-libbed and started painting, and *then* started to weep. He started to cry, and then he fell to the floor and rolled into the paint. It was beautiful. It was him kind of realizing that it's the end of the show. It was sort of the living embodiment of the show going away and how everybody kind of felt about it. He acted it out.

DAVID WEDDLE

He inspired everybody on the set to really rise up and be the best that they could possibly be. They all followed that. The star of a series can very much set the tone for the rest of the cast. The rest of the cast watches the star, especially the younger actors, and if the star acts out, if the star has temperament and rebels, then the other actors follow that, which can be hell for writers/producers. So that impressed me enormously.

RONALD D. MOORE

During "33," I remember Eddie wanted us to bring in someone who was an expert on sleep deprivation, and talked to the whole cast about the effect of sleep deprivation on people. Eddie wanted them to actually spend five days without sleeping. Some of the actors were going, "Really? We're not really going to do this, right?" Eddie did stay awake like twenty-four or forty-eight hours or something going into his scenes. Some of the others might have stayed up a night, but I don't think they had full sleep deprivation in preparation for the show.

EDWARD JAMES OLMOS

It was the head of British Columbia University. He came in and talked to us for hours. And, of course, some of the kids thought it was kind of funny, because, you know, we brought this guy in to tell them how to act? It was kind of weird and they weren't ready for it. Michael Rymer and the producers were there, because it was the first episode and we had been away from each other for almost thirteen months—they took forever from the pilot to the first episode we shot.

Anyway, this doctor said, "You guys are saying that the characters are under attack every thirty-three minutes, twenty-four hours a day for five consecutive days. If you're not getting at least ten minutes of sleep in that thirty-three minutes, you won't make it. It's impossible. Your brain will snap." And that was it. It was just amazing, because from then on out we knew what we had to do. I didn't sleep the night before we shot the opening sequence, and a lot of us had to do some method work on it and did. Some of us just saw what other people were doing and went further. Everybody was pushing everybody, which was really wonderful.

RONALD D. MOORE

Here's the thing about Eddie: He never gave me one note on the whole run of the series. He's the only cast member who never did that. Everybody else did, you know, to varying degrees. It was all fine, you kind of expect them to have notes or thoughts or, you know, "Does this line make sense?" or "Would my character say this? Why am I doing this?" You know, there's an ongoing dialogue that you just kind of expect as part of the production, which is completely fine. You want that. But Eddie, he never gave a note. He never questioned a line, he always did the script as it was written, and he was dedicated to that idea. And he held it all the way through the whole show. I'm still kind of amazed that he did that. He just respected the word. That was how he was trained and he just approached it from the point of view that his job was to bring these words to life, not to rewrite them or substitute his own judgment. That was just his point of view on the craft. He was willing to take a leap of faith on all of us as long as a bug-eyed monster did not come in the door.

EDWARD JAMES OLMOS

I was so honored to get those scripts, because I had no idea what was going to happen. No one did. No one knew, and I never complained once. If anything, they would complain to *me* about taking it too far. They'd say, "You *really* want to go there?" and I'd say, "Yeah, I'm an alcoholic as far as I'm concerned. You want me to take a drink? Watch." As we got into the third and fourth season, I took it away. I mean, Adama had lost it. It was the sadness, because there's our core, our admiral, and he was completely gone. Many times he was left on the ground, and yes it was devastating, and it hurt everybody. As I'd watch, I might say, "Well, this is really not healthy for everybody to see. We don't really want to know this about ourselves." And yet it was what drove the UN to say this could be the finest television series *ever*. I just sit back and go, "Oh my goodness," but it came down to one thing: the writing. Period.

DAVID WEDDLE

With some actors, there is a tendency to complain and to just criticize about their character, their part. There's none of that with Olmos. Consequently you didn't see that a lot with the other actors. I mean, there is definitely creative conflict and discussion with scenes, characters, story arcs, but it was all with the best of intentions. It wasn't about ego.

There was no place that we were going to send him that he was not going to go. We knew that. Like he's beating the Cylon Leoben to death. He was like, "Bring it on. I'll beat him to death with a flashlight; spray blood all over me. Go for it." He was like that with just about everything. We couldn't go too far with Eddie. Eddie would go as far as you wanted him to go and then some. I say this a lot, but it was an honor to work with Edward James Olmos. It was truly an honor and a privilege to work with someone like him.

MICHAEL ANGELI

We had our moments, too, where he got a little autocratic. He was acting in an episode where there was a cat, so we had to get a cat trainer. The cat had to jump up on Mary's desk, the president. We did seven takes and the cat just couldn't do it. Finally, Eddie comes up to me and says, "Dude, why don't you just write the cat out of the show? This is a beautiful script, a beautiful thing and it's ruining everything." I said, "Just one more time," and I literally took the cat and tossed it up on her desk. It worked, and Eddie's like, "You got away with it this time." He could be difficult, but you always ended up liking him. There's something about him that he's an extremely likable guy who's willing to do *anything*. He was in the movie *Wolfen* with Albert Finney. He played a shape-shifting Indian who worked on skyscrapers and whatnot. Actually does a full-frontal nude scene where he's running down the street. And he was like, "Stay on the cock." Like I said, he'll do *anything*.

Moore does admit that there was a moment of trepidation about Olmos during the making of the second episode of the series, "Water."

RONALD D. MOORE

The director of the episode, Marita Grabiak, did not have a happy experience that I remember. It was a problem with her and the cast, I think. Particularly Eddie. They just did not hit it off. It became apparent kind of quickly. I was doing something else in the studio lot and I was walking by the soundstage and I asked Marita how it was going and her response was, "I just think you're going to have major problems with Olmos. He doesn't listen, he's strongheaded and thinks he runs the set. I'm just telling you right now, you guys are in big trouble on this series" [*laughs*]. It was like, "Wow, what?" It was early in the show's run, because Rymer did the first episode, so she was the only person who ever directed him on the show other than Michael Rymer. Suddenly she was losing her shit . . . and didn't like it, thought he was a problem. That was the only time that had ever happened and we figured it was just Marita and she did not have a good experience for whatever particular reason.

But I will say, with Eddie sometimes you had to kind of roll with some of the things that he would try to do. He was *always* professional, but he would try things. Like there was a scene in that episode, in one of the conference room scenes, where he's talking and Adama's on his feet. He walks around the table, and over to a corner of the set without the light, driving the DP crazy and the director crazy. But they kind of were pressed for time and had to move on. If you look at the cut, it's still in there. Like he just walked out of the light, walked into the shadows because he was trying stuff. He wanted to experiment and he didn't want to be locked into a performance just because the lighting was set up that way. That was one of the beautiful things about the show as it developed and went on is we all were willing to play with stuff, not be traditional, you know, walk out of the light, shoot stuff on characters' backs. All that kind of stuff. It really threw Marita in that second episode.

EDWARD JAMES OLMOS

During the miniseries I remember telling Rymer, "I'm not going to stand where you want me to stand. I'm going to go be with all the crew. I'll be back there with the crew." We were all standing there and then when we started into it, I started to move and I said, "How many cameras do you have there?" He said, "I've got three." I go, "Great. Then I can move, right?" He goes, "Yeah." That's all I needed to know. I just started walking around the space.

DAVID WEDDLE

We won a Peabody Award, and the studio would pay for Ron and David Eick to go, but nobody else. So we all, as writers, because the show meant so much to us, bought plane tickets, we all bought hotel rooms, we all bought a table at the Peabodys. Which cost an enormous amount of money, by the way. After the Peabodys, after everyone accepted their awards, we had some kind of talk with journalists for something. Edward James Olmos got up and he said, "I just want to thank every writer on this show. The writers are the reason this is a great show. As a matter of fact, they care so much they all flew themselves in, and they are sitting in the audience right now, and let's give a standing ovation for the writers."

MARK STERN
(former president of original content, Syfy)

I remember when I called Eddie Olmos and told him we were picking the series up for season two and that there would be twenty episodes, he bawled me out. He said we were going to ruin it. "You can't do that many episodes and have them all be good." I had a lot of new experiences on that show, and this was definitely one of them. I'd never had anyone yell at me for ordering so many episodes before. Of course we ended up breaking up that order, so we actually did them as ten and ten, and did manage to maintain that consistent quality. Because he's right: If you're doing them all in a row, inevitably those middle few episodes just suffer, because you just don't have the time.

MARK VERHEIDEN

Adama has one of the greatest arcs, because he started out as part of a rivalry with the civilian side, with Roslin. Eddie Olmos always brought a great humanity to it, so I don't want to reduce him to archetypes, but the character started as the military man who was in command of these ships. His job was to protect these people and to maybe take the fight to the Cylons, but really it was to survive and he would do whatever it takes to protect his people. Roslin's side was, "Yes, but we have to do that in a way that continues to support the morality and the humanity that we had as people, so we can't just throw away everything, all the laws and rules that we had, because we're under crisis, or we lose everything that we were." That was the fundamental conflict, but in time what would happen is both of them evolved in a way. Adama had to loosen up a little bit as things went on. He had to learn to function with the civilian government. That the civilian government did bring something positive to the world.

MICHAEL ANGELI

The one constant that remained, and it was good that it did, was being this kind of solitary leader. That didn't go away, and I think that was important. Over time he started to wear his emotions on his sleeve more and allowed himself to feel a certain way, whereas he was very sort of buttoned up for the first few seasons.

DAVID EICK

My takeaway on the Adama character is you watch this commander and this man who's devoted his life to this, and having to compromise. At first with Laura. Having to learn to be a patriarch more than just a commander military guy. That these were people who suddenly needed not just a commander, but also a father. So you have to watch him develop the ability to be that, even though you saw roots of it, you knew it was a struggle. And then, ultimately, my favorite of many favorites that I would put near the top of the list, the way Eddie played Adama having to deal with Cain, and what that meant to not only his command and his ego, but to his family, which I feel Ron brilliantly placed under threat as well. It's not just that you're going to have your balls cut off, I'm going to hurt the things you love, too. So I really think it's his capacity of stooping to conquer, and watch him open his heart in ways that he never would think he'd have to in order to lead. I really struggled to believe any other actor could have pulled that off.

MARK VERHEIDEN

He went from the guy who wanted to kill the Cylons to wanting to make a deal with them somehow, and that's a *huge* shift for that character. Again, you went along with it, because there was an incredible honesty to every promise it almost gave, you could see the anguish he was in trying to work through these issues. You see that humanity in him trying to come out even in the face of Roslin doing things that he really didn't think were beneficial to their survival. You could see that conflict in him. You could hear some of the dialogue, too—to give the writers a little credit. His evolution was really fascinating and it was great to watch an actor of that caliber pull that off in the context of a show that's on a spaceship in outer space. What was really fun about seeing the reaction to the show was after a while, you forgot that's what they were and it became a show about characters and intense emotions and the worlds they were in. Less about the bells and whistles, though we loved the science fiction and looking at how they would survive.

That, to me, was Adama's journey. Roslin is interesting because she went the other way, which was in over her head to becoming almost doctrinaire in some respects. You know, "We're going to get rid of abortions" or "I'm going to manipulate the elections so I win," but then she couldn't do it. She went from over her head to becoming a very strong leader and staying there, so she and Adama were able to be two very strong leaders in charge of that fleet, which I think is beneficial to everyone there.

MARY MCDONNELL

I loved the encounter between Roslin and Adama in the miniseries, because I felt like it just had classic gender problems. Classic gender-power-struggle problems that kind of made me giggle a little bit, because it was sort of, like, "Hey, you two better get it together, because you've got bigger problems."

EDWARD JAMES OLMOS

Through the series, Adama went from being an extremely positive, uplifting commander who had served his time and fought his battles, and was very good at what he did. One of the best pilots there had ever been who was retiring. He was losing his strength in the world in respects of he had been retired, forced retirement, and his ship was becoming a museum. The world would get into a universal world war against the Cylons. So he becomes the hope for the advancement of humanity, the person who had to take care of it. Then the responsibility becomes so great as time goes on that he completely crumbles and becomes an alcoholic and a drug addict, and cannot even stand up anymore. Completely loses his sense of balance, only to rise from the ashes and, like the phoenix, continues forward and helps humanity survive. He comes back. I've never seen it in heroic terms, that demise of a character brought about that was so strong.

They didn't know I was going to take it to that extreme, but because I directed a lot of the episodes, they would see me in different episodes standing by the bar and drinking a lot, or I'd be dropping pills. People didn't register at the beginning too much, other than saying, "Well, you're just relaxing." But then as time went on, he becomes a total alcoholic and found himself just slobbering and throwing up, lying in his own vomit and unable to control anything anymore. He had lost it, totally.

Most of the time as a commander you don't really want to know your military. You want to be able to look at them as nothing but soldiers. You don't want to know them personally, because it becomes too difficult when you lose them. But on this show we were very tight with our military. We were very tight with our entire crew, so when somebody passed, it was deadly. When Dualla commits suicide, it's just very, very difficult for everybody. When we lost Starbuck, it was unbelievably difficult. When we thought that Lee had gone down with the president and everybody that blew up in Colonial One, it became very difficult to take. But there were so many moments where you just lost total hope and were just completely consumed by the reality that this is unbelievably difficult to take, but this is exactly what these people are living. And the challenge was to try and overcome that.

Laura Roslin was the secretary of education of the Twelve Colonies when the Cylons launched their genocidal attack. Through the rules of succession—despite the fact that she was forty-third down the line—she finds herself president of what's left of humanity. In the series bible, Moore adds about her, "Laura is an introvert by nature who's served in the public eye for most of her adult life. Uncomfortable with pressing the flesh and asking for support, she never considered a run for office, even though she has the rare ability to make a person feel as if what they're saying is the most important thing in the world at that moment. She listens extremely well, takes her time making decisions, and understands what makes people tick on a gut level."

Mary McDonnell was Moore's first choice for the character. With a background that has ranged from her Academy Award-nominated role in *Dancing with Wolves* to playing the first lady in the disaster film *Independence Day,* and her work on television in *Major Crimes,* she brought a combination of strength and vulnerability to the role of Laura Roslin.

ANGELA MANCUSO

My first choice for Laura Roslin was actually Alfre Woodard, because, besides her being one of the greatest actresses of our time, I really wanted diversity in the show. But she knew we were shooting in Canada and she still had kids in school and didn't want to go to Canada.

RONALD D. MOORE

I put Mary McDonnell at the top of the Laura Roslin list, because I had been watching *Donnie Darko.* I got turned on to that film and I was like, "Oh my God, what an amazing film." So I was watching *Donnie Darko* while I'm writing the mini, and I just fastened on to Mary, thinking she would be the perfect Laura Roslin.

MARY MCDONNELL

This is very cliché, but I was having lunch with my agents at Spago. I had gotten there early, which is highly unusual for me, and I saw Sidney Poitier there and had done *Secrets* with him, so I had been talking to him and was in a really good mood. I sat down; my agents came and said, "We're so sorry we're late, but an offer just came in for you and we wanted to get some information about it and bring it to lunch. We got on the phone with these people and the script isn't here yet, but there's an offer." I said, "Oh, great, what is it?" They kind of giggled and everybody pauses. They said, "Well, they're doing a remake of *Battlestar Galactica.*" I just started giggling. I said, "Preposterous. First of all"—not that I had that much knowledge of *Battlestar Galactica;* I'd maybe seen one episode, because it aired during my theater years in New York and I didn't have a TV—"why would anybody want to cast *me* in a show like that?" In anything remotely having to do with the pristine elements of outer space, I'm the Earth Mother. The Prairie Queen. They said, "We kind of thought the same thing, but they reassured us that it's actually quite amazing. It's a reinvention. The writer is excellent. We know his work. They're asking if you would just give it a chance. Give it a read." I said, "Of course. I think it's hilarious. Let's see what they want me to do."

I went back to their office with them after lunch, because Ron Moore's office said they would send it right over, and in fact it was there. I took it home and I read it that night after the kids were in bed. And I was absolutely floored. I could not believe how ridiculously ignorant my response had been. I've forgiven myself for it, but, honestly, it was just so delightful. I called my agent that night and said, "I want to have breakfast, or lunch would be fine, as soon as possible. Before we talk about this any more, I would like to meet Ron Moore and David Eick and Michael Rymer," who was already set to direct the pilot, "because this means me going to Vancouver. Leaving my home. I still have a son in middle school, a daughter in high school. This is going to be a lot of separation." This was going to mean a huge change, and even though it was just a miniseries, it was still a chunk of time. I said, "So I need to know that I like the people I'm about to work with, otherwise I'm not leaving L.A. under these circumstances." Two days later we had breakfast at the W in Westwood, and I loved them all.

RONALD D. MOORE

I started writing the part literally with her voice in my head. And then she agreed and that was fantastic. We had a *great* meeting with her. She brings with her a sort of innate intelligence. There's something very smart about Mary, in person and on camera. That was one of the reasons why I thought she would be a great president, because she just seems like a really smart person. A lot of her strength as a character flows from how smart she is. She's sexy and capable and can be fierce. If she yells, it kind of gets your attention. She just had all the perfect characteristics of the president. There was just something ideal about her. She was a great, lovely person. She laughs easily, she's funny and she liked jokes.

MARY MCDONNELL

I loved Ron's modesty, and his soft-spoken intelligence. He was definitely not a Hollywood type-A showrunner, although he's an extraordinarily strong human being. His intelligence has wisdom to it, so he's humble. He listens deeply, which is not necessarily a quality that goes with a Hollywood showrunner. He's just a beautiful spirit. That was delightful. David Eick was hilarious; very funny, very smart. Very interested in talking about the politics of the Laura Roslin situation, so that got me excited. Michael Rymer conveyed that everything was going to be a lot of fun, and edgy and cool. I was like, "Okay, these guys are very hip. Very young and very smart. It couldn't be better." It was pretty much that simple. I drove away from that breakfast knowing I was going to do it; I wanted to bring Laura to life. I wanted to be that reluctant president.

DAVID EICK

One of my faults is that when I talk about things like leadership and setting an example to the rest of the cast, I tend to talk about Eddie in that context, because I'm sexist and he's a good person. But the truth is, it really was Eddie *and* Mary. Eddie was louder and more aggressive about what was important and why it was so important, so I tend to kind of talk about him first, but we needed the balance of Mary, who is every bit Eddie's equal in terms of career accomplishment. Therefore, how she behaved and what she said and her reaction to material and all that kind of stuff was every bit as critical in terms of setting a tone and creating a sense of boundaries for the rest of the cast as how Eddie reacted. I think everyone fell in love with her on the pilot, and when I say everybody I just mean everyone who wound up staying involved in the show.

MARY MCDONNELL

I talk about this ad nauseam, but it was very important to me to explore a woman coming into power without a cultural training or support behind her as many women my age have experienced. Then it went from there in terms of Hillary Clinton and we were shooting this when Hillary was running [against Obama] and it became a very timely event for me. We started it not too long after September eleventh, so there was a deep emotional connection as well.

KATEE SACKHOFF
(actress, "Kara 'Starbuck' Thrace")

One of the fears I've always had in my life was how do you juggle motherhood and work? Mary was very honest about it. She said, "Sometimes you can't have it all. Sometimes you're going to have to choose your children." And that's what she did. She chose the kids, she walked away from the business, she disappeared for a while and raised her kids. And then she came back with *Battlestar,* because her kids were at an age where they were old enough to understand where she was going and come and visit her. She made that choice, because this business is not kind to aging women. Not only is it not kind to them, it's also not kind to women who disappear for a year, have a baby, and then want to come back. It's as if they've committed a terrible sin, and God forbid they need to breast-feed their kid at work. This is not a good business to try and age in and have children in. It *can* be done, and it has been done by so many women at a ranging level of success. But the beautiful thing about Mary was she was very honest about what it took from her, and her children are phenomenal. They're absolutely amazing kids. Granted she did it with her husband, but she was home with those children when they needed her, and she was willing to risk it all for her kids. I respected the fuck out of that.

REKHA SHARMA
(actress, "Tory Foster")

On my very first day as Tory, Mary was so generous and so open. I remember we did one or two takes and she just looked at me with this twinkling, expansive, Buddha-like love in her eyes and she just said, "You are *so* good." Very unusual in this world where people are so small-minded—not everybody, but you come across it where people are very competitive and small-minded. She was the antithesis of that. Everybody on this show was the antithesis of that, actually. I had never experienced so much fun on set working with someone the way I did with her. I learned so much from her in the years that we worked together, but on that first day, I went to my trailer at the end of the day when we wrapped and literally cried tears of joy.

MARK VERHEIDEN

Mary McDonnell is an amazing actress, and at first she brought that sense of, "I'm going to step up and I'm going to do this, but, oh my God, what world are we in now? This is uncharted waters. How do we even begin?" That determination that she had to hold on to the things that made these people human as opposed to giving it all up and just saying, basically, military law; you do what Adama says. Holding on to the things that made their civilization a civilization. She was able to just give such great voice to that feeling and that passion, which, frankly, as a writer, I very much agree with: Without really maintaining the humanity that you have, what are you? You're just out there going through the motions.

DAVID EICK

When she took the oath of office in the miniseries, there's something so terrified and brave about the way she stands with her hand in this very odd kind of position as she raises it to take the oath. It was like she really did have to become a leader, which was really weird, and I just remember people treating her differently. There was a little bit more awe around her, like, "Wow, you've really had to step in." It was like the story was informing the experience, and it was because of her performance. It was because of how compelling she was at delivering the reality of what the fuck would a schoolteacher do in this position. I think the love for Mary, and this is to take nothing away from just how she is as a person, came from her craft initially. I remember people gathering around the monitor when she was on, wanting to watch her prepare. She just really was a captivating actor, as a craftsperson. She was amazing to watch. And she was the most willing to struggle openly, and by that it's another way of saying complain. But I never felt it *was* complaining. She would question the material, but never in a judgmental way or with the assumption that she was somehow being short-changed. Her questions were always extraordinarily thoughtful, painful. About the cancer, about the loss of life, about having to restart humanity, having to restart the human race.

MICHAEL ANGELI

Where do I begin? I had never met her before, and in the beginning she would call and talk about lines and talk about the script. She made really good points. It was something that I hadn't experienced before, where the actor actually instead of seeing you on the set or whatever, they would get in touch with you to talk about their character. At first it was a little jarring. It sort of got my back up a little bit, but then I thought, "Well, what the fuck? She really wants to mine her character and figure it out." You know, "Why is she saying this and what is she feeling? What is she supposed to be feeling when she says this?" She makes you really nail it down, which was good. Then it got to a point where I couldn't wait for her to call. But then she didn't have to call as much, because what happened was you start writing *for* her, for her character, and figure it out. You just have to understand what she wants to be. Then it got to be she was my favorite character to write next to Baltar. I loved writing for her. It's astonishing she was never nominated, because she was just unbelievable.

RONALD D. MOORE

I probably got more notes from Mary than from any other cast member. Formal notes. She would want to meet and sit down and we would sit and go through the script, go through the pages. You'd have meetings like that with other actors. Most of them would be more casual or they wanted to talk about a particular scene or you might do a phone call or an exchange of emails. Every once in a while you might sit down and talk about it with the script in hand, but Mary did it a lot over the course of the series. She was always thinking about the character, where the character had been and where the character was going; what she wanted in this scene, a lot of "Why?" Why would she react like that or, "I don't think Laura would do this." It always made the show better, made her character better. She was able to connect the dots between this scene and something she had done the year before, and question whether or not that made sense.

DAVID EICK

She would get frustrated with Eddie, but a lot of that would be an extension of Laura's frustration with Adama. How to deal with that character would be a concern for her. She didn't want to look weak, yet she didn't want to pretend to be Linda Hamilton, when clearly she *wasn't*. That was a very delicate thing for her to try to handle: how to maintain not only her own strength as a character, but ensure that the character maintains her own sense of strength and self-respect and, by the way, femininity, *while* she's dying of cancer. I mean, the curveball you throw an actor like that, you just don't expect to be hit back with this sort of grace and chiseled nuance, and this was just a beautiful performance.

RONALD D. MOORE

We started focusing in a lot about how Laura Roslin was going to become the president and making her the secretary of education. I'd always liked those stories about the person that's designated as the sole survivor. For a State of the Union address, there's always that one person that's designated *not* to be in Washington, in case the whole U.S. government is wiped out. I thought, "Oh, Laura should be *that* person." She should be way down the chain of command and just have it handed to her out of nowhere. That's really fascinating and amazing.

MICHAEL ANGELI

She would say that she wanted to do justice to the script. Man, she did more than justice. She's one character that I think was ready to go. She lived an entire life through the life of the show, from being forty-third in line to being the president to leading them to a place where they could survive. And then dying. And so brave a character. When she was sick and bald and it was all makeup, it took six hours to get her to look like that. It was stifling and hot, and she just persevered.

DAVID EICK

I think of the episode "33," and her reaction at the very end of that episode is maybe one of my favorite moments of hers. It's when she's told that someone on one of the ships has had a baby. After all this horror and death and everyone being slaughtered, and then Billy [her assistant] comes in and says a baby was born on the *Rising Star* or something like that. If you didn't have that, that show is such a nihilistic downer. You'd watch it and then want to jump out a window. The fact that she does that "Yes!" motion at the end is why you want to watch the next episode, because you find yourself saying, "Hold on, this is more interesting than that. Oh, I see, so she'll ensure that the darkness doesn't ever get *too* dark, because she's going to be the heart of the show." And *then* she's suddenly throwing people out airlocks, and behaving like George W. Bush and outlawing abortion. Doing things that are *not* what we felt we were being set up for at all.

RONALD D. MOORE

I was surprised at how resolute and intelligent Laura was. You know, in my initial conception you saw more of the schoolteacher. You saw more of the secretary of education. You saw more of the woman that was like, "Wow, I wasn't prepared for this at all." Mary brought a deeper strength and moxie to it. She was more formidable, so that really started steering the character more strongly in that direction.

DAVID EICK

Mary was not a fan—maybe that's overstating it—initially of turning Laura toward a kind of martial-law direction when it came to the Cylons, because I think she, too, thought she would be the kind of hard-core commander, and yet as she discovered the richness of what was being written for her, she was both the heart of the show and yet had a point of view that many would compare with a much more reactionary individual. Once she understood it, it became irresistible to her and she took total command of it.

MARK VERHEIDEN

There were also her emotional stories dealing with Baltar, dealing with Apollo, and, of course, dealing with Adama. She was able to bring the humanity to those things. I remember one of my favorite scenes in the relationship between Adama and Roslin was in fourth season in the mutiny episode where they were in bed together and talking about getting coffee or something. I just thought, "Wow, how far we've come from them originally wanting to kill each other and now they're a friendly couple trying to figure out their day." That was fun.

DAVID EICK

You could imagine the number of times, in exhaustion, when someone pitches, "In the teaser, Adama and Laura wake up in bed. Oh no, what do we do?" I have to say, I'm so glad we never wound up going there, because it wouldn't have come from any place that would make sense. We were never building to that. I don't think anyone would've liked it; it was just the kind of temptation that happens when you're rowing and rowing and rowing and looking to land on the beach, so you're reaching for *anything*.

MARY MCDONNELL

That's why I say they were soulmates from the beginning, because he was an annoying, compelling foe at the beginning. When someone is that compelling to a woman who's intelligent, it usually means that there's something else there. And they very quickly switched the classic male/female response to life, and she becomes more of a hawk and he the dove. That idea blossomed in me, which is whoever this man is, is actually part of my world. Whatever we go through is going to have an afterlife. You go through things with a soulmate in life that could set you apart for the next three lifetimes. Then suddenly they're there again. It's like there was a deeper connection that they had and the universe sent them there together to accomplish this. No matter what they ran into, when it was time to take the next step, if that meant coming to agreement or a new agreement, they were both pretty willing to take it. Although I *was* a little pissed off when he threw me in jail. That was a tough season.

EDWARD JAMES OLMOS

Mary is a consummate artist and brilliant. Very committed. She and I took on our roles with a tremendous amount of passion, and she looked at the way I was doing it, of course, and I complemented the way she was doing it. That was very much a situation that grew, and it grew in such a strong way that it helped the character. It helped both the characters. We both became totally involved with the story, and it was wonderful to work with her. I fell in love with her. She's such a joy and to this day, fifteen years later, we're very close and dear friends. I'm friends with her family; I know her husband and her kids.

MICHAEL ANGELI

She was always gracious. I never heard her get angry or stomp her feet about anything. That's not true about a lot of people on the show, a lot of actors on the show. She's just such a sweetheart in so many ways. Eddie and Mary were the mother and father of the show. They were the parents. Everybody else were the kids. She played that role so well.

DAVID EICK

You got the sense that Laura Roslin had to develop her sensibilities on the fly; you didn't get the sense that she necessarily held them her whole life. But just as Adama has to force his heart open and realize he's not just an admiral, he's also Daddy around there and he has to figure that shit out because that's as important to their survival as the other. She's learning, "Okay, I'm a lover and now a fighter, and I never wanted any of this, but if you're putting me in this chair, here's what I think we've got to do." That pragmatism has to supersede your own nature sometimes, and you wouldn't have ever gotten there with a different actor in the role of Laura Roslin. That combination is what allowed us to do that. You cast a brute or a Nurse Ratched in that role, you go, "Okay, I get it." Then you cast some total softy in the role and you think "Bullshit" when she throws someone out an airlock. But Mary's able to do both, and that's the miracle.

The character was diagnosed with breast cancer in the miniseries, and that was something that plagued her throughout the series, on and off. At one point, the drugs designed to help her cope with her pain—which came with warnings of hallucinogenic side effects—led the character and the show itself in a different direction.

MARK VERHEIDEN

We wanted to play some of the reality of that, and clearly we had episodes where she's undergoing chemo and lost her hair and things were getting pretty dire. We really wanted to be true to that idea that there was no magical cure, though we did use Cylon blood [which put her in remission for a time].

RONALD D. MOORE

"Flesh and Bone" was an important episode for us. The "Laura Getting Visions" episode, with her tying into the prophecies, felt like that was going to be a big path forward for us. We started to talk about Laura and her role in the show as president; I kept referring to her as Moses. I would always talk internally about the fact that "I don't know when they're going to get to Earth, but when they do, she's going to be Moses. She's going to lead them to Earth, but she's not going to be able to go there." Like Moses was not allowed to go into the land of Israel when he leads the Israelites there. So that was always where I thought the character was. We just kept talking about her as Moses, and at some point, you start talking about if she's a secular character, she probably doesn't believe in God. In their system, the Gods. In their society, wouldn't it be interesting if she started to have prophecies and she is starting to see things, starting to believe that they're possibly true. And then you force the president to have to go to the very matter-of-fact, very secular Commander Adama and try to convince him to listen to a prophecy. And we thought, "Well, that's just great drama. That'll be a lot of fun in itself."

MARY MCDONNELL

I felt like Laura's whole experience was the universe asking her to stretch. This was just another example of that. Am I really having these visions, or am I actually seeing something that could help us survive? If so, where's the information coming from? Is this chamalla-induced or is the chamalla actually just opening me to be able to see what is actually here for us? You've got to understand, I was doing these psychedelic drugs inside a story where the actors know that in the very first episode, in the pilot, there's a woman walking around in a red dress who isn't really there. By the time we get to this question of whether or not it's a drug-induced hallucination or really information that the heightened awareness of the drug is allowing Laura to see—a survival road map—those negotiations were fun, because who knew? What I liked about Laura Roslin is that she clearly had the capacity to continue to innocently process new information and develop the courage to take action with no background in it whatsoever.

DAVID EICK

The whole messiah thing—I wouldn't do that now. I think there was something about the manifest destiny of Iraq, and the fact that it felt like we were following a messianic or religious trek, because there was no evidence, there was no attack, we're a sovereign country and we're doing this thing. And we've all had to kind of persuade ourselves that there's a moral righteousness behind what we're doing. So it starts to feel messianic. You have to rely on the fact that Bush has had a vision, or he sees into the soul of the bad guys and he just knows this. He feels it. And you start believing in feelings. I'm not even mocking any of this; I think this is all very real. A lot of this happened in World War II for the good. You know, my country right or wrong. So I think at that point, because of the eleven o'clock news, you could say someone's going to follow their vision, someone's going to follow not logic, not weapons of mass destruction, not evidence, but their visions. Their feelings.

Now I say I wouldn't do that today, because the zeitgeist is different, and I just think it would go down differently. Or at least it would to me. But at that time it seemed very much like an echo of what we were all doing as a culture anyway.

RONALD D. MOORE

When we came up with the idea of Cylon blood putting her cancer into remission, I did that because I was pretty determined that Laura was going to die by the end of the series, but there did come a point where we wanted to play it realistically and we wanted to go through all of the stages of it, dealing with the ramifications of it, but there was a point where it started to feel like it was going to take over her storyline. We just needed to press pause on that story; we'd gotten a little further down the line than I think we wanted to a little too fast. She would have gotten confined to the sickbay, which nobody wanted. So it was a total cheat, but here's this magic blood and it's Cylon blood and we'll cure her cancer and it'll come back later.

When the storyline came out, I said to Mary, "I'm not getting rid of this," because she was concerned. It was how you met her. It was one of the defining characteristics of the character. I said, "Don't worry, this isn't going away, but I need to press pause on this story for a little while. For now, let's play your character in terms of the miracle cure and what that does to her and how she looks at life differently after a moment like that. And how it influences her view of the Cylons, the Cylon baby and all of that."

MARY MCDONNELL

As a person, we started out with a woman who was a bit lonely and grieving the loss of practically everyone she knew. On top of that she's diagnosed with a fatal disease. In the beginning there was a sad, lonely person there, whose life had not really manifested much. Her life wasn't asking her to use herself much. Even though she was secretary of education, and I do believe that she was really good at it and very fulfilled, the little bit that we did learn about her on the way in flashbacks, etc. It became clear to me that she was living one of those mysterious lives that wasn't really full and out there. There were certain things about it that were secretive and she was having an affair with the president, but that wasn't out in the open. She didn't have her own children and she'd lost everyone. There were just certain ways in which her life was not really quite full.

By the end of the series, her last line is, "So much life." That killed me when I read it. That was not what the woman was experiencing at the beginning. By the end she had seen so much of the world inside this particular lens. She had seen so much about what she was capable of. She had done things that she was ethically in disagreement with as a human, but as a human had to make a choice for the greater good. She had fallen in love, probably with her soulmate. She had learned how to comprehend other realities. None of this was available to her as a human being. The idea that she had to become president is almost secondary—to me—to the fact that this particular woman went from living maybe her life at fifty percent potential to it took everything she had.

The alternative is that she could have died along with everyone else and not experienced any of it. Instead, she has to go on an obligatory trip that she already promised she would do, up to that stupid old battleship, and try and convince some stubborn old dude on a big ship that she be taken down, to let them use it as a learning tool for kids. Having gotten her news about the cancer, she could have said, "Excuse me, I can't come." How interesting that she didn't do that. Her life is radically changed and she is asked by the universe to use her mind, her heart, her courage. She has to discover and then develop a backbone of steel. She has to figure out how to *not* be intimidated by anything.

The relationship between Commander Adama and his son, Captain Lee Adama, was a difficult, tentative one at best, the backstory of which comes from the show's bible. Both Lee and his brother Zak were the children of divorce, admiring their father from a distance, seeing him only occasionally. Both nonetheless idolized the legendary commander. Lee quickly rose to the top of his class at flight school, with a great potential future for himself. Notes the bible, "It was about this time that Lee and his father began to have a falling-out. The boy's hero worship had turned into the young man's resentments at being abandoned and neither he nor his father knew how to bridge the gap, and so the visits became rare and the phone calls grew terse." His brother graduated the academy and wanted to join flight school, more to impress their father than anything else, and it was obvious to Lee that Zak wasn't cut out for the military. That seemed to become more evident when his application to flight school was rejected . . . until their father pulled some strings.

Continues the bible, "Then came another shock: Zak wrote Lee to tell him he was engaged to one of his instructors at flight school. Lee made time to visit and it was then that he met Kara Thrace for the first time. She was the polar opposite of Zak—where he was quiet, reserved, almost painfully sensitive, she was brash, loud, and had a thick hide. Lee liked her immediately. Maybe liked her too much. And he was pretty sure that she felt the same, but never seriously considered anything further. Lee wished them well and left to rejoin the squadron. Two weeks later, Zak's plane went down while he was flying a routine solo mission and he was killed. Lee's resentments and griefs boiled over at the funeral and he lashed out at his father, blaming him directly for his brother's death, saying in so many words that Adama had all but killed his own son. Father and son never spoke again. Lee spent the next two years focusing on his career, having no personal life and working to become the perfect fighter pilot. . . . He was at test pilot school when the orders came in to report aboard *Galactica* for her decommissioning ceremony."

Obviously this is where the miniseries picks up, with the Cylon attack and Lee remaining aboard the *Galactica*. Writes Moore, "He's a young man with a lot of anger, a lot of resentments and a lot of frustrations who knows not what to do with them. But he's also a fair and decent human being whose deeply felt sense of right and wrong have kept him afloat when so many around him have sunk. He's the kind of man few would call friend, but many would follow in the jaws of hell. He is his father's son."

Playing the character is British-born Jamie Bamber, who, prior to *Battlestar Galactica*, had been seen in the television series *Band of Brothers*, *Peak Practice*, and *Ultimate Force*, and the miniseries *Daniel Deronda*.

JAMIE BAMBER
(actor, "Captain Lee 'Apollo' Adama")

I'd done a body of work, but was still having to struggle, still hustling and working mainly in the U.K. I'd done *Band of Brothers* and some American stuff, but I'd never actually done a TV show in the United States, so I was pretty keen to do whatever it was coming down the pipe. Everything was an opportunity. I do remember at the time thinking, "Why on Earth would anybody want to remake *Battlestar Galactica*?" When my manager handed me this script over, I think I had just landed in L.A. and was staying in his studio apartment under his house. He poured me a glass of wine and then pushed this piece of paper across the table. I just thought, "Tell me Hollywood's got its own original ideas and isn't just having to do *this*," but then I read this mission statement that Ron Moore had written. Two and a half pages, I think it was, which was included with the script. I've since found out that Ron had never intended it to be included with the script. This was something he had written, obviously, to be kept to the executives and producers and stuff. But anyway, it was there with this script and I was really taken aback by the boldness of the ambition. It's what really sold it to me. Then I started reading the script and looking for the name Apollo and couldn't find him anywhere, because it wasn't there. There was loads of this character called Lee. Someone else called Kara, but on a quick glance Apollo and Starbuck weren't there.

So then I had to go back and read it, and I'd like to say that it immediately said to me this is absolutely the best thing I was ever going to be involved in, but because those names weren't in it, I was sort of stitching the childhood memories that I had of the show, which were very, very hazy, because I was very young when it came out. But that's really what I was doing, trying to work out what semblance this had to the one I had seen before. And then the more I read things like the idea of *Galactica* being turned into a museum and the ship being this old junked-up waste of space in a fleet that had moved on, and there were things like that, I suddenly went, "Wait a minute, there's something here." And it was the moment when Boomer was a Cylon that sort of got me going. Another moment was a line about the Cylons believing in one true God, and the humans not. I just suddenly thought, "Okay, he's doing what I like about storytelling and drama," which is turn what we naturally think to be right on its head and asking us to empathize with those that we expect to dislike and distrust.

And that was really the mantra of *Battlestar Galactica:* Anytime you thought you were comfortable, the good guys were going to do something worse than the bad guys and the bad guys were going to seem better than the good guys. As a result, you're forced to redraw all sorts of allegiance lines, and any show that does that is really using the most out of the dramatic form, which is about taking us to places of understanding that we can't achieve just by reading the newspapers. And, yeah, Ron did that, but on the first reading of the script, it was just a job for me. It was just an audition and I was desperate to get the part, though it was a long process. I had a few hoops to jump through, but there were two moments it became special. One, my then agent Michael Lazo called me and said it's the best thing he'd seen all year in terms of all the TV that he'd seen that season. Michael always had high taste barriers, so that shocked me.

And then it was when the very current political parallels started to be drawn between some of the stuff that Ron was writing about. The stories about torturing prisoners, the stories about things that were going on in Iraq, literally as we were filming. I suddenly got goose bumps when you realized that this show that was set in outer space is nothing but what we're doing to ourselves right now. You may have distilled it right down to the barest elements that made you think it's in another time and place, but it was the human experience distilled and made more shocking as a result. It was a bitter drink to drink as you watched the show. And it was really challenging to me. It was challenging to America at the time. There were some uncomfortable messages, and I loved that. I loved that we were trying to do something that's not safe, that's not easy, that's going to make people hopefully uncomfortable. And we did that.

RONALD D. MOORE

I'd say the biggest thing we struggled consistently through the years in terms of the story and characters had to do with Lee Adama. I sort of wanted to get him out of the cockpit early in the first season and make him a military advisor to Laura. I thought that would be kind of an interesting thing, and maybe there would even be a romance between the two of them. And *that* would be interesting, her being president and older. He's young and Adama's son. It felt like there was some drama to play there. I started edging around that a little bit, because I knew I didn't want to play Laura and Adama romantically for quite a while. I said in the show bible, if there's anything that's going to happen, it won't happen for a while. I was just looking for other colors to play and I thought, "Well, let's move Lee over and do that." But then, as the stories evolved, there was less and less of him to play with her, and there was more for him to play as the commander of the air crew. For a while he was kind of straddling both worlds, and then he kind of became more of a pilot.

JAMIE BAMBER

The nutshell of my experience playing Lee was the thing that I talked to Michael Rymer about all the time: just trying to avoid him being this slightly priggish Boy Scout, and to find steel in him. And not one that is just reciting what he *should* be doing, because he had a tendency at times to be a contrarian—to rebel against those around him for the sake of it, because he's got this problem in his past and this unresolved blame about the disintegration of his family and his brother's death. And to blame parents for things that happened in your upbringing is boring to listen to, because everyone does it. It's one of those tropes we all have a moment of doing, and if you keep doing that, any drama becomes tedious very quickly, like a boring friend who will not leave something alone when you go to the pub. You always have the same conversation about the same things.

So we were very keen to move him along from that, and different people in the creative process had different ways of expressing what Lee was within the show. David Eick called him the conscience of the show for a bit, and that's something that scared me as well, because, again, you can be stuck in a trope. But my thought for Lee is he was on a voyage of self-discovery. He was trying to find out who he actually is and was, because he didn't know.

He was defined only by relationships with others. He was defined as the son, as the potential girlfriend lover, and he was in a world that he never intended to be. He was on that battlestar for one afternoon begrudgingly, to fulfill a ceremonial function, but after that, he saw his life as anywhere but in the military with his dad, with Kara Thrace. He had no intention of being anywhere around these people. And *that* was the key to Lee, is he was someone trapped in his idea of Hell, which is this environment, but then realizing that his own rebellion had to come second when the survival of all the remaining human beings depended on him. Because he had a unique set of skills and he was there. He has to put his ego aside gradually, and I think that was the battle for Lee. It's sort of ego versus service, and you see that all the way through. He has this strongly defined sense of right and wrong and what should happen, and what shouldn't happen, but gradually he learns to put that aside in order to serve the needs of the greatest number of people.

MARK VERHEIDEN

It was trying to give him an identity that was more than Adama's son/fighter pilot. What unique thing was he going to bring to the *Battlestar* world. Jamie is a great actor, so it was never an issue about that. It was what could we do to make what the world he was in stand out.

JAMIE BAMBER

It was a struggle, because in a show like *Battlestar,* with so many wonderful characters and so many great actors, in a way we all are fighting for our corner of the story and to keep our little corner alive. I felt sometimes that Lee was not the most interesting character at the beginning. He didn't pull off the great moves in the Viper, he was by-the-book, and he was trying to keep people together. He wasn't the automatic choice to be the talisman of the fleet or anything. Gradually I learned the gift was to play that slightly misunderstood, stoic type who's not yet found his outlet and doesn't shoot from the hip, and thinks very hard about things and *doesn't* have the quip that's going to sort of button the conversation. But I never found the character easy. It was always a struggle, and I think that's fitting for someone who was fighting for his life, obviously, and the lives of those around him, but also for his identity within this changing world.

MICHAEL ANGELI

It seemed like he was always playing second fiddle to either Adama—his father—or Mary's character. He was on equal footing with Starbuck, but there was something kind of impassive for a long time about his character. It was tough. It was hard to find things for him to do. We failed a couple of times. When we went to *Cloud 9*, we had him running around in the walls of the ship fighting terrorists like the *Die Hard* guy. The intention was to give him something to do, but it didn't work. Until we decided to do the trial and have him represent Baltar in season three; that's where it kind of clicked. That's where it got better for him. It worked for his character, because he wasn't like Starbuck. He wasn't this sort of masculine warrior guy. There was something a little touchy-feely about him that we were trying to rid ourselves of. Having him use words to fight and to be in an unpopular situation where he's defending fucking Baltar! It gave him some controversy and for the audience you saw him in a different light.

JAMIE BAMBER

Basically I think the traditional role of the young masculine lead was taken by Kara in Ron's brilliant gender flip. That left Lee in a bit of a vacuum in terms of traditional male protagonists. So as an actor I think I struggled to find what it was that meant for Lee and his story role. I think the writers did, too. Initially I fought against it. It took a while to realize that the identity crisis is the opportunity. That *was* Lee's story. It was what makes Ron so good. Once we found that, then Lee becomes emblematic of what it is to be a male in today's world, when our traditional role models no longer work and we have to find a new definition of masculinity that includes feminine traits. Certainly with Kara, Lee is the silent, patient, traditionally feminine, passive partner. In all his relationships within the show, Lee is redefining and carving a new path than the one set for him. Consciously or not. By the end it was something we were aware of. I don't think we were at the beginning, because the focus was on changing Starbuck to a woman, and where that left Lee was not really addressed.

RONALD D. MOORE

Later on we tried to make him more of a marine or a special forces guy. And then eventually he kind of circles all the way back to politics and, ironically, *becomes* the president. But the truth is, you can plan all of this out, but the show demands something else. As a showrunner, one of the things you have to be able to do is be willing to recognize when that happens. This is what I thought it was going to be, but the stories are not working so well, so go another course. What's a better way to go? And being able to do that on the fly and just kind of reinvent the direction that the show's going.

MARK VERHEIDEN

Eventually it felt like taking him into the civilian side was what made the most sense in that it would disappoint his father "a little bit," but that he seemed to have a more humanitarian streak in him, so he would be drawn to the Roslin side of the equation. I also really enjoyed when he essentially was becoming Baltar's defense attorney later on. That seemed like the best fit, which came a little later, so it's the journey from fighter pilot to role in Roslin's government as the humanitarian voice in some of the discussions that were going on.

JAMIE BAMBER

It was sort of an outpouring of everything that he had bottled up all the way through. And then there was something of the truth in that, that he's defined as a son all the way through, but he remembers his grandfather and there's an idea that he could have been anything and something completely different in a world that had continued. In my mind, he was about to quit the military and do other things. So there's a lot of resentment attached to him still being in uniform, and then obviously when the opportunity opens up for him to leave the uniform behind and go and do other things, and then he gets the big court sequence where he represents the person that he despises the most in the world. It represents something, that he's discovered pragmatism. He's discovered a side of himself that he's never been allowed to express before, as a giver and follower of orders.

RONALD D. MOORE

A lot of things weren't jelling for him. In "Resurrection Ship" there's a point where he's floating in space, watching a battle play out. We kept reaching in the writers' room and thought, "We're going to turn the character in this beat." We thought, "If he goes through this experience, if he's hanging out there facing his own mortality, watching a war happen around him, and thinks maybe he's going to die, would that change him? What would that do to a person? He might come back from that experience changed." And so, we were hoping that that might be a pivot point for him. You see there is some aftermath of him lying in a bunk and him reflecting on the idea. We started talking about him becoming a marine. We were saying maybe he stops being a pilot and goes totally hard-core and becomes one of the special forces/marines in the fleet, and he's more associated with those guys and he's not a flier anymore, because that's following in his father's footsteps and it's also what Starbuck is all about, so then maybe he's looking for his own path. Ultimately we sort of started moving in that direction in subsequent episodes, but that didn't quite pay off for us either.

It was very frustrating, because we loved Jamie, you know? We loved Jamie Bamber. He's great and we liked the character but we kept getting to these places where you felt like the role of the pilot, the kick-ass fighter pilot, is sort of taken by Starbuck, like I said. Laura's the political person, Adama's the military commander, and Lee's role as a pilot and as a character, as sort of the fabric of the show, we kept losing focus of him. We kept looking for bigger solutions. We never gave up on it. Toward the end of the series, once Lee became vice president and ultimately president at the very end, it felt like that was a good path for him. But the only other way he could get on that path really was once you started taking Laura out of it.

Serving as executive officer aboard *Galactica* is Saul Tigh, a career soldier who fought in the Cylon war forty years earlier. Following the war, he wandered around aimlessly, eventually ending up aboard a freighter making runs between Caprica and Picon, which is where he met Adama, whom he bonded with immediately. Later, Adama rejoined the fleet and Tigh began drifting (and drinking) his way through life. But when Adama became a squadron leader, he pulled Tigh—who immediately cleaned up his act—along. Eventually they ended up together on the *Galactica*.

Notes the bible, "Saul is a fractured and damaged man. He's seen more combat than anyone aboard *Galactica,* including Adama, and the experience scarred him deeply. He's been avoiding responsibility ever since he returned to the Fleet, and if not for the patronage of Adama, he probably would've washed out years ago. But beyond the drinking and irresponsible behavior, there still lurks the man who fought Cylons hand to hand while standing in pools of blood made by his shipmates. Deep down, Saul Tigh is a warrior. The question is, can he reach down that deeply once again or has time passed him by?"

Canadian actor Michael Hogan has enjoyed a diversified career in a variety of mediums, including stage, radio, film, television, and even opera. While he appeared on a number of television series, *Battlestar Galactica* represents his longest time in a single role.

MICHAEL HOGAN

I almost didn't audition for *Battlestar*. I didn't have anything against the original show—I might have seen it walking through someone's living room—but it's not that I watched it or knew much about it. We saw that Michael Rymer was directing. My wife and I, we're Canadian, we do a lot of character-driven, low-budget independent films, and as we were watching *Angel Baby*, we went, "Wow, man. Who did this? What *is* this? This is an Australian film." And then the credit was, "Written, directed, produced by Michael Rymer." Who is this man? And then a few years later the audition for *Battlestar* came up and directing was Michael Rymer. Are you kidding me? And then Edward James Olmos is playing Adama? Whoa, whoa, whoa, whoa. What's going on here? So I went in to audition.

Now, Rymer loves working. He loves what he does. He loves creating with people that are of kindred spirit, and he loves working with actors. As the actor when you go in to audition, whether you get it or not, you get to read these great lines and you get to play for twenty minutes and then off you go. Whether you get it or not, the director and everybody else has had this great experience of working on this. That's what happened in the room with Rymer. Then a few days later I got a callback, so I went in. Once you start the callback, then we're getting serious here. This could be something. And then, after having spent the time with him, Rymer said, "I'm satisfied with the audition, but the network . . ." I guess the people down south had trouble that I'm too Canadian. Had trouble with the accent. I said, "Oh, there's no Canadians in space? Is that the case?" So I lost the accent and evened it out and ended up getting the role.

RONALD D. MOORE

There is something about Saul Tigh, this crotchety, abrasive guy who somehow you never dislike. No matter how much of a son of a bitch he was, there was always something appealing about him, and always something that you liked about him, and always something where you kind of saw his flaws. The flaws were worn clearly and obviously, but you wanted to forgive him for it over and over again, even when he was doing just really stupid things or behaving really badly or breaking trust with people or whatever. That's a really important characteristic in that character. Michael was a really easy, funny guy. He likes to drink, he likes to hang out, he likes to go to parties, he's very social, he's very friendly, very outgoing. You always heard his voice on the set. You always heard him cracking up or telling jokes about something. He and Eddie got along like gangbusters. They were just really tight, really good mates, and I think they hung out and did all kinds of stuff.

MICHAEL HOGAN

In the beginning, they didn't know what they were going to do with Tigh. They knew they were decommissioning the ship; it was going to be a museum. And there was alcohol. But that's basically all they knew during the miniseries. So I walked into the world right then. I'd been acting for thirty-seven years before *Battlestar Galactica* came along, so I'd been to National Theatre School, and in the early seventies we created, through local initiative, program grants, we created these alternative theaters in Toronto, and around Canada, and then slowly started doing film and television. I'd been around the block and I'd had a few series myself and had a great time. So when *Battlestar Galactica* came along, I was very aware. I think Eddie, Mary, and myself, being the oldest people in the cast, not that I equate whatever, but as being veterans of that, we all went, "Whoa! This is special." Of course, the younger people would think that it is now, but we knew that it was special then.

MARK VERHEIDEN

Michael Hogan was kind of like Aaron Douglas and Tyrol, though more seasoned, in that he brought an everyman quality. Saul Tigh's the grizzly guy you want at your side when you're going into battle. You sense the utter loyalty he had to Adama and the fleet. You could always give Michael anything and you'd know you'd get something better than you'd imagined when you wrote it.

DAVID EICK

In the miniseries, or maybe the first episode, you see Tigh measuring the precious few drops left in his liquor bottle, right? It's, like, "Holy shit, you've got a total alcoholic here." Now the world's been blown up. Where the fuck is he going to get his whiskey, right? It was great drama for that scene. You were forced to sympathize with the alcoholic, but soon after we had this decision to make: "Okay, do we want Tigh to be a dry drunk? Do we want Tigh to clean up and not have an alcoholism problem at all or do we want to say they find some bottles of booze on a ship sometimes?" The truth is, we love Tigh being drunk. So that's what we did.

RONALD D. MOORE

The other thing is that Michael reads older on camera than he was. He was bald, and prematurely gray in the hair he has. He's not quite as old as he seemed to be, which was a little good in terms of his relationship with Adama. I liked that Adama had this friend who was a pain in the ass and difficult and an alcoholic, whom a lot of other people would never keep around, but only Adama would. Adama saw value in him that nobody else did.

Moore's description of Lieutenant Sharon Valerii reads, "Sharon's first memory is that of crawling across the artificial grass in her backyard toward the family cat, Mr. Perkles. It's a vivid memory, one that she occasionally revisits in her dreams. It's also completely fake." She has a whole history leading up to her joining flight school and eventually getting her first assignment, on the *Galactica*, where she was aboard for nearly a year when the Cylons launched their attack. Says Moore, "Her relationship with her flight officer—Helo—was a close one, and the older man watched out for her as she struggled to make her deck qualifications. They almost pursued a romantic relationship as well, but then Sharon hooked up with Chief Tyrol. Helo was aware of the affair and the impropriety of it, but he guarded her privacy jealously and let it be known that he would exact a price from any pilot who caused trouble for her."

Most importantly, he continues, "Sharon is unaware of her true nature; unaware that, far from being the daughter of a mining family, she is in reality a Cylon sleeper agent, implanted into Colonial society. . . . Sensitive and shy, she puts on a tough-chick front for the benefit of those around her. In Tyrol she had found a man who is quite literally her first true love. What Sharon is doing on *Galactica* and why she was infiltrated into Colonial society will remain a mystery for some time."

A Canadian-American actress, Park had appeared on a variety of television series in guest-starring roles, among them *The Outer Limits* (the nineties remake of the sixties classic), *Dark Angel,* and *Stargate SG-1.* She was also a series regular on the 2001–05 drama *Edgemont.*

RONALD D. MOORE

Grace has an intense vulnerability about her. There is something about her person on camera that you feel protective of, you feel like there's a wound there, you feel like she's open emotionally in a way that a lot of people aren't on camera. She brought that to the character.

GRACE PARK
(actress, "Lieutenant Sharon 'Athena' Agathon / Lieutenant Sharon 'Boomer' Valerii")

For me, it wasn't the audition process that was grueling, it was my acting school and a class that I was in which really prepared me to be able to do *Battlestar.* It got my foot in the door essentially. I auditioned for the part of Dualla and I think it was a scene in the head. I had to be in my bra . . . I think I was washing up or something. I did the whole scene sideways, for some reason, as if the mirror was on the side. So I did it and then they're like, "Can you do the whole thing, but swing it ninety degrees?" So I did that. Now, my acting class really pushed us so hard . . . we called it being in a cult. Just an intense, unusually dark experience. So the audition room seemed minor in comparison, because it was, like, "Shit, I just need to get through this fucking audition so I can get back to study my shit for class," because you didn't want to get effed over in class. That was the problem, because she held the bar *really* high. It didn't matter how much you were pouring your heart out. You and the other actor might be sobbing onstage, and then she'd wait five seconds and say, "Get off." It's, like, "Stop wanking off up there."

So when you get used to that kind of "tough love," the audition room seems much simpler. Anyway, I was told to come back for Starbuck and I did go see the same acting teacher. When I read for that, she was like, "What are you doing? Are you doing all this weird stuff because it's a lead now?" When you go from going for smaller parts to principal parts, and then suddenly it's a lead, your subconscious is probably amped up and definitely nervous. So, yeah, she had to work me down from a number of those things. But I didn't have the process that Katee Sackhoff did, so after one audition, Michael Rymer gave me a note and I did it again. Gave me a note, did it again, gave me a note, did . . . eight times. Usually by the third note you're thinking, "Oh, I fucked up." Then *that* starts working in your head at the same time while you're trying to do the audition. Then with every added note it's just going to get worse. But somehow I was able to stay on track, even though I was pretty off.

The thing that Michael told me is maybe I just didn't get the gravity of how dark the series was going to be. After that, I went to L.A. and that's where I saw Katee and Jamie Bamber for the first time. If Katee and I and this Hispanic girl were going for it, it was obvious that the casting was pretty open. They weren't rigid on the ethnicity of the look, which was cool. When I went in for the screen test, I was told, "Okay, now it's not about the acting. They know you can act. That's how you got here. Now it's about getting through the room." That's all she had to say, and somehow it clicked and I got it. I was like, "Oh, this is a completely different test." Basically, are you going to crack or not? Everyone was brought up in different order, because it was as soon as your contracts came through. The girl that had left the room just before me was like, "I don't know what the fuck happened in there," and she walked out. Normally that would have made me nervous, but instead I was just feeling super ready. But the thing is, maybe I was too much in my own kind of space, because I went in with Jamie and there wasn't chemistry between us. That's one of the reasons—and I'm sure there are many—why I wasn't going to get Starbuck. But I suppose I offered enough of something for them to throw me a bone.

So I didn't get Dualla or Starbuck, but then when I was told I had gotten Boomer, I was *pissed*. I didn't like that. I was like, "Who the eff is Boomer?"

I didn't read the pilot for Boomer, and then we were shooting the miniseries and then also you do a little bit of research and realize, "Frak, I guess she's a Cylon." I asked Ron, "When did you change this? Was there something about me that made you change it?" She was always that and I just hadn't realized, because I wasn't reading for that and I wasn't picking up on the clues. But in the beginning, the character didn't seem interesting. Maybe I remember a general feeling of sadness or self-pity. More like sadness or melancholy, and it just seemed like the part was quite small. Whereas Starbuck seemed interesting and bold and more kind of fun to play. A brash character. Katee had said she wanted Boomer and I was like, "Why would she want Boomer?"

Park got a mistaken sense of the character's part in the hierarchy of the show when she and other cast members participated in a boot camp designed to give them a "modicum of militariness" in the way that they walked or saluted.

GRACE PARK

It was at that point that we'd watched an episode of the original *Battlestar,* and someone said, "By your command." It was to the ruler or whoever it was. I want to say "queen," but I don't know if it was a female. But at that point is when it dawned on me, "Oh my gosh, I'm the queen." Because Six says to one of the Eights, "By your command." So that's what I thought, though later, of course, I found out that I'm absolutely *not* the queen. Once again sent to the bottom.

RONALD D. MOORE

When she started out, she was very green and brand-new. I couldn't tell you if it was literally her first gig, but it was certainly one of them. You watched her grow into the role over time, and kind of quickly. It was a quick learning curve, and she just stepped up her game kind of fast.

DAVID WEDDLE

In the first season, Grace Park was good, but she wasn't the strongest actor, honestly. But by the end of the first season, when she tells Helo that she's pregnant, I remember thinking, "Holy shit, she's great in these scenes." She improved more than anyone in the cast. She really applied herself, and by the end of the series was as good as anyone in that ensemble, which is saying a lot. You could tell when she was playing Athena, you could tell when she was playing Sharon just by the way she walked or the look in her eyes, and that was an amazing feat for an actor who wasn't that experienced in the beginning.

MICHAEL ANGELI

When Grace started, she was really pretty, but she just was not very good. It was hard, but we asked her, "Listen, we really love you. We want to keep you for the show. Would you mind taking a couple of acting lessons?" She was like, "No, of course not." No pretense at all. And by the end of the series, she was amazing. One of the best actors on the show.

GRACE PARK

In the first season, Michael Rymer told Tahmoh and me that we improved a lot. We were feeling pretty good about ourselves, and affirmed. At that point he said something along the lines of, "You still have a long way to go, but . . . ," and we both were like, "Stop!" After the conversation was done, we kind of fact-checked with each other about, "Did you hear what I heard? I think we improved a lot this year." Then, of course, four years after that, we were just laughing at ourselves, rolling our eyes and thinking, "Can you believe we thought that we were pretty good at that point?"

When considering arcs for the various versions of her characters on the show, Park admits that she actually never recognized arcs because she was "too green" and was more concerned with individual scenes.

GRACE PARK

It's like how children look at really small things, and they're really big, but we can tokenize the entire situation and go, "It's a carnival, and there's a Ferris wheel and a roller coaster, and candy corn, and stuff," but they're, like, one thing is a world to them. So in a way everything was kind of expanded for me, so I was lost in each scene. So for myself, the Eights [her Cylon model] in general did not have an arc. They were just the Cylon prototype, kind of really neutral. It was really just Boomer and Athena that really had arcs. For myself, Athena really seemed like a side character for the first season. Whenever she was on the planet, she basically had to play a disguise that she was Boomer and getting this other raptor pilot to fall in love with her and she's not growing much. Everything is just a smoke screen. Meanwhile, Boomer was the one I had my hands full with, and she was conflicted, trying to kill herself, self-sabotaging. She didn't know what she was. I myself didn't even know what was going on. She would wake up and the word "Cylon" would be written on her mirror. I knew that it was her writing to herself, kind of giving herself signals and such. But I didn't even know how to play those scenes. It would be so much better if we were able to do it once again, kind of near the ending. So that character just seemed too lost in herself, and the conflict of who she was and her identity, how she fit in with the others, how she was an outcast.

RONALD D. MOORE

Grace would be one of the people that come up and ask questions about the mythology and backstory, even when I hadn't worked them out. She was always kind of surprised that I hadn't worked a lot of things out in detail, but she was always eager to ask questions, like, "What's going on here? When I'm doing this, what are they doing on *Galactica*?" Always trying to orient herself in the larger mythology of the show. I remember there was a sense of her being an intense student of her craft. Just a great spirit to her.

There was, however, a moment when Athena and Boomer had a scene together on the *Galactica* that would require split screen in which the actress would play both roles in separate camera passes.

GRACE PARK

I was not nervous for that scene, because I thought it was going to play as kind of how they did with James Callis when the two Baltars were in the scene together. But this version was trickier, because the camera was in one spot, and they were both in the same scene. Whereas mine, you cut from one version to the other, so it was actually way easier. But in my head I thought it was the worst possible version. I was so nervous about it, but I did the scene and I remember doing something with Boomer as a character. Michael Rymer once again comes over, totally bursts any bubbles, and he's like, "Why are you making her such a bitch?" And anything I was feeling was like, "prrew"—complete deflation. It doesn't mean you're right, but it's, like, you're trying to do something creative and someone's like, "That's dumb."

RONALD D. MOORE

The character of Sharon was sort of the vehicle through which I figured out we would do the different Cylons in a real way, because, A, she was the last one that we said "Oh, she's a Cylon" by the end of the miniseries, which was kind of surprising. Something David came up with and we put into a draft much later on. I hadn't given a lot of thought about where to go with that character. Right off the bat in episode two we started doing things, like, she's a sleeper agent and she's going to get into the water tank; that these Cylons cannot even know that they're Cylons in some instances. In the episode before that, "33," we start setting up that there's another Sharon on Cylon-occupied Caprica.

Now I had two of them. Over the first season, because I had two of them playing parallel stories, it was an opportunity to start figuring out how we're going to do this overall. Six was kind of in a different category, because she's in Baltar's head, we're not going to talk about what that is or what it represents. Let's play a lot of games with it. Let's make it a chip. No, it's not a chip. It's an angel. It's not an angel. Let's do all these different things and then we'll bring one on board, and that's mostly to screw with Baltar's head. With the Sharons, it was more, "All right, if we have multiple copies of all these, how would we delineate the differences between them? How would they be similar? Would they have certain characteristics that all of them share? How different could they be?" What would it be like in the show in editorial terms to be cutting between two of them? Are we going to confuse the audience if we've got these two actresses playing the same role? How would we differentiate them editorially and mood and so on? She was really the test case that allowed us to then branch out deeper and deeper as the show went on, because that taught us a lot of lessons about how to do it and how not to do it.

The Sharons were very similar up front, deliberately. We wanted the one on Caprica to be so similar to Sharon that Helo wouldn't know the difference. There weren't that many differences, but as you got deeper into that storyline, she actually acts on the feelings between her and Helo that had been buried all those years, and she hadn't acted on them. The other one's on a very different journey regarding Tyrol. That's where they started to branch out and then you started writing in subtle differences and their character voices and how one would respond and how the other would respond. A key insight, kind of a late-breaking idea in the middle of the season, was, "Oh, we're going to arc these two in the other direction. The Sharon that we know aboard *Galactica*, who has literally been there from the miniseries and is their Sharon that is established right away, she's going to go dark. And the one that's on the planet, she's going to go toward the light. She's going to be the one that we actually invest in and she's going to have a child and we're going to play the love story between her and Helo for real, and we're going to come to like her."

All that made us realize that not all the Cylons had to be villains, or she wasn't going to just screw over Helo and kill him or something once she got pregnant. It opened up the box in terms of what we could potentially do with all the Cylons. All the Cylon models, each one that we encounter, could have a different motivation, slightly. Could have different characteristics within a set of parameters, and then you could take them in any direction you wanted. You could redeem some, you could condemn some, you could have some that were weak and never figured anything out. It made them all interesting individuals.

Dr. Gaius Baltar, a brilliant scientist in artificial intelligence, is seeking to create an AI that could solve humanity's problems, while avoiding the situation that had in the past allowed for the Cylon uprising and subsequent war. His work moved to the next level thanks to the arrival of an enigmatic woman whom he connected with instantly. "She was beautiful, intensely sexual, funny, smart and with an intuitive sense of Baltar's every mood and thought," writes Moore in the show's bible. ". . . She understood how secret affairs both titillated and challenged him, so she told him she was from an unnamed corporation interested in defense contracts and that their affair was not only illicit, but probably illegal. She also shared his interest in A.I. systems and encouraged him to push the Defense Ministry further into computer networking than they were initially prepared for." Things progressed for two years, with Baltar inadvertently providing her with exactly what she was after: a means for the Cylons to try and wipe out humanity once and for all, with this woman revealing herself to be a Cylon just before the attack began.

"Gaius Baltar is not without conscience," notes Moore. "Indeed, he is aware of, and regrets the harm his actions have caused to both individuals and the society at large. While his guilt is not so keenly felt as to put himself at risk of discovery and punishment, it is important to remember that he is neither amoral nor sociopathic. He is a brilliant man, whose intellect usually finds a way to both justify his own behavior and yet at the same time condemn himself for those very rationalizations and obfuscations. He is weak without being craven, duplicitous without being untrustworthy, in league with the enemy without being treasonous."

Playing the character is British actor James Callis, who, before boarding *Galactica,* enjoyed great success in a number of West End productions in London. He wrote and directed the independent film *Beginner's Luck* (2001), and appeared in such films as *Bridget Jones's Diary* (2001), *Bridget Jones: The Edge of Reason,* and *Dead Cool* (both 2004), as well as a number of television series.

RONALD D. MOORE

There was a point during the run of *Battlestar* when I was nominated for an Emmy for a script. They had a nice little event somewhere in Hollywood for the nominees. I went there and met some of my fellow writers, which was very cool. I met with the creator of *Mad Men,* Matthew Weiner. The emcee of the event was Jon Cryer, and he would say nice things about each of us in turn. Then we got to me, and Jon went off on this whole thing about how much he loved *Battlestar Galactica* and how desperately he wanted the role of Baltar. That it was between him and James Callis at the very end.

Which was true: it was him and James. Jon Cryer was the *other* way to go, but then he went off and did *Two and a Half Men,* and it seemed that things worked out pretty well for him. It was very funny that he still thought about that, and how much he loved that character and how excited he was to have done the show or would have had a chance to do the show. It was very gracious of him to talk about that. Obviously his would have been a whole different take.

JAMES CALLIS

My friend Jamie Bamber was already cast as Apollo and I was in the States for the first time. I knew who Baltar was from the original story, so I had some trepidation about, as it were, stepping into those shoes. I was assured that it would be very different, and then reading the script of the pilot, it *was* very different. One of the people at the studio I knew was Angela Mancuso, who I had worked with on a show called *Helen of Troy* two years beforehand. She thought I would be great for it, so I went up for a series of auditions— though for the first audition I was there on the wrong day, which would probably explain why they didn't want to see me. In that case I was, as they say, fresh off the boat. Later in the casting process, I just went to some big meeting where there were five or six different actors who were all going up to be Gaius Baltar, and five or six different Sixes—young actresses going up to play Number Six—all in a room together, and we were paired off with each other to go and do a scene in front of the network executives. It felt like there were twenty people behind desks in the room. Then when they weren't happy with somebody or it didn't go somebody's way, then somebody would come out of that room, a bit like *Big Brother,* or one of these reality game shows, and tap somebody on the shoulder and say, "I'm terribly sorry, but it's not going any further today." And then that person would collect their stuff and leave.

That's what you do at a test like that, and it was quite an extreme situation. It seemed like a bad day; I want to say it lasted three hours. I know I was there beforehand an hour and then getting back is like five hours, and you *still* don't know what's going on. So it got to a point where I'd been auditioning for the same part for, like, a week and a half or two weeks. Since I'd arrived in L.A., I'd done almost nothing else. I was very excited to finally receive the phone call saying, "This is going ahead and you've got the job," but when I did receive the phone call, I couldn't enjoy it as much as I wanted, because I was physically exhausted from the stress of this whole thing. And for me, this would mean a big thing, because I was living in London at the time and it was filming in Vancouver. It was a question of what I was going to do with my family.

During those auditions, Tricia Helfer and I were paired together, which was very, very lucky for me. Insanely lucky for me. I don't think I was actually paired with anybody else from that collection of very lovely-looking people in that room. I'd seen Tricia before at another meeting at David Eick's when I'd been going into an audition, and she, I presume, had been leaving, but we hadn't spoken to each other. In fact, we didn't really know each other until our first day on set, pretty much.

But it was challenging. In the beginning I knew that Baltar was not good, or at least a spanner in the works. I'm trying to find the best way of saying bad things about the guy. So I know all of that, and that's a challenge. Then there's this person, this beautiful lady, who's in his head, which I really didn't understand. I just couldn't really get my head around it, because it was like, "How on Earth are they going to film that? How is that going to look believable? How are we going to make that real or look like it's credible?" Up to then, I'd not seen anything like that, but the only thing in my mind was, "That's like kids, isn't it? Having somebody in your head and you're talking to them? It's like your imaginary best friend." I brought that up to them and they said, "You've read the script. You've seen that millions are killed, right? It's *not* for kids."

I certainly got that. I'd gotten that from the auditions—they constantly had us auditioning the same scene, and it was the scene of Gaius Baltar in bed with another woman, found by Six. I just thought the whole thing was funny. I said to them, "You know, after the bomb goes off and he realizes that he's been implicated in this massive tragedy and possibly treason, his life is going to change. He's going to be a different person. But right now, he's somebody else. He doesn't think there are any consequences. It's all quite fun." I thought that scene was really fun in something that was very dark.

RONALD D. MOORE

James really surprised me the most, because the character of Baltar in the miniseries was not particularly funny. I didn't really write him that way. I thought he was morally ambiguous. You know, we talked a lot about the origins of Baltar, but I thought he was brilliant, egocentric, flawed as a person, ladies' man—all those kinds of things. I really didn't think he was funny, but James kind of brought this humor to the character that just made the whole thing wonderful.

JAMES CALLIS

Any actor, coming to a part, you've got a series of choices you can make, and I made them about this series. One of them is that early on they were talking about if you were going to be on the show, you were going to be in a boot camp. I was like, "What the eff. . . . Why? Why would I be in the boot camp? I'm not going to be in the boot camp. Somebody else can be. It's not even my character." They're like, "It's because you're aboard the battlestar," and I was like, "Read the script. I'm new to the battlestar. I'm from the planet." And then there were meetings on makeup and they're saying, "Cut your hair, it's military." "No, I'm a scientist. I don't have to." So the series of choices I made was that I was surrounded by a group of heroes, essentially. They were all heroic, to greater or lesser degrees. Mostly greater. Think about Adama and Roslin and Apollo and Starbuck and Helo and the chief. . . . Do you know what I mean? They're rounded and they're heroic, and they're heroic because they make sacrifices of themselves for other people. So I was placed in this thing where I was like, "Okay, I've got to be totally different to that." Essentially it's not even an antihero, it's just somebody who's not a hero.

He's his own man. He's dancing to his own rhythm. . . . I think they call that irritating, but it's beyond irritating. In some fashion he's kind of magnanimous, within his own mind. He's not really interested in playing politics. He's into science for the advancement of technology, science, the species. He's complicated and, like I always say, he's very bad on paper, but not *all* bad. In a more brutal or slightly more savage *Battlestar Galactica,* I'm sure that Gaius Baltar would've met his just desserts.

RONALD D. MOORE

James really changed that character. Now we started playing more of the humor, sometimes too much humor. Sometimes you'd just write straight-up comedic beats and he'd go, "You know, I'm not a joke. You know, we have to rein ourselves in." We knew James would just be so great with comedy that we started just writing comedy and the character becomes less mysterious. So we had to kind of watch ourselves.

MICHAEL ANGELI

James was kind of shy at first with writers, but then he liked what I had written, so we started to talk. His wit was just amazing. Really funny guy. His wife is from India and so they spend a lot of time there. He's totally into

Bollywood; I think he even acted in a couple of those films. I don't think anyone else could have played that character. I mean, Ron created the character, but he got the right actor. Somebody who could play it straight, but funny and venal at the same time. *That* was James.

MICHAEL RYMER

Ron was very tolerant and we would always try to honor the writers and do a take on a script and then if we knew a way to make it better, we would. Or try different ideas. And the writers usually were very non-precious, non-nerdy about it, and they're going, "Wow, that's great . . . ," and they would write to that. I think probably the biggest example is James making Baltar a comedic character. It was not that way on the page, and James just naturally played those beats. He was a bit of a genius in that he can play the humor, but never undermine the threat that is driving his situation in the story. It never became silly. It never became *Batman & Robin*. It's pantomime and brilliant pantomime. He was treading the line. For me, in a lot of ways, Eddie and Mary were the big guns, the big gravitas producers, and it was James and Katee that gave the show its fizz. You never knew exactly what they were going to do or say, and they were just very naturally entertaining as performers. I love watching those two do other things just to see what they're going to do with it.

JAMES CALLIS

I didn't mean to bring the humor. It just kind of happened and I'm cool with it. Like I said, that audition scene with Tricia, and Gaius caught in bed with another woman, I thought was funny. Also the whole idea of trying to explain it by saying, "Oh, I'm so sorry. It's not what you think. I'm not even in love with her." You know, it's ridiculous.

I kept saying to people, as it were the powers that be, this is not really the right scene that you should be watching to audition the character, because the character is going to change very, very much when he finds out actually what he's been involved with, isn't he? Essentially I wanted to bring somebody to the party that was not heroic. Who didn't know if they were going to move left or right. It's like walking down the corridor and everybody else walks with such purpose. They're on their way to something. Something military. So, what if there's somebody walking down the corridor who's like, "Did I have breakfast this morning? Is that important?" It was just a different energy. The writing was incredible and you started to fall in love with these people, but unless there was an element of humor or something, I'd have just been the person that you just hate totally. And what he was earlier involved in was monstrous. Totally monstrous. So if you knew what you were doing at the time, then that makes you a monster, and that *wasn't* what I wanted to be.

MICHAEL ANGELI

We had Head Six and then we did two Baltars—one being a "Head Baltar" the way we did Head Six—the idea for which was mine. Nobody liked it except James. He said, "Oh, man, I want to do this. I have to do this." Ron's like, "Okaaay," and we did it and it worked out really well. He went to bat for the character and for me. I thought it was great. I don't know if anybody else did. I think it kind of worked. The episode was really terrific.

JAMES CALLIS

I think that Number Six is one of the most brilliant creations in the show. Their relationship is the closest and the only time really Gaius Baltar came to love, and in loving there is something redeeming and redeemable, and that's a beautiful thing.

MICHAEL RYMER

Baltar was very sympathetic. *And* extremely selfish in a Machiavellian way. He is not evil. He is weak. He had a huge ego. He is lustful. He is a wonderful sort of human being who happens to bring down the human race [*laughs*]. I almost can't separate him now from the way James Callis played him. James made him extremely sympathetic and engaging, yet plausible.

JAMIE BAMBER

We all hated him, but we all loved him as well, because he was human. He's the most human character in the show. He's spineless, scared, and vain in equal proportions. We can all relate to that. When you actually put yourself in these situations that are life and death, maybe we're the ones that are the weakest and the most scared and we'd love to think we're the heroic, selfless types. But the way James brought this wide-eyed, almost childlike vulnerability and humor to it . . . he is a human being and he did evil things, but he did it from a place of weakness not strength, and as a result there's something redemptive in him.

With Baltar, you could see the self-preservation just seeping out of his pores, and there was something unnecessarily needy about him, even in the playing. But people like that exist and they can infuriate you, but they can waste your energy and all these things. Yet Baltar galvanized people and re-invented himself, a bit like Lee in other areas. He became the cult leader, the politician; whatever he needed to be, he became that to guarantee his own survival. I thought it was a wonderful performance, and I've always admired James's work on that show, particularly.

RONALD D. MOORE

Baltar serves such a key role in the original. He was the one human villain that you had in the piece, and it was only natural to figure out how I was going to work him into the show. The problem with the original is that I never understood why the hell he did what he did. I watched it a couple of times and was trying to figure it out. . . . All they really say is they promised him some kind of dictatorship over a planet or something. But they were going to wipe out all the humans, so who is he going to be dictator over? And why does he think that's attractive? "What's in this for Baltar?" was always such a tough nut to crack. And I just thought there's really no reason why a human character of any kind of depth, or any kind of intelligence, is really going to betray his entire race to genocide, regardless of what the Cylons promise. So that didn't make any sense.

We started to ask, "How could this happen? Maybe he's someone who betrays all of humanity without meaning to? How could that be a flawed character? He has weaknesses and he's prone to giving in to temptation. Maybe he has an ego issue. Maybe he's super smart and is intelligent, but he loves women and women are his weakness." I started just going down that route. So it became Baltar's ego is such that he betrays the human race without even meaning to. Once I got to that point, then I thought, "Oh, that's a great character." I knew people like that. I think there were elements of myself in Baltar. I mean, I've certainly liked women in my life, and there's a lot of me in Baltar in lies I've told other women. Situations of being caught by one woman while I'm with another. Setting yourself up as someone enjoying your fame and pretending not to enjoy your fame. There's certainly aspects of all of those things in Baltar. I mean, he's probably the one that I identify with the most in the show as closer to my own self. And my own perceived flaws. You know, I can be tempted into things and I can tell myself it's not such a big deal, I'm just going to do this one thing and then you find yourself in a difficult situation. Oh shit, how did I get here? And yet still trying to do the right thing. Still trying to tell yourself that you're a hero of your own story.

And I started to understand who this guy is, and started writing him as someone who likes fame, and someone who's comfortable being interviewed all the time. Someone who's getting a lot of awards. I'm starting to see this guy and I'm starting to like him. At the same time, I'm kind of being held captive by him, and I thought that was a fascinating mix.

MICHAEL ANGELI

Baltar was like a cockroach. He found ways to wiggle out of disaster constantly. That was by design. That's why he did survive until the end. He also had a nice arc where he went from betraying humanity to being sort of a good person.

DAVID WEDDLE

Baltar sort of starts out like a villain, somebody despicable, but then he became one of the best-loved characters on *Galactica*. And we all loved writing for him. James Callis was another amazing actor who could improvise moments and find dimensions in that character who could have been just like Dr. Smith in the original *Lost in Space:* cardboard cutout, you hate him, crazy coward. But James Callis brought such layers of emotion to his scenes that we wrote for that, too. We saw what he was doing. In our minds we all want to be Adama, but most of us are Baltar. You know, we're afraid, we run away, we don't do very well at things, we falter, we betray . . . I think people can really identify with that.

MARK VERHEIDEN

He was an incredibly nefarious spirit on the ship, but, it's funny, there's people in real life where I think if you ask, "How is it they keep walking around and yet others don't? How is it Baltar survived and so many others on that ship didn't?" He had a cutting way of self-preservation. He was useful to some extent being the scientist he was. The other thing is, when you have a finite number of people and a finite number of experts because of who those people are, who's left, what do you tolerate in terms of misbehavior or bad behavior—or, in Baltar's case, *extreme* bad behavior—to continue to use their expertise?

If you lost those people, regardless of how evil or ill-informed or mentally ill they are, what would the impact be? Was he better to keep alive than to just kill? I think that, yes, he was a nefarious person and tragic toward the end, but especially during the mutiny when he was trying to talk to Gaeta and trying to at least help a little bit, you got a sense that there was a little more going on. James Callis, by the way, was fantastic as Baltar, and maybe *that's* why Baltar didn't end up with a bullet in his head. Maybe it's because Callis played him in such a way that you wanted him to survive. You are involved in his story and he had a certain curious sense of humor and self-awareness about himself that was always fun to watch. I would have hated to lose that from the show.

MICHAEL RYMER

It never occurred to me that it was a story hole that they didn't kill Baltar. I guess because the show was an allegory and it was a fairly didactic allegory of who we are, how should we behave, what's acceptable, what isn't, and putting up with the Baltars of the world, owning them and so forth, is sort of who we are supposed to be. We don't execute people. We don't murder people. I know you could break that argument in a second by other moments in the show, but he's like Dr. Smith on *Lost in Space*. He's the man that you love to hate. He is the essential ingredient to our acute salvability as human beings. That selfish, frightened, greedy, self-aggrandizing sexual predator . . . all those things.

MARK VERHEIDEN

James brought in a character who could have been arch one side or incredibly dark on the other. He straddled the line in between. He had a self-awareness about his absurd relationship with Head Six, and then there was the fact that she would be giving him oral sex behind a table when someone would walk in and his pants would be off, but there's no one there with him. So it's, like, "What in the world is going on here?" but his reaction just busted in that situation. That was the sort of smoothness and yet self-awareness of how insane that was that he was able to bring to that. I thought that was really remarkable.

DAVID WEDDLE

As the series unwound, it became "The Nine Lives of Gaius Baltar." There's a resiliency in Baltar of reinventing himself constantly, which lots of us do try to do, hoping for some sense of truth, some sense of peace, some way to come to terms with our demons, so we might embrace different things. We might become born again. We might discard our religion. We might change careers, change marriage partners, move to a different place. It's all in a search for identity—who we really are—and Baltar eventually does find out who he is. And you sort of end up admiring the guy, because he had such resiliency, and in the end he's kind of redeemed. By being with these people, and the fact that they didn't kill him when they put him on trial, he sort of earns his place, finally, among the crew.

JAMES CALLIS

Basically the guy grew up. He started off life as an adolescent, almost, or like a child, and then that child is traumatized by his own actions. I've often said, when people are like, "Oh, he's really bad; he's really evil," I'm like, "I don't think he was evil. I think that he was very weak and narcissistic, and those are dangerous combinations." So over the course of the series, he grows up, but he grows up between the five stages of grief. There's denial for a large part of his journey on the trip, and then there's anger, and bartering and depression, and finally acceptance. He goes through a lot of colors and loads of different kinds of things, but that's one of the arcs that the man goes through.

ALESSANDRO JULIANI
(actor, "Felix Gaeta")

When we were on New Caprica, I worked closely with James and we had the most complete arc, I think, going from total hero worship to something a little more like family. It was a great time with James, who's up for anything, down for whatever and constantly a source of humor and fun, but rigorous, too. He wants to talk all the time. He wants to get in there. So many actors don't want to talk to you at all about what's going on. They just want to do it. But James is the opposite; he wanted to get in there and that was always a great pleasure. Particularly if we were working with a director who happened to also share that vibe. There were great discussions and great collaborations, and great changes that were made to scenes and script and moments based on those debates.

MARK VERHEIDEN

In "The Oath" episode, which was part of the season-four mutiny, Baltar was the one who suggested he call Gaeta and try to talk him down off the ledge. That was a late addition to the script, and turned out to be a great one, because of all the people that you would think to call Gaeta, it wouldn't be Baltar. But he gave it a try and I thought in that moment you saw a sense of humanity from him and a sense of regret over the fact that essentially so much of this was his fault. His attempt to try and fix something that was getting way out of hand was admirable. Although I would assume there's this element of self-preservation in that, because if this mutiny went as far as it did, I think Mr. Baltar would definitely be on the chopping block. I don't think he had a lot of fans on the ship at that point, so he had a really good sense of what his character might or might not do.

JAMES CALLIS

His decent side does win out in the end. So I don't think they were wrong about him, albeit as maddening as he could be and was. Of course, that's also the fun of the character, is making you want to strangle him.

"The woman as machine."

That, in its entirety, was Ron Moore's description of the Six character in the show's bible. Not a lot to work from for Canadian model turned actress Tricia Helfer. Acting was something she was just breaking into (the 2003 film *White Rush,* guest appearances on *Jeremiah* and *CSI*), and *Galactica* truly became the proverbial baptism by fire.

TRICIA HELFER

I had moved out to L.A. in the beginning of 2002, and that whole first year it was hard to even get an audition. I got a few, I did a lot of indie films, *CSI* and a couple of other things. It was really the next pilot season when I got *Battlestar;* I got the script a little before Christmas. I remember I took it home with me, I read it, and I *loved* it. It was my first audition back from the holidays. I think it was January 6, 2003. I met with David Eick and it wasn't a huge audition. Just two producers and a casting director or something. It went really well, but the feedback was really right there. I was a nobody. I was a model from New York. I would ask about it a few times, because there had been interest in me, but they were trying to find a "name." Two months went by and I just assumed it was done, yet I couldn't get rid of the script. It still sat on my desk, because it stuck with me. Then I got a call that I was to go back in again, and I did, and then I found out I was going to be cast on it. That I had a work session—I didn't even know what a work session was. Turns out it's with the director and not something that's always done, but sometimes before you have a cast that's in front of all the studio and network and everything . . . sometimes you audition for the studio first and then their choices go past and you test for the network. Sometimes they're all in the room together, which was the case with *Battlestar.* So you have a work session with the director, which helps with nerves as well and it ensures that you're on the same page.

This was the first time I'd actually met with Michael Rymer. I remember they were testing quite a few people, and this was the night before. I waited like two or two and a half hours. Everybody going in there was like forty-five minutes to an hour in there. And working with Michael Rymer, he was like, "Okay, let's do the first scene and then we can discuss it and do it again." We did the first scene and he goes, "That's it. We'll do that tomorrow. See you tomorrow." I was in and out. I thought it's either really good or really bad. I was kind of expecting a phone call that night saying, "You are no longer testing."

But I went in the next day and there were, I think, about eight girls and eight guys, and they had us each going individually. We all waited for a while, and then they came out and they dismissed a couple of the girls and a couple of the guys, and they started pairing us up. I went in with, I think, two different guys. And then I went with James Callis last. Each time you're going in, you're also getting different notes on this and that. I remember the casting director started to get ahead with filming and pulled me aside and was like, "Do what you did in the audition. Just forget everything now; you've been given so many different directions. Just do what you originally came in with."

And then when I went in with James, I assumed it was done, because I was taller than him. You're supposed to be a sexy character and all the other girls are in high heels and tight pants, and skirts and whatever, and I'm trying to be short, so I'm in flats and trousers. I'm *still* taller than him. I just assumed, even if I was good, my height lost me this one.

I remember after the test, because the test took half a day or something. We were the last to go in. At this point, I had no idea which way was up, sideways, whatever. I remember I left to go to Bristol Farms [a grocery store] and I went in and bought old-fashioned doughnuts and mashed potatoes, and I sat in my car and ate old-fashioned doughnuts and mashed potatoes. While I was eating, I got a call that they liked what I did in the test. So then I got called later in the day that we were heading the next day to Vancouver to film. Two days later we were filming in Vancouver, and the first thing we're doing is in Baltar's house where he hears the news of the attack and my spine is glowing red. A lot of intimacy. I had a particular outfit that had a lot of really fine snaps and patent-leather bra and panties. Patent leather kind of sticks and doesn't really do what you want it to do. They were probably worried I wasn't going to have this commanding quality, because I was sitting there, like, "I don't know what I'm doing. I'm going to be fired." Everybody's looking, you know?

RONALD D. MOORE

Trisha amazed us in that she was green as grass. She was a model, hadn't done a lot of work. Gorgeous. You know, very nice woman, but you weren't quite clear what she could handle.

TRICIA HELFER

Director Michael Rymer goes, "Okay, she has to be a little bit animalistic," and I'm like, "Okay, I can do that. That's fine." So we had to practice. Like, James had to practice disrobing me.

JAMES CALLIS

I've got to say, black plastic underwear is a bit of a handful.

TRICIA HELFER

He was getting nervous, I was getting nervous. We were both sweating, and all the execs and everybody were around the video village. It's the first day of filming; I'd barely ever been on a set before in my life. So finally I said, "James, there's a basement. Let's go downstairs. Let's practice the snaps. Let's practice the clasps." Then I just went, "Let's kiss." So we're downstairs in the basement and I planted a kiss on him.

JAMES CALLIS

It sounds really crazy, but genuinely it was a really good move, because we were both really self-conscious. We're going for each other in an animalistic way and actually feeling slightly self-conscious. More than slightly, because you're not in a room by yourself. You're being filmed. There's loads of people around, but I suppose that's part of the trick of acting, isn't it? That essentially was like a rehearsal, and then I think there was also the realization that we trusted each other. It's a thing about trust. That's what I think helped us and helped us establish the relationship, because some of that stuff—and being so close to somebody who you don't know—is obviously a lot of fun and very exciting, but it is intimidating. The very last thing that you want to feel on camera when you're trying to be real is to feel self-conscious. So it was a good move. What can I say?

RONALD D. MOORE

As concerned as we were in the beginning about Tricia, what started to happen was that as soon as we started asking her to play more than one model of Six, you suddenly realize, "Wow, she can really be different people without different makeup, and look exactly the same—it's clear you just put her in a ponytail or change her shirt and she's going to give us a different character." And that was an amazing thing. Once we started to be able to play that, we realized we really could play multiple models of all these guys. All of them could be distinct individuals with different characteristics, different character voice, and it just gave us a tremendous opportunity to really expand that part of the show.

TRICIA HELFER

The first one was Shelly Godfrey, and that was in "Six Degrees of Separation." I remember talking to Ron and saying, "She's written differently, can I play her differently?" Up until that point it had been Head Six, which I didn't understand who she was then. I was just playing her. I didn't understand until I watched the finale [laughs]. But after Shelly Godfrey there wasn't another one for quite a while, until the middle of the second season, with Gina. I saw them as different characters, and it's easier to play them when they are a different person. Their psyche, their mind, is different. Their experiences have been different, and so I saw them as the same base model, or like identical twins who have been raised separately. Their individual experiences, or how much contact with humans they had, altered them.

With Gina, I liked the idea of playing with the idea that a robot could have PTSD, and that it continued on once Baltar kind of smuggled her out, helped her escape and get onto the other ship. It was like a fantasy ship or something. There was one time where they finally got intimate, but she was struggling with it, because of the past that she had gone through. I also really liked Natalie, which was in the final season. She was the one that was trying to broker peace. She was the more political one. She was—Boomer ends up killing her, unjustly mind you, because she wasn't doing anything with Kara. After Natalie died, Sonia tried to step in and take her place, but that was kind of toward the end of the series. Then of course when Caprica came back around and downloaded, and we see her download into her new body. Then her struggle of seeing Baltar again, and then *loving* Baltar, but realizing she needs to side with her own kind and just embark on the resurrection ship or back on the Cylon basestar. Just trying to distance herself and shut down her feelings of having more empathy toward humans.

I tried to base them and structure them on their differences and their opinions that would be formed based on their interactions with humans. Caprica had this, I think, when she downloaded into a new body, and this is when she realized she actually loves this man that she had essentially used and manipulated for the Cylon mission. I really enjoyed her struggle as well, even though I didn't sometimes necessarily understand it. Her struggle of trying to be on the Cylon side and then ultimately ending up finding a way back to Baltar and finding herself alongside the humans at some point was great fun.

MARK VERHEIDEN

She was just amazing, and on a personal level, one of the nicest people you'd ever want to meet. Which was in contrast to her character, who on most occasions you probably *wouldn't* want to meet.

TODD SHARP
(production executive)

Basically the Six role came down to two people, Tricia and another person who was a more established actress. And there was a big argument between the studio and the network, and David, Ron, and Michael Rymer. They felt strongly that it should be this incredibly, spectacularly sexy Tricia, and the network was thinking maybe the better, more established actor. I certainly don't want to paint it as her acting wasn't good. Her acting was fine, but there was a more established actor who was attractive, but just not as stunning and striking, who originally the network had pushed hard for. In the end, Ron, David, and Michael got Tricia, and the big joke of course is that at first they [the network] fought against her, but then they made her the center-piece of the season-one [advertising] campaign in that red dress. We were like, "The other one you were looking to hire would *not* have been on the poster."

TRICIA HELFER

I swear, there were two reasons I became the centerpiece for the posters. One was that the red dress and the white hair stuck out in a show that was filmed dark and documentary style. Visually it stands out against everybody else that's in uniform and that type of thing. Also, I was really the only known Cylon in the beginning. Six is integral to the story, obviously, and I joke that the main reason is because I have a modeling background and I tend to have a lot more patience at a photo shoot. Actors almost all hate gallery shoots. For some reason they are super comfortable with a video, a filming, but once you get a still camera on them, it's like they become, "I don't know what I'm doing. This will capture a second in time and I might look really funny." Actors notoriously are *terrible* at gallery images; they are impatient. I had the patience, because I modeled for ten years with photo shoots. I just sat there while they just kept taking pictures.

DAVID WEDDLE

She's drop-dead gorgeous and does the vamp thing great, so in the beginning we just worked that, not thinking that she had any range beyond that. Then I remember writing a scene on Caprica and Athena has run off with Helo. She's pregnant and gone off the reservation, and they're talking about the fact that this has happened. That she's pregnant because she fell in love and that they need to find her. And Doral looks at her and says, "Do you envy her?" I forget the exact line, but she admits that she *does* envy them. I remember watching that daily, and Tricia *really* delivered it. I was like, "Whoa!" We started to realize she could do more and we started writing for that. She could play scenes with herself—two Sixes having arguments with each other—and you could totally tell that she was different characters. She turned out to have as much depth and dimension as anyone on the show. In "Pegasus," when she's a Six prisoner. My God, she played it. Everyone thought that she could do it, and she proved us right, because you could feel her trauma and her agony and her rage.

MARK VERHEIDEN

Think about it: She coopts Baltar into sort of destroying Caprica and reducing humans to this fleet running off into the distance. She started as a very malevolent character but, especially when we got into later episodes where the real Caprica was there and was captured, and was put in the same sort of abusive situations that the other Cylons were being put in, again, you could feel that there were different layers she was playing. Head Six was always sort of the same in terms of being this possible creation of Baltar's mind combined with what he thought she was. Later on, she became a fully realized character who underwent many changes as well. Mainly what I remember about Tricia Helfer was just what a great performer she was; someone who was so sharp in every scene and willing to really go for it, which is always fun when you're working with people.

There was a conscious effort to make the Head Six that would come to visit Baltar feel different than the reality of the Cylons that were in physical form. And the ones in physical form certainly could feel pain and be hurt, and had emotions. I don't want to say human, but they had emotions.

MARY MCDONNELL

That whole thing with Head Six. . . . You hear them say, "Rolling . . . ," and you go, "Wait, wait. Cut, cut, cut. Ron, David, Michael . . . somebody help me." They come running in and I go, "I really and truly don't know how to pretend I don't see Tricia. How does Laura Roslin *not* see her? You know, is she there? If it's an influence in the script, if it's an idea in the story and there's energies right on the other side, isn't there anything I can sense? I see Baltar looking at something." Well, eventually he just became a total nut job to me. It's pretty simple. I was told, "No, you don't see her. You don't feel her." So it became an interesting process of surrendering to the simple reality that the humans have to play in the story as opposed to the complex reality and ideas that were being played by the actors who were Cylons. It really was like playing two different worlds, but we were side by side and quite often in the same scene, so you'd have to try and not acknowledge some of the faces that James Callis has made.

There was a lot about *Battlestar Galactica* that centered on the relationship between Six and Baltar, though the writers admit that in the beginning they weren't sure how much mileage they'd be able to get out of it.

RONALD D. MOORE

I was hopeful, but I just didn't know where it was going to go. I loved the idea of him seeing her and continuing their sexuality and her sort of emotional and mental torture of him, and his own guilt. I just didn't quite know where the character was going to go and, as a result, where she was going to go. But episode by episode we would just invent a new little piece of business for them and try something different. What's the next trick to play? What's the next step in that relationship? And what *is* the relationship? You know, it wasn't for a while that we even sensed that there was a larger arc. You were just kind of doing it bit by bit by bit, hoping that later on it would amount to something. But the truth is that there weren't really many grand plans. If you read the show bible, you'll see that was the limit of what I had thought out. For instance, I knew that Laura would be in jail at the end of season one, but when and if they would get to Earth was something in the distance. I had no idea where I was going with Baltar. Was he going to become a flat-out villain? Was he going to become a trusted member of the family? Sharon, Lee, Kara . . . all of them. It was more like, "Let just start here and figure it out as we go along."

MARK VERHEIDEN

People will always ask me if Baltar had a chip in his brain or the Cylons had gotten to him, or is he just insane or . . . just what *is* his story? I don't know that we ever really answered that in terms of his relationship with Six. At least, Head Six—that's what we called her. There was Head Six and then there was real Six, the actual Cylons. He just had her in his head, and of course that turned out to be the linchpin in how everything went so south at the beginning of the series. Obviously it was some sort of Cylon something, but I think we also didn't feel the need to answer every single question.

TRICIA HELFER

I will admit I was getting a little tired of Head Six, because there was Caprica Six in the beginning, and once Head Six arrived and Gaius got up on the ship, it was really pretty much the rest of the pilot, the whole first season, and half the second season before the Gina episode and the *Pegasus* storyline. I was getting a little frustrated, because Six didn't have much of a storyline herself. Again, it was the start of the "God is love" and all these things. Well, there are only so many ways I can do this character, because she's kind of a little bit repetitive.

RONALD D. MOORE

In the beginning, I didn't want to settle on an idea of what their relationship was. I wanted to have a lot of possibilities. You know, what is she really? A chip in his head is the one we talked about the most frequently. Is she a manifestation of his subconscious trying to grapple with the enormity of what he's done, so it's all literally in his head? Is she an agent of an outside entity? Of God? Of whatever they believe God to be? What is it? I didn't want an answer to that. I didn't want to settle it. I wanted to be able to play different things for a while and not get an answer until much further down in the show. So early in the series, I just wanted to make sure that all of the above explanations were fluid.

DAVID WEDDLE

The spirituality aspect that Ron started to introduce gave that relationship a whole other dimension. It very much came out of the fact that we can't keep playing this dynamic over and over again; it's going to get boring. It started off physical but it became a much more dimensionalized, amazing kind of story. Then he's with them on the fleet, and then becomes part of the rebel Cylons—a lot of those big kind of turns that Ron came up with all so that we didn't fall into a rut.

RONALD D. MOORE

In the episode "Six Degrees of Separation," the other Six comes aboard. I felt I was deciding a couple of things. There was a great idea that somebody had in the room of just the thought that somebody would show up and it would be Number Six. That Six would walk into *Galactica* in the real world, and how would Baltar deal with that? So we loved that sort of notion of throwing him back on his heels right from the beginning. It was also a feeling that we needed to deal with what he did in the miniseries. That we hadn't really done too much with the fact that he had given information to the Cylons on the defense mainframe. That was the key element in their ability to pull off a surprise attack, and we wanted that to threaten him at some point. We wanted, suddenly, his biggest secret of all would be directly threatened and how would he deal with that? So it was just a very sort of sexy idea from the word go.

DAVID WEDDLE

In the end, Ron came up with the idea that Six really helped him with his father, who was senile, that she really did something emotional for him that meant a lot to him personally. So it wasn't about fucking even then, exclusively. That was part of his tie to her, and I thought that was a *great* revelation. You know, we start the series thinking Baltar's just a slimy womanizer, which he was, but his relationship with Six and his ties to Six were actually deeper even at the beginning, we just didn't know that as an audience and that gets revealed in that flashback with his father.

There's a certain irony in the fact that Kara "Starbuck" Thrace hates taking orders and military protocol but *loves* flying. Notes the show's bible, "Her record at the Academy and then at flight school was littered with demerits, reprimands and negative evaluations by her superiors. She drank too much, gambled too much, broke curfew almost daily, somehow always managed to be involved in any bar fight at the local watering holes and had a reputation for leaving a string of men with broken hearts and broken backs after sexual encounters that were more akin to a game of tackle pyramid than lovemaking. Simply put, she was a disaster as a military officer. But no one could argue with her flying."

She took a position at flight school, where she met and fell in love with Zak Adama. Writes Moore, "Zak failed a key flight test. A test Kara was administering. Zak was on the bubble as far as flight school was concerned and failing this test was a sure ticket out. It was Kara's duty to fail him. But she couldn't do it. Couldn't destroy Zak's dream of becoming a pilot like his father. She passed him and made a promise to herself that she would teach Zak everything he needed to know and make sure he became a great pilot. It wasn't enough." He ended up dying, though his death was chalked up to "pilot error" rather than attributed to instructor negligence. On the day of his funeral, Adama asked her to join him on *Galactica,* and she agreed; over the next two years the duo developed a father/daughter relationship.

Katee Sackhoff, a native of Portland, Oregon, got her start in acting by starring in the TV movies *Fifteen and Pregnant* (1998) and *Locust Valley* (1999). Some TV guest-starring roles followed, though she appeared in four episodes of MTV's *Undressed,* thirteen episodes of the series *The Fearing Mind,* and twenty-two episodes of *The Education of Max Bickford,* with Richard Dreyfuss, before becoming a part of the *Battlestar Galactica* ensemble.

RONALD D. MOORE

Making the character of Starbuck a woman was literally one of the first things I thought of, honestly. This was at a moment in time when we were just starting to see women in combat. You would start to see female fighter pilots for the first time. So it was kind of new, and I thought, "Oh, well, how would that play out? Wait a minute, she has all the same characteristics of the original Starbuck. She smokes cigars and she gambles, and she's the first one to throw a punch, and she's a little unstable." I thought, "I haven't seen that character before as a female fighter pilot. That's kind of cool." I thought it might be sort of a minor controversy, but I didn't really think it would be a thing. Then once it became a thing, then I was like, "Yeah, just stoke those flames, man. We need all the help we can get. Yell about it. Get angry. I need the publicity. Please. Go to chat rooms. More males demanding Ron Moore's head. Please. Give it to me!"

KATEE SACKHOFF

I was a lot younger than they had anticipated, or had been thinking about casting, or at least that's what I was told. When I read the script, it was this big thick thing and I was on a plane heading home for Christmas in 2001. I read this thing and I thought to myself, "Oh my God, I've been searching for this for, like, five years. I get to shoot a gun. This is amazing. My dad would be so proud. I have to do this." I called my people as soon as we got off the plane.

At the time, I was playing very stereotypical blond-chick roles and was sort of over it. I had just wrapped a series in New York, and really wanted to find something different to change the course of my career. We started looking and everything I was being offered was, like, "The chick in a horror movie that gets her head cut off." Been there, done that. So I read this script when I was, I think, twenty-one years old, and they had said, "You're way too young for this; they won't see you." I was like, "Okay, well, let me know if they change their minds, I love the script." About a month or two later, I got the phone call that they would see me. They were opening up a little bit, and I was like, "Okay." I went in and the entire time we just kept hearing back from them that I was too girly, and I wasn't right for it, and it wasn't the direction they wanted to go. It was just everything you *don't* want to hear when you really want a job. I just kept saying, "Will they please see me again? I'll go back and I'll do this and I'll change that." They'd say, "Hey, Katee, maybe you shouldn't wear heels to an audition to play a fighter pilot," and I was like, "Well, I feel like she would wear heels. I think she would not give a shit."

I auditioned like six or seven times. I cut my hair in the process. I took off my stilettos, because I guess Starbuck doesn't wear those. Eventually I got the part and I had no idea that it was ever going to be what it became. I tested against Grace Park for the role, and when I found out I got it, my parents just happened to be in town, and I turned to my parents and I said, "I feel so bad for the girl I met there. They should make her Boomer." And when it actually happened, I was like, "Oh, that's awesome!"

Come to find out they weren't testing her against me. They were probably testing both of us individually for those roles. The story goes that David Eick's ex-wife was watching the tapes sort of on silent, in the living room or his bedroom or something, the audition tapes, and his ex-wife walked by the tape and I guess he was begrudging the fact that they couldn't find Starbuck, and she walked by and said, "What are you talking about? That's her right there." So I guess that's how I got the job.

RONALD D. MOORE

I didn't know Katee before the role, but I always kind of thought, "This is a perfect marriage of actor and role," because, man, she seemed like Starbuck. There was a mischievous quality to Katee and a tough part. There was a "don't fuck with me" part of Katee; a somewhat dangerous part. It just felt so right that she played that role, and it just felt like she and the character became one.

KATEE SACKHOFF

I had never seen the original, so one of my best girlfriends and I decided to watch it, because I called my dad and said, "I found a role. You'd be so happy. It's *Battlestar Galactica*," and he's like, "That's great. Who are you playing?" I told him Starbuck and he said, "Do me a favor. Go to Blockbuster, rent it, watch it, and call me back." So my girlfriend and I were drinking wine, as you do, and we get ten minutes into it and they're talking about Starbuck and Starbuck's obviously in the room. She looks at me and goes, "Did we miss it? Where is she? Rewind it." So we rewound it, pushed play, and I went, "Oh, shit," and called my dad back. I was like, "I get that." So I marched down to the internet café, which was four blocks away. I paid my $11.99 for one hour, logged on to a chat group just to see what they thought about my being cast. I learned in that moment, "Fuck 'em." There you go.

RONALD D. MOORE

Katee was capable of doing almost anything Starbuck did. I wouldn't blink if she pulled out a gun in the middle of a fight or slugged somebody on the set. Not that she got into big fights like that, but just that the actress had this toughness and resiliency and this wicked sense of humor that was so close to what we were writing that you stopped thinking about whether you were writing for Katee or for Starbuck. It was really one idea that you were writing for. I don't mean that in a bad way at all. She didn't go off on binges, and she didn't actually hit crew people and she wasn't out of control, but there was this dangerous, unpredictable, mischievous part of Katee that you just saw the character through really easily. She *was* Starbuck. It was just that perfect in terms of casting.

KATEE SACKHOFF

I've been saying to people lately that I actually need to go and rewatch it, because I've actually never sat down and watched the series from front to back. I originally watched the directors' rough cuts, probably in my trailer while I was filming other things, and that's sort of how I saw every episode. I never actually watched it while it aired or anything. My experience of the show is purely just from an actor living it and not as a viewer yet. But I sure felt like Kara went through a lot. She grew a lot during the series, from the moments we first met her and she was one step above an angsty teenager. As time went on, we saw her maturing and realizing the magnitude of the responsibility that she had been given. In the beginning of the series, so many people in this world didn't understand this circumstance in anything other than history. So when it actually happened to them, I think that the responsibility for their position that they held took a while to hit some of the younger soldiers, Kara probably being the most evident of that.

When we were doing the pilot, I was told so many times that I was not right for this part that you get to the point where you think, "Oh my God, I'm not ready for this part." We're doing a scene in the Viper and it's the first time I've been in it. Part of me is going, "Oh my God, this is so cool," part of me is going, "Oh my God, it's like eight hundred degrees." Then the other part is like, "What the fuck is my dialogue? I don't know what any of this shit means. I don't know how I'm going to say it, because I don't know anything." I literally couldn't say the dialogue. We must have done it so many times, and I remember thinking to myself, "You stupid little girl, you're going to get fired." So I just put my dialogue right up on the screen, because I was like, "I'm just going to read it," and I did it for the rest of the series. All of my dialogue in the cockpit was on the screen, because I couldn't remember the science stuff. The one line I couldn't say was, "We've got violent decompressions radiating from the port flight pod." *Now* I can't forget it. It's in my goddamn head. It won't go away.

DAVID WEDDLE

I get choked up even just to talk about working with Katee Sackhoff, because she's one of the most phenomenal talents I've ever worked for. I say work for, because I wrote for her, and there's no greater thrill except maybe having kids and having your grandchild, but there's no greater thrill than to write for an actress of the caliber of Katee Sackhoff, and watching her bring that character to life was one of the greatest experiences of my career, and I feel that Bradley [Thompson] and I just really locked in to that character.

KATEE SACKHOFF

I lived in New York on September eleventh, and up until that moment I had, for the most part, lived a very sheltered life. I had lived on my own since I was seventeen, but nothing really terrible had ever happened to me that could have been potentially life-threatening. I think it was the first moment that I realized the fragility of life, and it was a lesson that hit really hard, really fast. It was a very similar thing that happened to a lot of the younger soldiers on the *Galactica* and in this world, because up until this moment, everything that she had been told about the Cylons had been read in history books.

DAVID WEDDLE

She was, in a way, me. Kara's father was, in a way, my father. Her mother was my father and me, and I know that sounds confusing, but those dynamics, those personal experiences were very much channeled through. When she talks about the story in "Maelstrom" when she says, "My mother was in a jungle fighting and she had this post-traumatic phobia about bugs, and I put rubber bugs in her closet, and she would try to smash them"—I did that to my dad, who was a marine in the South Pacific.

We wrote for a show called *The Fearing Mind,* which was Katee Sackhoff's very first show. She was a daughter in that show and I put all these scenes about my daughter and me, and Katee played my daughter in the material I came up with. You'd see her on "Maelstrom," and director Michael Nankin would say, "Do one now where her mother's dying. Cry your eyes out. Don't hold it back. Now smile as she tells you you're my daughter. It's a happy moment." Katee would do every color that Michael asked for. Oh, you know just fearlessly run into those emotions, and on an instinctual level is just an amazing actress and just such a thrill that I got to write with her. I love her with all my heart.

MICHAEL NANKIN
(director, "Maelstrom")

Katee and I had this great rapport right from the get-go. We just understood each other, and it was a sort of director/actor relationship that ran very deep. You know the stuff that she had to do and the places she had to go, and the stuff she had to dredge up to take the character where she needed to go. So it was a very intimate relationship, because you work in almost any other situation, you're not seeing your coworkers stripped to their core emotionally.

RONALD D. MOORE

Katee *was* Starbuck. So clear and perfectly created, that character in the miniseries, that then it became just keep going. She's set. We know who she is, *she* knows who she is, just write it.

MICHAEL ANGELI

Starbuck was in your face. She was tough. She didn't take any shit and got into it with everybody and mixed it up, right? Perhaps Katee being so moody and capricious and whatnot, maybe she was staying in character. Just to give her the benefit of the doubt, that could have been part of it, but I don't think so. I think she was Starbuck all the way through. I don't think she really had an arc. She got this big sort of smack down where we decided that we were going to kill her, and then she became something else. Then she became this more sort of ethereal, whimsical, mythical character. But she was kick-ass until the end. When you think about it, as far as a character arc, the conventional thing would've been she's kick-ass Starbuck and then becomes humbled and realizes that there's such a thing as humanity. That's a very conventional turn. We could've done that with her, but, like I said, that's kind of boilerplate. I like what we did. It was a great sort of violent right turn.

DAVID WEDDLE

Brad and I wrote "The Hand of God," "Act of Contrition." We did a lot of the writing on "You Can't Go Home Again," even though our names are not on the script. Then we wrote "Scar" in the second season. So we really kind of locked in on Kara Thrace, the reckless, self-destructive, yet brilliant Viper pilot. She was the best in the fleet because she had this sort of a reckless abandon; she would go right up to the edge of something that was suicidal. She didn't care, so you could set up perhaps a kind of death wish behind her bravado. That was very much Ron's take on the character, and Brad and I wrote to that in our episodes. The other thing that Ron had was a very strong idea that Kara would turn out to be some kind of guardian angel. Not that she would die—we didn't have that idea in the beginning—but that she would play a very critical role in leading the fleet to Earth, and she wouldn't realize she had this destiny or these abilities. His ideas were very strong on that, but how we were going to get there or how that story was going to un-fold, Ron did not know.

RONALD D. MOORE

Starbuck's journey started with something small, in a scene between her and Leoben in the episode "Flesh and Bone." He's tapping into the river and seeing things that no one else can see, that there's something special in her, and that she had a destiny and that she was unique. We didn't really know where we were going to go with that, but we liked the idea that Kara was special and Leoben saw it. Right away that meant whenever we saw Leoben, there was going to be a Kara story attached to it.

DAVID WEDDLE

In season two, I believe it's "Valley of Darkness," Ron did a rewrite of our script on that, like a polish, but he added a scene that turned out to be critical, though at the time it was just meant to be a slice-of-life moment. If you remember, Kara Thrace finds the Cylon Raider and goes back to Caprica, and she hooks up with Helo and there's a scene where they're on the run and they go back to her old apartment. Ron wrote that scene, conceived of it and everything. They wander into the wreckage of her apartment, and there's a painting on a canvas leaning against the wall of a giant mandala, and Helo says, "Who painted that?" And she says, "I did." Then a little bit later, she puts a record on the stereo and he says, "Who's that? What music is that?" And she says, "That's my father." Ron put those vital elements in, but not with any conscious idea that they were going to play out somehow. It was really meant as a kind of enigmatic little snippet or view into Kara Thrace's life, and a slice-of-life moment of these two lost people on this planet just sort of hanging out in what was once her apartment. That's all it was.

MICHAEL O'HALLORAN
(editor, *Battlestar Galactica* [2004])

I don't think it was intended, but that painting became such a huge part of the show. That was one of the great things; talk about a show building itself organically. That was one of those great moments. When I first got on the show, Michael Rymer asked me what I thought the show was about and I said, "It's 9/11 every single day to these people." In this episode, Kara has that moment where she says, "You know, after the attack, I realized"—I'm just paraphrasing—"I didn't care about another toilet that didn't work or the bad view of the parking lot outside." There she's lighting up her father's cigar that she finds in a little cigar box there. She just put on her father's flight jacket. She's just having that memory, and then she starts playing her father's music. It was just really, to me, everything that the show was.

DAVID WEDDLE

In season three, Brad and I are writing "Rapture," and Ron says the phrase "the Temple of the Five." We did a draft and then he was giving us notes on the rewrite, and he said, "What I would like is for Kara to be able to interpret something on the temple that no one else can." Because this was playing into his idea that she would be like a guardian angel. So he said, "Maybe there's some writing in an ancient language, nobody else can understand what it means, and Kara looks at it and can read it right away, and has no idea why." That was Ron's initial pitch, though he was just throwing it out as an idea. Brad and I mulled that over. It seemed a little too awkward or stilted if you did it exactly that way, but we knew what Ron wanted.

So we just start all of a sudden back to that scene in "Valley of Darkness," and the painting of the mandala, and thought that would be a more enigmatic, mysterious thing to tie to Kara Thrace. What if her mandala was on the temple? So we pitched that to Ron. He goes, "I love it. Do it." So we did it. Then of course at the end Helo says to Kara, "Do you have that picture of your old apartment?" And she pulls a snapshot out of a box, and he compares it to the mandala on the temple and says, "How did you paint a mandala that was on a five-thousand-year-old temple?" And she has no answer for him. So we wrote those scenes, and Ron loved that.

RONALD D. MOORE

David and Bradley have a lot to do with the way the Starbuck arc ultimately went. I was interested in the early Starbuck, the fighter pilot with the screwup, tragic backstory. The officer who would disobey orders at times, who would take a swing at her superior and yet worshiped Adama and had been mentored by him and then had been betrayed by him and vice versa. The betrayals involved in that relationship. I was interested in her relationship with Apollo, what that was about, and then ultimately with Sam Anders. I really liked the whole arc of her sleeping with Apollo and then marrying Sam. But they were *really* into her arc, and sometimes there's a point as a showrunner where you do kind of realize, "This one's better in your hands. You'll do better with this piece than I will."

BRADLEY THOMPSON
(producer, *Battlestar Galactica* [2004])

Katee was absolutely fearless about going to all these horrible, emotional places. The attitude was, "Can we make this character the most infuriating person ever?" Because she's totally self-sabotaging and tremendously talented. But a really, really big heart. All of these things that are fighting within her. Then we tried to come up with why would that be. What was her freight damage, so to speak, that brought her to this spot? It was a pretty incredible journey, especially if you're going to turn her into Christ or something that comes back from the dead and leads you to the promised land and then vanishes . . . I thought that was pretty cool.

DAVID WEDDLE

We didn't really know how we were going to pay things off yet, because it was such an organic process on *Battlestar,* and I was up for the preproduction in the first couple days of shooting on "Rapture" and "The Eye of Jupiter." Katee Sackhoff came up to me and said, "So what's the deal with the mandala? What does that mean?" Of course I didn't know yet, and I said, "Well, we're still developing that. It's kind of premature to talk about it." I was tap-dancing, and Katee said, "You know, I think that in light of seeing this mandala, and in light of knowing I have some other destiny"—because Ron had talked to her about that—she said, "Maybe there's something in my past. Maybe there's an event in my past that seems innocuous, never seemed important, but now in light of my mandala on the temple, I interpret it in a whole different way." So I said, "That's a really interesting idea, Katee."

I came back to the writers' room in L.A., and the story up on the board for the episode that they were going to have Brad and I write. In it, Lee and Kara are orbiting this planet with a lot of cloud cover, and while they're doing their missions, they talk about their fraught relationship. I said, "Well, we kind of have done that over and over. Can't we try to advance it in some way? And here's what Katee Sackhoff has to say." And I told them, and Ron just grabbed that and ran with it and said, "Yes. Let's do that." Then we got the idea of the cloud around the planet starting to look to her like the mandala, and then this whole theme of her always tiptoeing up to the edge of death. You know this might be a vehicle for exploring that.

RONALD D. MOORE

They were struggling with it and I wasn't in on the break. Then they pitched it, "You know, it just feels unsatisfying that in the end, she's just going to figure out a way to beat this thing. She's just going to come out smelling like a rose like she always does; it just feels like it's about nothing, and we had an idea. What if we killed her?" I was like, "What?" They're like, "We kill her. She dies. But we bring her back a few episodes later and she's been resurrected and she's some kind of guardian angel or prophet. We feed her into the larger mythology in some way; we shock the audience and really take her out of the show for a while. We let Lee and Adama and everyone deal with the ramifications of her death." I was really surprised and even said, "That's *really* unexpected."

DAVID WEDDLE

So we got the idea as it is in the show "Maelstrom," of her being drawn down into the mandala, and having a *2001* sort of vision and then pulling out again. So as we developed that, Ron said, "Why does she have to pull out? Maybe she goes all the way in and she dies." Which was an incredible, radical idea none of us would have ever dared to think of, and of course it plays into all the mythologies that's great about where *Battlestar* evolved to, and myths throughout every culture. Of course, most prominently Christianity, there is in every civilization with this death and rebirth, and a rebirth that offers a vision forward for the human race. So Kara was starting to jell as a character like that.

KATEE SACKHOFF

They didn't send the script out first and I got this cryptic phone call from Ron and David in my trailer. They were like, "So we want to talk to you about something. You've done nothing wrong." In my mind I'm thinking, "I totally did something wrong." "We're going to kill you, but we're going to bring you back, so don't worry. You're not going to be you. Don't worry about it. Everyone's going to think you're dead. We're going to take your name out of the credits. You're going to go home. We're not telling anyone anything." I'm like, "Okay. . . ." So I went to Mexico for a couple of episodes, but the problem was that I was lying to everyone.

RONALD D. MOORE

This was one of the stupidest things that David and I did in the entire run of the show. You're right at the cusp of social media and the internet starting to ferret out spoilers from shows. Various plotlines are getting blown online for the first time. This is becoming a thing that none of us had ever had to deal with before. Our feeling was this was only going to work if the audience thinks we mean it, and the characters mean it. We'll take her name out of the main credits, we want this to be a shock. Katee knows she's coming back and we swear her to secrecy, so then, of course, it just becomes a fiasco and Katee is telling everyone she's leaving the show. The script comes out and she's dead.

KATEE SACKHOFF

I'm like this child; I tell my mom, because I had to tell *someone.* My mom's on set. The crew were like, "So sorry about Katee." My mom's like, "I know. She'll be okay. She'll land on her feet."

MICHAEL ANGELI

We knew we were going to bring her back, so we wrote two endings for that script. One is that she *doesn't* die. *That's* the one that we circulated, because, first of all, we wanted it to be a surprise. Second of all, we didn't want to raise concern with the cast thinking, "Oh my God, they're killing her off. What *are* they doing?" Well, somehow the real draft got leaked, and there was just chaos. Everybody thought, "You're killing off Katee?" Leading the charge was Eddie Olmos. He was like, "This is preposterous. This is wrong. She's one of the signature characters in the show. What the hell are you guys doing?" Her mother even called, saying, "Why are you killing her? How could you possibly...?" Of course we had to explain what was going on, and come clean about everything. But it was astonishing how militant Eddie got about keeping her on the show.

RONALD D. MOORE

Eddie puts the script down after he reads it, and says, "The show will never be the same."

KATEE SACKHOFF

Finally I was like, "I can't do this anymore. I'm telling Eddie." So I called him and then he told everyone. We were doing the *Maxim* photo shoot and he stood up on something and he told the entire cast that I wasn't really dead, and I felt like such an asshole.

RONALD D. MOORE

While this is happening in Vancouver, David and I are getting calls in Los Angeles from the set saying, "They're really upset. You don't understand, people are freaking out that you're killing Starbuck." We're like, "Hey, it's working. Nobody's going to know. This is going to be the greatest prank of all time." A little time goes by and I get a phone call. Eddie's pissed, walking around saying, "This is the death of the show." It just spiraled completely out of control and we're like, "We're just trying to keep a secret on a TV show. We didn't want to upset anybody."

KATEE SACKHOFF

I don't even think we made it a week.

RONALD D. MOORE

It was just a matter of days and we were like, "Okay, call it off. Tell everybody. We're sorry."

DAVID WEDDLE

We did a break where we talked about her visions in the clouds before she "died," and everything was pitched out from Lee and Kara have sex on the hangar deck and all the other characters are in bleachers. Every kind of bizarre thing was thrown up on the board, and then Brad and I went off to write it, and it just seemed too gimmicky and over-the-top. But one of the things that had been talked about in that, and that I felt very strongly, I think I brought it up, was her mother.

Obviously Ron laid in this whole thing of the abusive mother. He never came out with why the mother abused her, who she really was. So we just decided to center on that. That was going to be the vision. It's going to be the mother, and we came up with the idea of maybe it was the last time she saw her mother. So we wrote the first version of it. She goes to see her mother and her mother's had a stroke and cannot talk, and it is Kara Thrace just venting toward her mother who had abused her. In the middle of it, tears start to come out of her mother's eyes, and she goes, "Don't. Stop crying or I'll give you something to cry about. Remember that? I do." Then she does this whole venting and she runs out, and it was the last time she saw her mother. So we wrote that in a draft and Ron said, "This is the best script you guys have ever written for me." And I was overcome with emotion about that, and thought, "Wow. That was an incredible affirmation." Then Michael Nankin came on to direct it. He'd directed "Scar." Brad and I were already really close with Michael, and loved collaborating with him. The three of us became a kind of team on *Battlestar*. But I didn't love him this day. All of a sudden he wanted a conference call for the script that Ron loved better than any script we've ever written, and Michael Nankin starts saying, "I don't understand the relationship between Kara and her mother. I don't understand why we're doing this flashback. Blah, blah, blah." Ron defended our version for a long time, and then suddenly turned and said, "Maybe Michael's right. Maybe we need to see the lion roar one more time. Maybe she goes to see her mother after the day that her mother has gotten a notice from a doctor that she's dying of cancer, and Kara discovers this. Then we can get the back-and-forth with the mother and understand the relationship. Then maybe that can show us . . . maybe you can tie in the mandala and her cosmic destiny into that."

Then Michael and Ron said, "So what do you guys think?" And we had like four days before prep started, or three days I think it was. I said, "Well, it all sounds great but I don't know how we do this in three days. . . ." Michael Nankin laughed and said, "Oh, you guys can do it. You wrote 'Scar.'" So Brad and I, as we often did trying to solve *Battlestar* episodes, walked the entire backlot of Universal, through the Western street, the New York street, talking about this, and came up with a bunch of bad ideas of how to tie the mandala in. None of them were good, and Ron then pitched his ideas, none of which were good. I didn't sleep that whole night. I felt like I had a fever, and suddenly hit on the idea of the mandala being in a scrapbook, because my mother kept scrapbooks on me, and I thought, "What if the mandala's in the scrapbook and she painted it when she was like two or three and didn't even remember this painting, and her mother had it and shows it to her?"

So we went in to pitch that to Ron, and he said, "That's fantastic." And we had more discussions about the mother, too, with Ron, and he said, "Maybe it's, you know, like with my parents, they always felt that I was special, that I had special abilities. Therefore nothing I ever did was good enough. Maybe she had a feeling about her daughter. She knew she was special, but the way she communicated it was kind of fucked up, because she had been in the military and been in combat, and had all these demons. She knew something true about her daughter, but communicated it in a very dysfunctional way." So that's how "Maelstrom" came together. It wasn't pre-planned. It all kind of sprung from this scene that Ron wrote in season two that had these clues and these elements that were potentially powerful. The way we started to write the show was to look back at what's happened and build on that, or expand on that, or go to the door of a scene that had certain clues in it.

Then of course in the last season, they said to us, "What do you want to write for the last episode?" Because we had been so intimately involved all the way through, they let us kind of choose what we wanted to do, and I said, "I want to do her father in that very same scene in her apartment she plays the music, you hear her father's music. Now let's see the father. Let's complete Kara Thrace's story and let's use the father to do the final steppingstone of her destiny." And Ron said, "Great. Go for it."

So of course we're talking about "Someone to Watch Over Me," and that's what it became, and Mark Verheiden had the idea of the father not as a . . . You know, we started with flashbacks, the way we had done kind of Socrata Thrace, like see flashbacks, and then what we'd done on "Act of Contrition." A series of flashbacks to sort of fill in the father's story. But Mark said, "What if it's a ghost story, like he's playing a piano in the bar and you don't know he's not real. Only Kara sees him." We loved that idea, and that was a brilliant idea of Mark's, and then Ron really helped with the notes of the music. The notes of the music would correspond to the coordinates for Earth. Ron came up with that.

It was this wonderful wedding of the cosmic destiny of the character, the spiritual dimension of the character, to her personal story. So by the end of "Someone to Watch Over Me," you have all of Kara Thrace's story from the beginning to the end. So that's an example to me of the whole organic process of writing *Battlestar Galactica*, which I think was one of the real keys to it being such a great show.

Not a lot of character background was available on Lieutenant (eventually Captain) Karl "Helo" Agathon (an electronic countermeasures officer), as he was a character that wasn't supposed to go beyond the *Battlestar Galactica* miniseries. For a variety of reasons, though, he was kept alive, his story unfolding on Cylon-occupied Caprica, where he is paired with Grace Park's Sharon Valerii, unaware of what she really is. Like much of the young cast of the show, the Canadian-born actor in the days prior to the miniseries had spent much of his acting time appearing in small feature film parts and guest-star appearances on television.

MARK VERHEIDEN

The character of Helo was a really grounded guy. This sounds a little corny, but the everyman soldier feeling I got from Helo, that he was just trying to have a family and get on with some version of life, whatever you can have in this situation, is something I really enjoyed. And Tahmoh is a great actor and was always great to work with, but it's good to have a character in there that is the grounded guy you could go to if you wanted an honest answer about where things are really at.

RONALD D. MOORE

I would have to say that the actor that changed the conception of the character the most, now that I think about it, is Tahmoh, who played Helo. We never had any intention of keeping him in the show. He was a guest-star character. He was supposed to come in the miniseries and he was going to die on Caprica. There was no such thing as Cylon-occupied Caprica. That wasn't even part of the story or part of the bible. You were never going to cut back to Caprica. What happened was when we saw the miniseries all put together at a DGA screening—we were watching the show projected on a big screen, and it was a *huge* moment. I remember after it was over, David Weddle—who I saw there with Bradley Thompson, first time since *Star Trek*—and I were having a conversation about, "God, Helo was really fucking good, wasn't he?" "Yeah, it sucks that we killed him. . . . Is there any way . . . ?" We kept talking that night and then it just kept coming back up in our discussion about, "Is there any way we can bring Helo back in the show?" Because we really liked him. "What if we cut back and saw Caprica?" At the same time the network was pressuring us to do some planet shifts so that everything wasn't claustrophobic on the ships. And I didn't want to have a *Star Trek* series where they just kept running into these Earthlike planets and go down and have an adventure.

TONI GRAPHIA
(co-executive producer)

Early on there were a lot of discussions about the fact that this could be a very claustrophobic show if it only takes place on the ship. But then there was Helo left behind on Caprica. I think there was a plan that at some point he would get picked up, but we started thinking, "Geez, it would open the show up more to just leave him on the planet. Have him there for a while so we could use the sun, the trees and daylight." But then we were like, "But there's radiation down there, so how is that not killing them?" And we literally had to make up—and it sounds a lot easier than it was—antiradiation meds, and they give themselves shots. It protects them against the radiation, like a vaccine. We just made up those fixes as they went along, and there had to be a certain amount of believability or we would have lost the audience there. But having Helo on Caprica? A *great* addition to the show.

MARK STERN

Going back to pick up that story was great. One of the things I loved about the show was they really respected all their actors. You would spend time with all these different characters and really flesh their lives out and see all different facets of them. It was a true ensemble in that respect. Also, if you sit down and kind of binge them, you really see how these actors grow. Tricia Helfer probably most of all, but Grace Park as well. When they play multiple versions of themselves, it really pushes them as actors and you can see their development, which is really cool to watch.

RONALD D. MOORE

So then we started saying, "Well, if we cut back to Cylon-occupied Caprica and told a story with Helo, that would get the network off our back and then we get to have Helo in the show again at the same time." And so it kind of came out of our desire to have him.

TAHMOH PENIKETT

I didn't expect to come back after the miniseries. As far as I was concerned, I was playing a very heroic and upstanding moral character and then he dies at the end. The planet is supposed to explode, so I didn't expect to come back. I was having a good scene with Grace Park and I remember Edward James Olmos approaching me on the day, and he was there just observing us. He wasn't actually acting that day. We were shooting in Aldergrove and were doing this incredible scene with Grace Park and the planet's about to explode and there's only so many seats on our Raptor. I feel like I'm not going to survive, or I feel like Gaius Baltar's life is better than mine. I make a very heroic and selfless decision, and Helo gives up his seat.

So I thought I was done, but Edward James on that day that we were filming, came to me and I remember him saying, "Listen, the producers love you. They're going to bring you back." Even early on in my career I knew that I couldn't put any weight in that. I was very gracious and very accepting of that huge compliment from this legend who I'd always looked up to, but I didn't depend on it. I actually went and did a Canadian television cop series right after that, which ultimately ended up getting canceled. When I did get the call from Ron's office saying we want you back, we've got an idea for a storyline, I was more than flattered and excited. I was over the moon and just couldn't wait to do it.

RONALD D. MOORE

I remember the early writers' room meetings where they were asking me "So where are we going with this story" and I was like, "I have no fucking idea." It's just something we came up with. I wrote "33," all I knew was he was on the run, they were chasing him, he had to have antiradiation medication in order to survive, and he was going to run into another Sharon and *that* was going to tell us that, "Oh my God, there's more than one Sharon? He doesn't know!" I knew that was a great setup to . . . *something.* That Sharon coming at the end of that story and rescuing him from another Six, that the audience would kind of go, "Wow. What does *that* mean?" And that's *all* I knew. We didn't stroke out the master arc, we just sort of did it episode by episode. It was, "Okay, what's the next step? What should they be trying to do in this episode? We know that she's a Cylon, he doesn't. When is he going to find out? How long can we hold that off? What's the plan? Well, there has to be a plan. They're after something. What are they after?"

CARLA ROBINSON
(writer, *Battlestar Galactica* [2004])

I came onto the show with virtually no knowledge of anything regarding *Battlestar Galactica.* I remember on the old show they wore capes, and Lorne Greene's eyebrows, which I thought were a character themselves. But I remember on my first day in the writers' room I said, "Okay, these Cylons, the humanoid Cylons, they're full-grown. We see them. They're already made. Can they get pregnant?" It got really quiet in the room. I remember thinking to myself, "Oh, Carla, you just suggested that a robot get pregnant. How stupid!" At that point I figured I might as well ride it off the rails and I said, "How about if we get one pregnant with a human?" Again, it got this weird quiet. And Ron just said, "We're going to look into it." We walked outside and David and Bradley were with me, and they said, "I think he liked that thing you said." I said, "Well, I hope it wasn't too stupid." I had no idea at the time that the human-Cylon hybrid baby would become such a point of direction for this show.

DAVID WEDDLE

Going back to the idea that the Cylons can't reproduce, Ron says, "They have the equipment to reproduce and they fuck like crazy, but they can't have babies, so maybe the occupation of Caprica is a ploy." It's an experiment that they're coming up with to try to sexually reproduce, because maybe they get a theory that what they're missing is, biologically, they can't experience love. So maybe if they use a Sharon and she becomes a girl in danger, Helo falls in love and maybe they can make a baby and maybe it works. She gets pregnant, but what the Cylons don't understand is that if she gets pregnant, she falls in love with him and goes off the reservation and is no longer with the program.

RONALD D. MOORE

While we were talking about that, there was chemistry between the two of them. We had played that in the miniseries that there was sort of a quasi kind of thing going on between them, but it hadn't really been acted on. Now they're alone, they're isolated. Why would the Cylons do this? What could they possibly want from Helo? He can't know where the *Galactica* is, he has no idea, so that can't be it. He doesn't know some supersecret military intelligence, he's just a navigator. What else could it be? Why would they set up this scenario? Why would she kiss him? Why would they sleep together? What if it's about having sex? Why sex? Well, sex is a big thing with the Cylons; we've been playing that. What if it's about reproduction? Wait a minute, reproduction! It's about having children. Maybe they can't have children. Maybe that's the thing. Maybe the desire to have children is a biological imperative and it's what would make them closer to their conception of God. That's what it is! It's about the Cylons can't have children. It just came out of many hours in the writers' room and arguing different ways of going at it.

It's the best part of what we do. I love the improvisational nature of that. The joy of discovery. You're there together, you're working at a problem, you're hearing different ideas, you're trying them out. We put things up on the board and take them down, because they would fail, but you kept hunting, you kept searching, and you find it. It's just unbelievable. It's a high. Everyone's just excited and thrilled, and then you're just scared that someone's going to say no. Then you're scared the network's going to hate it or something. If they do, then you've got *that* battle to fight. But that's the great thing in the writers' room, man. There's nothing like that. There's nothing like coming in there with nothing and going "What the hell are we going to do with this guy?" and you just create it out of nothing. Wonderful, wonderful experience. It changes so much. Just like, "God is love" changed the mythology of the show. It was just such a small one, but the show pivoted on both those moments.

TAHMOH PENIKETT

Caprica's a nuclear wasteland. It's done. They're moving on. You see in "33" everyone's trying to escape, which is why that episode is so brilliant. Now you're in space, you're trying to get away, and when it cuts to Helo, I think the audience is just like, "Oh my God, we did not expect to see that guy again, this is fantastic." Not to say it was monotonous in any way on the ship, but it really broke the almost claustrophobic confines that the directors and the writer and the actors really captured, where there's only forty thousand of us and we're running for our lives. We're in a bunch of spaceships stuck in deep dark space.

But Helo's arc over the course of the series was huge, man. You see examples of who this man potentially could be, who he was at his heart, but he's still a young man. He didn't make those decisions without fear and trepidation and doubt. When he gave up his seat, that's all there. That was what was beautiful about him: that fear, that conflict was there. Most of us have that in life when we make really big decisions. It's rarely a hundred percent. Because of that, we saw him continually be challenged when he would go against the grain, because he was incapable of doing wrong. He's often referred to as a moral compass on the show, and it's a suitable term, because he really could see both sides of an issue. Both sides of the war, the battle, the conflict.

He was in love with a Cylon, who he was having a child with. That conflict, that prejudice, that bigotry that they faced was a continual thing against him, a continual challenge. But as a man his perspective was always broadening and being forced to grow, because he was married to a Cylon, because he had a child, because he potentially was a prime example of what the future could be, which was love, and harmony and tolerance. Like I said, it was not an easy ride and he faced doubt and people doubted his loyalty and his conviction many times. But he was arguably the most solid and grounded individual on that ship.

There comes a time when Helo is faced with whether to be complicit and allow biological warfare to be used against the Cylons to wipe them out, and he can't do it. You see that conflict between him and Roslin, him and Apollo. I'd see people at conventions when things like that were happening and they're like, "You know, I hate you. I don't like your character," and then other people would say, "I love you so much, you're the bravest character I've ever seen." But every time I say, "Do you realize that the show would have been done if I didn't do what I did? We wouldn't even be here right now discussing this. The Cylons would have been gone." Again, that speaks volumes about how much people believed in the show and how moved they were by the performances. They got really passionate about it, man.

Arising from the Sharon/Helo relationship on Cylon-occupied Caprica was her pregnancy—something that *shouldn't* have been able to occur. It creates a serious divide on *Galactica,* between people thinking the birth should be aborted for humanity's sake, and others believing it was Sharon's decision (despite the fact that she's a Cylon). As a result it examined the whole abortion issue, with Roslin deciding for the sake of their species, abortion needed to be outlawed regardless of her personal feelings on the subject. Of course, this being *Battlestar Galactica,* the path from there was not a smooth one, with the baby being born, then, under Roslin's orders, Sharon being told the baby had died and been cremated (she wasn't, just placed elsewhere). That betrayal would become an issue later on in the series. At one point, when their child is taken to a Cylon ship, Helo has to shoot Sharon so that she will download again on the vessel and find their child.

RONALD D. MOORE

The pregnancy became a huge part of the mythology; that idea of the Cylon drive toward Cylon reproduction became one of the defining characteristics of the whole show and the whole race.

MARY MCDONNELL

When Roslin made the choice to ban abortion, obviously you're trying to save the human race. There's got to be babies, right? That was very hard for me personally to get behind. I made the assumption that the secretary of education, a woman who was deeply invested in the education of children and the promotion of life, and teachers being able to live their lives, and young women being able to protect themselves, obviously would be pro-abortion. My thought was that Laura had to go against something that had been a given for her. To make those decisions requires a cutting off of the rest of her, which would force her to hesitate and therefore the quality of ruthlessness developed. It all came back to her ideas about how to survive as a species. Those moments came from learning how to separate the actions from the self. She did not have that quality going into the situation.

MARK VERHEIDEN

I remember when we talked about it, there was a show called *Everwood* that had done an episode that dealt with abortion. It turned into kind of a cause célèbre for a little while about doing that sort of hot-button topic on a show. We had no problems. I don't recall any issues with actually tackling that particular subject, because, again, we were one step removed. We're not saying it's about your little girl in Middle America. We were talking about a completely different situation where President Roslin had to make a difficult choice that went against her personal morals. A choice she felt she *had* to make for the survival of mankind. Again, we did things we were able to do or at least not run into as much trouble doing, because of the one step removed of science fiction.

RONALD D. MOORE

As soon as you see the word "abortion," it's controversial, so the network and the studio certainly started getting a little nervous when it was brought up, but they didn't really, to their credit, pressure us not to do it. The trick for us was, it was interesting about Laura, the liberal president who, forced into this situation, would look at this with different eyes and come to a conclusion that she really despised, but that made sense in terms of the survival of the human race.

GRACE PARK

The whole baby thing had a fantastic setup, including the idea that they were going to abort it. So when it's dead, there's the grief and you're fighting for something. You're thrashing against something. And *then* the absolute betrayal when you find out the baby is alive and was taken from you. Yet the joy and the brilliance that the baby is still alive; it's the hope that ideally pulls you through.

The man with the wrench on *Galactica* was Chief Galen Tyrol, who, having risen and fallen elsewhere owing to a tragic mistake made by his deckhands, found himself on the battlestar, more or less starting his career over. Writes Moore, he tried to "keep his head down and forget about what had happened. But he didn't stay anonymous for long. Adama liked to walk the flight line every day, checking out his birds as part of the morning routine, and he soon spotted Tyrol and his affinity for the fighters and the deck gang. It wasn't long before Adama restored his rank and made him Chief of the Deck. . . . Tyrol had found his home and his place."

The same could be said for Canadian actor Aaron Douglas, who had scored a few guest roles and bit parts in films prior to being cast on the show, but truly got to demonstrate his acting prowess as the chief.

AARON DOUGLAS
(actor, "Chief Tyrol")

In 2001 or 2002, I guess I didn't really have a career, I was a reader in casting sessions. I would be the person standing beside the camera reading opposite the person auditioning. I was reading for a woman named Maureen Webb, who is a Vancouver casting director. She was in negotiations to do *Battlestar Galactica,* but it was Bryan Singer's *Battlestar Galactica,* the continuation reboot or whatever it was. That went okay, and then I was a reader for these casting directors who ultimately cast our show, Coreen Mayrs and Heike Brandstatter. They were having the Vancouver search for all the characters. I was a reader in the session and afterward they'd go, "Oh, Aaron, it's your turn to read for Apollo." I originally read for Apollo, which I didn't get, which is great, because Jamie had to go to the gym and I didn't.

Then I get a callback. That would be November–December 2002. And then I got a callback in January 2003 for the role of Gaeta, which I also didn't get. Which is great, because Alessandro Juliani is a fantastic actor and does a great job of Gaeta and he's got all that tech talk, which I don't like to do.

I was on the outside looking in and they got to the end of one of the sessions, and Michael Rymer turned to Eick and said, "You know, you got a lot of old dudes in the show. You should find some more younger guys." Because Chief Tyrol was supposed to be a contemporary of Colonel Tigh. Eick said, "How about Aaron Douglas? He doesn't have a role right now and we really like him." Then I obviously got it, read the pilot, and the chief character was pretty small. Rumor has it that the chief was supposed to die early in season one. Chief finds out that Boomer is a Cylon and she whacks him before he can run off and tell anybody. But they liked me, because I ad-libbed so much and they liked what I was doing. So they decided to keep him around. The rest is history, as they say.

RONALD D. MOORE

Aaron's a very instinctual actor. I don't know if he was formally trained; he just went by instinct on a lot of things. He'd just show up and be like, "Okay, let's do it." He just did it from the gut and it gave Tyrol this very grounded, very man-of-the-Earth kind of quality. That was an interesting characteristic of Aaron and of the character. They just were both so blue-collar, middle-class, guy next door thrust into extraordinary circumstance. He never really lost contact with that all the way through. There was always this internal brooding quality to Tyrol that I thought was interesting.

MARK VERHEIDEN

You need that grunt-level guy who was making the ship run. He was the guy with the wrench. As the show went on, his character gained way more dimension, which is a credit to Aaron and what he brought to it. And what we realized we could do with him. So Chief Tyrol became a very important part, and the thing about Aaron is that underneath the surface he comes across as sort of the middle-class guy who's got the wrench, and just wants to keep things going. You get a feeling that he goes back to his bunk at night and pulls out the bourbon and sits there.

There's a darkness inside that character that we saw come out. That was the surprise in watching him evolve from being the cheerleader, almost, of the flight deck, "Let's keep these planes going," into something much richer and darker as the show evolved. Aaron's a personal friend, but that doesn't matter. He just did a great job on the show. I don't think that character would be as rich as it was without the reality that Aaron gave Tyrol. You feel like he *could* fix your ship. If he says he can fix it, I believe him. On the other hand, when the dark side came out, you were like, "Wow, there's an undercurrent of something going on with this character that is really interesting to explore."

RONALD D. MOORE

When he does the show where they have to kill Crashdown, when they're down on Kobol and there's all the scenes where Tyrol has to rein himself in and he knows Crashdown's screwing it up and he knows this guy is not qualified to lead the mission, but he's got to support him and he's got to tell the other guys to pipe down and shut up, and it's all just boiling within him, it's all fantastic work.

AARON DOUGLAS

I viewed Chief Tyrol as a blue-collar, honest guy and sort of the heart of the show. I don't want to rewrite history and cast my mind back with the information I have now, but he was a military guy. We had Sergeant Ron Blacker, retired U.S. Army Ranger, instruct us, "This is how you stand, this is how you walk, this is how the military does it." I'm from Canada and my grandfathers fought in the Second World War, but other than that I have *zero* military history. I'm fascinated by it, I read about it, but I don't have any understanding of what these guys actually did. But he put us through a boot camp and all of that.

So with Tyrol I wrapped my head around, "Okay, he's a military guy and he believes in what he's doing following orders, but he's also got to have a little bit of self-assuredness and be a bit of a freethinker." But like I said, it wasn't until after season one that they even came to me and said, "Okay, we want to offer you a contract." I was just a day player up until then. They set up a five-year deal. I realized that, okay, this is a character that is going to stick and they wanted to do something with him. At the beginning, once I got settled into the hangar deck as my domain, even though the officers outranked me they're now in my sandbox and they can come in and they can swing their dicks around all they want, but at the end of the day I can punch them in the dick and throw them against the wall and tell them to get out. And they go back to their officers' rooms and play cards and drink and smoke and fight, but I get to say what goes on in my hangar deck, because it's my playground.

With the chief, here's a guy trying to do his best, but life just kept coming up and punching him in the face. The universe was just one thing after another. He just kind of got to a place where it was like, "What the fuck is the point? Why are we doing this?"

Prior to further revelations that would come later in the series, Sam Anders is a sports legend when it comes to the game pyramid (a card game in the original series, as opposed to triad, which was inadvertently confused in the writing of the new show), and he's someone enjoying fame with his teammates. Until *everything* is changed when the Cylons launch their attack and he suddenly finds himself transformed into a freedom fighter. He also ends up getting romantically involved with Kara Thrace, which goes about as smoothly as one would expect. Playing him is California native Michael Trucco, who, beyond scoring some guest-starring roles on TV shows, was also one of the stars of the series *Pensacola: Wings of Gold*.

MICHAEL TRUCCO

Early in the process I initially auditioned for the role of Apollo, and rumor has it that I got very, very not close at all. I had done this show years ago called *Pensacola: Wings of Gold*, where I played a firefighter. I was like, "I was on a syndicated television show with James Brolin, dammit. I should be on this show." Apollo, I just wanted that so desperately and I didn't even get close to it. Coming up a year later, I still remembered this audition for what was supposed to be two episodes. So as you do as an actor, you go in for a guest shot and recurring. I was just lucky to be there, and so I said, "Yup, this is great," and went in for this character called Anders that was meant to meet the girl, sleep with the girl, fall in love with the girl, and then get kicked in the ass out the door by the girl. *That* was the arc of the character. It was just sort of a deflection from the Starbuck and Apollo love story. I was going to be this third leg in that triangle for a couple of episodes, but something incredible happened: The majority of the people fucking hated my character. They hated me, and I think that fueled Ron more than anything. He was like, "Oh, you don't like Anders?"

RONALD D. MOORE

Now he's coming back!

MICHAEL TRUCCO

I mean, talk about the chat rooms in the early days of the internet. People are mean, man. *Really* mean.

RONALD D. MOORE

They're *still* mean.

MICHAEL TRUCCO

They said some horrible things, and that just kind of fueled the storyline. Then it became, "Well, you're going to come back for another episode." I said, "Oh, cool, I'm doing three." They go, "Might be two, could be four, but five at the most. No more than six. Seven. Could be eight episodes. Just the first four episodes of the next season, but that's it." Then it just kept growing and growing and suddenly I found myself in this club—in their sandbox—and getting to play with this family. My first contact was Gracie and Tahmoh and Katee, and they treated me like one of their own from day one. That has resonated with me to this day.

I always looked at Anders as the Tom Brady of the *Battlestar* game pyramid. So he was a put-upon hero. An unsolicited hero in a way, not meaning to save the day, but this team that I was working with in the mountains was doing high-altitude training and that's when the bombs started dropping. We're a bunch of pampered athletes, looking for our team trainers to get us out of there, and now there's bombs dropping. So now these characters had to shake a whole life of celebrity and privilege and athleticism and all the things that go along with it. It was all gone. From there we had to pick up guns; my character had never shot a gun before. So Anders is wielding these guns and being in a situation where I'm going to put on the strong face; I'm the team leader. You know, all that bullshit talk. But underneath he's just shaking. It was being out of my element. It wasn't the military like Starbuck and Helo or Apollo. Those people are trained for that. My guy was an athlete. So I had to evolve into this freedom fighter to fight the very thing that I would eventually be revealed to be.

13.
ROOM SERVICE

"The story of Galactica isn't that people make bad decisions under pressure, it's that those mistakes are the exception."

By the time he been hired to write and produce *Battlestar Galactica*, Ron Moore had acquired a great deal of experience, much of it coming from the rich creative environment of *Deep Space Nine*. Early staff hires for the new show's writers' room were David Weddle and Bradley Thompson, the team Moore had worked with on *DS9*; Toni Graphia, whose credits before then included *China Beach, Cop Rock, Chicago Hope, Dr. Quinn, Medicine Woman, Wolf Lake,* and, with Moore, *Roswell* and *Carnivàle;* and Michael Angeli, who prior to *Galactica* had worked on *Now and Again, Cover Me: Based on the True Life of an FBI Family, The Twilight Zone, Playmakers, Touching Evil,* and *Medium*. Angeli had worked with Moore previously, hiring him for *Touching Evil,* and worked with David Eick on *Cover Me* and a pilot they had done with Shaun Cassidy.

RONALD D. MOORE
(cocreator/executive producer, *Battlestar Galactica* [2004])

What I learned was the fundamentals of trying to have a room that could function as a team, you know? That was really important to us on both *Star Trek* shows. Especially *Deep Space Nine*, where it was a tight group of guys, and we were very loyal to each other and to each other's shows and to the show in general. We hung out a lot, we ate lunch together, we fought and laughed, and cried and did all that stuff in the writers' room. It was a really formative experience for me as a writer and a producer. As I looked to put a staff together for *Galactica*, I very much wanted to replicate that experience.

TONI GRAPHIA
(co-executive producer, *Battlestar Galactica* [2004])

The staff the first year was really only me, David Weddle, Bradley Thompson, and Carla Robinson. And Ron. I liked the way Ron ran the writers' room. Most of the time when you're on staff, it's way more people. Maybe twelve or thirteen people on a drama staff, and you usually have to sit around a big conference table, like a boardroom table. But we had a couple of couches, some club chairs, and a very small whiteboard. It was very intimate, probably the most intimate staff that I had been on. We went to lunch every single day, and we took a walk—we were on the Universal lot and we would take a walk around it every day after lunch. A lot of our best ideas were not even *in* the writers' room. They might have come while we were taking a walk. We would still keep talking about the show, because it wasn't the kind of show you wanted to get away from.

MICHAEL ANGELI
(co-executive producer, *Battlestar Galactica* [2004])

There was a lot of competition in that writers' room, because all the writers were really good. I've been in writers' rooms where that's just not the case. That's the exception that we had a room full of really talented writers. So there was competition, but it was friendly.

TONI GRAPHIA

The show was kind of a mystery in the beginning, but Ron had such a strong vision that we were just there to support that vision. And he gave us a lot of freedom. He believed in our talent, and he had handpicked us, so he trusted us.

RONALD D. MOORE

With *Galactica*, the solution was to go to people that I'd worked with before. People like David Weddle and Bradley Thompson, and then Toni Graphia. I'd never worked with them in the same group, but I'd done two shows with Toni before that and then I'd done *Deep Space* with David and Brad. So I had a shorthand with all of them and it was easy to kind of picture us all in a room together. I figured we would get along; the staff for season one was very small. But it was a good group and we added people to it as time went on over the life of the series.

Eventually Toni left. David and Bradley stayed through there the whole run, and they were kind of the foundational writers because of that. I heard when I wasn't in the room that the writers would be going at each other. Some of them didn't get along, but generally when I was there everybody played nice and there was definitely a team spirit that we were all in this together, even if there were personality differences between some of them in later years.

DAVID WEDDLE
(producer, *Battlestar Galactica* [2004])

I'd been a journalist for years and had written a book on director Sam Peckinpah. Ira Behr loved that book and invited me to Paramount to walk through the sets, which was amazing. Brad—I went to film school with him—was a *Star Trek* fan, and I asked him if he wanted to pitch *Deep Space Nine,* because Ira had said we could. So we went in and pitched the show. Ira Behr was incredibly generous to us and spent a lot of time with us, and we sold a story. Then the next year they gave us a teleplay, which they loved, and then we sold another teleplay and they put us on staff. So it was very happenstance that I ended up a science fiction writer, but I have grown to love the genre since I've been in it. I love Westerns. In fact, in the *Battlestar* room I was constantly referring to Westerns, because I think that there are tremendous parallels. Westerns are existential dramas, because people are moving across an uncharted territory, a frontier. Roddenberry made these analogies with *Star Trek* and there's no civilization in place to say, "Here is the moral structure. Here are the laws that govern your behavior and the decisions you make." Instead, you're traveling through an existential void and you have to make choices for yourself about what is the moral choice? What is the ethical choice? I was *constantly* referring to Westerns for archetypal patterns and structures/templates for telling stories.

BRADLEY THOMPSON
(producer, *Battlestar Galactica* [2004])

The influence of real-world military on this show was tremendous. Both David and I studied history; both of us came from families that have veterans in them. I've always been interested in it. Actually at the time I had started teaching military tactics. I learned to fly. I was a combat shooting instructor back then. Not for the military, but for a civilian organization. We wanted the guys to behave properly, getting them to behave in a real way. To not have people swinging gun muzzles around. Give the fighter pilots an actual language of their own, which they got to use. For example, a lot of the stuff with the brevity of language our fighter pilots use is actually Air Force brevity language.

RONALD D. MOORE

I'd done a science fiction series with them before. They were conversive in the genre itself. I also knew that they were both interested in history, and that Brad in particular had a lot of military knowledge and a lot of contacts. He was very well versed in a lot of military aspects of things for the show. I just knew what it was like to sit in a room with them and pitch ideas, and they were both willing to mix it up and try different things. I like a very improvisational room where everyone's just kind of pitching some stuff out. The best story, theoretically, should win, and I knew that they could thrive in that kind of environment and that their first drafts would be solid first drafts. As the show went on, I wanted to get them more in touch with the production side of things so they could be producers and go up to Vancouver and produce their individual episodes. I wanted them to step up and sort of experience responsibilities.

DAVID WEDDLE

With Ron there's a quality of trying to harvest the mind of the room, and getting the group to focus on a problem and solve it together. If you have a really good writers' room, it elevates everything beyond something even Ron Moore could come up with. Ron wanted you to have ideas of your own; he wanted to innovate. With drafts of scripts, he *wanted* you to surprise him. And that's quite unusual. There are a lot of showrunners where you do something that wasn't in the story break at all, and he might say, "I don't want to go in that direction," but he'd never criticize you and say, "What the fuck?" In fact, a lot of times he would say, "That's fantastic," and it was something that wasn't even in the break at all and it could be a radical difference and Ron would embrace it. In the case of some of the writers he let go, he said, "You never surprised me. It wasn't that you were a bad writer, but you never surprised me."

That's a key difference with Ron. I've never known anybody quite that adventurous and encouraging. The writing experience became a journey of discovery, and instead of having everything mapped out, he knew what the big milestone episodes were. He knew how he wanted the series to end, more or less right from the beginning. He knew in the middle of the series he wanted to find Earth and it was a smoking radiating ember; a dead civilization, but he didn't know how the journey went. He knew from the beginning that he wanted Starbuck to be a kind of guardian angel who has more to her than *she* even realizes, but he didn't have a concept of how that would play out. We discovered that all together.

CARLA ROBINSON
(story editor, *Battlestar Galactica* [2004])

All the writers had a voice in the room. Even if they were bad ideas, you were allowed to share them and every idea was considered, explored. Sometimes, sure, they would go down some divergent path and sometimes we'd follow along to see how far we could go with it and then realize, in some cases, I just remember blurting out, "I hate the way this is going." Somebody else spoke up: "I don't like it either." And I think it was Ron's idea: "What if we make Lee Adama a Cylon?" "No!" We were all free to do that, which is something I loved about being there. We all had the same goal in mind, to make a good show and service the characters living in their world. And every writer who worked on this show had a real respect for the fans. We knew our fans.

MICHAEL ANGELI

We were given so much latitude with what we wanted to break. Things that just out of nowhere we decided we wanted to do, and this is without Ron.

Ron would come, and we'd pitch it to him. You know, "We want to do this," and he gave us so much freedom. He had such a great bedside manner, too. If he didn't like something, he had a really droll way saying, "I don't know about that . . . ," and you'd just get it right away.

RONALD D. MOORE

Toni, just a great, pure writer. She's always impressive, she always delivers really great stuff on the page from the first draft on. She's really capable of throwing it out and doing a page-one rewrite if you ask her to. I just kind of knew that you needed that kind of person on staff that, no matter what, was going to give me a great draft. She has a good sense of character and a good sense of story. I'd worked with her on *Roswell* and *Carnivàle* before that, so she and I had a shorthand. I knew her strengths. She was a little over-whelmed by the science fiction aspect of the show and it took a while for her to get to a place where she was comfortable writing it. At first she kept thinking of it as such a different genre; that she had to be a "sci-fi writer." I kept trying to emphasize to her, don't worry about that, just write it as a drama. And then you also had the military aspect on top of that, which she was also not as familiar with. I think she had to work hard to catch up to sort of feel comfortable in what she was doing.

Michael Angeli is a fascinating guy. There was an interim period when I was at Universal before they picked up *Galactica* to series. I was on a deal and just waiting, and they said, "In the meantime, we want you to go help out on this show called *Touching Evil*," which was a U.S. version of a U.K. show. Michael was running the writers' room and I came over to do a script. That was the context in which I met him. He was funny, cynical, really well read. He used to be a journalist. But he has great chops in terms of writing on the page. There's an intensity to it and a beauty to the language. He's a writer's writer, like Michael Taylor, who came aboard later. You read their stuff and you're really drawn into it . . . sometimes to the detriment of the show, because you're reading it and you're like, "Wow, this is unbelievable." Then you have to step back and go, "Wait a minute. Does this work as an hour of television?" It's that kind of thing. But Michael is fun in a room. He's got a vivid imagination. He's not afraid to pitch out crazy ideas, things that are really transgressive or challenging to the show. So he became one of the members of the staff.

MICHAEL ANGELI

There was some diversity in that room. Like Bradley was kind of a super conservative gun freak and heavily into the military, which is strange because he was a rocker. In fact, we play in a band together; an incredible bass player. Then there were people like me—we were, like, crazy, radical liberals. Then there were people who had families. It was just a really eclectic mix of people, and somehow it worked out. It was a perfect storm. In the time that I was there, I think two people were fired, or their contracts weren't renewed. I've never been on a show either prior or after where there just wasn't a huge turnover of writers. It really was an unusual place.

RONALD D. MOORE

Carla Robinson was an intern on the show. She was wild and funny and you loved having her in the room. You kind of got the sense that she was out of her mind, but that's why we kept her. She would just have tales . . . she was bawdy, she would tell the dirtiest jokes but with the sweetest voice you can imagine. You couldn't believe some of the stuff that would come out of her mouth. She would start telling you the conversation she had with some one-legged prostitute that was outside her apartment last night. Like, "What?" She was a character and kept the room lively.

One of the paramount rules of the writers' room was to avoid the technobabble that had somehow become a substitute for genuine science fiction on other genre shows.

RONALD D. MOORE

Technobabble was such a bane of my existence in *Trek*. I mean, it got so crazy in *Next Generation*. Just pages of it. I'm writing dialogue and it has the word "tech" all over the place. You know, "Mr. La Forge, can we tech the tech main engines?" And Geordi would say, "Well, Captain, if we tech the tech then the tech will overload and blow the ship apart." Data would say, "Captain, there is a theory that if you tech the tech with an alternative tech, using the tech from the tech, you might be able to actually make it work." "Will it work, Mr. Data?" "It's just a theory, Captain, but I'm willing to try it." It was just *such* bullshit. At the time, fans complained. The actors *definitely* complained. But we were kind of straitjacketed in certain aspects, because Rick Berman really thought that that's what gave authenticity to it, and that's what gave it credibility as science fiction—as a *science* fiction piece as opposed to the fantasy. It just became a crutch on the show, where you're going to tech your way out of all kinds of bizarre situations. You're sitting in the writers' rooms having these long, tedious arguments about what the warp drive can and cannot do, and I just didn't want to do that anymore. I was sick of it.

One element that he wanted to embrace was the military aspect, raising the question of whether or not the show was based on true military history.

RONALD D. MOORE

Actually, a lot of it was drawn from my memory of military history. I was someone who was always interested in military history, and especially U.S. naval history. I had read a lot of accounts of the Carrier War in the Pacific in World War II. And I'd read accounts of Vietnam, and I was always fascinated with naval aviation and aircraft carriers and the military and marines. So I knew a lot of that stuff. When I remembered a story, I could go back and get more of the details either through books I already owned or could get. A lot of the way the *Galactica* operates was based on my knowledge of aircraft carriers and how they worked, especially in the Second World War. From the way the squadrons were organized and the relationship of the captain—the CAG, the commander . . . you know, how they launched attacks with fighters protecting bombers and torpedo bombers. All that kind of stuff was just happening. I knew it pretty well and could kind of inject it into all the different stories.

DAVID WEDDLE

We watched some documentaries on aircraft carriers and their crews, and Ron talked about how he really wanted the show to be analogous to our own armed forces today, and for the ships to have lots of real-world problems. There were not going to be any replicators that could make food, like on *Star Trek*. There weren't going to be dilithium crystals so that they wouldn't have to worry about fuel. So right away they're running out of shit and stuff breaks down.

TONI GRAPHIA
(producer, *Battlestar Galactica* [2004])

Ron would always say, "To me, a great episode is . . . what if they run out of paper? What would you do if you ran out, because there's a finite amount of paper on the ship and you can't produce more." We never wrote what we called the paper episode, but we *did* write an episode about running out of water and them having to go to the water planet. But Ron liked focusing on the small things, even though those small things became a big crisis because of the situation they were in. He was interested in the minutiae of life on that battleship.

MICHAEL ANGELI

As you know, the military is a very organized system. It felt at one point that the show became more and more left-leaning and rule-breaking, with mutinies and so on. In the beginning, it was really buttoned-up from a military aspect. It made me a little edgy. I know where the influences came from; there were probably two of them. One of them was Ron himself, who was in ROTC, an experience that stayed with him. He was able to capture some of the verisimilitude of the military. And, like I said, Bradley was just a total theater-of-war and weapons freak. He knew every type of weapon imaginable. He knew military history backward and forward. We used to say that he could disassemble a German tank and put it back together again.

RONALD D. MOORE

In the second season we did an episode called "Fragged," about these guys stranded on a planet with Baltar and then a character named Crashdown being the de facto leader and trying to act like a leader. There was something fascinating about taking a character like Crashdown, who was really fun and had been really great in the show—a beloved character there for humor and some fun beats—and suddenly have him unable to step up and to command. The traditional way you do this story is that guy, the funny guy, is suddenly in command of the squad behind enemy lines. At first he stumbles; then the squad members lose faith in him and then he remembers some sage advice from Adama or something, and he steps up and by the end of the show everyone rallies around him and he goes back to the *Galactica* a hero.

We didn't want to do that. I wanted to go against that normal narrative and go with the idea that he would be unable to lead this group. He really *wasn't* that guy. So, yes, he'd gone through officer training and he had all the basic infantry tactics, but then suddenly behind enemy lines you have to rally these people to you and you have to carry out this plan that he just wasn't up to. And that ultimately he would have to get to the place where they would have to kill him. We were drawing on stories from the Vietnam War. You know, the term "fragged" is a war hero's term for when the guys decided to put out an officer that was putting them in danger. They would throw a grenade into his tent, or do something like that. They would frag it. So that's where the title came from.

MICHAEL ANGELI

Tigh, of course, in a lot of ways was the face of the military. He was like MacArthur in a lot of ways, and some of the audience loved him and some of the audience hated him, so it worked both ways, but you'd watch it anyway. As the show became sort of more egalitarian as far as the military goes, I really began to enjoy it. In fact, the last season with the mutiny was my favorite.

RONALD D. MOORE

In "Resurrection Ship" there's the scene where Lee is floating in space as the war plays out. One of the inspirations for that was a real incident that happened during the Battle of Midway in the Pacific, where a U.S. Navy pilot was shot down early in the Battle of Midway. He survived, got a life raft, and literally was in the water and watched the American dive bombers destroy the four Japanese carriers and turn the course of the Pacific War. He was an eyewitness there, bobbing in the water and watching it happen around him.

TONI GRAPHIA

History itself was a big influence. In season two I wrote "Resistance," where Sharon Boomer has recently been found to be a Cylon. When we broke the story in the writers' room, the ending was supposed to be that she was being taken out of her cell to be transferred to another ship to do some testing on her, because she's a Cylon that looks like a human. The end was just that she's taken in handcuffs and kind of walked through this gauntlet of everyone. But when I was writing it, somehow that ending wasn't satisfying. Now, this is something that writers rarely do, because you have to follow the outline that has already been approved by the powers that be, but I knew that Ron was a history buff like me. We were both very obsessed with the Kennedy assassination, and the conspiracy theories around it. It occurred to me that while you would never kill on TV a main character without checking with your boss or the network, I thought the Cylons were a unique situation, because if we kill one of them, we can have her again, just in a different body.

So I made the decision when I was writing the script and took direct inspiration from Jack Ruby shooting Lee Harvey Oswald. And then I said that everybody on the ship hates Boomer right now and is really angry at her. But I'll take the lowliest person, who was the character of Cally. And even though she seems like a really meek and mild, soft-spoken, timid, young kind of not-very-high-up person, have it be her, that she's so angry over what's happened, and I made it a Jack Ruby situation, where she comes out of the crowd and unexpectedly shoots Boomer and kills her. I was nervous doing it, but thankfully Ron loved it.

Both Moore and David Eick were determined that the directorial style of Michael Rymer, which had been such a standout on the miniseries, would carry over to the weekly show as well.

DAVID EICK
(cocreator/executive producer, *Battlestar Galactica* [2004])

During the miniseries, I remember talking to and debating with Rymer a lot about trying to figure out how to describe the show to directors. The director's care package that they would get before they get on the plane should consist of DVDs for *2001, Blade Runner,* and *Black Hawk Down.* Those three films, you put them in a blender and *that* was *Battlestar Galactica.* We took

forever to settle on that, but by the time we did have a series and had directors coming in, I could sit down with every one of them and explain to them
exactly how each of those films applied to what we were trying to do. I think
a lot of them found that really helpful.

MICHAEL RYMER
(director, "Daybreak")

As much as there were science fiction references I turned to, there were war
movie references, because it struck me that this was as much a war movie as
anything else. *Black Hawk Down* was a film that I had greatly admired as
well as *Band of Brothers,* which are basically very docu-style treatments of
recent war events. So I looked very carefully at the way those things were
shot, and I always try to approach the visceral quality that those films have,
but those films have an extremely high body-part count, and planes being
shot out of space is a little more remote. But we tried very hard to show that
when someone dies, there are consequences. That there is a body in there
that is destroyed. Not to be gratuitous, but to make it feel real and not like a
video game where the violence has no consequence.

Like I said, a lot of those things were shot docu-style, long lens, there is
some grain in there, no one is worried about fill light, they don't mind if
something is silhouetted; war correspondents don't worry about good lighting. Hopefully that's how the show feels. One of the things that I was working very hard to do was show that outer space is an extremely hostile
environment. You are not meant to be out there. There are all these people
floating around in these tin cans being bombarded by radiation and living
in air-conditioning with no windows and no light for years. We wanted to
try and get a sense of that. The thing that I admire now has mostly to do
with things that ground us, connect us with our world, whether it's relationships, politics on the ship, or the fact that we see Eddie Olmos with a
mouthful of noodles when he's interrupted. Just little details. We even
showed a scene, which didn't make it into the cut, of him on the can.

That's one of the other things that I love about it: Half the bad things that
happen to the human beings are self-inflicted. They certainly in the larger
sense created the Cylons, but there is a sequence where Adama is nearly
killed in an accident as they are loading ammunition. We spent a lot of time
researching the reality of what it's like to live on an aircraft carrier, and these
are extremely dangerous places to be. People as we were shooting were dying

on routine exercises, and that's true in this story. There is a sequence which he had to cut for time which was where two characters are out putting this new window into the landing bay, because it's being made into a museum. Bitching and moaning about how battlestars don't have windows, and their welder gets loose and slices open his space suit and he decompresses, dying in a gruesome way. That was in the opening act and it was saying that bad shit happens in this place, because it's a hostile, scary place to live—it's like living on an oil rig somewhere.

DAVID EICK

In television at the time—it was starting to change—directors were not very respected. There were some, obviously. There were the handful that you could get a pilot made if you got them, but other than that, you didn't really build your pilot sale around a director or the director that was going to be there when you got the series made. Now that's become very important. That's become almost a critical piece of any package; if you really want to go in and create an auction situation on a pilot, you need that. However, I cut my teeth working for a film director—Sam Raimi. I always liked directors and like their input. Even on TV things when it wasn't popular to do, I liked them and liked talking to them and including them. I found that they worked harder, because they were pleased to finally have the opportunity to do something other than direct traffic.

MICHAEL NANKIN
(director, "Maelstrom")

Ron Moore was a man who hired people who he respected and let them do their jobs, which is rare. *Battlestar* afforded me the ability to work in film the way I thought it should be, no one looking over my shoulder. I had only collaborators. Ron Moore's marching orders to the director were, "Go make a movie." We would talk a lot about the script in prep, and then he would just wait for the dailies. I had a lot of collaboration with the writers. I did a lot of David Weddle and Bradley Thompson scripts, and we bonded instantly and had pretty much a love affair on set.

DAVID EICK

That was one of the things that Ron shared. It was unusual, because Ron came from more traditional television, where directors get beaten up a lot. He shared that sense of, yeah, the guy's smart, and if he's a real filmmaker and he's not just a traffic cop, but he has stuff to offer, we weren't precious. There are guys in my job, in Ron's job, who will tell the directors what lens to use, whether to be on a dolly or sticks or Steadicam. We didn't do any of that, not just with Rymer but with any of the directors. There were ranges and boundaries and parameters that I would sit down with them and explain, but we would invite input. Rymer was the first to show us that that could work. You didn't have to have it all figured out like some dictator. Before you got there on the set, you could say, "Hey, what do you think we should do here," and really listen and get some great ideas that way.

RONALD D. MOORE

In some ways, the beginning of the series were the most fun days, because I had a strong sense of where the show should go that first season. I knew we were moving inextricably toward this place where Laura is going to be thrown in jail and Adama is going to stage a military coup by the end of season one. That was a pretty solid direction and everybody was into it. I'd written that whole show bible, so there was a lot of depth of stuff for the writers to dig into with everybody's backstory—who Adama was, who Kara Thrace was. You had a lot of great characters to work with, and at the outset we told ourselves that there were going to be different stories. It was going to be that we'd go to the hospital ship, and we'd go to the prison ship, then we'd go to the ship where there's a serial killer on the loose. We'd go to the ship with the murder mystery. There was just this idea that the fleet was going to generate all these episodic stories, and then within that we were going to tell the longer arc, and then the shorter character arcs.

But we quickly realized that that wouldn't work, because of our budget, because once we did the prison show with Tom Zarek, it almost broke our bank in terms of the fact we were way over budget and had to pay for it in subsequent episodes to make up the deficit that we'd suddenly incurred. Building the new sets was one thing, but then building a new ship that wasn't the *Galactica* was really difficult. We realized we couldn't do this every week at all, so it forced the story back onto the *Galactica*. More long-term storytelling, much more about the pilots. Much more about Adama and Tigh and Kara and Laura. People that you could shoot on standing sets. So that forced the storytelling in season one to be much more character-oriented. It goes less and less plotty over time. It became much more about the core family.

DAVID WEDDLE

At the end of the first regular episode, "33," Ron threw in this scene where Helo is trapped on Cylon-occupied Caprica. He was left behind. He's in the woods and then Number Six approaches him and there are all of these Cylon Centurions, and it looks like he's going to be killed. Then, all of a sudden, Six gets her head blown off and there's a Sharon who he thinks is his Sharon. She says, "You're in great danger, Helo. We've got to get out of here, right now," and they run off. So we all read the script—Toni Graphia, Carla Robinson, Brad, and I—and we go, "God, that was a great scene. Why did Sharon come for Helo? What's that all about?" And Ron said, "I don't know. I just thought it was an interesting thing to throw in at the end." And he did that a lot. I don't mean to make it sound like Ron was haphazard or arbitrary. He had that creative instinct for writing scenes and not knowing exactly what they meant yet.

RONALD D. MOORE

The first season's very difficult for the other writers, because I'm still figuring out the show. Often times I would send them off to do a draft. They would send me back the draft and I would go, "This doesn't work," and then I would rewrite it completely, only because I still haven't figured out the show. Not that they didn't do what I asked them to do, or that they're bad writers, but there were a lot of times where I literally didn't quite know what the episode was or how the characters should behave or what their proper voice was until I took it myself and started to just, like, do it. Sort of like, "There's a car, go fix the car." But sometimes you've just got to get your hands dirty and you have to take apart the carburetor yourself to kind of realize what the issue is. And *then* you can teach somebody else how to do it.

That is traditionally the way showrunners are. And for a reason, because the showrunner is expected to hold the vision of the show and the voice of the show. There's an expectation that it's going to go through your typewriter at some point. Even on *Outlander,* year one, I rewrote every script to varying degrees. To small degrees, to large degrees, as I'm figuring it out, I've got to do it. Everyone expects that as part of the game. The network kind of wants you to do it, because to them and the studio you're the guy. You're the one who's responsible, and when it's turned in we assume that you have taken a pass at this, so you stand by it and this is what you want the show to be. They don't want to hear you say, "I had problems with it, but I didn't change it." They want you to just go ahead and make the changes.

The balancing act becomes at what point are you just making a change to make a change? And at what point is it a change that's necessary to the show? That's the key question. So what happens, in an ideal situation like *Galactica,* is season one I rewrite everything. Season two, I'm still rewriting quite a bit, but I'm doing less. Season three, now I'm starting to let writers take more and more of the burden of taking it all the way to the end and doing their own notes, their own redrafts and all that. And then the fourth season, I'm pretty much just diving in and out on little things here and there, and concentrating on my episodes that I might be writing. Doing more producing, and spending more time in editorial. And then the show is over.

But long before it was over, there were the battles—particularly early on—with the network, which oftentimes could get quite acrimonious.

TODD SHARP
(production executive, *Battlestar Galactica* [2004])

The studio has its interests. The network has its interest. The network is going to pay a license fee. The studio is going to take on the deficit. There are many, many shows that aren't seen by anybody on the network, but make a fortune for the studio. There are also shows that are seen by tons of people on the network side, and don't make any money for the studio. There are different goals on each side, and in this case the studio was making the show for the network. Mark Stern was the network executive who would give notes on scripts, but so would the creative executive and the production executives on the studio end. Sometimes, as it is in most places, it's going to be done separately.

It's not like you send the show out to everybody and then you get all the notes and you compile them. The show will go from the producers to the studio. The studio will take a whack at it. The studio will give their notes. The producers will make changes. *Then* the show will go to the network. Then the network will give notes. Now the studio and the producers will decide which of these notes are we going to or not going to do. There is that tension born out of separate interests and separate goals, and separate needs and separate opinions, and you hope that everybody comes together. I would say as a general rule that Mark Stern is one of the smartest executives in town. He's a very smart and savvy and passionate guy. He feels very strongly about his convictions. His goal was to make a show that would appeal to the broadest possible audience. The producers' goals aren't always in line with that.

RONALD D. MOORE

Like I said, I sold the show under the idea that each episode was going to be really episodic and self-contained. And the first season *is* kind of reflective of that. But it evolved and just kept going in the direction of making it more and more serialized, just like *Deep Space* did. But the network didn't like it. They were not happy with the show generally the first season. There was a difficult relationship, and they hated the first episode "33." To be fair, Mark Stern, when we he first saw it, called me and said, "My God, what you did. This is *West Wing* in space. I can't believe it." He was *really* blown away.

MARK STERN
(former president of original content, Syfy)

I don't care what anybody says, there was a lot of nervousness about *Battlestar* at the channel, from a lot of different sources about what we were trying to accomplish, including from me. But it was one of those things where you knew that you were uncomfortable, but it was the right kind of uncomfortable. It pushed you outside of your limit and you really had to steel your spine and say, "Okay, we're going to do this."

RONALD D. MOORE

The higher-ups at Sci-Fi and the Sci-Fi network were not so thrilled, and they thought it was too depressing, too down. You know, "No one's going to watch this show." They started talking about whether we could reedit the episode so that "33" would be the fourth or the fifth. It was one of those things, which was interesting. We never even took it seriously. We just said no, because there's not even a chance. But they *were* fearful, and, "Oh my God, the show is just so dark and crazy. No one will watch it. It's a huge flop."

DAVID EICK

The note we would bristle the most at would be "It's not fun . . ." or "It's not likable" or "She's not likable, because . . ." To us, the whole point was to do something in the genre where you weren't stumbling over yourself to remind people that it was fun. By the way, that remains a hurdle and a challenge today as I know for both of us, as we continue to develop work on other stuff. You're *always* fighting the fact that they buy, and to a certain degree the audience is trained to expect, a genre thing has a certain escapist component to it. Now, this is being said without really taking into account what's happened with *Jessica Jones* or *Daredevil* and a lot of shows that have obviously not erred on the side of being silly or escapist. They really tried to make a heartfelt or pathological kind of character piece. I commend that. I don't get a chance to watch a lot of it, but I commend it. But that doesn't mean it's easy. If you have Marvel, that obviously buys you a lot of leeway, but if you're just trying to sell something in science fiction as a space opera or anything that has to do with fantasy, horror, sci-fi, and that kind of thing, you're always facing a little bit of a struggle ensuring that people will allow you to do it seriously, that you can approach it from a place where you're attempting to say something, not just entertain. Very, very difficult.

ANGELA MANCUSO
(former president, Universal Cable Entertainment)

Mark Stern and I definitely disagreed a lot; he always thought the show was too dark. And added into the mix was Michael Rymer, who had never done television before and he is not someone who puts a lot of levity into his work. Michael tends to be more serious in the tone of his pieces, and Mark was more on the side of lightening it up. We were more on the side of letting it be a little dark, a little scary and a little foreboding. Needless to say, there were definitely some disagreements on what the tone of the show should be.

RONALD D. MOORE

In "33," there was a lot of argument about whether there were any people aboard the *Olympic Carrier,* which has to be destroyed at the end to avoid further tracking by the Cylons. We actually shot people in the *Olympic Carrier* where Lee is flying down the side of the ship and he looks in the windows. We shot them. There were all these people looking out the windows at Lee. The word came down that we couldn't do that. There couldn't be anybody on board that ship, and that was their hill to die on.

MICHAEL RYMER

What we tried to show was that there were times when you had to sacrifice the few for the many. The tough call, and I'm sure in real life it's a lot worse than we imagine. You have a lot of blood on your hands. If you are not prepared to act decisively, if you are afraid to make decisions, you could cause a lot more damage. You have to take responsibility where the consequences are extremely high for a lot of people who don't even know you, and that's a big weight.

MARK STERN

There was a real involved discussion with the folks in New York, who, when they first saw "33," got really nervous, because it's a very atypical episode in terms of traditional television. So you've got all your cast and they're exhausted, and they look like hell, and it's a pretty dark episode. Then you've got one of your main characters who has to destroy a civilian ship. There was a certain amount of pushback from New York about wanting to move that episode down in the order, but we couldn't because we were told it was a serialized show so it had to be in sequence. So there was a real gut check there. We changed it so the windows were empty, just to give us a little bit of breathing room there. So you don't know if it's filled with people or not, but we don't need to see the little kid in the window crying when he gets blown up by Apollo in the first episode of your series.

RONALD D. MOORE

They just wouldn't allow it. Finally David and I conceded on that. So David, with visual effects, put in some movement behind the windows. Little flickers suggesting that things *might* be moving in there, but we really felt there were people on that ship, because the story has no teeth to it if you don't do that.

MARK STERN

By the way, that was just a back-and-forth discussion. It wasn't like Ron and David were like, "We need to see those kids in the windows." It was more like, "Look, guys, we're all with you on this, but we're seeing people." It was a good example of a bit of give-and-take. Of, "We're going to that place with you guys, but let's just take a little bit of the edge off."

TODD SHARP

This was a battle that Ron went toe-to-toe with the network on, and ultimately backed down. Now, that's a situation where somebody might say, "I hate Mark Stern, because he made us lose that." The truth is, Mark has interests that he has to represent and defend, which is about growing the audience for the show. What's the good of making a show if you're not going to have as many people watching it as possible? Between producers and the studio the tension is usually about money. For producers and networks, the tensions are usually about creative. In that case, it was very strong-willed people on both sides who felt strongly that we should either cross the line or stay just to this side of the line.

DAVID EICK

We had to make a couple of calculated decisions about the happy factor; not to accommodate a network note about make them nicer, because if you're going to write a drama about the Holocaust, you're probably going to have this scene where they sing a Hanukkah song on Hanukkah, because the tragedy comes from human spirit struggling in spite of all the hardship. So you need those scenes, too.

DAVID WEDDLE

Back on *Deep Space Nine*, we saw Ira Behr heroically pushing the envelope and breaking the rules as often as he could get away with. *Battlestar* started as a reaction toward *Star Trek*, then it grew into its own unique, organic show.

BRADLEY THOMPSON

The key is to take chances. That was the biggest thing. Ron was also encouraging in that he was like, "I want you to surprise me." He was confident enough to say if that surprise wasn't enough, he could push it back.

DAVID WEDDLE

In season two of *Battlestar* we had an episode called "Valley of Darkness." Chief Tyrol and others were on Kobol and they had to get medicine to a guy who's been hit. Tyrol and Cally have to go back to their landing site all the way across this planet . . .

BRADLEY THOMPSON

Where they left the med kit.

DAVID WEDDLE

And they lose a guy who gets killed on the way. I can't remember if there was an endpoint carved out or not. But Brad and I were given the freedom to write it however we wanted to. So we wrote that they go through all this shit and then somebody dies. They get back and the guy is already dead. We eventually changed it to he's dying and it's too late. But I remember Ron's note was, "The guy's already dead. It was for nothing? Awesome!" We had that kind of freedom. We were allowed in drafts to just do stuff like that and let Ron see it and see what he thought. It was a logical extension of the *Deep*

Space Nine aesthetic, because now we were free, because we weren't with a franchise. We didn't have all these inhibitors.

MARK STERN

There were definitely conversations about how far to take certain things. The mix of light and darkness. One of my favorite stories about the series is that there was a constant dialogue with Ron and David about the balance of where does this show become hopeless versus just a struggle? And where do you start to maybe detach from that struggle because it's so hard? You always wanted to go there and not pull your punches, but there was definitely a discussion back and forth about, "Let's give ourselves things to hold on to while these people are going through their struggle," which obviously got pretty dark. Early on I remember saying, "You know, even though things are difficult on the ship and everything's a struggle, life goes on and people have birthdays and celebrations and we should see some of those things."

RONALD D. MOORE

The network wanted birthday parties. We're in the first few episodes. I get this call. They'd seen the story outlines of the scripts and they say, "The show is just too depressing. It's too dark. It's too down. Why can't these people go to a birthday party or go play basketball once in a while to get away from their troubles?" I'm like, "These people just went through an apocalypse. Billions are dead, they're running for their lives, and you want them to have a birthday party?" "Yeah, we just think you're being too precious with the show. This isn't what people want to see, and you're underestimating the impact of what you're doing," blah, blah, blah. So basically I told them to go fuck themselves.

MARK STERN

So this pilot achieves a certain a number of flights, and there's a celebration. Yeah, they hoist him on their shoulders and then, in the middle of the celebration, a bomb shakes loose and rolls into the room and blows everyone up. And with that I was like, "Okay, got it. Won't be asking for that again."

That was their little "fuck you" to the network, which I appreciated. It was like, "Okay, it's not all going to be hearts and flowers." Truth is, you always got nervous when you'd read a script and there would be something happy happening, because you knew, "Uh-oh, it's not going to last."

RONALD D. MOORE

The network got their draft and I get this call saying, "Okay, we get it. No more birthday parties." And then they promptly said, "But does it have to be twenty pilots dead? Can't it be fifteen?"

Ironically, this was similar to an argument that the producers on *Deep Space Nine* had in the final season where they wanted the Ferengi character to lose his legs in a war, but were told he could only lose one of them.

RONALD D. MOORE

It's the *same* argument. Somehow *that* makes it better for you? Fifteen or twenty? Favorite phrase was, "It's just the tonnage. It's not any individual thing, it's the tonnage of how much depression and horror that's in the show. It's just the tonnage of it; it's so severe, you just can't handle it." I just kept hearing the mantra all year one about how dark the show was, how no one's going to watch this, why can't you lighten up and be more fun? And we just kept fighting it. David and I, fighting it tooth and nail.

We had a *huge* fight with Mark Stern about the episode where Kara is interrogating the Cylon Leoben and puts his head in a bucket and all that. Mark didn't want to show it. He didn't want torture on the show. Can't have the characters torturing anybody. They're heroes, they have to act like heroes. And this was right in the middle of the whole thing that was going on in Guantánamo and waterboarding, and all this kind of stuff. It was in the news. And we were like, "No, we are doing this show *because* this is an important thing. We're doing the show to talk about things like this."

Had a *really* volatile argument with Mark on the phone, the bulk of it us getting really pissed at each other. Eventually there was a compromise. There's a moment in the script where Kara literally hit him and knocked out some teeth. I took that out, but kept the bucket and the waterboarding and all that in. That was enough to kind of satisfy Mark, but that was a touch-and-go kind of thing.

TODD SHARP

This was way, way too dark for Sci-Fi. They already aired the miniseries, which aired as a backdoor pilot. So it's not like people didn't know that the show was living in a dark world, but for some of the executives that was a little bit too far over the edge. They didn't want it to be *that* dark. Frankly, I don't think Sci-Fi got permission to embrace the dark until the reviews started to come in, and the accolades and the Peabody, and the *Time* magazine cover calling it one of the best ten shows on television. As soon as that started to happen, Sci-Fi was able to trust more in what Ron was trying to do in terms of the dark and the ugly and the moral questions.

RONALD D. MOORE

You'd have to ask them. I *think* they heard what I was pitching, but then they didn't believe that I meant it on some level. I think they just thought, "Well, once we get into the series, there'll be a little more action/adventure. It'll be more fun. It'll be a little more games in space." No one was fighting for the whole version of the show. I wasn't getting that note, but they were not prepared for how seriously we took the premise and how seriously we took what we were doing. And that we were going to hold that line trying to make it realistic, and trying to deal with people at war and taking losses, torture and security and suicide bombings and all that. I just don't think they thought that we really meant it.

DAVID EICK

Believe me, because we didn't know so much about where we were going with the mythology, and where we were going with the religion and where we were going with Laura and who the Cylons were, all you really could sell was, "Well, they'll run out of water and they'll run out of ammo and they'll run out of food." Because you didn't know what else you were going to do.

RONALD D. MOORE

It reminds me of an incident on the miniseries. I was producing *Carnivàle,* but at one point David called me up and he said, "I need you to be on the phone for this one call, because we've gotten to a place with the network where I think it's going to get kind of ugly. I may need you to kind of be the rational voice here." "Okay, what's going on?" The scene in the miniseries where Adama and Leoben are on the space station together and Adama, you know, beats him to death with the flashlight. Mark *hated* that scene. He wanted to lose it. It had to be more kung fu or it had to be more of a fight. He was relatively new at the network; it was definitely a period of transition. But that scene was going to be shot, and they were having a confrontation about it.

DAVID EICK

We start shooting this scene between Adama and Leoben. They're walking and talking and Adama's growing suspicious. Finally we get to where the fight's going to be, and it's late; Eddie's tired. We've always envisioned this as this kind of guttural, intimate kind of fight anyway, right? So Eddie just kind of starts pitching, "Well, why don't I just get him down here on the bottom of this stairwell, and as soon as he gets there, I'll hit him in the back of the head with this brick or whatever and he falls, and I just jump on top of him and bash, bash, bash, bash." And that's the fight. No acrobatics, no stunts, no wire work. Just one guy behind another guy in a stairwell clobbers him. Guy falls, first guy jumps on top of him and keeps clobbering him until his face is hamburger. So that's what we did, and it was fucking great. Eddie was scary as shit. There was a flashlight, and even as he lifted the flashlight to deliver the last blow, it was like he was savoring it. He was just, like, "Fuck you, fuckers!" It was so great to see your hero sating the audience's need for vengeance, right? One of those great moments, and we're beyond thrilled. Creatively, we feel like we did something kind of artful. Something Scorsese-ish. You know, we're kind of jerking ourselves off a little bit.

So we get to the next day and they see the dailies, and Mark Stern calls and he's apoplectic that . . . I can't even remember what the phrase was that was being thrown around, but there was some sort of accusation along the lines of bait and switch, or not living up to the spirit of the agreement. It was getting kind of ugly; like we had done something either underhanded or just plain incompetent. And Michael Rymer loses his fucking shit. We're on a conference call getting these notes verbally . . . Rymer's in the car on the way home. I'm in the Vancouver office. Stern's in L.A., and he says, "You're going to reshoot this. You're going to reshoot this as scripted, and I want the fight scene that we talked about. And it's going to be at your expense." And we're totally getting our knuckles rapped. Remember, it's the end of the day, so we're beat. Everyone's exhausted and has been shooting fourteen hours and they've gotten the day, at least from them. Then Rymer says, "I don't think you would know a good show if it landed in your lap. The fact that you want us to turn something like this into a ridiculous, fanciful piece of shit like the kind of shit you would do is beyond me!" *Then* he added, "And the fact that you're in charge makes me terrified for the future of this show."

MARK STERN

These *were* very early days for me at the network and my relationship with these guys, but in that fight in the miniseries between Adama and Leoben . . . When you saw Eddie Olmos as the man he used to be, as the warrior, as opposed to the retired kind of man in his decline, when I saw dailies of that scene it was a very tame, kind of a-couple-of-punches scene. I said, "I really think this scene needs to be more brutal than that. I really think we need to see Adama being *it*. This is where we see who he can be." And they didn't disagree with me.

RONALD D. MOORE

Michael Rymer was refusing to back down, and they'd already had one go-around about this. So now we were going to have a *bigger* go-around. A bigger conference call that I was on. I hadn't really been participating in these fights, because I was producing another show and kind of took a back seat. I remember Michael and Mark just going at it, and Rymer getting so pissed about, "You don't know what show you're making. You don't even understand what the hell you bought. *This* is the show and you don't know what you're talking about!" Finally, Rymer really hung up on the network. I remember Mark being startled [*laughs*], and David and I were quite amused. So Rymer hung up.

DAVID EICK

I'm just laughing at this point, because it was just *so* awesome that Rymer said that. Then Stern calls back and Rymer won't take the call, so now I've got to handle it, right? But that's my job. So I'm talking to Mark and I'm explaining that, at the end of the day, he didn't have to say what he did. That we were really proud of what we did, we don't want to reshoot it because we can't afford it, we can't schedule it, we had the factory for one day and that day is gone. It was all these interruptions, complications, and expenses, and I couldn't get him off of it. So some compromise happened where I rewrote the fight to some kind of specification that Rymer thought we could get, that Eddie would do, that wouldn't violate the tone of the show, but that would deliver a little bit more of what the network was looking for. And, of course, Eddie starts out with, "Well, fuck him. Tell him I'm not showing up." And so I've got to talk Eddie into it, and explain to Eddie that I'm going to rewrite the fight, we're going to make it cool, we're still going to keep it guttural.

So finally I'm able to kind of get everybody on board with this thing, but Rymer's caveat is that we decided we're going to shoot it on a fucking Saturday, one of our precious days off and we're able to get this factory again. Rymer says to me, "You tell Mark I'm not rolling camera until he's sitting in the seat next to me." Meaning Stern is going to get on a fucking plane and if he wants it exactly like he wants it, then he'd better be here to supervise it. And Stern, to my dismay, was like, "Fine, I'm happy to hop on a plane on Saturday and go to fucking Vancouver to oversee a fight scene." Psycho. Anyway, so now Mark's got to come, we've got to shoot on a fucking Saturday, I've got to rewrite this fight.

MARK STERN

They made me fly up to Vancouver—I kind of feel like there was a bit of retribution in this—for when they shot it. Now, obviously there's a great practicality to that, because what they *didn't* want to do was go through this elaborate stunt sequence and then have me look at the dailies and go, "Oh, that's not what I meant." But we also happened to be shooting that scene in probably the most disgusting location I've ever been in.

DAVID EICK

[*laughs*] It was just toxic and awful.

MARK STERN

It was an old sugar factory and it was coated with a burnt-molasses-like sticky black sugar. And it stank. I'm like, "Of course you would want me here so that I would have to sit on your set and never bother you again with my ridiculous notes."

DAVID EICK

We all show up on Saturday, everyone's ready to go . . . and Stern's not there. Rymer stands up, turns around, and he walks out. I'm like, "I can't believe this. Now we're *not* going to shoot." So I beg Michael to come back. I get on a phone and find out that Stern's renting a car and he's just late. Finally Stern gets there, walks in, shameless, smiling: "Hi everybody," he's just showing up to a part. "So what are we doing?" And so he sits down, we start doing the fight. As the day goes, Mark can appreciate the complexities involved in shooting in this particular location, the sort of tonal awkwardness of some of the stunts that didn't really feel like it fit the tone of the show; Eddie's resistance. He could feel Eddie's hatred. I think "brrrr" went through the back of his head every time Eddie sat in his chair. And I know that, for a fact, we not only wound up cutting out a lot of what we had planned to shoot that day, and simplifying it even further, but by the time we got to the editing room, and got done with it, it is near or exactly the very thing we had when we got done with it the first time.

TODD SHARP

You'll find me the defender of Sci-Fi and Mark Stern. Don't get me wrong, they made some boneheaded decisions, but they had the best interests of the show at heart, which were how do we grow an audience so that this show can have longevity. I commend Mark Stern for his passion, and I commend Ron Moore and David Eick for their passion. With them it was good cop/

bad cop. David would be the bull in the china shop and pave the ground for Ron to come in and fight that creative battle and say things like, "It's got to be 'All Along the Watchtower,'" or "I've got to end the show *this* way," or "Kara has to disappear behind the bushes at the end of the finale for *this* reason." Ron was able to save it for those load-bearing creative battles that ultimately he won most of, because Ron was a visionary. But he couldn't have fought those battles as well as he did without the partnership of David, who also was a creative force. And Sci-Fi was as good a partner as you could hope to have when you have such a dark and challenging show that is trying to find what voice is acceptable. Nobody had ever seen anything like it before. There was a process of kind of figuring it out. Once everybody figured that out, I would say that it was largely smooth sailing with the network.

MARK STERN

But, you know, it's really a pleasure when you have exec producers who know what they're doing, are passionate about what they're doing, and who know their stuff. It keeps you on your toes. You really have to come to them with smart, knowledgeable notes. You feel like you're very much partners on that process, which is probably the best circumstances for making a series. You know, I had been a producer just six to eight months prior, so a lot of the things they were saying and doing with me, I would've said and done with the network executive that was giving me those kinds of notes with the best intent. It's really just about putting your executives on notice that you're going to take them seriously, and you expect them to take you seriously. You need to be able to back up what you're talking about and defend it, and you need to be respectful of the process. So it wasn't a situation where it was like, "Goddamn these guys." It was more like, "Good for you, guys. Push back, believe in it." And I really believe that.

DAVID EICK

There were a couple of bad ideas he talked us out of, and I think there were a couple of good ideas he talked us into. I would never take that away from him. But I think Mark's style, at times, could be micromanaging, which everyone would tell you. He would tell you that about himself. And there was not always a taste connection. There were times when it would feel like Mark would insist on doing things that were not of this show, so there could be a struggle getting him on the same page with the show we were doing. I would say that lasted the first season, and then we had less of that kind of problem.

RONALD D. MOORE

The network never admitted it was wrong in so many words. But what happened was, once the show was on the air we talked about the miniseries and the success of the miniseries, and how that changed the conversation. And then, season one of the show got a tremendous amount of critical acclaim. It started getting awards, started getting attention and Peabodys. Suddenly we were in a different ball game. Suddenly we were the prestige show on the network, so it definitely changed their attitudes. I don't think they ever came back and said, "You were right, we were wrong."

DAVID EICK

Before *Battlestar*, my career was as a nonwriting producer. It was only because of some of the "necessity is the mother of invention" situation that that changed. There was a time in particular where Ron got so frustrated with notes from the network on a scene that he threw up his hands and was like, "I'm going to fucking quit." I don't think he really considered it, but he was pissed off. So I wrote it and he liked it. I thought, "Oh, I can write a scene that Ron likes. That means I can try writing an episode," and I did. Now I'm a writer/producer and that's what I do for a living, but writing on the show was because there was so much friction in the very early going, trying to let this show be about stuff other than we're out of shit. And not just for me. A lot of folks on that staff blossomed because of the hardship of that friction. Folks who we stay in touch with now and are off running their own shows who were vital to that little chapter of difficulty. And so made the show a lot better that we had those fights. It also paved the way for people to come out of their shell a little bit, too, which was great.

RONALD D. MOORE

The network did start backing off, but there were still flare-ups and fights, but we didn't have quite the same sort of trench warfare we had in year one where they were no longer arguing about the fundamental tone of the show. I'd still have arguments with them about the tonnage and how many people have to die in the scene, how much blood we were going to show, does the ending have to be this downbeat . . . they never really let it go, but it became less fraught and less harsh. They kind of had to resign themselves to, "This is the series, and we're also kind of proud of it at the same time." They embraced it.

Suddenly I'm going into executives' offices for meetings, I'm looking at the wall and there's, you know, an AFI Award for *Battlestar Galactica*. Or a magazine with our actors on the cover on their desk. You could just keep walking into their offices and bit by bit, you start seeing more of our stuff around and you realize that they were proud of it. They were like, "Hey, we're making a hell of a show here and it's getting recognized." They were very proud of what we were doing, even though they disagreed with a lot of the reasons why and how we got there. But eventually they did kind of come around, and by the end they were very much our supporters.

In its first season, the *Galactica* is still being pursued by the Cylons, which seem to be tracking a particular ship, which has over one thousand civilians aboard. Apollo gives the order to destroy the vessel, sacrificing the passengers to save the rest of the fleet.

After the *Galactica*'s water tanks are sabotaged, Boomer begins to question her true nature. She's programmed to think she's human, including elaborately constructed memories and records. Rumors spread throughout the fleet that the Cylons now look like humans, and that they have operatives in place on board the *Galactica*. As evidence mounts, Tyrol becomes suspicious of Boomer, eventually ending his relationship with her. The rumors are, of course, true. Roslin and Adama ask Baltar to build a Cylon detector, but his spectral Six (more popularly known as "Head Six") tells him he needs a nuclear warhead to complete the device. Adama gives him one, and Baltar uses it to build a functioning detector. Colonel Tigh's wife, Ellen, suspiciously reappears in the fleet, but by that point Baltar is too afraid of Cylon reprisal to report the true results of the test.

Starbuck faces her own fear and admits to Adama that she was responsible for Zak's death. Despite this, Adama risks the future of humanity to rescue Starbuck after her Viper crash-lands on an uninhabitable planet. Later, Starbuck is tasked with interrogating another copy of Leoben, who tells her that she has a destiny. President Roslin blows the Cylon out an airlock. But Cylons aren't the only threat to Roslin's administration. Tom Zarek, a revolutionary leader, makes a bid for the vice presidency. With no other option, Roslin nominates Baltar for the position, and he wins it.

On Caprica, Helo is rescued by another copy of Sharon Valerii. They travel through destroyed cities and abandoned buildings, pursued by Cylon Centurions. Helo realizes that there are Cylons who appear human, but doesn't realize that Sharon is one of them. Over the course of their journey, they fall in love. When they finally reach a spaceport, Helo spots another Sharon. He shoots the woman he thought was Boomer, suddenly unsure who to trust.

Roslin, afflicted with terminal breast cancer, begins taking a hallucinogen called chamalla and seeking the spiritual counsel of the priestess Elosha. She comes to believe that she is the "Dying Leader" prophesied about in the Book of Pythia, who will lead humanity to Earth. The Boomer on board the *Galactica* discovers a habitable planet, which Elosha believes to be Kobol, the birthplace of the Thirteen Tribes. Tyrol and Baltar lead a team to the planet to investigate, but are shot down by Cylons. During the planning of a rescue mission, Roslin's religious fervor conflicts with Adama's atheistic pragmatism. Against his orders, Roslin sends Starbuck to Caprica to retrieve the Arrow of Apollo, which Pythia foretells will guide them to Earth. Adama retaliates by ordering her arrest, but Apollo disobeys the command and is arrested himself.

Starbuck arrives on Caprica and finds the Arrow. She's forced to fight and kill a Number Six copy, then reunites with Helo. She sees the Sharon that he's been traveling with, and realizes that she's a Cylon. Starbuck tries to shoot Sharon, but Helo stops her. She's not just any Cylon. She's pregnant with Helo's child.

Boomer, armed with a nuclear warhead, flies into the Cylon ship orbiting Kobol. A dozen identical Sharons greet her, confirming her worst fear. Nevertheless, she completes her mission and returns to *Galactica*. Shaken, she reports to Adama that the basestar was destroyed. Without warning, she pulls out her sidearm and fires two bullets point-blank into Adama's chest.

RONALD D. MOORE

The episode "Water" got us into a conversation about the *Galactica* herself and how it functioned. It has a big recycling plant, so it was pretty much independent. But maybe the other ships of the fleet wouldn't have the same facilities. *Galactica* would have to be the big water tank and be topping off the other ships periodically, but they'd still have to find sources of water out there in the galaxy.

DAVID EICK

We originally thought the show was going to be much more about how do people survive in space when there's no water and there's no booze and there's no farms. We got bored of it. We did some good ones, but we just didn't care. It just wasn't interesting to do a show that was all about that. In a way, it meant you were constantly focusing on housekeeping shit, and you weren't getting into interesting character shit.

MARK VERHEIDEN

I enjoyed dealing with the infrastructure of how you would survive in this diminishing-returns world you're in. At first, basically they still had everything that they needed to keep going; some of the basic comforts of life. They could pretend a little bit that they could still live life like they did before, but as we went further into the show, obviously things got much more desperate and dire. In some ways, it felt like their situation had become darker and a little more real, because that's really what that situation would have been.

I think of a show like *Star Trek: Voyager,* where they're seventy-five years from Earth. I thought the reality of that is that they would just be killed. An entire ship would be taken over by pirates and they'd go to hell in twenty minutes, because I don't have a high opinion of human nature sometimes. I felt like we played with the reality of that on *Battlestar Galactica.* Not to the point of everybody being killed, but certainly, in later seasons, mutinies and talks of colluding with the Cylons becoming a huge flash point for people. I just found those very rich and really great worlds to play in.

RONALD D. MOORE

We saw an opportunity to set the table on a bigger scale. Okay, what kind of show is *Battlestar Galactica*? "Are they going to run into aliens" was one of the quick questions we wanted to answer. Lying to rest that sort of vision of the universe, there's a speech by Colonel Tigh where he kind of talks about, "Look, the universe is pretty much a barren, empty place. There's not much out there. Most planets aren't habitable, there's very little life, and it's a big empty universe." I wanted to put that in the audience's mind early, so that we took off the table the whole notion of not only aliens, but also that there would be a planet of quality for the series. That it wasn't going to be a series about continually pulling out to a new potential home and then having to have a plot that told us why that one wasn't going to work. I wanted the audience to realize that that really wasn't going to be part of the story. It was another effort to set the show apart from *Star Trek* and, to a certain extent, from the original *Battlestar*. I was definitely still in the mode of walking away from anything that felt like *Trek*.

DAVID EICK

It looked like we were abandoning the original plan, and the network was like, "Well, then what is the show? You guys told us it was going to be a show about we're out of shit, and if it's not that, what is it?" That made it a little more difficult.

RONALD D. MOORE

I remember Toni Graphia was writing the script for "Bastille Day" and we started talking about the fact that I was on the lookout for a character that could be right for Richard Hatch. As the story started to develop into an Apollo story, that was going to be sending Lee out to deal with the prison episode, it felt like the perfect opportunity to bring in Richard to play the leader of the mutineers, Tom Zarek. Then we'd get to have these scenes with old Apollo and new Apollo that we got excited about. It just felt like a really unexpected way to go, to bring him in and to have him be the character voicing skepticism about everything that they were doing. There was just a lot of fun in that idea. That Richard, who vocally had *not* been supportive of this iteration of *Galactica,* would then be the guy to be in the show and saying a lot of those kinds of things. The redirection of *Galactica* and questioning the people doing it and running everything. We just thought that was a lot of fun.

BRADLEY THOMPSON

Ron's concept of Zarek was as the guy that would say all the bad things that Ron thinks we're doing with the show and the people, and him being right about a lot of it. I thought that was brilliant. It was fun to write him that way, as the gadfly, the revolutionary, and the fact that he was right about so many things really helped. It's one thing to create a villain that's twisting his mustache and saying, "I'm going to kill everybody and I'm going to dominate the world!" Instead, he's the guys that says, "You know what? You're acting like a petty despot," and Laura Roslin's going, "Yeah? Well, there's a good reason for it."

It gets you into instead of a comic book character, you've got the problems that Abraham Lincoln had, which is, "I've got a civil war going on here. You know what? Habeas corpus does not serve here. I need to put all these Confederate leaders in jail without any actual charges other than that they're making me annoyed and I'm worried about them." Basically he got rid of habeas corpus for all of that. Then again, he had the balls to say, "We're in the middle of a civil war, but I'm still going to hold an election." That is a multifaceted character. Zarek was pointing out, "Hey, wait a minute, Abe, you're doing some wrong things here." She may have good reasons, but does that make those reasons correct? "Do you deserve to have your society or are you just going to be another petty despot? In which case, do you swear you're going to have free elections once the crisis is over? How many times have I heard that?"

The show needed that, and Adama did, too, though he's coming from the military point of view. And the military mind is mission, whatever it is. What's going to accomplish the mission? He had a conscience about it in terms of the witch hunts. Why we have posse comitatus laws is that the military is trained to fight enemies, but now they're working with your civilians and patrolling them as police. They start to see the civilians as the enemy and that's *not* a good thing.

Ron and David, coming from political-science backgrounds, had a heavy interest in politics. All of those things kept coming up. It's, like, "How do you design a government?" You see that every day on the news. You're still trying to figure out whether they were right or wrong in setting this up. You've got the two sides saying, "Well, it can be whatever we want it to be, because we're the majority." They're going, "Wait a minute. No! These rules were set up a long time ago to protect the minority against your majority." What is a representative republic as opposed to a democracy? All those questions are still valid and they're still being argued today.

JAMIE BAMBER

When I was a kid, America was the promised land of everything that was good. All the best food, all the best toys, all the best movies. They all came from America, and *Battlestar* was on TV. I remember it distinctly. We rented a home in Old Lyme in Connecticut for the summer, while my dad was doing some work in New York City, and I watched *Battlestar*. And so to then meet the guy that was from this world, so far away from mine, it was amazingly special. And on my first experience of doing an American TV series! So the whole thing was romantic and glamorous and exotic, but on the flip side of that, Richard had been sort of outspoken to the press about his antipathy to what we were doing. So there was the added pressure that not only was this guy, this figure from my childhood, there, but he didn't like me.

I was terrified and a bit resentful, to be honest, if I'm really open about why I was the character chosen to have to come across his alter ego. Why couldn't it have been Herb [Jefferson] and Boomer or Dirk Benedict and Starbuck? Why couldn't it be somebody else? But I could see why Ron had done it. I could see what he'd gone for in the story to create another dysfunctional mentor-pupil relationship to sort of mirror the father-son relationship he got in there with Adama. And there were so many metatextual kind of references to a freedom fighter that I had admired, but was disappointed to meet in person. And he saw something in me within the story of Zarek and Lee Adama.

JAMES CALLIS

I always thought Richard was a prince of a man. He was kind and generous, gentle and thoughtful. He had a certain quality that you couldn't quite say exactly what that thing was, but that's why he was who he was. I remember just thinking of him as a real hero, watching him as Apollo in the original—I just thought he was pretty incredible. Playing Tom Zarek was something I think Richard loved and enjoyed, but it certainly brought some challenges, because Zarek was nothing like Richard at all. I hope people realized it was just acting, because he wasn't that guy.

I had some funny scenes with Richard, because when he came in for the first time and he had a scene, he wasn't quite sure how Head Six was going to work. Like, with Tricia coming out from behind the scenery. That was just amazing, in the sense of us all falling apart just laughing. The whole thing sometimes is rather silly. You're doing this very serious thing, and it's, like, "Wait a minute, is she coming from behind the scenery? Can I see her?" We're like, "No, you can't see her. You're not allowed to look." He's like, "Well, that's a bit tough," but we said, "No, sorry, Richard, you're not allowed to look at Tricia."

MARY MCDONNELL

My memory of Richard is watching him so gracefully surrender to the current *Battlestar*. He did it with such dignity. He was a very kind, wise human being, so to watch him slowly surrender to this situation and also begin to realize that the more he did, the more Ron Moore got excited by his performance and this character became such an interesting force . . . I'm just very happy it was a part of his life.

RONALD D. MOORE

I just called Richard up and I said, "Look, we talked about this at one point, now it's happening and I want to send you a script." I think he was a little skeptical, but he really liked it. He responded to it; it was a great role for him, so he said yes and we brought him aboard. I have to say that Richard was one of the most professional actors we ever worked with. He was really a pro.

The table read on *Galactica* was usually like the day before shooting the next episode, and the cast was almost always brought in on their lunch hours. So we've only got an hour and we're crammed in and they're eating and flipping through the pages and reading their lines. They'd seen it before, because they've seen all the pages, but never really focused on it. But Richard comes in and he's off book. He's playing it, and they all notice. He was *that* guy. He was really well prepared on the set and never gave anybody a problem. He embraced the show so completely that he then became an advocate for it. He was telling fans how great it was. Just an amazing transformation.

JAMIE BAMBER

I'd come in especially for the read-through, and when I walked into the room, there was only one person I could see there, but I deliberately tried not to walk straight up to him, but just to sort of act like I normally would. And then I thought, "No, I'm going to go straight up to him. I'm going to tell him how much I admire his work." And I was going to just get in there first, make sure I started this thing off in the right way. But he beat me to it, because he's such a nice, nice man. He was someone who was so warm and generous. He was so thrilled to be there, by the end. And in our many years since, he's been so encouraging and positive about everything that I've tried to do with my career, and he's shared experiences from his career in a very generous, very humble way in the way that he was. I told him straightaway, there is only one Apollo—I'm playing Lee Adama. As far as I'm concerned, he's a different character and I wouldn't try and imitate what you tried to do and what you did so successfully, and you're a huge part of my childhood and everything like that.

He then ended up, over the years, saying to me, "Jamie, I'm so envious, because all the things that you're getting to do with this character are the things that I really wanted to do, but obviously our program and television at the time wasn't ready to do it yet." He then said, "I'm enjoying playing Tom Zarek more than I ever enjoyed playing Apollo." Even though my performance is different from his, he's a latent part of it. There's no way in which I can disassociate what I did from what he did, even though I tried not to think about it too much while I was doing it, but there is that nobility that he created that can't help but be part of the light that shines through what Ron wrote, and what I then brought to the screen was the candle of an honest soul that he brought to that character.

RONALD D. MOORE

In "You Can't Go Home Again," they're searching for Starbuck. This was a great opportunity for us to really get inside the characters. I remember thinking I really wanted to show Adama and Lee going too far. The way you traditionally tell that story is, "We're going to find our man no matter what!" and, lo and behold, we do. And no one really questions whether it's worth the time and resources to do it. I really wanted to push that as far as we could in the show, so that ultimately Laura has to say, "This is ridiculous," and Tigh supports her, surprisingly. And then get to that place in the scene where Lee says, "What would you do if that was me down there?" and Adama answers, "You? I'd never leave." Which I thought was a really great thing, especially since up until then the whole thing we had been playing pretty much was just conflict between father and son. That was a turning point in their relationship, for Adama to say that, and for Lee to really hear it and believe that he truly meant it.

The episode "Litmus" brought with it the idea of suicide bombers, a subject that remains sadly as relevant today as it was back then.

RONALD D. MOORE

We were looking for a bottle show, something that would stay on *Galactica*, because we were looking for ways of making up the deficit for the prison episode. So the idea of doing some version of a trial episode is an easy one to do, because it's going to be one of the basic sets. So we were looking for that concept. It was our first foray into the notion of suicide bombers on the show, which we thought was going to be a loaded idea. I was prepared for a big fight with the network about it, but it never came, to be honest. It was not a big deal to them. Again, what was a big deal was the graphic nature, how much you were going to see and were there body parts flying through the air? Blood! Very little about the political nature of the show, which I was grateful for. That really sort of laid the groundwork for the rest of the show. I had very few, if any, arguments on any sociopolitical aspect of the show, religion of the show, or any of that. It was always about graphic content. And how depressing the show is. But the big ideas seldom had any arguments.

Moore also believes this episode served as the opportunity to get further into the Cylons themselves, through our first inside look at a Cylon Raider.

RONALD D. MOORE

I didn't have a lot in the show bible about the Cylons, and I didn't really anticipate we were going to get to know them so deeply and intimately as we did, as quickly as we did. So this forced to the surface some pretty fundamental questions. You know, what would the inside of one of these Raiders be like? What *was* the Raider? What was the Raider in relationship to the humanoid Cylons? Did it have an intelligence? Was it sentient like they were? And if not, why not? And how did that work? And how could Starbuck use one to get back to *Galactica*? So we started talking about maybe they're more like animals, more like horses to the humanoid Cylons. Or were almost pets. You know, so they could be trained to do tasks and would do them until they were destroyed, but had no self-awareness, no true sentience of themselves. The humanoid Cylons would not have conversations with them, for instance. But there would be room inside of it for Starbuck to get inside, figure out how this thing worked, and then be able to fly it. That was the fundamental idea, which got us into this melding of organic and biomechanical infrastructure inside of Cylon Raiders, which later would lead to the development of the Hybrid. The Hybrid that ran the basestars was sort of born in this idea that there were these forms in the Cylon world that were cybernetic.

DAVID WEDDLE

"Flesh and Bone" was a key episode for us. What we were fascinated with, and I can tell you that from the beginning I was a big proponent of this, was the idea that because they are robots, it's easy to say that the Cylons aren't legitimate life forms. In the miniseries there are all of these derogatory comments about Aaron Doral, "You're just a robot, you have gears and circuits and you don't have feelings." I don't remember the exact dialogue, but it was a put-down of Doral, and I wanted to make that a theme, because I felt this was very much about war. This is what human beings do to each other in every war. We make the enemy "the other." The way we say, "They're not like us; they don't have the same values, they don't have the same feeling as us."

The Japanese in World War II were considered to be animals who don't care if they live or die. Unlike us. We say that to this day about ISIS, and they say it about us. The Japanese said it about us. So it was great to explore that with the Cylons, because it was easy to do. Like I said, they're just robots, killer machines. They don't have feelings, so then it was interesting to challenge that assumption and do a thing about what we do to our enemies during war.

TONI GRAPHIA

One of my favorite parts of the episode is when Kara eats a sandwich in front of Leoben during the interrogation. That was Ron's idea. He was like, "Do something you don't do in a normal interrogation scene. Throw a curveball in there. Like, a regular interrogation scene you wouldn't think of doing that, because a person's human. But that's one way she could be testing him to see if he's human. Is he hungry?" So Ron said, "Just have her eat a sandwich in front of him, and see what he does." I remember being like, "What kind of sandwich . . ."—I felt like I was taking his lunch order. He was like, "Just a big sloppy sandwich. And she just eats it; enjoys it in front of him." And we came up with a few other things, like does he sweat? He's sweating during it and she's watching his forehead.

The end scene where they throw him out of the airlock—there were lots of discussions about that. About whether President Roslin should stop the execution, or condone it. I love at the end that *she's* the one who does it. It's kind of like good cop/bad cop, because Laura Roslin goes in there and berates Starbuck for, like, "How could you do this and treat this guy this way?" And then she talks to Leoben, gets the information she needs, and is like, "All right, throw him out the airlock." I thought that was awesome, because *that* was her role. She had to do it.

RONALD D. MOORE

To me it was a small thing, but it was important in terms of telling the audience that these characters are not just cookie-cutter heroes. They are capable of lying. They are capable of doing things that are ethically questionable. I wanted characters to occasionally do the wrong thing for the wrong reason, and for us to kind of go, "Ugh, Laura. Jesus." You know, the good-guy character never does that. That was important for me, to sort of lay out a marker of, again, what these characters are capable of. To sort of say this is not a traditional show.

MARY MCDONNELL

I thought Katee and I were going to get fired over that scene, because we literally could not stop laughing. It was horrifying. I mean, we were really upset. We were backstage crying, because we couldn't stop laughing. Then we promised each other that we wouldn't laugh . . . and we would laugh and laugh.

EDWARD JAMES OLMOS

It wasn't a funny scene.

MARY MCDONNELL

It wasn't funny at all. I was supposed to be ejecting Leoben and we couldn't stop laughing. Poor Callum [Keith Rennie] is trying to figure out how to act the scene and these two women are just losing it. . . . You notice we didn't have too many scenes like that.

RONALD D. MOORE

"Flesh and Bone" was where Leoben was waterboarded. When we were working on that episode, it was, like, well, we're going to really lean into this story, too. We're going to have our characters do this. And they're going to do it to a Cylon. And doing it to a Cylon, what's the ethics of that? Is this a person? It is a machine? If it's a machine, why do we care whether it cries and screams in agony or not? And if it's a person, then why are you doing it? So it was just a great way to illustrate some of the core ideas of the show, one of which is that we've cast human actors to play the Cylons, but we're saying that they're not people. But if it acts like a person and feels like a person, cries like a person, at what point is it a person?

TONI GRAPHIA

The end, where Starbuck puts her hand up to the glass to meet his, that was very much inspired by *Dead Man Walking*. It was kind of like Susan Sarandon and Sean Penn in that film. The thing is, the more you get to know someone, even if they're guilty, even if you know or think they did this crime and they deserved this punishment, they have become more human to you. And so Leoben, more than his sweat and more than whether he was hungry and wanted that sandwich, what made him really seem human is the fact that he got Starbuck to care about him in some bizarre way. There's a moment where he says, "I want you to be there when I die. I want you to witness my execution." *That* was inspired by *Dead Man Walking*.

KATEE SACKHOFF

The interesting part about Kara in the early part of that scene is the callousness and the immaturity that she's bringing to it as well. Which was such an interesting thing, because a lot of times we take for granted how young soldiers are forced into situations that are so adult, and so big. There are moments where we hear about the terrorizing of prisoners, and there is an immaturity that goes along with that. That was something that Kara had in that scene the whole time. When people are going through things in real life, very rarely do we realize the weight and magnitude of what we're actually living until afterward. Hindsight is such a beautiful thing.

DAVID WEDDLE

He gets humanized, and at the ending we're just not sure: Is he really just a robot? At the end Kara isn't sure if he really is just a robot. Toni Graphia wrote an excellent draft, and Ron did a polish, and he had the concept that Kara had a destiny, that she was kind of a guardian angel and didn't know it. And he put in all of these things that were insights about her and her mother, and Leoben saying that she thinks of herself as a cancer that destroys the people she cares about, because her mother told her that. When we read it as a staff, we were really kind of scared of that stuff. You know, "What is Ron doing?" I can't answer for him, but right there he started making the Cylons even more complex. He wasn't just human, he had insights that we didn't. He had spiritual insights, and the whole metaphysical and spiritual dimension of the show became a huge theme as it went on. It started right there.

TONI GRAPHIA

It's really poignant at the end. I believe she goes back to her locker and says a prayer for him, for his soul. *That* was the whole question: Does this guy have a soul? Because that would be what made him human. We don't know if he has a soul, but the fact that she prayed for his soul, to me that means that he has one. It's a human connection, and you can't make a human connection if you're not a human. It stirred the pot of all those really fascinating thematic questions.

DAVID WEDDLE

It took it beyond its initial concept and the show got even more complex and more profound because Ron introduced that. And once he introduced that, it naturally evolved that we would explore that with the Cylons. He thought from the beginning that we were monotheists and polytheists and it was an exploration about how monotheism is not necessarily the superior religion, which we in the Judeo-Christian world think—that we've gone beyond that polytheism, which is obviously pagan or primitive. That was what we used to start exploring these things, and then he did that thing in the first-season finale at the Opera House, where Six is showing Baltar the shape of things to come. That she's prophetic and raises the question of whether or not she is just a chip in his head, or is she a guardian angel? Where all of this was going, I didn't understand at all, but it was Ron expanding on making the Cylons more organically complex, and they were growing beyond our initial concept. And a lot of it started with "Flesh and Bone."

RONALD D. MOORE

When we were doing "Tigh Me Up, Tigh Me Down"—the return of Ellen Tigh—the network was still on my ass about lightening up the show, and this episode was indicative of how tired I was of fighting with them. At that point I was fighting with them about the tone and the feeling of the show almost daily. Weekly at least. And it was getting to me, you know? And this is before the show's on the air. This is when the network's at their most nervous and least likely to be cooperative, because they're scared of what people are going to say. They haven't really seen an audience reaction, so this is when it's always tough.

So we were struggling with this episode, trying to figure out the meaning of bringing back Ellen Tigh. Was she a Cylon? Wasn't she a Cylon? What was really the point of it? We were just struggling internally with how to make it work as an episode. It had gotten to the point where I did a page-one rewrite. Eddie was going to direct that one, but while rewriting I decided to turn it into a comedy. I rewrote it with an eye toward making it the first time we should try to do a lighter episode. It would be more overtly comedic and start to play the French farce of it. You know, like them sitting around the table and Ellen Tigh's foot going up Lee's pants. Crazy stuff in the hallways, and just having a little bit more fun with it. I remember Eddie being really taken aback by it. We ended up swapping the episode order on him or something at the last minute, so he was going to direct a different episode, a heavier, more serious episode. Suddenly he was going to direct the French farce episode and he just kind of swung with it and said, "All right, we'll lean into it. We'll make this one as good as we can." But that's why that episode is the way it is.

Things were definitely more serious—but not too much so—in "The Hand of God," which was about Starbuck leading a mission to capture a fuel-rich asteroid from the Cylons.

RONALD D. MOORE

"Hand of God" came out of David Eick's desire to do what he would call a Big Mac episode. He'd be like, "It's all great we're doing all this really intense and philosophical deep drama, but every once in a while I just want a Big Mac." You know, popcorn. Empty calories. Let's just go do an action piece. I want to find a target, I want to blow it up, I want to enjoy it. So we went, "You know, there's a validity in doing a Big Mac." David and Bradley wrote this one, and this was a perfect one to hand them, because it was all about, "Okay, how do you reinvent some of the language of the space battle and a lot of the tropes that have gone before, and make it really interesting and make it fun and just have it be unusual?" They came up with a lot of the detail work in that episode. This is also where we introduce the table models. You know, the big war table with the models of the Vipers and so on on top of them. Which I thought was a great device to use. It works really well in those World War II movies and it made perfect sense for us, because we were sort of antitechnology. I'd also tried a couple of times in *Star Trek*, in similar situations, to do it with animation on a big screen with a map and dots, and logos of ships moving to attack positions. It never really worked very well in *Star Trek*. It was always disappointing what you ended up with. It never told the story very visually. There's something about those three-dimensional models on a tabletop and people moving them that just kind of somehow brought you into the story a little more easily, and it was just more fun to look at.

The popcorn action was important, because it allows you to expand the story. Anything that can keep you out of having to do core mythology shows allows you to extend, ultimately, the life of it. This was another chance to sort of get into the religious thing with Baltar and Six. Him literally just pointing randomly at the board at where he thought the key vulnerability was, and having that be the actual key vulnerability. Moments like that were built in to kind of say, "Look, there is something at work here. There is another power that has to be acknowledged that does appear to influence the events and lives of our characters." It's the classic fate versus destiny. Or free will versus destiny. So you want to be able to play that question of, "Are we in our lives just fulfilling destinies that are written for us or do we have free will?" You want to be able to search the evidence of both.

Things were more political in "Colonial Day," which had Tom Zarek seeking the office of the vice president, but Roslin nominating, instead, Baltar, who wins.

RONALD D. MOORE

"Colonial Day" was a tricky one, because it was an unabashed political show, which, of course, made everybody nervous at the network. I think even David was a little nervous about it. I thought it was kind of cool. Let's deal with things like elections and let's deal with Parliament, and let's deal with how these people are governing each other. I was fascinated with the concept of what people out there in the fleet were doing day-to-day. And coming up with this idea of *Cloud 9* [a domed ship containing a casino, spa, fancy restaurant, and so on], which allowed us to go shoot it, because we could just get a location and say that it was inside a big dome. It was really a cost-saving thing. Like, "Okay, if we set it in a big dome made to look like a planet, then we can shoot it at BC University or something." So that's where that came from.

But I liked the idea of talking about all these people out on these ships that were just still kind of going through their lives as if nothing had changed, because they didn't know what else to do. That speech of Tom Zarek where he says, "Look around. The gardener over there, every day he's still acting like a gardener. The lawyers are still acting like lawyers, you know? The teachers are still acting like teachers, as if the world they knew is still around. And they're doing it out of inertia. It's not a choice. It's just, that's what they do, because they don't know what else to do." I thought that was just fascinating. I thought it was really an interesting take on what all these thousands of survivors were really doing day-to-day.

Somehow in the course of that episode we came up with this idea of making Baltar the vice president, which was just kind of fun. We knew that he and

Laura would have great scenes together. I'm not even sure how many scenes he and Laura had together before this point. I think just a handful. But we knew that there was a great duo to put together and that by making him an important political figure, he would have to deal with Adama and all of our bigger characters. So that's kind of the reason why we decided to go down that road. And I just thought it was a great way to kind of talk about the colonies.

The political scientist in me sort of was fascinated by coming up with a new political system for these colonies and kind of saying that they were sort of in a federalized system where each planet had its own government. Its own culture, but they had a council and a president over them. Each colony was much more independent than each state in the United States was, for instance. That the colonies probably used to fight among themselves. That they had wars against each other, and that the idea was that the first Cylon war was the instance that united the Twelve Colonies into this federal structure that has held ever since then. It's like one thing implies another. That, to me, is how world building works in TV and film. You say she's the president and you say there are colonies. Well, how would that really work? And the more authenticity you can bring to that, the audience starts to feel more and more like it's a real place.

With "Kobol's Last Gleaming," I said right at the beginning of the show bible that the end of the first season was going to be the coup with Adama putting Laura in jail. So I knew that's where I wanted to go. So, bit by bit, over the course of the first season, you kept seeing these two in conflict. We kept seeing Laura being the hawk and, ironically, Adama being the little dove. And Laura's willingness to do anything it took to protect the fleet, running afoul of Adama's view of civil liberties and rights, and right and wrong. And that eventually she was going to go a step too far and he was going to have to lower the boom and pull her back. So I always knew that's where we wanted to get to.

This was much bigger at one point. Like way too big. We were going to have the guys go down to the planet's surface. It was going to be a whole thing down on the surface of the planet. It was originally going to be a different cliffhanger, because there was going to be Apollo, Tyrol, Cally, and some others actually got down to the planet and they found a big temple right on Kobol. And the idea was that they were going to get into this temple, and I was looking for something to come out of left field and really surprise the audience at that point. There's a draft of the show that does exist where they get inside the temple and Baltar's there to walk down a corridor. It's like a pyramid or something. I was, again, trying to sort of touch on some of the iconography from the original series. So there was a pyramid-shaped temple that they found. They got inside, Baltar's going down some corridor, and suddenly he's enveloped in darkness. A voice comes out and he turns . . . and there's Dirk Benedict, and Dirk Benedict says, "Hello, I'm God," and that was the cliffhanger.

Now I look back and I think, "God, I was out of my mind." But at the time, it was coming out of Baltar's vision and the religious aspects that were going on. The whole "all of this happened before, all of this will happen again" idea roaming around in my head. I was reaching for an idea that was saying that this story is the wheel of life. It comes around, is told, is retold many, many times in many different forms, and that there was some connection between the original *Galactica* series and our series. They were both turns of the wheel in different universes or different parallel existences. Like a multiverse, but nobody was fond of this idea. It was shot down rather quickly. There were all these religious things that are still in the show: the Arrow of Athena, Laura telling Starbuck about her vision, Starbuck going against Adama's orders and going back to Caprica and all that stuff. So it was sort of part and parcel of all this other religious stuff that was going on.

DAVID WEDDLE

It was here that Six brought Baltar to the Opera House, and the way Michael Rymer directed it, with the swirling camera moves, the music and the weird archetypal white cradle, and suddenly it's elevated into something that's kind of beautiful and mesmerizing and you're not sure what's really going on. That brought things to a whole new level, and they're talking about the baby, which is going to be a theme as things continue, and the child ultimately becomes the progenitor of what becomes the human race at the end of the series.

RONALD D. MOORE

David might be the one that came up with the idea of Sharon shooting Adama at the end as a shock moment and making that the big cliffhanger. Then that was an element to sort of work in eventually—that she would come in, get into the right position in CIC and really holding the cards, the gun in her hand, until she lifted it up. All that took a lot of detail; a lot of fine-tuning work.

We can probably say the same thing about season one as a whole. Season one, I think, fulfilled the promise of the miniseries. I think the miniseries set up a promise of what the show could be, and season one fulfilled it. The miniseries sets in motion all these characters, sets up this premise, establishes a way that we were going to shoot this stuff. But can you actually do that every week? Can you actually be true to that vision? Will it be entertaining? Can you make it interesting enough to pull the audience through? Can you really live up to these kinds of goals that you set for yourself, or will it kind of fall off and just become another normal sci-fi piece of an action-adventure sort that comes and goes? And I think season one really took the miniseries and kept going and really made it even more challenging, even grittier, and even more shocking in many ways. A lot of the characters deepened the backstory, expanded the universe, and met our goal of going beyond the miniseries.

14.
I AM LEGEND REDUX

"Commander, why are you launching Vipers?"

As the second season begins, Adama, having been shot by Boomer, is bleeding out, and everyone now knows that the Cylons look like humans. Colonel Tigh takes command of the fleet, keeping Roslin and Apollo imprisoned. Tigh tries to hold the fleet together, but after Roslin announces that she's been diagnosed with terminal cancer, many in the fleet believe that she is indeed the Dying Leader from Pythia's prophecy. She is rescued from her jail cell and hidden by her former enemy, Tom Zarek. Colonel Tigh, sensing control slipping from his fingers, declares martial law.

Starbuck and Helo are abandoned on Caprica when Sharon steals Starbuck's ship. After stopping for supplies at Starbuck's old apartment, they head into the wilderness. They encounter Sam Anders, a former pyramid star and leader of the human resistance. After spending a raucous night with Anders, Kara is captured and subjected to experiments in a Cylon breeding farm. She escapes from Simon, her captor, and is rescued by Anders, Helo, and the pregnant Sharon. Starbuck retrieves the Arrow and says good-bye to Anders, with a promise to return for him and his people.

On Kobol, Tyrol, Crashdown, and Baltar are fighting a guerrilla war against Cylon Centurions. Crashdown orders the crash survivors on a suicide mission to destroy a Cylon installation. At the last moment, Baltar shoots Crashdown in the back, saving their lives. After being rescued, Tyrol is interrogated by Colonel Tigh about his relationship with Boomer. While being transferred, Boomer is shot and killed by Cally. Egged on by Ellen, Tigh's iron-fisted tactics lead to a massacre of civilians. When Adama returns to duty, a third of the fleet has jumped away, following Roslin back to Kobol.

Starbuck and Helo return with the Arrow of Apollo and join Roslin on Kobol. Starbuck, Apollo, and Roslin represent the only semblance of family Adama has left, and he can't let that family fall apart. He goes to Kobol, and together they find the Tomb of Athena, which contains a map of constellations as seen on Earth. Apollo recognizes a nebula, giving them their first signpost on the road to the Thirteenth Tribe.

While they jump toward salvation, the fleet encounters the battlestar *Pegasus*. Another miraculous survivor of the Cylon holocaust, the *Pegasus* once shepherded her own civilian fleet. That is, until Admiral Cain took vital components from the civilian vessels, abducted "useful" passengers, and abandoned the rest to fate. Cain is a counterpoint to Adama, a hard-edged warrior whose conscience never instructed her to forgo revenge and preserve human life. Since she outranks Adama, she is now in command of the fleet. Cain assigns one of her officers to interrogate the pregnant Sharon, and things get out of hand. With Tyrol's help, Helo stops the attempted rape, but Cain's officer is accidentally killed in the scuffle. Cain sentences Tyrol and Helo to death, which leads to a standoff between the *Pegasus* and *Galactica*. Kara stops a bloodbath by returning with images of a resurrection ship, the Cylon technology that allows them to be reborn. Adama and Cain agree to a joint mission to destroy the resurrection ship, but each secretly plans to have the other assassinated.

Baltar gains crucial information about the resurrection ship from Gina, who is a copy of the Number Six model and a prisoner on the *Pegasus*. Baltar forges a deep connection with Gina, and as the battle rages around them, he frees her. The resurrection ship is destroyed, and both Adama and Cain call off their assassination plans, but Cain is hunted down by Gina and killed anyway. Roslin promotes Adama to admiral, since he now commands two battlestars.

Roslin is at death's door, with only days left to live. In her near-comatose state, she remembers seeing Baltar and Six together on Caprica the day before the attack. She's left with serious doubts about his ability to lead the fleet, and expresses them to Baltar. Outraged, he hands over the nuclear bomb from his Cylon detector to Gina, who is now in hiding with a group of Cylon sympathizers. Despite their disagreement, Baltar cures Roslin's cancer using stem cells from Sharon's half-Cylon baby.

Starbuck is overwhelmed with guilt for having left Anders behind on Caprica. When Kara resolves to rescue Anders, Lee is given command of the *Pegasus* after her previous commander is killed. This complicates his budding relationship with Dualla, *Galactica*'s communications officer.

On Caprica, Anders continues to wage a war of attrition against the entrenched Cylon forces, which are starting to use human buildings and live out their lives as if they were human. Boomer, whom we haven't seen since she was killed by Cally, has yet to accept her true nature. D'Anna, another of the Cylon models, convinces Caprica Six (the Six who seduced Baltar and infected the CNP code) to speak with Boomer. When Anders's resistance group bombs their building, Boomer and Caprica Six come to an understanding: Maybe humans and Cylons are better off working together.

Roslin doesn't share that opinion. Sharon gives birth to her hybrid child, Hera, but the child is stolen. Cottle tells them the child died and was cremated, but Roslin arranges for Maya, a woman who lost her own child, to care for Hera. Another child-related debate is started when Roslin outlaws abortion in the fleet in the interest of increasing the human population. Baltar uses that as an excuse to oppose her in the upcoming presidential election. Roslin has the support of the religious sects, but the discovery of a habitable planet sways the votes to Baltar's side. The planet, dubbed New Caprica, is hidden in a nebula that will prevent the Cylons from discovering it. Roslin wants to continue following the path laid out in the Book of Pythia, but the promise of breathing fresh air outweighs the hope of Earth, and Baltar is elected president. Remembering her vision of Baltar with Six on Caprica, Roslin is terrified of a Baltar presidency. She conspires with her new aide, Tory, to steal the election. Adama's conscience won't allow it, and he convinces Roslin to accept defeat.

In the midst of the election, Starbuck returns to Caprica and rescues Anders and his resistance fighters. When they return, Tyrol recognizes Cavil, a priest traveling with Anders. Cavil is a Cylon, and he brings a message of peace. The Cylons are leaving the colonies, and think that man and machine are better off leaving each other alone.

When Baltar is sworn in as president, he decides to settle the fleet's population on New Caprica. Gina isn't pleased, and as Baltar makes the public announcement, she detonates the nuclear warhead, destroying Cloud 9 and several other ships. As Baltar reels from the attack, we jump ahead one year. Baltar's presidency is a failure, Tyrol (now married to a pregnant Cally) is a union leader representing the disaffected workers, and the crews of the Galactica and Pegasus are gradually mustering out into the civilian population. Starbuck and Anders are married, Apollo has grown fat and complacent aboard Pegasus, and Adama has a mustache. Then, the Cylons find them. Baltar has no choice but to surrender, and Adama and Apollo have no choice but to jump away.

RONALD D. MOORE
(cocreator/executive producer, Battlestar Galactica [2004])

I remember that between seasons one and two they made us sweat out the pickup, which they did every year. We were worried that they weren't going to pick up the show, and then they did some kind of market research, and so you get all this network bureaucratic stuff back. You know, the things they're considering. The show's dynamic, and blah, blah, blah. But we'd gotten significant amount of critical acclaim at that point even off of the first season, so it was pushing them to want to pick it up even though they were sort of harping on our numbers and the fact that they wanted us to appeal to more women in the second season. That was actually a thing. Sort of like a "condition" of the pickup is that you expand your female demographic. We nodded and said, "Sure," and promptly ignored them. You know, what does that mean anyway? How are we going to expand our female demographic?

But it was good in that it was a bigger order so that there were twenty episodes the second season, which was good news and bad news. Good news, sort of a sign of success. Felt like no matter what they were saying on the one hand about us not having good enough numbers, they were also willing to order a lot more for the second season. So that was good. It also made it easier, just in terms of producing the show, in a lot of ways, because with more episodes you amortize certain costs over more episodes, which brings down the per-episode cost. So it just makes it kind of easier to do the show. But, yep, that meant more scripts to write. That meant more stories to break. It's a longer, more daunting haul for everybody. But I do remember starting the second season kind of feeling like we had a little bit of a wind in our backs finally. You know, the skepticism had finally been put aside. Definitely starting to make noise and it was going to be a positive year. That was kind of the mind-set I remember starting out with.

Our goals were to expand on what we had done in season one. I was proud that we accomplished what we set out to do. I wanted to deepen that. I wanted to make even tougher choices for the characters. I wanted to challenge who they were and have them make more mistakes and really screw up a lot of the relationships we had formed in the first season. To push the envelope in terms of the style of shooting it and the style of storytelling. I definitely wanted to be more serialized in the second season. First season you could see that we were still kind of trying to be somewhat episodic while maintaining a bigger arc. Second season I was trying to move past that completely. Let's just do a straight-up more serialized show, which they were still not overtly saying "okay" to. So there would be times when we had to call things "part one" and "part two," and that always made them nervous. They didn't like it. It was, "How many of these two-parters are you going to do?" So we always had to talk them down off the ledge when we were doing that. In the meantime, they weren't even really noticing that all the other episodes were becoming more serialized even without formally saying that they were two-parters.

A significant change to the writing staff in season two was the addition of co-executive producer Mark Verheiden, who at that point had already worked on such shows as *Timecop, Freaky Links,* and *Smallville.*

MARK VERHEIDEN
(co-executive producer, *Battlestar Galactica* [2004])

When I was asked to become part of the show, I sat down and watched the miniseries and the first season. What drew me in was the seriousness with which they approached the science fiction concept in the show, and the sheer inventiveness of some of the character stories. Six being the key one. Where did that come from? *That* is amazing. I think the episode where I said I absolutely wanted to be a part of it was "Act of Contrition," where Adama learned that Starbuck may have been involved in his son's death. That's a scene that could have gone a lot of different ways. It's a scene where Adama could have said, "I forgive you," or pick any number of ways you could have done it. I was so impressed that they went the really human, emotional way, which was to have Adama tell her he never wanted to see her again, which just destroyed her. What they managed to do in that scene was take this world of science fiction with spaceships and being chased by what are essentially killer robots, and in the middle of that create a scene of such dramatic intensity and it felt so real. Science fiction show or not, that would have been a real angry scene in *any* show. It was an episode where I just thought this was a show trying to do something in the world of science fiction that I had not seen on television before.

RONALD D. MOORE

Mark was an incredibly calming presence in the writers' room. He was the guy that was going to get it done, and he never worried about getting it done. I could let him run the room; I could leave and go do something else, take a call, and Mark would make progress and he could wrestle all that ego. He wasn't threatened by any of it. He was confident in himself and his storytelling abilities. And he could just sit back and let people yell and argue, but then kind of say, "Okay, well, we still need to solve this problem, guys, so let's just solve it." He would do it in a very matter-of-fact way, and the other writers respected him and liked him. He was pretty personable, and you really like Mark when you meet him, and then he's just got a warmth to him. He had good story chops and was a really important member of the show once we brought him on.

MARK VERHEIDEN

I think in some ways that was my job. Look, there were many great writers there. So to say that was my job, I was nominally the head of the writers' room seasons three and four when Ron and David weren't there. Obviously it was Ron and David's show, but I was there to keep the stories going forward. My theory of that, and that's gone on to where I'm running shows now, is that there are no bad ideas. However, there are ideas that are maybe not worth pursuing very long or ideas that we could come back to later. The mutiny in season four being a good example. I have a five-minute rule, that basically any idea we're talking about for five minutes and it's not working out, there has to be a voice that says, "That's interesting, but let's put that aside and let's try this or let's go this other direction or let's see if we can pursue this this way, because that's a direction we want or a direction that Ron has pushed us toward."

What was fantastic about the writers' room was you could come up with stuff that you would be nervous about pitching in terms of this is pretty out there, and they would be totally receptive to hearing that and there'd be no "Are you out of your mind?"–type recriminations, which if you've been on other shows, that can happen. Often the crazy idea may not be the one you do, but it points you in the direction that is something you never imagined until you entertained the crazy one.

MICHAEL TAYLOR
(co-executive producer, *Battlestar Galactica* [2004])

Ron Moore had an incredible vision for the show, yet at the same time you could say there's a nautical metaphor that comes to mind: He kept a loose hand on the tiller. He hired a lot of writers who were all wonderful writers and loved working together, and he would see what would happen. He'd come in and give us his thoughts and then give us his notes. His notes were sort of lines that nothing is ever truly finished. In that first episode I wrote, "Unfinished Business," there was a scene in which originally the chief and

Adama duke it out in the boxing ring. I was going to have, in my first draft, Adama beat him up; the old man manages to beat him up to sort of teach him a lesson. Ron said, "Well, what if it was the other way around? What if Adama gets his ass kicked? Somehow there was still some lesson, some wisdom being transferred or offered?" That was so cool and I just completely redid it. Ron would consistently do that. He would consistently question things that even seemed good or great. How could they be better? How could they be less predictable, more unexpected?

MARK VERHEIDEN

I think back to season three, where we had a few episodes where Roslin was off with the Cylons and split away from Adama, and he thought she was dead. We actually wrote her out of the show for a while. Well, that's insane in television, but it was an idea that just came up in the room, where we're like, "Wow, we've got to get her back. We can't have her out of the show." But then we were saying, "Well, why do we have to bring her back? Why can't we play out what happens to Adama when his emotional linchpin of his life is gone? Let's play that. Let's play that we don't know if she's coming back," and so you pitch that and in some rooms they go, "Are you nuts? She's our lead! What are you talking about?" But we did that, which was one of the fun things.

MICHAEL TAYLOR

Ron was always open to any kind of change that he hadn't anticipated. He enjoyed working with writers who might have ideas that he hadn't had. He would also constantly question our choices, to see if we could come up with something even better. That process could be very challenging for writers and enmeshed in an artistic process to the end, never a sense of an assembly line, of a blueprint being fleshed out, as on many other shows—good shows—but a sense of really just being in through the very end. The final edits.

When it came to the writers, directors, and actors–particularly in season two and onward–Moore had yet another anti-*Trek* sentiment he wanted to enforce when it came to dialogue being changed by actors during production.

RONALD D. MOORE

On *Star Trek* there was a strict rule that the actors had to say the lines *exactly* as they were written. I mean, *exactly*. If they were going to change the lines in *Star Trek,* they literally had to call. It got to the point where there were beeper days. There was a writer's beeper that whoever had a show on the stage that week had to carry around twenty-four/seven, because if the actors down on the stage wanted to change "there is" to "there's"—I'm not kidding—that beeper would go off and you had to call the soundstage. The AP would say, "Brent wants to say it this way. Patrick's pushing this line that he wants to change." It was hard-core. That was Rick Berman's rule. I don't think any of the writers thought it was necessary, but that was the rule.

So at *Battlestar,* from the outset I said that I didn't want to do that. "You guys know the characters, you're going to know the characters, and you need to say the lines so that they fit in your mouth, so that you feel comfortable with it. I'm totally open if you want to improvise, if you want to play around, you want to try different things, go for it. But there always has to be one take where you do it as written so that if I get in the editing room and it doesn't work, I've always got that one to go back to." That was *our* rule.

MICHAEL RYMER
(director, "Pegasus")

Ad-libbing by the actors became part of the show in that loose way that I think was also very well done by *Friday Night Lights,* where you would have a very loose shooting style, where basically the camera guys are shooting the rehearsals. And you're shooting it like a documentary. All the time we were putting the camera guys in stress positions to try and find their shots as if they were really in the room, and it was also encouraged in the acting. There would be overlapping dialogue, people wouldn't finish sentences, there would be a looseness at times, as well as something that at the time was forbidden on television, which was silence.

I kept saying to the cast, "Slow it down. You don't have to steal every available space; we can take it out later if we need to."

TV acting at the time was quite different from film acting. You had to keep moving and you had to keep it snappy. And don't get too heavy. I remember the first day I worked with Michael Trucco was the day that Starbuck goes to rescue Anders. He has this line where he sees her in the forest after a year or whatever and says, "What took you so long?" There's a jokey, Bruce Willis–y way to deliver that line, and he did that. And I go, "Great. Now do it like you mean it. Do it like you haven't seen her for a year. Play the circumstance," and it was much better. The irony is that underneath it you could still get a glimpse of it and it was great.

Many times during the filming of the show, we were constantly just trying to find the tone from season to season; trying to push the boundary of what we were doing in terms of performance, naturalism. We were not opposed to nice chunky, juicy acting. Often, like a lot of James Callis's stuff, he would do very broad takes and then I'd let him go for a while and say, "Okay, give me one where you do that. Give me one where you do nothing," and that was always the take that was in the show. But all that other stuff was preparation for that take where he threw it away.

RONALD D. MOORE

Some actors like to improvise more than others. James Callis *loved* it, and he would do all kinds of stuff. It was like he was doing another show; he was riffing all kinds of things. Some of it was fantastic, some if it was insane. But it was always sort of interesting to watch what he was going to do with it. Eddie just read the line.

MICHAEL NANKIN
(director, "Faith")

I was mostly a gushing fan of Mary McDonnell and totally intimidated by her résumé, so it was very important to me that when I did my first scene with her, that she like me and think I was a good director. So we did this scene with Doc Cottle. She's had her tests done for her breast cancer, and she's coming to the sickbay to get the results. And it's, like, a two-and-a-half-page scene, all medical jargon. We start rehearsing and it's playing like a soap opera scene. There was nothing going on; he's just rattling off all this shit about the cancer cells. It's *not* an emotional scene; it's not what the scene is really about. So I said to Mary, "You're the president. He's got this clipboard with all the answers on it, so why don't you just take the clipboard out of his hands and read it? Why does he have to? Then the bad news comes in. There's this bed here, so why don't you back off and put the bed between you two? Like you're protecting yourself." She liked that idea. And then they had these semitranslucent privacy curtains around each bed, and I said, "You know what? If I put a light behind the curtain, then you go behind the curtain to collect yourself. You don't want to lose it in front of this doc. I'll see it in silhouette if you go behind the curtain." And she liked *that* idea.

So she takes a minute behind the curtain and we see her, and she takes a deep breath and becomes presidential, comes out and asks the big question: "How long?" So I'm watching this and it's looking good, but it still sounds dull and everyone on the crew's standing around, staring at me, saying, "When are we gonna get to work?" And I'm trying to solve the sort of stodgi- ness of the scene. I thought, "Okay, let's do an experiment. Just play the scene, but no one say anything." And Doc Cottle, who had the most dia- logue, said, "What do you mean?" I said, "Don't say anything. No dialogue." So we try it, and a chill goes through the room. She walks in, we know why she's there. She takes the clipboard, she reads it, she steps back. She collects herself, she comes out. She hands the clipboard back, she walks out. And it's beautiful. But this is my first episode on *Battlestar Galactica*. I know that if I eliminate all the dialogue, they're going to fire me tomorrow. So we shoot it two ways, one with dialogue, one without. In editing, I just cut out all the dialogue except for the last lines. So she comes in, does all the pantomime, everything works without dialogue. She comes out from behind the curtain and says, "How long have I got?" And he says, "Four weeks." That's the end of the scene. And the producers loved it. And Mary McDonnell thought I was a good director. So mission accomplished.

The difficulties on the show usually came down to how do we elevate this beyond the traditional approach to a scene. That was the challenge all the way through *Battlestar*.

MICHAEL RYMER

There's not terribly many circumstances I think of since—maybe *Hannibal*— where you really have the time to noodle with a cast of professionals who have their characters down and are now going, "Oh, okay, we're stuck on this ship." That was always a constant challenge when I did the show: How do you shoot these things to keep them looking different, looking fresh for yourself? We were pulling walls and going with long lenses. We were going extremely wide one season, developing shots, and just really trying to mix it up as much as we could at a time where the technology was not up to scratch. Even that is part of the texture now, the fact that to make it look like a film, we actually just pushed the gain. You would never do that now. You would find other ways to create the texture.

MICHAEL NANKIN

The other thing to keep in mind is that *Battlestar Galactica*'s essentially a submarine picture. It all takes place on the ship, except every once in a while we go somewhere else. But the advantage of being on the same sets all the time and not having to light them from scratch afforded us an enormous amount of time to play with the scenes. In a lot of ways it became like a repertory theater. It's the only show I've ever worked on that you could get forty-five minutes or an hour into a scene and stop and say, "You know, this is not working. What's your thinking?" And there would be enough time in the day to extract yourself from the wrong path and rethink and start over. So it became about the scene work. The average length of the editor's first cut was usually about twenty minutes too long. So an episode that needed to be limited to forty-three minutes was sixty-five minutes. That was the average.

The reason that that happened was because the writing on *Battlestar Galactica* encouraged the actors and directors to capture moments. The show lived in the space between the lines, so things would expand and you'd find moments and chase them down until you pulled them to the ground. Ron, God bless him, would not cut all those moments out and just stick with the dialogue. He would just throw out stories and preserve the work that the actors and the directors had done.

RONALD D. MOORE

We started the year with "Scattered," and we were essentially picking up with Adama in the hospital and Tigh's in command. Stepping into the season, I knew I didn't want to do a quick reset to the events that had happened at the end of the season. I didn't want to get Adama out of the hospital quickly, get him back in command and sort of set everything back to the way it was. I wanted it to feel that we were definitely moving forward, and that when big events like that happened, they had consequences for all the people involved. So we kept Adama in that hospital bed for quite a while.

He didn't even speak. It's like the original *Godfather,* you know? Vito Corleone gets shot, he's kind of out of the story for a good chunk of time. I wanted to play it like that. Eddie was totally down for it. He was great. Didn't want to play how easy it would be to recover from a gunshot wound like that either. So we were very much on the same page.

And I liked the idea of Colonel Tigh being the commander, declaring martial law, starting to squeeze too tight. So you could start to see the difference between him and Adama and realize why he wasn't the right guy to command a battlestar on his own. It was sort of the reverse of the way we always played this dynamic in *Star Trek.* And in *Star Trek,* the captain goes down, the first officer takes over, and it's never a big deal. Whether it's Riker or Spock, or whoever, the first officer always steps in. There's always a little thing about, "Well, we miss Picard, but Riker's great." I didn't want to play that at all. I wanted to really go the other direction. Like, oh shit, Tigh's in command, this is a real big problem. And that Tigh, absent the sort of cooling and calming presence of Adama, would realize he'd have to back off. I really enjoyed playing that, because I think that it was an expectation at that point to the audience that we're just going to reset the show. That it would kind of magically just go away. And we opted not to do that.

MICHAEL HOGAN
(actor, "Colonel Saul Tigh")

I loved that stuff where Adama was almost killed and Tigh is in command. Well, he doesn't even want to wake up in the morning. He's seriously hoping he has drunk himself to death, because he does not want to be responsible for anything. He never wanted a command. Adama brought him back into the service. And when Adama is on his deathbed, they gave me that wonderful speech where I say to him, "Don't you die on me. I never wanted to command," etc., etc.

RONALD D. MOORE

With "The Farm," that was another one that David Eick really pushed the writers' room to do. We wanted to do something that was a little odd, a little more horror-oriented. Something that sort of changed up the format from the combat war movie to more of a genre piece. A little bit more horror. Strange things are happing on this farm. Kara is taken there and not quite knowing who to trust. Just giving a creepier, stranger vibe.

We also wanted to do a love story for Kara. That's where Michael Trucco as Samuel Anders, who was introduced in "Resistance," came in. He was introduced as this sort of on-the-ground resistance fighter, one of the last ones left. And that she would be a good match for him. The idea was to set him up in a lot of ways like a better match for her than Lee was.

Even though there'd always been this kind of budding sexual tension between her and Lee, let's introduce one that's a little more like her, a badass fighter, resistance leader. More of a grunt, and that they would have a little bit more in common, and see how that all plays. We knew that she was going to leave him behind, but we definitely wanted to leave the door open to revisit that character later. So we didn't see him get killed. We had no idea how we were going to get him back to *Galactica* later on, but we wanted to set it up so that we could pay it off some future day.

MICHAEL TRUCCO
(actor, "Samuel Anders")

I had auditioned for the role of Apollo in the miniseries, which I didn't get, but then this came up as a guest star with recurring appearances to come. Anders was this athlete who meets Starbuck and Helo on Cylon-occupied Caprica. A lot of the description didn't really have much meaning for me; I didn't know the lore of the show. Before I went to Vancouver, I watched a couple of episodes and was like, "Holy crap." So I get really excited, I go to Vancouver, I meet Katee Sackhoff and Tahmoh and Grace Park, who are the first two people I worked with. Katee, on my first rehearsal, our first meeting, was on an empty soundstage with a stunt coordinator. It was the three of us and we had to come up with the choreography for this game called pyramid, which doesn't actually exist.

So we're banging into each other and going head-to-head, and shoulder-banging, and we kind of land on each other and there's that moment of locked eyes and sexual chemistry that happens. And, man, we just had the same sense of humor. We just clicked, you know? There was something that felt really easy. It was tough coming onto somebody else's show as a guest actor and you're kind of an outsider. I remember I had no delusions of grandeur that this was going to be any more than one or two episodes, but these people were so welcoming. And I bring up the chemistry, because Katee told me that the original idea was that the two characters meet, they sleep together, and then she was going to kick me to the curb and that was going to be the end of Anders. It was just another obstacle in the relationship between Apollo and Starbuck, right? Then we get the call saying, "You're going to be in the next episode."

MARK VERHEIDEN

Michael Trucco came in a little later into the show. First of all, as I've said with everybody, he brought a real strength as an excellent actor, but, again, that person you felt really could be with Starbuck. The star-crossed romance between Starbuck and Apollo, I think for various reasons, we never really wanted to consummate. Not really for the TV reasons, like if they get together somehow something changes in the show that you can't bring back. It just didn't feel like where we wanted to go, but it did feel like we wanted to give both Starbuck and Anders an emotional life. So his character became very connected to Starbuck. They got matching tattoos and all that fun stuff, which must have been really fun to paint on every morning when they went to work.

RONALD D. MOORE

We dug deeper into the mythology with "Home." This is where we return to Kobol and they discover the secret with the constellation. We needed to sort of complete the arc that had really begun with the shooting of Adama, where the fleet is split. There's different warring factions: Laura Roslin has gone renegade, Adama has thrown his coup, Tigh had taken command, Lee had gone against his father . . . we had all these sort of divisions in the ranks, and so "Home" was designed to bring them all back together. To put the family back together again, and give them the next piece of the puzzle in terms of "Where is Earth?" With the idea of the Arrow of Apollo, we just decided to lean in to the Indiana Jones of it all. It's, like, okay, we've got this ancient artifact, this physical arrow that has been brought all the way back from Caprica . . . what do you do with it? And we didn't know what to do with it until this episode. David felt it was Indiana Jones, that we were going to put the arrow into some crevice or into some old broken piece of statuary, and the room's going to change and we're going to get a big cookie.

It was also part of the evolution of figuring out the big mythology of the show. You know, like I've said before, I didn't really have it all worked out in my head when we started. You know, where is Earth? Are they ever going to find Earth? How will they get there? What does it all mean? And I was taking pieces of the original *Galactica* and sort of combining them in different ways and trying to make it all make sense. In the original *Galactica,* they did go to Kobol and Adama found a clue that pointed the way toward Earth. So I wanted to say, "All right, we're going to do a similar kind of gag here. We're going to go to Kobol again, and Adama's going to get a clue. What is the clue? Why is there a clue? What could the clue be?"

I had these long talks with Gary Hutzel and our science advisor. I had this idea about, okay, if the clue here is that Earth is the place where you can look up in the sky and see all twelve constellations, that's the way to figure it out. Like, okay, so you walk in this room, the room changes. Suddenly you're looking into this night-sky scene from Earth and there's little markers—twelve markers all the way around you, and one says Caprica and above that is the constellation of Capricorn. A spacefaring people could triangulate and figure out the mathematics and go, "Well, if Earth is where you can see these stars in this alignment, that's a big navigational help. That's what we're looking for: a place where you can see all twelve of these constellations at the same time."

It was interesting to work in the sci-fi mythos to a show that dealt so much in military themes. There were all these bubbling things that we had been referencing. You know, Gaius has visions and in "33" God came to help the plan work in some way. Our characters have this mythology about Earth and the lost colony. So there's all this other stuff bubbling around the edges of the combat. It felt like we got to bring that in and integrate it, too, since we'd already done Laura Roslin's prophecy. We'd already done those kinds of things. So it felt like we needed to kind of integrate this all so it all felt like it was of a piece. And that the characters in the show would have the reaction that we would. Some of them would be fervently religious believers, some of them would be devout atheists and skeptics, some people would be in the middle. I wanted to be able to play all those different colors, so that you could watch a group of people that were representative of us work through these problems and try to grapple with things like, "Really? The Tomb of Athena? The Arrow of Apollo? That nonsense actually has meaning?"

It's not that different from the Shroud of Turin, and people put a tremendous amount of faith in all kinds of things that sound crazy.

It all felt of a piece to me. That there was a way to do this. I mean, the Tomb of Athena is a direct reference to the original *Star Trek* episode "Who Mourns for Adonais?" because he tells that great story of Athena spreading herself on the wind when they all realized that their godhood was at an end. Athena goes out and spreads herself on the wind until she's no more. I think I wrote something similar, a similar story in their mythology of how Athena died. I wanted to touch on that same kind of piece in the *Star Trek* lore as well.

In the episode "Final Cut," Lucy Lawless (*Xena: Warrior Princess*) appeared for the first time in what would become a recurring role, the Cylon D'Anna Biers. Only in this case, she was a TV reporter assigned to shoot a day-in-the-life-type documentary aboard the *Galactica*.

RONALD D. MOORE

From the very beginning we said this show was like a documentary series. We talked about doing a docu-style show, handheld. The idea had been kicking around the writers' room for a while of, "Well, let's do a documentary." Mark Verheiden wrote it, and it was shot as if it was a piece of film. It eventually broke down; it was too much to wrap our heads around how to do that. I was thinking a lot about the *M*A*S*H* episode where a documentary crew comes in and the whole episode is shot black-and-white as though it's a documentary film. I was like, "Let's do it like that," but it just was wildly complex. And how do you do that for an hour show? Trying to write the dialogue that's supposed to feel so natural? We realized we would use a lot of the documentary footage in the show, but we're not going to do it completely like that.

MARK VERHEIDEN

I think it shows sort of my obsession, which was a chance to go behind the scenes of what was keeping the fleet going. To see people in situations that weren't quite as ultradramatic, where you would see them in whatever situation Lucy Lawless's character found them. The upshot that she's a Cylon was fun. But for me that was a chance to explore another aspect of the show that in a way wasn't quite as fraught as "We're under immediate attack today, and the ships are going out" or something. It was a way to look at the infra-structure of how this world works.

One of my favorite moments was in the episode. This is going to sound funny, because I've said I wasn't a huge fan of the original show, but at the end of the final cut of the documentary within the episode—and I don't know who put this in—but they showed a sort of montage of people mop-ping up and doing things on the ship, and they put the original *Battlestar* theme underneath it. Even I got chills, man, because that was such an in-spired idea. I wish I could take credit for it, but that was such a nod to the other show. It just worked on so many levels for me.

And then there's Lucy Lawless, who is an incredibly kind, incredibly good actress, and just such a pleasure to have added to the show.

RONALD D. MOORE

Lucy Lawless brings this sort of devilish quality to everything she does. There's something you see in her eyes and in her smile. There's always a little bit of the devil in there; something wicked and something fun at the same time. She just kind of carries that with her as a person, and it always comes into characters on camera. I'm pretty sure that Lucy's casting came from David, because David's first experience in the business goes back to *Xena*.

MARK VERHEIDEN

I could be wrong about this, but I'm not sure we anticipated she would be-come sort of a regular that would last through the entire series. She was a semiregular, which is how much we loved that character.

Another beloved character who returned to the genre after his long tenure on *Quantum Leap* (and, of course, David Lynch's *Blue Velvet*) was Dean Stockwell as Brother Cavil.

RONALD D. MOORE

My vague memory is that when we were casting the John Cavil character there was another one of those lists with big names on it, and Dean Stockwell's was there. His agent responded positively, got him the script, and he said yes. I didn't have any conversations with him before he took the role. I just talked with him a few times during the run of the show, and he was just great. Such a pro, and he'd been around forever and done so many things. He was just really respected on the set. The cast really liked him and he was easy to work with. He brought this really interesting gravitas and quirky edge to everything he did. The character really allowed him go dark. The only note I ever got from him in the whole thing was in the finale. He wanted to just shoot himself; that was his idea. I can't remember what it was in the draft—I think he got killed by somebody else or something. Thrown over a banister or something by one of the characters. But he called me up and he said, "I think that my character, he would look around, realize it's over, and just pull out a gun and blow his head off. He would just recognize that would just be 'it.'" That was brutal and quick, and we could do that.

In "Flight of the Phoenix," Chief Tyrol builds a stealth Viper out of spare parts. The ending of the episode was particularly powerful as far as Moore was concerned.

RONALD D. MOORE

Our department had this cockpit that was kind of a stripped-down cockpit that they used for certain shots of Vipers. We'd used it before. It wasn't a full Viper, literally just a cockpit. It was used in certain scenes when they were flying. You could put the camera right in their lap and get it much closer, because it wasn't the full vehicle out there. So they had this sort of cagelike cockpit, and that was what we used to sort of build the Phoenix from. It was built outward from it. They were very excited about it, because they really liked it. I remember the art department really digging the Phoenix; the aspect of watching it being built through the show was really cool.

I do remember also on this particular show I was on the set, and there's a scene where Laura comes down toward the end of the episode. She's there and they unveil it to her, and they revealed that they named it *Laura* in honor of the president. It was this very emotional, touching moment in the show.

MARK VERHEIDEN

The idea that they would name it in honor of her was one of those moments, too, where you felt like the walls between military and government were beginning to fall a little bit, despite a bunch of hell yet to come.

RONALD D. MOORE

She had come down to them and, given all the problems that had gone back and forth between the president and grunts and military and all this, this is like a really healing moment. It was such a lovely scene. I remember watching it. I was standing over in Video Village and I got very emotional. There were tears in my eyes and I was very, very moved by it. I hadn't been on the set for a while, and Mary and Aaron came over to talk to me. They said, "How's it going?" and I literally couldn't speak. I sort of backed away and I was very choked up. I put my hand on my heart and just waved or something. They were kind of startled. It was just one of those moments where you really stopped and smelled the roses. I was like, "Wow, this is an incredible show I'm doing. This is an amazing experience. The people are special. Look at what we're doing here." I was just really overcome.

One of the strongest arcs of season two was the arrival of the battlestar *Pegasus*, a re-imagination of a storyline from the original series with Michelle Forbes (Ensign Ro from *Star Trek: The Next Generation*) in the role of Admiral Cain, a promotion from Lloyd Bridges's Commander Cain, who was junior to Lorne Greene's Adama in "The Living Legend." In this case, Admiral Cain was senior to Adama, which was at the heart of much of the triptych arc's searing drama, consisting of "Pegasus" and the two-part "Resurrection Ship."

RONALD D. MOORE

When I looked at what stories we might be able to use from the original, I don't know if there really was another one that worked, because the original show went in a very *Star Trek* direction where they would pull up to a planet. You know, "This week we're going to do *Shane*." They were constantly planet-of-the-week kind of tales, and we just weren't doing that style of show. But "The Living Legend" I knew was a great story. When we got into a second season, it just was on the table and we just kept talking about how cool it would be. I said, "Let's not do another *Galactica*. Let's make this a bigger, badder, and more modern warship." Because our backstory was different. Our backstory was that the *Galactica* was an old ship. It was getting ready to become a museum piece. It wasn't state-of-the-art. So we said, "Let's do a battlestar that *was* state-of-the-art. What's the up-to-date version going to be like?"

RICHARD HUDOLIN
(production designer, *Battlestar Galactica* [2004])

The problem with the *Pegasus* sets was that we had this crappy little stage for them. It wasn't wide enough, and it wasn't high enough and it wasn't long enough. It was just a rotting old building that they called a stage. So I was forced into getting my ship in this kind of setting. I mean, I couldn't do the figure-eight trick, because the stage wasn't wide enough. So I came up with the corridor, and then I said, "The admiral's going to be in these quarters down there, and then, this is over here, that's over there." I could modernize, because it's a different class of ship. That one just kind of came together really quickly. It was a little different feeling in the ship, and especially in her quarters, and the way the doors open and close and all that kind of stuff. We had the main elements. We had the same kind of central cable with the overheard monitors and such. Lots of places to go walk and talk. It was totally different than *Galactica*.

RONALD D. MOORE

We wanted to have *Admiral* Cain in command of *Pegasus*. In the old version he was just another commander, and he and Adama were equals. What I thought would be fun is if the other battlestar shows up and Cain is an admiral, and Cain *immediately* takes over command, because it would go down that way. Wouldn't even be a question. Like the admiral shows up, he or she is in charge in the story. That's great, because the suddenness of that would have an emotional impact on all of the characters as they try to adjust to it. Now make her a woman, because that was one of our things. And a hard-ass. She'll have a completely different take on everything in life, and it kind of just sprung from there. We also wanted to communicate really quickly key differences between the two ships, key differences in the commanders and their style of command, and how their ships functioned. You wanted a sense of, "Uh, wait a minute. We've all gotten kind of comfortable here." The characters and the audience were like, "Oh, we love Adama and we love our battlestar and we love the way it works." It's kind of this crazy group of misfits who are stuck on this old bucket and they have the old man in charge. There's a lot of love around here even though it gets hard. Not anymore. Now guess who's in charge, and you're going to all act like that. That seemed like a real great way to shake up the show.

JAMIE BAMBER
(actor, "Captain Lee 'Apollo' Adama")

The *Pegasus* definitely represented an alternate vision of reality. It reminded me of *Watership Down*, when they come across this other rabbit warren halfway through the film, which is this regime of authority and secret police. It's kind of like East Germany in the Cold War. Another version of how it is to exist and another solution, another response. It was also a really cool moment in the story to create another storytelling possibility and the clash between the two, and humans were more of an enemy than a friend. Ron was always bisecting and cutting things in half, and so just when you think you've been made whole again by finding more people, they are the very thing that's threatening you.

RONALD D. MOORE

Then we started talking about the *Pegasus* crew torturing a Cylon. What does that mean? What's that about? It will be another one of the Six models, so now we're getting back into all that kind of territory of torture; what's right and wrong for a prisoner of war. Go back to the idea of, are the Cylons people? Are they machines? Do they have rights? Do we have sympathy for them?

TRICIA HELFER
(actress, "Number Six")

On *Pegasus* I was Gina, tied up on the floor. Tortured. When it turned on my coverage in one take, I just broke down in heaping sobs. We'd already done James Callis's coverage, and I was very much more kind of comatose as the character. In this one particular scene, it turned around on me and Michael Rymer gave me a different tone and, I don't know why, I just broke out in sobs. He lets it roll a little longer and then we cut. I'm still laying there, because I didn't move the entire time we filmed that scene. I stayed chained up. They changed angles and changed lights and worked around me. Michael comes in, he just looks at me and he goes, "Did you mean to do that?" That was his version of saying, "That was really good." Then he's like, "Okay, we're using it. That was good."

After that episode I got an email from David Eick, and he complimented me on my work and was basically saying, "We didn't know you had this in you." I remember thinking at the time what an honor it was getting an email like that from the producer. It's a lovely email to get, but then I'm also going, "Why is it such a surprise? Give me stuff; I can prove anything," because Head Six was so limiting. "Give me more!"

MARK VERHEIDEN

I remember the challenge Grace had doing "Pegasus," which was a very brutal episode for that character. I don't care who you are, it's difficult to go through those experiences even when you're "pretending" to be raped. The very brutal sort of attacks that she suffered there . . . She went through a lot. She got killed! She had a number of very intense scenes. But you always felt that humanity inside of her. When she realized she was a Cylon at the top of season two, and was torn between what she was going to do or not do.

One of my favorite scenes in the whole series was between her and Adama, where they're having a conversation about who she is and how could she do what she'd done. It was very low-key, because Adama had an affection for Sharon. There was something about watching that happen live that was so interesting. To see the pauses, the sense of reflection both in Sharon and Adama. That scene took, like, twenty minutes, and it *wasn't* a twenty-minute scene. But the pauses, and the thoughts that were going into it, were fascinating. Once you cut it down, it wasn't twenty minutes but it would be interesting to actually go back and watch those dailies with all the moments in it. Not to use a current reference, but when I think about it now, I think about the pacing of the new *Twin Peaks*. Now everything is very somnambulistic. David Lynch lets everything play out *forever*. There's a new sense of reality you get when you just let scenes play with enormous pauses in them. They become almost unnatural pauses in *Twin Peaks*.

Between Sharon and Adama, the pauses were not unnatural, but it was a real conversation. It has pauses, and has digressions, and moments where you're reflecting and trying to figure out what to say next. It was a really nice piece of acting from both of them in that moment. On that show there was a responsibility to be prepared and bring your best and all that sort of thing. She, like everyone else, brought her best in some very challenging stuff. Playing multiple personalities isn't easy.

RONALD D. MOORE

I wanted that Cylon to be *really* sympathetic. I wanted her to be horribly abused. Physically abused, mentally abused, so that we're shocked and not sure how to feel about all this. Really push the audience into very difficult circumstances. We did have big fights with the network about the rape of Number Six. And the attempted rape of Sharon. It was pretty tough stuff, especially for basic cable in those days.

GRACE PARK
(actress, "Sharon 'Boomer' Valerii")

I remember that it was very clear in the stage directions of that script. It had said "no penetration" or "before penetration" in bold type. It was really clear what they wanted, and I was quite fine with that. When I went to do the prep, I borrowed the movie *Irreversible,* a French movie done in chunks backward, with Monica Bellucci, which has a seven-minute uncut rape scene. It is so graphic and intense that people were leaving movie theaters. I was watching that in my trailer just before shooting the scene, and Michael Rymer knocks on my door. Usually the directors aren't coming to your door; you usually get called by one of the ADs. And he said, "Are you ready?" Then he added, "So how do you want to do this?" I said something like,

"Well, it's *Battlestar Galactica* and it's you, so let's go do it." The meaning was, "We're going to shoot a rape scene."

For prep, it was supposed to be "before penetration," but I'm not going to be wearing underwear where you can see the sides, because they'd have to cut that out with CGI. We hadn't told the other actor that I would basically be wearing a double-stick taped triangle to the front and underneath. So the other actor is pulling down your pants on the profile and it just looked like, "Oh, she's not wearing any underwear." But he didn't know and here's this respectful actor, on the day, and it's, like, "Oh, shit," and he tried to pull them back up. But we shot it like a full rape scene and, timing-wise, Helo and the chief come in. The rape has happened and then they burst in, grab the guy and whatever else happens. So we shot everything as we did, fully, and we didn't listen to the stage directions. I remember that so much of *Battlestar* was *so* intense. It was draining in a lot of ways because of that intensity.

MARK STERN
(former president of original content, Syfy)

The moment with Boomer almost getting raped in the cell, they had scripted that originally as a rape. At the script phase we said, "Look, if you're going to rape this character, then that is something you need to deal with in terms of a multi-episode arc where she grapples with that and we see her go through that. And if you want to do that, we're all for it. Let's take that one and all the brutality of what that is and how that changes that character, but you need to have that depth." They decided, ultimately, that wasn't really where they wanted to go with the character, and so they rewrote it without the rape, where it gets close and then it gets interrupted. But when we saw the first cut, it was *rape*.

GRACE PARK

The weird thing is that while we were shooting it, I remember *not* feeling like, "Oh, I need to be in this space or get my mind and emotions in this head space." But the weird thing was, while I was filming it, the song "Somewhere Over the Rainbow" was going through my head. But I wasn't doing it on purpose. It was just this weird thing, and what I think happened is that

I just disconnected from that scene. Some part of your head is like, "I'm just going to sing a nice little light tune," because you have to disassociate to some degree. Even talking about it at this point, I feel goose bumps and I'm actually kind of sweating. The scene just went to this whole other level, and I'm actually happy we did that, because of the reaction I had during it. You almost allowed yourself to play the whole thing fully, and even if you subtract that one piece, you're still telling the whole story. It's still horrifying and freaky. But then, not to air it the way we shot it . . .

RONALD D. MOORE

It was a pretty knock-down, drag-out fight about it; about how it was depicted, whether it was going to happen or not. How far it would go, how graphic it would be. I felt strongly that if you were going to do a story that had that as a moment in it, that you shouldn't shy away from it. You shouldn't just look away and cut quickly. It should be brutal and ugly, because it's a brutal and ugly thing and it was important to the characters to understand how ugly things had gotten on *Pegasus* and what kind of people we were dealing with.

GRACE PARK

I was feeling so powerless when the cut went in and everyone freaked out. Okay, we take it back. Crop a little bit more. They send it over. The network loses its shit. Shave off a little bit more. And then they're like, "What the fuck are you doing? We cannot rape one of the leads." But at that point I was completely uninvolved. Plus I'm actor number seven; you don't have *any* power.

MARK STERN

I get on the phone with David, and I think it's the only time I lost my temper, and was like, "Guys, we don't give you many notes, because you've earned that. The notes we give you, we feel very strongly about. And this one in particular was very important to us, and to feel like you just went ahead and did it anyway, even when you'd written it otherwise, is *not* okay." So they changed it, but that's one of the few times when I really think we actually ever got into any kind of a back-and-forth about anything. Generally what we talked to them about were things that we thought would just help liven it, make it better or, you know, give them some perspective from the outsiders' point of view.

RONALD D. MOORE

He might be right about the way the scene was shot. I don't really remember. I know that we argued through the script phase and that there was another fight after he saw the dailies, and another fight after the edits. They all kind of blur together as one long fight about the scene.

GRACE PARK

I thought to myself, "We're throwing people out of the airlock, shooting people, killing loads of people, and yet *this* happens?" Why is something like this not allowed anywhere in here, and yet this other end of violence is all over the place? It's a point when I definitely felt like this was something they were trying to squash, and I really didn't like that. It's a human story. Why are we telling all these other human stories, but not this one? Because this one also has a path of grief, of helplessness, or powerlessness and of shame.

RONALD D. MOORE

We knew that Cain was a big juicy role, so you go through that same process where the network says, "Well, we should talk to Susan Sarandon." And you're going, "God, how much time are we going to waste trying to get Susan Sarandon? Can we get to the *real* list?" So Michelle Forbes's name was on the real list. I saw it and I was like, "Oh, I know her. And she would be great," and knew she just has a certain toughness to her character. I thought she could play it really well. She brought a real sense of power, which was an important characteristic. She had to be Adama's superior and Adama had to say yes to her and back down initially, ceding control of the fleet. You had to believe not only that, but that she had commanded this battlestar and seen it through some horrific things and made them do horrific things. There had to be a real sense of presence and gravitas that just communicated, "Wow, the new commander in chief is here." Michelle really brings that. She can walk into a room and command a room really quickly. She just has this certain presence and force of personality when she wants to play that. It's the old thing about playing a king onstage. There are certain actors who can just command the stage, and Michelle is one of those. When she's in charge, or something like that, you say she is the admiral, she *is* the admiral and it just clicks. It was just an immediate thing.

DAVID EICK

I'm particularly proud of that bit of casting, because it was a total lark. I'd only seen Michelle in *Swimming with Sharks,* which had been over a decade earlier. But I never forgot that performance; it was the bull's-eye balance of strength/sexy/scary/mysterious we were looking for. We got early word she wasn't interested, and I panicked. I got her agent to give me her number, and I cold-called her and basically just begged. I found out her reluctance had something to do with a *Star Trek* arc she'd done years earlier, and she worried that the fan base in sci-fi was a bit rabid. I assured her we were nothing like *Star Trek* and then probably proceeded to say whatever I thought she needed to hear before I heard yes—which, to the great benefit of our show, I eventually did.

She's absolutely brilliant in the role, and in person couldn't be more of a polar opposite to Cain. She's really funny and vulnerable, intellectually curious, with zero attitude or affect. It was almost like she didn't know how awesome she was, but she's certainly my pick as the best "guest casting" we ever did.

RONALD D. MOORE

In part one I wrote the sequence where we're cutting back and forth between Adama talking to Starbuck and Cain talking to somebody, and each of them is plotting to assassinate the other commander. And they're each finishing each other's sentences. I really liked the way it was laid out, because Adama would start the sentence and then we'd cut to Cain and she would complete the sentence. And then she would start a sentence and Adama would complete it. I just had this epiphany and wrote it. It was all about rhythm. The rhythm of the dialogue, who would start the line and who would complete it. I just wrote the whole sequence in, like, ten minutes. I loved it when we cut it together.

We had it in mind from the beginning that when we first brought the *Pegasus* and Admiral Cain into our series, at the outset we talked about maybe it gets destroyed or disappears again, which didn't feel right, even though the original series did it. So we started talking about the idea that the *Pegasus* would stick around even after Cain was gone. We all got kind of excited about that, that it would change the dynamic of the show in certain ways to have another full battlestar, new crew, new Vipers. We could really start playing around with different elements of the show. So we really liked that. "Resurrection Ship"'s primary function was ultimately to sort of take Admiral Cain out of the show and leave us with the *Pegasus*.

The problem became that it was hard to use it too much. Even though we had a set, we had the CIC and Admiral Cain's quarters as sort of semi-standing sets, we didn't really have the rest of the ship. And because we had boxed ourselves in a little bit and said that the *Pegasus* was a very modern battlestar and was a completely different style and it didn't look like *Galactica*. It just meant it was really hard for us to go back and use *Galactica* sets and say they were *Pegasus* sets. Also, it had to be a whole new cast, it had to be new visual effects. So it was cool having that second battlestar for a while, and part of me wanted to keep it even longer, like all the way to the end, but it became problematic on a production basis week-to-week. But I loved what it gave us in terms of story. It gave Lee something specific to do, and later we made him commander of it. I thought that was cool. Giving Starbuck the CAG responsibilities, just all that stuff was really great.

JAMIE BAMBER

Having Lee take command of *Pegasus* was a massive buzz. Every change that my character went through, in terms of the jobs that he did, I just couldn't wait to get going, just to find the whole new world that's suddenly it, and it's always exciting to push a character to a different place. It's weird how your chest swells slightly when suddenly they're calling you commander rather than captain, and it's sort of irrational, but we're weird as actors and quite vain. Just getting a new outfit and being measured for it is part of the fun.

RONALD D. MOORE

Season two was angling toward finding a new home, the election and the year jump forward. We started talking conceptually about that—to jump the show ahead a year was something I had always kind of had in the back of my mind, because it was a notion for something I was going to do at *Carnivàle,* if I had stayed with that show. That was just interesting, to take the audience out of the linear timeline where they were. In that case, I was going to go backward. I wanted to start the second season back in the 1920s or the teens and see how the carnival itself had started. I just wanted to open the season apropos of nothing, just sort of shocking the audience, and you're in a completely different time frame, and just play a bunch of episodes like that.

DAVID EICK

When we get closer to season three, I have to take you back a beat. Season one was the culmination of a thirteen-episode first season, which was just grueling. It was tons of fights with the network, it was a lot of struggle just to get it on its feet for a whole host of reasons. It was just deeply challenging in ways other first-season shows don't reach. I mean, it was *really* fucking hard, okay? And the network turned around and said, "Do twenty season-two episodes." Well, we barely had caught our breath. We begged them not to do twenty. *We* didn't want to do twenty; they insisted. So we have to figure out how to break the show and expand the staff. We do twenty and it's really great, but we're just done. It was a year to do the miniseries, it was a year to do season one, year to do season two. And I'm not even the head writer at this. That's Ron. So I'm done, but Ron is *really* done. Ron's like, "Fuck. This. I'm. Done. Don't even talk to me. I don't want to talk about the show."

RONALD D. MOORE

Yeah, there was a bad moment in time where I was truly just brain-dead. I had rewritten every episode of the first season and the second season, and it had become an all-consuming task. And the difference between doing thirteen year one and twenty the second was *enormous.* It was exhausting and

I was profoundly tired by that point. It was all that time in the writers' room. Then all the time writing the scripts, then all the time in postproduction and sets, and the ongoing, never-ending arguments with the network about *everything*. Then there was the budget and sweating out the pickup. Just a long, long battle. There was a time when David and I went to Disneyland and Club 33. I had a couple of drinks at the club and was like, "I can't do it; oh my God." It was just a low point. I was mind-fried. He did help me get back on the horse.

DAVID EICK

As per our usual routine, we have these early kind of meetings. For this one we went to Disneyland and Club 33. We met there at like ten in the morning or something like that. Whenever they open. The reason you go to Club 33 is that's the only place they got a bar at Disneyland. So we started drinking, and Ron says—I think he was half kidding—"Hey, Eick, I'm really not ready for this." Turns out, he's *not* kidding. He's like, "No, dude, I don't have it. I don't want to do it. I'm not into it; there's nothing left to do." And through that kind of gallows humor we wound up talking. Like, what's the thing we could do that shakes it up the most? One of those things became Ron's idea for a time jump.

RONALD D. MOORE

I remember as we got into the second season, I started thinking more seriously about the justification for a time jump. And then, separately, we had sped up in season one that there was going to be an election at some point; in the prison ship episode and the deal Lee Adama struck with Tom Zarek was that there would be a presidential election in the fleet. That was a great marker we knew we would pay off at some point. And with the way we were starting to get Gaius Baltar more involved in the political aspects of things. We quickly started talking in the second season about bringing all these different elements together. So then you can kind of see there was sort of an effort toward generally arcing the show in that direction. So that by the end of the second season we could do something dramatic. Laura could lose the election somehow, Baltar could be in charge and maybe we'd do a big time jump at the same time. So all of that was kind of in place.

TODD SHARP
(production executive, *Battlestar Galactica* [2004])

Ron and I were always on the same page throughout the series, except for this one instance, which was the one-year-later jump that is now TV lore. It's the moment in the last episode of season two where Baltar puts his head down, and he pulls his head back up and it's a year later. Well, that episode was having some financial challenges. We were at a place where we essentially ran out of money as we were budgeting it, before we shot it. I told Ron and David that I didn't think we could afford to do that bit, that we should end the season *before* that jump in time, and we'll make the jump going into season three. And Ron said in a very passionate, but very nice, way, that this was a load-bearing wall for him. He said, "I am *not* going to end the episode prior to that." So we all put our heads together and made the economics work. I said it then and I'll say it now, Ron was right. Because not only was that episode better for it, not only was the series better for it, but it was considered one of the boldest things that ever happened in television. People talked about it then, and they talk about it now.

15.
ALL ALONG
THE WATCHTOWER

"Fear gets you killed. Anger keeps you alive."

With the start of season three, in the four months since the Cylon occupation of New Caprica, Tyrol, Anders, and Colonel Tigh have created a resistance group. Their efforts have landed Tigh in a detention cell, and cost him his right eye. Ellen sleeps with Cavil in exchange for Tigh's release, but the colonel's freedom comes at a high price. Cavil convinces Ellen to give up the secret meeting place where Adama's returning forces are going to meet Tigh's resistance fighters. Tigh is forced to poison Ellen to prevent her from suffering a worse fate. In response to a series of suicide bombings, the Cylons decide to round up and execute troublemaking humans, including Roslin, Tom Zarek, and Cally. Tyrol is able to stop the execution thanks to the help of Lieutenant Felix Gaeta, who is working as an informant inside Baltar's government.

Adama leads *Galactica* back to New Caprica, where they engage in a daring atmospheric jump that leaves the *Galactica* burnt and scarred. With the help of Sharon (now given call status and the call sign Athena) they are able to evacuate the colonists from the surface and jump away. Anders rescues Starbuck, who has been held in an eerily domestic prison by Leoben. There, Leoben convinced her that she had a daughter (Casey), the result of Cylon breeding farms on Caprica. In truth, Casey was the abducted daughter of another human woman.

While providing cover fire for civilian ships, the *Galactica* is overwhelmed by Cylon forces. Moments from destruction, *Pegasus* arrives and draws fire away from *Galactica*. Apollo sacrifices his ship to save his father (and the rest of humanity) and the *Pegasus* takes several basestars down with her. With Baltar gone, Tom Zarek is technically the president, but he steps aside for Roslin to return to power. There's a celebration on *Galactica* as the heroes return, but for some of the crew, life has been irreparably changed.

Baltar, no longer welcome with the humans, leaves with the Cylons.

To secure his place, he hands Hera over to them, despite the implications. Several of the models don't trust him, and he has to prove his worth. When the Cylons contract a fatal illness, he takes the opportunity to investigate for them. The disease is highly contagious (but only to Cylons) and was spread by a beacon left by the Thirteenth Tribe. The *Galactica* stumbles upon an infected baseship, leading them to realize that the virus could destroy the entire Cylon race. Roslin and Adama decide to go ahead with their plan, but Helo sabotages the effort by killing the infected prisoners before they can download to a resurrection ship and pass on the disease.

Running desperately low on food supplies, the *Galactica* and the rag-tag fleet jump through a dangerous stellar cluster, losing several ships along the way, to reach the algae planet. They are able to recycle the algae into edible forms, working around the clock to harvest it before the Cylons find them. During the mission, Chief Tyrol is inexplicably drawn to the Temple of Five, an abandoned monument built by the Thirteenth Tribe. The scriptures say that the Eye of Jupiter is contained inside the temple, and that it will lead them to Earth. Unfortunately, the Cylons arrive before they can find it. D'Anna calls Adama's bluff and sends a team to the surface, which starts a ground war with Apollo and Anders's team. Starbuck is injured, and Dualla risks her life to save her. D'Anna reaches the Temple of Five just as the nearby star supernovas, revealing that the star itself is the Eye of Jupiter. D'Anna is granted a vision of the Final Five Cylons, a group that the other seven are programmed not to think about. She recognizes one of them, but Cavil deactivates the entire D'Anna line before she can tell anyone her secret. The *Galactica* is barely able to jump away to avoid being destroyed. Baltar is abandoned by the Cylons and brought back to the *Galactica* to face trial.

During the crisis, Athena learns that Hera is still alive and being held by the Cylons. Helo shoots Athena and she downloads aboard the Cylon ship, where she kidnaps Hera. Boomer, who has been caring for Hera since New Caprica, has been unable to console the child. Caprica Six helps Athena escape, and they return together to *Galactica,* where Caprica Six is put into the brig that once held Athena.

After Athena returns, Helo shows Starbuck a picture of the temple interior. There was a marking on the wall in the shape of a mandala—the same mandala that Starbuck drew on the wall of her apartment. Later, Starbuck spots a Cylon Heavy Raider in the clouds of a gas giant. She follows it and begins to have strange visions of Leoben and her mother. She approaches a massive storm on the planet's surface, which also has the appearance of the mandala. Leoben tells Starbuck that she's ready to see what's on the other side of the storm. While Apollo looks on, she plunges her ship into the storm and is apparently destroyed.

While mourning for Starbuck, Adama realizes that life must go on. That includes the trial of Gaius Baltar. Apollo is pulled off of combat duty due to his barely contained emotions, and instead is assigned to protect Baltar's lawyer, Romo Lampkin. As Baltar's trial heats up, Lee decides that the fleet is better served with him out of the cockpit, and he joins Baltar's defense team. Considering the ill will toward Baltar, it will be an uphill battle, especially with Admiral Adama as one of the judges. Roslin is put on the stand, and Lee forces her to reveal that she is again taking chamalla, a hallucinogen, to treat her cancer relapse. Lee gives an impassioned speech, reminding the fleet that many sins have been overlooked, and that Baltar should be treated no differently. Baltar is acquitted of the charges and freed, although no ship but the *Galactica* will have him.

The *Galactica* reaches the Ionian Nebula, the next signpost on Pythia's path to Earth. Colonel Tigh, Chief Tyrol, Sam Anders (who is now training to be a Viper pilot), and Tory Foster are hearing a strange melody, as if it's coming from *Galactica* itself. The melody draws them together just as power is lost across the fleet. All of them come to the same conclusion, but Tyrol is the first to admit it: They're Cylons. They're four of the Final Five, and they have been from the beginning. A Cylon basestar appears and launches an attack, and the four scramble back to their stations, suddenly unsure of both their pasts and futures. Lee Adama watches as pilots rush to their Vipers and decides to join the fight himself. Once in the air, he spots another craft in the distance. He's amazed to find Starbuck at the helm of a pristine Viper. She assures him that it's really her, and that she's been to Earth. "I know where it is, and I'm going to take us there."

RONALD D. MOORE
(cocreator/executive producer, *Battlestar Galactica* [2004])

What that time jump ahead one year gave us, and this was important, was a whole new world. I don't remember when the lunch with David took place, because the way the seasons and the overlaps are, we may not have even finished season two when we actually had that lunch. The show might have still been in production, so I don't think I'd seen the finale of season two yet, because I know when I *did* see it, I was so excited about how well the jump forward worked that I was really excited about playing out those stories in New Caprica. I found myself thinking, "How long can I keep a stamp on New Caprica?" So it's a blur about the sequence of events, but the New Caprica thing, I got really jazzed by the fallout from it. All the repercussions about who collaborated with who once they get back to *Galactica*, and the rescue potentials and how that was going to reset the decks in terms of all the character relationships, and gave us a chance to really invent the show in a lot of ways. *That* was really exciting.

DAVID EICK
(executive producer, *Battlestar Galactica* [2004])

Out of all that talk during our lunch came the idea of telling season three from the Cylons' point of view. We build the Cylon ship, we go inside the Cylon culture, we present the Cylons in a way we haven't gotten to know them yet. We're writing brand-new characters, dealing with their whole system of interaction. Everything about their culture we would get to invent and explore. And *that* seemed to shake off enough of the cobwebs that we were able to at least tell the network that we weren't going to abandon a third season. To open that season in a kind of occupied territory was just so strong from an eleven-o'clock-news-metaphor standpoint that you couldn't help but get excited about it. Even as we started breaking the season, that was just so powerful and so timely and it felt urgent. It made you feel like you were writing something important.

JAMIE BAMBER
(actor, "Captain Lee 'Apollo' Adama")

I loved the Cylons, I really did, but it was a bit like the shark in *Jaws*. The more you see the shark in *Jaws,* the less the film holds up for me, and I felt that the Cylons were much more interesting in a Cylon-to-human context than they were in a Cylon-to-Cylon context. I don't know if I'll still feel that when I watch it again, but at the time that's really what I felt. I felt it was worth holding the point of view as a human point of view, rather than trying to go inside that world where it becomes a bit more sci-fi, a bit more futuristic. If the Cylons were really coveting man's relationship with God, they would be even more into something that we would recognize. Let's not forget, Cylons aren't aliens, they are creations of Man. They are technology, and I just felt they should have sat more within what it is to be human and, when they got their consciousness, not necessarily to strive for something strange, which that basestar felt to me. But I am more than happy to be wrong when I watch the show again.

BRADLEY THOMPSON
(producer, *Battlestar Galactica* [2004])

One of the things we really liked was when we *didn't* know about the Cylons, but they kept giving us more seasons, so it reached a point where you have to say, "Okay, it's now time to let us know what's going on with them." But it was fun to explore. They probably do not have the same morals, so to speak, as we do, because they're machines. They're not doing biological re-production, do they have the same sexual kind of things? Is it fun for them to do that? Why is Baltar in bed with two Cylons—outside of their appeal to us and totally horrible male fantasies? It was also, *how* different was it? Do they care about wearing clothes all the time? It seems that they wouldn't. There are only however many models we had, so there's not going to be any real differences. Do you need controls to run the ships? Do you pick up a telephone and call somebody or would they have something else set up? All of that was tremendous fun.

TRICIA HELFER
(actress, "Number Six")

I don't think I enjoyed the stuff when we eventually got on the Cylon side of things, inside their ship. That always felt more sci-fi and harder to get into, when our hands were all on this console with the lights and there's a little bit of water. There were some elements that were great. It felt like a different show. Filming it definitely felt more sci-fi, and there was more green-screen stuff, more technical stuff that didn't feel as grounded.

Prior to *Battlestar Galactica*, a time jump on a series had only been done twice before, during the final season of the Vietnam-era *China Beach*, which shifted to 1985; and in the second-season finale of *Alias*, which saw that show's spy Sydney Bristow (Jennifer Garner) mysteriously finding herself two years in the future.

MARK STERN
(former president of original content, Syfy)

We had a bit of a ritual where we would have this call in which Ron, David, and their team would get on the phone with us and tell us what they wanted to do to end the season. I loved those calls, because they were inherently un-nerving. You knew that they were going to break something that was not going to be comfortable. They did that all the way through the show. That moment where he said, "Okay, we jump to a year later, and he lifts his head up and we're now in the full occupation," was revelatory. That was awesome. Scary as shit, right? Like, "Wait a minute, what are you doing?" but for the right reasons. It was *so* bold and cool, and it really went right there. You knew it was going to be a real moment.

RONALD D. MOORE

For us, it was a bit of an unknown quantity. Like, "Wow, what would this do to the show?" The reasons that we did it were very specific to *Galactica*, because I really liked the idea that they would find a planet and a potential new home, and go there. Which was an idea that got pitched in the writers' room all the time: "Well, they come across an Earthlike planet and they want to stay." You knew that it was definitely going to be one of the shows at some point, but I kept pushing it off and pushing it off, because I wanted it to have meaning. It's like we're only going to do this once. I didn't want to keep finding new potential homes and then be like, "Oh, this one's riddled by volcanoes; this one's radiated, and then the bad guys . . ." You know, you could never really have a true home, because it would go against the con-cept of the show. So if you're going to do it, it felt like you were going to do it one time and it should really have meaning.

DAVID WEDDLE
(producer, *Battlestar Galactica* [2004])

Ron had this idea, what if they found a planet that was somewhat habitable? And what if that became a presidential campaign issue? Then he wrote that finale where the Cylons just come in, and then we cut to a year later. Super influential episode that's been copied, and that device used by many other shows since, but Ron Moore was one of the first to do it. It was incredibly dra-matic. It was great. Ron had those brilliant insights to knock all the chess pieces off the board, and then we as writers would have to reassemble them. For us it was always anxiety-producing, like, "Jesus, where do we go now?" But what we would quickly discover is he gave us all these new stories, and Ron had the idea that we, bam, cut a year ahead. When we start season three, we don't answer all the questions right away. He wanted to hold off for a while.

MARK VERHEIDEN
(co-executive producer, *Battlestar Galactica* [2004])

It was definitely a fun way to put everyone in a different environment. The whole New Caprica story had to be very carefully conceived, because it was quite expensive to go to that place, so we knew we had to get there, do it, and get out of there to stay on budget. A lot of thought went into those episodes.

BRADLEY THOMPSON

I thought the jump was great. It saved us a lot of what we would call shoe leather, because the other obvious way to do that is we get there and civilization happens and relationships change. Ron's gift was, let's just knock all the pieces off the board, set them up in a new place, and then figure out how we got there. All of a sudden, Starbuck and Tigh are best buds. How did that happen? Why is Lee running around in a fat suit? It was spectacular, because we were all doing some amazing stuff. Everybody in there was top of their game at that point. You had somebody you totally and utterly respected as a storyteller running the thing. You're sitting there beating your head on something and it's feeling a little bit conventional, and Ron would just come in and go, "You know, I'm trying to get here with you, what if . . . this?" Why the hell did we not think of that? Because it's totally unexpected.

It's like when we did "Exodus," and we pretty much came up with a military tactic. What we wanted to do was distract everybody and bring these guys from *Galactica* in. Ron took a pass on it and came up with the whole idea of just dropping the *Galactica* in the middle of the atmosphere, which was totally unexpected. That's what he was looking for. That was his gift that he could do that.

RICHARD HUDOLIN
(production designer, *Battlestar Galactica* [2004])

The challenge was finding a location to represent New Caprica. We had this area that we called the Dunes, which was basically a big dumping pit of sand. And we said, "Okay, A, how are we going to do this? And, B, what's it going to look like?" And that's where we came up with the idea of using all of the scaffolding to create the whole city. Almost like a boardwalk or a Western town. Just to be able to walk around and stuff was great. I pulled elements from all over the place, and we set it in this wonderful location. With the help of effects, it looked even bigger. So it was a bit of a hodgepodge of design elements that we stuck in there. Some were hard, some were soft.

You sit there and go, "What am I going to do now?" Then you get together with your art director and the construction coordinator and whoever we're talking about, and say, "What have we got a lot of?" Obviously there's a budget there, so what can we deliver? And how much time, how much money do you need? Because I was seeing this as a pretty big thing. So, anyway, we evolved all of that, and then we started doing some drawings, sent them up to Ron and the boys and they bought it, so we were off and running.

RONALD D. MOORE

If we were going to make a go of it on this world and Baltar is going to be president, we were going to let that play out and you had to give it months. They had to spend a lot of time down there. Because if we made a big deal out of this and said, "Wow, this is the potential new home and this is what the election's all about," and they make a big announcement, but then the Cylons show up next week, it just meant it was all kind of bullshit that didn't go anywhere. So in order to make it work, they had to be down there for months if not a year, just to really see if they can make a colonization effort. What *would* Baltar's government really be like?

However, the show is *Battlestar Galactica*. It's not *New Caprica*. So you kind of felt at the same time that you didn't want them building on the planet's surface while the *Galactica* circled overhead in orbit for hour after hour. I honestly don't remember whose idea it was, it might have been mine but it could have just been something I threw out there and the writers glommed on to, but then we started saying we should jump ahead and get to the good stuff. You just wanted to get to the point where it's all gone to hell. Baltar is a failed president, there's a lot of dissatisfaction and disaffection among people. *Galactica* hasn't been doing anything for a very long time, and then the Cylons show up. Because that's really the juice of the fun. Plus it would shock the audience and they'll think that it's a big dream. Or that we don't mean it. Or that we take it back.

MARK VERHEIDEN

I enjoyed how we would occasionally subvert the military reality of the series. The specific case was when our guys landed on New Caprica and we did that year jump and then we see that the Cylons are in control and the humans are under the Cylons' thumb and the humans have become the suicide bombers to try to stop the Cylons. That was not trying to make it a fantastically on-point allegory about anything, it just felt like it's interesting to see the fight from the point of view of the resistance that's been driven to the point of doing this.

DAVID EICK

The politics of *Battlestar* were always a bit inadvertent, or kind of a delicate analogue. The third season we just went for it. We were just, like, "Fuck it, this is on the front page of *The New York Times*. We're doing this!" We were going to do occupation and insurgencies, and we're just going to go for it. And it just shook the hell out of the show.

RONALD D. MOORE

We were just going to own it and see what happens. And then we really started getting excited about that in the writers' room, because it also meant that there was an entire year of backstories and things to make up and that we could scramble the relationships. You could suggest certain things that had happened and explore them later. Other things would be a mystery. Suddenly you had a whole giant chunk of story that was fun to play with, but we didn't really have to delineate and outline in great detail before we did it.

MARK VERHEIDEN

From a creative standpoint, those were really fun episodes, because we came in on season three pretty early. Maybe six months out from production, which is quite early for a show. Four or five of us sat down and wrote about a seventy-page document that would be the first five episodes of season three before we even got started on writing the scripts, and really broke down the whole New Caprica adventure. Part of that was we needed to do that for production, because going to New Caprica was an expensive production situation and we had to know what we were going to shoot, what we needed to get there. So going into it, we could play, but also it just gave us a chance to really work through what we wanted to have happen in those episodes. That's how we got to Tigh losing his eye, and becoming the suicide bomber, and the arguments between them about whether that was a valid strategy, Baltar is the world's worst president, etc.

DAVID EICK

When that year started out, it really felt like we were riding a motorcycle with the kickstand down, but then it got going. We had that bizarro Disneyland experience. We got drunk, we went on Space Mountain, and then we went home and it was like, "Hey, we've got a season three." We were exhausted, but we were galvanized by these new ideas. We were being more aggressive in terms of the sociopolitical metaphor. It did add pressure to the process, and I think it did create more conflict during development of stories and arguments about cuts and stuff like that, because it felt weightier. Suddenly the argument felt a little bit heavier, a little bit more like you wanted your point of view known perhaps more than in the first two years.

MARK VERHEIDEN

We were able to subvert the idea of who's the good guys and who are the bad guys in terms of our guys being essentially the suicide bombers, the resistance, and that was fun. It was an interesting opportunity to look at what a resistance against a more powerful force might look like if you're on that side of the equation, which from the United States' perspective, we're rarely on that side of the equation. For American viewers, it was probably, like, "Wait a minute, what's going on here?" But we just thought it was interesting to look at it from the other point of view. I don't think we were trying to say any point of view was morally better or worse—suicide bombing is not good—but that was where they had been driven to by the desperation of the situation.

MICHAEL HOGAN
(actor, "Colonel Saul Tigh")

Before we started shooting season three, I got on the phone with David Eick and asked him what was up in the new season. He said, "Well, Tigh's incarcerated. And he's tortured." "Tortured? How is he tortured?" He said, "Well, he's tortured." I said, "No, David, you can't just say that. We owe it to all the people in the world who *are* tortured. We can't just randomly go, 'He's tortured. He's limping.' You've got to be more specific." And he says, "We're thinking that he loses an eye." I laugh out loud and said, "David, you know what? Phone me when you figure it out." So then I get the script for the first episode, and the first scene is a beautiful scene with Cavil, Dean Stockwell—who'd have thought you'd be sharing a scene with Dean Stockwell? Anyway, I'm reading through the script and I go, "I have no eye." I call David up and say, "You took out my eye. An actor's main tools are their eyes. On the movie screen it's one thing. On the stage it's another thing. But on television you're in close-up. Your eyes are your tools and you've taken away fifty percent of my tools." But it was brilliant, because you knew that they wanted something permanent from the torture, and it's something you never get over: you will always think of the Cylons and the taking out of his eye.

Early on I also had a problem with Tigh going down to the planet. I totally disagreed. I happened to be reading a book called *Seize the Fire,* because I'm a research junkie. It was about the Battle of Trafalgar, and I was amazed at reading how similar the British navy was to the battlestar *Galactica* and our whole fleet, because they would leave port and go for years at a time making sure everybody was safe in their dominion and fighting off and discovering new lands, etc. And they would come back to port, disembark, go home to the farm or whatever, see the family, give them the money, have more kids if they can, get back on the ship, and go again for years. Tigh, of course, was one of those career soldiers who would go off, get loaded, and then get back on the next night or whatever. He would go and get back on because that's his life. He has nothing. So I'm in the middle of this book when I read the script where I'm down on the planet. I said to Ron, the guy wouldn't do it. He's *glad* Ellen's down there. He certainly does not want to go and be with her. Period. He wants to die. He doesn't want any more responsibility, and now he just can't die because these responsibilities keep coming. And you will find a lot of military people, or human beings, going, "I wish I could just walk away." But he's got responsibilities, and responsibilities to humanity. They rely on you. But having a chat with Ron, I realized

I needed to see what happens, because this was not going to just be a blind leap of faith.

JAMES CALLIS
(actor, "Gaius Baltar")

The thing about the occupation is that it was bending to their will, and breaking to it. For Baltar, there's the moment where I have to sign the death warrants. The whole thing is very involved in the sense of he needed *a lot* of prompting to sign that letter. There was this excellent thing that was written where a Caprica Six comes up to him and pleads with him, but it's still not enough. Then Doral just shoots her through the head and says, "Listen, the thing is, she's going to come back, but when I stick this through your brain, *you* won't." Well, there were lots of conversations; I was very nervous about it. I wrote to them initially about him needing to be brutalized into signing the thing. It's got to be a big, big deal. It's got to be very, very difficult. And we went that way, and filmed it in a very menacing way that worked for everyone. I mean, we're creating something and we're all acting, but having somebody thumping a gun against somebody's face and screaming and seeing their blood everywhere . . . we were all like, "This is getting very fraught."

Then when I saw the edit, all of the stuff with Tricia, Number Six, Caprica Six coming up to Gaius and appealing to him, and being shot through the head, had been cut, so that the episode ran as kind of like, "Sign it, sign it," and there was a bit of blubbering and then he did. I was just taken very aback and found it worrying, because he really has just rolled over. I actually was devastated on his behalf and I wrote to Ron and David and said, "You know, the whole thing about Caprica Six being killed first is so important, because it's a message of she can download, but you won't. It's more like psychological torture to sign the death warrants, otherwise I don't care about him anymore, because then it's too easy for him to just sign those things, and who cares about anybody like that anymore?" And they were like, "We totally understand where you're coming from, but we sent the cut out to everybody, even to the journalists. Not only that, we've got certain amounts of time for people to work on it. The edit suites are hired at certain times with certain people and we'd have to scramble, we've also signed off with it with the network," etc.

RONALD D. MOORE

I do recall this. James did fight for the coercion and then again after he saw the cut. I think I did put more of it back, but I can't recall why it was cut differently to begin with. It was probably either a director's cut he saw initially or maybe I had cut it down for time in the producer's cut. Either way, he was right.

JAMES CALLIS

I kind of got over it, but over the weekend they changed it back. I'm not sure why they changed it, and while there are so many things about that show that I'm grateful for, to Ron and David I was very grateful for that, because I thought that that was a really amazing thing for them to do for me and the character.

ALESSANDRO JULIANI
(actor, "Felix Gaeta")

It had been clear from the beginning of the series that we were doing something a little bit different. We were trying to make a drama that just happened to be in outer space. But I think those storylines on New Caprica is where that went to the next level. In terms of my involvement in it, it was great. It was sort of a darkening and a deepening of the relationship between Gaeta and Baltar. It added another level of toxicity to things, which is always fun for an actor. Then to just get to be able to be the person who, again, is just trying to do the right thing in all of it. Even being on the ship the whole time in the first season, and then getting to be outside, getting to be in a new environment, it changed everything for all of us, too. For those of us who were down in New Caprica in the tent city, being in a new environment was a sea change for all of us.

RONALD D. MOORE

New Caprica was so important for the Gaeta character. He befriended and looked up to Gaius Baltar early on in the run, so we had that relationship early, and then when you go to New Caprica and you do the jump ahead a year and Gaeta is one of his key advisors, he's still with Baltar, and he's trying to do the right thing, but now he's part of the occupation government. But at the same time he's also trying to help the resistance, but doesn't want to give himself away. So he's a man trying to dance on both sides there, and then after they're all rescued, then he's nearly killed for his collaboration.

MICHAEL TRUCCO
(actor, "Samuel Anders")

I remember my first reaction to the one-year leap was, "What the hell? You're just going to arbitrarily throw us ahead a year?" It was just that knee-jerk, selfish actor reaction of feeling like you were being gypped, denied the drama that had played out. Then it was, like, *trust*. Let the powers that be do what they do. As it turned out, Anders got deeper. Suddenly he's more embedded with the crew and the gang, and the people. It was the first time that I felt that I had been a part of the family, of the *Battlestar* lore. It was easy to feel like an outsider and thank you for bringing me back for another episode, but I always felt like it was their show and I'm just playing here. When that jump happened, I was like, "Oh, okay. They've mixed me into the bowl."

Physically, I loved getting in the dirt in that location. I loved that I had welts all over my back that I thought were fire ants, but because I'm a lefty, when you shoot a semiautomatic gun—they're quarter rounds that are blanks, but still bullets—the empty shell casings would eject out across the front of me. If you're right-handed, they go to the outside of you, but if you're left-handed they go right across your face. I was up against the dirt and we're shooting the guns and these hot shell cases were hitting the dirt, rolling back down the embankment, and sticking to my bare arms [*laughs*]. They were stinging me, making little welts, and I thought I was being eaten by fire ants.

RONALD D. MOORE

The experience of New Caprica really scarred a lot of the characters in pretty deep ways. It's interesting, because the show starts out with an incredible attack and the people are all scarred from the initial moments of the Cylon genocide of the human race. But somehow what happened to them all on New Caprica felt like it ran deeper in some ways in terms of the characters. Maybe because you'd gotten to know the characters over two years and had deepened their relationships and the cast knew each other better, and we knew the characters better. So we had a firmer grasp on who they were two years in than we did at the very beginning. When suddenly a big traumatic event like this happened midway, it just felt like the characters were more deeply wounded. They carried the scars a little more visibly. Everyone was a little angrier, a little more bitter. You'd sensed that they had really gone through an additional trauma beyond the one that had sent them on this journey to begin with.

MICHAEL HOGAN

When Tigh finally comes back up after the planet, Adama meets me as I'm coming off and says, "Good work. You brought them back." And I said, "Not all of them." And that's all. Nothing is ever said about that, but that still brings chills to me, because that is dead on. This is life. They're working soldiers.

RONALD D. MOORE

After the resistance was over and they were back on the ship after the New Caprica story, it made perfect sense that Starbuck would be leading the charge to track down and take vengeance on all the collaborators. I thought that was fantastic.

MICHAEL TRUCCO

There was a great movie called *The Star Chamber* starring Michael Douglas, and the idea was the same: Judges got together and the cases that got thrown out on a technicality, they would retry and send a hit man to knock these guys out—rapists and murderers that got off—and that's kind of what we were doing. It was our own little Star Chamber and our own vigilante circle and picking people that sided with the Cylons. They wrote Anders with a conscience and he recuses himself eventually. That it had gone far enough. I struggled with that a bit; on whether or not it was perceived as weakness. And then I've got Starbuck calling me a pussy, so I had to work to strike the right tone and balance. I guess kind of being pushed back on your heels like that as an actor is probably the best.

RONALD D. MOORE

The execution-squad idea came out of our discussions of, "Okay, historically what would happen after these things?" There was a lot of discussion about what had happened in post–World War II France after the Allies had liberated the villages and the way they paraded people through the streets or shaved the heads of the women that slept with the Nazis and shot some of them and killed them, and how people in this situation, who had been under occupation for all this time, there were some who had fought and some who had collaborated and people remembered. Once they were all free, there would come a reckoning and was there going to be a council of reconciliation, like they did in South Africa? Probably not. How were they going to go through this? Some people would take the law into their own hands, and that was a great story. It should be brutal, it shouldn't be pretty, and who would be on it?

MARK VERHEIDEN

What was so liberating about *Battlestar* in so many ways is that we were able to approach situations that would be incredibly hot-button to do if you did them on a regular set in America or in the Middle East. This was a science fiction background and they were essentially robots versus us, so we were able to do a lot of things because of being that one step removed. That's what the best science fiction always lets you do is take that one step removed and look with a different eye at situations that feel real to us as human beings, and as citizens of the world, but you take that one step back and you're able to look at it in a slightly different way. It becomes less charged, less immediately going, "I don't like this, because it took this political stance." Taking that one step, you don't feel as invested in being angry about it, because you're not actually saying it's Republican or Democrat or something like that.

DAVID WEDDLE

Of course, by that time we had the Iraq War going and were witnessing all the stuff in the Middle East. We wanted to mix it up. Ron's whole thing is never make it a one-on-one; that even if we were inspired by current events, we didn't want it to be a transparent commentary on current events or take a political side of anything. The thing about New Caprica and the drama there is it really fit for an occupying army anywhere. Germany occupying Russia and all of Europe. Or the Romans occupying the Middle East themselves. We wanted to write about an occupying force and to look at that dynamic from an angle that the public doesn't normally look at it. You don't have your heroes being suicide bombers or blowing up cafés or doing anything they can to push these occupiers out. Then people are forced to look at the ramifications of their actions, and then the Cylons start thinking, "Hey, what's wrong with these people? We've been decent with them, we didn't annihilate them, why are they sabotaging us at every turn?"

RONALD D. MOORE

It was kind of easy to figure out who would be behind it. It was really easy to go, "It's going to be Saul, it's going to be Starbuck, and they're going to be hunting them down and they're going to be passing sentences." It was really dark, but it seemed true. It seemed like this was the reality that we wanted to paint, because all through that storyline, we really wanted to play how people really behaved, how they really act in these circumstances, and it just felt like that was where our characters would go.

DAVID EICK

We were doing things to the characters that were extraordinarily risky. Our protagonists were leading an insurgency and hiring suicide bombers. Our antagonists were running for their lives. The visual effects were incredibly challenging, because we were in a broad-daylight scenario versus our usual kind of inky black. There were tons and tons of fights and arguments and redo's—all kinds of R and D and headaches and nightmares that just exacerbated all of it. It was a much harder season than anything we had done.

And I don't care who you are—you can be Gandhi—you're going to argue more when you're doing that kind of thing under those conditions.

Prior to the characters' return to the *Galactica,* the New Caprica storyline concluded in spectacular fashion with an epic two-parter called "Exodus" (episodes three and four of the third season), but as originally conceived it was supposed to be a single episode. The shooting style of the show changed that.

FELIX ALCALA
(director, "Exodus")

"Exodus" was supposed to be a one-hour episode. After we shot it and it was being cut together, the editor called after speaking to Ron and told me we had too much material. I had done all the explosions, I did this war stuff with the arrival of *Galactica* and all. I made a meal out of everything. We put it together and I said, "Look, cut a movie out of it." And we ended up with a really long cut which was only short of a two-hour episode by very little. The editor called Ron and then he spoke to me and he said, "We can make this a two-hour. It'd be fantastic." And then Ron calls me and said, "Look, I'm going to write another scene. We have two more scenes we can pick up and stick in your movie. We'll have a two-hour special." And so I ended up, for the price of a one-hour, giving them a two-hour.

RONALD D. MOORE

That's a little bit of an exaggeration, but not by much, actually. It was just a big script, and then Felix shot it really well. The run time was way over the hour mark, and so you got to a point quickly where you saw the first cut where you realized, "What are we going to do with this?"

TODD SHARP

The first cut of the episode came in thirty minutes over, and it was all great. Everybody's saying, "How are we going to cut this down to size?" The answer was, we don't have to. Why don't we add another episode? We had to add about twenty more minutes of material and shot for three more days and we had a whole extra episode out of it.

RONALD D. MOORE

That first cut wasn't quite enough to get to two hours, and Sci-Fi really didn't like to do the ninety-minute format, because it gave them scheduling problems and financial issues. So we did say, "Well, we could make this into a two-parter if we just added a couple of scenes here and there." So we did make that decision on the fly and just went for it, and it probably did save us quite a bit of money in the scheme of things.

DAVID WEDDLE

When Brad and I broke the episode, we knew that it was too much material. We'd done that a couple of times on the show, where we expanded things into two-parters. I remember we were on a plane going to Vancouver—Michael Rymer, our producer/director, was with us—and he read the script for "Exodus." When he was finished, he looked at us on the plane and said, "There's no way you can do all this in one episode. This is two episodes." We smiled and said, "We know." As it turned out, that's exactly what happened.

TODD SHARP

With *Battlestar* in general we shot much more material than we were ever able to use. In episodic television, you really want to shoot only about three, four, or five extra pages or minutes of material to be able to cut a fine-tuned show. You don't want to shoot an extra ten or fifteen minutes, because that's a day or two of photography that ends up on the cutting room floor. But we did that. We did shoot episodes that are ten or fifteen minutes over. You see on the DVD there are tons of deleted scenes. But we did that by intent, because David Eick made a very strong case early on. There was a moment that Mark Stern loved in the miniseries between Adama and Tigh, and Adama's shoving noodles into his mouth. It's a dim, kind of gross, but very human moment. When the studio was saying, "Look, guys, you're leaving a lot of money on the floor every episode here. Think of how much more you could put on the screen if we weren't throwing away a day of photography." To his credit, David said, "But if I'm not shooting an extra ten or fifteen minutes of material, I'm not going to be able to give Mark Stern those great moments, like Adama shoving noodles into his mouth." There's something about all the excess that we shot that allowed us to be able to craft the show.

RONALD D. MOORE

We would usually shoot way more material than we could cram into our forty-minute box. The network did start going, "We're wasting an awful lot of money." They would call it wasting. Todd Sharp would try to voice this and say, "It's a problem and I really think you guys should dial back. It hurts you later, in fairness, when you ask them for extra money for big shows, when you're doing a bigger show like the New Caprica storylines or the finale or something. You go to them and ask for extra money, and they're like, "Well, maybe you'd have more money if you hadn't spent all this other money on footage that didn't even make it into the show," which is a fair argument. *My* argument, and still to this day, is that I still do shows that are too long. My scripts are always too long on any show and the cuts are always long. I just think it helps to cut down. It helps to figure out what works and what doesn't later.

I'd rather just shoot it all, put it together, and then realize, "Oh, this section doesn't work" or "I'm having problems with this one and I've got material." I like having more than enough to play with and don't like making the final decision on stuff at the script stage. I'd rather shoot all this stuff knowing it's not all going to fit in the show and, yeah, it's going to be wasted footage. Yeah, it's too much money, but you know what? *So what.* It's just money. In ten years when I'm having conversations like this one, no one's going to give a shit. No one will care. We don't care today, and we're not going to care tomorrow and it's going to make the show better, so just shut up and leave me alone.

DAVID WEDDLE

Being able to cut from New Caprica to *Galactica* and *Pegasus* was fantastic. One thing I remember is that we wanted to play Lee getting fat physically and emotionally. Also, when Adama decides to go back to New Caprica, we wondered what we would do with Lee. I used the example of the Sam Peckinpah film *Ride the High Country,* where Gil Westrum, Randolph Scott's character, escaped but in the end he's the guy who turned on his friend. But his friend is provoked, challenged him morally, and in the end he has to come back and rejoin the fight and shows up as kind of a surprise at the end of the film.

I brought up the idea of Lee coming back with *Pegasus* as a surprise, and Ron said, "Yeah, that's like *Star Wars,*" which I'm actually not that familiar with, I'm sorry to say. But George Lucas probably got the idea from Westerns. So I remember it was Brad, me, and Ron who came up with the idea of *Pegasus* showing up all of a sudden, coming in and helping Adama. Ron came up with the idea of Battlestar *Galactica* coming down into the atmosphere, which I know the fans went nuts over. That was a completely Ron Moore inspiration. It was *such* an audacious and risky move on *Galactica's* part that threw the Cylons into chaos. And it probably would have led to Adama's death, except that Lee then came back with *Pegasus.*

DAVID WEDDLE

Felix Alcala was the right director for "Exodus." He's like a field marshal on the set and did an amazing job of that, and all the stuff on New Caprica with the fight that happens until the human race escapes. And Harvey Frand, who was our line producer, one of the best line producers I've ever worked with. They built an entire city out there on what was, I think, a sand dune. It was all this loose dirt that they built the city on and I remember going there with Brad for "Exodus" and it felt like a movie. We had an entire city built out on this sand. It was a thrilling thing to be a part of. You felt the show just growing in terms of what it was able to achieve.

And for Gary Hutzel and his crew to make all of those sequences work so fantastically. Gary was a genius and I think that he always looked from the point of view of making the visual effects sequences different from what he had done on *Star Trek,* where everything was very objective when you saw a space battle. It stayed stilted in a way. Gary revitalized the whole approach to space battles by thinking like a filmmaker and about point of view when he created those battles. Which gave them a vibrancy and visceral power that had been lacking in television space battles certainly before that.

In "Exodus" there is also a climactic moment when everyone is leaving New Caprica, and Saul Tigh has to take action against his wife, Ellen, for her seeming betrayal of the humans to Cylons during the occupation. His plan is to have her drink poison.

FELIX ALCALA

Now, the scene is very difficult to do. It's difficult, because it's emotional and then she realizes what he's going to do and she takes the cup from him. She says, "No, I'll do this myself. I want to save you from doing it." And that's the kind of shit Ron would write. It was *so* heavy. There's so much information of this woman and what they're going through and she doesn't want her husband to suffer even though she fucked him over and she's going to do it herself.

RONALD D. MOORE

In the aftermath of New Caprica, Lieutenant Gaeta certainly went through a big change. You know, he was the loyal officer on the flight deck or on the CIC until then. And he started to raise objections to things here and there, but once he started helping with the human government and throwing himself firmly into that camp and then being accused of being a traitor and all the ramifications . . . The repercussions that happened to him after the New Caprica episode ultimately aligned him with Tom Zarek and led to his death in season four. It was a decisive turn for that character, and Baltar as well. Baltar becomes president and it's a major thing for him. We also saw, in those episodes, him struggling with his own moral dilemmas probably more deeply and profoundly than he had, even in the two years leading up to that.

JAMES CALLIS

What was interesting about him being president is that if you don't have quite the understanding or the respect for the office, it shows immediately. The whole thing about Baltar and politics is it's not his idea. This is a wider agenda. This is Number Six. She teams him up with Zarek. They spot chinks in Roslin's armor and the planet becomes a rallying cry. And Baltar, in his naïveté, thinks that he's doing the right thing initially. He doesn't realize he's being played. Not that that would be much of a defense in court, necessarily.

RONALD D. MOORE

And then there was Colonel Tigh, certainly deeply scarred by New Caprica physically and emotionally. They were all affected in different ways, but those were probably the big ones. The Apollo/Starbuck/Sam triangle gets scrambled a lot. She marries Sam, then throws over Lee, and that sort of psychic and emotional scar never really healed between those two characters. But that felt, in some weird way, almost like that was going to happen whether they were down on New Caprica or not. You know, you kind of felt like that wasn't so much about that particular experience as it was that that was the road that these three characters were going down. Yes, it was Lee and Kara were sort of soulmates in some weird way, but she couldn't quite embrace that, so she was going to go for Sam and break Lee's heart. And he was going to be embittered about that. Look, if it was someone else, eventually they would try to make their way back to each other, but by the end of the show they never quite made it. That probably wouldn't have been their arc whether we'd gone to New Caprica or not.

Overall, season three was meant to be a lot of fallout and repercussions of the New Caprica experience. They had divided themselves. Some had aligned themselves with the Cylons, some had not. There were war crimes and accusations. We wanted to do a lot about collaboration and a lot about what people did due to circumstances, and how other people would judge them for that. You know, how some of those wounds would never heal. We didn't really have a clear sense of what the end of the season was going to be for quite a while. At the beginning, yeah, we were more focused on, "This is great. We love all these New Caprica episodes." And then, "Let's do fallout after that. What's the next big thing that would happen to them as a result of what happened on New Caprica?" It wasn't until probably midway through the season that we started really thinking about where this was going.

The next big thing, dramatically, was the dual exploration of the Baltar character and Cylon society by having him brought aboard a Cylon basestar.

RONALD D. MOORE

There were two things at work there. Part of it was the journey of Gaius Baltar. The man who never intended to do most of the things that had happened to him. Never intended to really betray the human race, didn't think he was going to be a survivor, didn't intend to have this relationship with Number Six in his head, gets pulled into politics without even really intending to, becomes president—almost out of spite for Laura Roslin—then is a Cylon puppet and at the end he has no choice but to go live among the enemy. How does that journey play out for him?

JAMES CALLIS

For Baltar, politics was not important. Politics was only the art of the possible, essentially, or it should be the art of the possible. But look at it, it's so internecine, the battles between whoever the diametrically opposed parties are, and then becomes more about fulfilling one's party agenda over another, and that would infer and incur planning. Like real planning. And Baltar was not a planner. He's like a pinball in one of those machines, getting socketed from one thing to another, and some of them are literally his own making as he's kind of fizzing around. If he only had planned, his journey might have been a bit easier. It's a character *and* a character strength. He's working on his wits and his science and he doesn't need to plan ahead, or whatever, in that way. Or at least planning ahead isn't improvising in the moment to get out of a situation. Surely planning ahead is like you've got at least a six-month, a year, or five-year plan. I don't see Baltar planning things out more than an hour. He's like this feral creature, constantly afraid that he's going to be stabbed in the communal bathroom.

RONALD D. MOORE

The second thing is that it forced us—and me—to sit down and really put together my thinking about Cylon society for the first time. How does the basestar operate? Why do we only see so many Cylons? Once we decided that Baltar wasn't going to be arrested at the end of the occupation and he was going to go off with the Cylons, you immediately go, "Well, all right, so now what are we going to do?" Because once you go on a Cylon basestar, you're either going to run into all twelve Cylons quickly and give them all away, or you have to have a reason why you're only showing some of them. So I came up with this idea that maybe there's a reason. Let's preserve the mystery of revealing the Cylons, because that was such a great part the series was playing, "Who could be a Cylon and which among us might have been a Cylon all along?"

JAMES CALLIS

Having Baltar go over to the Cylons was like stalking new territory. It was slightly exposed, in more ways than one. It felt like we were really creating something or trying to create something with lots of visual ideas—loads of things—how to play with this thing. There's lots of reasons for that, and why we're thinking about it in the sense that when you're on the battlestar and you were in the CIC, or walking down those corridors, the scene played out and you knew how that was going to work. Walking around the Cylon ship, or being in the Cylon ship, or talking to the Hybrid or things like that, were more complicated. Initially the fun was in the idea of "I've been abducted by alien robots." The idea was that I was going to be naked, initially, and I had to roll down my boxer shorts. I've seen now it just looks like I'm wearing my boxer shorts really low, but it was supposed to be that you've been taken totally out of your comfort zone and anything can happen. I suppose the thing is the Cylons are initially the big bad enemy, and now we're on this ship and we're going to show bits of them.

In any horror movie or genre like that, in some fashion, the less you see the monster, the better it is. So the more you reveal the monster, the monster is potentially less threatening. *Unless* threatening things happened to you while you were on the ship, and thus, for example, Baltar was tortured by Gina. That was an important part of essentially keeping the threat level up. I think the show kind of suggested, and I certainly said in an episode to Boomer, "Believe me when I tell you, there are far worse things than death." I believe now, having gone through them, just as an actor, being tortured is one of them.

RONALD D. MOORE

Then I came up with this idea of the Final Five; that we had seen seven of them, but there were five remaining. And let's say that there's a particular mystique to the Final Five; that they have a meaning in Cylon mythology that is greater than what you know. So there's this reason why that gives us a bigger backstory. It enriches Cylon society, and it also just meant that we could tease out the reveals for a while. So now you had the Final Five and you were telling the audience, "Okay, now who are the last?" You could really dig into that.

That was a big groovy thing that we came up with at the beginning of season three, and then as you got deeper into talking with Richard Hudolin and various directors about what the inside of the Cylon basestar was going to be, we started really throwing around different ideas. I didn't want it to just look like a generic spaceship. I wanted it to really look and feel differently. I wanted it to operate differently. I wanted it be as alien to our way of thinking as it possibly could. I think we were successful to a large extent. Some of the ideas didn't quite play out the way I wanted them to.

RICHARD HUDOLIN

I went with a very clean look, with the red line in the Cylon environment. And water was a big element, because that's the essence of all life. And there were lots of big spaces. For some directors it worked really well and they loved it, but for others they'd walk in and go, "What the heck? How am I going to shoot this?" "Well, I'd love to show you." I don't know if I'd call it a complete success or a complete failure, but I thought it was pretty cool. It was also a nice contrast using the rib and the peak red color, and designing stuff for the Cylons. It was a lot more cerebral than the *Galactica*.

RONALD D. MOORE

There was an idea that the Cylons, when they're walking around the ship, could mentally imagine themselves in any environment they want. They're machines, so they could be in a room, and essentially be in a virtual-reality space where they think that they're out in the woods. That's just how some of the Cylons prefer to think of their environment. They're completely aware of where they are. They know that they're really on the base station. They know where every object in the base station is, but they prefer to feel like they're standing out in the redwood forest. So let's do that. And at first I thought that was going to save us money. I was like, "This is a great way to save us from having to build all these sets, and we'll put them out in the woods. We'll film on location," and, of course, it became very expensive and difficult and time-consuming. So you only saw us do it a few times here and there to sort of sell the idea. And then you kind of went away from it.

It's Lucy with the football with production, always trying to figure out how to save money for the show, and inevitably it comes back, "Well, you didn't save anything and maybe it's *more* expensive." And it's just so frustrating, because the people who work on the production side always think that the writers live in ivory towers and don't care about money. It's, like, "You guys just write stuff and you don't think about how hard it is to make," and we actually spend a lot of time trying to imagine ways to save money for production or make things easier. The problem is, what sounds good or what seems logical, you get into the practical craftsmen and artisans and they come back with these answers that usually shock you: "What do you mean it's *more* expensive to do it this way? This is a way of saving money, can't you see that?" But apparently it doesn't.

For both Grace Park and Tahmoh Penikett, an important moment—and not just for their characters—was when a plan was devised for Helo to kill Athena, thus sending her back into download mode on the Cylon resurrection ship where she would be able to rescue their daughter, Hera.

TAHMOH PENIKETT
(actor, "Captain Karl 'Helo' Agathon")

That's one of the heaviest things I've ever done to this point, but because I had such trust with Grace Park, because I had such chemistry with her, because she was such a friend, and we both came up as young actors on this show, we both came from the same acting school, and we were always willing to go to that truthful place. We didn't have to do a lot of takes. It's an emotional scene, but I knew I could go to that place, because that storyline affected me. That said, I was a young enough actor that it was hard for me to shake those heavy scenes.

GRACE PARK
(actress, "Sharon 'Boomer' Valerii")

We knew it was going to be heavy, but it's weird because she was a robot and she would be coming back. But I think what it represents is trust and faith. That whatever you're trusting in is really the right thing, because you're still killing somebody. When we were doing it, there was a lot of flexibility in terms of where we put the gun, do we start it like this, are we sitting? All that kind of stuff. Part of it was also that Tahmoh was really just pure and vulnerable as well. He's a generous actor and we always were really great at working these scenes together, which is something I've always appreciated.

TAHMOH PENIKETT

I would sometimes be in a place for days afterward, because you're going to a powerful dark place and you have to experience it. I didn't know how to turn it off or leave it where it was. I think with a heavy scene like that you've got to pay it service, to give it the time and respect, and then shake it off and move on. That was hard then. But Grace and I, the moment we met we just clicked. There was an understanding. We were definitely siblings in another lifetime.

GRACE PARK

You definitely do scenes where you're like, "That was amazing," and then you'll watch it and be like, "Hmm, that didn't translate. I guess I'm just going to leave with my memory of it, because that was better." And there are other times where you do something, it's not that great, but when you watch it, you're like, "Shit, those guys are so good in post." You just realize that you're just one of the many pieces holding the web together.

RONALD D. MOORE

The second part of the season was about revenge and forgiveness. And justice. You know, what do you do after you've liberated a people from an occupation or you've freed a country, but everyone's kept score and waited for their moment. "Now I'm going back and get the person that killed my father!" Or,

"Those guys down the block, they were collaborators and I'm going to finger them." We were fascinated with those ideas, and they kind of dominated our thinking, in large part because of what was going on in Iraq. The American occupation was well under way and there were all these sorts of sectarian and tribal feuds that had been suppressed during the Saddam Hussein years, and suddenly the Americans come in and now was the chance of a lot of those people to get revenge for all the bad things that had happened to them under the previous regime. What was justice like in those sorts of circumstances? Could you ever forgive what people did when they were under an occupying power? And who's to say what's right and what's wrong when you have no choices? Another country, another power comes in and is controlling your land and your people. Who are the good guys and who are the bad guys? And when that force is suddenly taken out, how people just quickly bring out the long knives and start going after their enemies. We found that fascinating and wanted to watch our characters grapple with that.

We sort of knew from the beginning of season three, once we started talking about New Caprica and the occupation and the occupation is going to end, Baltar is probably going to go on trial. The question just became, *when* were we going to do the trial episode? As we got into it, we decided we didn't want to do it right away. It felt like a big idea, the trial of one of our key characters for treason and the possible execution and all that. So we sort of put a pin in it and said, "All right, that's going to be the season finale. We don't really know what's going to happen between here and there, but somehow Baltar's going to get captured or he'll be traded back to them or something. Through some mechanism, our characters will get their hands on Gaius Baltar again, and then we're going to have the trial of the century. *That* will be the end of the season." And we just left it at that.

It sort of hung out there on the writers' board. That was really the only pointer that we had toward what the end of the season was going to be. Everything else was kind of embroidering on the fallout from New Caprica and continuing to advance different character relationships and plot ideas. Just always in the back of our head saying, "Eventually we'll end the season with a trial."

MARK STERN

When the idea of the trial was pitched to us, it just didn't feel like it was big enough. Or special enough to end the season. What they came up with instead, I absolutely loved.

RONALD D. MOORE

We had done an initial break on the finale—on the trial—and the writers were pitching it to me in the room. I remember just feeling like it wasn't enough. I was kind of dissatisfied. It worked perfectly well as a story, but it didn't feel like it was a season finale. It just wasn't big enough, which I think surprised me and surprised everyone, because we'd been assuming that was the big, slam-bang ending to the season. I said that it felt like we should reveal a Cylon or something, but that wasn't very big. Then I said, "Maybe we should reveal four out of five of them in one big shock moment," and people were taken aback, because the four would be among the crew.

MARK VERHEIDEN

So the enemy was living amongst us the whole time. *That* really threw an emotional wrench into all the relationships. Not just people who had specific relationships with those characters—the last Cylon characters—but also the relationships between the crew and their commanding officers. How could you have let this happen? How could you *not* have known? Were you in league with them this whole time? Who else is going to come out as a Cylon?

Ron and David had come to us and said, "We think we should pick X number of significant crew members to realize they've been Cylons the whole time, under deep cover." That led to a three-day summit in Lake Tahoe, where all the writers got together. We sat down with a whiteboard and we're trying to figure out what would be the most interesting combination of characters to have this revelation be about; who could we use that would be the best way to achieve what we wanted to achieve by making this big series-changing revelation. That was a really fun exercise in running through all the options we had.

RONALD D. MOORE

I literally sketched out this image. I said, "We can just cut to four characters in different parts of the ship, and they all start going toward one room, you know? They just all walk into that room and they look at each other, and suddenly they're like, 'We're Cylons,' and that's how we would do it. They were all called by some unknown force or some trigger and we just really shock the audience." People were surprised in the room, and some of the writers were reluctant that it might be too many, but as we talked about it, we got more excited.

MARK VERHEIDEN

After that, it became planning on how to get to that place, and choosing who would be the best people to be Cylons, knowing that there were a few cast members who would absolutely not want to play that part. They were never on the table, really. Mr. Olmos, for example. I don't think that would have flown. I don't think President Roslin was interested in being a Cylon.

RONALD D. MOORE

We sat there for a few hours and dug through all the possibilities—the whole cast and recurring cast. We got to the core group of four kind of quickly, and then just kept talking about other possibilities.

Those who *were* chosen to be a part of the final four of five Cylons turned out to be Aaron Douglas's Chief Tyrol, Michael Trucco's Sam Anders, and, most surprising of all, Michael Hogan's Saul Tigh and Rekha Sharma's Tory Foster, a character introduced as a presidential advisor to Laura Roslin, who, more than the others, truly seemed to embrace the sudden revelation of what she is.

BRADLEY THOMPSON

We knew that we were eventually going to have to explain who they were. I was actually up in Vancouver when they were doing a lot of that. We put everybody up on the board. Everybody was a possibility. It was like, "Who would give us the best stories if these guys turned out to be Cylons?" That's how we picked them. Ron wrote them on the board and said, "Okay, these are the guys." After we'd done all our discussions about it, he said, "Sleep on it, because tomorrow that's going to be real."

RONALD D. MOORE

People came in and out, but we sort of figured that Tyrol was a good one, because he was such a human character. He was just such a guy. The idea was mind-blowing, but we hesitated, fearing we might lose that quality about him, but we didn't.

AARON DOUGLAS
(actor, "Chief Tyrol")

My initial reaction to being one of the Final Five was that you're taking somebody that the fans love and you're going to turn him into somebody that they don't; they're going to hate this guy. But I didn't really understand the nuance and just how bloody smart sci-fi fans are that they can vacillate between, "Okay, now I'm on their side. Oh, now I'm on these guys' side," and just go back and forth. You know, "Okay, I like the humans, but what they're doing right now is just full dick mode. I'm going to hope that the Cylons do something cool here and put them in their place."

Ultimately what I've come to is that if you want to humanize the Cylons, I don't think anybody does a better job of that than Colonel Tigh and Chief Tyrol. The chief is such a likable guy and he's not nefarious and he doesn't have the ulterior motives. He's just trying to do the best he can and he's a fairly simple guy. Shit just goes wrong and he keeps plugging away. He's kind of an easy guy to root for and then you find out he's a Cylon and you go, "Oh, shit, can I still like him? Yeah, I can." It makes them not ultimately just evil for the sake of being evil. A lot of us were just doing the best we could with the hand we were dealt, and it doesn't matter that we were born tens of thousands of years ago or created whenever.

I thought you need to play him the same way. He fundamentally doesn't change in one way, but in another he still wants to do what's best by everybody or do the best that he can. I'm really happy that they discovered it when they did, and told us when they did, because if we had known from the outset, that would have really changed how the role was played. You know, if they said early on, "By the way, you're a Cylon, but we're not going to reveal it until season four." That would have detracted from the character for sure.

RONALD D. MOORE

Rekha's character of Tory was kind of an easy one, because it was, "Okay, another character that joined us later and, oh, she's been really close to the president; that's a good position to be in."

REKHA SHARMA
(actress, "Tory Foster")

That character, I felt, was very much about the brutal reality we lived in. And, for me, supporting a female president was awesome, especially being her right-hand gal and blatantly saying things that don't want to be said. It's all about these tough calls. She's someone who has to learn to be brave enough to do the job, because she's never done this before. All of the people in our story before the war began were doing regular jobs, and everything changed. I can't remember what Tory was before, but it was certainly not the chief of staff to the president. It's, like, okay, a big opportunity and these are big shoes I've got to fill, and this is a big crazy time in the world and I've got to step up. It was this balance of creating a rapport and a friendship and really getting to know the president. *Then* finding how we trust each other and how we work together and being strong enough to say, "Actually, *don't* do that."

The revelation that she is actually a Cylon was a total shock. I knew something was up the day I read it, beginning when I was getting ready for work and Eddie said to me, "Have you read ahead?" I was like, "No." Then he just laughed, sat in his chair, just laughing. "Better pull up your socks and get ready." I was like, "What's he talking about?" He said, 'You go to the office before you leave today and you get the next script. You take it home and you read it. Just you wait. Just you wait, little girl." So I went in and got the script, took it home, read it that night, and literally squealed with joy. I couldn't believe what I was reading. Then we proceeded to have no idea what it means. Many theories were going around. Nobody would say whether or not it was true. I thought maybe they planted a chip so that we think that we're Cylons, but we're actually not, and it's a whole ruse to take us down or something. We didn't find out until moments before we actually shot the scene.

Then, she almost became afraid of herself in the beginning. It took her to this very still place, where I was almost afraid to do anything. You just stay still, you don't move too much. All of these feelings were arising inside of her. One thing, for instance, was sexuality. She was all of a sudden having an affair with Anders. We were, like, what the hell is going on? Clearly in the world, he's not her type. He's a jock, she's an intellectual. But they were inexorably drawn to each other. So she's coming alive in an unknown way to herself. Then she starts to feel strength, power, that she's been so afraid of coming from the outside, and now she realizes she has that power. She decides to embrace it. From that point, she was just looking for truth.

I love the metaphor of it. To learn that you're your own enemy and the thing you've been fighting against your whole life, but filled with the fear of annihilation, because I'm surrounded by people who would like to kill me.

RONALD D. MOORE

Sam was kind of an easy one, because we met him on Cylon-occupied Caprica and that was just an easy way to posit that he was a Cylon. Then the question became, what would that do to his relationship with Starbuck?

MICHAEL TRUCCO

I'm deeply gratified I got to step into that role as a Cylon and take that character on that much of a strange journey. That could've been a very one-off, ancillary character. Could've been the eye candy that she sleeps with and then she kicks to the curb. But I was given the permission to inhabit this character and given the storylines to make something of them. I look back now on the journey, and ending up to be one of the Final Five was like being knighted. I felt like, you know, take a knee and have a sword touch both shoulders, because you're going to be part of the lore of this show for the rest of its life.

After he realized it, I remember a scene specifically in the little hallways when Starbuck was like, "If I ever find out you're a Cylon, I'll put a bullet through your head." Suddenly Anders was filled with paranoia. His confidence shifted to one of fear. So I was initially confused, but other people had different reactions. Michael Hogan was just *pissed*. He was like, "C'mon . . . are you fucking kidding me?" He was genuinely mad. If you ever watch Tigh as a Cylon, he's just mad. Aaron Douglas was, "Of course the chief's a Cylon." With that sort of resigned irony. Me? I was like, "Whoa, whoa,

whoa. Time out. Ron? David?" I call them on the phone and I'm like, "What about all those things where I was fighting?" They're like, "Yeah, you know, you're a Cylon." So I had to take that confusion and I realized that I played Anders more paranoid. My biggest fear was my own life, because I believed that if Starbuck found out I was Cylon, she *would* put a bullet in my head.

As a character, nothing felt different inside. That was the genius program of the Cylons: that they were, for all intents and purposes, human. They had the flesh and the blood and the bones and they had the soul and minds. All that programming was so sophisticated that we thought we were human. If they didn't click that thing in our heads, we'd still be going on as humans. But then you find out you're a Cylon with emotions and feelings, and feeling pain.

RONALD D. MOORE

When Adama was shot in season one and Tigh took over and ran into all kinds of problems, we thought there might be repercussions between the two of them, but thought it more important that Adama give him a pass, and that said more about their friendship than anything else. He just wasn't going to call him on the carpet for any of the things he'd done; Adama was just going to keep up and keep moving. Then, of course, when Tigh revealed himself to be a Cylon . . . The thing to shake him deepest was to threaten his ship and the friendship and trust he had in Saul. We went right at them there toward the end.

MICHAEL HOGAN

There's the wonderful scene in the CIC after I find out this news, wondering what am I going to do? Terrified. Adama gives me an order and says, "Tigh, are you all right? I gave you an order." "Oh, I never felt better in my life." Lifts up a gun and shoots, and I think he shoots Adama, right in the eye, by the way, and down he goes. And that's the nightmare that Tigh is living with ever since, right? The fear he could actually do that.

RONALD D. MOORE

Saul was a tough one. That was the one where we were like, "Boy, what are we doing here? What does this do to his relationship with Adama once we do?" The thing that attracted me the most to him was what it did to that character who had been the most anti-Cylon of all of them. He had led the resistance. He had lost an eye, for God's sake. It just really turned that character inside out.

MARK VERHEIDEN

Tigh was the one that was maybe the most difficult to finally land on, because, just from a structural standpoint, and what we'd established from his life and his history with Adama, it took a little bit of backfilling to make it clear how he could have been a Cylon, and then all this time has essentially been a sleeper agent within the fleet. The others had come in a little later, so it didn't feel quite as tricky to do that. I think we actually did episodes where we saw them in their younger days. I can't remember if Tigh was in the episode where we met Adama's wife or not, but we certainly suggested that they'd known each other for many years. That was the logic issue we had to deal with when considering the change of making Tigh one of the Cylons.

EDWARD JAMES OLMOS

No one knew who the Cylons were going to be ahead of time. There are a couple of people that said they knew because they had gotten to read the script earlier than anyone else. I believe that, but in essence the majority of us did not know who the other Cylons were. So they wrote it and we started to do a table reading and people got *very* angry. The most anger came from Michael Hogan. He said, "This is bullshit. I'm not going to do this. I'm not doing it," and he stood up and walked out. He was very angry and frustrated. He couldn't believe that they had done this to him. He ended up bringing that anger to the performance. If you watch him when they finally meet inside the hangar, the four them, he is *so* angry. He hates the Cylons, but as time goes on, he learns that he's actually the father of all of them. He was the first one. He helped create Cylon number one.

MICHAEL HOGAN

At the time, someone told me there was a poll online of all the people that had been on *Battlestar Galactica* that could be Cylons, and apparently Tigh was second to last. Just least likely. And on set, everybody's teasing each other and it was close to zero hour to find out who were the Final Five. At that point Eddie looked at me and said, "You're hearing the music." "Come on, Eddie. Frak off, man. Not you, too, for God's sake. Let's get on with it." Then Michael Rymer was there and he said, "Ron Moore hasn't talked to you?" I said, "Rymer, not you, too, man." Then Ron flies to Vancouver to talk to me, and in the long run, I think it's absolutely brilliant they chose Tigh, because if he's not chronologically the oldest human being alive . . . seriously, there's only some thirty-thousand-odd of us left, so if he's not the oldest he is certainly the most dangerous. He's got more battle combat than anybody in the fleet. He's fought the Cylons hand-to-hand, etc. And he's the most loyal. So he's dangerous. So you're like, "What's going to happen here? Tigh's a Cylon?"

RONALD D. MOORE

What would call them in? What do they hear? What would it be? And somebody said, "Music. What if they heard a song?" I immediately said, "And it's going to be 'All Along the Watchtower.'" That was something I'd wanted to do in an episode of *Roswell*. Never got made, but I'd become sort of quasi-obsessed with that song. I said, "The lyrics are crazy and weird and it's perfect, and we can have all kinds of interesting things going on. And there are coded messages in the lyrics." It had something to do with all of this has happened before, all of it will happen again. Next thing you know, we all got really excited by it and that became the big thing that we were going to do at the end of the season. Which is so ironic, because now most people probably think of the ending for that season as the revelation of the four out of five Cylons, and they forgot that was the trial of Baltar.

MARK VERHEIDEN

It just made things infinitely more tense when we did that, and it also made the Cylons, again, more like they are just people that were treated badly and rebelled. They're constructs, but they didn't care for being pushed around as much as anybody does. What you also ended up with was that the Cylons, for better or for worse, had been introduced into the highest levels of the command structure, both civilian and military, when Tigh and Tory turned out to be Cylons. Which really motivated later on the mutiny with Gaeta and Zarek.

DAVID WEDDLE

We had such a great team of writers by the last couple of seasons. You know, Mark Verheiden, Michael Taylor, Jane Espenson, Michael Angeli. All were great, phenomenally talented writers who brought different colors to the show, and they each took their shows and their shows added slightly different character and sensibility, and yet it fit into the whole sensibility. Everybody was able to do that, to write the show and write their own episodes and bring them all the way through with notes from Ron. So this team, this incredible team that was assembled, when it came time to write something like "Rapture," there's a scene where Tigh is going to confess to Adama that he's a Cylon. He's been knowing it, he's been holding on to it, and we were supposed to write that. I, not having an experience in my life of having to confess to somebody that I'm a Cylon, a killer robot, really was intimidated by writing that scene. So at first we tried to skip over it in the draft. We had Tigh go, "Bill, there's something I've got to tell you." Then we cut away to another story and come back and Adama's slapping him across the face and calling him a Cylon and dah, dah, dah. Ron read the draft, he goes, "No, I want to see him tell Adama."

I didn't know how the fuck to write that. It seems silly, right? Like, how do you write the dialogue in a way that's not silly or weird? So in desperation, I followed Mark Verheiden to his car; he was going home. I go, "I just don't know what to do with this scene." Mark came up with the idea of Adama first trying to not take it in, saying, "They did something to you. They put an implant into you. Let's go to the doctor. We'll get you checked out." And Tigh goes, "No, I'm telling you, I'm a Cylon." That was a good piece, something I could grab on to. Then I ran to Michael Taylor's office to talk about it some more, and he goes, "Maybe Tigh could say, 'I lied to you. I lied to you, because I didn't know how to tell you. I didn't know what you'd think.'" That was another great little element to the scene that he added.

Having those elements, suddenly I could write the scene, because you could give it a build, Adama's denial, Tigh's forcefully making him face the truth, and then Adama's breakdown, which was what was so amazing about writing for Eddie Olmos, who never had notes on any script of mine. He might have notes on the set, or talk to you about how he's going to do it. Instead of airlocking Tigh, he can't do it because it's his best friend. He can't do it. Instead he breaks down. He punches the mirror. He becomes a blubbering mess on the floor, and Edward James Olmos showed up on the set and just said, "Ah, another great day with Adama." So we rolled the cameras and he did it. I have so many stars that I could tell you would never, ever in a million years do that. "What, I'm weak? I break down? I can't do it." You know?

EDWARD JAMES OLMOS
(actor, "Commander William 'Bill' Adama")

There was an incredible amount of courage and real security by everybody. The writers, the actors, the directors. Everybody had a secure feeling about what we were doing. So much so that you could explore situations that were not even really brought out. You'd go there, and you'd touch it, and you'd go, "Whoa, that's crazy. That's good." One of the situations was Admiral Adama taking pills and lying on the ground, then throwing up and he just became a mush. Here's our hero and, you know, he became nothing. That wasn't really written. I took him there and I said, "This is going to be the most difficult situation for all who love Adama; it's going to be heartbreaking to see him groveling on the ground, throwing up and the whole thing." I remember when I did, the producers didn't know I'd shot that. I was in the bathroom painting the thing, and I had learned that my son had been killed by Starbuck, and my best friend was a Cylon.

It was over. As far as I'm concerned, I gave up. How many times do you ever see Kirk give up? Never. How many times have you ever seen your hero give up? We all felt it when we saw him. I remember getting the phone messages from military leaders who thanked me for bringing about the understanding of how difficult it was. How they could not take it. They had never been able to see themselves the way that they really were until they saw themselves in me. They saw that what I was doing, they had done. They had broken down, but kept it quiet. They didn't let anybody know that they were having a nervous breakdown, because they were the heads of the military. That took courage on behalf of the producers, and especially the writing team, because they augmented it. They said, "Let's really go there." So they let me completely destroy Adama.

BRADLEY THOMPSON

Adama has to be able to accept the enemy that he has fought all his life as essentially his equal, so to speak. He had to go through the death of his son. He had to go through the fact that his favorite girl caused the death of his son. We just kept hitting him. His best friend was his deepest enemy. All those things. The guy had to learn to accept a lot of shit.

DAVID WEDDLE

In "Sometimes a Great Notion," Adama is nudging Tigh into shooting him, wanting to die over Dualla's body in season four and Lee saying, "Why would she do this?" The first couple of drafts I wanted Adama to try to explain it, and Ron said, "Maybe he just doesn't know." So I finally put in this thing where he's getting drunk and he looks at Lee and goes, "I don't fucking know." Olmos just played that so fearlessly, so great. You could see Lee looking at his dad and feeling put off and let down. Those were great experiences in terms of writing, but I wanted to tell you about that one, about Tigh's confession, because it shows you how a writing team helps each other. You know, if you didn't know how to do something, you run into another writer's office and you go, "I don't know what to do with this scene." Through talking it through, you come up with a solution together. When you have a great staff of people, it's like a great jazz band, and that was the best staff I've ever worked with, those people.

MARK VERHEIDEN

The Cylon reveal that was the hardest was Colonel Tigh, but, boy, he did such an amazing job with that. A great actor. His own horror at realizing that's what he was, then having to turn that around somehow. And Adama's reaction, which, again, was hard, sick, and fraught with potential violence. That was fun stuff to work on. When we got toward the fourth season and it's revealed that Anders is one of the Cylons, and we get into the ending where he's a Hybrid and been put into this tub, it was a game performance in a very difficult situation. My feeling on Anders was, he just again gave us a guy with a lot of strengths who, when you reveal that he's a Cylon, is also forced to deal with how did this happen to my life? How did everything get turned upside down? He was able to play that really well.

MICHAEL TRUCCO

I was in a car accident! We had finished midseason four and the writers went out on strike. We didn't even know if things would be continuing. So I was back home in L.A. on a Sunday morning at about ten thirty. I was in a car with my agent at the time, and we were going to a car show in Thousand Oaks. We were in his Ferrari and he was taking the scenic route up to Cayman Road, up to North Park Highway, and he fucked up and we went across the road, the car flipped and I broke my neck in three places. I was airlifted to a hospital where they rebuilt me. It should've killed me, or at the very least I should have been in a wheelchair, breathing into a tube, but I got lucky. In truth, I was lucky across the board, because not only did I live, not only was I *not* paralyzed, but the writers' strike made the show go dark for four months and my recovery was four months. In that way it could not have worked out better; they would have had to have written me out.

There was a scene where Anders was jumped; they put a hood over my head and then I end up getting shot in the back of the neck. Then Starbuck's cradling me and that's what put me in the hospital. They had to shave my head, and that storyline was, I believe, informed by my physical condition. They were like, "Well, what are we going to do with him?" That led to him becoming a Hybrid and I got in the tank with all that goo and started speaking gibberish. I didn't see *that* coming. Six months earlier I was pretty sure that if the show was going to be coming to an end that Anders would be one of the guys out there, guns blazing, but because of insurance they were like, "Get in the goo and shut up" [*laughs*]. And by the way, a little footnote: That was a bald cap that they put on for the last four or five weeks of filming. What a pain in the ass that was; had I known, in retrospect I just would've shaved my head. It would have been a lot easier.

Before the reveal of the four Cylons, there was the even more audacious death (or, more accurately, apparent death) of Starbuck in the episode "Maelstrom," as well as the trial of Gaius Baltar, in which veteran character actor Mark Sheppard (who was interviewed for this book at length and, in true Lampkin form, subsequently asked not to have it included) played the sleazy, cynical, but brilliant Romo Lampkin, who put *Star Trek*'s Samuel Cogley to shame.

RONALD D. MOORE

It was interesting to play a lawyer character like that, and a different way to go in the series. We didn't have anyone in that profession and we didn't really have people, other than court-martial scenes, where we had done the sergeant major and stuff in the first season. There was something fun about this lawyer in this context. "What does a lawyer do in the Colonial fleet at this point?" It was a great question and kind of funny. It was great to imbue him with the smarts and the cynicism of the character. The episode where he's carrying around the dead cat in his briefcase. That went through so many changes and revisions. We struggled with it, the network didn't like it, and we went back and forth on it, and I can't remember who wrote that, if it was Mike Angeli or Michael Taylor. I think I might've been the one that made it the dead cat in some moment.

I'm not sure if anyone grasped what I was quite going for, but I liked the idea of him hauling around this cat as an expression of his internal guilt. There was something I liked in that it was such a broken character, psychologically, that he was still attached to it. He was still attached to things that had happened back in the colonies, during the original attack. I thought that was great, too. I liked that we had someone on board, who still hadn't left the attack in some proud way; that had never moved beyond that moment for some crazy reason. Even after all the things, all these people and these four years, the basic psychological wound of the original attack was still unhealed for the vast majority of these people. I thought there was something great to dramatize that in this one man.

JAMES CALLIS

During the trial, there was lot of it that I really didn't enjoy, because I'm Baltar and every time somebody looked at me and sneered at me, or whatever, it was personal as it can be. But you're acting, and when they say "Cut" you can all smile at each other a little bit. The people who were speaking against me in the trial, we were chatting beforehand. One of the things about the trial was, and this is the really great thing, Baltar is not allowed to speak, for really the first time in the whole show. It's so good. You just don't hear him for a while. The very few things that I did speak, I ad-libbed in the sense that they weren't scripted, because I just wasn't supposed to say anything for the whole time. But I just couldn't resist in the moment of doing that thing that I really enjoyed, which was at a great moment of great importance and everybody's there to see, and there are people being astonishingly worthy, and there's somebody talking about something really petty. Something like, "You're a butterfingers." It's, like, "What? Is that your defense, you idiot? You tried to stab me through the neck and you missed." Like, "What the fuck are you doing? That's *so* stupid."

JAMIE BAMBER

For Lee there was a resentment attached to him still being in the uniform, and then obviously when the opportunity opens up for him to leave the uniform behind and go and do this other thing, and then he gets the big court sequence where he represents the person that he despises the most in the world. It represents something; he's discovered pragmatism. He discovers a side of himself that he's never been allowed to express before as a giver and follower of orders.

JAMES CALLIS

Jamie was very interested in the nature of the trial, and he had this thing of, "Well, let's really make it like a trial." The whole thing with the show was, "Well, we've got certain parameters, because it's television, so we've got to address this and we've got to finish like this, and there's only so long we've got." Jamie was like, "Well, then it's got to go into the next episode, but we need the two parts, because this is a wider thing and it's actually talking a lot about what we were talking about all the way through."

JAMIE BAMBER

When Lee calls everybody out and describes things as he sees them in the courtroom, it came from me, too. It was kind of an outpouring of the character who has been restrained and he's about to unshackle, and he's going to just let it rip. I felt very excited by that opportunity. I ended up asking Michael Rymer, the director, if I could write some of the speech and I used what Mark Verheiden had written and then expanded on it, and wrote it, and came up with a whole chunk of that.

You know, I can't think of any other American or British TV series where I would be allowed to do what I did that day. Michael said, "Go for it. Say whatever you have, don't tell me what it is now. I don't want to know. Just do your thing and I'll let you know if it worked or not." I'll never forget; we didn't really rehearse. I just said, "Okay, well, first time I'll do it . . ." and did it and then there was a big silence at the end. Michael said, "Cut!" and then the whole place just erupted. It was amazing. I look at it and in a tiny little way for me, as an actor who had some experience, but I wasn't hugely experienced at the time, it was a big risk for me to take with a set full of all the lead characters in the show and hundreds of extras, and it was a big expensive day. For Michael to let me do it, and then it stayed in. Every single line.

I felt the character needed it, because he had been tight-lipped and he had explosions, but basically he was repressed. By the situation, by his own idea of what you do in a situation, by his dad's expectations. There was more to him and I always felt that. I know Ron said they had struggled with him, and I struggled with the writers together. I think the virtue of the character was the pressure cooker. It was the fact that he was under a lot of pressure and he doesn't necessarily need to vent, but vent we did in the end. That scene was cathartic.

JAMES CALLIS

Mark Sheppard's another genius. Lovely guy and a brilliant actor. Coming into a show that's already on and you've been doing it for a while, you've got to find your feet for a few days, or it can be a bit intimidating. We didn't have any of that with Mark. He was right at home from the first moment. He's quite in-your-face in that way as Romo Lampkin, but in real life he's very softly spoken, very thoughtful. It was always a very interesting difference when they said "Cut!" and Mark would become Mark.

JAMIE BAMBER

Mark's a great friend and he came in to steal the show, there's no doubt about it. He would say jokingly, but not jokingly, "It's all about me." He was disarmingly charming. He came up to all of us and said, "Look, I love this show, it's the best show on television. You guys are so lucky you've been doing this show," but he came with intent and we loved that. We loved it when people came with all their game, and he certainly did. I loved working with him; he was a new, fresh energy, which is needed in shows like that from time to time. Just to react to something new.

RONALD D. MOORE

Lee played really well with Romo; it was one of the reasons we used Romo as much as we did. We got a lot of juice out of those scenes, and it felt like it was bringing the Lee character to life as well.

TODD SHARP

When Mark Sheppard first appeared on the show, there was some magic there. The writers knew to write more to that magic. And someone like him and the character of Romo Lampkin are the little discoveries along the way. I mean, look, through all of the planning that Ron did and for all the vision that he had, and he did—he knew where this series lived and where it was going. But even then, there were all sort of discoveries along the way. This character was one of them.

JAMIE BAMBER

All you ask for as an actor is someone to bring it all and say, "Let's get it on." The scenes between me, James Callis, and Mark were great fun, and we were all on it. It was cool.

In the end, Baltar was acquitted of the charges against him, Starbuck died and miraculously returned, claiming that she had found the way to Earth; and there was still some question as to whether or not year four would be *Battlestar Galactica's* last on the air.

RONALD D. MOORE

Sometime after the wrap of the show, when we started thinking about year four, was when I started feeling like this was it. It just had this sense that we'd entered the third act of the story. We had revealed four of the five Cylons. We also had Starbuck coming back and saying she knew the way to Earth, and it just felt like we had moved the story so far forward that I didn't feel like it could sustain going much further than another season.

DAVID EICK

In a way, the decision to end the show goes back to what we were doing in the first year. You know, there's a version of *Battlestar* that's still on. If we had done it in a particular kind of way—and I don't mean without any mythological kind of invention, but if it had been built more like a traditional space opera—who's to say *that* show's not still on TV? That's not the best version of the show. I'm not arguing that I wish that that's the version of the show we had done. But that version of the show was possible, and it would have been more like a *Star Trek*–type show that went on and on. Adama retires, Lee takes over; Baltar gets killed, you bring on his son. All of that shit, right? You could've totally done it, year after year after year.

But really I think what happened after the end of season three were a couple of things. One, we realized the show was never going to be that. If we know it's not going to be that, and we know that we continue to fight with the network about fundamental things—not blisteringly, but it's an ongoing struggle. We know the ratings have been slipping. And what we *don't* want is to have a situation where we're *told* the show is off the air, because then who's to say we're in a position to end it the way we want? Who's to say *when* that decision comes, so why don't we just call a spade a spade here? The show's run its course; it's never going to be the ten-year or twelve-year *Star Trek*–ian type of show, so let's end it now. And that's what we decided to do.

RONALD D. MOORE

I talked to David Eick and we called the network and said, "We think the next season is it." They were surprised, but they didn't really try to talk us out of it. That was because of the ratings. The truth is, they didn't spend that much on the show, so it really wasn't that expensive a show.

MARK STERN

One of my laments about the show, and I'm sure David and Ron feel the same way, is I felt like it was just before its time in terms of the world we're in now. Today the audience is so immersed in this kind of serialized storytelling, but it was never a huge hit for Sci-Fi, but it was a solid performer for us. It was a huge critical hit and a huge hit within the network. It really did put us on the map and set the stage for us in terms of what we were trying to accomplish. So we were disappointed when Ron and David called us and said they were going to end it. Which was a weird conversation to have. I've *never* had anyone cancel their own show before. Seriously.

DAVID EICK

They were shocked, but it was tempered a bit by their acknowledgment that the numbers were slipping, so it wasn't a hundred percent shock, but deep shock. It was not what they were expecting to hear at all.

MARK STERN

The first response to them wanting to cancel the show is tremendous respect. You know, to go out when you want to go out. And in the way you want to go out. But it was definitely weird and disappointing. When they came to us, it was still in the middle of the run and the show was still clearly creatively hitting its stride. It's a different situation if a series is starting to tread water, which that show clearly wasn't.

DAVID EICK

I think if they felt strongly that we underestimated the longevity, or the ratings, or any potential of it, they might have tried to continue it without us. But we already knew that they were probably going to see some core value in ending it. Remember, if the creators are ending it on their own terms, that creates tremendous promotional value for them, because they can promote the end of the show as "Three more . . . two more . . . One more. . . ." You do all that, and there's an upside. The downside is we're not going to have a season after this one, but they looked at the ratings and the nature of the show had narrowed, which I'm sure in no small part had to do with what was going on with the ratings.

RONALD D. MOORE

They were a network that didn't really want to be in the space business anymore. The show was sort of flying in the face of everything else they wanted to do as a network. They wanted to stop doing space science fiction, they didn't want to do dark stuff, they didn't like that it was on and on and on. But it got all this critical acclaim and it had a passionate following and all that. But the ratings were sort of on the bubble. The ratings were not the best. The ratings were always a little sketchy. As I've said, at that point the industry didn't care about DVR numbers.

There was a point where David Weddle and Bradley Thompson went in for a development meeting at Sci-Fi while the show was on the air, and they told them, "You know, we're still proud of *Battlestar Galactica*. It's an amazing series and an incredible thing you guys have done . . . and we're never going to do a show like that ever again" [*laughs*]. They were sort of really taken aback, because that was the opening statement. Now, of course, they're always saying they're looking for the next *Galactica*.

DAVID WEDDLE

One slight clarification: Sci-Fi didn't say that they did not want to do science fiction. They said they did not want to do complex, dark, intricately plotted science fiction, with layered characters that were deeply flawed. They wanted simple, straightforward science fiction that would be light in tone, wholesome, and simple to follow. Bradley Thompson said to them, "Oh, so you want the kind of shows where people can walk out of the living room, go to the refrigerator and get some ice cream, come back to the living room and still be able to follow the plot." They said, "Exactly." Consequently, Brad and I never pitched them a pilot.

16.
THE RAZOR'S EDGE

"Sometimes you have to roll the hard six."

The fourth season of *Battlestar Galactica* debuted with the two-part "Razor," which in itself had actually been a made-for-DVD film later aired on Sci-Fi Channel (the show's continued success on home video had helped sustain the series despite less than stellar ratings on the cable network). Told through a number of flashbacks combined with footage from previous episodes, it serves as a prequel to season two's "Pegasus" storyline, chronicling Admiral Cain's response to the Cylon attack that wipes out most of her people, and her transformation into a ruthless military leader. In the present, Lee Adama, serving as the Pegasus's executive officer, has to come to grips with Cain's legacy.

RONALD D. MOORE
(cocreator/executive producer, *Battlestar Galactica* [2004])

Home video saw an opportunity to sell *Razor* as a DVD, because DVD sales were very strong on the show and this was at a point when DVD was very big. In fact, DVD sales were propelling a lot of the revenue and there was also an international play to make it as a two-hour movie. So it kind of came out of Universal Home Video wanting this and then Sci-Fi Channel seeing that there was a market for a two-hour version as well, so both of them came to us and said, "Look, we're interested in doing a two-hour movie. Would you guys be interested in doing it and what would it be?" I threw it to the writers' room right off the bat and asked, "What do you guys think? What possible story could we do?" It was tricky, because it had to be part of the show, but it couldn't be just two episodes put together. It wasn't going to be part of the actual season; it had to be kind of a standalone, which meant it couldn't really be part of the strongly serialized story that we were telling.

So that took a bit of thinking, and ultimately we go to the story of *Razor*, because everyone really liked Admiral Cain, and she had been such a great character. We somewhat regretted killing her off, even though we *had* to kill her off. We couldn't keep that character in the show without fundamentally changing the show. But everyone missed her. She was just so great and there were great stories to tell with her. So the idea came up of, "Why don't we tell the story of the battlestar *Pegasus* and what it was before it got to the *Galactica*?" Everyone kind of got excited about that. Plus we had the sets, so they could be used and it kind of went from there.

Writer Michael Taylor, another veteran of *Deep Space Nine* and *Voyager,* who had joined the show in season three, was chosen to write the script for the film, which, it turns out, was actually inspired by the film *Patton,* which had starred George C. Scott as the military general.

MICHAEL TAYLOR

Ron and David came to me between the third and fourth seasons and asked if I wanted to do a movie. It was a wonderful experience trying to find a story that could bridge the gap and also a chance to sort of, for me, hark back to the original series, which I watched back in my college years—I'm *that* fucking old. You see the old Cylon Raiders and the old Cylons, and I thought it was really cool. I got to write a movie and it was a movie; they actually showed it in theaters as a promotional stunt.

RONALD D. MOORE

There's a scene early in *Patton* where he's just taken command in North Africa and the command is a mess. The soldiers aren't looking like soldiers. They just got defeated by the Germans and there's a moment in there where Patton says, "I'm gonna turn them into razors." The phrase kind of struck me, something about turning them into razors. So I said that to Michael as we were talking about Admiral Cain, and she was based in part on Patton. Back in the original series, Patton was definitely a strong influence on the way they did the original *Pegasus* storyline, so all of those connections are there. Then it became, all right, let's talk about her as a literal razor and talk about what her backstory was, tying it into the Cylons and the first Cylon war. It was a pretty in-depth conversation in mythology. It was a lot of fun. It was just a really interesting story. It was great to see a battlestar run in a completely different way than *Galactica*, by a different commander.

FELIX ALCALA
(director, "Razor")

There's a scene where the *Pegasus* crew invades a civilian ship to loot their supplies and equipment for the war and one lady says, "You can't do that." Our lead gal comes over, makes her get on her knees, and executes her. What I remember is the Vietnam War and that famous photograph of the general shooting the guy in the head. We literally duplicated that shot. We said, "Literally, let's do that moment in time when this guy looks around and very casually reaches over and, boom, kills this woman." And she did. It was really great.

RONALD D. MOORE

In addition to getting into who Cain really is, we wanted to get a sense of who Gina—Tricia Helfer's Cylon—was as well. I remember Michelle Forbes calling me up at one point after she had gotten the script and her saying, "Talk to me a little bit about this lesbian thing with Gina and what that's about." I said, "Here's the deal. I'm not trying to do it for a salacious way or to make it just sort of shocking." I was looking for a reason for why she acted. Her reaction to this woman when we met her in the original episodes was so strong and she had taken *such* strong security measures, that there was a sense of betrayal in it. And there were references, too, that Gina wasn't just some person. That she was someone pretty important. And I thought to understand the viciousness of what happened, and the sadism of it, and the profound *anger* of it, it felt like there had to be a relationship there. That this was something else. This was like a personal betrayal as opposed to a military one. Then Michelle was aboard. It came from a character point of view and made sense in the story.

With the *Razor* telefilm being written by Michael Taylor, it fell to Moore and Eick and the rest of the writers' room to engineer a satisfying final season for the series, a goal that eluded many other high-profile shows of that era.

DAVID EICK

(executive producer, *Battlestar Galactica* [2004])

It's really important to note that we met in Vegas before we opened the writers' room for season four, and we agreed on a few things that the season was going to accomplish. The first thing we agreed on was that it was going to be the end. So the show *wasn't* being canceled, we were canceling it. So when you know you're going to end something, that's more definitive. There's less wiggle room. You're less inclined to say, "Oh, yeah, it could go five different ways." No, man, it really can only go *this* fucking way. It *really* can only go this way, and Ron and I definitely had some disagreements about it. So just the nature of ending a show is narrower and has less wiggle room. Also, at the time I had sold another show and was being pulled away for other reasons. It just seemed more reasonable to defer to Ron. I know he appreciated it, but I don't mean to say I abdicated or bailed. I absolutely own and stand by all the decisions of season four, despite the fact that I know some of them were controversial.

RONALD D. MOORE

Then, going into season four, it was a very different kind of game, because we set out to say, "Okay, this is the last season. This is what we're gonna do. Let's map out the whole thing." We took a writers' retreat to Vegas. Took all the writers there for a couple of days, rented a big conference room at the hotel, and did a couple of all-day sessions where we just talked, overall, on the whole story. We went through just a lot of big-picture "Okay, where's the show going? What is the meaning of . . . What's it all about? Where are we ending up?" I had said over the past couple of years that I thought the show was taking place in the distant past, as opposed to the distant future, or having anything to do with today. So I sort of started leaning in that direction over the course of the series, and so now it was time to say, "Okay. I really think that when they get to Earth, it's probably the distant past, and we're gonna get there . . ."

And then we talked briefly about all the various scenarios. Do we get there during the time of the Egyptians and tie it into the original series in some way like that? Are we getting there . . . What period? And we kind of started moving toward even further into the distant past. It felt too cute to do the Egyptian thing. And also, *Stargate* was very strongly associated with that. So we kind of had at least as a marker that we were gonna get to Earth a long, long time ago, and I also liked the idea that in some way, shape, or form, our characters were the ancestors of us today. I wanted that to be the thread that tied the audience to the characters and the revelation that they were related to us. That was kind of the beginning of a lot of conversations.

DAVID EICK

The point of conflict, not necessarily between me and Ron but between the fans and the show, oftentimes boiled down to people who were fans of the deeper, more esoteric kind of ambiguous mythology versus fans of family Adama and the interactions of characters. It's not that they were mutually exclusive, but the episodes that leaned more toward that deeper mythology or more ambiguity, in my opinion felt less satisfying. Any difference that had to do with how many of those kinds of episodes are we going to do versus the other kinds of episodes was the rub. If left to my own devices, I guess the show might have maintained the mythological aspects at a greater distance than perhaps was Ron's taste, to allow it to more sort of carry the show in the fourth season.

RONALD D. MOORE

The writers' room and I were looking for something new in the show. There was always a search for, "How are we moving the show forward?" I don't think we were ever really satisfied with where the show was. It was always about, "What's the next thing? How can we move the storyline? Let's do something bold, let's go into this other direction." And there was this natural progression. Once Baltar ends up on that Cylon basestar, then you're going to start telling Cylon stories. You're going to start opening up that world, and that's how the Final Five were born and all of that. But once you start moving into that head space, and we started talking about it in the writers' room, all these possibilities started opening up. You're like, "Well, the Cylons, they could be like this, they could be like that."

At the same time, and on a parallel track, we had lost touch with the underlying mythology of the series. The beginning of the series has to do with the lost planet called Earth, the sacred scroll, the prophecies, and there was this mysticism and stuff that had been there all along, but we hadn't really stayed on it. And it felt like we should go back to that and try to embrace that part of the show. Our view was, "Let's bring that to the fore-front and stretch, let's not just keep doing the same war story all over again." Because it felt like we had done that. We had done this pretty solid, great war story, then we got to New Caprica and had gone through this traumatic story of the occupation and resistance and the escape, and it didn't feel satisfying to any of us to just start doing the old show. It felt like doing the old show again—not the original show, but our old show.

But there was a part of David that argued, in fairness, "But that's part of the great thing of the show. Some of our best episodes, and the audience loves that, and I love that. Let's get back into doing shows like 'Hand of God,' and let's do some of those big things and do character stuff like that." As a group we felt, "Been there, done that. Time to try something different. Time to push the boundaries." Okay, we're a show that's dealing with religion and God, and doing these sort of existential ideas. Let's lean into that. Let's see what we can find in that, let's do something that science fiction typically shies away from. Let's see what's out there for us in that direction." And that's why we did it.

As things continue, the fleet is outgunned and on the brink of annihilation. Anders flies into the fray, but finds himself unable to fire at the Cylon ships. One of the Cylon Raiders scans Anders's eye, recognizes him as a Final Five Cylon, and retreats to the basestar. Unable to continue the attack, Cavil's forces jump away. Roslin and Adama are both wary of Starbuck's sudden reappearance, especially since her path to Earth doesn't coincide with Pythia's. Adama decides to take his chance on both women and gives Starbuck command of Demetrius, a sewage-recycling freighter. She takes a small crew and heads out on a path to Earth.

Cavil is enraged by the Raiders' apparent free will. The Cylons hold a vote—should we lobotomize the Raiders and remove their ability to make high-level decisions? The vote is deadlocked until a single Sharon—Boomer—casts the deciding vote: lobotomize them. Natalie, a copy of Number Six, responds by giving the Centurions even greater self-awareness. Their first action is to kill all of the Cavil, Doral, and Simon models on the basestar. In response, Cavil lures the Sixes, Sharons, and Leobens out of resurrection range and opens fire.

On the Galactica, Baltar's manifesto (essentially his views of the universe and all that he has undergone) has given him a large following. His sermons about the Cylon God attract Tory's attention, and she is soon one of his devotees. Her true beliefs are clouded, however, by her new Cylon identity. When Cally learns Tyrol's secret, Tory kills her and makes it look like a suicide. Soon after, the Baltarites attract the ire of the Sons of Ares, a militant polytheist group, leading to a vicious attack. Lee, now a member of the Quorum, uses the opportunity to confront Roslin about her controversial political decisions, including a measure meant to shut down Baltar's "sex cult." Roslin, now in full treatment for her breast cancer, is frustrated with Lee for taking the high road instead of the smart road.

Starbuck's mission takes a disturbing turn when they find a Leoben stranded in space. She agrees to follow him back to his basestar, where he claims the Hybrid will show her the way to Earth. That is not a popular decision among *Demetrius*'s crew, forcing Anders to shoot Gaeta in the leg to prevent a mutiny. Kara takes a small team to the basestar and meets with the Hybrid, who tells her that she's the harbinger of death before spouting a cryptic message about the Dying Leader. They use the Raptor's computer to jump the basestar back to *Demetrius*, but they arrive too late and Gaeta's leg will have to be amputated.

The basestar jumps back to the Colonial fleet, putting the entire population on edge. The Cylons are embroiled in a vicious civil war, and the Sixes, Sharons, and Leobens are losing. They want to reunite the Cylons with the Final Five, and they need *Galactica*'s help to accomplish that mission. In exchange, they'll help destroy the Resurrection Hub, the central server required for Cylon resurrection. Without it, Cylons would be mortal. Starbuck repeats the Hybrid's "Dying Leader" babble to Roslin, who goes to the basestar to hear it for herself. At the same moment, Athena has an Opera House vision (like the ones she has been sharing with Caprica Six and Roslin) wherein Hera is kidnapped by Six. Athena finds Natalie (a Six) hovering over Hera, her worst nightmare come to life. She shoots Natalie, killing her, prompting the basestar to jump away with Roslin, Baltar, and half of *Galactica*'s air wing aboard.

Adama is distraught over Roslin's disappearance. The Colonial government is in shambles, with no clear line of succession. Everyone knows that Adama will not accept Tom Zarek as the new president. An emergency vote names Lee Adama the new president of the colonies, but it's a bitter victory. His father decides to stay behind in a Raptor and wait for Laura's return . . . even if that return never comes.

Meanwhile, the basestar jumps toward the Resurrection Hub. Once they reach it, they plan to resurrect D'Anna (who knows the identities of the Five) and then annihilate resurrection forever. Their mission is successful, and they begin jumping back to the *Galactica*. On the journey, Roslin tends to a wounded Baltar, who finally admits to his role in the fall of the Twelve Colonies. Roslin has a vision of the priestess Elosha, who tells her that to lead humanity to salvation, she has to be able to love. Despite everything he's done, Roslin forgives Baltar.

Once the basestar reaches the fleet, D'Anna takes control of the situation and holds Roslin and the air wing hostage until the Final Five surrender themselves. Tory willingly joins the Cylons, with the excuse that Laura needs her medications. To break the stalemate, Tigh admits to Adama that he's a Cylon. Adama is devastated, and leaves Lee in command. Lee threatens to launch Tigh out an airlock, but D'Anna is ready to call his bluff. Simultaneously, Tyrol and Anders begin hearing the same haunting melody that activated them. They're able to localize the source—Starbuck's pristine Viper. Tyrol and Anders are thrown into the airlock with Tigh, but Starbuck stops Lee from executing them. There's a signal coming through her Viper's emergency radio. Humans and Cylons converge on the Viper, and both sides agree that it is pointing them toward Earth. They decide to travel there together.

JAMES CALLIS
(actor, "Gaius Baltar")

When I think about that storyline—that Baltar cult, as it were—I find myself thinking of a few things and they all come out at the same time. One is that things are made for television. This is something that we spoke about while we were doing the show, and had we had, I suppose, more years or longer to tell the story. We could have done more. Some episodes are so multipacked, I used to think, "My God, just one of these elements could be an episode, really, and then I could have four more episodes." One of the discussions we had was that prophecy takes thousands of years to come true. When we look at the history of our own planet and see the clues that have been left—for example, fossils—and decipher that information by carbon dating it, the things that we find out that were important were millions of years in the making. So there's a certain aspect of television that these things need to happen a bit quicker, because otherwise what are we going to do?

I don't know how many episodes there were that particular season, or how many more there could have been, but you may have had some episodes where Baltar disappears for a couple of shows, and you see him picked up, you see the journey toward this place. On some level it makes perhaps more organic sense. Totally opposite to that, look at the real world. The chance of somebody today beating a trial and having some dreadful things said against them, but beating that and winning out, and *then* becoming leader of a cult is possibly *not* so unusual.

BRADLEY THOMPSON
(producer, *Battlestar Galactica* [2004])

One of my favorite things I ever saw in the dailies was when James Callis comes down and they've rescued him, his cult. He comes in and he sees that big altar of Baltar. There are takes in there that are just astounding. Of course, you didn't get to see all of them like we did. It was just such a wonderful moment, there was this thing where James is going, "Really? Really? This is everything I ever wanted, but really these guys are nuts." What is it to be admired by all of these people? In one way this guy deserves a bullet, but then one of the most annoying things to do is make him a god. There's a certain perversity of "Can we take the audience on this ride, too?" Everyone knows he did all this, despite his rationalizations. It's just, like, "All I want to do is get laid and get a lot of money." All his goals are human goals. They're not "I am the embodiment of evil." It's more like, "I just wanted to do this and it seemed like a good thing to do at the time. I'm kind of a little bit of a sociopath in the sense that I'm not really thinking about how it's going to affect other people."

JAMES CALLIS

So I think the powers that be needed to have him in the mix. I remember when the idea had come up, that Baltar was basically going to be abducted after the trial, it was, like, *who* was going to abduct him. They didn't want it to be some terrorist or fringe unit, because that would mean putting it on another ship, and that would mean building another set, etc. So then they were like, "Let's think of something very unusual. Like, you think these people are out to kill him, but . . ." I remembered then about so many people who might be in prison for the one offense or another, sometimes dreadful offenses, and they're developing a kind of cult. There are some women who fall in love with this particular person.

So it was this idea that through the trial, there had been a silent minority of people who were following him and wanted him and felt like he had something to give them. We tried to have as much fun with that as possible, in the sense of that thing of, "Do as I say, don't do as I do." Sending out some spiritual message, being very venal, I think the word is in real life. I suppose there was a transformation in there somewhere, where Baltar is beaten to bits in front of Lee and starts saying, "The Lord loves you as you are . . ." I'm not sure how long he remembers that.

BRADLEY THOMPSON

What could we load on him that would just spin his head around? He thinks he wants that. Then you give it to him and it's, like, "Do I *really* want that?" Because here it is, Gaius Baltar. You wanted all this from back on Caprica and now you've got it. Now it's in the bowels of the ship. You just barely got out with your life from the whole thing. The Adamas saved you. It's just nuts that we could go there. Obviously it's entertaining, too. It's like, "What do you do when you put this guy in this cult with all these people?" Again, this isn't the National Society of Scientists saying, "You're wonderful." This is a bunch of whack jobs.

The cult of Baltar was about as "light" as things would get in season four as the show pushed itself, the story, and the characters toward their collective resolution.

MARK VERHEIDEN

Basically season four is the fleet is coming apart, both emotionally because of the realization that we're going to have to make a deal with the Cylons, and that we had Cylons in command positions inside of the fleet all this time. And infrastructure-wise, we're running out of everything. The ship is starting to crack down the middle.

DAVID WEDDLE
(producer, *Battlestar Galactica* [2004])

In the end, a faction of the Cylons rebelled and joined our side and it made them complicated and it really made a statement about war. You dehumanize your enemy, and usually in that process of dehumanization, you do that so you can feel okay about killing them. And, really, it's a fiction. It's a fiction that we create so that we can come to terms with killing fellow human beings. So by gradually revealing the human elements in the Cylons and opening questions about, "Well, are they really that different from us? Are they really just machines or are they a legitimate life-form?," it made all the issues and the drama more complex, and complicated it, and so it was great. I'm glad that we did it. Initially we were reluctant to do it. But in the end, it's a group of Cylons and humans that find Earth, and it's a hybrid child— Hera, the child of Helo and Sharon—that becomes the Eve of the human race. Which is all pretty amazing stuff.

BRADLEY THOMPSON

That's an old science fiction trope. This goes back to *Star Trek* when the emotion grabber has taken over the *Enterprise* and Kirk and the Klingon leader are beating each other up [in "Day of the Dove"]. Then they realize that this enemy is feeding on their anger. They're never going to get rid of it as long as they're shooting at one another, so they have to make nice. We're all humans even though we've got differences. Well, if we all are the same, do we have the same principles? Or at least can we unite for survival? In history, we have done that, deciding to align with Stalin against Hitler. It's, like, "Okay, we'll do this, solve that problem. Then we'll go back to the problems we had with each other."

TRICIA HELFER
(actress, "Number Six")

It's interesting that you think the humans are going to be the ones to logically and philosophically deal with everything, but, no, there are two sides to it. Two sides between you and your enemy. If you only see your enemy as a certain way, you're not taking full advantage of their abilities. You're not understanding them fully.

DAVID EICK

There was some talk that this was an allegory to what's gone on in Iraq. It was half and half. We're news junkies and history junkies, so there was always an initiative to inform the work with current events and sociopolitical realities, and an allegory for our times. But what was interesting was to take what audiences would expect . . . you say, "Okay, we're going to do a metaphor for our own reality, therefore the good guys are going to be the Americans and the bad guys are going to be the Iraqis."

Instead, we had the good guys be the polytheists, who were suicide bombing, and the bad guys be the monotheists, who were trying to orchestrate some sort of a détente with the humans.

And that is when it became interesting. In a way it freed us from the need to feel like we were Dick Wolf on *Law & Order*, ripping the headlines from *The New York Times* and saying, "Let's do this episode." That was never really the approach. It was really based on story, based on character first, and sort of the continuation of whatever story arc we'd established and whatever cultural or political sort of world relationship the stories had was subtle and tangential. It was sort of a delicate influence as opposed to a deliberate adaptation.

MARK VERHEIDEN

Another part of them working together concerned the *Galactica* itself. I'm kind of a nut about infrastructure, and playing with those ideas in context of a science fiction world, so I always want to know, where is the food coming from? Who's making the oxygen for you? Who is creating the booze? We had an episode where they start discovering giant cracks in the hull of *Galactica*. It's starting to give. It just won't last any longer. Well, that is *exactly* what would happen to a ship that's been battered by all these battles, and has been pressurized for how many years. Again, playing with the idea of the reality of this just can't go on, because, frankly, it's just going to fall apart at some point. It will not hold. It's just a piece of machinery. I loved the detail that once we discovered there was a crack down the middle of *Galactica*, we didn't just say, "Oh, they fixed it." Or, "They welded it, now it's better." We played that. It's, like, "No, it's getting worse." And then we ended up using Cylon technology to help with repairs. Now they're *saving* us. Season four got *very* interesting.

RONALD D. MOORE

That was a big deal for us, because we're four seasons in and we're aware that this is the third act. Everything in fourth season is with an eye toward the endgame. I said, "Let's start developing cracks in the *Galactica*. The show is going to die, the *Galactica* is going to die." The ship was symbolic of the show, so the *Galactica*'s on her last legs. She can't last much longer. What else does the old girl still have in her? So we were using that metaphorically in the show. And then Adama, being the one most married to the ship, would care the most, and it would be the hardest for him of all the characters to accept Cylon help and technology on that ship.

One of the very first scenes that he has in the entire show is his refusal to allow Laura to put networked computers on this ship. He laid that line down really early as a character. It was great to now be able to make him have to accept not just networked computers but Cylon technology on his ship, and what that would do to the man. We just really wanted to take him apart as best we could in that last run. To really challenge the hero of the show and break down the leader of the whole thing, which is, again, in the spirit of, "Let's do something different. Let's do something other shows don't do." The writers all went, "Yeah, let's go ahead. Nobody fucks with their hero. Nobody takes Picard apart."

DAVID EICK

Eddie so rarely would have notes on script or big things that he wanted to change. But I do remember how anxious and fervent he was about Adama's point of view about putting Cylon technology in the ship. It's Archie Bunker getting a blood transfusion from an African-American. We never would've hit it as hard as we did had he not been as vocal about it. I was worried it would be over-the-top, but Eddie was like, "No fucking way; I don't want those motherfuckers anywhere near the ship"—you know, talking about it like they were Nazis and just the epitome of evil. So you sort of get it and you sense it'll be fun. And it was. It was fun playing him under such duress having to endure that. So that particular story point had a lot of Eddie Olmos in it.

RONALD D. MOORE

We wanted to take Adama to a really dark, bad place, and the same thing for his ship. Eddie was totally up for it. He's up for everything. But that's the thing, too: for Adama to suddenly be surrounded by his best friend, by these other people who he served with all these years, and they're Cylons, and he's been working with them. That's got to change his perception of Cylons in general.

MARK VERHEIDEN

There were several occasions where characters would reflect on where they were at and begin to wonder if there was a point to this; if there was any end to this. Adama certainly. I do remember Lee having thoughts like that. Even though Lee was in government at that time and was negotiating some of the deals, I guess for lack of a better word, with the Cylons, he still expressed doubt about whether or not this was the right move. He wasn't an avid supporter of let's make a deal with these guys but he realized it was the only way to survive, so he was holding his nose a bit while he was doing it. But he was as frustrated as anyone else, I think, that they were reduced to this or forced into this.

I don't remember the exact scene, but I know that sentiment certainly began even in season three. Certainly there were elements of it all through the show. You can almost put your finger on the beginning of the series with the competing military versus political faction, civilian faction, which is that whole, What are we? What do we hold on to to be the people that we were before? How much do we have to give up to just survive, and what does that leave us with? What are we when that happens? That certainly became stronger toward the end when everything's really coming down around their ears.

RONALD D. MOORE

We were taking the audience and the characters on this journey that was going from the genocide of the pilot to a place where they would actually have to work with and embrace some of their most profound enemies that you could possibly imagine. That was important to us; it was part of what the show was about. It was a redemptive quality to what we wanted to do that was a sense of compassion and understanding for that which you hate and that which you despise, and trying to be able to bridge that gap and get to that place. For the humans to accept the Cylons as people was the biggest journey. *That* was the big one, because that was always the line: "They're not people, they're copies, they're not true, they're not real, they don't have sentience, they're something that has been created to mimic us."

As season four moved toward its midpoint, there was a very real chance that the show could have ended with episode twelve, "Revelations," when the united humans and Cylons reach Earth, only to find that it's a burnt-out nuclear wasteland. Hollywood feared a similar fate when it became increasingly likely—and did come to pass—that the Writers Guild of America would be going out on strike that year.

RONALD D. MOORE

What I remember most is the strike landing right in the middle of our final season, and it was a big sort of shock. What stands out the most to me is I felt like I had to go up to Vancouver and talk to the crew on the eve of the strike, once it became clear that everyone was going out the next day. I flew up and back down the same day.

When I arrived, I had production get the whole cast and crew together, and they all assembled in the CIC, since it was the biggest space and the only place you could literally get the entire cast and crew together. Once they were all there, I walked in to CIC and there was the entire family, everyone in the round on both levels. I talked to them for ten to fifteen minutes, and I started off by saying that when Admiral Cain was being attacked in the original Cylon attack on Caprica, she did a blind jump and that's what we're all about to do here. We're just going to do a blind jump to somewhere. They all laughed. I said, "The writers are going out tomorrow and I'm going with them, and that means there aren't going to be any changed pages and the scripts you've got, that's going to be the script." I said that—I believe it was—Michael Rymer was directing, so he and Harvey Frand were in charge. I said, "The line of authority after this moment will go from God to Harvey Frand." Then I added, "And to be clear, there are no issues here about crossing picket lines. There's no picket line outside the gate to Vancouver Film Studios, so that's not what this is about. I'm not expecting people not to show up. I want you to show up and do your job . . . and get all the overtime you can get. . . . I trust you and hopefully this will all end soon and I'll see you after the jump."

I walked out and it was very emotional and people applauded and hugged and all that on the way out, then I got back on a plane and flew to L.A. and was on the picket line with the writing staff literally the next day. It was just surreal that the show was kind of going on without us. That was a weird moment in the whole thing.

GRACE PARK
(actress, "Sharon 'Boomer' Valerii")

Shooting that sequence on Earth was really eerie, because that really could have been the end of the series. It wasn't expected, but it wasn't just some random side episode about Tigh and Ellen getting drunk. It really could have been it. On top of that, Eddie told us it *was* the end. Years later I said to him, "It's the only thing that you'd said that didn't come true," and he said, "I had to tell you guys that to prepare you in case."

RONALD D. MOORE

You didn't *really* think that Sci-Fi was going to cancel the show, but you start talking about it more and worrying about it more. It was in the air. In retrospect, you look back and realize they probably wouldn't have canceled it unless the strike went on for a year or something. But at the time, it was the uncertainty of it all that was really a big deal.

MARY MCDONNELL
(actress, "President Laura Roslin")

I remember the day we shot that, because it was a very funny situation in that there we were in a nuclear wasteland, and we were sort of walking amongst the ruins and there was a big crane shot happening. Every time they said, "Cut!" all the actors pulled out their cell phones, because it was the beginning of the writers' strike and we were trying to figure out what we would do. Suddenly they'd be, "Okay, rolling," and everyone's phones would go away and there we would be again. But it just came to me that on that day on the set, when we were trying to figure out where we were on this planet, we were trying to simultaneously figure what the future of our industry was. The feeling was like, "Wait a minute, are we shooting our final scenes?" Everybody was calling their agents in between trying to get somebody to figure it out, because honestly no one knew. But it had this spooky kind of synchronistic life-as-art-is-life feeling, and that kind of stayed with me as my overall image.

JAMIE BAMBER
(actor, "Captain Lee 'Apollo' Adama")

That was definitely a false ending, where we thought it all might be taken away from us and we were never going to end this thing, because of the writers' strike. That night we celebrated like it was the end—I even stole my costume just in case. But, of course, we got a second life and we got to come back to get the perfect curtain call.

AARON DOUGLAS
(actor, "Chief Tyrol")

We shot that thing where we finally find Earth and it's a burned-out mess, and there's that long, slow panning tracking shot. I'm thinking in my head, how would Chief react to this? Every single person is devastated and they're shaking their head and they're looking at each other, and some of them are crying and stuff. I made the choice that I just stood there giggling to myself. Camera rolls past me and nobody said anything. A couple of days later I got a call from one of the writers and they said, "I can't tell you how much I loved that. It's the perfect Chief reaction." That reaction is, like, "Hey, we found Earth, and *of course* it's a fucking burnt-out shitshow and we can't live there." It's the great cosmic joke. *Of course* we're not going to be able to do the thing that we want to do. *Of course* it's just going to get worse and shittier. It got to the point where he expects this to happen. He's the worst-case-scenario guy—"the glass is half full" is just gone. The glass is empty, screw you guys. And then there's the decision toward the end there, too, where he just says in his last scene, "You know what? I've had enough of you guys and I'm going to an island off the northern continent and I'm going to call it Scotland and I'm going to build a castle, and I'm going to have sex with sheep and make Scotch. *That's* my plan."

RONALD D. MOORE

Eddie would have been very happy if that was the ending. His pitch for the last episode was we get to Earth, everyone is excited on the *Galactica*. You know, "We made it, we made it, we made it." And then, all of a sudden, you cut to the White House and in the Oval Office is George W. Bush and somebody comes in and says, "Mr. President, there's a spaceship in orbit," to which Bush replies, "Launch the nuclear missiles." They destroy them and that's it. *There's* a barn burner.

Two episodes into the second half of the fourth season, Moore wrote and made his directorial debut on the episode "A Disquiet Follows My Soul," which, among other things, takes a closer look at the growing human/Cylon alliance, and the dissent—flamed by Tom Zarek—that will soon lead to mutiny.

RONALD D. MOORE

It had come up through the years, was I going to direct an episode. My standard answer was always, "Well, I'm still kind of learning this job and that's taking on a whole other set of responsibilities." I always kind of pushed it down the line, but as we got into the last season I think it was kind of now or never. If I'm going to do this and do it for the first time, I should do it on my own show when the crew is well into the run and everybody knows what they're doing and do it toward the end so that I can step out of showrunning for a few weeks. Because that's *really* what it requires. I had to focus on prep and then shooting it and cutting it, and so it kind of took me out of prep and post in other episodes. At that point in the series, I just kind of felt like, okay, it was time to do that and I could do it. So I put myself on the list and just decided I'd direct and write. And what I wrote was just a character piece of these people and the aftermath of the disappointment of finding the nuclear Earth and what are they going to do next, and starting to plant just the seeds of what was going to explode shortly thereafter.

The strangest thing about the whole experience was that I found it relaxing. I realized later that that was because showrunning is all about constant interruption. I can't focus on one thing. I can't focus on this script, because I have to answer this email or I'm going to get a phone call or now I've got to go jump to this other story, I've got to go to post and work at this other episode; oh, the writers want to pitch me a new version of that episode; and, oh, they're calling from the set. Am I ever going to get back to my script? You're constantly juggling and constantly multitasking all these things, from prep to shoot to post, every day. But when I was directing, they don't want you to do anything else. The whole system is designed to make space. All I had to do was focus on this scene, and talk to these actors about this, and it was just freeing. The cast was great, the crew was very supportive and helpful. They would catch me if I was going to do something dumb, or give me a suggestion on how to do something a little different. It went great.

In some ways it may have gone *too* well, in that on the last day of directing, he went home to the house he and his wife were renting in Vancouver, went outside, sat on a rock, and cried. It was, he says, the weight of the fact that he and David Eick had volunteered the end of the show.

RONALD D. MOORE

It was so great and we were ending the show. I was just, like, "What am I doing? Why am I ending this thing I love so much and these people I love so much? What a fool I am." I was just devastated. *Then* I got over it and I wrote the crew a letter that went out on the call sheet the next day, just thanking them for making it such a great experience and then telling them about that experience and how much I loved them all and loved the show. I knew that ending the show was clearly the right choice, but it just hit me emotionally what it was going to mean to really walk away from it.

Prior to that episode was "Sometimes a Great Notion," which dealt with the aftermath of the discovery of the irradiated Earth. One result was Lee Adama and Anastasia Dualla, former communications officer of *Galactica* and his estranged lover, being drawn back together romantically, and after a wonderful time with him, she nonchalantly commits suicide by shooting herself.

MARK VERHEIDEN
(co-executive producer, *Battlestar Galactica* [2004])

I think back to Dualla's suicide; that she preferred to go on that note rather than the note of chaos that was overtaking the ship. This was right before the mutiny happened. The reason that scene was so powerful is because there were three and a half seasons of Dualla playing this role as Lee's lover, and as an incredibly competent lover. When I say Lee's lover, by the way, it could also be that Lee was *her* lover. You'd gotten to know that character, so to see her do that was so powerful, because I think that was the episode where you thought, "Okay, this fleet is really about done. They are really coming apart." Then we made it worse with the mutiny, but it was really a culmination of the bad that had been seeping through the entire fleet.

AARON DOUGLAS

When I think of the show, I think of things like Kandyse McClure, who played Dualla; when she had that affair going with Apollo. They finished dinner and she goes back to her quarters and is humming. I know it's coming, but in my brain I completely switched off the part of knowing, having read the script. I'm watching and she opens her books, looks in the mirror, kind of smiles at herself, and then just pulls out a pistol and blows her head off. I literally jumped in my chair, and just was horrified and screamed, "No!" It was just so powerful and so beautiful and just heart-wrenching. Just absolutely gutting.

MARK VERHEIDEN

Because of the strike, we had to stop writing as of episode thirteen. That was a *terrible* strike. When the strike was over and we came back, we watched all thirteen episodes. When you watch them back-to-back and you get to Dualla's suicide, we realized, "We have *really* gone to a dark place with this show." Maybe it didn't hit the others as much as me—or maybe it did—but I just went, "Whoa, the crisis level on this ship is sort of beyond belief." Some theaters in Los Angeles were showing these episodes, or we would rent a theater to bring friends out, but a theater actually showed the episode where Dualla died. It was a packed house and no one knew this was coming. It was absolutely heart-stopping, and you could hear a pin drop when that happened.

It was one of the more powerful moments I've had with something I was involved in to watch, because it was so dramatic. It came out of nowhere but made sense when you thought about it that she had finally had one last good day with Lee, and figured that was the *only* last good day she had in her. I don't necessarily agree with that attitude, but that's the attitude she had. She's someone who went from being the person who essentially gave you information—she was on the command deck—to this fully evolved, emotional life.

RONALD D. MOORE

The seeds for the mutiny came out of, "What happens once they get to Earth and it's a radioactive cinder? All their hopes have been destroyed." It felt like that was the moment of touching bottom for everyone. Everything they had pinned their hopes on since the pilot was to not be. They literally had no idea what to do next. Earth was a disaster and at that point it felt like things would start to come unraveled, and that people would start questioning authority. People would start rebelling, people would start to fight against the power that had been in place all this time, and they would start to tear at each other. So out of that, somebody was going to lead a mutiny and it felt like a natural story, because a mutiny is one of those ideas that gets tossed around all the time in a show like that, because you're on a ship and it's just one of the natural things you go to.

BRADLEY THOMPSON

We figured that sooner or later a mutiny had to happen, and at one point we had it done by Tigh, and that would have been earlier in the show. At that point, each of them thought they were Cylons. So we were trying to get to that, but the more we tried to work on that, the more we thought Tigh is never, ever going to think Adama is a Cylon. It's just not going to happen. Even if he were, he's *so* loyal to the guy.

MARK VERHEIDEN

In an odd way, the mutiny episodes, which were a bit more of action, were a way to lift us out of this incredibly dark place we were at, even though those episodes were very dark, too. But people were in movement. I guess the darkness led to where we could do a mutiny; where we could do sort of that ultimate betrayal of everything. It was such a dark, hopeless place that the idea that former colleagues could turn on one another like that finally made sense. We talked about doing a mutiny as early as season two, but it just came down to feeling like it was too early. We didn't earn that yet.

RONALD D. MOORE

I kept pushing the idea away, saying, "No, we're not at that place." And for something like that to happen, it has to be a big deal. You just shoved it away, but it was always a viable concept if you found the right story. In the same way that New Caprica was always a viable concept. People were always pitching, "What if they find a planet that maybe they could settle on?" I knew you could only get to play that card once as well. So the mutiny was always sort of in the air, and this was the moment to do it.

MARK VERHEIDEN

It was also pointed out that mutinies are a *huge* thing to even attempt regardless of the situation you're in. In terms of *Battlestar,* you're on the run and you're on your own. There's really no court system that's quite so valid, although Gaeta and Zarek certainly got in trouble. But we really felt like that fourth season was the right time to finally approach it, because we knew those characters so well. It was interesting that in the second episode of the mutiny story I had originally written in a flashback from the miniseries that showed how loyal Gaeta had been to Adama, just to show how far they had gone and see how this relationship had gone completely off the rails. We couldn't end up shooting that for time reasons, but the idea that Gaeta had gone so far that he could turn against the man that he admired and respected more than anyone was very interesting.

BRADLEY THOMPSON

Then when Zarek showed up, we're going, "Okay, we now have the conditions that are right for a mutiny, let's do it. What should it be?" We were taking Gaeta down that dark road, blowing his leg off and all. The evolution of Gaeta was great, in the sense that he used to be the guy saying, "This is what the computer is telling me," to the guy where he finally got pissed off at Tigh. Everything we threw at him he could handle, and then some. It was from that moment of abuse, questioning whether this was making any sense at all and whether you could make a deal with these guys, he would go, "You know what? The guy's consorting with Cylons. His executive officer is a Cylon. This has got to stop." That was when our cast just gave us those things. The ability to go those places; you never saw it in the beginning. We wanted to do *Red October* real early. We wanted to do *Crimson Tide*. That came up many times, but we just couldn't take those two guys—Adama and Tigh—there. We finally built the other two characters, Gaeta and Zarek, enough so that they could hold their own against our guys.

RONALD D. MOORE

Gaeta was one of the characters that writers tended to give interesting bits to whether they were in the outlines or not. You would often read drafts and there was always something for Gaeta. The roots of the mutiny in Gaeta were just seeds that sprung naturally in that direction. And we kept putting him against the other characters, because you got great drama out of it. It was just great. We had this great conflict between Gaeta and Kara, and Gaeta and everyone else. You just kept playing those scenes because they were fun scenes to play. And then when you really got to the point where, "Well, who's going to be one of the lead mutineers?" it was so obvious. It was like, "Well, clearly it's going to be Gaeta." And also it was going to hurt so much, because he was an original member of the family. He was with them from the very beginning, so there was a great unexpected way to go at the same time.

ALESSANDRO JULIANI
(actor, "Felix Gaeta")

My expectations were nothing when I became a part of the show. I didn't expect to come on set, to push buttons on the console and for them to actually light up. That was *crazy*! I was happily just soaking it in at that point. I never, in my wildest dreams, ever thought that the character would eventually go as far as he did. One of the great things about the show was the trust that the producers and writers had, gradually entrusting us with more and more as they watched and saw what we did. I suppose it's like that on any show, but at the time I didn't know that. As things began to expand, it expanded our universe, too, and the challenge was great.

RONALD D. MOORE

You can outline the arc of the character quite well. During New Caprica we talked about him in the room as being the flunky under Baltar who saw him in idealistic terms and blind to all this and that. But as the drafts started to develop, and as the writers sort of took all those drafts and embroidered on them, Gaeta became something greater than himself. From New Caprica forward, he became this much more complex character who had really sacrificed, who had extended himself and put himself far out there for ideals that he believed in. I remember different discussions in the writers' room about where we could take that character.

ALESSANDRO JULIANI

Gaeta started out as a real company man. And certainly a bit of an idealist, believing in the leadership and the hierarchy and how the world just seems to work. And as a person who had been a sort of scientist, he had a healthy that side of the brain that determined a certain logic to how things would happen. And a sense of order and of morality. I suppose like many of the characters in the show, that was completely uprooted and shaken over the course of the series. He certainly had mentor figures and idols, which he chose and who proved false. He began to see that the world was probably a lot more complex than when he started out.

DAVID EICK

Well, you know, the actor, too, has something to do with that. If Gary Burghoff in *M*A*S*H* had been responsible for coordinating an attack on the United States by the North Koreans, you would have gone, "Radar is the one?" And we had that option with this actor, because he was so versatile and he started off being sort of, you know, Sulu. But by the end he had really evolved into this very multidimensional actor. Writers are inspired by and helped by what they see onscreen. How they view their jobs can be made, if not easier, then at least more interesting by what actors provide them with. And AJ, as we call him, is an actor who was reading off jumble jargon and scientific coordinates, and yet there was a quality that made you go, "Wow, there's something about him that we can take chances with that guy."

JANE ESPENSON
(co-executive producer, *Battlestar Galactica* [2004])

It's one of my favorite things to do—to take a secondary or tertiary character and put them in the center. Nobody in real life is a supporting character. Everyone's the hero in their own story, so we can tell those stories. They're often the most interesting stories, because they're a character that you've never looked closely at before.

JAMIE BAMBER

Very few people are actually evil. I think most people are well-intentioned. They can be delusional and dishonest with themselves, they can have all sorts of problems, but essentially they're trying to sleep at night. They're trying to do the right thing in difficult situations, and they may make terrible mistakes, and that's what *Battlestar* really did. There were very few baddies. We had weak people, we had scared people, and Zarek is the perfect example of that, where you could read that on the page and it could be an archvillain— someone very broad, out for their own ends and nobody else's—but that's not what we got, because we had Richard Hatch, who is a noble person, in charge of that. Although he struggled with the whole mutiny storyline.

RONALD D. MOORE

Richard had one note about when Zarek orders the execution of the Quorum, and how that happened. In the original draft, he goes in and he asks them for a vote of confidence or something, or no confidence. And the vote went for him, if I'm remembering this right. He was surprised that, at the moment, the Quorum actually supported him, supported Zarek. Then he walked out the door where the guards were and said, "I'm surprised they supported me, but we've still got to get rid of them." And he ordered the soldiers to go in and shoot them anyway, which is pretty dark. I just thought that there was something interesting about, "It didn't really matter if they supported him or not. They were the old regime, and the old regime had to be wiped away so they can succeed."

Richard objected to that. He was like, "Look, if he's gone in there and they've given him what he wants, I just don't think he's going to kill them for the sake of killing them." He thought it made him look too bloodthirsty and too maniacal, and I went, "All right, I get it. I was trying to go for some irony to it, but, yeah, maybe I'm thinking one level too far." So I rewrote it so that the Quorum vote went *against* him and then he executed them. And it plays fine.

JAMIE BAMBER

Richard liked and believed in Tom Zarek, and you have to do that as an actor. Anybody who then takes that character and goes, "Oh, I can really be evil here; I can really go for it," you're going to fail, because the reality is that people don't think that way. I don't think even in North Korea, the regime there—even there—I don't believe are consciously trying to be evil. Even though in the West, we have that perception of them. From beginning to end with Ron, there's no character that hasn't been shaded with every hint of gray, from near white to near black, and everything in between. It's my sort of modus operandi as an actor to find that in every character. If someone's coming across as good, then find what's really a problem. And if someone's coming across as bad, then find the good and play that. You've got to fight for the character, and Richard did that to the very end with Zarek. He was really disappointed that Zarek could be seen as a bad guy by the end. He fought against it all the way.

ALESSANDRO JULIANI

I'll never forget sitting side by side as Richard and I were about to be executed and sharing that moment with him. It wasn't literally my last moment on the set, but it was close to it. There was so much going on for us as characters, but as human beings what a journey for Richard, at that point, and for me, someone who was just still at the very beginning of their career. I knew that it was the end of something massive and seminal in my life. As the years go by, that only intensifies, that memory, that sense of "What a thing!"

RONALD D. MOORE

Executing them was hard, and it was obvious. I really felt that if they did this mutiny, heads would have to roll. They would just have to. They couldn't just send them into jail. It felt like we would be cheating if we did that, and the show was ending. There wasn't a problem doing it, it was whether or not we were going to see it. And whether or not you were going to be there with them. Or should they die in gunfire when the rebellion is put down and they die a quasi-heroic death? Or should they be executed? Do we see Adama execute these two men? And I said, "Yeah, we do. We're going to go right to that—we're not going to shy away from it. We're not going to be TV, we're not going to give them the easy out, and the easy out is they just take a bullet somewhere in the fight for control of the ship, and they just end up dead. But the tougher one is Adama executes them, and he executes two characters that we really like."

The network blanched over that a little bit. Mark Stern was a little, like, "Really? You really want to see these guys get executed? Is that necessary?" There were qualms, but we just pushed it through.

MARK VERHEIDEN

We really tried to build that so it didn't feel like it was coming out of nowhere. It felt like a character turn that made sense, and Zarek was further along that path. He was easier to get there, but with Gaeta, we really wanted to understand his disappointment with Adama and how this desire to make a deal with the creatures that were making their lives an utter misery and wanted to destroy them, how the man he respected was going to try to do that would destroy his faith. This guy that he respected became the core of that series of episodes.

ALESSANDRO JULIANI

When you get that unexpected call from Ron, then you know, "Oh, shit, I'm not gonna make it to the end of the series after all this." But, then, when we got on the phone and he told me what they were planning for the next four or five episodes . . . well, what a great frakkin' way to go. Without putting too fine a point on it, I think that ultimately Gaeta's actions shook everyone out of their various stupors and in a way saved the fleet. Saved them all.

Without that mutiny, things were kind of inexorably doomed. In a strange way it galvanized everyone and bonded them together.

DAVID EICK

When you're nearing the finish line, you have to start casting people in bronze. The characters are about to become what they'll always be known for, and you're about to resolve them in a way that in some respects is kind of permanent. To that extent, I think you find yourself making less-nuanced choices, because when you think of the character, you tend to think in simple, bold, loud terms. What stands out about that character, you're not thinking about the time they did three things that are uncharacteristic.

My point is, I think Tom Zarek was a damaged guy and he was a Machiavellian guy. While I think Zarek had compassion and understood, we wanted the character to understand and be sensitive to human pain and suffering. That still doesn't trump the Machiavellian impulse and the lust for power, and the sort of insanity that occurs when you can't get it. Again, you get to the end of the run and you have to start saying, "This is who this guy is." When you look back, this is who this guy was. So in a nutshell, with Tom Zarek you're talking about a dark guy. Now if we talk about him longer, there's a lot of beveling and nuance, but in a thumbnail sketch, yes.

MARK VERHEIDEN

One thing that I actually tried to do in "The Oath," which was the second mutiny episode, was to inject a little bit of the fighting spirit that our guys had. Specifically, there's a scene where they're about ready to shoot Lee Adama as he gets off of a diplomatic shuttle. The people on *Galactica* that are mutinying, they don't have any interest in negotiating with the Cylons and they know Lee's been doing that, and they're just going to shoot him. They're going to kill him as he gets off the shuttle. You hear a bang, and there's Starbuck standing there with a gun. She says, "Let him go." Another guy draws a gun, she shoots him, too, and says, "I could do this all day."

Basically they have to let Lee go, and as she's leaving she says something like, "Follow me. Please." I think the audience was hungering to see the Starbuck who would fight for Lee, who would defend herself, who would do the right thing, and basically we were able to do a little more . . . action's the wrong word, but the movements that earlier shows had in terms of the struggle they were having. I really wanted to capture, "Okay, Starbuck's back. Good. Yay," after her being in a bit of a fog, because she didn't know who she was, either. What she *did* know is that she wasn't going to let people shoot Lee Adama and she wasn't going to let them fuck with her ship. That's who we knew she was.

RONALD D. MOORE

Part of the fun of doing the mutiny was watching the power slide back and forth. It's control of a discrete thing, a ship, as opposed to a political mutiny or a cop, where you're trying to take over the reins of government. Whether you're killing Hitler and trying to get the troops to do things in Berlin, it spread all over the place, and there's lots of weight power centers and lines of communication. It's a very complicated thing, but when it's on a ship, it's very specific and you can control the power and you can control the weapons. You can lock things, you can cut off certain corridors so it becomes very tangible, and you can watch on camera as certain things are shut off to them, and then somebody gets control and, yes, someone's locked up and then someone's released. You can really dramatize it in a very literal way.

MARK VERHEIDEN

With mutinies, there are a lot of negotiations that have to go on. We tried to play that it wasn't just this monolithic black-and-white situation. Once you've turned into a mutineer, that's it. Now, some of the characters were that way, but there's a scene where Tigh and Adama are being escorted to basically a prison cell or something, and clearly there were some arguments happening between the guards that are leading them along. That escalates to a point where Adama is able to take advantage of that, basically using his Edward Olmosness, being a guy you don't want to mess with, and actually sort of turned the tables on those guys. The greatest part of that entire story is that Gaeta was actually right. What were they doing trying to make a deal with the Cylons? The murkiness of saying that we like Adama better than we like him, but here's Adama's best friend and first officer who is a Cylon. I would have a hard time wrapping my head around that as a crewman myself. So it was a really fun one to work out. I thought we got some really interesting and, frankly, fun places in those episodes. With dark scenes at the same time.

RONALD D. MOORE

The mutiny grew out of real issues. There were good people on both sides, and there were characters you cared about on both sides. We had started the thing with Gaeta. We started putting him at odds with the rest before we ever thought that he was going to end up as a mutineer, which really made it work, because there was an organic quality to his story in particular that made you believe where he was going. And Tom Zarek, way back, all the issues that came that they were focused on were true. They weren't wrong. Adama and Laura had led them all to nothing, to ruin. They had legitimately pissed away the whole thing, and so the rebels really had a strong point and you could understand completely why people would get behind that banner and follow it, because, man, you couldn't really argue with what they were saying.

ALESSANDRO JULIANI

To the bitter end, Gaeta certainly stuck with whatever his moral sense was. He definitely went down thinking he had done the right thing, all the way to the airlock. I think there was a sense of peace, if you will, by the end for him. Which, given some of his actions, it's a long way to that point. What a complex character. He was like the most reliable, faithful, consistent, and dependable guy in practically the whole fleet. For him to then be turned, or to think that the leadership had been so corrupted there, mutiny was the only choice for him. It was like he was the only one who had retained his sanity in all of this. Which, to be frank and from his perspective, I totally get it. Even through all the craziness, the shifting allegiances, the inconsistency, at times, of leadership, I totally sympathized with him. All the way to the end. He just didn't really pick his allies particularly well. That was his big flaw.

MARK VERHEIDEN

As an aside, there was a theater in Portland, Oregon, that would play the episodes off of the Sci-Fi Channel feed. They'd fill the theater up for free, because the theater sold beer, which is how they made their money. I went up for that to catch my episode of the mutiny and watch it with a crowd of about five hundred people. That was awesome, because you could see the visceral reaction people were having to this these. These are true fans who are just caught up in every moment. As was I. To see them respond so positively to this show. The episode ended with one of the mutineers rolling a hand grenade in on Adama, and then it stated it would be continued. Well, the place just erupted. That was one of the more fun moments of my time on *Battlestar,* to see it with the crowd.

The last major piece of the puzzle to be revealed in the series was who the final Cylon was. The revelation did not disappoint when the curtain was pulled back to reveal that Kate Vernon's Ellen Tigh was the last of the Final Five Cylons.

RONALD D. MOORE

One of the early paths was talking about who was the final Cylon. Who was it? And we went through all the possibilities. Through the whole cast, right? Who could be the Cylon? A guest star from the past or a brand-new character? We went through all of it. But I think Ellen Tigh just kept coming up. She was the character that we just kept gravitating back to for a variety of reasons. One was everyone loved Kate Vernon and it was hard when we decided to kill her character, and everyone kind of missed her. So you kind of felt like there was a missing part of the family going into the home stretch. It was a good way to bring her back and it also allowed us to get into that character one more time and look at the relationship between her and Saul in a different way. Now you're talking about two Cylons in a relationship and we could play that out as they had a turbulent, *Who's Afraid of Virginia Woolf?*–type relationship for eons. There was something really interesting about that, about what it said about these two characters who seemed to have this bizarro marriage between the two of them, but once she said they were both also Cylons, you started thinking, "Well, that takes us deeper into some interesting backstory." I was really attracted to it for that as well.

MARK VERHEIDEN

Look, everybody's got their opinion. Again, we ran through many permutations on who would be the Final Five Cylons. And that's the other thing: No decision is bulletproof. I guarantee if you ask the writers, there'd be writers who worked on the show that would say I didn't agree with that, but I went with it, because that's where we were going. It's never a hundred percent acclamation, but we were pretty much on the same page working through the show.

MICHAEL HOGAN
(actor, "Colonel Saul Tigh")

You never know when you sign on to a series—and not necessarily just *Battlestar Galactica*—what the writers are going to come up with. Who would have thought Tigh would be a Cylon? And the same with Ellen? Where does *that* come from? I know that Kate Vernon was ecstatic about it, because here's this different take on the character.

RONALD D. MOORE

Ellen Tigh was also sort of the one that gave you a big shock, because we had killed her. We hadn't been doing a lot of flashbacks with her or anything, so it would be a big surprise to suddenly have Ellen Tigh resurface. And then her backstory itself kind of lent it . . . It was cloaked in mystery. She was not with them originally. She had come to *Galactica* late in the first season under mysterious circumstances. Her story was a little suspect. Adama overtly suspected her of being a Cylon, so we'd already sort of gone down some of those paths. And someone inoculated her from that. It just felt right. There was also something about, "If Tigh is one, maybe Ellen's another," and then you're in a situation where, "Well, okay. So who were they really?" and "What's the nature of the Final Five?" Once you started talking about, well, if these core five characters are the Final Five, why were they special? We had to kind of face that question finally. What makes them special? What is their backstory? How did that all come about?

In the end, *Galactica*—with Adama leading a coalition of humans and Cylons—manages to defeat the plans of Cavil, ending the threat of Cylon attacks forever. Then Starbuck—whose resurrection became one of the major mysteries of that last year—uses enigmatic musical notes to lead the fleet to another habitable planet, which turns out to be our Earth in the ancient past. It is here that the collective crew settles, dispersing and planting the seeds that will lead to the future of humanity and our current world.

DAVID WEDDLE

In the fourth season, Brad and I wrote "He That Believeth in Me," "Sometimes a Great Notion," and "Revelations." "Sometimes a Great Notion" is where Kara finds her body down on planet Earth. The idea behind that was never wanting to concretely say, "Yes, Kara Thrace is an angel from God or from the gods, sent to guide us to Earth." We never wanted to make that concrete, so we wanted to leave multiple ways of interpreting it. So by her finding her own body, it not only asks, "Am I really alive or what else am I?" But is it some kind of weird theory of relativity through a black hole, you know, a doppelgänger created by the mysteries and the physics of the universe? So that was the idea of finding the body down there, and then it throws Kara into real doubt about who the fuck she is. She comes back, sort of, "Hey, it's me, but I don't know what happened. I can't remember." But by the time she finds that, it throws her into a crisis of—which is kind of the final movement of her character—"Who am I?"

DAVID EICK

The real thing that was a point of contention for everyone was the death of Starbuck. When I say I might have pulled the leash less toward something kind of ambiguous and mysterious, that's an example. That's not to say I didn't approve it. I remember we talked about that at our big meeting. I kind of threw up my hands and said, "Let's see if we can make it work." It's the most controversial, because, on some level, it feels to some people like we didn't have an answer, so we just didn't give it to them. I can confirm we *did* have the answers. We had the answer from the beginning of that season. Whether the audience accepts that or thinks that it's a terrible idea or not, I had to own that right along with Ron.

RONALD D. MOORE

When she came back, it kind of works. She comes back and goes off in the freighter, and she's drawing the mandala in her cabin. It did feel like we wandered there a bit; I know we were trying real hard to bring focus into that, and it felt like once you had resurrected her, she had to have a huge storyline that justified that—that it was important then to the rest of the show. But I do feel like we never quite brought that into focus. It feels like those episodes do wander around a little bit as she's on this vision quest, and trying to find answers. The point where it did come into focus for me, ultimately, is when we do the episode with her father and the piano. She realizes there's a message in the music, and that pays off in the finale when the musical notes then get translated to the coordinates that take us to Earth. *That* I love. So I love where it ended up, but I was never quite happy with the first half of season four with Kara.

DAVID WEDDLE

I can tell you that in the writing room, there were multiple theories as to who Kara Thrace really was, how did she come back, why did she disappear in the end. We never answered those concretely, nor do I think we ever should. The opinions of the writers in the room are just like the opinions of the viewers. It's open to interpretation, and there are multiple ways to interpret it. It's a fantastic journey for the character, and I'm so proud of it.

DAVID EICK

If you ask me what I would have done, I probably wouldn't have veered in quite as inexplicable direction, but I don't think I would've had the idea to kill her, bring her back, and then have to decide what to do with her. So it cuts both ways, you know? It's easy to complain that there wasn't a more satisfying solution to the character, but as you're complaining about that, you have to acknowledge that you enjoyed the shit out of several episodes where you were made to think she was dead and then made to think she came back, and couldn't figure it out. So, you know, you live by the sword, you die by the sword. I can say, "Gee, I don't know if I would've done that, even though I absolutely approved that and absolutely own it." At the same time, I have to say I may not have made or presided over as many compelling, juicy, nougaty episodes that sprung from her death that we did benefit from.

MARK STERN

The only thing that really bugged me about the ending of the show was Starbuck as an angel, or whatever the hell happens there in the wheat field. But sometimes you just have to give your folks a gimme every now and then. For all the cool stuff they did with her, the fact that they didn't quite, in my opinion, have a real answer for how to resolve her storyline is, like, "All right, if that's your worst sin, go with God." It is kind of lyrical, though, isn't it?

KATEE SACKHOFF
(actress, "Kara 'Starbuck' Thrace")

They wanted to leave it ambiguous and they wanted to give the viewer the ability to determine what the show was for them. So they had to leave some characters open in the sense that they couldn't wrap it up with a pretty little bow. I had said to Ron the entire time, "Please do not have Kara walk off into the sunset with Lee Adama. She will *not* be happy. This is not this character at peace. This character at peace is back at war. *That's* who she is, that's where she's comfortable." I didn't want her to have a pretty ending, so for me to have her disappear was actually perfect, because it was such a metaphor, in my opinion, for everything that she had been through. And how history would have painted her as the person who led humanity to the New Earth, but ultimately it doesn't matter. It doesn't matter who led them, because she's not there anymore.

The irony is that she doesn't get to experience it with them, because she's not there. I thought that it was a beautiful thing. One of the truths of death that we have such a hard time understanding as people, is that when you're gone, you're gone. People remember you, but life carries on almost instantaneously. That is the circle of life, so it made complete sense that she fulfilled her mission and then left. I also thought it was such a beautiful thing, too, that she left as soon as Lee started talking about the things he was going to do.

DAVID WEDDLE

I know a lot of people were pissed off with how it ended, where she just vanishes, but I love that. You know, I think our least successful episode was where we tried to explain the Final Five, and let's answer every little detail of it, which was not a good impulse, I think. We felt the need to do it, but in the end, I think we would have been better off not doing it. Ken Kesey, who wrote the novel *Sometimes a Great Notion,* which that episode is named after, has a great quote about fiction. He says, "Don't look for the answer, look for the mystery." I've seen people find what they think is the answer, but when they do, they stop thinking. So the job is to look for the mystery. To plant a garden in which mysteries bloom, and if you're pursuing a mystery, you'll always be searching. So that aesthetic, I think, was a fundamental setting of *Battlestar Galactica.*

RONALD D. MOORE

We debated various options. There really wasn't a good one, because every definitive answer felt deflating. If you had said, "Oh, she's literally a guardian angel," you go, "Oh, she's a traveler from another dimension. She's from the future." There were all these alternatives that you could come up with, and none of them felt as interesting as just not answering the question. Making it ambiguous that she was truly representational of a power that could not be understood. God could not be understood by man, and Kara had touched that; it was part of that, and she had been brought back by that power. For a time and a place, and a purpose that was somewhat mysterious, and then was taken away. I just think that's a much bigger statement on her than to try and answer it definitively. It's just a more memorable ending. Starbuck disappeared, and what did that mean? I think it's a great question and I'm happy to leave her character on a question.

KATEE SACKHOFF

One of her main concerns and one of the things that she was doing was that she was sort of wrapping up and saying good-bye to the people that mattered to her. For her, when she said good-bye to Lee and she asks him what are you going to do now, and he starts to explain what he's going to do, she realizes he's going to be okay and she leaves, because her job is done. He doesn't need her anymore.

RONALD D. MOORE

Similarly, at the end Baltar has a speech in the CIC where he says, "We all have seen stuff, things have happened, and it can't be denied that there's something else. We don't know what it is, but there's something else at work that has some connection to us, and some interest in what is happening in our lives." And that's as far as I thought you could go, because it didn't feel like you could answer the question, "Are the Colonials right? Or are the Cylons right? Is there one god, many gods, or are there *any* gods?" It just felt the show could go as far as saying, "Well, there's something else. There's some other something; some greater power. Some other entity with an intent in their lives, that had some connection to it." For purposes that we cannot comprehend, for motives we cannot understand, and whose actions may not always make sense to us. But there is something there, and that felt like that was also about as far as you could go without becoming too cute, or without giving it a really simple answer that becomes unsatisfying. It felt right to leave it on a tone of mystery, but acknowledge that it existed, whatever it was.

DAVID EICK

I'll give the other side of my feeling about these sort of mythology issues: Had I been more successful at choke-holding the mythological esoterica, so to speak, in the late first and early second seasons, I don't think the show would've had nearly the appeal. I think I would've been too conservative in trying to keep it more on the rails of a traditional type of conflict and so forth, as opposed to getting into metaphysical things. The show not only benefited from but, in an existential sense, *needed* that element in order to elevate it from an excellently done *Star Trek* or an excellently done *Stargate*. And so, as I say I might have argued at times to pull it a little less David Lynch, I also understand that had I succeeded every time I wanted that, the show wouldn't have been as special.

RONALD D. MOORE

This is the downside in a lot of ways of the method that I preferred to do the show in. I really liked the improvisational nature of the show. I liked figuring things out and making it up as we go along.

MARK VERHEIDEN

I've always equated the process to wanting to go to Seattle. Well, you can take the scenic route or you can go to the Grand Canyon, or you can take many different roads to get to that place. To shut yourself off from being open to the creative impulse that comes when things are evolving during the actual writing of a season is, I think, crazy to stick to some sort of pre-ordained plan that you may have come up with because you just decided to do that and not take into account as you're watching episodes go by and you say, "Wow, this relationship between these two characters is really getting fraught and interesting." Or, "Boy, wouldn't it be interesting if we'd go this way or that way." It's a long way of basically saying that things like we want to make five people that are very close to our cast into Cylons was, admittedly, not planned from the beginning, but it was something that felt like we could get into it in season three once we made that decision to go there. After that, it became planning on *how* to get to that place.

MARY MCDONNELL

Ron was completely open to the new information that was coming to him through characters, through some of the ideas of the other writers, and in that way, if it's a really strong journey, it steers itself at moments. The very, very confident writers embrace that, and he did.

RONALD D. MOORE

I've talked about this before. I love the surprise of it. I love the spontaneity of it, to create a frisson that you sort of get in the writers' room, and you find all kinds of things you never would have thought of if you mapped out everything in advance. Well, the downside is then you get into these kinds of situations where you backed yourself into certain corners, and you're like, "Okay, now I really have to straighten out this mythology and really figure out how it all works."

DAVID EICK

A lot of head writers don't have that discipline. They say either we're going to map it out so painstakingly and specifically where there's no room for improvisation—jazz is not allowed—or, hey, let's just make it as we go along. I started writing on this show, I wasn't a writer before *Battlestar,* and one of my most painful and yet I have to say most instructive quotes from Ron was, "I know that's what we were saying then; this is what we're saying now." And it was *really* instructive. Because you have to be willing to borrow from or be adherent to the spine that you've set up, and we always got together to set up what that spine was, and were pretty religious about it. So there were rules, and yet within those rules there was a great flexibility and freedom. Or, what I like to call "infecting the staff with accountability." If they feel as responsible for the success of the show as we do, then we're not going to lie awake in bed at night wondering, hey, they're actually contributing and worrying about it, and in a very profoundly personal way. The age of "Do it my way, write it my way, write the show in specific terms" is dying, and we're heading toward a much more collaborative or certainly flexible and fluid medium.

RONALD D. MOORE

The vision of the Opera House on Kobol is a great example. A lot of these were images or thoughts or ideas that were either born in the writers' room, in discussions among the staff or somebody sort of creating them on the page, or someone had a suggestion and it worked its way into the fabric of the show. We would say, "That's an interesting idea. I'm not quite sure what it means, but I love the iconography of it." The Opera House was something that actually Michael Rymer came up with as a place to put Baltar, whatever the original iteration of that was. But there were various versions. And then later the challenge of doing a series like this, in my opinion, is then to sort of take those inspirational ideas where you're throwing something against the wall, you think it's pretty, you think it's an interesting place to go, and then to make a mosaic out of that. Say, "Okay, well I heard something here and didn't know what it meant, but now it's a part of the picture and what can I do to make the picture fill in, making the picture interesting?" And then, how do we get to the Opera House? What does the Opera House ultimately mean in this circumstance and how can I bend the story sort of back to there and give it meaning and make it feel satisfying and make it feel like it was all valid? Because in my opinion, whether you sit down at the beginning of the project and say "I'm now going to map out everything that happens over the arc of this story" and you follow it, or you invent it along the way, improvisationally, like jazz or something, either way is valid. All that really matters is what you end up with.

DAVID EICK

In the last days, while we were identifying who the Final Five were going to be revealed as, everybody's name was on the table. There was debate about it. I don't think anyone came away from the debate feeling upset that we had done anything wrong, but there was certainly debate about it.

RONALD D. MOORE

So the deep backstory of the Final Five and their previous selves was very complicated, and the problem was, every which way we turned it was always complex, and it was always hard to follow, and it was never a simple story. And that was always the bugaboo. I always wanted it to be easily digestible. I wanted to be able to just tell the audience the story and move on, because the show wasn't about that. It wasn't about that secret, but we had elevated the mystique of the Final Five to the point where we really did have to answer this question, and all the writers felt very duty-bound that we were going to answer this question. We had done this and, by golly, we were going to figure it out. Somehow.

We pitched various versions to each other, to David. We went to the network a couple of times with versions of it, and it just kept changing over and over and over again, until we finally got to the place where it works. It's kind of rickety. It's certainly not the easiest backstory to understand, but it felt like it encapsulated everything that had kind of been established. And at the end of the day, it felt like, "Okay, it may sound a bit weird that this is the backstory, but it does hold up, and it is kind of consistent with everything that we had laid out," which is not that satisfying an answer. But in the scope of things, looking back at the show, I'm less satisfied with that part of what we did. I understand why we did it that way and how we got to that point, and I'm not sure I would've done it differently. I'm very sure I would not, if I had to do it all over again, I would not have tried to lay out the mythology first. I never would have come up with so many things that made the show very special, so I think I just liked what we did, and there are flaws in it and this is one of the flaws, and I'm willing to sort of accept that flaw.

The flaw is the complications of it. I think it's a complicated kind of convoluted backstory. It's not exactly what you feel like the Cylons are all about. You know, that there was an original set of Cylons and humans. It sort of feels like it's part of the all of this has happened before and all of it will happen again. It *does* fulfill that idea, the circular nature of these events. So it plays into that very well. But I'm not sure that ultimately it's that satisfying. I think it works. It works logically. It's just not a "Ooh wow, that's such a great story" moment.

It's almost like we're tying up loose threads to satisfy the audience that's paying attention. So we were duty-bound to kind of do that. One of the things we did do, going into the fourth season, is we took a white dry-erase board in the writers' room, and we listed every plot thread that had not been tied . . . that needed to be tied up, every question that had been asked, and every bit of backstory that felt chaotic or unfulfilled. So that we wanted to check each one of those things off before we went off the air. It was very important to us that we be consistent, that we honor the continuity of the show, and that at the end, all the big questions were answered, and that no one could accuse us of having ignored things, and pretend that things didn't happen.

MICHAEL TAYLOR
(co-executive producer, *Battlestar Galactica* [2004])

I remember we were trying to plot out this big thing in the writers' room and we had the revelation that it's not about the plot, it's about the characters. Ron went and wrote these wonderful little vignettes that were sprinkled through the story. That, to me, was what the finale was all about. It was weaving together all these character threads from past and present and future. Laura Roslin and her sisters in her youth; Starbuck and Lee and Lee's brother; Starbuck was an angel or something.

MICHAEL ANGELI
(co-executive producer, *Battlestar Galactica* [2004])

What worked for us with the show is that we just tore everything—every expectation, every cliché—apart, so that by the time you got to the finale, you just didn't know what to expect. And speaking of the finale, Ron showed me his first draft of the finale and I told him, "Dude, this is the best thing you *ever* wrote. This is just fucking amazing." He said, "Really? I left a lot of stuff out." So he went back and he added it. Then we had a two-hour finale. Then other people read it and the network read it, and we had a three-hour finale. Then they realized it was going to be too expensive, so it was back to being a two-hour and it was just stunning.

MARK STERN

I loved it. Look, it's very hard to end a series of caliber. I kind of feel like you're on a ride, and I thought it was very in keeping with the rest of the series. Bringing it home to us, so you couldn't just kind of resolve it as, "Oh, well, that was a whole other story, with a whole other group of people." Instead, it's, "Are *we* the next Caprica?" We kind of are. It's a cautionary tale and, without hitting it too hard on the head, it was like, "Yeah, this is a cycle. The whole show is about cycles repeating themselves. Here's another cycle." It felt appropriate.

KATEE SACKHOFF

One of the beauties of *Battlestar* is the fact that ultimately, in the end, the Cylons and the humans do come together, and they do bring sort of a utopia that, granted, we know in the end it's going to happen again, it's going to go to shit at some point, but it is interesting to watch through all the conflict and everything else that has gone on, they ultimately put their differences aside and they are together on Earth. I think it's a hell of a message.

SCOTT MANTZ
(film critic, *Access Hollywood*)

It's very hard to do a series finale. Sometimes they ruffle feathers, like the ending of *The Sopranos,* where people were infuriated over the way that show ended. You have a show like *Breaking Bad,* which was perfect. I think the ending of *Galactica* was perfect. Just that coda; it happened once, it can happen again. They get to Earth, and clearly, we sprang from them, which I can't say was a surprising development. They did that in the comic book once, but who read that?

RONALD D. MOORE

All this has happened before and all of this will happen again, which is a line from the Disney version of *Peter Pan.* I was watching with my kids, and I went, "I love that line," and it was something interesting and it kind of felt, at that point, as sort of a nod toward the original series. It was sort of acknowledging in some subtle way that there was an original series, and we were telling the same story all over again. But as we got deeper into the show and started thinking about that idea, it was in their version of the Bible. It was a piece of prophecy. It had a deeper resonance, and I started feeling, "Well, this is a cycle of man. This is a cycle of technology turning against itself, and awakening," and there were existential questions within it, and there was something interesting about then getting to the finale and basically saying, "And it will happen here, too."

Optimistically, there is the feeling that the repetition of certain things toward some goal feels like there are key things that you get better at in an ideal world. Practicing, doing things multiple times, you learn more the second time through. You perfect things through repetition, through practice, and the cycle of time that we were positing. Eventually this was moving toward a place of higher understanding. It was a positive circle of time.

And looking at our current society, where the machine is evolving to the point where sex robots are not too many years away from becoming a reality for ordinary people, it's a message that seems to have brought with it a bit of prescience when it originally aired.

RONALD D. MOORE

I think it's exciting and disturbing all at once. I remember when we were doing *Galactica* and I was in Vancouver, [my wife] Terry and I happened upon a documentary that was talking about those Japanese sex robots, at that point. I was fascinated with it, and certainly, like, "Wow! This is crazy." The thing to me that speaks most strongly, though, was the movie *Her.* That was an emotional connection to an artificial intelligence without the body. So it was strictly like an emotional and intellectual relationship that was established with this synthetic person, or this true AI. And I thought that was fascinating, because that felt very close to the world that I'm starting to live in now. I talk to my Alexa, and I hate Siri, but I've used her on occasion. You kind of start to see how this is going to change as your relationship with technology and with AI is going to change. Not quite clear that we get to the walking-around humanoid synthetic person yet. Sort of a question of why you would want to build that. Like maybe it gets built because people just want to do it. But it's one of those, "It's because it's there and somebody does it."

In the series *Caprica,* we tried to sort of lay out the steps that took you down that path in some ways. The tools to soldiers to people who are quasi-slavelike to you. But I'm fascinated to watch that the society I live in is actually moving in the direction *Galactica* was starting to talk about.

KATEE SACKHOFF

I just had one of my girlfriends tell me that the problem with dating when you're divorced and you're in your forties is that the men your age want younger women, and the older men that are sixty-five don't have the energy to actually hang out with you anymore, so you're sort of fucked. So maybe sex robots would be great, because she said, "Honestly, I really don't need anyone but my girlfriends, but I am a little lonely and could use a handyman." Maybe the Japanese are on to something. We should just have sex robots for all the divorced forty-five-year-old women who don't want a sixty-five-year-old and don't want to just go fuck thirty-two-year-olds.

RONALD D. MOORE

When we did the episode in season one where Starbuck is interrogating Leoben—and the whole crux of that show was "Is he a person or is he a machine?"—he's acting like a person. He's acting like he's in pain and like he's suffering, and you start to feel sorry for him, because he seems to be emulating all of the human signs of someone in distress and suffering. So it becomes this complicated thing where one part of your brain is saying, "Yeah, it's just mimicking human response. Don't be fooled." And the other part of your brain is being stimulated to feel like, "Well, this is a person in front of me, and how do I ignore their suffering?" And in *Her*, that was the moment when he's talking to her on the AI, and I think he starts to realize that she sounds like she's upset or she's feeling bad and it gets into this really complicated place where, well, once you imbue them with feeling and thought and sentience, are they sentient by definition? Or is there still some objective way of figuring it out? It's fascinating territory once you go down these paths.

I tried to leave them all in a place where they were about to embark on a different chapter of their lives in different ways. Adama has lost the woman he's come to love and his soulmate in a lot of ways. And now he's alone. And it kind of felt like Adama would want to remain alone. He had left it all behind. He wasn't going to seek out his son. He was going to live alone up on that ridge in the cabin and talk to Laura at her grave, and it was very sort of bittersweet and kind of an ending. It reminded me of *She Wore a Yellow Ribbon*, where John Wayne's character lives at the fort, and he goes out and talks to his wife's grave at the beginning of the movie, and it's implied that he's been doing this ever since she passed away. I sort of always liked that image and loved that movie. So it was reminiscent of that. So Adama was in the last chapter of his life. He was going to live out his life in this little cabin and talk to Laura until he died.

MICHAEL TAYLOR

I remember when Roslin and Adama got high together, lying under the stars and her talking about the cabin she wanted to live in. The connection between them was just so lovely, and that relationship came to an equally lovely and even more affecting and tough conclusion with Mary's character's death at the end. You felt you've been on a real journey with these two, and that journey comprised my tenure on that show, from the episode of the two of them out there becoming intimate in a way, and that conclusion. For me it's that journey. That finale was a very apt conclusion to the journey for all the characters. And for the writers and cast.

DAVID EICK

That relationship was one of those things that could only end that way. It's like putting the last brick in the house, and it fits perfectly. So I loved it. I loved the pain of it, the sadness of it, and the fact that, in a way, it was like he had lost his wife. And that makes me love Adama more. I just thought it was perfect.

MARY MCDONNELL

In that very first breakfast with Ron Moore, I said to him, "You've got to be honest with me. Is this a long job or do I die fast?" He said, "She'll go back and forth. She'll feel very healthy some days, and she'll have a hard time others. She will probably at all costs try to hide it from the people, but I'm thinking that she'll probably die once we reach Earth." Now neither he nor I knew what that meant, but we found out four seasons later. What became obvious to me is that he did understand the bigger arcs, but he was interested, fascinated, longed for the *how* of the journey.

DAVID WEDDLE

You know, that love story between Adama and Laura Roslin I don't think was envisioned at the beginning at all. In the beginning, it started out as the classic confrontation between the schoolteacher/liberal politician and the admiral. So they kind of started in a place that was pretty familiar. But as we watched that chemistry between Mary McDonnell and Edward James Olmos in the times that they would forgive each other and come back together and realized they needed each other, we started to see a chemistry in that. We started to see the way he kind of admired her and admired her strength. That was something that sort of evolved as we wrote it, watching those two actors together, and it wasn't a planned thing that we do a love story. It just sort of organically evolved as we watched them. It became one of the most moving, powerful things in all of *Battlestar*.

MICHAEL ANGELI

When Laura was sick toward the end and she was bald because she had lost her hair from treatment, Adama embraced her. They lay down together and he just held her. They talked. It was a gorgeous scene, but that is *not* the Adama from season one and season two. At the end, it's this weirdo *Driving Miss Daisy* thing where he's just going to stay with her until she dies, which is another un-Adama kind of quality where he's going to be kind of a spiritual custodian. That's how I think that character changed the most.

DAVID WEDDLE

What an amazing love story, that he gets her to Earth and she can barely make it. This was Michael Rymer's idea, that we go over the Earth and see all the plentiful game, and the wild, unspoiled land, and that's her last vision. And then he ends up building her cabin beside her grave . . . I'm getting emotional just talking about it.

That was something where you just saw the themes between the actors and began to build on it. And then Olmos's willingness to be harsh and vicious enabled us to do this relationship with both Kara and Lee that we could play the evolving of a father/son relationship and a father/pseudo-daughter relationship that was really more like real families. Equal parts rage and love.

MICHAEL ANGELI

The end of the series for Adama was kind of bittersweet. Sensing his own mortality, but still feeling as though there was other business to attend to. There was something wanting about him in the end, I do believe. I don't think there was any kind of sense of, "Wow, I've done everything. I've fulfilled all of my aspirations. It's time for me to ride off into the sunset."

RONALD D. MOORE

Tyrol, I remember loving the idea that he was going to go out into the Scottish Highlands and become the über-Scot. That was where he was going to go. Helo and Sharon felt like, okay, we're moving them into the family. They're going to be a family unit. That the surprise at the end was going to be that Helo survived, because it kind of felt like, as we were plotting the story, he felt like an obvious person to kill or sacrifice and so we shied away from that, because we kind of felt like everyone's going to be expecting to kill Helo, so let's not do that, because that's a fun surprise. And then they would have a strong family all the way, and that their child would then become our distant ancestor.

The one, though, I think we shortchanged was Tigh and Ellen back together, being a married couple. They're the only two that didn't really get a good-bye scene in the finale. I think it was shot and it was cut for time or something. But I'm trying to really remember. I don't remember specifically if we talked too much about what their future was going to be. It was just we were more interested in putting them back, that after everything they had gone through, it was something interesting and ironic that Ellen and Tigh were the most solid couple of all. It was, like, through the millennia, these two just could not quit on each other and just kept coming back, and could not put that love away. I always loved that idea.

Lee kind of felt like he really would be the great explorer, and he was going to try to go around the world. I remember thinking maybe he was going to build a boat or something, and he would go out onto the ocean, and would try to map Africa. You know, I had these just vague ideas of him as the first great explorer of Earth.

JAMIE BAMBER

Being there was kind of a release for Lee. It was like the first day of summer. They're free. Finally. And I remember a lot of people going, "Free to do what? There's nothing there." Well, there's *everything* there, there just isn't the stuff that we're used to in the modern world, and that these people have been dealing with. But green grass and air was all the paradise these people ever dreamed of in whatever time frame they were all enclosed in; in a prison in space. So I thought it was a massive release and it felt like it as an actor, too. Art and life go hand in hand. This show is wonderful, but at the time I remember feeling the responsibility of opportunity and not knowing what's coming next. So it felt to me like we'd done it, we'd finished and it was an amazing, emotional moment. And, yeah, there's a bit of me in there, I think, too.

GRACE PARK

In my mind, the series was always going to end on Earth. The new Earth, with Adama, and the president dying, Starbuck kind of disappearing, and Helo, Sharon, and Hera and everyone most likely going off onto the different continents to start their lives. To me, I always make that the ending, because that was really the heart and soul of the family. You don't know exactly where they went, but you have an idea. To me, that's why we followed the show. They're the ones that went through a lot of the things, and I love that not everybody made it.

BRADLEY THOMPSON

Again, if you ally with the Russians, what's that going to mean? If you ally with the Soviets, then downstream they're going to have tentacles into your system. But sometimes people are honorable. As dark as *Battlestar* got, we always wanted to keep the glimmer of hope that basically humanity, under the right circumstances, can do the right thing. Or even under the wrong circumstances.

RONALD D. MOORE

Baltar and Six were, like, the first couple on the show, so ending with them together seemed right. Again, and in terms of there's a certain amount of irony there, and there was also something sweet about finding that that meant a lot to Baltar and taking him back all the way to his roots. So he did grow up on a farm, and then he actually knows how to farm and that that's actually . . . For once in his life, that's a useful skill, and that there was some kind of homecoming for him, too, and I really liked that.

JAMES CALLIS

I think that everything in *Battlestar* is kind of subversive and slightly insidious, and not quite on the page how people think it's on the page. I'd say that the ending is a similar case in point, where it's actually slightly elliptical and it's not exactly stipulated. Having previously arrived on the planet and leaving it, there's one way out of it, isn't there? Well, there are two options. The battlestar is blown up into space and that's it, or you're going to have survivors and the survivors are going to colonize a planet. I know which one I'd prefer to see, and it's the one we did.

BRADLEY THOMPSON

Baltar is someone who built this whole persona out of something he didn't want to be. He didn't want to be the farmer from wherever it was that colony of his came from. He had that accent that he got rid of. He became this huge public figure. Again, parallel to the Cylons. Then he went back to who he was to start with. He was going back to be a farmer. All the ego stuff in the end didn't make him happy.

MICHAEL RYMER
(director, "Daybreak")

In some ways we were trying to portray a parallel world where the people spoke English, they had presidents and all of these things. It was, I think, part of the genius of it. It forced the audience to suspend disbelief in a much more childlike way. You've made them buy the lie so deeply that they're just much more into it. Ron Moore and I used to talk about various episodes that maybe had too many coincidences and too many bits of serendipity. He would say, "Look, the audience will give us one chance to see if they can buy or not," and I think one of the great buys of *Battlestar* was that there was a parallel galaxy with twelve planets where they spoke English and had a very similar world to ours. The notion that this was the original god Apollo or the original god Athena, I always thought that was a stretch. I argued during the finale that the show, in reality, was two train tracks that should never cross. I lost that argument and we ended up back literally in our world. Which makes it harder to buy it all in some ways.

MARY MCDONNELL

That ending completed the circle and it gave us a stop. It gave us a place to stop and go back and watch the whole thing again. I like how it brought us back to wanting to go back to the beginning. Here we are in New York City, and huh? What is that about? Where are we in time? That's what I liked about it. I was suddenly unsure of where I was in time, and that I actually found intriguing. It made me want to do the whole thing all over again, and I think that was awesome. It was hard for me to really receive in full, because when you finish in a series yourself, and then you try to watch the rest of the story, you're not an innocent observer. Your observation is a bit tainted. I thought it screwed around with us one last time in terms of time and space; all this happened before and will happen again.

EDWARD JAMES OLMOS

The concept of a human/Cylon child drove so much of the series, and I think that Ron knew that the coup of coups was to really infuse the understanding of how close these two different cultures could relate and come together. To me it's stunning. And you go to the end, and that's where Baltar and Six are walking through Times Square and Six says to him, "This has happened before, it's going to happen again." And he says, "I don't agree. I think humanity has learned its lesson." And then it cuts to a little robot and they go walking off into the streets of 2008 in downtown New York. What we're saying with that one stroke is that humanity came from another galaxy, arrived here and mingled with the human elements that were here, and then spread and evolved the humanity that we know today. So we all come from that combination of cultures.

MICHAEL ANGELI

With Baltar and Six on modern-day Earth, what we were going for was a string theory/alternate reality kind of thing. Them going into a movie theater and all that other stuff—we didn't see him as an angel—certainly not—but this being science fiction, we just felt like we could play fast and loose with string theory, where there are nine realities that coexist of individuals in time, and how time becomes warped. That's what we were going for, *and* it left us open if we wanted to continue—which we didn't.

I had no problem with the ending myself. Our fan base, they flipped out. They were like, "This is an outrage." They were comparing it to *The Sopranos*' ending, which I think was great, too.

JAMES CALLIS

Those entities represented by Baltar and Six on modern-day Earth were supposed to be angels. Essentially Ron had kept the mystery going for myself and Tricia all the way through. He was like, "Whatever works for you, and you think works for you." We'd had a conversation about the Lord's Prayer earlier on, and when he explained to me at the end, the way he was thinking, he was like, "But surely you knew. We had that conversation about the Lord's Prayer, and 'forgive me my trespasses as I forgive those who trespass against me.'" So for a man to say, "Forgive me my trespasses," it was like, "God Almighty, what have you gone and done?" And he was like, "This is what the thing is like. Those voices in your head, or him and Six, the apparitions, they are energies of light, and they're not necessarily corporeal when you see them." Looking at the robot in the window, we're not quite sure.

TRICIA HELFER
(actress, "Number Six")

I was happy with those final moments. Of course, when we were shooting what was the finale, there are so many emotions going on, because it was coming to the end of our five-year family. Every time somebody would say it was their last scene or whatever, there'd be tears or one scene just hit you funny and somebody breaks into tears.

MICHAEL RYMER

Emotionally, Ron got it right. He went for character and he went for depth. We learned more about these people's past, and I loved the structure and the cross-cutting sectors of the early days, but I think once we got to the planets it would've been better to have left it unsaid. I love the planet they ended up on and I love the way they dispersed and the fact that it *could* have been our world. You know what I'm saying? On some level, it could have been. There were just certain things that could've been left unsaid. When I handed Ron the director's cut, it went from flying over the world in a Central Park, and then you just saw a crowded street and Baltar and Six walking through the crowd. And that was it. You didn't know what that meant. Have the Cylons come back? What did it mean? It was open-ended. Now there's quite a bit of explanation about what exactly it means and doesn't mean and so forth.

Ron always had a genius for the popular gesture. He'd also make an argument saying, "That makes no sense," or if there was a better way to do it, if we were a bit more realistic, and he's going, "No, we're telling a story. It's mythology. I don't feel as bound by that," and I think that's interesting.

SCOTT MANTZ

They knew by the end of the second season that the show was going to be done after four seasons. The show didn't go on, it didn't wear out its welcome like *The X-Files*. It didn't have ridiculous seasons like *Lost*. There's not a bad episode in that bunch. I loved the show. I was staying home every Friday night to watch it on Syfy. I thought it was great.

Beginning on March 13, 2009, and concluding a week later, Syfy aired the series finale of *Battlestar Galactica*. A show that the network had reluctantly put on the air, initially fighting against but ultimately embracing all of the things that frighteningly separated this show from most of the others on the air, but ended up making it the science fiction series by which all others would be measured. And nothing could have driven that point home harder than, just three days before it all ended, the show being celebrated at the United Nations in New York. It was an unprecedented event, promising to examine issues like human rights, children and armed conflict, terrorism, and reconciliation and dialogue among civilizations and faiths.

RONALD D. MOORE

They invited our cast, David Eick, and me and it was hosted by Whoopi Goldberg. At the UN there's the big classic hall where they give the speeches for the General Assembly, but there's a couple of rooms where you can fit the entire assembly in. We were in one of those rooms and went up to the dais. On the tables, where normally there would be all the names of all the different nations of the world, they had replaced with the names of the Twelve Colonies. It was like, "Oh my God!" . . . and completely mind-blowing.

Then we sat up there and the conversation was about what *Galactica* was talking about and how they were also things that served the UN's mission, talking about terrorism, talking about human rights, talking about freedoms and democracies. It was a fascinating discussion, because it was about all the themes and ideas that we dealt with in the show, but talking about it in this very rarefied forum. There were some ambassadors there. Some UN officials. There was a high commissioner for, I think, terrorism there. Then there was a reception afterward and I met lots of delegates and staff and ambassadors to the UN and they were fans of the show. They were like, "The show is really talking about things that matter to us here a lot. We just think it's a really interesting opportunity to do this kind of thing." They had classes and students that came and sat in the audience to listen. It was one of those amazing moments. It was really something. That's the sort of thing that makes up for the lack of more mainstream Emmy recognition.

SECTAR FOUR

GALACTICA & BEYOND (2009)

Bears. Beets. Battlestar Galactica.

17.
HATCHING THE PLAN

*"Earth is a dream . . . one we've been chasing
for a long time. We've earned it."*

Although *Battlestar Galactica* was winding down as an episodic series, there were several attempts to sustain the franchise over the subsequent years, first in the form of the 2009 made-for-DVD film *Battlestar Galactica: The Plan*. Designed to show the events of the miniseries and the first two seasons from the Cylons' perspective, this sci-fi *Rashomon* follows two versions of Dean Stockwell's Cylon, Cavil, offering up points and counterpoints on the validity of the Cylons' planned attacks. A number of actors from the show reprised their roles for the film, which was shot after the series wrapped.

JANE ESPENSON
(writer, "The Plan")

I look at *The Plan* as being nice for completists. It's really only a joy to those who are interested in some creative tying up of loose ends. I don't know that it really works on its own. You have to be not just a fan of the show, but a pretty obsessive fan of the show, to get what we were going for with *The Plan*. I loved doing it, and working with Eddie. The scope of it was just very hard to keep in my head working on it.

What did Baltar whisper? How did that Six escape down the hallway? Just little fun things that you wouldn't even know were loose ends. "Oh, look, they re-created the shot of Boomer from the 'Water' episode." They did a lot of re-creating of shots so that we could add dialogue. That was a lot of fun. I don't think it really worked a hundred percent, but little moments in it worked great.

BRADLEY THOMPSON
(co-executive producer, *Battlestar Galactica* [2004])

There were a couple of things I wish we hadn't done, and *The Plan* was one of them, because I like the plan being a mystery. I didn't want to explain anything. But they wanted it, it worked, and a lot of us were driven by having to pay the rent. We were trying to say, "If it did exist, what would it be?" That was a challenge and could we do it? In retrospect, I would rather these things stayed a mystery.

DAVID EICK
(executive producer, *Battlestar Galactica* [2004])

It wasn't viewed—internally or by the *BSG* fans—as successful as *Razor*, which I wholeheartedly agree with. In retrospect, Ron and I might've been better off passing on that deal, but at that time we were also committed to supporting other writers and directors from the show, and that project kept many of our people employed during the off-season.

A year after *Galactica* left the airwaves, the newly rechristened Syfy Channel produced a single season of a prequel television series called *Caprica*. Starring, among others, Eric Stoltz (*Mask*) and Esai Morales (*La Bamba*), it was set on the titular planet about fifty-eight years before the events of the main series. The focus is on the creation of the Cylons as told through the Adama and Graystone families. Despite the success of *Galactica,* the prequel series failed to connect with viewers in the same way.

Initially, Ron Moore was keeping his distance from the show, so veteran TV writer Jane Espenson (*Once Upon a Time, Buffy the Vampire Slayer*), who had joined *Battlestar Galactica* in its fourth season, was picked as showrunner, a position she was reluctant to assume.

RONALD D. MOORE
(executive producer, *Caprica*)

It's the great missed opportunity. It had a lot of potential, but for a variety of reasons it just didn't click. Creatively it was pretty close, and you can see it kind of finding its way through season one. We got really lucky with the cast again; we just lucked into another great group of actors that were really good in the show. It was a strong ensemble we could build on. But the problem was the behind-the-scenes issues just kind of infected the show. It lacked a certain focus of what it wanted to be in that first season.

JANE ESPENSON
(executive producer, *Caprica*)

My feelings about the show are guilt. I took on a project that I wasn't ready for. I was not reared to run a show, and I think *Caprica* deserved better than what I was able to give it. I gave it my heart, but I am not a showrunner and I didn't realize it yet. Ultimately I ended up stepping down, and Kevin Murphy took over at the end and did a beautiful job. When I was asked to be a showrunner, I couldn't turn it down because I loved *Battlestar* so much and thought that every time I have succeeded at something, I've also felt very reluctant to try. So maybe I'd get in there and discover that I could do it. Well, no, my original instinct was right. It wasn't for me.

RONALD D. MOORE

I know Jane blames herself, and that's unfortunate, because ultimately I'm responsible for making the decision to put her in that position, and she told me right up front when I asked her about it. She said being a showrunner hadn't been one of her ambitions. She said she liked being a writer, she liked being a personal attendant. I should have listened to that. Like, "Okay, wait a minute, you're telling me right at this moment, this isn't really something that you want to do, but you'll do it and you're a good soldier." That may not be the best choice for the showrunner. It just isn't. But I just wasn't in a place where I could hear and think clearly about that.

I kind of feel like the key problem, probably, was at that moment in time I just didn't want to be showrunning. I was in a different headspace. I was very tired by the end of *Galactica*. I had also started questioning whether or not I wanted to keep going in television. *Galactica* had become such a thing. It was so great and exceeded my expectations on so many levels. Just an amazing run, and then I had this sense of, What do I do next? How do you top yourself? The Orson Welles curse: You make *Citizen Kane* and then what do you do?

JANE ESPENSON

Kevin was better at recognizing when the room had the right idea. I got a lot of direction from the network, and every story that the room bought into, I was like, "The network's not going to like this." I remember the first day Kevin took over, the room was like, "What if we did this?" And he said, "Great. That sounds good. Let's do it." I saw right away I should have been trusting this room of very good writers more than I was. I was second-guessing them, because I was anticipating everything that the network might not like when I should have had more confidence of, "You have a smart idea, let's sell it." Instead of saying, "Yeah, but what if the network doesn't like it?"

RONALD D. MOORE

Eventually the show gets there, but we just kept starting and stopping so many times. It was so difficult to get the show made and approved and to get the scripts approved. We were constantly having to go back and rebreak stories and throw out storylines, redo everything over and over again and it just became chaotic. As a result, when you look at it as a collective whole now, it probably starts in one direction, kind of zigs and zags through that first season, and then toward the end you can just kind of sense an almost desperate quality as we're trying to get the network off our backs. Trying to do different things and trying to get a pickup there by the end. We didn't.

MARK STERN
(former president of original content, Syfy)

Caprica was a heartbreaker, because I felt like it really carried the themes of *Battlestar* forward in a different way. They found really cool ideas in there. There's a lot you could say postmortem about *why* it didn't work. My personal feeling is that it was two main things. One, the marketing campaign didn't work. We were too clever by half. We tried to ignore the fact that it was *Battlestar* so that we could hopefully pull in other people. We did this very obscure campaign with this half-naked girl eating an apple. You're like, "What the fuck's that about?" We didn't talk about what the show was about in marketing, because we were a little afraid, so we didn't really communicate effectively to a larger audience. And the *Battlestar* fan was kind of confused about what the hell the show was, and we weren't talking to them.

JANE ESPENSON

The show told the story of the Cylons, it told us all that the genocidal impulses came from one angry teenage girl who became the first Cylon, and that's fascinating. It talked a lot about really interesting meditations on what it means to be conscious and what it means to be you. Are you you, if your brain is in a different body? How much humanity depends on having a human body, if any? My favorite part was the world building, the cultures of it. What would it mean to have these colonies so close to each other, but on different planets with different climates, different religions, different approaches to religion? Different cultures. What does popular culture feel like on a planet that's Earthlike, but not Earth? If you're going to write a show about a new culture, why give it all the limitations of the old one? I thought *Caprica* really lived up to that. It showed us a culture that had its own problems, but didn't have all the same limitations as the culture we already know. I was very proud of that.

MARK STERN

What ultimately killed the series was it was trying to do too many different things at the same time. It was more intellectual than emotional. The dilemma of this girl trapped in this virtual world was hard to relate to or connect with. The themes of the nuns and what they were trying to accomplish, and the larger themes of what their plot was of apotheosis, were really confusing and, ultimately, kind of a big shrug.

RONALD D. MOORE

Jane got stuck in the meat grinder with the network, and Syfy was consciously being at their worst at that point. They were approving things and then changing their minds, and then approving something else and then throwing it all out. You'd be three or four episodes into writing scripts and then they wanted a whole new direction. I'd come back in and argue with Mark Stern about it, but I'm fighting on ground that's not really my own, and that's a harder game to play. I'd try to support them, let them get down the road a little bit, and then the network blows that up again.

It just became this ugly cycle of constant stress and constant straining trying to just get Syfy to stick with what they had agreed to. That was a *big* source of frustration. They'd agree on something and change their minds, or they would pass the buck and say, "Yeah, we approved this, but now New York has weighed in." Weeks would go by and you'd get really far into the creative process, and *then* New York would suddenly wake up and say, "Oh, we hate all this. We don't want to do any of it." So we'd start all over again. It was maddening.

MARK STERN

I guess the bottom line is that it took an attack on some really cool themes and ideas, which is one of the things I loved about it. But it did it in a way that didn't connect to you emotionally, didn't feel compelling. The thing about *Battlestar* that was part of its secret sauce was you could talk about all those different things, you could talk about spirituality and mandalas and destiny, and cycles of love and whatever, yet every now and then a Cylon would pop up and try to kill you. It was a struggle of survival. It was a struggle to get somewhere safe. Those two elements really balance each other well, giving you something that was smart, erudite, and thought-provoking, but also emotionally compelling. *Caprica* just wasn't able to achieve this.

RONALD D. MOORE

The whole situation was crazy. They were only sort of supportive, like they were with *Galactica* in the beginning. *Caprica* wasn't really the show they wanted to do, but they had green-lit and then they were pregnant with it, but they kept messing with it. Then they just gave us a hard time about the ratings all the way through. In fairness, okay, the ratings were *not* stellar and we were on the bubble, but I felt—and I'm pretty sure David did, too—that we had earned the right to get a little slack.

We had created *Battlestar Galactica* for them. We had put the channel on the map in a way that it had not been before. We had delivered the goods and we had earned the awards and the acclaim and we'd made something that was really, really special. And it felt like, at the end of the day, none of that counted as they punted us out the door at the first opportunity. It just felt like we had earned the right to get a second season, and they wouldn't give it to us. That was *very* frustrating.

Following the short-lived *Caprica*, there was *Battlestar Galactica: Blood & Chrome*, a ten-part webseries that would eventually air as a two-hour 2010 movie on Syfy. Designed as a pilot for another prequel series, it cast Luke Pasqualino as a young William "Husker" Adama during the first Cylon war.

RONALD D. MOORE

The idea of doing another show had come up while I was on *Caprica* and still at Universal. I had some conversations with Mark Stern about was there another series. "Is there another show, another spin-off? What else can we do?" And it was really funny. Like I keep saying, they didn't love us while we were there, but once *Battlestar* ended, there was a sense of them suddenly having the attitude of, "Well, we do kind of want to keep this going somehow, so can we keep talking about another project?"

So there was *Caprica* and then they started talking about another show, and I said, "Well, the thing that would interest me, that would be different, is there is this block of time. There is this story in our past of the first Cylon war." And my idea was to do the story of the *Galactica* during the Cylon War, and what that meant to me was, you would start with the *Galactica*'s commissioning and you would take her through the Cylon War sort of episodically, and mixing up the timeline. *Not* doing it chronologically and changing the cast a lot. There were a group of fighter pilots at the beginning and there was her original commander, but she would kind of like mix it up. And you would have actors talking to the camera; we were going to break the fourth wall, like they're being interviewed. And it would be their memories of being aboard the *Galactica*.

It's really about the ship and the people that went through her halls over the course of the Cylon War, with their different perspectives, battles they won or lost, people who died, cowards, heroes, traitors, all that kind of stuff, and do it in this sort of nonlinear kind of way. I *really* liked that idea, but they were less enamored of that idea, and it sort of didn't go anywhere. But then they kept talking about it. Like, "We still want to do this other thing." And they never quite wanted to pull the trigger on, "Let's talk about a story."

Or "Let's really get a formal pitch together." It kind of limped along. And then, eventually, *Caprica* was canceled, my deal ended with Universal, and I decided I didn't want to. I was going to go work on some feature projects for a while, and eventually go to Sony.

DAVID EICK

I'd just been through a lousy breakup and was on the plane, probably on my third Scotch, and started sketching out a story about a woman who crushes a man's heart by betraying him. I swear, that's the stupid origin story for *Blood & Chrome*. I knew that generally the network was interested in another prequel and there had already been discussions about what that might be. Perhaps by that point the notion of "Young Adama"—a fairly obvious concept—was already swimming around in my head with the booze.

I jotted down some ideas about how that premise might inform some critical aspect of Adama's worldview—his sense of brotherhood with those who are loyal; his sense of caution and distrust among potential enemies. But the real opportunity, in the minds of the folks at Syfy and Universal, was to use the *BSG* brand to break into a new form of programming. In this case, they wanted a *BSG* spin-off that could premiere on Xbox—I'm serious—and in success spin out into a weekly series on the network. That meant the concept needed a "game-ish" vibe, something that would feel at home in that medium.

They wanted an action piece—not too dense or mythological—so the pilot story was designed to be a hundred minutes, broken into ten ten-minute cliffhanger segments ("game chapters"), that would ultimately work as a standalone movie with enough of a final cliffhanger to tease another movie or one-hour series or whatever.

MICHAEL TAYLOR
(writer, *Blood & Chrome*)

This was after *Caprica*. David Eick came to me and said we had an opportunity to write a webseries, because that's what it was conceived of at the time. I was able to bring in David Weddle and Bradley Thompson to help plot it out. Once they got the script, they saw that it could be a pilot. I actually wrote a thirty-page outline for a first season and into subsequent seasons, and it brought back some of the old cast. Honestly, it would have been just fucking insanely cool, but it didn't happen. It at least got to be a fun TV movie. I had more of a sense of that being almost like a World War II movie, with elements of propaganda films and a basic war story and wartime espionage. And characters being used by higher powers, possibly for good reasons, but still being used. A lot of classic themes of a lot of movies I love. That was a real cool experience.

DAVID EICK

When the network saw the script—codeveloped by myself with David Weddle, Bradley Thompson, Jonas Pate, and Michael Taylor, with the teleplay written by Taylor—they really flipped. But at about the same time, the Xbox deal was falling apart. Rather than abandon the project, Syfy elected to proceed with it as a traditional pilot, which meant we could bail on the "ten cliffhangers" structure, which was frankly a bit contrived. . . . The bad news was we were still stuck with the "experimental budget" we'd been saddled with.

This forced us into another design conceit, which was to use the expertise in green-screen CG we'd spent the past decade perfecting to substitute for all practical locations and most practical sets, which are two extremely expensive categories of production. We had digital photos of all the *BSG* sets—taken years earlier, before we dismantled everything—and used those as a guide. The result was a pilot shot entirely on a green-screen stage, including vast epic shots of frozen tundras along with all the spaceships and robots and monsters. At six-hundred-plus visual effect shots, nothing on television like it had been attempted before—or since. It proved to be a totally different look from *BSG* or *Caprica* and gave *Blood & Chrome* a gleaming, hypervisual style unto itself.

MICHAEL TAYLOR

I was there for two months in Vancouver on a kind of disco stage where everything, in a way, was virtual. All the sets were these very spare kind of jungle gyms, and everything was flown in digitally with the help of a remarkable visual effects coordinator, Gary Hutzel, who ran his own ship, which was sort of created with Ron on *Battlestar*.

DAVID EICK

Once the network saw it all put together, their enthusiasm was off the charts. Michael Taylor, Jonas Pate, the director, and I set about breaking season one, and a pickup seemed imminent. Then, I think, the reality of *Caprica*'s poor showing in the ratings began to set in. The network seemed to slowly sour on the *BSG* brand, almost like they just wanted a break from it. Maybe it was to prove Syfy's programming independence of the *BSG* moniker.

MICHAEL TAYLOR

Sort of interesting, in some small respect, is that after *Battlestar*, the network auctioned off all the props. I got a prop from *Razor*, like the backup knife that Admiral Cain had as a young girl to try and ward off Cylons. I've got the old rusty knife. I think it was the backup prop. When it came time to do *Blood & Chrome*, we had to rent back props from fans who had bought them.

Currently in development at Universal Pictures is a new feature film of *Battlestar Galactica* that would reboot the franchise yet again. An attempt by the studio to once again capture the excitement and stratospheric grosses of *Star Wars* clearly proving once more that this has all happened before and will all happen again. Lisa Joy, one of the creators of *Westworld* with her husband Jonathan Nolan, is writing the film for the studio.

RONALD D. MOORE

They've talked about it for years. They talked about it while I was still at Universal, much to my surprise. One of the worst days I had at Universal was picking up the trades and seeing that they were talking about doing a *Battlestar Galactica* feature film, and reading it in *Variety* at my desk. That's how I found out. They never called. All of these fiefdoms at Universal are very, very separate, so the feature people had nothing to do with the TV side, and they had the rights from Glen Larson, or still had an option on the rights from Glen Larson, or something. Some convoluted thing. So they were on a completely separate track and they made that announcement, and it was a shock.

I was very upset. I just went home. Syfy called me up and they were like,

"Oh, we're so sorry. This wasn't well handled." And I was like, "Fuckin' A, it wasn't well handled. What are you talking about?" It's, like, you're gonna do a reboot of the show? We're *on* the air! It might have been during *Caprica*, but it was right there toward the end. I said, "The body's not even cold yet, for fuck's sake."

As has been proven since *Battlestar Galactica* ended its run, that "body" has yet to cool off even some ten years later. Its impact, influence, and importance continues to be felt not only by the fans, but by the cast and crew who were brought together to bring it to life in the first place and find their bond stronger than ever.

EDWARD JAMES OLMOS
(actor, "Admiral William 'Bill' Adama")

The connection I felt and feel with everyone involved with the show is something I've never felt before, and I've been in some great ensembles. This became something else; we went to another place. The feelings were real. We lived it. Okay, we're actors and we have to do that. That's part of the whole experience, and you hear it from everybody. I mean, *Hill Street Blues, ER, The West Wing*—they all have incredible feelings about their relationship to one another and to the show. But because of the nature of what we experienced and where we took it in respect of the responsibility of really understanding that we were documenting human behavior in one of the most difficult situations known to humankind: the extermination of humanity.

We were in Vancouver, so we kind of cocooned ourselves off into totally our own space. That's why it came out the way it did. From the opening scene of Starbuck running through the hallway of the ship—a scene that never seemed to stop. If you look at that scene, you're going to say, "Holy crap, there's no edits. It just keeps on; characters are introduced and then move off and another character comes on." But you felt that right from the beginning there was a tremendous understanding; that we all understood as a unit.

JAMIE BAMBER
(actor, "Captain Lee 'Apollo' Adama")

The show was like making an independent film where our voices as actors were appreciated and heard and we weren't just hired and told to stand in the right place and say the words. We were on this journey with everyone else and we were all there to make it better. So it really taught me a lot of things about this business and storytelling and acting and responsibility to those around you. For me, it was right place, right time, right moment in my career. But also an experience the like of which I haven't had since in terms of the media and the public response and the way it seemed to just fire people's bellies.

TRICIA HELFER
(actress, "Number Six")

I'd been acting for a year when I got the show, and for me personally it was a brand-new experience. I definitely got lucky having an amazing experience as the first one that didn't sour me on the business. The show represented a combination of things, between the incredible writing and the story that is actually there, and knowing you are doing something special. And knowing you are doing material that, even though it's fiction, has a heavy core to it. It *means* something.

When you are talking about the annihilation of human rights and what it's like to be in war and what it's like to be fighting for your lives and all that type of thing, it hits you heavier. To have that and to know you are doing good material, but also mixed with a team that's just really bonded together. We became really close and it became a special project for us all. Children were born during the beginning of *Battlestar* and during the run of *Battlestar*. You'd all have birthday parties and the kids' parties and Sunday barbecues. Just amazing.

RONALD D. MOORE

The show is bigger than all of us. It really touched people and challenged them. It's not like any other program. It was and is unique. It's just a special piece. When you watch it, you're sort of pulled into this other world and it's nothing like *Star Trek*, it's nothing like *Stargate*, and it's nothing like *Star Wars*. It's its own unique animal, and people really responded to it and got emotionally involved with those characters and the story. It just really touched a nerve.

TAHMOH PENIKETT
(actor, "Captain Karl 'Helo' Agathon")

Deep meaning. Resonance. Love. These are the words that come to mind when I think about the show. Absolute joy. I had such a deep and ever-growing bond with this group of individuals that I had the pleasure of working with on the show. The beautiful thing about it is that it continues to grow. Many of us are still very, very close. I don't think anyone had the foresight to be able to tell what this thing would become and how meaningful it would be for all of us and how it would bind us all together in a sort of way.

AARON DOUGLAS
(actor, "Chief Tyrol")

I've got about a hundred credits, give or take a few, which means that I've done *a lot* of TV shows and films, but I don't keep in touch with anyone from any other show like I do with *Battlestar*. Not even remotely close. The genuine love and the genuine affection that we all have for each other and for the show and for our shared piece of it, is something remarkable. For some reason, the fans have that same shared love and camaraderie and sense of family that we do.

GRACE PARK
(actress, "Sharon 'Boomer' Valerii")

For myself, it evokes an era of a time when things were more innocent, though I'm sure they'll always be more innocent in the past to some degree. But the five years that spanned the time we shot the series I grew a lot as an actor. There were a lot of challenges and growth, but also the people that were a part of it from onscreen, behind the scenes, the creators, producers . . . It was jelling with everyone finding out how we were going to be with each other, how Eddie was leading us, how talented and supportive the crew were. It just seemed like a really special time where these things were coming together. And we really had no idea how good it was going to be. I'm sure Eddie will say that he knew or Mary will say that she knew, but it was definitely my biggest job to date and I really had no idea. Eddie had to tell us multiple times to get ready, that this was going to be the best thing we would do for forty years, so we should make it special.

How much more special can you make it than just to be as present as you can be? Meanwhile, these things are being thrown at you and you're doing your best to juggle and stand on all these balls and remain balanced; keep your head above water. It was just all these things at the same time. People would say, "You were the actor that grew the most," and I was like, "That's meant as a compliment, I suppose," but the way my brain works, it's like, "Oh, that means I was the shittiest at the time." I guess I got less shitty?

KATEE SACKHOFF
(actress, "Kara 'Starbuck' Thrace")

Truthfully, Tricia Helfer was just at my house for four hours hanging out. We are a family. I see Michael Trucco all the time and James Callis. I'd see Bamber more but he had to move to France. We're a family and I think part of it was the fact that we were all in Vancouver. It was a really good place to be. There was no judgment. It was a completely supportive environment where everyone from the grip to the director to the art department to the AD department . . . every single person on that set was respectful of the process that the actor needed to go through and the freedom that it required, and the time that it took. We created something really great, because everybody sort of respected that. It was really great.

Battlestar Galactica is the biggest gift I could possibly have ever given to my career. I never dreamed that the show would give me a career. *Battlestar* was the fourth or fifth series that I did, and I never dreamed that some remake of a sci-fi show that some people remembered and some people didn't at all would actually give me a career in the sense that it's had this longevity because of this character. That's something that people in this business fight for.

MICHAEL HOGAN
(actor, "Colonel Saul Tigh")

A lot of people talk to me about *Battlestar Galactica* on different film sets. It always takes a couple of days before they bring it up; some people aren't saying it right away, but eventually the director of photography or somebody will say, "I know you're tired of hearing about it, man, but *Battlestar Galactica.* . . ." And I always say, "You know what? I'm not tired of this. Quite a while since we did it and I love talking about it, so anytime during the shoot if you want to ask me something, feel free, because it brings back these great memories for me." It's just one of the shows that everybody involved is so incredibly proud of the product, incredibly proud of their work as opposed— not that there's that many—to some shows that one is involved in where you, "Oh, you want to talk about *that*?" *Battlestar* is, "Oh, yes, bring it on." There's no question, and I think that everybody involved means that. *Battlestar* was a movie that took us five years to shoot, and what a gift as an actor that is.

ALESSANDRO JULIANI
(actor, "Felix Gaeta")

I think of *Battlestar* as a life changer. Childhood wish fulfillment. It's a rare thing to get to actually become the things you played with as a child, so that's totally what it was for me. When booking the series, I didn't really believe it. But going into my basement and finding my old *Battlestar* action figures, and my board game, and thinking, "This is pretty fucking cool." So what instantly comes to mind is, "Wow, what a cool, atypical thing to get to experience as an actor." And to then have action figures of yourself in that same universe is pretty wild.

JAMIE BAMBER

I think about *Battlestar Galactica,* and I think about all those wonderful people that we got to know so well. It's the people, really, and the fact that we were all in one place together, many of us away from home. Brought us closer together and it's a period in time for me and it was a very key point of my life. I got married, had three kids up there, basically. A golden few years of a journey that I had no idea we would ever go on, and the further it retreats in the rearview mirror, the most halcyon those days seem, because they were very special.

At the time, Edward James Olmos said he felt sorry for the younger members of the cast, of which I include myself, because he said, "It's happened to you too early in your careers and you're never going to have another experience like this." He's definitely been right. When you're in the middle of anything, it's very hard to appreciate every moment, but it's wise advice to live in the moment as much as you can.

GRACE PARK

The show evokes that time where we were all thrown into it together with this wonderful script. But the writers were figuring it out as they were going along. So there was something about the show, but it's hard to tell if it was just the script. Was it the people? Was it being in my twenties and thirties? There were a lot of magical little pieces. Even the making of it was pretty special.

MICHAEL TRUCCO
(actor, "Samuel Anders")

If you were playing word association and said *Battlestar Galactica,* it conjures up so many images. I see Eddie in the CIC with the microphone in his hand; the gravitas and the weight and the charisma that that man brought to Adama as a microcosm for what our show was. I *don't* think people saw it coming. The caliber of storytelling and the acting. The tone that was set by guys like Eddie and Mary and Michael Hogan and James Callis. These are heavyweight actors that brought the level of talent and—there's that word again—gravitas to the show.

MARY MCDONNELL
(actress, "President Laura Roslin")

Not only did we collectively engineer a whole new idea for the elegance of *Battlestar Galactica,* without betraying the first one, but while we were shooting and it was airing, this brand-new business was emerging that we all are part of now with the new platforming and literally transitioned from film to high-definition video. We also made the transition from your acting space being sacred and no one ever got to come visit you unless it was a very special event, to people sending out pictures and message of life on the set that day. Everything was changing right before our eyes; as we were shooting it, our whole reality was changing. We were going through the primary between Clinton and Obama . . . just so much change in the air and so many different ideas happening, but every time you heard "Rolling," the focus would instantly be in this galactic universe where we were trying to explore these very same ideas through.

JAMES CALLIS
(actor, "Gaius Baltar")

We've been saying this kind of stuff for a while now. *Battlestar* is worth more than the sum total of its parts. You only look good when you're next to other people who look good. Otherwise, nobody's watching it and it's not any good. It's one of those things that I think you're right to highlight it, that again it's something that I suppose I slightly took for granted, that everyone was just phenomenal. Your imagination or what you're bringing to the party is enhanced, supported, generated, by the other people around you and your interaction with them. Whenever I think about the show, essentially I think about all the people, and there were a lot of us. The cast and the crew and the postproduction and the executives who made it happen. I see faces more than anything else. I would imagine that every person in the show wants to acknowledge as many people as they possibly can, because every person in the show was so instrumental in making the show what it was and is.

AARON DOUGLAS

Once you get to a place where you know that you're making something extraordinary, you can't take your foot off the gas. It's like we're the ultimate team sport. You don't want to let your fellow cast members down or the writers are trying to out-write each other, and the actors are trying to out-act each other, and the grips are trying to out-grip each other. Everybody knew that this is a really special thing. Don't show up hung over. Don't mail a scene in, don't take any time off. Just put your head down and keep going. I've seen so many other shows where you can tell that they're just tired of doing it and there's no oomph left. But I don't think we ever lost our oomph, and that's from everybody at the top in L.A. all the way down through where we were filming and down to the person guarding the parking lot. They were proud to be on *Battlestar Galactica.* It was a very cool thing.

TRICIA HELFER

I hope to be working for many more years to come, but when people say, "Do you ever get tired of hearing and talking about *Battlestar,*" I'm like, "Not at all." Not only was it an amazing experience, but the fact is that audiences are still finding it and still passionate about it, and there are new people finding it all the time and still passionate about it; it shows that it doesn't have a time stamp on it, so to speak.

TAHMOH PENIKETT

Sometimes things are just kismet; they're brought together because they're a beautiful project. It's a very timely project and this group of people were meant to work together. I don't want to speak in religious aspects, but it's as if a greater hand had something to do with this, and not many actors in this industry can say that. They might have one experience in their career, or if they're lucky they may have numerous ones, where they've formed that bond and they never lose it. Because they worked on a project that was so relevant and it meant so much to them, that even with the passing of time and not having seen that castmate, or that writer or that director, for a long time, they still have that. They still have that shared experience.

JAMIE BAMBER

Battlestar Galactica was like the little hammer on the patient's knee in the doctor's office. We just hit the right spot and the knee jerked to hit that spot within the world of television and cable TV and the media, and just to get a reaction from people. I've never worked in anything else that has had that reaction, that immediately hit the tone right for the time that we were in, and that everyone was talking about. I've done shows that have been great and things that people have admired, but nothing that really captured the imagination of a global audience in those years, the way *Battlestar* did, and is obviously still being talked about. Just for the last few weeks I've fielded several requests for reunions and get-togethers and retrospectives and things like that. So obviously it's something that's touched people and that made people reflect a bit on the world that we were living in at that time, and are still living in. And entertain them, too.

ALESSANDRO JULIANI

It tapped into something deeper. Something about our basic humanity. Anything I say right now is not going to really do justice to it, but any great piece of art, or any great thing, reflects back on us. *Battlestar* must have done that in an expected genre, maybe in an unexpected way. We must have all seen ourselves in the show in some capacity for it to have inspired so much of life beyond its short little run. When we go to these reunions and things, I remain sort of flabbergasted at the longevity of it. The people who watched the show when it was first out, they are now showing this show to their kids. So their kids are discovering it on their own and so now families are coming and the kids are now dressing up, or the teenagers. So there's this sense now that it's going to go on forever. It's going to perpetuate itself and beget itself. What a remarkable thing. What a phenomenon.

RONALD D. MOORE

From the outset, one of the first things that David Eick and I talked about was the fact that we wanted the show to be relevant. That we thought to do a science fiction show that isn't purely escapism, that isn't about people and civilizations that mean nothing to us. Let's do a show that's more along the lines of older and more traditional science fiction that's sort of common to the audience and contemporary society through this interesting prism.

DAVID EICK

Most of the things that were created and now are being analyzed by the United Nations and others were dreamed up in sports bars. It's surreal for me to contend with that, but we were averse to attempting to adapt headlines. That wasn't what we wanted to do.

RONALD D. MOORE

I think that while we're both sort of historians and science majors, we also decided that the show was not really a soapbox for our particular political viewpoints. You can't help but let your own worldview leak into what you do—I don't think any of us can fool ourselves into thinking that it wouldn't—but it was important to us that the show was not really just an opportunity to say, "This is what we think the right answer is, and this is what the answer to these difficult political and moral questions is." It was really an opportunity to examine them, to ask questions or look at them from a slightly different point of view and say, "Here's a group of characters that we are now going to ask you to invest what you will in." As we got into the series, we started dealing with more and more of these kinds of things.

DAVID EICK

There was a sense, of course, of this fairly restrictive administration and a period of time when it seemed like human rights and freedoms were being restricted and that we were not clear about *why* we were doing things that we were doing, and why our sons and daughters were being lost. That just uniformly indoctrinated itself into the world, and the work was all about drama and about trying to make people feel what we were feeling in the room, what we were feeling as we discussed things with each other, and it wasn't that dramatic, it wasn't that situationally specific. It was really about just trying to tell good stories and finding ourselves amidst this period in time in America where those good stories were being informed by the sick and upsetting world. And in the final analysis, that has borne itself out, that there's a sickness and a darkness and a tortured quality to the heroes of *Battlestar Galactica*. If we had done this show ten years later, that never would have happened.

RONALD D. MOORE

I took the approach that we were going to try to represent all of the sides of these debates fairly. We would try to sort of take Lincoln's phrase of "With malice toward none, with charity for all" and make *that* what the show is about. We were going to give everything their time and their place, and we would give these very difficult, very thorny issues a hearing and sort of watch how characters like Adama and Laura Roslin would grapple with these issues, but not pretend that it was a simple or a political instance, one of the two. We didn't want to say, "Well, the liberal point of view is there, therefore the show is going to promote that." And at the end of the episode, the captain will say, "This is what the right answer is." It's always going to be difficult to get to anything resembling a right answer in these very complicated questions.

TODD SHARP
(production executive, *Battlestar Galactica* [2004])

Did we know that people would love it? Did we know that people would watch it? Did we know that we'd still be talking about it all these years later? Did we know there would be a United Nations panel with cast and crew? Did we know that we were going to be at the Peabody Awards? We were making a show for Sci-Fi Channel, for crying out loud. I don't think anybody was thinking about that at all. Actually, Eddie Olmos was. He was the guy going around telling everybody you have no idea how this show is going to grow over time. "It's like *Blade Runner*," he said. "Twenty years from now, this show is going to find a brand-new audience and people are going to embrace it all over again." Sure enough, it's happened.

MARK STERN

A lot of people adopt successes after the fact—"I always knew it was going to be a hit"—but none of us knew what *Battlestar* was going to become. That it would become a phenomenon. I don't care what anyone says, you don't really ever know. But what we *did* know is that it was different, and we knew that it was special. We knew that there was something about it that really resonated, and that it deserved the best shot it could get. It was really one of those things where you wanted to make sure it had the time it needed, that these guys had the support they needed and that they had the best possible talent we could find.

DAVID WEDDLE
(producer, *Battlestar Galactica* [2004])

Battlestar Galactica was a product of everybody getting so excited about going to work, and knowing they were doing something so innovative, that *everybody* pushed the envelope. Every department. I can remember seeing set guys building flats, talking about how they were pushing the envelope on set design. It's a rare thing that every department and everybody on the crew were all together. There was such a high morale and such a feeling we were doing something extraordinary and everybody trying to go beyond just doing a job. It was *thrilling* to be a part of all that.

JANE ESPENSON

The power of the show comes from a combination of everything. I like shows that mix tones and goals, and this had this mixture of tones where Baltar could be hysterically, broadly funny, and you had action—"33" has this very tense situation where the Cylons are attacking every thirty-three minutes—and incredibly actiony, tense, suspenseful stuff. I'd never seen a show before that dealt with things as honestly as this show had. The notion that the right answer was to run away. We've *never* seen that, because it's not the normal thing to do, but it is if it's the only way to save what's left of humanity. Then that becomes very much the right thing to do. Most people in the drama business would say, "Yeah, but why depict that? It's not dramatic, because the choice to run away is so unsatisfying." So it had a mixture of tones, and then it also has these really high aspirations. That it wasn't going to settle for just being a ripping yarn, but it clearly was there to say something.

BRADLEY THOMPSON

We tapped in because when we were making it, we were going, "This is probably the coolest thing we're ever going to do, because we got to tap into all this stuff and everything was working." We had these great actors, we had a studio that more or less backed what we were doing. We had incredible visionaries running the thing. We had Gary Hutzel making stuff happen that nobody had ever seen before. It was just this conglomeration of really cool stuff all at once. I'm glad that still sells and people still react to it. We were talking about things that were real even in the best science fiction. I've always loved talking about real things in a wacky place, so you can divorce yourself from your own biases and look just at the issue itself. You're never looking at it as the issue, you're enjoying the life with the characters. Then you go, "Oh, wait a minute. What did they just do? Why was that a good or a bad thing, and how do I feel about that?" I cared whether Sharon got to keep her baby and all those kind of things.

MICHAEL RYMER
(director, "33")

When people say to me, "*Battlestar* was the first of the great competent TV shows, good TV shows. Not the best of them, not up to *The Sopranos* level, but certainly part of that wave," I agree. It was the writing and that we had a feature-level cast who were acting and creating behaviors. It was much better than what anyone was used to seeing in science fiction. Then, of course, Ron was writing much more human, complex stuff that you weren't seeing on *Stargate* or all these other shows, which were good, but this was more a saga for the ages.

KATEE SACKHOFF

Star Trek and *Next Gen* had this thing where they talked about real issues, which is so important in television, but I think that *Battlestar* was the first time it was talking about current events as they were happening in real time, and making people take notice, in a science fiction show.

RICHARD HATCH
(actor, "Apollo"/"Tom Zarek")

My experiences on *Battlestar,* classic and reimagined, have provided me with the love, support, and sense of family that I missed in my childhood and given me a home where I could finally grow into the actor I always knew I could be. The original cast of *BSG* was truly a family, led by the gracious Lorne Greene, and this current family of Colonial actors has only taken the true meaning of family to an even more elevated and rarefied place. I love both *BSG* series and feel very blessed to have been part of two great shows. Art is about life and exploring our wildest imaginings. It's about touching the infinite and exploring what's possible if we only believe. *Battlestar* embodies all of this in the most personal and intimate way and she will always be in my heart.

AARON DOUGLAS

It's the reflection of the drama of humanity and that we are not white hats and we are not black hats. We're gray hats. You can believe in your heart and in your mind that you are a certain way, but when presented with information that fundamentally changes your worldview, your view of self will change. You really have to sit back and go, "Oh, shit, what *am* I? What do I mean? How am I going to go moving forward?" When you watch a show like *Battlestar,* you see the characters going through these crazy shifts, because they're presented with new information that totally offends their view of the world, themselves, the people that they love, the people beside them.

You live beside people all of your lives and the people beside you just happen to be Jewish or Muslim or whatever. Then 9/11 happens and you're looking at your neighbors going, "Wow, so what are you up to?" The most nonsensical, idiotic thought you can have, but people's natural reaction is to have that, because all the news stations are going, "Oh, look at what happened. These terrorists are bad people." The people who live beside you are the same damn people they've always been, and they're lovely. It's not their fault there's a couple of assholes out there. *Battlestar* held that mirror up. I always come back to Ron Moore's desire to hold a mirror up to the world and say, "Now what do you think?" *That's* the power of the show.

JAMIE BAMBER

Battlestar Galactica is good storytelling. It's all the elements of what it is to be a human being, distilled down to their rawest and most essential forms. You take a human race and human history and you distill it down to fifty thousand people, the size of a small village. The kind of community where you can know every significant member of your community, personally, and you stick it out in space, which is the ultimate realm of romance. Looking for home, there are so many stories from biblical to before that, to the modern story of America and the settling of the West and people stretching out into unknown territories, against unknown threats, fleeing something from their past to find the future that will offer them the chance to express and be themselves. It's elemental storytelling, yet told with such specificity and boldness and prescience. The fact that the story was really a vehicle for Ron to talk about the world as it was, in a very specific time, ironically is what makes it timeless. In removing it from the actual context and yet having it be a specific reaction to 9/11, to our invasion of Iraq, to our colonizing of a foreign country and the seeds of discord that we unwittingly sowed in doing that, that's a very specific thing that he was writing about. But he's done it in this beautiful, universal way.

MICHAEL NANKIN
(director, "The Ties That Bind")

One of the best working experience I've ever had. We were making a show, but we were also building a family. That doesn't happen very often. People in television live a gypsy life, especially in the last ten years, when production has gone so international. But as dark and as tough as the show was, we were all fans of the show we were making. The other thing is we were allowed to go crazy. It's a show about people pushed to the edge. There's people getting in their way. A lot of people are being pushed to behave in ways that normal people don't get a chance to. It's exciting and compelling to watch these episodes and think, "What would *I* do in that situation? Is there a point that I could be pushed to poison my wife, or betray my colleagues, or drop a bomb on someone?" It's delicious to imagine yourself in these situations, and it's kind of safe, because it's a sci-fi show.

JAMES CALLIS

It's about trying to make great television, and telling a story. An allegorical story, a story for our time, in a very deft way. One of the things that possibly we did accomplish as a team is that we made people care, and I think care deeply, for fictional characters in a way that you possibly hadn't done in the same way before. And so they became important to you. They were certainly very important to us, but you had to believe them, and you had to believe the situation that they were in, so that the whole edifice, the whole thing that's created and that you watch, is just a great example of great television. A great television show. It's almost kind of a secret alternative history, because it is the world reflected through a different glass.

ANGELA MANCUSO
(former president, Universal Cable Entertainment)

In any of the best television, you relate strongly to one or more of the characters. And I think the vulnerability of those people in that situation connects to everybody in a way that they feel about the world. That we're vulnerable, we don't know what's going to happen, we don't know who's coming for us. And the idea that you have to circle the wagons in order to survive—that's a very powerful idea. I also think we were very lucky to have words put into the mouths of fabulous actors that pulled it off and always made it real. There was never a wink at the camera. It was always real. The threat was always real, the emotions were always real. *That's* what makes the best television.

EDWARD JAMES OLMOS

The writing of this show was really thought-provoking and very intelligent, and led us into a world that made people, when they were watching it, think about the world that they were living in now. It's even more poignant today than it was ten years ago when we finished. There's no comparison. It's going to become even more significant as time goes on. I've said it a couple of times now, and it's something that causes people to step back a little bit when I do, but it's a truth: The people who have seen this show, and have taken the journey from the beginning of the pilot all the way through to the very last film, will be able to understand if we ever have a nuclear holocaust and they lose everything; they will be able to reflect on the story and understand that they have to move forward, that they have to keep going no matter what. You know, when you've lost everything like was expressed in this storyline, and it was in the original also, but the way that it was reimagined was so profoundly direct. The annihilation of humanity to the point where there are less than forty-nine thousand people left alive.

MARY MCDONNELL

The idea that humanity could be reduced to fifty-five thousand people all of a sudden and force a collective group of people to have to see each other as one, to me, is something that continually resonates. With *Battlestar* we have a reminder that it could go down that path. I think we're unfortunately living on the edge at the moment on this planet. Perhaps we can stop dividing each other and see each other as one, because there is no difference.

EDWARD JAMES OLMOS

We're on the verge of probably the most difficult moments in technology that we've ever had. Meaning that our technology today is our biggest asset and our biggest deficit. No two ways about it. Our sense of security is put forth in a big way by way of feeling secure, feeling that we have computers that can regulate messages coming from outside of our hemisphere and outside of our stratosphere and moving out into the world with satellites and be able to protect us. But in the same way they become the third eye out there in space. They can pinpoint a license plate from thousands of miles up in the air. And then all of our phone systems are now nonexclusive. There's no privacy, yet everybody wants to be protected, so they're thankful that there are people who are listening in on everybody else and protecting us from ourselves. That being said, the worst part of the whole thing is that we're at one of the most crucial times in the history of humanity with a person who literally has no conceptual understanding of how to deal with the situations as they're materializing, the biggest one being North Korea. We are very close to having probably the worst nuclear disaster in history, even more intense than would have been as a result of the Bay of Pigs and the

Cuban Missile Crisis. But this is much worse, because our weaponry is so much stronger now than it was then.

MARY MCDONNELL

I just thought there was so much relevant human behavior inside this very big story; that it would be a wonderful place to collectively try to reflect some of what we were actually experiencing culturally and historically on the planet. Right from the beginning, I loved the pilot in that it also presented us with, instantly, a kind of fascination, love, and terror of the other and the unknown. My character has breast cancer—wait a minute, we're not that far advanced. It was kind of this giant stew of past, present, and future all at once.

EDWARD JAMES OLMOS

Even Ron Moore, who is a critical thinker and an extraordinary storyteller, went to the jugular with it and said, "Okay, let's see what we're going to do here; how much can we actually move the needle to understand that we are really headed into catastrophic, monumental misunderstanding about technology?" He went all the way. He left nothing untouched. He annihilated everybody.

GARY HUTZEL
(visual effects supervisor, *Battlestar Galactica* [2004])

Battlestar Galactica was like serving in a great war. The strategy is set, the forces are tasked, and then you are dropped behind enemy lines. At first there is a sense of hopelessness to the task. Long page counts, huge cast, giant set pieces, constant schedule changes, no money, no time. But almost from the beginning there was a feeling that we are a part of something much greater than our own contributions, and even as the burden became greater, it actually felt lighter. Now I look back and marvel at the men and women that I served with, their sense of duty, strength of character, and willingness to laugh when the going gets tough. To all those whom I have served with on *Battlestar,* I say truly, it has been an honor.

KATEE SACKHOFF

The show was cathartic for a lot of people in the sense that at the time *Battlestar Galactica* and science fiction were not taken seriously. It's still not *really* taken seriously, because one sort of thinks about science fiction and fantasy as not being real. Our creators and our writers and the network and the studio were able to allow us to do things that other shows couldn't do. We were allowed to do it, because it wasn't real. We were allowed to depict suicide bombers in a very real way, because it wasn't real. People were able to experience the loss in a safe fantasy world that helped a lot of people through war. It's one of the things we hear from soldiers all the time, that they watched *Battlestar Galactica* while they were serving abroad in the midst of a war, and watching it was cathartic for them while they were actually living something that was so harrowing.

AARON DOUGLAS

I have so many military people come up to me and say, "It got me through Iraq, it got me through Afghanistan, because Friday night on the base we'd all rush back from whatever tour we were on, because in the hangar they'd put *Battlestar* on at 9 P.M. and if you were late, then suck it, you were late. If you didn't make it, you run around telling everybody to shut up, because they're talking about it and you'd have to wait your turn to finally get to see it." For them it was just this really amazing moment. Other people have talked about how they were battling cancer, were bedridden, and *Battlestar* was the thing that they'd wake up every morning and be excited to power through. I don't know; it just has that grip and that hold on people. Next week I'm doing a movie and the day after I finish, I go to HawaiiCon, because they still want to sit down and talk about *Battlestar*. I've done so much since then, it's almost been ten years, but they just want to talk *Battlestar Galactica*. I'm certainly not complaining.

TONI GRAPHIA
(co-executive producer, *Battlestar Galactica* [2004])

It was the theme of survival and family that drew me in, and what I believe drew the audience in. When you have a crisis, such as the apocalypse that happens in *Battlestar*, it strips everything else away and down to what *really* matters. The essentials of life and relationships. You're thrown into this situation with people that you don't know that well, but you become a family. You do what you have to do to survive. Everything becomes hyperreal, and everything matters in a way that you can't squander *anything*. That's because everything becomes way more important, because it means the difference between life and death.

MICHAEL O'HALLORAN
(editor, *Battlestar Galactica* [2004])

Battlestar was the epitome of a well-written, well-told story. It's probably the best science fiction show ever made. To me, if HBO had done a science fiction or space show, this would have been it.

TODD SHARP

There's a universality to *Battlestar Galactica*. It's about war, it's about family, it's about humanity, it's about our place in the universe, it's about things that don't just matter to people on the left or people on the right. It's a show that I think transcends any particular political point of view. The show plays just as well and has just as much to say under a Trump administration as it does under an Obama administration. The show has just as much to say to somebody who writes for *National Review* as it does to somebody who writes for *The Nation*. And I think it has as much to say to an eighteen-year-old as it does to a seventy-year-old.

RONALD D. MOORE

People have asked me how I felt when the show was coming to an end. I'm always aware of sets being struck. Of models being put away. The nature of TV is just the constant churning through things. The sets are going to be discarded, that prop will go away and we trash the bridge. I'm hyperaware of the transitory nature of it all. Being at *Trek*, after doing five years on *Next Gen* and then suddenly it's over . . . that's, like, "Wow, I'm not coming to work and talking about Picard and Worf anymore. I'm coming to work and talking about Kira and Sisko." And then realizing at the beginning of *Deep Space Nine* that this will end, too. *And* I realized with *Battlestar Galactica*, this also has its arc.

But the afterlife of *Galactica* is enormously gratifying. When you write and produce these things, and sweat them, you tend to forget that there's a big audience out there. You're not projecting it into a theater every week. You don't have that experience of standing in the back of the auditorium and watching the crowd react. You make them, you show them to your wife, show them to your friends, and then you do the next one. And so your circle of audience feedback is very small. Then you go out in the world and someone will stop you and they'll say, "Did you work on *Battlestar*?" Or you mention it and they react. It just means everything, because it was just so much effort. You were fighting so hard for a particular vision of what you were trying to do. And ultimately you had to tell yourself that, whether or not anybody else likes it, *I* like it and I'm satisfied with that. But, you know, there's a big part of your heart that's hoping that there's those people out there that respond to that, understand or are moved, are touched by that and that it matters in their lives. To this day, I *still* have people coming up and telling me how much that show meant to them, and I love that. That means the world to me.

MARY MCDONNELL

When Ron and David and Eddie and I appeared at the United Nations, that was a pretty big indication of the connection the show was making. The show also served as the impetus for the public relations department of the United Nations to say, "Hey, this might be a good way to bring the public into awareness of what we do here. It might be a really good way to get students here." The place was *packed*. It was absolutely extraordinary. My feeling about the reach of this show is that it's not as popular as *Star Trek*, and I don't think it will ever be quite as popular, but there's something really profound going on with this show as a mirror to life. I *don't* see the world getting that much better. The mirror that we're presenting, or presented back then, is only going to have more resonance as we go forward until we work out some of this stuff.

EDWARD JAMES OLMOS

I think back to that first day when we were all together, where I unexpectedly led everybody through the chant of "So say we all." It was the first time we had all been together standing in a room, and it became really evident that, boy, this was going to be a journey that we would never, ever be able to understand again. This was one of a kind, and it proved to be exactly that: one of a kind.

ACKNOWLEDGMENTS

First and foremost, this book would not exist without the work and decades of diligent scholarship of **Steven A. Simak**, the world's foremost *Battlestar Galactica* historian. ("Galacticaspert" just doesn't have the same ring.) Steven has been covering *Battlestar Galactica* since he first wrote about it as a teenager for the *Galactic Journal* in the mid-eighties, and we are deeply appreciative for his friendship and willingness to share his extensive archives with us for this volume.

All the interviews for this volume were solely conducted by Altman, Gross, and Simak with the exception of Jack Gill, Sarah Rush, David Stipes, and Claude Earl Jones, which were generously provided by GalacticaTV .com webmaster, **Marcel Damen**. Supplemental Lorne Greene and Maren Jensen quotes were drawn from the original 1978 ABC press kit.

Additional special thanks to archivist **Rob Klein, The Archive of American Television, Eddie Ibrahim** and his team at Comic-Con International, **Grant Moninger** at the American Cinematheque. **Nick Hornung** and **Zack Ferleger** for being our conduit to the stars (and producers), and especially to everyone who took the time to be interviewed, sometimes for many, many hours, for this volume.

The other person who needs to be profusely thanked by us is **Ronald D. Moore,** who provided his complete cooperation and assistance in assuring that we could cover his series comprehensively in this volume as he did previously for *The Fifty-Year Mission*. In addition, his help with contacting the entire cast and crew of the 2004 *Battlestar Galactica* was instrumental in completing this volume. We are deeply grateful for his support and encouragement . . . as well as the bottle of Dom Perignon he sent Altman for the world premiere of his film, *Free Enterprise*.

As always, our gratitude to senior research assistant **Jordan Rubio** for his help throughout the process as well as the assistance and encouragement of Brandeis University professor **Thomas Doherty** and New York University professor **Andrew Goldman**.

Also, our eternal gratitude always to **Brendan Deenen**, our editor and enthusiast in chief, Tor Books' **Christopher Morgan**, as well as **Laurie Fox**, our literary agent at the Linda Chester Agency.

And, of course, our most profound thanks and deep appreciation to the late **Glen A. Larson**, whose contribution to television history speaks for itself (where would we be without being able to make jokes about *Manimal*), as well as the unheralded genius of **Leslie Stevens**, who, much like the late, great **Gene L. Coon**, did not live long enough to tell his story and take a well-deserved bow. Rest assured, your visions live on.

To reach the authors or to inquire about promotional and personal appearances, email them at 50yearmissionbook@gmail.com.

ABOUT THE AUTHORS

MARK A. ALTMAN is a television and motion picture writer/producer/ director who most recently served as co-executive producer of TNT's hit series *The Librarians*. Previous TV credits include *Agent X* (TNT), *Castle* (ABC), *Necessary Roughness* (USA), and as executive producer and creator of *Femme Fatales* (HBO), for which he also directed several episodes. In addition, he directed the comedy special *Aries Spears: Comedy Blueprint* for NBC/Universal.

In addition, Altman has sold numerous pilots, including to USA Networks, and, most recently, developed pilots for Beacon Pictures, El Rey Network, and Sony Pictures Television. Altman has also sold feature scripts to such studios as DreamWorks SKG and Constantin Film.

Altman produced the $30 million film adaptation of the bestselling video game *DOA: Dead or Alive*, which was released by Dimension Films. His first film was the award-winning *Free Enterprise*, starring William Shatner and Eric McCormack, which he wrote and produced and for which he won the WGA Award for Best New Writer at the AFI Los Angeles Film Festival prior to its theatrical release. He is also a producer of the House of the Dead movies, based on the popular video-game series from Sega, released by Lionsgate. In addition, he produced James Gunn's feature film *The Specials*.

His bestselling two-volume book written with Edward Gross, *The Fifty-Year Mission: The Complete, Uncensored, Unauthorized Oral History of* Star Trek, was released by St. Martin's Press in 2016 in hardcover to unanimous critical acclaim, including raves in *The Wall Street Journal, Booklist,* and *Publishers Weekly.* Their follow-up on *Buffy the Vampire Slayer* and *Angel, Slayers & Vampires,* was published last year by Tor Books.

Altman is also a former entertainment journalist. In the past, he has contributed to such newspapers and magazines as *The Boston Globe, Geek, Written By, L'Cinefage, Film Threat, The Manchester Guardian, The Boston Edge, Cult TV, Computer Player, Brandeis Magazine,* and many others, including *Cinefantastique,* for which he launched their independent film division, CFQ Films, which produced numerous successful genre features for DVD and VOD release.

He has also written numerous comic books for DC and Malibu Comics, including issues of *Star Trek* and *Star Trek: Deep Space Nine*. With Steve Kriozere, he cowrote the critically acclaimed graphic novel *Elvis Van Helsing* and *The Unknowns*.

Altman has spoken at numerous industry events and conventions, including ShowBiz Expo as well as the Variety/Final Draft Screenwriters Panel at the Cannes Film Festival. He was a juror at the prestigious Sitges Film Festival in Barcelona, Spain. He has been a frequent guest and panelist at Comic-Con, held annually in San Diego, California, and a two-time juror for the Comic-Con Film Festival. In addition to being a graduate of the Writers Guild of America Showrunner Training Program, he is a member of the Television Academy.

Twitter: @markaaltman

EDWARD GROSS is an entertainment journalist currently serving as executive editor for film and television for the Bauer Xcel Media Digital Network, senior editor of *Geek* magazine, and executive editor, U.S., for *Empire* magazine's empireonline.com. His nonfiction books include *Planet of the Apes Revisited* (with Joe Russo and Larry Landsman), *Rocky: The Ultimate Guide, Spider-Man Confidential,* and, with Mark A. Altman, the bestselling two-volume *Star Trek* oral history *The Fifty-Year Mission,* and the *Buffy the Vampire Slayer* and *Angel* oral history *Slayers & Vampires.*

Twitter: @EdGross